Lecture Notes in Computer Science 13337

More information about this series at https://link.springer.com/bookseries/558

Gavriel Salvendy · June Wei (Eds.)

Design, Operation and Evaluation of Mobile Communications

Third International Conference, MOBILE 2022
Held as Part of the 24th HCI International Conference, HCII 2022
Virtual Event, June 26 – July 1, 2022
Proceedings

 Springer

Editors
Gavriel Salvendy
University of Central Florida
Orlando, FL, USA

June Wei
University of West Florida
Pensacola, FL, USA

ISSN 0302-9743   ISSN 1611-3349 (electronic)
Lecture Notes in Computer Science
ISBN 978-3-031-05013-8   ISBN 978-3-031-05014-5 (eBook)
https://doi.org/10.1007/978-3-031-05014-5

This Springer imprint is published by the registered company Springer Nature Switzerland AG
The registered company address is: Gewerbestrasse 11, 6330 Cham, Switzerland

Foreword

Human-computer interaction (HCI) is acquiring an ever-increasing scientific and industrial importance, as well as having more impact on people's everyday life, as an ever-growing number of human activities are progressively moving from the physical to the digital world. This process, which has been ongoing for some time now, has been dramatically accelerated by the COVID-19 pandemic. The HCI International (HCII) conference series, held yearly, aims to respond to the compelling need to advance the exchange of knowledge and research and development efforts on the human aspects of design and use of computing systems.

The 24th International Conference on Human-Computer Interaction, HCI International 2022 (HCII 2022), was planned to be held at the Gothia Towers Hotel and Swedish Exhibition & Congress Centre, Göteborg, Sweden, during June 26 to July 1, 2022. Due to the COVID-19 pandemic and with everyone's health and safety in mind, HCII 2022 was organized and run as a virtual conference. It incorporated the 21 thematic areas and affiliated conferences listed on the following page.

A total of 5583 individuals from academia, research institutes, industry, and governmental agencies from 88 countries submitted contributions, and 1276 papers and 275 posters were included in the proceedings to appear just before the start of the conference. The contributions thoroughly cover the entire field of human-computer interaction, addressing major advances in knowledge and effective use of computers in a variety of application areas. These papers provide academics, researchers, engineers, scientists, practitioners, and students with state-of-the-art information on the most recent advances in HCI. The volumes constituting the set of proceedings to appear before the start of the conference are listed in the following pages.

The HCI International (HCII) conference also offers the option of 'Late Breaking Work' which applies both for papers and posters, and the corresponding volume(s) of the proceedings will appear after the conference. Full papers will be included in the 'HCII 2022 - Late Breaking Papers' volumes of the proceedings to be published in the Springer LNCS series, while 'Poster Extended Abstracts' will be included as short research papers in the 'HCII 2022 - Late Breaking Posters' volumes to be published in the Springer CCIS series.

I would like to thank the Program Board Chairs and the members of the Program Boards of all thematic areas and affiliated conferences for their contribution and support towards the highest scientific quality and overall success of the HCI International 2022 conference; they have helped in so many ways, including session organization, paper reviewing (single-blind review process, with a minimum of two reviews per submission) and, more generally, acting as goodwill ambassadors for the HCII conference.

This conference would not have been possible without the continuous and unwavering support and advice of Gavriel Salvendy, founder, General Chair Emeritus, and Scientific Advisor. For his outstanding efforts, I would like to express my appreciation to Abbas Moallem, Communications Chair and Editor of HCI International News.

June 2022   Constantine Stephanidis

HCI International 2022 Thematic Areas and Affiliated Conferences

Thematic Areas

- HCI: Human-Computer Interaction
- HIMI: Human Interface and the Management of Information

Affiliated Conferences

- EPCE: 19th International Conference on Engineering Psychology and Cognitive Ergonomics
- AC: 16th International Conference on Augmented Cognition
- UAHCI: 16th International Conference on Universal Access in Human-Computer Interaction
- CCD: 14th International Conference on Cross-Cultural Design
- SCSM: 14th International Conference on Social Computing and Social Media
- VAMR: 14th International Conference on Virtual, Augmented and Mixed Reality
- DHM: 13th International Conference on Digital Human Modeling and Applications in Health, Safety, Ergonomics and Risk Management
- DUXU: 11th International Conference on Design, User Experience and Usability
- C&C: 10th International Conference on Culture and Computing
- DAPI: 10th International Conference on Distributed, Ambient and Pervasive Interactions
- HCIBGO: 9th International Conference on HCI in Business, Government and Organizations
- LCT: 9th International Conference on Learning and Collaboration Technologies
- ITAP: 8th International Conference on Human Aspects of IT for the Aged Population
- AIS: 4th International Conference on Adaptive Instructional Systems
- HCI-CPT: 4th International Conference on HCI for Cybersecurity, Privacy and Trust
- HCI-Games: 4th International Conference on HCI in Games
- MobiTAS: 4th International Conference on HCI in Mobility, Transport and Automotive Systems
- AI-HCI: 3rd International Conference on Artificial Intelligence in HCI
- MOBILE: 3rd International Conference on Design, Operation and Evaluation of Mobile Communications

List of Conference Proceedings Volumes Appearing Before the Conference

39. CCIS 1582, HCI International 2022 Posters - Part III, edited by Constantine Stephanidis, Margherita Antona and Stavroula Ntoa
40. CCIS 1583, HCI International 2022 Posters - Part IV, edited by Constantine Stephanidis, Margherita Antona and Stavroula Ntoa

http://2022.hci.international/proceedings

Preface

With the rapid technological advances of mobile communications, mobile applications are not only changing people's living style but also changing organizations', industries', and governments' operation, management, and innovation in a new way, which further impacts the economy, society, and culture all over the world. Human-computer interaction plays an important role in this transition.

The 3rd International Conference on Design, Operation, and Evaluation of Mobile Communications (MOBILE 2022), an affiliated conference of the HCI International conference, addresses the design, operation, evaluation, and adoption of mobile technologies and applications for consumers, industries, organizations, and governments. The purpose of this conference is to provide a platform for researchers and practitioners from academia, industry, and government to discuss challenging ideas, novel research contributions, and the current theory and practice of related mobile communications research topics and applications.

The papers accepted for publication this year provide a good overview of currently active themes and topics in the field of mobile communications. Several contributions pertain to design procedures and aspects of mobile applications and services addressing a variety of fields, such as health, well-being, tourism, culture, entertainment, and human collaboration. A considerable number of papers address topics related to user experience evaluation of mobile communications, as well as their acceptability and adoption, encompassing issues relevant to privacy, trust, ethics, and user loyalty. In an era when social media are omnipresent, several papers focus on approaches and findings from studies of mobile commerce and social commerce, as well as social media advertising and influencers. Finally, the prominent topic of mobile interactions with agents as well as other recent and emerging technologies in the field are included in the papers that readers can delve into.

One volume of the HCII 2022 proceedings is dedicated to this year's edition of the MOBILE conference and focuses on topics related to designing mobile interactions and systems, user experience and adoption of mobile communications, mobile commerce and advertising, and mobile interactions with agents, as well as emerging mobile technologies.

Papers of this volume are included for publication after a minimum of two single-blind reviews from the members of the MOBILE Program Board or, in some cases, from members of the Program Boards of other affiliated conferences. We would like to thank all of them for their invaluable contribution, support, and efforts.

June 2022

Gavriel Salvendy
June Wei

3rd International Conference on Design, Operation, and Evaluation of Mobile Communications (MOBILE 2022)

Program Board Chairs: **Gavriel Salvendy,** University of Central Florida, USA and **June Wei,** University of West Florida, USA

- Abdellatief Abouali, Elshrook Academy Computer Science, Egypt
- Emad Abu-Shanab, Qatar University, Qatar
- Ahmed Wasiu Akande, Beihang University, China
- Ramiz Aliguliyev, Azerbaijan National Academy of Sciences, Azerbaijan
- Mohammed Amin Almaiah, King Faisal University, Jordan
- Mohammed Alsalem, University of Mosul, Iraq
- Hilal Özen, Trakya University, Turkey
- Akram Zine Eddine Boukhamla, University of Kasdi Merbah Ouargla, Algeria
- Mahmoud Brahimi, Mohamed Bouduaf University of M'Sila, Algeria
- Astrid Carolus, Julius-Maximilians-University Wuerzburg, Germany
- Yuangao Chen, Zhejiang University of Finance and Economics, China
- Ramesh Cheripeli, G Narayanamma Institute of Technology and Science, India
- Alain Chong, University of Nottingham Ningbo China, China
- Yee Lee Chong, Universiti Tunku Abdul Rahman, Malaysia
- Marisol B. Correia, University of Algarve and CiTUR, Portugal
- Gonçalo Dias, University of Aveiro, Portugal
- Amir Ekhlassi, University of Tehran, Iran
- Zhongwei Gu, Shanghai Dianji University, China
- Shangui Hu, Ningbo University of Finance and Economics, China
- Omar Hujran, UAE University, United Arab Emirates
- Min-Shiang Hwang, Asia University, Taiwan
- Zurida Binti Ishak, Management and Science University, Malaysia
- A. Y. M. Atiquil Islam, East China Normal University, China
- M. Sirajul Islam, Örebro University, Sweden
- Cynthia Jayapal, Kumaraguru College of Technology, India
- P. S. JosephNg, UCSI University, Malaysia
- Ali Kazemi, University of Helsinki, Finland
- Hanaa Khadri, Ain Shams University, Egypt
- Hyun K. Kim, KwangWoon University, Korea
- G. Kousalya, Coimbatore Institute of Technology, India
- Jianwei Lai, Illinois State University, USA
- Guoxin Li, Harbin Institute of Technology, China

- Manlu Liu, Rochester Institute of Technology, USA
- Leonardo Madariaga, Federico Santa María Technical University, Chile
- Phung Minh Tuan, Ton Duc Thang University, Vietnam
- Solomon Negash, Kennesaw State University, USA
- Wilson Nwankwo, Edo State University, Nigeria
- Sunday Olaleye, University of Oulu, Finland
- Challiz Omorog, Camarines Sur Polytechnic Colleges, Philippines
- Jaehyun Park, Incheon National University, South Korea
- Shaun Pather, University of the Western Cape, South Africa
- Renato Pereira, ISCTE Business School, Portugal
- André Pimenta Freire, Universidade Federal de Lavras, Brazil
- S M Sohel Rana, Independent University, Bangladesh
- Blerim Rexha, University of Prishtina, Kosovo
- Maruf Salimon, Universiti Utara Malaysia, Malaysia
- Muhammad Sarfraz, Sabah Al-Salem University City, Kuwait
- Omair Shafiq, Carleton University, Canada
- Don Shin, Zayed University, United Arab Emirates
- Hatem Ben Sta, University of Tunis El Manar, Tunisia
- Su Mon Chit, UCSI University, Malaysia
- Sanjib Sur, University of Southern Carolina, USA
- Chee Ling Thong, UCSI University, Malaysia
- Sacip Toker, Atilim University, Turkey
- Abderrahim Tragha, Université Hassan II de Casablanca, Morocco
- Christos Troussas, University of West Attica, Greece
- Thiruvaazhi Uloli, Kumaraguru College of Technology, India
- Fuhong Wang, Shanghai Jian Qiao University, China
- Ari Widyanti, Bandung Institute of Technology, Indonesia
- Kusum Yadav, University of Ha'il, Saudi Arabia
- Shuiqing Yang, Zhejiang University of Finance and Economics, China
- Zhijian Yang, University of Illinois Urbana-Champaign, USA
- Ravi Sekhar Yarrabothu, Vignan's University, India
- Shubin Yu, Peking University, China
- Abdelhalim Zekry, Ain Shams University, Egypt
- Peiyan Zhou, Jilin University, China

The full list with the Program Board Chairs and the members of the Program Boards of all thematic areas and affiliated conferences is available online at

http://www.hci.international/board-members-2022.php

HCI International 2023

The 25th International Conference on Human-Computer Interaction, HCI International 2023, will be held jointly with the affiliated conferences at the AC Bella Sky Hotel and Bella Center, Copenhagen, Denmark, 23–28 July 2023. It will cover a broad spectrum of themes related to human-computer interaction, including theoretical issues, methods, tools, processes, and case studies in HCI design, as well as novel interaction techniques, interfaces, and applications. The proceedings will be published by Springer. More information will be available on the conference website: http://2023.hci.international/.

General Chair
Constantine Stephanidis
University of Crete and ICS-FORTH
Heraklion, Crete, Greece
Email: general_chair@hcii2023.org

http://2023.hci.international/

Contents

Mobile Interactions with Agents

Emerging Mobile Technologies

Designing Mobile Interactions
and Systems

Identifying Interaction and Awareness Services in Mobile Collaborative Applications

Maximiliano Canche[1,2], Sergio F. Ochoa[1(✉)], and Daniel Perovich[1]

[1] Computer Science Department, University of Chile, Beauchef 851, Santiago, Chile
{mcanche,sochoa,dperovic}@dcc.uchile.cl
[2] Faculty of Mathematics, Autonomous University of Yucatán, Mérida, México

Abstract. The interaction and awareness services play a key role on the impact that mobile collaborative systems have on their application domains. Identifying these services at early design stages is not only challenging, but also mandatory to determine the feasibility and scope of the system to be developed. Based on a literature review, this paper presents a set of interaction and awareness services that helps designers determine what services to embed into mobile applications, depending on interaction needs that must be addressed.

Keywords: Computer-mediated communication · Interaction and awareness services · Interaction design · Mobile collaborative systems · People-driven collaboration

1 Introduction

December defines Computer-Mediated Communication (CMC) as "a process of human communication via computers, involving people, situated in particular contexts, engaging in processes to shape media for a variety of purposes" [1]. Examples of CMC are social interaction through social media [2], mobile collaborative work [3] and people-driven collaborative processes [4].

For many years, the Computer-Supported Cooperative Work and Human-Computer Interaction research communities have studied the CMC processes from several perspectives, trying to understand its implications mainly on the social, educational and business domains [2, 5]. However, few research efforts have been done from the software engineering perspective, to determine the interaction requirements that should be considered when designing applications that support these processes.

Today, the identification of interaction requirements, particularly, the interaction and awareness services required to support people-driven collaborative processes (PDCPs), is done in ad hoc manner following guidelines from participatory design [6]. This means the interaction services identification depends on several factors, like the skills of the people performing the elicitation, the size and complexity of the PDCP being addressed, and the capability of the users to participate in the elicitation and design of interaction services. Consequently, the results of the services elicitation are highly unpredictable and error-prone, and also it tends to be slow, expensive and difficult to replicate [7].

G. Salvendy and J. Wei (Eds.): HCII 2022, LNCS 13337, pp. 3–16, 2022.
https://doi.org/10.1007/978-3-031-05014-5_1

In order to address such a challenge, the authors proposed a visual modeling language, named Computer Interaction Modeling Language (CIMoL) [8], which allows designers of mobile collaborative systems to represent and characterize the CMC mechanisms (i.e., interaction and awareness services) required by participants in people-driven collaborative process to interact among them. These participants can be human beings, software agents, information repositories, and also end-users utilizing commercial applications. The interaction requirements between different types of participants can be also different; therefore, this is an aspect that software designers have to address when conceiving and modeling these applications.

This article presents a review of interaction and awareness services reported in the literature, which can be used to support mobile workers participating in PDCPs. Next section presents the background on PDCPs and also on the systems that support these processes. Section 3 describes the stereotypes of actors that can interact with these systems. Section 4 presents the communication and awareness services that can be used to support interactions among the participants. Section 5 shows a correspondence matrix that relates interaction services with the types of users roles participating in PDCPs. Section 6 presents the conclusions and future work.

2 Background

Collaborative processes can be classified according to their level of structuredness, ranging from tightly framed (structured) to fully unframed (unstructured) processes, as shown in Fig. 1. Next, each class is described according to the definitions presented in [9, 10].

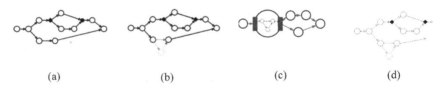

| | | | |
| (a) | (b) | (c) | (d) |

Fig. 1. Level of structureness of collaborative processes [10]: (a) tightly framed processes; (b) loosely framed processes; (c) ad-hoc framed processes; (d) fully unframed processes.

- *Tightly framed processes.* These processes are well structured, fully predictable and highly repetitive. In this process type, the activities performed by the participants as well as the activities workflow are completely predefined. These workflows pass through the same predetermined order of steps over and over again, very often it consists of routine activities. Figure 1.a shows the structure of these processes; typical examples of them are found in production and administrative processes.
- *Loosely framed processes.* These processes capture standard ways of performing tasks (Fig. 1.b). They have a completely predetermined workflow with some exceptions. An example of a loosely framed process is the processing of consumer credit applications, where there is a clear workflow, but also some exceptions depending on the particular customer request or customer type submitting the application.

- *Ad-hoc framed processes.* These processes capture structured fragments that are then composed on a per-case basis (Fig. 1.c). Processes in this category contain a predefined workflow, but also parts of them being ad-hoc planned and executed. An example of an ad-hoc framed process is the solving of software problems. In this scenario, a standard guide to develop the solution of the most software problems can be pre-established, however, some of them have to be planned and solved on-the-fly.
- *Fully unframed processes.* These processes are fully unpredictable and highly non-repetitive. That is, the activities performed by the participants, as well as their workflow cannot be predefined at design time. This kind of process frequently involves urgent, short-lived, exceptional, and/or confidential activities, which are typically performed considering participants' roles. Figure 1.d represents this type of process; examples of them are hospital work, disaster relief efforts, and global software development.

The two latter kinds of processes (ad-hoc framed and fully unframed processes) are usually also known as people-driven [11] or knowledge intensive [12]. The main characteristics of a people-driven collaborative process (PDCP) is the presence of roles played by the participants, and a lack of a pre-established workflow (or part of this workflow) that coordinates the actions of the participants. As mentioned in the introduction, the participants decide on-the-fly how and when to conduct the coordination activities, by considering several context variables, such as, the content of their to-do list, or the priority/urgency of their pending activities. The modeling of interactions in this process type is the focus of this work.

2.1 Mobile Collaborative Systems that Support PDCPs

A collaborative process involves people (users) playing predefined roles and interacting among them to reach common goals (usually, group or organizational goals) [13, 14]. These processes are commonly supported by several types of software applications, e.g., cloud-to-mobile collaborative systems [15], as a way to make the people's participation more flexible, and improve the efficiency of the processes.

The design of these applications involves four major design dimensions (Fig. 2): communication, coordination, collaboration, and awareness. The communication dimension identifies the channels and mechanisms required to support interactions among the participants in a PDCP. This dimension also determines the basic services required to coordinate the people's activities, and integrate and share the interim results. The communication and coordination services are usually required to allow collaboration among the participants, and thus help them reach their individual and group goals.

The awareness dimension includes the mechanisms (usually through visual representations) that keep participants informed about the joint work, and mediate the communication, coordination, and collaboration among these people. Coordination, collaboration, and awareness are design aspects that depend on the communication support provided by the PDCP. Designing the communication aspect of a collaborative system (i.e., the interaction services) is mandatory to then address the other design aspects.

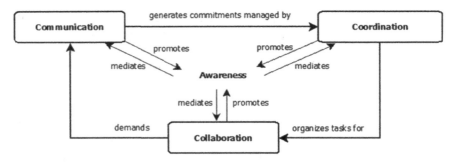

Fig. 2. 3C model adapted from [16, 17].

2.2 Using Mobile Collaborative Applications in PDCPs

We name "human-machine unit" (HMU) to a mobile worker that uses a collaborative application to participate in a PDCP. Typically, these HMUs perform loosely-coupled work [18], i.e., the HMUs work autonomously most of the time and carry out sporadic on-demand collaboration processes. Once finished the collaboration activity, these units return to autonomous work [19, 20].

Figure 3 shows two HMUs interacting; they play the role A and B respectively, and use a shared workspace (e.g., the mobile app of Uber) to participate in a PDCP. For instance, let us suppose that a sales company contracts Uber to transport their salesmen with minimum delay among several places they have to visit during a working day. In this case, the role A could be the salesmen and the role B can be a particular subset of Uber drivers. Both roles can use a particular flavor of the Uber application to coordinate the pick-up and drop-off times, monitor availability of the counterpart, or estimate trips duration.

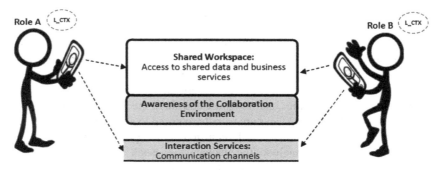

Fig. 3. HMUs interacting through a mobile collaborative application

The front-end of the application usually represents the major part of the shared workspace; therefore, it changes with every application. The information and services available to the user, and also the way to visualize them, is ad hoc to the PDCP being addressed by these HMUs.

Figure 4 shows the Uber workspace. It embeds awareness mechanisms that allow drivers and potential passengers to know what is happening in the collaborative environment (e.g., what cars are in the area, or where is the current location of the assigned driver).

In this sense, the application usually provides to HMUs contextual information (usually as visual awareness) about the collaboration environment. However, each HMU has information of its own local context (L_CTX in Fig. 3), which is kept in the users' mind. The HMUs use both context information to determine their next action, therefore, their workflow is defined on-the-fly.

Fig. 4. Interface of the Uber workspace

The HMUs participating in a PDCP perform several activities depending on their own needs, or address the requests of other units. When the HMU needs to interact with others, e.g., to perform ad hoc coordination activities, the collaborative system should provide them: 1) particular services that support the interaction between every pair of roles, and 2) awareness information that allows the HMUs to determine when and with whom to interact. Therefore, the design of the interaction support to be embedded in the mobile application must identify these services.

Typically, it is done as part of the requirement engineering and preliminary design stages. Consequently, the languages used to model interaction scenarios should allow representing these services, since they are part of the agreement and shared understanding between the stakeholders and provider.

3   Stereotypes of Users in Mobile Collaborative Applications

As mentioned before, several types of actors can participate in the interaction scenarios involved in PDCPs, and the visual languages used to represent them should allow specifying the types of participants. Figure 5 shows a more complete interaction scenario, where we can identify internal and external users. The first one are actors (end-users) that utilize the application being developed, as an instrument to interact with others. Different actors types, and also different roles, can access different functionality of the mobile application.

The internal users can be human beings, but also information repositories or software agents. The repositories are passive actors that act as intermediary between other participants. The software agents are autonomous components that have a set of services predefined to interact with others. It is assumed that repositories and software agents have high availability to perform interactions; in this sense, their uptime is considered similar to a cloud regular service.

As shown in Fig. 5, agents and repositories do not have a local context as the human being. Their local context, if there exists, it is part of the shared data space.

On the other hand, the external users are human actors that interact with others using a system that is different to the mobile application being developed. For instance, a user can utilize the regular Telegram or Whatsapp system to communicate with actors that use the ad hoc mobile collaborative application.

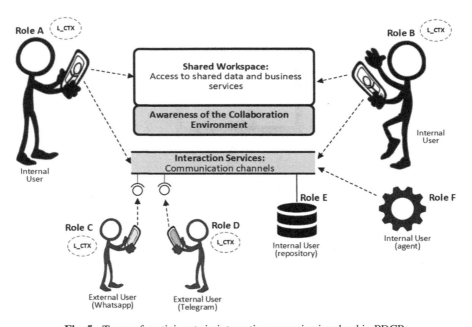

Fig. 5. Types of participants in interaction scenarios involved in PDCPs

Having external users allows the participation of people that are not willing to install the ad hoc collaborative application in their devices. For instance, a physician (i.e., a particular mobile worker) can participate in several PDCPs using Whatsapp, regardless of whether other users utilize an ad hoc application to interact with him/her. When external users are going to participate in PDCPs, the collaborative system should provide a software interface (usually an API) with external applications to allow the interaction with those users.

4 Interaction Services

As any software system, the applications supporting a PDCP usually require a communication interface to an information environment that is shared by the participants, in order to enable them to achieve group and individual goals. Designing such an interface requires identifying the suitable interaction services (particularly, communication and awareness mechanisms) to support the collaborative work.

Researchers recognize that identifying interaction services when a scenario is being modeled is a challenging task, due it depends on both, the task to be supported and the interaction context [21]. Such as described in [22], groupware services (i.e., those involving multiuser interactions), differently from functional services, are often known by users but not clearly visible for most developers, whereby the elicitation of groupware requirements may have to involve people with some experience in the design of collaborative tools.

Some works have proposed methods to perform this activity and they also have described typical services involved in mobile collaborative applications. The following subsections describe some of the main services found in the literature. It is worth mentioning that this work does not intend to present a comprehensive catalog of services, but a relevant list of them. Such a list should help engineers identify interaction requirements (interaction services) to be embedded into the system being designed.

4.1 Communication Services

Communication is the most important aspect to foster collaboration, since only through communication other collaboration aspects (e.g., coordination) may occur [21]. To identify communication requirements, the system designers must know which communication aspects should be provided in each particular collaboration context.

Typically, the complexity of such an identification process increases when diverse communication services are required. For instance, a single CMC activity (e.g., a meeting) often contains many types of information with diverse channels that may be activated. This was empirically revealed with a study showing that those who frequently communicate or engage in important information exchanges tend to combine the use of diverse media [23].

A review of the typical communication services was performed in order to provide a helpful list of them to engineers developing mobile collaborative systems. Table 1 contains such services that can be used to support interaction scenarios in PDCPs.

Table 1. Typical communication services that can be in systems supporting PDCPs

Communication service	Description	References
Email	Send and receive emails	[21, 24, 25]
File transfer	Exchange of digital information (files). It can include the transmission of heavyweight data types, such as *images*, *video* or *audio files*	[3, 24, 26]

(*continued*)

Table 1. (*continued*)

Communication service	Description	References
Boards	Exchange of information through electronic boards. Also referred to as *discussion forums* or *bulletin boards* in the literature	[21, 24, 25]
Audioconference	Perform an audio conference among two or more participants	[21, 24]
Videoconference	Perform a video conference among two or more participants	[21, 24, 27, 28]
Message exchange	Exchange of electronic messages with particular (ad hoc) formats	[3, 21, 24, 29]

According to the participants' needs, diverse communication services can be required depending on the time the interaction among participants takes place. For instance, when a synchronous interaction occurs, both participants need to be available and prepared to interact at the same time, and they should have access to the necessary communication services to carry out the interaction process. Conversely, in an asynchronous interaction the time is more flexible, and the participants do not necessarily have to be available to interact at the same time. In this scenario, the participants do not know when the messages will be received or sent until these messages arrive at the destination [21]. Moreover, whether the interaction is synchronous/asynchronous, different communication services must be identified and defined.

4.2 Awareness Services

As described previously, identifying awareness services (as part of the interaction services) is a difficult task. Similar to the previous subsection, a review of the main awareness services considered in the development of collaborative applications was performed. This provides a helpful list of services, which are likely to be included in an application during its design.

In this review, several interesting and useful works were identified. For instance, [22] presents a method that helps designers of mobile collaborative applications to identify awareness mechanisms to support nomadic users that perform a particular collaborative activity. In such a work, a list of useful awareness services is identified from literature. Similar to that study, [30, 31] provide different kinds of awareness obtained from reviews of a significant number of proposals from the literature. Moreover, going further Collazos et al. [32] present a review of several awareness mechanisms, frameworks and uses proposed in the literature from a software engineering perspective. They also propose the definition of a framework that could assist groupware engineers to incorporate awareness mechanisms in the development of collaborative systems. The most widely accepted awareness services, which also can be considered to be embedded in mobile collaborative systems that support PDCP, are presented in Table 2.

Table 2. Main awareness services that can be embedded in systems supporting PDCPs

Awareness service	Description	References
Location	Awareness related to the physical or virtual location of a user. It includes awareness about different aspects related to location: *distance* regarding other users, and *displacement* from the other user	[22, 26, 30, 31, 33]
Availability	Indicates whether the user is busy or available to collaborate with co-workers	[21, 22, 31–33]
Presence	Indicates the presence of the user in the interaction. This service includes awareness about *connected / disconnected users*, and *transitions* between connection and disconnection	[19, 22, 33, 34]
Communication log	Awareness related to the interactions' history	[3, 21, 31]
Messages status	Informs the user when her/his messages are sent/delivered to the target users	[22, 32]
Incoming call	Informs the user when a call is incoming to her/his device	[33]
Identity (user representation)	Provide information about the co-workers	[31, 32]

It is important to mention that although the literature shows additional types of awareness services, potentially useful for collaborative applications, our aim is to identify the services required by participants in people-driven collaborative processes to interact among them. For instance, a type of awareness named *activity awareness* [22], indicates the individual activities the users are engaged in (at their device), or another type of it named *workspace awareness*, which refers to the capability to utilize determined cues to understand the activities being carried out in the workplace [30].

4.3 Complementary Requirements

Besides typical interaction services (communication and awareness services) that are useful to support a PDCP, we have also identified in the literature relevant requirements supporting communication or data transmission when CMC takes place. Among them, we can mention the following:

- Communication directionality [21, 24, 29]
- Explicit "reply-to" relations [29]
- Roles definition (external users, agents, work groups, etc.) [21, 26]
- Number of participants (not per roles, but researchers acknowledge the lack of them) [21, 26, 29]

Table 3. Matrix showing the possible services required by each user type in his/her interaction with the counterpart

To / From	Human being (external user)	Human being (internal user)	Repository (internal user)	Agent (internal user)
Human being (external user)	• Email • File transfer • Boards • Audioconference • Videoconference • Message exchange • Location awareness • Availability awareness • Presence awareness • Communication log awareness • Messages status awareness • Incoming call awareness • Identity awareness	• Email • File transfer • Boards • Audioconference • Videoconference • Message exchange • Location awareness • Availability awareness • Presence awareness • Communication log awareness • Messages status awareness • Incoming call awareness • Identity awareness	• Email • File transfer • Audioconference • Message exchange • Location awareness • Availability awareness • Presence awareness • Communication log awareness • Messages status awareness • Identity awareness	• Email • File transfer • Audioconference • Message exchange • Location awareness • Availability awareness • Presence awareness • Communication log awareness • Messages status awareness • Incoming call awareness • Identity awareness
Human being (internal user)	• Email • File transfer • Boards • Audioconference • Videoconference • Message exchange • Location awareness • Availability awareness • Presence awareness • Communication log awareness • Messages status awareness • Incoming call awareness • Identity awareness	• Email • File transfer • Boards • Audioconference • Videoconference • Message exchange • Location awareness • Availability awareness • Presence awareness • Communication log awareness • Messages status awareness • Incoming call awareness • Identity awareness	• Email • File transfer • Audioconference • Message exchange • Location awareness • Availability awareness • Presence awareness • Communication log awareness • Messages status awareness • Incoming call awareness • Identity awareness	• Email • File transfer • Audioconference • Message exchange • Location awareness • Availability awareness • Presence awareness • Communication log awareness • Messages status awareness • Incoming call awareness • Identity awareness
Repository (internal user)	• Email • File transfer	• Email • File transfer	• Email • File transfer	• Email • File transfer
Agent (internal user)	• Email • File transfer • Audioconference • Message exchange	• Email • File transfer • Audioconference • Message exchange	• Email • File transfer • Message exchange	• Email • File transfer • Message exchange

- Cardinality in interactions (combinations to represent communication with one or many persons) [21, 26]
- Participants privacy [21, 26]
- Speed of communication [29]

These requirements could be relevant if the application must support some specific needs from the participants' interactions. Of course, if a modeling notation considers visual components for all of them, it could become excessively expressive to the designer (i.e., the end-users of these notations), and probably jeopardize its usability. Therefore, the inclusion of visual components to model these aspects should be carefully evaluated before including them into a new or existing notation.

5   User Stereotypes versus Interaction Services

The correspondence matrix shown in Table 3 relates interaction services with the types of users roles participating in a people-driven collaborative process. In that, concordance combinations become apparent and also trade-offs are identified. This matrix can be used for identifying participants' needs in correspondence with their roles.

In such a table we can observe the possible interaction services that can be required by each user type. For instance, a *human being* (independently if he/she is an internal or external user) interacting with another *human being* (also internal or external user) can require all or part of the communication services listed in Table 1 and all or part of the awareness services listed in Table 2. However, if a *repository* is interacting with a *human being*, the former only can require the email or the file transfer service to communicate with the latter and no awareness service (i.e. the awareness services regarding its counterpart are useless for the repository). A similar situation happens with an *agent*, it can only require part of the communication services and no awareness about its counterpart.

6   Conclusions and Future Work

This paper presents a review of interaction and awareness services reported in the literature, which can be used to be embedded in applications supporting mobile workers participating in people-driven collaborative processes. Also, this work can help designers to get a deeper understanding of the communication and awareness needs in order to define more suitable supporting requirements. With the typical interaction services shown in this article it is possible to organize and use them in the requirements engineering stage using existing elicitation techniques and modeling notations. Moreover, it describes the stereotypes of users that can utilize (or interact with) the mobile application supporting PDCPs. Based on the characteristics of them, a correspondence matrix was developed, which illustrates which interaction services can be used for each kind of user according to who he/she communicates with. It helps designers of mobile collaborative systems to determine, at early development stages, which communication and awareness services to embed into the applications.

The future work considers to assess the actual services supported by modeling notations and languages, in order to determine their suitability and completeness to model mobile applications that support PDCPs.

Acknowledgements. This research work has been partially supported by Fondecyt (Chile), grant: 1191516. The work of Maximiliano Canché was funded in part by the PRODEP Mexican Program, grant number PROMEP/103.5/16/6096 and the Ph.D. Scholarship Program of Conicyt Chile (CONICYT–PCHA/Doctorado Nacional/2019- 21191825).

References

1. December, J.: Notes on defining of computer-mediated communication. Comput. Mediat. Commun. Mag. **3**(1) (1997)
2. Rains, S.A., Wright, K.B.: Social support and computer-mediated communication: a state-of-the-art review and agenda for future research. Ann. Int. Commun. Assoc. **40**(1), 175–211 (2016)
3. Herskovic, V., Ochoa, S.F., Pino, J.A.: Identifying groupware requirements in people-driven mobile collaborative processes. J. Univers. Comput. Sci. **25**(8), 988–1017 (2019)
4. Antunes, P., Baloian, N., Zurita, G., Pino, J.A.: Supporting people-driven, dynamic and geo-located work processes. In: Proceedings of the 10th International Conference on Subject-Oriented Business Process Management, pp. 1–10 (2018)
5. Wright, K.B., Webb, L.M.: Computer-Mediated Communication in Personal Relationships. Peter Lang, Bern (2011)
6. Nolte, A., Prilla, M.: Anyone can use models: potentials, requirements and support for non-expert model interaction. Int. J. e-Collab. (IJeC) **9**(4), 45–60 (2013)
7. Canché, M., Ochoa, S.F.: A survey of development strategies for collaborative systems. In: 23rd IEEE International Conference on Computer Supported Cooperative Work in Design, CSCWD 2019, Porto, Portugal, 6–8 May 2019, pp. 261–266 (2019). https://doi.org/10.1109/CSCWD.2019.8791934
8. Canche, M., Ochoa, S.F., Perovich, D.: CIMoL: a language for modeling interactions in people-driven collaborative processes. Technical report TR/DCC-2021-3, Computer Science Department, University of Chile (2021). https://www.dcc.uchile.cl/TR/2021/TR_DCC-202 11115-003.pdf. . Accessed 18 Nov 2021
9. Cardoso, E., Labunets, K., Dalpiaz, F., Mylopoulos, J., Giorgini, P.: Modeling structured and unstructured processes: an empirical evaluation. In: Comyn-Wattiau, I., Tanaka, K., Song, I.-Y., Yamamoto, S., Saeki, M. (eds.) ER 2016. LNCS, vol. 9974, pp. 347–361. Springer, Cham (2016). https://doi.org/10.1007/978-3-319-46397-1_27
10. Huth, C., Erdmann, I., Nastansky, L.: GroupProcess: using process knowledge from the participative design and practical operation of ad hoc processes for the design of structured workflows (2001). https://doi.org/10.1109/HICSS.2001.927236
11. Dorn, C., Dustdar, S.: Supporting dynamic, people-driven processes through self-learning of message flows. In: Mouratidis, H., Rolland, C. (eds.) CAiSE 2011. LNCS, vol. 6741, pp. 657–671. Springer, Heidelberg (2011). https://doi.org/10.1007/978-3-642-21640-4_48
12. Di Ciccio, C., Marrella, A., Russo, A.: Knowledge-intensive processes: characteristics, requirements and analysis of contemporary approaches. J. Data Semant. **4**(1), 29–57 (2014). https://doi.org/10.1007/s13740-014-0038-4
13. Ellis, C.A., Gibbs, S.J., Rein, G.: Groupware: some issues and experiences. Commun. ACM **34**(1), 39–58 (1991). https://doi.org/10.1145/99977.99987
14. Smith, R.B., Hixon, R., Horan, B.: Supporting flexible roles in a shared space. In: Proceedings of the 1998 ACM Conference on Computer Supported Cooperative Work, New York, NY, USA, pp. 197–206 (1998). https://doi.org/10.1145/289444.289494

15. Deng, S., et al.: Toward mobile service computing: opportunities and challenges. IEEE Cloud Comput. **3**(4), 32–41 (2016). https://doi.org/10.1109/MCC.2016.92
16. Ellis, C., Wainer, J.: A conceptual model of groupware. In: Proceedings of the 1994 ACM Conference on Computer Supported Cooperative Work, New York, NY, USA, pp. 79–88 (1994). https://doi.org/10.1145/192844.192878
17. Fuks, H., Raposo, A., Gerosa, M.A., Pimentel, M., Filippo, D., Lucena, C.: Inter- and intra-relationships between communication coordination and cooperation in the scope of the 3C collaboration model, vol. 1, pp. 148–153 (2008). https://doi.org/10.1109/CSCWD.2008.453 6971
18. Churchill, E.F., Wakeford, N.: Framing mobile collaborations and mobile technologies. In: Brown, B., Green, N., Harper, R. (eds) Wireless World. Computer Supported Cooperative Work, pp. 154–179. Springer, London (2002)
19. Pinelle, D.: Improving groupware design for loosely coupled groups. Ph.D. thesis, Citeseer (2004)
20. Pinelle, D., Gutwin, C.: A groupware design framework for loosely coupled workgroups. In: ECSCW 2005, pp. 65–82. Springer, Dordrecht (2005). https://doi.org/10.1007/1-4020-402 3-7_4
21. Miranda, I., de Araujo, R.M., Borges, M.R.: Discovering group communication requirements. In: CIbSE, pp. 107–120 (2007)
22. Herskovic, V., Ochoa, S.F., Pino, J.A., Antunes, P., Ormeño, E.: Identifying the awareness mechanisms for mobile collaborative applications. In: Antunes, P., Gerosa, M.A., Sylvester, A., Vassileva, J., de Vreede, G.-J. (eds.) CRIWG 2013. LNCS, vol. 8224, pp. 241–256. Springer, Heidelberg (2013). https://doi.org/10.1007/978-3-642-41347-6_18
23. Haythornthwaite, C., Wellman, B., Garton, L.: Work and community via computer-mediated communication. In: Psychology of the Internet, pp. 199–226 (1998)
24. Bubaš, G.: Computer mediated communication theories and phenomena: factors that influence collaboration over the internet. In: 3rd CARNet Users Conference, pp. 24–26 (2001)
25. Spitzberg, B.H.: Preliminary development of a model and measure of computer-mediated communication (CMC) competence. J. Comput.-Mediat. Commun. **11**(2), 629–666 (2006)
26. Ochoa, S., Alarcon, R., Guerrero, L.: Understanding the relationship between requirements and context elements in mobile collaboration. In: Jacko, J.A. (ed.) HCI 2009. LNCS, vol. 5612, pp. 67–76. Springer, Heidelberg (2009). https://doi.org/10.1007/978-3-642-02580-8_8
27. Wittenberg-Lyles, E., Oliver, D.P., Demiris, G., Baldwin, P.: The ACTive Intervention in hospice interdisciplinary team meetings: exploring family caregiver and hospice team communication. J. Comput.-Mediat. Commun. **15**(3), 465–481 (2010). https://doi.org/10.1111/j. 1083-6101.2010.01502.x
28. Oliver, D.R.P., Demiris, G., Day, M., Courtney, K.L., Porock, D.: Telehospice support for elder caregivers of hospice patients: two case studies. J. Palliat. Med. **9**(2), 264–267 (2006)
29. Li, H., Kraut, R.E., Zhu, H.: Technical features of asynchronous and synchronous community platforms and their effects on community cohesion: a comparative study of forum-based and chat-based online mental health communities. J. Comput.-Mediat. Commun. **26**(6), 403–421 (2021). https://doi.org/10.1093/jcmc/zmab016
30. Antunes, P., Herskovic, V., Ochoa, S.F., Pino, J.A.: Reviewing the quality of awareness support in collaborative applications. J. Syst. Softw. **89**, 146–169 (2014). https://doi.org/10.1016/j. jss.2013.11.1078
31. Dirix, M., Le Pallec, X., Muller, A.: software support requirements for awareness in collaborative modeling. In: Meersman, R., et al. (eds.) OTM 2014. LNCS, vol. 8841, pp. 382–399. Springer, Heidelberg (2014). https://doi.org/10.1007/978-3-662-45563-0_22

32. Collazos, C.A., Gutiérrez, F.L., Gallardo, J., Ortega, M., Fardoun, H.M., Molina, A.I.: Descriptive theory of awareness for groupware development. J. Ambient. Intell. Humaniz. Comput. **10**(12), 4789–4818 (2018). https://doi.org/10.1007/s12652-018-1165-9
33. Ljungstrand, P.: Context awareness and mobile phones. Pers. Ubiquit. Comput. **5**(1), 58–61 (2001)
34. Oyekoy, O., et al.: Supporting interoperability and presence awareness in collaborative mixed reality environments. In: Proceedings of the 19th ACM Symposium on Virtual Reality Software and Technology, pp. 165–174 (2013)

Application of Virtual Simulation Technology in Dragon Boat Race Teaching and Cultural Promotion

Wenmei Dong$^{(\boxtimes)}$ and Wanqing Yu

Minzu University of China, Beijing 100081, China
dongwenm@163.com, 20302146@muc.edu.cn

Abstract. To solve the problems of the traditional classroom-based dragon boat race teaching, such as the lack of venues, facilities and experienced instructors, as well as the loose course design, etc., this paper proposes a web-based teaching system that applies the virtual simulation technology. Based on the theoretical and practical knowledge of the dragon boat race, this paper has found the specific information-based teaching methods that are useful for teaching this sport, with the hope to enhance the experiences and outcomes of teaching and training.

Keywords: Virtual simulation technology · Dragon boat race · Virtual reality

1 Introduction

The dragon boat race, commonly also known as "hua longchuan" ("rowing the dragon boat"), is a folk sport event that is popular both in China and among the Chinese-speaking world, particularly in the provinces in the southern part of China, such as Fujian, Guangdong, Jiangxi, Hunan, Guizhou, Taiwan, and Hubei [1]. The dragon boat race, a Chinese folk culture with a long history of more than two thousand years, has attracted people around the world to experience its unique charm. Today, beyond its original nature as a local folk culture and sporting event, the dragon boat race has now become a new platform for people across the world to meet and exchange cultures. As for the young people, to organize the dragon boat race activities in schools and universities can enhance students' team spirit and, at the same time, allow them to experience this fine cultural tradition.

With the rapid progress of the global information technology, the information-based teaching methods emerging in the "Internet Plus" era are transforming the traditional teaching. This paper proposes to apply virtual simulation in dragon boat race training, which follows the current trend towards information-based teaching in physical education. The proposed system will not only promote the dragon boat race culture and teaching, but also provide a teaching model for the training of other folk sports.

Awarded by Research Special from Minzu University of China.

《The Role and Innovation of National Traditional Sports in Forging the Conscious-ness of the Chinese Nation's Community》(Subject number: 2020MDZL23).

G. Salvendy and J. Wei (Eds.): HCII 2022, LNCS 13337, pp. 17–25, 2022.
https://doi.org/10.1007/978-3-031-05014-5_2

2 Virtual Simulation: Definitions and Applications

2.1 Virtual Simulation

In 1965, American scientist Ivan Edward Sutherland, known as "the father of virtual reality", put forward the idea of building a virtual world by computer, which started the research of virtual reality [2]. Regarding the definition of virtual simulation, researchers have different ideas. Some think virtual simulation is a rising discipline, and most regard it as a technology; however, both views agree on its essential features [3, 4].

Wang Weiguo, et al. collected and reviewed the literature, documents and Internet resources about the application of virtual simulation to experimental teaching in the universities outside China, and identified ten information technologies that are commonly used in virtual simulation teaching; they are multimedia, man-machine interaction, visualization, simulation, virtual reality (VR), virtual simulation, augmented reality (AR), virtual world, 3D printing, and telepresence. Among them, virtual simulation is the result of the developments in multiple technologies, such as multimedia, virtual reality, man-machine interaction, Internet, and communications; it is a more advanced simulation technology which integrates simulation and virtual reality (VR), as well as other technologies [5].

2.2 Research Status of Virtual Simulation in Physical Education

Wang Weiguo, et al. reviewed the current situation of virtual simulation experimental teaching in the universities outside China, and listed the cases in the US, UK and Canada. They concluded that the rapid development of information technology has provided strong support for the establishments and applications of virtual laboratories, virtual simulation experimental systems, collaboratory platforms, immersive experimental software and open education resources, which has triggered reform in the concepts, modes, methods and means of experimental teaching [6].

Regarding the use of virtual simulation in physical education, Shao Ruifang et al. have found two types of teaching methods after reviewing the relevant literature: using virtual simulation to make courseware and using virtual simulation to create man-machine interaction [7].

Some researchers have adopted virtual reality to make courseware. Zhao Xiaokun did a teaching experiment, in which the experimental group incorporated Flash courseware into the traditional teaching and the control group only used the traditional method. The results show that the method used by the experimental group effectively improves the students' focus and movement proficiency; also, it also gives quick feedback, which helps the students better master the key and difficult techniques and more engaged in learning [8]. He Kun and Wang Ying, used virtual reality to create courseware in their respective teaching experiments; the results show that virtual reality courseware significantly improves students' engagement and learning outcomes [9, 10].

Some researchers have used virtual simulation for man-machine interaction in their teaching. Song Wei applied virtual simulation called TRACK MAN GOLF in his teaching experiments, which got the data of the clubhead speed, angle of attack, swing path, club face angle, and shot distance. The results show that the TPI teaching method helps the beginners perform better in the clubhead speed and shot distance than the traditional teaching method does; in addition, it increases the students' swing stability [11]. Pan Yonggang applied KUDU movement analysis system in his golf teaching experiment, with the number of the experimental group and control group being 14 and 15, respectively. The results show that the 7 iron club in the experimental group shows higher weekly ratio in shot distance, ball speed and clubhead speed than those of the control group. Moreover, Pan concluded that the inquiry-based golf teaching that applies virtual simulation helps the learners better master the correct techniques, significantly improving the golf teaching results [12]. Lu Jie used the golf simulator to integrate virtuality and reality in his teaching. He used the methods of experiment, questionnaire, and comparative teaching; the results show that the experimental group do significantly better in general physical training, movement techniques, and swing stability than the control group. Lu concluded that virtual simulation can enhance student engagement and self-motivation, better achieve the teaching objectives, improve the teaching efficiency, and help the students master the key techniques [13]. Jiang Qinxian used 3D video motion capture system to record the golfer's torso forward-inclination angle, side-inclination angle, clubhead speed, club-shoulder angle, and shoulder-hip angle, to check the consistency in movement and clubhead speed between non-ball swing and ball swing. The results show differences in the data of both movement and clubead speed [14]. Han Li and Liu Qi used the motion capture technology in their experimental teaching with the 2012 Volleyball Class at Liaoning Normal University. The experimental group used the real-time man-machine interaction system based on virtual simulation, and the control group were taught in the traditional method; the experiment lasted for 16 teaching hours. The results indicates that the motion capture technology had a significant impact in improving students' technique performance and the teaching quality [15]. Covaci A. et al. developed a virtual basketball free-throw system by using the motion capture technology, which allowed the students to practise free throw without the presence of the instructors [16].

2.3   Virtual Simulation in Dragon Boat Race Teaching

Significance of Teaching Dragon Boat Race in China. Zhao Cibao et al. studied the importance of teaching the dragon boat sport in China from the perspective of cultural dual-core theory. They points out that the teaching content and models are the key issues of training dragon-boat talents in China; they suggested that the teaching content of the dragon boat culture include six sub-cultures (dragon boat spirit, racing culture, educational culture, entertainment culture, material culture, and business culture), which encompasses twenty specific cultural aspects in total [17]. Chen Linhua and Gao Jierong believe that the dragon boat race reflects the traditional Chinese concept of respecting nature and developing in balance; they advocated to design the teaching based on the ecological view of curriculum, arguing that the course should offer teachers and students an open teaching and learning space and an opportunity to get closer to water and nature, and that the course should have a positive influence on students' personal growth and teachers' professional development [18]. The dragon boat race, being regarded as a folk sport that reflects China's socialist cultural values, has been introduced into China's higher education and seen rapid development, which is of certain significance in promoting Chinese folk sports, carrying forward the national spirit and culture, and achieving the rejuvenation of the nation [19].

Challenges in Dragon Boat Race Teaching. Wu Guangjin investigated into the key difficulties in university dragon boat teaching, which include the lack of training venues and facilities, fundings, and experienced trainers [20]. Lin Li points out that the main challenges for teaching the dragon boat sport lie in venues, fundings, experienced trainers, and the balance between students' academic learning hours and dragon boat training hours [21]. Lin Yaohui also found that the external circumstances, venues and facilities, fundings, and qualified trainers are the key aspects that hinder the development of the Dragon Boat Clubs in China's universities [22].

Applying Virtual Simulation to Dragon Boat Race Teaching. The dragon boat race, with its nature as a folk culture and a folk sport, is inevitably constrained by the external circumstances in its development. The information-based teaching methods can help the students better memorize the knowledge about the dragon boat race and enhance their engagement and motivation, offering them a better learning experience than the traditional classroom teaching do (Fig. 1). The virtual simulation dragon boat teaching system has several advantages: first, the virtual simulation teaching can break the restrictions of time and space; second, it can visualize the optimized real-time movement techniques to the students while they are doing the training; third, the rapid development of the technologies will lower the cost of using new media in teaching. In a word, to some extent, the proposed virtual simulation system can solve some of the above discussed main problems facing the dragon boat teaching, such as the lack of venues and facilities, fundings, experienced instructors, and good course design, etc.

Fig. 1. The information-based teaching

3 Basic Ideas of Virtual Simulation Dragon Boat Teaching System

3.1 Design of the System

This system applies virtual simulation to dragon boat race teaching; it integrates such technologies like 3D model, imitation, man-machine interaction, etc. to dynamically simulate and visualize the real-life dragon boat racing scene (Fig. 2). For people of any age groups and professions, such simulation can help them visually get to understand this sport and "how to row" the boat. Furthermore, this system can also add VR gears and motion-sensing devices to offer the students the realistic-looking experiences. Besides, in terms of the specific strength training, this system, for its advantage of learning by imitation, can provide students better learning experiences in not only theorical knowledge, but also actual strength training.

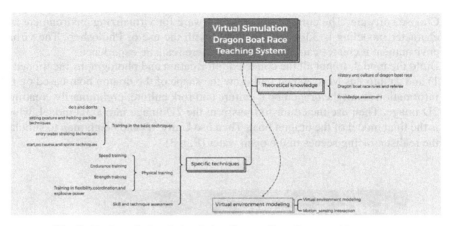

Fig. 2. Design of virtual simulation Dragon Boat Race teaching system

3.2 Benefits of the System

Its main benefits include

1. In terms of the knowledge learning, it can help students better grasp the knowledge of the Chinese folk sports and learn the dragon boat race rules and umpire rules.
2. In terms of the specific techniques, it can help students better master the basic holding-paddles and stroking techniques, understand how to do the general physical training, and see visualized movement structure and characteristics.
3. In terms of the learning outcomes, for the students who have access to the offline dragon boat racing venues and facilities, introducing virtual simulation teaching can enhance their understanding of the key and difficult points of the classes, which can increase their learning efficiency. As for the students who have no access to the offline racing facilities, the web-based teaching system can not only increase their interests, but also allow them to timely check how well they have learned by doing the simulation-based tests after each web-based class.

4   Collecting Information and Building Virtual Simulation Model

Modeling of the dragon boat virtual environment includes race-lane modeling, ambient environment modeling, character modeling, and the rendering of the sky, ripples, and virtual environment. Before building the virtual simulation teaching model, we need to collect information.

1. Collect the dragon boat race venue information. Collect and sort out the information about the dragon boat training and racing venues through the methods of literature review, interviews with experts, and field research, to maximumly re-create a real racing scene to enhance the experience.
2. Get the dragon boat model diagrams. Frist get the model diagrams of the dragon boat, dragon head and tail, then take close shots of them with a high-definition camera for the details, which is important for the modeling and laminating at the later stage.
3. Choose software. The currently popular software for virtualizing environment and character modeling is 3ds Max, combined with the use of Photoshop. The virtual environment it creates can offer students a more realistic experience.
4. Build the model. Imput all the collected information and photographs mentioned in 1) and 2) into 3ds Max, which will draw the shape of the dragon boat based on the information about the dragon boat culture and fork culture, preliminarily creating a 2D image. Then use the editor to transform the 2D image into a 3D model, which is the final model of the dragon boat. Then use Unity 3D and heightmap to simulate the realistic racing scenes in the open water (Fig. 3).

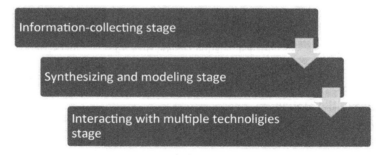

Fig. 3. A flowchart showing the process of virtualizing the Dragon Boat Racing scenes

5   Realization of Virtual Reality Interaction in Dragon Boat Race Teaching

5.1   Realization of the Virtual Effect

Input the prepared racing scene, the dragon boat model, and ambient information into Unity 3D (Fig. 4); at the same time, add the prepared 3D model, materials, and components into the scenes to synthesize multiple files, then adjust the model features like location and situation to model the scenes [23]. This system uses 3D Max and Unity 3D to build the virtual environment for the dragon boat race teaching; it uses the 3D Max rendering function and Unity 3D Shaderlad to further render the virtual environment effect [24, 25].

Fig. 4. Virtual scene of Dragon Boat Race

5.2   Realization of the Immersive Effect

The immersive effect is achieved through watching the images on mobile phones with VR devices (commonly seen in the market like VR glasses) (Figs. 5 and 6). As the basic

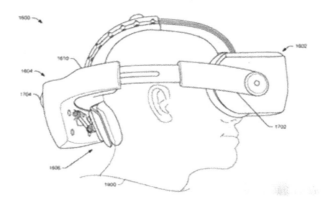

Fig. 5. The VR device

conditions for achieving 3D effect is to split screen and watch them through two separate lenses, so that both eyes can watch the same image to reduce the sense of visual overlap caused by binocular angle overlap. For the same reason, the key to realize VR interaction in the dragon boat race teaching is to display the real-time image from the Unity 3D on PC onto the mobile terminals in the split-screen mode [26].

Fig. 6. A student with VR glass

6 Conclusion

Folk culture is the culture of the ordinary people, which comes from life and shows features of inclusiveness, continuity, and persistence. As an inexhaustible source of folk culture, the dragon boat race, for its casual and lively cultural elements and long history, should be learned and carried forward by the young Chinese, and should be regarded as an embodiment of national spirit and a way of body building. To incorporate immersive VR into dragon boat race teaching is not only important for promoting this cultural tradition, but also, as a good example of the trending teaching method based on VR, useful for the education, transformation, and development of other folk cultures.

References

1. Wei, X.: The origin of the dragon boat race. J. Sport Hist. Cult. (01), 45–46 (2002)
2. wapbaike.baidu.com
3. Chen, P.: Research on the Applications of Virtual and Simulative Technology in Clothing Technology Teaching, p. 65. Hunan Normal University, Changsha (2009)
4. Chen, Y.: Research on Simulation and Virtualization Based Virtual Overlay Network Model, p. 122. Shanghai Jiao Tong University, Shanghai (2008)
5. Wang, W., Hu, J., Liu, H.: Current situation and development of virtual simulation experimental teaching of overseas universities. Res. Explor. Lab. **34**(05), 214–219 (2015)

6. Ibid
7. Shao, R., Zhang, H., Jin, W.: A review of virtual simulation technology in sports field. Zhejiang Sport Sci. **40**(05), 108–112 (2018)
8. Zhao, X.: Modern Education Technology Application in the High School Physical Education and Health Course Teaching Research – A Middle School in Nanchang City as an Example. Nanchang University, Nanchang (2015)
9. He, K.: Research on Application of Virtual Reality in Creating Shot Put Courseware. Wuhan Sports University, Wuhan (2007)
10. Wang, Y.: Wushu Courseware Design Production and Teaching Result is Analyzed. Hohai University, Kaifeng (2011)
11. Song, W.: The Research of the TPI Technology Effect on the Full-Swing of the Golf Beginners. Hebei Normal University, Shijiazhuang (2016)
12. Pan, Y.: A study of the application of the KUDU movement analysis system in golf teaching. Guide Sci. Educ. **10**(3), 39–41 (2010)
13. Lu, J.: Research on the technology of VR based sports teaching practice – taking golf as an example. China Sch. Phys. Educ. (High. Educ.) (8), 36–39 (2016)
14. Jiang, Q.: Difference of kinematic parameters on club head speed between B-Swing and NB-Swing. J. Tianjin Univ. Sport **29**(5), 433–438 (2014)
15. Han, L., Liu, Q.: A study of the volleyball teaching model based on motion-sensing technology. Chin. J. ICT Educ. (4), 77–81 (2015)
16. Covaci, A., Postelnicu, C.-C., Panfir, A.N., Talaba, D.: A virtual reality simulator for basketball free-throw skills development. In: Camarinha-Matos, L.M., Shahamatnia, E., Nunes, G. (eds.) DoCEIS 2012. IFIP AICT, vol. 372, pp. 105–112. Springer, Heidelberg (2012). https://doi.org/10.1007/978-3-642-28255-3_12
17. Zhou, C., Wang, L., Wei, Y., Liu, M.: Research on the content logic and paradigm of Chinese dragon boat sports cultural inheritance in the perspective of cultural dual-core theory. J. Guangzhou Sport Univ. **36**(03), 33–38 (2016)
18. Chen, L., Gao, J.: Research on the establishment of dragon boat curriculum group in China's universities. Sports World Sch. (08), 20–22 (2011)
19. Xu, F.: SWOT analysis and the countermeasures on the implementation of dragon boat race in college and university. J. Huaihai Inst. Technol. (Humanit. Soc. Sci. Ed.) **11**(07), 115–118 (2013
20. Wu, G.: An analysis of the development and status quo of dragon boat sports in Chinese colleges. J. Guangxi Univ. Natl. (Philos. Soc. Sci. Ed.) (03), 98–101 (2007)
21. Lin, L.: Dragon boat problems and development strategies in colleges. Sports Sci. Res. **18**(06), 49–51 (2014)
22. Lin, Y.: An investigation into the challenges and solutions for China's university dragon boat club teaching. Youth Sport (12), 88–89 (2017)
23. Jiang, L., Chen, J., Feng, J., Huang, T.: Research, design and development of VR folk games: case study of dragon boat race. China Educ. Technol. Equip. (04), 51–54 (2019)
24. Mao, J.: Application of college P.E. based on VR, AR and MR. **51**(9), 76–80 (2017)
25. Mao, J.: Application of college swimming teaching based on Kinect motion-sensing technology. Sport Cult. Guide (6), 100–103 (2016)
26. Mao, J.: Development and Application of Swimming Course Teaching System Based on VR. Beijing Sport University Press (2021)

Research on the Promotion of Excellent Sports Culture of the Chinese Nation Based on AR Technology—Take Ansai Waist Drum as an Example

Wenmei Dong[✉] and Tutong Tian

Minzu University of China, Beijing 100081, China
dongwenm@163.com

Abstract. Sports intangible cultural heritage is an important part of China's excellent traditional culture, and it can strengthen the development of sports culture and promote its prosperity. As an art with the characteristics of the Chinese nation and the continuation of the red revolutionary culture, Ansai waist drum has the reputation of "the first drum in the world", "victory waist drum" and "the soul drum of the Chinese nation". The Ansai waist drum was included in the first batch of national intangible cultural heritage in 2006, which made the Ansai waist drum once again enter the public eye. In order to better inherit and develop Ansai waist drum, which is an excellent sports culture of the Chinese nation, this paper aims to explore the application of AR technology to promote the spread of Ansai waist drum. While introducing AR technology and Ansai waist drum, this paper analyzes the role of AR technology in promoting the excellent sports culture of the Chinese nation, summarizes the advantages of AR technology in promoting the spread of Ansai waist drum, and proposes strategies for AR technology to accelerate the promotion of Ansai waist drum. It is hoped that AR technology can better advance the efficient popularization of a series of Chinese excellent sports culture such as Ansai waist drum.

Keywords: Ansai waist drum · AR technology · Cultural promotion · Intangible cultural heritage

1 Introduction to AR Technology and Ansai Waist Drum

1.1 AR Technology

Augmented Reality (AR) is a technology that calculates the position and angle of camera images in real time and adds corresponding images [1]. The goal of this technology is to organically integrate the virtual world and the real world, and then interact in two

Awarded by Research Special from Minzu University of China.

《The Role and Innovation of National Traditional Sports in Forging the Conscious-ness of the Chinese Nationâ€™s Community》(Subject number: 2020MDZL23).

© The Author(s), under exclusive license to Springer Nature Switzerland AG 2022
G. Salvendy and J. Wei (Eds.): HCII 2022, LNCS 13337, pp. 26–34, 2022.
https://doi.org/10.1007/978-3-031-05014-5_3

directions. And it is presented in the field of vision with the help of display technology. Augmented reality is a new and hot research field in recent years, causing numerous technical and theoretical studies. As for the definition of augmented reality, different experts have given different descriptions. After a comprehensive comparison and sorting out, the same conclusion is reached: Augmented reality (AR) can integrate virtual things and information into the real environment, such as graphics, video, sound and even the touch that people can really feel and all of these can be superimposed through specific devices or methods [2], while allowing users to interact with virtual things and information to a certain extent. Then virtual things and information are used as supplements to the real scene to achieve the effect of augmented reality [3].

1.2 Ansai Waist Drum

Ansai waist drum originated in Ansai District (formerly Ansai County), Shaanxi Province. It has a huge influence in Yan'an area and even the entire Shaanxi Province. It is deeply loved by the masses and was selected as the first batch of intangible cultural heritage in 2006. Ansai waist drum is a comprehensive sports activity project, which is a comprehensive presentation form of sports, music and dance [4]. Ansai waist drum has a long history and is characterized by the Loess Plateau. In the process of development and evolution in recent years, Ansai waist drum has integrated modern dance, traditional martial arts, gymnastics, percussion and performance of folk songs. Its content and form are rich and diverse, and it is suitable for a wide range of people. The Ansai waist drum was performed at the founding ceremony of the People's Republic of China in 1949, the 3rd anniversary celebration, the 50th anniversary celebration, the 60th anniversary celebration, the 70th anniversary celebration and other large-scale events. It is an integral part of the culture of the Yellow River Basin. As a folk-art project, it is a mass physical fitness activity. Besides, the Ansai waist drum has the function of strengthening the body, and its movements include twelve elements such as twisting, running, jumping, turning, kicking, dodging, dodging, shaking, straddling, angling, jumping, and celerity. At the same time, the Ansai waist drum is also an integral part of the Yellow River culture, it has unique regional characteristics. Therefore, the cultural charm contained in the Ansai waist drum is even more memorable [5].

According to the "Classic of Mountains and Rivers", the drum was invented during the war between the Yellow Emperor and Chi You, and it was widely used in the war a long time ago. During the Qin Dynasty, the soldiers defending the city regarded the waist drum as a weapon of equal importance to the sword, bow and arrow. At that time, when the enemy was attacked, the soldiers would play drums to remind other soldiers, so that the soldiers quickly entered a state of combat readiness. At the same time, the corresponding information can be transmitted with the help of different drum sounds, thus realizing the confidentiality of military information. When the two armies are fighting fiercely, the sonorous and powerful sound of drums can boost morale and act as a deterrent to the enemy at the same time. The Ansai Waist Drum in the "Yan'an Period" is also known as the "Victory Waist Drum". From October 19, 1935 to March 23, 1948, this was the thirteen years of the Central Committee of the Communist Party of China in Yan'an. At that time, the role and value of Ansai waist drum, a folk- art activity, also changed, and it was mainly used to publicize the party's policies and guidelines.

With the beginning of the National Liberation War in 1946, the Ansai waist drum also was spread to the north and south of the motherland. The military and civilians used the Ansai waist drum to express and celebrate the joy of the victory of the revolution.

There is a saying in Ansai, "Whether it is a ninety-nine-year-old old man or a child who had just learned to walk, everyone knows how to play the drum". Now that people's living standards are improving day by day, and waist drum performances are performed among neighbors or in the same village in their spare time. With the popularity of waist drums in Ansai showing a trend of spreading out, more and more young people join the team of learning and inheritance. Wang Peng from Ansai District Intangible Cultural Heritage Protection Center said, "At present, Ansai District has established an electronic archive of Ansai waist drum successors and an Ansai waist drum training center. Ansai District also holds a school-wide waist drum competition every year. The popularity rate of the waist drum in schools has reached more than 85%. We welcome fans from all over the country and even the world to come to exchange and learn the Ansai waist drum." At present, the physical education classes of Ansai waist drums entering Shaanxi Province's universities, primary and secondary schools are in full swing. There are more and more fans of Ansai waist drums, and foreign friends are also crazy about it, which fully demonstrates the excellent culture of the Chinese nation.

In 1989, the Song Dynasty portrait brick "Ansai Waist Drum" unearthed in Ansai Country.

1.3   The Artistic Core of Ansai Waist Drum

Ansai waist drum is an excellent sport of the Chinese nation. The essence of its performance, "six strengths" respectively refers to: shaking the head with strength, swinging the hammer with ruthlessness, kicking with brute strength, turning with fierce strength, jumping with strength, and the whole body exerted strong energy [6]. With the prosperity and development of the motherland, the Ansai waist drum has long since faded away from the traces of war and sacrificial times, and replaced it with a new form of celebration, physical fitness, entertainment and rehabilitation. Ansai waist drum closely combines sports, literature and art, also it is an important resource of folk sports culture.

The waist drum is an important way to reflect the "spirit" of the Chinese people, and it also represents the spirit of the times of the Chinese nation's perseverance and daring to fight.

Ansai Waist Drum in the 1940s.

1.4   The Analysis of Combination of AR Technology and Ansai Waist Drum

The application of AR technology to promote Ansai waist drum is an opportunity in new era. And it is also a new attempt, breaking the traditional cultural promotion model. By downloading the APP software equipped with AR technology, with AR technology glasses, and loading the resources of Ansai waist drum culture and technology, fans can freely choose different Ansai waist drum performance clips, so that they can understand the Ansai waist drum immersive. The Ansai waist drum culture can also be understood by more people with the help of AR technology. AR technology can decompose the complex movements in the Ansai waist drum. With the help of experiential teaching, learning Ansai waist drum is more interesting.

2   The Role of AR Technology in Promoting the Excellent Sports Culture of the Chinese Nation

2.1   Enhancing the Simulation of the Excellent Sports Culture of the Chinese Nation

Cultural promotion has undergone a major shift with the advent of new technologies. AR technology collects, summarizes and presents body parameters during exercise, and combines with interactive motion capture devices to provide real-time feedback on body movements, analyzes and virtualizes the learning process of sports technology, and helps fans enhance their sports experience. AR technology allows fans to intuitively feel and control the dynamics of sports activities such as Ansai waist drum to gain cognition. What's more, AR technology can help fans shape the learning situation of sports cultural projects, as if they are in a multi-person sport. Especially for enthusiasts, AR technology can make people quickly enter the simulation scene of sports, enhance the sense of reality experience and stimulate interest in learning.

2.2 Promoting the Formation of the Chinese Nation's Excellent Sports Culture Immersion

The research of the famous psychologist Trechler shows that the amount of knowledge acquired by means of sight, hearing and touch is 83%, 11% and 1.5% respectively. From this, it can be seen that there is a high correlation between acquiring teaching knowledge and physical sensory experience, and immersion is mainly shaped by the environment to achieve the resulting experience. AR technology can effectively promote the organic combination of vision, hearing and touch, therefore sports culture fans can quickly immerse themselves in the interaction between virtual and real situations. AR technology can break the constraints of region, space and language, so that enthusiasts can devote themselves to activities. AR technology can break the limitation of sports cultural space in the process of technical teaching of sports activities such as Ansai waist drum, encourage enthusiasts to interact and feedback with virtual learning content, improve participation and control in order to stimulate enthusiasts to improve their professional skills. By shaping the physical education teaching process, creating a practical stage space simulation, and outlining the process of physical education and the space for its special development and changes, the full function of perception can be obtained.

2.3 Stimulating the Independence of Participating in the Excellent Sports Culture of the Chinese Nation

Physical culture programs are also effective collections of multiple motor skills. Learning new skills is a process. Many difficult sports activities will make fans feel intimidated, and VR technology can help fans to evaluate their learning according to their own conditions, and capture actions through a video interface to increase their participation in sports. The combination of enthusiasts' self-learning, theoretical study and sports practice has become an inevitable trend in the reform and development of physical education, which is also the emphasis of AR technology. It can effectively help students develop the habit of playing sports independently, which is also an important goal of sports culture promotion. Integrating VR technology into the excellent sports culture of China can encourage fans to learn and play sports by their own according to their actual conditions, create a variety of virtual sports situations, enrich sports information resources, receive various feedback data in a timely manner, and fully stimulate sports culture enthusiasts to participate into physical activity with high willingness.

3 The Analysis of the Advantages About AR Technology in Accelerating the Spread of Ansai Waist Drum

3.1 AR Technology Reduces the Technical Difficulty of Ansai Waist Drum

Ansai waist drum has a strong sense of rhythm and many essentials of movement. It is an extremely particular sports art in the excellent sports culture of China. It also integrates martial arts, dance, music and percussion. The performance was initially conducted by the lead drummer with the whistle, who later became the conductor of the band. The drummer's suit and props were originally in the style of ancient warriors, but white kerchief shaped like lamb belly and red belt have become the clothing feature of waist drum performers, which has been applied to this day [7]; the drummer's drumstick is about 25 cm, and the red silk is around 40 cm; the red silk that is used to bind waist drum is up to 2 m, the drum body is made of red wood, and the ends are covered with cowhide. The Ansai Waist Drum vividly displays the scenery and land forms of the Loess Plateau through the changing and blurred movements of running, jumping, twisting, turning, kicking, flashing, stomping, straddling, angling, and jumping [6], with the help of the drummer's body to constantly change within a certain area.

It is difficult to learn the movements of the Ansai waist drum, especially in the early stage of learning in which the multiple movements of the Ansai waist drum should be connected. The problem can be effectively solved by AR technology that brings fans into the real situation of Ansai waist drum and slowly decomposes the action with their own learning, largely reducing the difficulty. At the same time, AR technology can help Ansai waist drum to seize the opportunities of the times, take advantage of the current scientific development concepts, and form the characteristics of Ansai waist drum promotion and teaching. The method about adding traditional waist drum to rich multimedia technology can attract more young people to participate in this activity. While protecting and inheriting the pure essentials of the Ansai waist drum, AR technology also combines tradition and modernity which brings traditional culture to enter society and life. AR technology can fully decompose the steps of Ansai waist drum, helping more young enthusiasts to use modern equipment to reduce the difficulty of learning and increase the fun of learning, so that the fans can easily enter the Ansai waist drum situation without going to Ansai, and improve the efficiency of learning.

3.2 AR Technology Fully Demonstrates the Ansai Waist Drum Culture

In the early stage of the large-scale promotion of Ansai Waist Drum, AR technology can effectively make up for the deficiency of Ansai Waist Drum realistic experience, helping more fans to experience the atmosphere of multi-person participation of Ansai Waist Drum without limitations about time and place. Ansai waist drum is an excellent national traditional sports culture in China. It can be seen from its cultural functions, characteristics and value that waist drums can not only improve physical fitness and delight both body and mind, but also preserve and inherit excellent cultures such as the Loess Plateau and the Yellow River. AR technology can selectively design the development mode of Ansai waist drum according to its own actual and local cultural characteristics, and integrate the local features of traditional culture, which is helpful for the development of Ansai waist drum in different regions.

Most of the primary and secondary schools in Yan'an City and Yulin City in northern Shaanxi have already carried out the Ansai waist drum school-based curriculum. In particular, Ansai County began to make the waist drum into the campus activities in the primary and secondary schools in the region as early as 2002, which won the love of many physical education teachers and primary and secondary school students. The project has become the characteristic and shining point of school sports, and it has fully certified the feasibility of integrating Ansai waist drum into the school sports curriculum. If AR technology can be fully applied in the process of introducing Ansai waist drums into the campus, students can use AR technology to understand the charm of Ansai waist drums, and make primary and secondary school students immersive. On the basis of fully understanding the excellent Chinese culture and revolutionary red culture of the Ansai waist drum, people first like the Ansai waist drum, and at the same time use the regional sports and cultural resources to give full play to the teaching and educating people, cultural education, sports fitness and game entertainment of school sports, which is of great practical significance. In addition, with the rich and colorful AR resources of Ansai waist drum, more people can contact with Ansai waist drum, which is conducive to the popularization and socialization of Ansai waist drum, and can promote the spread of Ansai waist drum culture.

4   The Strategy of AR Technology to Promote the Spread of Ansai Waist Drum

4.1   AR Technology Improves the Learning Strategy of Ansai Waist Drum

AR technology can complete the multi-dimensional presentation of the Ansai waist drum integrating martial arts, dance, folk songs and percussion, making it easier for fans to learn the essentials of the original Ansai waist drum. Costume beauty, song beauty, health beauty and cultural beauty are integrated and presented to fans with the help of AR technology. At the same time, the development of Ansai waist drum AR learning resources can realize the improvement of Ansai waist drum aesthetic education in daily life and learning. Modern AR technology can improve the influence of aesthetic education, and enable fans to correctly master the coherent movements of Ansai waist drum, advance cultural connotation, and master the essentials of Ansai waist drum movements. Relying on AR technology can help fans to easily master their own Ansai waist drum learning status, and learn other companions' perception of Ansai waist drum, as to stimulate their learning motivation through the companion effect. The effective combination of AR technology and the spread of Ansai waist drums achieve the goals of making a professional skill popularized and life-like, and encouraging more enthusiasts to participate in the learning of Ansai waist drums in their spare time.

AR technology integrates the small waistband, large waistband, waist wrapping over the crotch, jumping legs over the block, kneeling and turning around, worshiping Guanyin (a kind of action in Ansai waist drum performance), pairing drums, harvesting steps, two-person crossing, etc., making it easier for fans to comprehend the essentials of the action [8]. After learning the basic technology, one person can carry out classification and arrangement, including transformation of the formation of the queue, so that one person can also complete the training of queue and formation during the learning process, and can participate in the learning of Ansai waist drum at any time with the help of AR technology in the team [9]. Basic skills are an essential part for Ansai waist drums. Only by laying a solid foundation, can we carry out the later combined rehearsal. Then, AR technology can carry out targeted technical training, adjust the training content according to the individual differences of the learners, and help adjust the learners' mentality. Then, learners will realize that learning the Ansai waist drum is a better method to inherit the national intangible cultural heritage and promote the excellent sports culture of the Chinese nation.

4.2 AR Technology Advances the Communication Strategy of Ansai Waist Drum Culture

Ansai waist drum is a treasure of traditional Chinese culture, and the focus of its inheritance lies in people. Relying on AR technology to learn the Ansai waist drum, not only can you learn the technical essentials, but also learn the humanistic feelings and cultural essence integrated in the Ansai waist drum, so that the beauty of the Chinese nation contained in Ansai waist drum can be presented, and the cultural self-confidence can be fully reflected. People learn the Ansai waist drum, and they love the Chinese nation and inherited Chinese culture. The development of Ansai waist drum courses through AR technology can allow more and more enthusiasts to understand the Ansai waist drum culture and appreciate the spiritual charm of Ansai waist drums. We will strengthen cultural self-confidence and carry forward the national spirit through modern technology; make independent innovation in inheritance, make the Ansai waist drum more vigorous, push the Ansai waist drum to more regions, develop and inherit the excellent sports culture of the Chinese nation, in order to enhance the culture Make new offerings with confidence.

It is recommended to use AR technology to efficiently carry out the propaganda work of Ansai waist drum culture, and effectively combine virtual and reality. Ansai waist drum carries the unique spiritual connotation of the Shaanxi-Gansu-Ningxia border region, and the confidence and spirit contained in Ansai waist drum culture help people to overcome their many difficulties, also the power of this spirit is still growing. With the help of Ansai waist drum, more people can be inspired. The large-scale promotion of Ansai waist drums can be implemented efficiently thanks to the strengthening of cultural assistance and cultural facilities in our country. AR technology will definitely play a more prominent role in the promotion of traditional culture, which will improve cultural self-confidence and help local places find special fulcrums, so that more people can deeply understand the cultural connotation of Ansai waist drum. The Ansai waist drum has a long history and the profound humanistic charm of the Chinese nation. In the promotion, the "intangible cultural heritage" education is combined to arouse the fans' concept of inheritance, and at the same time, let the fans feel the unique cultural spirit substance of the Ansai waist drum.

5 Conclusion

The Ansai waist drum has nearly 2,000 years of cultural accumulation and artistic precipitation, also contains the profound excellent culture of the Chinese nation. Ansai waist drum has gradually grasped public attention, and more and more fans have participated in the inheritance of Ansai waist drum. AR technology can meet the needs of cultural inheritance and development in the new era, and promote the scientific promotion of Ansai waist drum in the process of organic integration with Ansai waist drum It is expected that AR technology will spread the Ansai waist drum culture widely, promote the diversified development of sports and cultural undertakings while enhancing the people's physique, improve the people's awareness of cultural heritage, let the Ansai waist drum culture continue to be inherited and developed, so that this sonorous and powerful drum sounded throughout the land of China.

References

1. Lizhi, W.X.: Research on the application points of AR technology. Sci. Technol. Vis. (32), 98–100 (2021)
2. Guo, Z.: Research on the communication of traditional Chinese culture based on VR/AR technology. Comp. Study Cult. Innov. **5**(32), 50–53 (2021)
3. Wang, Y., Yang, H., Tang, W., Hu, X.: The application of virtual reality and augmented reality technology in anesthesiology teaching. China Med. Educ. Technol. **35**(06), 673–676+680 (2021)
4. Zhang, Y., Du, C.: Research on the educational inheritance and development of Ansai waist drum. Youth Shanxi (07), 30–31 (2020)
5. Zhao, D.: Research on the development prospect of Ansai waist drum from the perspective of intangible cultural heritage protection. J. Shaanxi Univ. Sci. Technol. (Nat. Sci. Ed.) **29**(03), 183–186 (2011)
6. Sun, S.: A Study on the Inheritance Mode and Changes of Ansai Waist Drum. Beijing Sports University (2017)
7. Du, C., Li, H.: Feasibility analysis of the integration of Ansai waist drum into the characteristic physical education courses in Shaanxi colleges and universities. J. Yan'an Univ. (Nat. Sci. Ed.) **34**(04), 100–104 (2015)
8. Yang, C., Yang, Z.: On the historical origin and development status of Ansai waist drum. J. Yan'an Univ. (Soc. Sci. Ed.) **36**(05), 114–117 (2014)
9. Zhao, D.: The role of Ansai waist drum in national fitness. Sports Sci. Technol. Lit. Bull. (04), 79–80 (2008)

Evaluating Intertwined Effects of Emoji and Message Framing to Vaccine Communication Strategy

Tingyi S. Lin(iD) and Yue Luo(✉) (iD)

Department of Design, National Taiwan University of Science and Technology, No. 43, Keelung Road, Sec. 4, Da'an Distict, Taipei City 10607, Taiwan
{tingyi,d10810802}@mail.ntust.edu.tw

Abstract. Under the circumstance of continuous variation of COVID-19 virus, verified the temporariness of the vaccines made by various countries. One cannot expect permanent protection by accepting only one dose of vaccine. In order to prepare and respond to the pandemic, many countries are applying different strategies to increase vaccination rates. The WHO appeals to the world to take the vaccine booster shot for community immunity. Relevant authorities then have to provide and spread visual health messages on the booster shot to keep the public informed. This study examine how unofficial organizations can guide and persuade people to adopt relevant health actions more effectively (such as continuous vaccination) by introducing emoji with different emotional valences in different message framing. An online experiment adopted a 2 (emoji: positive versus negative) × 2 (message framing: gain framing versus loss framing) design to investigate the effects of contrary emoji on people's self-efficacy to continuously take the booster shot. In total of 240 university students were recruited to participate in this study. Within two types of message framing, the experiment simulated 4 pieces of health messages on the COVID-19 booster shot released by an unofficial organization, together with emoji of two emotional valences. The results showed that health messages with negative emoji result in stronger self-efficacy to user. Moreover, there is an interaction effect between emoji and message framing on self-efficacy. This study is intended to provide meaningful insights for health communicators, visual designers and health practitioners concerned.

Keywords: Emoji · Message framing · Emotional valence · Self-efficacy · Health communication

1 Introduction

The COVID-19 pandemic caused by the novel coronavirus outbreak is affecting the public's health and livelihood. The widespread variation cases all over the world result in successive pandemic situations. It is out of question that the public health communication is confronting tremendous challenge. In order to confront the pandemic, nations worldwide actively research and develop vaccines, and use various strategies to increase vaccination rate. However, scientific research and clinical trials prove that the pandemic vaccine effectiveness has its time limit. One cannot count on the protection of one dose forever. Hence, the WHO appeals for people of all nations to take the booster shot for herd immunity. During analogous public health crises, it is extremely important that departments concerned provide and communicate relevant information on the booster shot to update the public, so that they can determine better decisions for their health's sake (Cooper and Roter 2000; Ho et al. 2013; Ye et al. 2021). Being helpful to largely prevent and decrease morbidity and mortality of diseases, vaccination has always been an important achievement in public health (CDC 1999). However, achieving a high vaccination coverage level is a critical issue and an urgent thing to do. An investigation by Pew Research Center (2020) shows that even though COVID-19 vaccines are available, 49% of people will not or may not take them. Thus, designing effective vaccination messages for communication to influence and persuade the preference of the public can affect positive change in preventing COVID-19.

Making use of visual strategies to ameliorate the quality of health communication can reduce messages imbalance caused by message spread barriers during public health crisis (King and Lazard 2020). This also indicates that it is worthy to delve into the interaction factors and connection between visual elements and health message communication after they are intertwined together. Emoji, which is a visual language expressing emotion or supplementing text content in digital messages, has become very popular in the world and has been used in numerous mobile terminals and digital platforms (Lu et al. 2016; Smailović et al. 2015). Scholars gradually realize that using emoji of different emotional valences can effectively stimulate users' behaviors (Das et al. 2019), such as accessing restaurants' cleanliness (Ray and Merle 2020), recognizing and predicting mental issues (Marengo et al. 2017), and increasing consumption intentions (Das et al. 2019). Existing investigations, as well as our previous study, have proved that health messages with emoji can strengthen people's wills to adopt prevention action, especially when the messages are released by unofficial organizations. In other words, besides messages released by official authorities, messages released by unofficial organizations have become the main source from which people obtain health advice. Furthermore, besides the visual stimulation, people will also have different responses and different preferences to the ways in which messages are expressed when they are making decisions on health. Years of research have concluded that when emphasizing benefit or risks, health messages can have important and different influences on people's wills and preferences to adopt health behaviors (Tversky and Kahneman 1985; Rothman et al. 1999; Yu et al. 2010). Although concrete advice on how and when to use visual measures to deliver scientific risks and health messages is needed badly, not many strongly persuasive ones exist. In addition, some individual differences that may affect message reception and the characteristics of health behaviors themselves have not been fully explored (Rimal et al. 2011), for instance, interior difference (including self-efficacy and risk perception), exterior environments and culture, and contextual features etc. This study therefore aims to discuss the persuasion that different emoji possess when messages are used to promote COVID-19 vaccine booster shots. This effort is to figure out how people's self-efficacy on accepting COVID-19 vaccine booster shot are impacted by different emoji and different message framing so as to examine emoji's effectiveness. Three research questions raised in this study: (1) whether embedding positive and negative emoji in health messages will generate different persuasion to people's self-efficacy to take the COVID-19 vaccine booster shot? (2) whether messages in a gain framing and a loss framing will have different persuasion to people's self-efficacy to take the booster shot? (3) whether emoji's emotional valences will intertwine with message framing and impact on people's self-efficacy to take the booster shot? This study hopes to provide helpful insights for health communicators, visual designers and relevant health practitioners.

In Fig. 1, the conceptual and theoretical model were explained which guide the research motivation of this study.

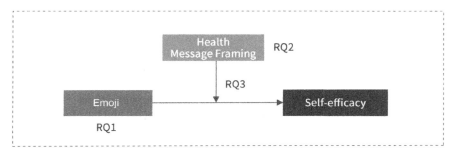

Fig. 1. Conceptual overview and framework of the study

2   Theoretical Background and Literature Review

2.1   Emoji and Emotional Valence

Along with the exponential growth of communication through social networking sites and software, in the field of digital message, the role of emoji had translated from the initial expression of basic emotions to the present, and the usage of them kept in a more common manner compared to nonverbal cues as well as gestures in face-to-face interaction (Gawne and McCulloch 2019; Lo 2008). Users relied more on digital communication during the epidemic, emoji had extraordinarily replaced the usage of facial expressions in non-face-to-face communication. In addition, most researches relevant to emoji came up with emotional valence of emoji, and their emotional mechanism might be exceedingly equivalent to the traditional facial emotional ex-pression (Kaye et al. 2017), and supported that emoji proved a concept of emotional signals (Gesselman et al. 2019). Moreover, emoji with different emotions had a large opportunity to have various effects on users' attitude and behavior (Kaye et al. 2021). Generally, when receiving messages, the emotional response of users in an automatic manner tend to occur, which could be made use of as a directional mechanism to guide message processing (Slovic et al. 2005; Zajonc 1980). Kralj Novak et al. (2015) created an Emoji Sentiment Ranking containing 751 emoji and and provided algorithms and models for emoji-based emotion analysis (demonstrated in http://kt.ijs.si/data/Emoji_sentiment_ranking/ for details).

Accordingly, the purpose of these studies was conducted so that the emotional valence of emoji could be used more accurately in messages.

Kaye et al. (2021) drew a conclusion that compared with words with neutral, words with emotional have more processing advantages, and individuals can expect emoji to possess the same processing advantages, and the processing speed of message recipients towards facial emoji proves strikingly faster than that of written characters. Consequently, the interaction between emoji and the accompanying text, as well as the pattern of reading had a theoretical impact on the common's psychological feelings and subsequent behaviors. Moreover, when reading the message, readers never failed to interpret emoji and integrate it into the sentence connotation. Emoji, as an exceedingly effective tool to evaluating emotions, could be selected as part of users' specific and informed decisions (Jaeger et al. 2018). In light of the research of Spinelli et al. (2015), the main characteristics of the emotional field kept valence (positive/negative) as well as arousal (active/passive). Thus, the role of emoji in health messages could be discussed from its positive as well as negative. Lo (2008) demonstrated an instant messaging software emotional text conversations towards a user, and these conversations showed either presented in plain text or followed by some positive or negative emotions. The receivers evaluated the emotion, attitude and attention of these dialogues, and they found that the addition of emoticons affected people's perception, strengthened the emotional intention of all messages, and made them tend to the value of emoticons. Pinto et al. (2020) concluded that generally, emoji expressing positive emotions (e.g., 😄 and 😊) could promote consumers' confidence in consumption and purchase intention, while negative emoji (e.g., 😣) could bring a passive correlation. Ray and Merle (2020) clung to the perspective that the smiling emoji (🙂) could make the public feel that the restaurant remained hygienic and willing to grab a bite, however, emoji expressing disgusting (🤢) could boost people's motivation to stay away from the restaurant. Our previous studies detected that those emoji relevant to negative or disease (e.g., 😷 and 🤮) could enhance people's intention to adopt preventive behavior. In particular, it is used in health messages issued by unofficial institutions, which had strengthened the perceived risk and fear. Furthermore, these researches all drew a conclusion that emoji could have an impact on the folk's behaviors and attitude. However, in the field of health communication, the role of emoji could under no circumstance proved to be analyzed in a full manner. In addition, compared with other health-related prevention behaviors, the difference in the vaccination mainly was to have some possibilities to bring side effects as well as risks, resulting in some persons unwilling to go on vaccination (Ye et al. 2021). Therefore, the research will make a further experiment in order to test whether the health information introduced into emoji could work in public's self-efficacy, which will make an investigation from two emotions: positive and negative.

2.2 Health Message and Message Framing

Under the current background of epidemic and infodemic, the issues faced by health communication proves no longer the deficiency of information transmission or the amount of information collected, but it is in a correct as well as effective manner that whether the heath information can be sorted, designed and presented to the common. The research demonstrates that health messages had clues relevant to action suggestions, including health knowledge, risk expression, preventive behavior suggestions and so on (Chang 2015; Kaye et al. 2017). By using different types of message framing, health communication organizations can effectively guide and persuade people to take health behaviors (such as vaccination). Those health messages providing the framework arguments about gain or loss had various impact on behavioral decisions (Rothman et al. 1999). Messages in the gain framing, generally, could trigger preventive health behavior in a more effective manner, which proved to keep health and minimize the risk of health issues. Additionally, messages in the loss framing, in a more effective manner, could promote the detection behavior, involving the risk of discovering health issues (Tversky and Kahneman 1981). People deal with health message not completely rationally. It illustrated that only making research on the source of information or the confidence from the common could under no circumstances in an accurate manner measure the persuasion of health message, and the decision-making preference towards information by private individuals could be affected by the expression as well as presentation of information content (Ye et al. 2021). In light of the Framing Effect Theory, the presentation of health information could have an impact on individual decision-making preference, resulting in the increasing or decreasing of behavior (Plous 1993). Therefore, mastering the interactive process between message and receiver and designing effective messages to affect people's decision-making process can produce positive effects when communicating during the public health crisis. Some researches had poured a good supply of energy into making research on whether one framework could be more effective than another. The initial research on vaccination advocacy revealed the framework of gain could be more effective (Rothman et al. 1993). Other researchers had been convinced that the messages in the loss framing might be more effective due to vaccination might be assumed risky or side effects (such as, Abhyankar et al. 2008). Recently, some studies have suggested factors that moderate the effectiveness of the message framing. A meta-analysis (O'Keefe and Nan 2012) claimed that there existed no significant difference in vaccine persuasion between the two frameworks, but they stressed the need to further determine whether there remained regulatory factors interacting with them. Moreover, if the influence of specific moderator variables cannot be determined, the size of framing effect might be masked (Covey 2014). Although researchers above have carried out various discussions on the message framing and come up with the need for the introduction of moderator factors, there has remained exceedingly scarce studies about the message framing cross over the visual factors.

In order to shape private individuals' decision-making that frameworks and visual aids or images might work together (Garcia-Retamero and Cokely 2011; Seo et al. 2013). A review of past studies proved a conclusion that in the health messages, the usage of various visual effects, including graphics/illustrations (Houts et al. 2006), data visualization (Ancker et al. 2006) and photographs (Gibson 2003), could have some impact on the result of message receivers' interest towards those topics relevant to health. The role of these various visual effects was found visual action cues in health messages. In addition, based on the Health Belief Model Theory, the existence of action cues was stressed as an extraordinarily indispensable behavior trigger (Rosenstock 1974; Rosenstock et al. 1988). However, during the novel coronavirus pneumonia mutation, we need to explore what kind of health message can provide the most effective clues, whether in visual or textual language. Although those previous studies have revealed the effects of health messages towards the common' behaviors, this paper hopes to make an exploration on whether emoji and message framing can form more effective action clues and encourage more confidence in continued vaccination, which proves conducive to fill the gap in this aspect of visual health communication.

2.3 Self-efficacy and Behavioral Intention

In addition to action cues, Health Belief Model (HBM), Theory of Planned Behavior (TPB) and Protection Motivation Theory (PMT), etc., considered self-efficacy as an indispensable factor to guide behaviors (Glanz et al. 2008; Ajzen 1991; Floyd et al. 2000). The self-efficacy, as an approach to ameliorating private individuals' healthy living ability (Koelen and Lindström 2005; Mackintosh 1995), might have an impact on the common's cognition, decision and choice towards activities, and even further influenced their efforts towards healthy behaviors (Bandura 1977, 1996; Gözüm and Aksayan 1999; Sheeran et al. 2016). There remain some current researches pointing that via boosting their sense of self-efficacy, the common's ability to address health problems can be enhanced. For instance, the meta-analysis of health messages by Witte and Allen (2000) demonstrated that the message content resulted in the message receiver's self-efficacy, which could prove conducive to the behavior intention. Compared with in plain text, prevention messages in vivid schema could create a more significant sense of self-efficacy (Chang 2013), and in terms of boosting self-efficacy, those smoking cessation messages that could cause human beings' emotion and wake-up response proved more effective as well (Helme et al. 2007). As a result, in the health messages with behavior suggestions or preventive knowledge, the common may tend to obtain a sense of self-efficacy.

Multitudes of news media claimed that the COVID-19 vaccine side effects, which resulting in vaccination considered as a risky behavior. Those suspected cases relevant to vaccination or deaths caused by negative reports all can bring a social distrust towards the vaccine to the common. In the empirical researches relevant to the health issues, considerable attention was poured into the impact of self-efficacy towards behavioral intention, and it was between self-efficacy as well as behavioral intention that it was drawn a conclusion that there remained a positive relationship. For instance, the message of preventing heart disease could enhance individuals' self-efficacy and then trigger them to take preventive actions (Maibach et al. 1991), and the message of promoting influenza vaccine could ameliorate self-efficacy to promote vaccination as well (Prati et al. 2012). Other studies having demonstrated that once the behavior affected by self-efficacy has health risks, self-efficacy had a negative impact on behavior intention (O'Connor and White 2010). The research makes an exploration on the comon's self-efficacy of COVID-19 "booster shot" vaccine.

3 Materials and Methods

This study adopted a 2×2 between-subject experiment design with emoji (positive versus negative) being the independent variable, message framing (gain framing versus loss framing) being the moderate variable and the self-efficacy to accept the booster shot being the dependent variable. We mainly discussed the role played by the emotional valence of emoji in the abovementioned self-efficacy and the moderation effect of the message framing. Moreover, we also examined an interaction effect.

3.1 Study Design and Participants

An online experiment was implemented in this study, following a 2 (emoji: positive versus negative) $\times$ 2 (message framing: gain framing versus loss framing) design. Young participants who had accepted at least one dose of COVID-19 vaccine were recruited by the online group of WJX https://www.wjx.cn/) (similar to Amazon's Mechanical Turk and Prolific) through purposive sampling. Participants were invited to visit a website and sign an informed consent. Our previous study shows that health messages with emoji strengthen people's will to adopt preventive action, especially when they are released by unofficial organizations. Thus, this study continues to explore how unofficial organizations introduce emoji of different emotional valences in different message framing to more effectively guide and persuade people to accept the vaccine booster shot. On the experiment website, we introduced a fictitious unofficial organization named Vaccine Health Manager, which devotes itself to health and medical messages communication, especially the recent information about COVID-19 vaccine. Once the participants agreed to take part in the experiment, they would be randomly assigned into one of four scenarios. Firstly, they were asked to report the COVID-19 vaccine they had known. Secondly, they were shown a health message about promoting to take a COVID-19 vaccine booster shot, which was manipulated in a gain framing or a loss framing. In addition, the emotional valence of emoji used in the message were also manipulated (positive or negative). After reading the message, the self-efficacy of taking the booster shot were tested by the 7-level Likert scale. Finally, Participants' demographic information were collected, including age, gender and education background.

220 youth from Hong Kong, Macao and Taiwan consisted of the final experimental samples, including 85 males and 135 females. They, who were between 18 and 45 years old ($M = 27.42$, $SD = 6.32$), were all traditional Chinese users with an education background of high school or above. All of them had practical experiences reading posts on Facebook in the past.

3.2 Stimuli and Measurement

In order to better simulate the scenario of communicating messages on accepting the vaccine, the experimental stimulant was designed as a facebook post. The post was written in traditional Chinese with introduction to COVID-19 vaccine booster shots and advice on vaccine acceptation. Different emotional emoji were used in the message in different message framing. According to the emotional value of Emoji Sentiment Ranking created by Kralj Novak et al. (2015), 😊 and 😆 were chosen as representatives of positive emoji, and 😕 and 😟 as negative emoji, placed in the middle and the end of the post. Furthermore, in accordance to the studies of Rothman and Salovey (1997), and Tversky and Kahneman (1981), messages in a gaining framing emphasize the benefit and positive effect of the booster shot, while those in a loss framing highlight the disadvantage of not taking the booster shot. Messages in four different scenarios were shown—using positive emoji in gaining framing, using negative emoji in loss framing, using negative emoji in gaining framing and using positive emoji in loss framing.

Participants were randomly assigned to one of the four scenarios. Before testing relevant variables, a manipulation test was performed to examine the efficiency and reliability of the message stimulant. There were two dimensions of the manipulation test. First, we tested whether participants recognized the emotional valence of emoji. Second, we tested, between positive and negative expressions, as which expression participants regarded the message. For instance, we listed questions such as: do you think the message uses positive emoji? Do you think the message emphasizes the benefit of accepting the vaccine booster shot? In addition, the self-efficacy measurement was adapted from the study of Stout et al. (2020), containing options such as "I'm confident with the COVID-19 vaccine booster shot, even though it is expensive". Within 4 items, the higher score, the stronger self-efficacy of vaccination. In the end, participants reported demographical variables (Table 1).

Table 1. The reliability of the measurement.

Construct	Items	Cronbach's alpha
Self-efficacy (Stout et al. 2020)	I'm confident with the COVID-19 vaccine Boost shot, even though: • It is expensive; • It may generate some pain; • It may cause allergies or side effects; • It needs me to make tedious appointment and to queue up	0.817

4 Results

To test the research questions, three analyses were conducted. Firstly, we analyzed the manipulation check to observe whether participants perceived the manipulated variables. The main effects of emoji and the moderation effects of message framing were second examined, after which the interaction effect between emoji and message framing was inspected. All analyses were performed using analyses of variance (ANOVAs).

4.1 Manipulation Checks

Manipulation checks were conducted on emotional valence of emoji (positive versus negative) and message framing (gain framing versus loss framing) using a series of Independent Sample t-tests. The results showed that the message with positive emoji was perceived to focus more on expressing positive valence related to miniature ($M = 4.78$, $SD = 1.752$) by participants than the message with negative emoji ($M = 2.32$, $SD = 1.755$, $p = 0.00$). Moreover, participants in the gain-framed message condition ($M = 4.58$, $SD = 1.582$) were more likely to perceive the message as describing a positive content related to vaccination than were those in the loss-framed message condition ($M = 5.41$, $SD = 1.388$, $p = 0.00$). Therefore, both manipulations were successful.

4.2 Main Effects and Interaction Effects

We studied the influence on self-efficacy to accept the booster shot of message receivers, by the emotional valence of emoji (Table 2). The results indicated that emoji in vaccine promotion messages has a statistically main effect on self-efficacy (F (1, 216) = 8.428, $p = 0.004$). Specifically, in terms of the emotional valence of emoji, compared with messages with positive emoji ($M = 4.166$, $SD = 0.131$), messages with negative emoji ($M = 4.707$, $SD = 0.132$) are more likely to increase self-efficacy of participants to accept the booster shot. This result answered the RQ1. Negative emoji can increase people's self-efficacy to accept vaccination. On the other hand, the message framing has no significant main effect on self-efficacy (F (1, 216) = 0.054, $p = 0.816$). In other words, be it gain-framed vaccine messages or loss-framed ones, they cause no difference on people's self-efficacy, which answered RQ2. The interaction effect between the emotional valence of emoji and message framing was examined and a significant interaction effect (F (1, 216) = 5.166, $p = 0.024$) on self-efficacy was observed (see Fig. 2). Receiving gain-framed messages, people sensed stronger self-efficacy when they saw negative emoji ($M = 4.940$, $SD = 0.173$) than positive emoji ($M = 3.975$, $SD = 0.192$). However, positive and negative emoji exert no significantly different influence ($Mpositive = 4.356$, $Mnegative = 4.473$) in loss-framed messages. That is to say, the emotional valence of emoji in vaccine health messages is moderated by message framing and the emoji effect only exists in gain-framed messages, which answered RQ3 positively.

Table 2. Means and standard deviation related to research questions 1–3.

	Source	DF	MS	F	p	η2
Self-efficacy	Emoji	1	15.897	8.428	0.004*	0.038
	Message framing	1	0.102	0.054	0.816	0.000
	Emoji × Message framing	1	9.745	5.166	0.024*	0.023

*p(significance) < 0.05, meaning significant difference observed

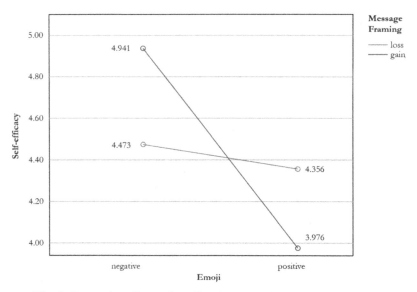

Fig. 2. Interaction effects of emoji and message framing on self-efficacy.

To sum up, it is valid to use emoji in vaccine promotion messages to affect the self-efficacy and the vaccination intention of message receivers, especially negative emoji.

5 Discussion and Conclusion

This study is one of the few research projects that investigate the effect of the emotional valence of emoji and message framing on promoting COVID-19 booster shots in vaccine messages. To be specific, using negative emoji in vaccine promotion messages can generate higher self-efficacy of message receivers than positive emoji. Also, using negative emoji in gain-framed messages can better increase people's self-efficacy than in loss-framed messages.

The core argument of this study is that negative emoji used in health messages can better promote people's self-efficacy than positive emoji, which carries on our previous study results and echoes the perspectives of Lo (2008) and Jaeger et al. (2018). We believe that it is consistent with the possibility of emoji affecting people's behavior. Emoji can guide the perception and behavior intention of receivers onto its valence. Because negative emoji can evoke the risk perception and fear index of the public and drive them to adopt low risk action (Ray and Merle 2020). Learning from the Prospect Theory, although the public regard vaccination as an action that contains certain risks, they prefer to adopt actions that contain less risks (Ye et al. 2021; Weimer and Vining 2017). The results of this study provide a new insight for using emoji to promote health communication. We can use emoji to stimulate people's self-efficacy and guide them to adopt health behavior.

Another result is also revealed by this study. There is no significant difference between gain framing and loss framing in promoting vaccination self-efficacy, which is consistent with the research results of O'Keefe and Nan (2012). However, we discover that the message framing can moderate emoji's effect on self-efficacy. Using negative emoji in health messages can help to establish the public's self-efficacy, which is extremely significant in the gain framing. But when a health message is written in a loss framing, the emotional valence of emoji has no significant effect on self-efficacy. This moderation effect verifies the viewpoints of Garcia-Retamero and Cokely (2011), as well as those of Seo et al. (2013): framing and visual images work together to shape people's sense of efficacy in the context of health behaviors. Hence, to better shape the self-efficacy, with the effect of negative emoji, health messages expressed in a gain framing contain the most persuasiveness.

This article introduces different emotional valences of emoji in health messages expressed in different framing to discuss the influence on self-efficacy of the public. It not only adds academic theories to the role of emoji in health communication but also provides practical reference of health message design and communication to concerned practitioners such as health communicators and visual designers. The message framing discovered by this study may not be the only moderated mediation factor. Future studies may dig in moderation and mediation variables that contain higher correlations. Although there is more work to be done in visual health communication, this study provides phrased advice to emoji use in health communication and plays a certain role in vaccination campaign in the pandemic background.

References

Abhyankar, P., O'connor, D.B., Lawton, R.: The role of message framing in promoting MMR vaccination: evidence of a loss-frame advantage. Psychol. Health Med. **13**(1), 1–16 (2008)

Ajzen, I.: The theory of planned behavior. Organ. Behav. Hum. Decis. Process. **50**(2), 179–211 (1991)

Ancker, J.S., Senathirajah, Y., Kukafka, R., Starren, J.B.: Design features of graphs in health risk communication: a systematic review. J. Am. Med. Inform. Assoc. **13**(6), 608–618 (2006)

Bai, Q., Dan, Q., Mu, Z., Yang, M.: A systematic review of emoji: current research and future perspectives. Front. Psychol. **10**, 2221 (2019)

Bandura, A.: Self-efficacy: toward a unifying theory of behavioral change. Psychol. Rev. **84**(2), 191 (1977)

Centers for Disease Control and Prevention (CDC): Impact of vaccines universally recommended for children–United States, 1990–1998. MMWR Morb. Mortal. Wkly. Rep. **48**(12), 243–248 (1999)

Chang, C.: Seeing is believing: the direct and contingent influence of pictures in health promotion advertising. Health Commun. **28**(8), 822–834 (2013)

Chang, C.: Motivated processing: how people perceive news covering novel or contradictory health research findings. Sci. Commun. **37**(5), 602–634 (2015)

Cooper, C.P., Roter, D.L.: "If it bleeds it leads"? Attributes of TV health news stories that drive viewer attention. Publ. Health Rep. **115**(4), 331 (2000)

Covey, J.: The role of dispositional factors in moderating message framing effects. Health Psychol. **33**(1), 52 (2014)

Das, G., Wiener, H.J., Kareklas, I.: To emoji or not to emoji? Examining the influence of emoji on consumer reactions to advertising. J. Bus. Res. **96**, 147–156 (2019)

Floyd, D.L., Prentice-Dunn, S., Rogers, R.W.: A meta-analysis of research on protection motivation theory. J. Appl. Soc. Psychol. **30**(2), 407–429 (2000)

Garcia-Retamero, R., Cokely, E.T.: Effective communication of risks to young adults: using message framing and visual aids to increase condom use and STD screening. J. Exp. Psychol. Appl. **17**(3), 270 (2011)

Gawne, L., McCulloch, G.: Emoji as digital gestures. Lang. Internet **17**(2) (2019)

Gesselman, A.N., Ta, V.P., Garcia, J.R.: Worth a thousand interpersonal words: emoji as affective signals for relationship-oriented digital communication. PloS ONE **14**(8), e0221297 (2019)

Gibson, R.: Effects of photography on issue perception. In: Communication and Emotion, pp. 331–354. Routledge, London (2003)

Glanz, K., Rimer, B.K., Viswanath, K. (eds.): Health Behavior and Health Education: Theory, Research, and Practice. Wiley, New York (2008)

Gözüm, S., Aksayan, S.: The reliability and validity of Turkish form of the self-efficacy scale. J. Anatolia Nurs. Health Sci. **2**(1), 21–32 (1999)

Helme, D.W., Donohew, R.L., Baier, M., Zittleman, L.: A classroom-administered simulation of a television campaign on adolescent smoking: testing an activation model of information exposure. J. Health Commun. **12**(4), 399–415 (2007)

Ho, S.S., Peh, X., Soh, V.W.: The cognitive mediation model: factors influencing public knowledge of the H1N1 pandemic and intention to take precautionary behaviors. J. Health Commun. **18**(7), 773–794 (2013)

Houts, P.S., Doak, C.C., Doak, L.G., Loscalzo, M.J.: The role of pictures in improving health communication: a review of research on attention, comprehension, recall, and adherence. Patient Educ. Couns. **61**(2), 173–190 (2006)

Jaeger, S.R., Lee, S.M., Kim, K.O., Chheang, S.L., Roigard, C.M., Ares, G.: CATA and RATA questions for product-focused emotion research: five case studies using emoji questionnaires. Food Qual. Prefer. **68**, 342–348 (2018)

Kaye, L.K., et al.: How emotional are emoji?: Exploring the effect of emotional valence on the processing of emoji stimuli. Comput. Hum. Behav. **116**, 106648 (2021)

Kaye, S.A., White, M.J., Lewis, I.: The use of neurocognitive methods in assessing health communication messages: a systematic review. J. Health Psychol. **22**(12), 1534–1551 (2017)

King, A.J., Lazard, A.J.: Advancing visual health communication research to improve infodemic response. Health Commun. **35**(14), 1723–1728 (2020)

Koelen, M.A., Lindström, B.: Making healthy choices easy choices: the role of empowerment. Eur. J. Clin. Nutr. **59**(1), S10–S16 (2005)

Kralj Novak, P., Smailović, J., Sluban, B., Mozetič, I.: Sentiment of emojis. PloS ONE **10**(12), e0144296 (2015)

Lo, S.K.: The nonverbal communication functions of emoticons in computer-mediated communication. Cyberpsychol. Behav. **11**(5), 595–597 (2008)

Lu, X., et al.: Learning from the ubiquitous language: an empirical analysis of emoji usage of smartphone users. In: Proceedings of the 2016 ACM International Joint Conference on Pervasive and Ubiquitous Computing, pp. 770–780, September 2016

Mackintosh, N.: Self-empowerment in health promotion: a realistic target? Br. J. Nurs. **4**(21), 1273–1278 (1995)

Maibach, E., Flora, J.A., Nass, C.: Changes in self-efficacy and health behavior in response to a minimal contact community health campaign. Health Commun. **3**(1), 1–15 (1991)

Marengo, D., Giannotta, F., Settanni, M.: Assessing personality using emoji: An exploratory study. Pers. Individ. Differ. **112**, 74–78 (2017)

McClain, C., Rainie, L.: The challenges of contact tracing as US battles COVID-19| Pew Research Center. Technical report, October 2020 (2020). https://www.pewresearch.org/internet/2020/10/30/the-challenges-of-contact-tracing-as-us-battles-covid-19

O'Connor, E.L., White, K.M.: Willingness to trial functional foods and vitamin supplements: the role of attitudes, subjective norms, and dread of risks. Food Qual. Prefer. **21**(1), 75–81 (2010)

O'Keefe, D.J., Nan, X.: The relative persuasiveness of gain-and loss-framed messages for promoting vaccination: a meta-analytic review. Health Commun. **27**(8), 776–783 (2012)

Pinto, V.R.A., et al.: Health beliefs towards kefir correlate with emotion and attitude: a study using an emoji scale in Brazil. Food Res. Int. **129**, 108833 (2020)

Plous, S.: The Psychology of Judgment and Decision Making. Mcgraw-Hill Book Company, New York (1993)

Prati, G., Pietrantoni, L., Zani, B.: Influenza vaccination: the persuasiveness of messages among people aged 65 years and older. Health Commun. **27**(5), 413–420 (2012)

Ray, E.C., Merle, P.F.: Disgusting face, disease-ridden place?: Emoji influence on the interpretation of restaurant inspection reports. Health Commun. 1–12 (2020)

Rimal, R.N., Lapinski, M.K., Turner, M.M., Smith, K.: The attribute-centered approach for understanding health behaviors: initial ideas and future research directions. Stud. Commun. Sci. **11**(1), 15–34 (2011)

Robus, C.M., Hand, C.J., Filik, R., Pitchford, M.: Investigating effects of emoji on neutral narrative text: evidence from eye movements and perceived emotional valence. Comput. Hum. Behav. **109**, 106361 (2020)

Rosenstock, I.M.: Historical origins of the health belief model. Health Educ. Monogr. **2**(4), 328–335 (1974)

Rosenstock, I.M., Strecher, V.J., Becker, M.H.: Social learning theory and the health belief model. Health Educ. Q. **15**(2), 175–183 (1988)

Rothman, A.J., Martino, S.C., Bedell, B.T., Detweiler, J.B., Salovey, P.: The systematic influence of gain-and loss-framed messages on interest in and use of different types of health behavior. Pers. Soc. Psychol. Bull. **25**(11), 1355–1369 (1999)

Rothman, A.J., Salovey, P., Antone, C., Keough, K., Martin, C.D.: The influence of message framing on intentions to perform health behaviors. J. Exp. Soc. Psychol. **29**(5), 408–433 (1993)

Sheeran, P., et al.: The impact of changing attitudes, norms, and self-efficacy on health-related intentions and behavior: a meta-analysis. Health Psychol. **35**(11), 1178 (2016)

Smailović, J., Sluban, B., Mozetič, I.: Sentiment of emojis. PLoS ONE **10**(12), e0144296 (2015)

Slovic, P., Peters, E., Finucane, M.L., MacGregor, D.G.: Affect, risk, and decision making. Health Psychol. **24**(4S), S35 (2005)

Spinelli, S., Masi, C., Zoboli, G.P., Prescott, J., Monteleone, E.: Emotional responses to branded and unbranded foods. Food Qual. Prefer. **42**, 1–11 (2015)

Stout, M.E., Christy, S.M., Winger, J.G., Vadaparampil, S.T., Mosher, C.E.: Self-efficacy and HPV vaccine attitudes mediate the relationship between social norms and intentions to receive the HPV vaccine among college students. J. Community Health **45**(6), 1187–1195 (2020). https://doi.org/10.1007/s10900-020-00837-5

Tversky, A., Kahneman, D.: The framing of decisions and the psychology of choice. Science **211**(4481), 453–458 (1981)

Tversky, A., Kahneman, D.: The framing of decisions and the psychology of choice. In: Wright, G. (ed.) Behavioral decision making, pp. 25–41. Springer, Boston (1985). https://doi.org/10.1007/978-1-4613-2391-4_2

Weimer, D.L., Vining, A.R.: Policy Analysis: Concepts and Practice. Routledge, London (2017)

Witte, K., Allen, M.: A meta-analysis of fear appeals: implications for effective public health campaigns. Health Educ. Behav. **27**(5), 591–615 (2000)

Ye, W., Li, Q., Yu, S.: Persuasive effects of message framing and narrative format on promoting COVID-19 vaccination: a study on chinese college students. Int. J. Environ. Res. Publ. Health **18**(18), 9485 (2021)

Yu, N., Ahern, L.A., Connolly-Ahern, C., Shen, F.: Communicating the risks of fetal alcohol spectrum disorder: effects of message framing and exemplification. Health Commun. **25**(8), 692–699 (2010)

Zajonc, R.B.: Feeling and thinking: preferences need no inferences. Am. Psychol. **35**(2), 151 (1980)

TimeAlone - The Stress Relieving Android App that Combines Diary and Music

Di Lun Liong, Su Mon Chit[✉], and Chee Ling Thong

Institute of Computer Science and Digital Innovation, UCSI University, No. 1, Jalan Menara Gading, Taman Connaught, Cheras, Wilayah Persekutuan, 56000 Kuala Lumpur, Malaysia
`chitsm@ucsiuniversity.edu.my`

Abstract. Various applications related to mental health continue to appear and constantly innovative psychological applications or the use of traditional relaxation methods combined with technology have become new choices in people's busy lives. In recent years, the rate of adolescents suffering from mental illnesses such as depression and suicide has been increasing. Adolescents in this age group do not have good stress management skills. This research paper is to design and develop a suitable decompression application with a combination of the diary as expressive writing and music. The objective of the paper was to study and explore the impact of expressive writing and music on stress. Then determine suitable music and color for the application with the use of the quantitative method. Design and develop the application which meets the objective and aim and evaluate the application based on users' experiences.

Keywords: Expressive writing · Music · Stress · Mobile health application · Diary · Android app

1   Introduction

The simplicity and ease of use of mobile devices have caused people to pursue and pay attention after they were invented. According to NEWZOO's "Global Mobile Industry Report 2020", by 2020, the number of mobile phone users will reach 3.5 billion [1]. And it is expected that with the advent of the 5G era, mobile phone users will reach 4.1 billion in 2023. Especially in recent years, the number of people with mental health problems has increased, causing people to attach great importance to mental health. For example, depression can increase the risk of coronary heart disease in healthy adults [2, 3] and the mortality of patients with coronary heart disease [3, 4]. Especially since the outbreak of the Covid-19 epidemic, not only people's health has been threatened, but psychological problems have also appeared. Many scholars continue to pay attention to the psychological impact of Covid-19 on humans. It can be said that Covid-19 has had a major impact on our lives. These influences will undoubtedly bring huge challenges and pressures to people. The endless lockdown and isolation also make people prone to panic and anxiety. Therefore, in order to reduce or even solve people's mental health problems as much as possible, use application as a new strategy, combining traditional

G. Salvendy and J. Wei (Eds.): HCII 2022, LNCS 13337, pp. 49–59, 2022.
https://doi.org/10.1007/978-3-031-05014-5_5

stress reduction methods with application, hoping to effectively reduce people's stress and anxiety. So in this paper will include section for literature review, methodology, result and discussion and the conclusion.

2 Literature Review

2.1 Stress

Stress is a perception of emotional or physical tension and in most definitions of stress is often used in conjunction with negative life experiences or life events. Most people are being stressed and there is a number of incidents that leads to negative emotion in one's life. It can be positive at times, or contras. If people are in a state of adapting to stress, they will show behavioral defense and change one's cognitive process and emotional landscape. However, prolonged stress will lead to the emergence of diseases and mental health disorders [5, 6].

Even though stress is an inescapable part of life for a wide range of populations with no regard to their age, gender, educational status, or economic status. Despite this fact, stress is a prevailing mental health problem among teenagers. As teenagers, they often need to adapt to different environments and these difficulties will affect their psychosocial well-being and learning outcomes. Especially nowadays in a competitive, other than the expectation of themself, teachers and parents also burden the students with a lot of pressure of getting good grades. Other than that, most students still need to participate in extracurricular activities, because the current expectation for them is to be all-rounders. All the demanding attitudes from parents and teachers leave the student creating more stress [6, 7].

But it is worth noting that not every student is able to handle this pressure and if they face negative life events in this context can confer a risk of depression or suicidal thinking. All of this statement actually can be supported by the data given by ACHA (American College Health Association) in 2019. This study found that 8.6% of students reported seriously considering suicide at least once in the past 12 months period and 1.4% of students attempt suicide. Among the common cause of death in teenagers, suicide is currently the seconds [8].

Especially since the spread of COVID-19 to the entire world at a terrifying speed in 2019, has caused catastrophic problems everywhere. Most countries have adopted strong blockades in order to curb the spread of diseases. After the large-scale outbreak of the virus in Malaysia, corresponding measures were also taken, that is, a national "movement control order" was announced to prevent the further spread of the virus. Although the blockade has greatly slowed the spread of the virus and is a necessary measure to protect health, long-term social isolation and different lifestyles have caused most people to fall into anxiety, irritability, and fear of the virus. In particular, the reasons for the economic downturn caused by the lockdown have caused people to experience physical and psychological shocks, and the suicide rate remains high [9].

Many scholars also urge people not to ignore mental health. Many articles at home and abroad have also studied people's mental health and the need for immediate intervention. Especially for students, in addition to the pressure mentioned above, the emergence of the virus is also completely changed their way of life and learning. In the modern era with advanced information, we can have various channels to contact information, but the ubiquitous negative news will undoubtedly gradually erode the psychology of students. In the [9] study, it was found that nearly 29.8% of students experienced different levels of anxiety and the results were similar to the results in [21–23]. At the same time in [24, 25] was also found that the average probability of anxiety of female students is higher than that of male students. This may happen to be aggravated or aggravated by the virus because women can express emotions better than men [9].

2.2 Mobile Application

In recent years, due to the ubiquity and popularity of users, mobile applications are growing at an exponential rate. In [10] pointed out in this article that the number of mobile applications has reached 2 million, and the number of downloads has exceeded an astonishing 140 billion times. All this proves that mobile applications have been greatly developed. One of the reasons for this rapid growth is that users spend approximately 90% of their time on mobile applications compared to mobile networks [11]. In another article, the author also believes that over time, it can be inferred that most websites will be replaced by apps. In fact, it can be seen from our lives that people are more inclined to download related applications to use or solve problems than mobile networks. And the categories of mobile applications are different, there are thousands of different applications, such as games, health status. News or tools. Users can always find suitable programs and download applications through the corresponding operating system. No one can deny the benefits that applications bring to people.

At the same time in [14], the author defines the term "mobile application", "mobile application" as a kind of mobile application or just the abbreviation of application, which can be used on smartphones, tablets, and other mobile devices Running design. The application software on the device". And because the application has been downloaded and installed on the phone, some applications can even be used offline. The author also recommends if the goal is to interact with users or provide more features than the website Similar to a running computer program, the application is meaningful or desirable [14].

Most developers will encounter different problems when developing mobile applications. One of them is which platform to choose as the first platform because the hardware and software of different platforms are different and cross platform development tools are too complex to deal with. And different platform development will have their own limitations. In today's application market, IOS and Android can be called department stores in applications. App Store and Google Play occupy almost all market shares every year. Although there are many operating systems, in fact, most applications provide the same functionality [30].

Android operating system has become the most used OS in the world due to its large user base and can be executed on most smartphones. It is pointed out in [12] that ANDROID, like all operating systems, enables applications to use hardware functions through abstraction and provides a defined environment for applications. In most research, Android is the first choice for most people because it is a free and open-source mobile platform and can be used in any form of smartphone developed by any manufacturer. In addition, because it is implemented using developed source code, the Android framework allows hardware manufacturers to build custom user-friendly interfaces to meet individual needs [12].

In addition to choosing an operating system, the usability of mobile applications is a point that developers often overlook, but this determines the success of the application.

Five attributes of usability are determined in his article:

- Efficiency: Resource consumption related to accuracy and completeness which users achieved their goals.
- Satisfaction: Get rid of discomfort and have a positive attitude towards using the tool product.
- Learnability: The system should be easy to learn so that users can quickly start use the system to complete the work.
- Easy to remember: The system should be easy to remember so that casual users can return to the system without using it for a period without learning everything started again.
- Error: The system should have a low error rate, so that users make few errors during the use of the system, if they do make a mistake, they can easily recover from them.

2.3 Writing Therapy

Diary writing may sound very old fashioned, but the habit of it can help individuals keep track of their daily lives. In the past, people only used diaries as a medium or tool for expression and recording, without realizing that expressive writing helped improve personal health and mental state. This statement was first put forward by James W. Pennebaker in the 1980s. He pointed out that using writing to express the thoughts and feelings of uneasy or traumatic time can effectively help people. In the past few decades, there have also been empirical confirmations of negative expressions through writing. Emotional benefits. As for the term expressive writing, I will quote the definition mentioned in [13].

"Expressive writing is a form of therapy in which the individual writes down thoughts and feelings related to personal stress or traumatic life experiences. Expressive writing is sometimes referred to as written disclosure because the author is required to disclose personal information, thoughts, and feelings. Unlike communicative writing, expressive writing is personal, free-flowing, and informal, usually without regard to style, spelling, punctuation, or grammar."

It means that diary was first considered a very intimate personal activity but under the rapid development of the Internet, the diary entered the fuzzy area of public and private [14]. This is because with the support of technology, for example, the emergence of blogs allows people to express their thoughts or feelings or some anonymous forums on a regular basis, and these are based on traditional pen-and-paper diaries. The author also expresses that no matter what kind of diary, it is regarded as a means of thinking [13]. also put forward the same opinion, but believed that although blogs provide all the same opportunities as diaries, their privacy and confidentiality will make most people uneasy [15].

In [15], the author stated that written emotional disclosure (WE1D) is effective in producing beneficial results both physically and psychologically. For example, WED reduces the number of doctor visits for people with breast cancer and effectively reduces depression and anxiety. In addition, the results of [16] showed that the stress level of students has decreased after receiving the treatment of expressive writing. At the conclusion of the article, the author also urges students to try to express their feelings, whether they are good or bad, can help improve their physical and mental health. At the same time, the results of [17] also pointed out that writing therapy has a certain effect on reducing students' stress and depression. This is because writing therapy helps students understand and accept the current situation and is self-motivated because writing will stimulate the brain to help people organize their thoughts and feelings.

In addition to the benefits of physical and mental health, diary is actually regarded as a tool to enhance personal learning and self-development. Research [18] pointed out that diary helps students to reflect on themselves and cultivate students' critical thinking skills. In addition, self-reflection when writing a diary can effectively improve students' ability to analyze and solve problems. The author also pointed out that feelings and emotional responses are particularly important for students and can have a significant impact on students' learning and interpersonal relationships. Therefore, it is necessary to express students' stress and emotions through diaries. In [19], the author also gave a very interesting statement, that is, because writing is a recursive behavior, we will read what is being written. And knowing may in turn affect us when we are writing, and thus affect what we write next. So from this perspective, the simple act of writing is therapeutic in itself.

2.4 Music Therapy

Compared with other languages, music can be regarded as a universal language. Sometimes you can feel the emotion and power it expresses without understanding the lyrics. Especially in recent years, the use of music as a treatment method has become more and more popular. The research [26] proves that music affects many areas of the brain including emotions, cognition, feelings, etc. At the same time, music can stimulate the reward centre in the brain, arouse positive emotions and relieve many symptoms related to mental health problems. In general, music is a powerful stimulus that can regulate emotions and has a long history of using music as a treatment method. Most articles indicate that music has a relaxing effect and can reduce anxiety [27].

In a recent meta-analysis, [39] had reviewed 72 randomized controlled trials and concluded that music is a significant help in reducing postoperative anxiety and pain symptoms. Music can be considered as an emerging treatment option for mood disorders that have not yet reached their full potential. Many researchers have reported the beneficial effects of music, such as enhancing awareness and sensitivity to positive emotions, or improving mental symptoms. It is also stated that music seems to have a major impact on the lives of teenagers, so the use of music lyrics and expressive writing can promote disclosure in the writing process [20]. It is also suggested that the combination of music and expressive writing may help reduce the stress of bullied teenagers.

In addition, there is ample evidence that people use music every day to improve their mood in daily life and music therapy [29]. The article also pointed out that music is not a panacea that can immediately solve negative emotions, nor is it always helpful, so more experiments and research are needed for a second discussion.

3   Methodology

The main purpose of this section is to introduce the research methodology for this quantitative-based theory study regarding design and develop a suitable android based diary application that also combines music function which aims to help teenager relieve their stress. This approach allowed for an understanding of the user's need for a good diary application and their stress level and stress management skill level. Besides that, this also can understand their opinion on the relationship between stress and writing therapy. The applicability of the model framework and other approaches for this study are discussed in-depth in this section.

3.1   Research Methodology

Survey questionnaires is used as the quantitative data collection method in this study. The preliminary survey is conducted to gather early data requirements regarding the project. An easy-to-understand Google form was used to collect basic information, stress level, and user requirement. Google forms were sent to 30 students of different schools/universities and were asked to fill the forms. At the start of the survey question also inform all the participants were provided with information concerning the research purpose, confidentiality of information, and the right to revoke participation without prior justification.

The survey questionnaires have used different types of questions such as multiple-choice checkboxes, the linear scale options, and the single-choice button. There has an option "Other" in certain questions to allowed participant to write down their own idea. This questionnaire mainly gathers information to know the user requirement or expectation of mobile diary application so can help in UI design and the application functionality.

A quantitative survey was used in this project because it is more scientific, fast, and acceptable for this project. The quantitative approach can gather and analyzed a large amount of data without bias. Other than that, a quantitative approach can get data that is more precise and data collection using the quantitative method is relatively quick and easy especially during the pandemic covid-19.

3.2   System Development Methodology

The model framework/method of the project chooses iterative and incremental development because it is a discipline based on the production of the deliverables development systems. The basic idea of this method is to develop the system by repeating the loop (iteration) and a smaller part (increment) at a time. In this approach, different parts of the system are developed at different times and integrated according to their phases, while in iterative development, the various parts of the system will be re-examined to modify and improve them.

This method is ideal because the operating system involved in the mobile application can be constructed flexibly and can be completed with minimal hardware and tools. In addition, the time limit is not a problem, because the given time is enough for the room to iterate through the stages as necessary. So, research can focus on continuously improving the system to ensure that the project goals are met.

3.3 Preliminary Result

According to the overall results and findings of the preliminary survey, most interviewees have optimistic and positive ideas about diaries and are willing to try as long as the application meets and satisfies their preferences. At the same time, most of the interviewees never wrote a diary because they didn't know how to start, what to record and there was no time. Therefore, it is recommended that respondents who try to write a diary do not necessarily have to record daily and use more methods they like. In addition, according to the survey of respondents, we can know and understand their desired functions and interface design.

4 Results and Discussion

After all the testing has been done, it will be deployed to some end-user to test the system and get feedback. User Acceptance Testing (UAT) is testing the system or application by the user to determine whether it can be accepted or not and this is the final testing after the unit, integration, and system testing. The test was given to 15 tester to test for the final prototype of the application after the development. This section will show the summary result on the UAT test. Following table is the demographic of the tester (Table 1):

Table 1. Demographic

Gender	Number
Male	3
Female	12
Age group	
18–21 years	15
Education level	
Bachelor's degree	15

The UAT test done by 15 tester with the questionnaire prepared and as the table shown,most of the tester are female and all of them from 18–21 years and study in bachelor degree (Figs. 1 and 2).

From the analysis of the result of UAT, the overall satisfaction given by user was good. Most of them are feeling the application work well but at the same time they also give some suggestion and comment for the future improvement. First they feel well on the interface of application juts hope there more choice of font, music and theme.For the function part they will hope can taking photo and upload directly also allow upload multiple submission. Other than that, automatically save function also needed for them to avoid the data loss. They feel satisfied of the display and the introduction page make them know more clearer about the application. The last was the security protection part which they hope can have email authentication for register and reset password. With this

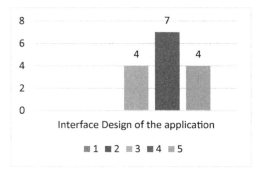

Fig. 1. Interface satisfaction

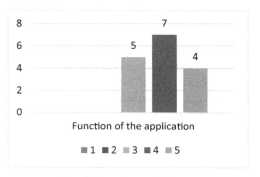

Fig. 2. Function satisfaction

ways, their data will be protected more securely. On the other hand, they comment that the idea was good and combine with the music they feel relaxing, and expect changes or improvement on it. With the user acceptance system to collect users' opinions and suggestions on this application, many improvements can be completed in the future.

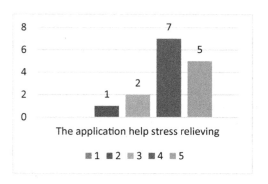

Fig. 3. Help in stress relieving

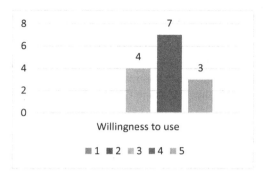

Fig. 4. Willingness to use

At the same time, Fig. 3 shows that the result of asking the tester is that the app helps relieve stress. Most people agree and comment that the app is good. They can use it to record their emotions or life, which also helps them. Introspect. But there is also one tester who disagrees with it because he feels that this is hard to insist on for him and he expects other ways to relieving stress. Music functions are also good, but they want more choices. The last Fig. 4 shows the user's willingness to use, most of these users will use the application in their lives and expect improvement, 4 testers are neutral on this.

5 Conclusion

In conclusion, this project has been researched and repeatedly tested to ensure that the goals and objectives set in the proposal stage are achieved. After the project is developed and tested, the goals set out before are generally met.

The main output and development of this project is the designed system and psychological mobile application which combined with the way of writing diaries. This mobile application is developed using JAVA and runs on the Android platform. The project mainly uses the method of writing a diary, supplemented by music, fonts and interface design factors so that students can use this method to reduce or relieve stress. This is also the way to achieve the main goal of the project.

The goals proposed at the beginning of the application planning process have been achieved one by one in various stages and in various ways. First, I used the survey to understand the prevalence of diaries among modern students and the students' understanding of diaries. At the same time, the function and design of the ideal diary application of the students are also obtained through the survey. Due to the epidemic, this survey used online questionnaires which is GOOGLE FORM to distribute to higher education students in different institutions. This method can more comprehensively collect and analyze the opinions and ideas of various students.

After collecting the project requirements information, start to find some related journal articles, or books, papers, and websites as documents to help the project research and understand the development of related topics. The purpose of the literature review is to learn more about the current up-to-date information about the project, so the articles we found tried to limit it to nearly five years.

After consulting the literature, the collected survey results will be further analyzed to better understand and identify the functions and interface requirements or preferences envisaged by the students in the diary application. In addition, through the analysis of the survey results, we can further understand the students' views and understanding of diary writing.

When all the data is analyzed, the development and coding of the application begin. In the development process, developers must perform some tests, such as unit tests, to ensure that each object of the developed application can run normally. In addition, run integration tests to ensure that all units communicate with each other. The next test is the system test to check whether the entire system is operating normally without any abnormal problems or crashes. The last test is the user acceptance test, which is the end-user to determine whether the developed application meets the user's expectations and needs. Using this method, developers can directly collect data and feedback from users to understand the limitations of the project and some suggestions for improvement. The final conclusion is that the goals established in the planning stage have been achieved in different stages and the above-detailed introduction of all stages and processes of developing this application.

References

1. Newzoo: Newzoo Global Mobile Market Report 2020—Free Version—Newzoo, Newzoo (2021). https://newzoo.com/insights/trend-reports/newzoo-global-mobile-market-report-2020-free-version/. Accessed 08 Feb 2021
2. Pan, A., Sun, Q., Okereke, O., Rexrode, K., Hu, F.: Depression and risk of stroke morbidity and mortality. JAMA 306(11), 1241–1249 (2011)
3. Shi, S., Liu, T., Liang, J., Hu, D., Yang, B.: Depression and risk of sudden cardiac death and arrhythmias. Psychosom. Med. 79(2), 153–161 (2017)
4. Barth, J., Schumacher, M., Herrmann-Lingen, C.: Depression as a risk factor for mortality in patients with coronary heart disease: a meta-analysis. Psychosom. Med. 66(6), 802–813 (2004)
5. Rosiek, A., Rosiek-Kryszewska, A., Leksowski, Ł., Leksowski, K.: Chronic stress and suicidal thinking among medical students. Int. J. Environ. Res. Publ. Health 13(2) (2016). https://doi.org/10.3390/ijerph13020212
6. Jain, G., Singhai, M.: Academic stress amongst students: a review of literature. Prestig. e-J. Manag. Res. 4(2), 58–67 (2017)
7. Yikealo, D., Yemane, B., Karvinen, I.: The level of academic and environmental stress among college students: a case in the college of education. Open J. Soc. Sci. 06(11), 40–57 (2018). https://doi.org/10.4236/jss.2018.611004
8. Editorial Board: Spring 2019. Cornell. Int. Aff. Rev. 12(2) (2019). https://doi.org/10.37513/ciar.v12i2.517
9. Sundarasen, S., et al.: Psychological impact of covid-19 and lockdown among university students in malaysia: implications and policy recommendations. Int. J. Environ. Res. Publ. Health 17(17), 1–13 (2020). https://doi.org/10.3390/ijerph17176206
10. Li, D., Guo, B., Shen, Y., Li, J., Huang, Y.: The evolution of open-source mobile applications: an empirical study. J. Softw. Evol. Process 29(7), 1–18 (2017). https://doi.org/10.1002/smr.1855

11. Anwar, N., Rizal, M.A.M., Mustamum, H.A., Taib, K.M., Razak, A.A., Nordin, Z.: Mobile application development: a preliminary study. In: Proceedings of 2020 International Conference Information Management and Technology, ICIMTech 2020, no. August, pp. 951–956 (2020). https://doi.org/10.1109/ICIMTech50083.2020.9211289

12. Okonkwo, W.C.: Critical success factors of mobile application development supervisor, November 2015

13. Thatcher, C.: In dialogue: how writing to the dead and the living can increase self-awareness in those bereaved by addiction. Omega (United States) (2020). https://doi.org/10.1177/003 0222820976277

14. Ковалишина, О.Р.ШИВ.ИО.В.: Using writing as a therapy for eating disorders: the diary healer and the process of using personal diary excerpts to write a book to assist people with eating disorders. Вестник Росздравнадзора 4(March), 9–15 (2017)

15. Hibsch, A.N., Mason, S.E.: The new age of creative expression: the effect of blogging on emotional well-being. J. Creat. Ment. Heal. 6(4), 511–521 (2020). https://doi.org/10.1080/15401383.2020.1820925

16. Mukhlis, H., et al.: The effect of expressive writing technique to stress level decrease of new student at Al-Falah Putri Islamic Boarding School, Margodadi, Tanggamus. Ann. Trop. Med. Public Heal. 23(6), 758–766 (2020). https://doi.org/10.36295/ASRO.2020.23624

17. Istiqomah, Z.N., Erawati, E., Suyanta, S.: Life writing therapy decreases depression in late adolescence. J. Ners. 13(2), 207 (2019). https://doi.org/10.20473/jn.v13i2.4686

18. Reljić, N.M., Pajnkihar, M., Fekonja, Z.: Self-reflection during first clinical practice: the experiences of nursing students. Nurse Educ. Today 72(February 2018), 61–66 (2019). https://doi.org/10.1016/j.nedt.2018.10.019

19. Catarina, A., Viegas, M.: Expressive and creative writing in the therapeutic context: from the different concepts to the development of writing therapy programs (2021)

20. De Oliveira, I.M.: Music and Expression: An Adlerian Approach to Healing Wounds of Childhood Bullying, pp. 1–14 (2017)

21. Cao, W., et al.: The psychological impact of the COVID-19 epidemic on college students in China. J. Psychiatry Res. 287, 112934 (2020)

22. Wang, G., Zhang, Y., Zhao, J., Zhang, J., Jiang, F.: Mitigate the effects of home confinement on children during the COVID-19 outbreak. Lancet 395, 945–947 (2020)

23. Azad, N., Shahid, A., Abbas, N., Shaheen, A., Munir, N.: Anxiety and depression in medical students of a private medical college. J. Ayub Med. Coll. Abbottabad 29, 123–127 (2017)

24. Mirza, I., Jenkins, R.: Risk factors, prevalence, and treatment of anxiety and depressive disorders in Pakistan: a systematic review. BMJ 328, 794 (2004)

25. Thoma, M.V., La Marca, R., Brönnimann, R., Finkel, L., Ehlert, U., Nater, U.M.: The effect of music on the human response. PLoS ONE 8(8), e70156 (2013). https://doi.org/10.1371/journal.pone.0070156

26. Koelsch, S., Jancke, L.: Music and the heart. Eur. Heart J. 36, 3043–3048 (2015). https://doi.org/10.1093/eurheartj/ehv430

27. Hole, J., Hirsch, M., Ball, E., Meads, C.: Music as an aid for postoperative recovery in adults: a systematic review and meta-analysis. Lancet 386, 1659–1671 (2015). https://doi.org/10.1016/S0140-6736(15)60169-61

28. Cheong-Clinch, C., McFerran, K.: Musical diaries: examining the preferred music listening ofaustralian young people with mental illness. J. Appl. Youth Stud. 1, 77–94 (2016)

The Effectiveness of Smart Tourism in Malaysia in Covid-19 Post-pandemic Era: A Case Study

Chee Ling Thong[1(✉)], Lee Yen Chaw[1], Aswani Kumar Cherukuri[2],
Abdulrahman Jalil[3], Su Mon Chit[1], and Chiw Yi Lee[4]

[1] UCSI University, 56000 Kuala Lumpur, Malaysia
chloethong@ucsiuniversity.edu.my
[2] Vellore Institute of Technology, Vellore 632014, Tamil Nadu, India
[3] University of Computer Science and Engineering, 63000 Cyberjaya, Malaysia
[4] UCSI College, 56000 Kuala Lumpur, Malaysia

Abstract. The use of technology in supporting business processes has become an integral part of business in the post-pandemic era. This study focuses on two aspects of technology which are digitization and digitalization of business processes in tourism industry in Malaysia. Due to movement constraints in Covid-19 pandemic, most of the related studies are conducted based on media report, peered review articles and research letters or empirical articles. There is a lack of case study to examine the effectiveness of various factors and how these factors impact the recovery of the post- pandemic tourism industry. A research case in earlier study implies that digitization and digitalization have an impact in recovery of tourism industry and insight gained motivates this study on effectiveness of smart tourism in Malaysia. Hence, this study aims to investigate effectiveness of smart tourism by using a self-developed mobile application which enables multiple trips organize in Kuala Lumpur, Malaysia. Test cases are conducted among eleven managers in travel agencies and positive feedback are collected on system quality, perceived mobility, mobile usefulness, mobile ease of use and usage intention. Findings show that ICT has a major role in reviving business processes when tourism enters recovery phase. The study also discovered the importance of understanding the new patterns emerging which may include new tour packages or travel destinations that are emerging in future. In future work, artificial intelligence or machine learning based smart tourism models are introduced to analyse the new pattern emerging.

Keywords: Smart tourism · Travel agency · Post-pandemic · Mobile application

1 Introduction

In post-pandemic era, the use of technology become an integral part of businesses. Information Communication Technology (ICT) bring smartness into organization particularly in tourism industry and societies. [1] opined that individuals are exposed as information makers, filtering the existing options for tracking their position by having smart tourisms. According to the research [2], COVID- 19 has negatively impact on the overall tourism

G. Salvendy and J. Wei (Eds.): HCII 2022, LNCS 13337, pp. 60–73, 2022.
https://doi.org/10.1007/978-3-031-05014-5_6

industry but it also promoted smart tourism to some extent. A combination of traditional tourism and "smart" technology is a new way of tourism model and new path for development of tourism industry. Various terms have been used to define smart tourism and it includes IT, mobile communication, cloud computing, artificial intelligence and virtual reality for developing innovation tools and approaches to improve tourism industry [3]. It also provides benefits of tourism informationization and consists of digital intelligent and virtual technology based tourism to provide variety of end-user services and devices to tourists, enterprises and organizations [4].

According to study conducted by [5] on the effect on tourism and hospitality industry in Malaysia, one of the resurgence strategies suggested/discussed from both the experts of academic and industry is the focused-on digitization of the tourism industry. [5] opined that digitization is transforming the integrated spectrum of the whole tourism industry through leveraging ICT for entering smart tourism and it can impact the recovery of tourism in post-pandemic. However, the limitation of their research is only based on media report, peered review articles and research letters/empirical articles. This study is conducted to overcome the limitations of the said study by doing quantitative studies to examine the effectiveness of digitization as well as digitalization of tourism industry by using a self-developed mobile application (app). In this study, effectiveness is measured by perception towards usage intention by manager of travel agency of the mobile app. Measurement criteria of effectiveness are system quality, perceived mobility, mobile usefulness, mobile ease of use and usage intention. The research question of this study is: what is the acceptance of mobile app in terms of effectiveness in facilitating the work of manager in travel agency?

2 Literature Review

This section presents various definitions and models of smart tourism, definitions of digitization and digitalization as well as its applications in tourism industry; and criteria use for measuring effectiveness in this study.

2.1 Smart Tourism Model

Cloud Tourism is one of the smart tourism models which emerge together with Virtual Reality (VR) parks. As field travels are restricted during the pandemic, cloud tourism and VR parks attracts tourists' interest and satisfy their travelling needs which promotes tourism market [2]. As offline tourism activities are restricted, tourism products are also in the risk of low sales. In order to avoid that, a new smart tourism mode of "Tourism+ Livestreaming" has been introduced to promote, endorse, and attract traffic to tourist destinations. This new method can promote tourism products via online without needed to have face to face contact. Another way of tourism using appointment is also widely used to control the crowd at the scenic spots at the designated time. This can not only control the crowd to reduce the pandemic, it also can be used as a data source for contact tracing.

Technology based tourism model such as using AI and VR in human-machine interactive devices have positive effect on service quality as well as lead to satisfaction and loyalty of tourists [6]. Hence, there are more collaborations required not only at public level, but also private level using Internet of Things (IoT) to accelerate the formation of smart cities. The relationship between innovation and smart cities has become the main contributing factor in tourism industry [7].

Technology has been widely used to address the impact caused by COVID 19. There are a variety of approaches has been planning to apply ICT in tourism industry in post pandemic era. A comparison study conducted on tourism and ICT solutions in COVID-19 post-pandemic era between two countries, Japan and Sweden discussed the difficulties faced by the tourism industry in these countries [8]. It was found that in Japan, there is a discrimination based on place of residence and in Sweden, there is race-based discrimination. In the post-pandemic era, the research promote tourism in using location-based games and contact information applications to prevent people gather and to provide secure environment for the tourists. Smart tourism using technology has potential to be widely accepted by some industry especially in smart cities. A study shows that current adoption of smart tourisms in museums are slow and there is also a high potential for the use of it [9].

2.2 Digitization, Digitalization and Application in Tourism Industry

According to Information Technology Gartner glossary, "Digitization is the process of changing from analog to digital form" (URL: https://www.gartner.com/en/information-technology/glossary/digitization). "Digitalization is the use of digital technologies to change a business model and provide new revenue and value-producing opportunities; it is the process of moving to digital business" (URL: https://www.gartner.com/en/inf ormation-technology/glossary/digitalization). In order to formulate business strategy, understanding the key terminologies of digitization and digitalization is essential. Some of the benefits of digitization are rapid access to useful information and historical data in a business environment. Digitalization brought in efficiency and productivity to a business as well as better decision making for managers.

There are various applications adopted in tourism industry. One of the mobile applications introduced is Smart Doaa [10], it displays recommended Doaas which can be determined by using search function, and GPS in identifying the holy place based on current location of visitors or determining the holy place by analysing an image taken by the visitors using a Deep-Learning (DL) based method. It supports both online and offline processing where the training models are deployed on client devices with the use of Automated Machine Language (Auto ML).

Amar Bangladesh [11] served as the first tourism-based Android-mobile apps which embeds Google Maps API and Machine Learning (ML) to find and display the shortest route to reach the point of interest in Bangladesh. The apps use Android built-in GPS tracker to track the real-time location of tourist and display the nearest tourist spots to them. Besides, the Apps implements Dijkstra algorithm to find out the shortest path and route to the tourists. Linear Regression is used to study the preferences of tourist by checking the most frequent clicks on attraction spots and hence recommend the most preferable point of interest to them.

VisitMalopolska mobile application [12] was developed under m_MSIT project. The main focus of the project is supporting trips in Malopolska region by providing and access information which enables independent sightseeing. The application uses beacons-sensor to communicate with a Bluetooth-enabled devices and requires activated GPS location tracker. The application also implements AR that enables user to connect with the virtual world through simulations by pointing their mobile phone camera to a selected tourist attraction. It also enables behaviour of users such as viewed- places, events, routes or planned trips to be observed and analyzed.

PekanBaru Guide [13] is an Android-based Apps which use GPS location tracker to locate point of interest in Pekanbaru city. It provides information such as tourist attractions, hotels, restaurants and shopping spots in Pekanbaru city. In addition, K-nearby algorithm (KNN) is also implemented in determining the closest route to reach the point of interest.

The Smart Tourist System (STS) [14] was developed to facilitate tourists' activities in historical places in Kingdom of Saudi Arabia (KSA) while keeping tourist privacy safe. Besides handling the shortage of having multilingual tourists' guide, it also helps to cut expenses needed to prepare KSA to be a tourist attraction. The project employs the usage of Quick Response (QR) codes technologies to access the video-based or textual-based information of historical spots in KSA and provides location services where it allows the Android-based App to connect to the Global Positioning System to locate users' current and nearby location. Table 1 shows the summary report of selected applications used in tourism industry, their common and special features as well as limitations.

Table 1. Summary of selected application in tourism industry

Mobile app	Common features	Special features	Limitations
Smart Doaa [10]	GPS tracker to identify Doaa based on client location	Using Deep-Learning (DL)-based method	Complicated method as too much algorithms and theories due to framework and libraries are new
Amar Bangladesh [11]	Built-in GPS tracker in Android phone to locate the nearest point of interest	Implement Dijkstra algorithm to find out the shortest route and Linear Regression in Machine Learning to recommend place of interest based on students frequent click on certain point of interest	

(*continued*)

Table 1. (*continued*)

Mobile app	Common features	Special features	Limitations
VisitMalopolska mobile application [12]	Built-in GPS tracker	Using AR enables users connect to the virtual world. allowing users to connect reality with the virtual world	There may be a technical support issue in future when the application are downloaded for more than thousand times
PekanBaru Guide [13]	Built-in GPS tracker	Implements K-nearby algorithm (KNN) to determine the closest route to reach the point of interest	Not identified
Smart Tourist System (STS) [14]	Built-in GPS tracker	Use QR code to display the video-based / textual based information of historical places in KSA	Did not support any charged Google map service and only cover Arar ancient Mosque

2.3 Various Factors in Measuring Effectiveness

There are many factors in measuring effectiveness. In this study, effectiveness is measured by system quality, perceived mobility, mobile ease of use and mobile usefulness. The following sections present more relevant literature.

System Quality. According to [15], system quality refers to the extent of consistency in the system performance in terms of its functionality, reliability, availability and etc. The system is expected to perform according to the function built and therefore meeting users' expectation. In current advances in mobile technology, mobile apps are getting popular as a tool to source information. As a result, to promote smart tourism, system quality plays an influential role over how users evaluate a system or an app which lead to usage intention. In this study context, tour managers may find the smart tour mobile app is a relevant tool to use if he/she seldom encountered or experienced very minimum disruption while using the mobile app for getting trip information. Besides, the app is reliable and always ready for users to download tourism information. Studies such as [16, 17] have shown the relationship between system quality and usage intention on mobile technologies and social networks. System Quality of mobile apps can contribute to smart tourism effectiveness by enhancing tour managers on-site work experience.

Perceived Mobility. [16] posited that perceived mobility is an essential attribute in mobile communication environment as it allows users to access as well as to communicate seamlessly via wireless networks. [17] described perceived mobility as "the degree to which users are aware of the mobility value of mobile services and systems" [17]. This is particularly important for tour managers who are very much depending on mobile technology to function their daily work effectively especially in the current pandemic situation. Tourism industry has been very competitive, and mobile technology is capable of minimizing direct human contact and achieve efficient communication even in the pandemic situation. Given the unique mobility feature of smart tour mobile app, tour managers can now access the app anytime and anywhere to manage multiple trips/activities either through WIFI or mobile network. This helps to achieve two important goals of the study on smart tourism: virtual connectivity and precision which translate to smart experience that specifically focus on technology-mediated tourism experience to travellers. In accordance to the empirical study [16] that perceived mobility has influence over tourist' mobile social tourism shopping intention as users see the value offered by the mobile technology.

Mobile Ease of Use and Mobile Usefulness. Mobile ease of use and mobile usefulness are the two main constructs introduced by [18] in the mobile technology acceptance model (MTAM) to suit the context of research in mobile technology adoption. Mobile ease of use refers to "the ease of use in relation to the use of a particular system" [19]. In other words, the lesser effort is required by users to operate the system or application the more likely the usage of it. In this study, it is believed that tour managers will be motivated to adopt the smart tour mobile app when attributes such as easy to learn and easy to use are the contributing factors to attract them to adopt the app. Mobile usefulness is defined as the overall evaluation on the usefulness rendered to users during the process of adopting mobile technology [18]. When a user is able to accomplish a task effectively and efficiently provided by the mobile app, this will raise perceive usefulness by user. Furthermore, mobile usefulness has been validated in recent studies [18, 19] in the mobile commerce arena. [20] empirically found that ease of use and usefulness influences the behavior intention to adopt branded mobile applications. In the current study, the tour managers are the users of the mobile app who perceive mobile usefulness from using smart tour mobile app. For example, the app enable the tour managers to generate report of multiple trips in various locations, enables manager to plan multiple trips/activities with confidence and etc. When tourism is supported by technology in this case mobile app to transform data into on-site experiences, it potentially contributes to efficiency, sustainability and experience enrichment not only to tour managers but also tourists [21].

3 Methodology

The research objectives are achieved using quantitative research. Firstly, a mobile app is developed based on business requirements gathered in earlier study [22, 23]. When app code is completed, unit testing, integration testing and system testing are performed by developer. Any effect or errors are fixed during the testing process before rolling it out in actual testing environment by users. The main objective of the app testing is two-fold: 1) to ensure higher user engagement; and 2) to determine effectiveness of app among users (who are managers in travel agency). They are eleven travel agency managers who are registered members of Malaysian Association of Tours and Travel Agents (MTTA) participated in this study. They are contacted via email and required to follow two simple steps below to complete the process:

Step 1: All participants are given briefing individually via email on the main purpose of developing mobile app which enables manager in travel agency to monitor multiple trips and track trip status when driver start/end the trips. At the same time, they view video provided in order to understand the key functionalities of the mobile app.

Step 2: All participants participated in the online survey. There are six sections in the online questionnaires covering personal information, system quality, perceived mobility, mobile usefulness, mobile ease of use, usage intention and open-ended questions (provide comments). The questions are designed based on research model in Fig. 1.

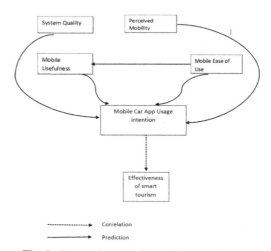

Fig. 1. Research model for mobile app adoption

Since data collection phase falls within post-pandemic period (when Malaysia implemented Movement Control Order 2.0 and Movement Control Order 3.0), there are constraints such as unable to meet up with users in person and demonstrate/test the app. Furthermore, based on news in Straitstimes.com on 14th March, 2021 (https://www.straitstimes.com/asia/se-asia/malaysias-travel-agencies-turn-to-selling-fruits-food-and-even-plots-of-land-as-borders), since tourism industry in Malaysia hit badly by Covid-19 pandemic and most travel agencies have collapsed and diversified their business to selling fruits or other products instead of tour packages. Due to this constraint, snowball sampling techniques until saturation point is used in this study. The selection criteria of participant are travel agency manager who have at least two years' experience in managing multiple trips in Malaysia. In the survey, the Likert scale is constructed to achieve the research aim, which is to understand the opinions/perceptions of users/participants related to the acceptance of the mobile application in terms of the effectiveness in facilitating their work in travel agencies. It is devised in order to quantify subjective preferential thinking, feeling and action in a validated and reliable manner [24]. The participants need to indicate their level of agreement ranging from 'strongly disagree' to 'strongly agree' on a metric scale. Last section of the questionnaire asked respondents to provide their comments or suggestions pertaining to the use of the mobile application. To analyze the Likert-scale data collected from the survey, descriptive analysis is used to describe and summarize data points in a meaningful way [25]. The analysis recommended for ordinal (type of data collected in this survey) measurement scale items include a mode (the most frequent response) or median for central tendency and frequencies for variability [26]. The findings, conclusions and recommendations of this research apply only to the population of respondents and should not be generalized to other populations.

4 Results and Discussions

This section presents the descriptive results which are analyzed from the survey.

4.1 Demographic

Basic demographics for the respondents are presented in Table 2.

Table 2. Demographics of travel managers

Category	Response	n	%
Gender	Male	7	63.6
	Female	4	36.4
Age	18–21	1	9.1
	26–29	1	9.1
	30–35	2	18.2
	>35	7	63.6
Years of experience	2–3 years	1	9.1
	>3 years	10	90.9

Most of the respondents are male (63.6%). Seven of them are aged more than 35 years old (63.6%) and two of them are between 30 to 35 years old (18.2%). The remaining is less than 30 years old. All of the travel managers classified themselves as having more than 3 years' experience of working (90.9%) except for one.

4.2 Measurement Criteria

System Quality

Figure 2 shows the travel managers responses regarding the system quality of the mobile application. Most of the respondents (36.3%) provide Neutral response when asked about any problems or issues faced by them when using the application to get trip information.

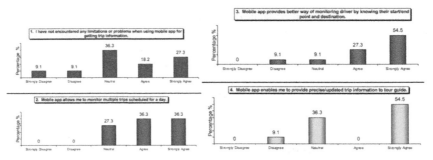

Fig. 2. Responses for system quality

In combination, most of the respondents (72.6%) are Agree and Strongly Agree that the application provides them the capability to monitor multiple trips scheduled in a daily basis. Obviously in the figure, most of the respondents (54.5%) Strongly Agree that the application provides better way of monitoring driver and precise/updated trip information to tour guide.

Perceived Mobility

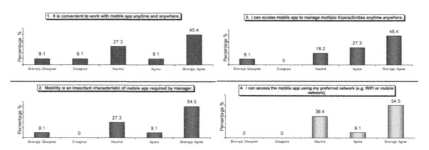

Fig. 3. Responses for Perceived Mobility

Figure 3 shows the responses from the travel managers in terms of their perceived mobility. Most of the respondents (45.4%) think that it is convenient to work with the mobile application anytime and anywhere and most of them (54.5%) also perceive that feature is really important for the application. Jointly, large percentage (72.7%) shows that they are Agree and Strongly Agree with the capability to access the mobile application to manage multiple trips and activities. Majority of them (54.5%) can access the application using their own preferred network (e.g. Wi-Fi or mobile network).

Mobile Usefulness

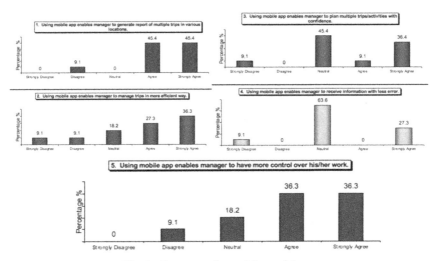

Fig. 4. Responses for mobile usefulness

Figure 4 presents the responses from the travel managers regarding the criteria of mobile usefulness. Equally (45.4%), the respondents Agree and Strongly Agree that the mobile application enables them to generate report for multiple trips in any location. Combined (63.6%), Agree and Strongly Agree that the application enables them to manage the trips in more efficient way. However, most of them provides Neutral response when asked about their confidence in planning multiple trips with the application (45.4%) and whether they are able to receive information with less error (63.6%). Finally, most of them collectively (72.6%) Agree and Strongly Agree that the application enables them to have more control over their work.

Mobile Ease of Use

Figure 5 presents the responses from the travel managers regarding the criteria of mobile ease of use. Most of them (54.5%) think that it will be easy for them to learn to use the mobile application in order to receive information related to drivers. Together, most of them (63.6%) Agree and Strongly Agree that it does not require a lot of mental effort to use the application to receive that type of information. Obviously, a big number of them (63.6%) think that it would be easy for them to become skilful at using the application to get drivers' current location. Nevertheless, majority of them (45.5%) provides Neutral response for being able to use the application to receive drivers' information without calling them. Interestingly, the response received from the respondents for indicating

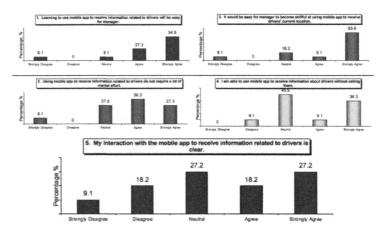

Fig. 5. Responses for mobile ease of use

clear interaction with the mobile application to receive drivers' information is quite scattered (18.2% for Disagree and Agree, while 27.3% for Neutral and Strongly Agree).

Usage Intention

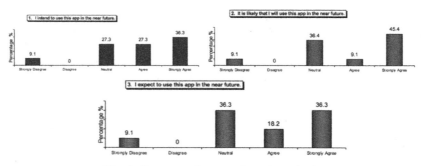

Fig. 6. Responses for usage intention criteria

Figure 6 presents the responses from the travel managers regarding the usage intention criteria. Jointly, most of the respondents (63.6%) have the intention to use the mobile application in the near future. While most of them (45.4%) are likely to use the application, 36.7% of them provides Neutral and Strongly Agree responses respectively for anticipating using the app in the near future.

5 Discussion and Implications

The findings of this study provided some insights that shed lights on current and future tourism in Malaysia particularly in adapting to new normal after Covid-19 post-pandemic. In this section, the following insights are discussed:

1. The practical implication of [5] research work has assisted tourism or travel agency manager a partial view of current and forthcoming challenges in the tourism industry in the post-pandemic era. However, in this study, the researchers have verified in a case study that the challenges mentioned can be addressed by introducing smart tourism in Malaysia rather than maintaining the current tourism trajectory in the post-pandemic era or new normal. This study suggests to tourism industry to adapt to new normal by incorporating IT innovation (digitalization/digitization concepts/theories) in planning business strategies, activities and policies and it may assist travel agency manager to rebuild or transform their business after hitting badly by Covid-19 pandemic. Tourism industry has start selling their tour packages by embarking on the smart tourism after gaining insight of the effectiveness of smart tourism in this study.

2. Based on the findings of this study, mobile app which leverages on the mature technologies (GPS) in acquiring trip information such as real-time location-based information of the bus or car drivers; and generating report of multiple trips containing bus start/end time and destinations. The key highlight in this study is the use of technology in multiple trips planning is more cost effective. Moreover, based on the results on usage intention presented in Fig. 6, technology acceptance by travel agency manager is high (more than 50%). This has also answered the research questions on the acceptance of mobile app in terms of effectiveness in facilitating the work of travel agency manager. However, the results presented in this study cannot be generalized due to limited sample size. This limitation can be overcome in future study when tourism industry enters into recovery phase.

In the nutshell, the practical implication of this study is to assist the travel agency manager to discover the two 'C's. The first 'C' stands for challenge, which is current challenge in facing the tourism industry that bad-hit and forthcoming challenge in recovering the tourism industry into good-shape. The second 'C' stands for cost, which is cost effectiveness when offering activities or tour packages in the recovery phase. Both 'C's are able to apply smart tourism in planning business strategies, activities and policies to adapt to the new normal. As mentioned, technology is the heart of smart tourism, the smart tourism models selected (but not limited to) are technology-based tourism models which include cloud tourism and so forth.

6 Conclusion

As a conclusion, this research has successfully investigated the effectiveness of digitization and digitalization in tourism industry by adopting a self-developed mobile application to enhance the travel agencies business processes such as monitoring and organizing multiple trips. The research has found that the use of the mobile application by the travel agent could provide more effective way to monitor and organize trips for tourist in Covid-19 post-pandemic era. Nevertheless, as a future work, the mobile application could be more improved possibly by implementing AI/ML features in order to provide advice and suggestion for the travel managers to plan a trip by learning the historical data pattern of the previous trips.

Acknowledgement. This research work is supported by UCSI University under Pioneer Science Incentives Fund (PSIF).

References

1. Dias, A., Santinha, G., Rodrigues, M., Queirós, A., Rodrigues, C., Rocha, N.P.: Smart cities and accessible tourism: a systematic review. In: ICT Tools and Applications for Accessible Tourism, p. 19 (2021). https://doi.org/10.4018/978-1-7998-6428-8.ch005
2. Yang, T., Yan, Z., Wen, J.: Impact of COVID-19 pandemic on smart tourism, **167**(Ermi), 90–93 (2021)
3. Rodrigues, J.M.F., Cardoso, P.J.S., Monteiro, J.: Smart Systems Design, Applications, and Challenges, p. 22 (2020). https://doi.org/10.4018/978-1-7998-2112-0.ch00
4. Zhang, L., Yang, J.: Smart tourism. In: Jafari, J., Xiao, H. (eds.) Encyclopedia of Tourism, pp. 862–863. Springer, Heidelberg (2016). https://doi.org/10.1007/978-3-319-01384-8_175
5. Khan, Md.A.A., Hashim, H.: The effect of covid-19 on tourism and hospitality industry in Malaysia, resurgence in the post-pandemic era: a conceptual criterion. Int. J. Tour. Hosp. Rev. **7**(2), 54–62 (2020). https://doi.org/10.18510/ijthr.2020.726. e-ISSN 2395-7654
6. Van, N.T.T., et al.: The role of human–machine interactive devices for post-COVID-19 innovative sustainable tourism in Ho Chi Minh City Vietnam. Sustainability (Switzerland) **12**(22), 1–30 (2020). https://doi.org/10.3390/su12229523
7. Fernandes, S.: Which way to cope with COVID-19 challenges? Contributions of the IoT for smart city projects (2021)
8. Ide, A.: Tourism and ICT solutions in the COVID-19 era: a comparison between Japan and Sweden. Rev. Socionetw. Strateg. **15**(1), 195–211 (2021). https://doi.org/10.1007/s12626-021-00072-x
9. Naramski, M.: The application of ICT and smart technologies in polish museum - towards smart tourism. Sustainability (Switzerland) **12**(21), 1–27 (2020). https://doi.org/10.3390/su12219287
10. Boulila, W., Abuhamdah, A., Driss, M., Kammoun, S., Ahmad, J.: GuideMe: a mobile application based on global positioning system and object recognition towards a smart tourist guide. arXiv preprint arXiv:2105.13426 (2021)
11. Ghani, T., Jahan, N., Ridoy, S.H., Khan, A.T., Khan, S., Khan, M.M.: Amar Bangladesh - a machine learning based smart tourist guidance system. In: 2018 2nd International Conference on Electronics, Materials Engineering and Nano-technology (IEMENTech), pp. 1–5. IEEE (2018)
12. Manczak, I., Bajak, M.: Tourist mobile applications: evaluation of the VisitMalopolska app. Turyzm/Tourism **31**(1), 29–38 (2021)
13. Nugraha, N.B., Alimudin, E.: Mobile application development for tourist guide in Pekanbaru City. J. Phys. Conf. Ser. **1430**(1), 012038 (2020). IOP Publishing
14. Al-Omari, A.H., Al-Marghirani, A.: Smart tourism architectural model (Kingdom of Saudi Arabia: a case study). Int. J. Adv. Comput. Sci. Appl. (IJACSA) **8**(10), 76–81 (2017)
15. Chaw, L.Y., Tang, C.M.: What makes learning management systems effective for learning? J. Educ. Technol. Syst. **47**(2), 152–169 (2018). https://doi.org/10.1177/004723951879582
16. Hew, J.J., Leong, L.Y., Tan, G.W.H., Lee, V.H., Ooi, K.B.: Mobile social tourism shopping: a dual-stage analysis of a multi-mediation model. Tour. Manag. **66**, 121–139 (2018). https://doi.org/10.1016/j.tourman.2017.10.00
17. Kwon, S.J., Park, E, Kim, K.J.: What drives successful social networking services? A comparative analysis of user acceptance of Facebook and Twitter. Soc. Sci. J. **51**(4), 1-11 (2014)

18. Ooi, K.B., Tan, G.W.H.: Mobile technology acceptance model: an investigation using mobile users to explore smartphone credit card. Expert Syst. Appl. **59**, 33–46 (2016). https://doi.org/10.1016/j.eswa.2016.04.015
19. Tan, G.W.H., Lee, V.H., Hew, J.J., Ooi, K.B., Wong, L.W.: The interactive mobile social media advertising: an imminent approach to advertise tourism products and services? Telematics Inform. **35**(8), 2270–2288 (2018). https://doi.org/10.1016/j.tele.2018.09.005
20. Stocchi, L., Michaelidou, N., Micevski, M.: Drivers and outcomes of branded mobile app usage intention. J. Prod. Brand Manag. **28**(1), 28–49 (2019). https://doi.org/10.1108/JPBM-02-2017-1436
21. Tsaih, R.-H., Hsu, C.C.: Artificial intelligence in smart tourism: a conceptual framework. In: Proceedings of the 18th International Conference on Electronic Business, 2–6 December, Guilin, Guangxi, China, pp. 124–133. ICEB, Guilin (2018)
22. Too, W.G., Thong, C.L., Chit, S.M., Chaw, L.Y., Lee, C.Y.: Features of mobile tracking apps: a review of literature and analysis of current apps compared against travel agency requirements. In: Salvendy, G., Wei, J. (eds.) HCII 2020. LNCS, vol. 12216, pp. 107–120. Springer, Cham (2020). https://doi.org/10.1007/978-3-030-50350-5_10
23. Thong, C.L., Chit, S.M., Chaw, L.Y., Lee, C.Y.: Design city trip management app in the Kuala Lumpur context during pandemic Covid-19: a preliminary research case. In: Salvendy, G., Wei, J. (eds.) HCII 2021. LNCS, vol. 12796, pp. 100–112. Springer, Cham (2021). https://doi.org/10.1007/978-3-030-77025-9_10
24. Joshi, A., et al.: Likert scale: explored and explained. Br. J. Appl. Sci. Technol. **7**(4), 396–403 (2015) Sciencedomain.org. https://doi.org/10.9734/BJAST/2015/14975
25. Marshall, G., Jonker, L.: An introduction to descriptive statistics: a review and practical guide. Radiography **16**, e1–e7 (2010). Elsevier Ltd., Lancaster. https://doi.org/10.1016/j.radi.2010.01.001
26. Boone, H.N., Boone, D.A.: Analysing Likert data. J. Extension **50**(2) (2012). http://www.joe.org/joe/2012april/tt2p.shtml%5B8/20/2012

Towards the Implementation of a Versatile Mobile Health Solutions for the Management of Immunization Against Infectious Diseases in Nigeria

Maudlyn I. Victor-Ikoh[1][(✉)] ⓘ, Anasuodei Moko[1] ⓘ, and Wilson Nwankwo[2]

[1] Department of Computer Science and Informatics, Federal University Otuoke, Otuoke, Nigeria
{imegiim,mokoaa}@fuotuoke.edu.ng
[2] Software Engineering and Cyberphysical System Unit, Department of Computer Science,
Edo University Uzairue, Okpella, Nigeria
nwankwo.wilson@edouniversity.edu.ng

Abstract. Immunization against infectious diseases is a lifelong engagement requiring proper record management. In recent times, following the outbreak of COVID-19, it has become imperative that immunization records done locally should be accessible as substantial accessible proof internationally, anywhere, anytime and for future use. Apart from the Electronic Management of Immunization Data (EMID), an initiative of the National Primary Health Care Development Agency (NPHCDA) in response to the outbreak of COVID-19, that schedules and captures individual's data for COVID-19 vaccination, the management of other Routine Immunization records in Nigeria is presently done manually with each immunized individual given an immunization card as proof of immunization, and for follow up on other doses of the vaccine. This method is not without its plethora of challenges. Leveraging mobile health solutions, especially one that places the individual at the centre will benefit the management of the immunization process in Nigeria. There have been a few mobile solution initiatives in Nigeria to address issues associated with managing the immunization process, but they have been fragmentary and have suffered setbacks. This study takes a holistic approach to the management of immunization and proposes a mobile healthcare technology framework using USSD (Unstructured Supplementary Service Data), Short Message Service (SMS) and Mobile Application (Mobile App) towards the implementation of a versatile Mobile Health Solution for the management of immunization in Nigeria. Existing works of literature were reviewed, and interviews conducted amongst health workers and mobile developers. This framework serves as a launchpad for future mobile system Implementation that will continuously enforce scheduled vaccines, provide accurate population immunization coverage data, and combat vaccine hesitancy through effective communication and community engagement approaches.

Keywords: Immunization · Mobile solution · USSD · SMS · Mobile Application

© The Author(s), under exclusive license to Springer Nature Switzerland AG 2022
G. Salvendy and J. Wei (Eds.): HCII 2022, LNCS 13337, pp. 74–81, 2022.
https://doi.org/10.1007/978-3-031-05014-5_7

1 Introduction

Immunization is the safest proven method for protecting against life-threatening and infectious diseases. In Nigeria, Routine Immunization (RI) provides individuals access to vaccines against infectious diseases for the control and eradication of vaccine-preventable diseases. Routine Immunization (RI) is the process of timely vaccination regularly with vaccines considered important for a given country to reduce morbidity and mortality [1]. RI is enabled by a country's healthcare system and managed through a set of management subsystems needed to continuously enforce scheduled vaccines, monitor their safety, control population immunization coverage, measure their epidemiological impact and report to international bodies [2]. The National Primary Health Care Development Agency (NPHCDA) of the Federal Ministry of Health (FMoH) of Nigeria coordinates RI policies and strategies while the Local Government Areas (LGAs) are responsible for the implementation of RI services [3].

It is the responsibility of the government to secure its public health via immunization its citizens against infectious diseases. Carrying out a large-scale immunization campaign in a densely populated country like Nigeria can be difficult and requires good data management and administration to be successful. As a result, immunization information systems are recommended. Immunization information systems are secure, population-based computerized databases that track all immunization doses given by participating clinicians to people living in a specific geopolitical area [14].

One thing the COVID-19 Pandemic has brought to the forefront is that immunization is not only for children but individuals of all ages. A Nigerian child is considered fully vaccinated if he or she has received the following vaccinations: 1 dose of Bacille Calmette-Gue'rin (BCG) against tuberculosis, 3 doses of Pentavalent (Penta) vaccine to prevent diphtheria, pertussis (whooping cough), tetanus, hepatitis B, and Haemophilus influenzae type b, 3 doses poliovirus vaccine (OPV), 1 dose of inactivated poliovirus vaccine (IPV), 1 dose of measles vaccine and 1 dose of yellow fever vaccine [4]. At any stage from teenage to adulthood, a girl is required to take the Human Papilloma Virus (HPV) Vaccine against Cervical Cancer [5]. All pregnant women are given routine tetanus toxoid (TT) to prevent maternal and neonatal tetanus (MNT) [6]. Hence Immunization against infectious diseases is a lifelong engagement that requires proper record management as in recent times, immunization record done locally is now required as substantial accessible proof internationally and for future use.

Apart from the Electronic Management of Immunization Data (EMID) [15], an initiative of NPHCDA in response to the outbreak of COVID-19, that schedules and captures individual's data for COVID 19 vaccination, the management of other Routine Immunization records in Nigeria is presently done manually with each immunized individual given an immunization card as proof of immunization, and for follow up on other doses of the vaccine. The healthcare facility also manually keeps a record of all those vaccinated in their facility and submit a monthly/periodic report to the state ministry of health. This method is not without its plethora of challenges. They include: Immunization card records can be easily misplaced or lost; erroneous data record by immunization staff; missed or overdue immunization due to forgetfulness; incongruous immunization records due to immunization done in multiple healthcare facilities.

Leveraging on mobile devices, especially mobile apps for immunization, places the individual at the centre of care [7]. Mobile Health Solution is the delivery of healthcare support via mobile technologies. Mobile solutions can do a lot of good to managing the immunization process in Nigeria. There have been a few mobile solution initiatives in Nigeria to address issues associated with managing the immunization process, but they have been fragmentary and have suffered setbacks.

Hence, this study takes a holistic and integrated approach to the management of immunization and proposes a framework towards the implementation of a versatile Mobile Health Solution for the management of immunization in Nigeria. This framework creates a launchpad for future mobile system Implementation that will continuously enforce scheduled vaccines, provide accurate population immunization coverage data and Combat Vaccine hesitancy through effective communication and community engagement approaches.

2 Literature Review

Previous research studies in Nigeria have linked low vaccine uptake, and likely predictors for completion of full vaccination in children to a variety of issues such as the awareness of when to begin and finish vaccines, knowledge of vaccine safety and efficacy was extremely low, birth facility, mother's level of education and place of residence (rural or urban) [8, 9]. [10] identified barriers to immunization coverage amongst which are Low or nonexistent community engagement, Poor access to hard-to-reach communities, unreliable or invalid administrative data, Unclear protocols and inadequate training of staff for appropriate data collection and utilization, data are not being used for decision making and the lack of basic data collection tools such as the State-provided registers.

Every year, UNICEF, and the World Health Organization (WHO) publish fresh estimates of immunization coverage for 195 countries, including Nigeria. Following each immunization coverage operation, a comprehensive assessment is performed to determine the degree to which every child was reached and immunized. Such statistics can assist highlight where progress has been made or where it is needed, where reversals in immunization coverage are occurring and where there are areas of success. UNICEF in 2018 reported that 4.3 million Nigerian children still miss out on vaccinations every year. As alarming as the figure may look, [11] in a survey result suggest that administrative RI data do not reflect true vaccination coverage for Nigeria. Several factors can contribute to inaccurate and inconsistent administrative data. Which includes erroneous data reporting from health facilities, incomplete data reporting, delays in recording summarizing vaccination data after RI sessions and poor review and use of RI data locally [12]. All these lapses call for proper management immunization system.

[11] a pilot study demonstrated the use of SMS to daily report the results of routine immunization sessions as opposed to end-of-the-month reports. Their study showed that daily SMS reporting can be used in the management of immunization services such as monitoring routine immunization data more frequently and facilitating timely interventions for improving the quality of data collected by the program; providing supervisors with an alternative source of information to identify areas where routine immunization services are suboptimal; and to help, decision-makers identify which healthcare facility did not report sessions conducted and ensure prompt follow-up.

Studies from [13] identified some aspects for realizing mobile healthcare solutions in developing countries. One aspect is the use of the appropriate technology; technology that is most suitable and compatible with the targeted populace. The study submits that while SMS is a very effective and cost effect mobile technology for healthcare solutions; it is, however, not a universal preference. Hence to obtain long term positive results across the populace for which the mobile health technology is for, researchers must investigate the prevalent technology amongst the populace and take appropriate action. Another aspect that must be addressed to realize mobile healthcare solution is the problem of health information fragmentation and interoperability issues amongst healthcare facilities. Fragmented health information hinders effective healthcare. Therefore changes are needed to create mobile healthcare solutions that solve the problem of fragmentation of health data [13].

RemindMe, a product of the Innovation Corner, is an offline data management and reminder system for immunization using USSD/Voice Technology [16, 17]. RemindMe addresses the foremost problem of vaccine uptake due to forgetfulness. Some parents in rural areas had difficulty determining where, when, and how frequently their children were supposed to obtain immunizations. Because of the uncertainty, vaccines were delayed and repeated, increasing the risk of baby and child death from preventable diseases [16]. Via a personal interview, one of the co-founders of RemindMe stated that since the launch of RemindMe in Nigeria 2018, it has suffered many setbacks and has stalled. One of the limits of RemindMe was that it was deployed from the state level (not from the federal level or NPHCDA that is responsible for immunization initiatives in Nigeria) hence the change of state governments affected its implementation. Secondly, the project became an object for politicking.

Another mobile healthcare initiative for immunization is the Electronic Management of Immunization Data (EMID) [15] an initiative of NPHCDA. EMID is the registration platform of the Federal Ministry of Health for COVID 19 Vaccination which was in response to the outbreak of COVID-19. It captures individuals' data and schedules individuals for COVID-19 vaccination. Unlike RemindMe, EMID is the brainchild of the Nigerian Federal Government hence, was deployed from the federal level by NPHCDA and is in use by all COVID- 19 vaccination centres in every state in Nigeria. This factor made the rollout of EMID a huge success. While EMID is evident that immunization management system can be deployed from the federal level and implemented by states, it however does not manage other Routine Immunization.

3 Materials and Methods

Pieces of literature on similar topics were reviewed, interviews were conducted with healthcare vaccination workers and developers of other immunization mobile solutions to gather data and the working modalities of immunization in Nigeria. Data gotten were assimilated to model the existing system using computer-aided software. The proposed framework was consequently modelled with computer-aided software to showcase areas mobile technology can be used to improve the existing framework.

3.1 Existing System Analysis

Figure 1 represents the present method of managing immunization in Nigeria. Each immunized individual is given an immunization card as proof of immunization and for follow up on other doses of the vaccine. The healthcare facility also manually keeps a record of all those vaccinated in their facility in a register and submits a monthly/periodic report to the state ministry of health. The National Primary Health Care Development Agency (NPHCDA) of the Federal Ministry of Health (FMoH) of Nigeria creates and rollout strategic policies for activities concerned with routine immunization while the Local Government Areas (LGAs) under the regulation of the state ministry of health are responsible for the implementation of Routine Immunization services. Healthcare facilities, both private and government-owned are the centres where immunization is given and data collected and collated for forwarding to the NPHCDA hence the federal government of Nigeria. Data received are used for planning immunization coverage, the number of needed vaccines and sent to global health organizations.

The present method is not without its plethora of challenges. They include:

1. Misplaced or lost immunization card records.
2. Missed or overdue immunization due to forgetfulness.
3. Incongruous immunization records due to fragmented immunization data from immunization done and stored in multiple healthcare facilities.
4. Erroneous data record by immunization staff.
5. Delay in transmitting immunization records to the relevant authorities for real-time decision making.
6. Immunization registers are susceptible to damage without the guarantee of data backup hence causing the unavailability of immunization records for future reference.

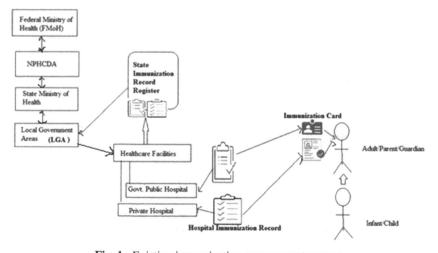

Fig. 1. Existing immunization management system

Immunization against infectious diseases has become a global concern. Managing the immunization record of a populace is a critical venture that will probably become a necessity for global interaction. Therefore Nigeria requires a shift from its current way of managing the immunization process, to something more robust and sustainable into the future by leveraging technology.

3.2 Proposed System

The proposed framework anchors on mobile technology for the management of immunization in Nigeria, especially the versatility in mobile solutions comprising of SMS, USSD, and Mobile Apps. The proposed framework integrates these versatile solutions into one solution to allow users to decide on which is their preferred mobile solution for managing and engaging with their immunization process. Following the setback suffered by RemindMe, and the success experienced with EMID, the mobile framework proposes that mobile healthcare solutions for managing immunization be rolled-out from the federal level and implemented by states. Immunization data are consolidated in real-time from multiple healthcare facilities into a single record that will make available official immunization records for individuals, the local and state government, and ultimately the federal government.

Figure 2 is a representation of the proposed framework for managing immunization in the Nigeria Healthcare system. There are four key players to this system they are: the Government, healthcare providers and the individual seeking to be vaccinated and Mobile healthcare solutions synergizing immunization activity.

1. **Mobile solution:** The solution provides an integration of both offline (USSD and SMS) and online (Mobile Application) modes of immunization process management. That can be easily accessible at any location, and at any time.
2. **The Individual:** This framework caters for individuals of all ages willing to be vaccinated. In the case of a child/toddler, such minor can be registered by parents or guardians and their account managed until old enough to manage his/her record and continues with that account with the required adult vaccinations. The user registers queries
3. **Healthcare facility:** The framework gives aggregated immunization histories for use by a healthcare facility in determining scheduled vaccines at the point of clinical treatment.
4. **The Government:** This framework provides a structure for centralized data reporting, that will empower the government to be able to provide statistically accurate and up to date immunization records to international health bodies.

This framework offers the following benefits include:

1. Versatile means for individuals to access their immunization record via USSD code or mobile app offering an advantage over traditional immunization card record.
2. It allows the user to check and verify their immunization record in real-time at the place of immunization and on-demand.

3. It can help individuals set reminders or be reminded via SMS of the next immunization appointment avoiding overdue or missed vaccinations.
4. Mobile health solutions can enable reporting of immunization records independent of the healthcare facility as information captured at multiple healthcare facilities can be accessed via a web service for a lifetime.
5. Another possible advantage of leveraging on Mobile Health Solutions for managing vaccinations is the opportunity to boost vaccination confidence, rates, debunk myths and ease vaccination hesitancy due to unfounded religious beliefs via enlightenment.

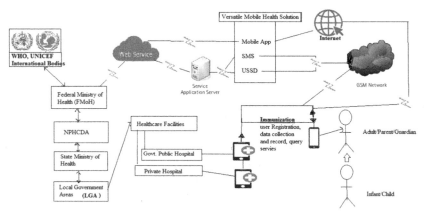

Fig. 2. Proposed versatile mobile health solution framework for managing Immunization in Nigeria.

4 Conclusion

This paper has examined the current practice and challenges with the management of immunization data in Nigeria as it affects lifelong record keeping, access by individuals and the prospect of versatile mobile health solutions to improve the state of things. A mobile immunization solution framework is proposed. The framework would provide discourse towards the implementation of a mobile solution for the management of immunization against infectious diseases.

References

1. Intellectual Concepts: Routine Immunizations. IT Consulting, 26 February 2019. https://intellectualconcepts.com/consulting-services/public-health/routine-immunizations/
2. Shen, A.K., Fields, R., McQuestion, M.: The future of routine immunization in the developing world: challenges and opportunities. Glob. Health Sci. Pract. 2(4), 381–394 (2014)

3. Eboreime, E., Abimbola, S., Bozzani, F.: Access to routine immunization: a comparative analysis of supply-side disparities between Northern and Southern Nigeria. PLOS ONE **10**(12) (2015)
4. Ophori, E.A., Tula, M.Y., Azih, A.V., Okojie, R., Ikpo, P.E.: Current trends of immunization in Nigeria: prospect and challenges. Trop. Med. Health **42**(2), 67–75 (2014)
5. Igomu, T., Folorunsho-Francis, A.: HPV vaccine, the cervical cancer prevention most Nigerian women don't know. Healthwise, 9 February 2020. https://healthwise.punchng.com/hpv-vac cine-the-cervical-cancer-prevention-most-nigerian-women-dont-know/
6. Immunization_tetanus.pdf. https://www.who.int/reproductivehealth/publications/maternal_ perinatal_health/immunization_tetanus.pdf. Accessed 20 Dec 2021
7. Wilson, K., Atkinson, K.M., Westeinde, J.: Apps for immunization: leveraging mobile devices to place the individual at the centre of care. Hum. Vaccin. Immunother. **11**(10), 2395–2399 (2015)
8. Tagbo, B.N., Eke, C.B., Omotowo, B.I., Onwuasigwe, C.N., Onyeka, E.B., Mildred, U.O.: Vaccination coverage and its determinants in children aged 11–23 months in an urban district of nigeria. World J. Vaccines **04**(04), 175–183 (2014)
9. Oluwatosin, O.A., Brown, V.B.: Socio-demographic factors associated with childhood immunization uptake in Akinyele local government area, Oyo State, Nigeria. Afr. J. Med. Med. Sci. **41**(2), 161–167 (2012)
10. Wonodi, C., et al.: Landscape analysis of routine immunization in Nigeria: identifying barriers and prioritizing interventions. In: IVAC (2012)
11. Akerele, A., et al.: Improving routine immunization data quality using daily short message system reporting platform: an experience from Nasarawa state, Nigeria. PLOS ONE **16**(8) (2021)
12. Schwebel, F.J., Larimer, M.E.: Using text message reminders in health care services: a narrative literature review. Internet Interv. **13**, 82–104 (2018)
13. Latif , S., Ali, A., Qadir, J., Rana, R., Imran, M., Younis, M.: Mobile health for the developing world: review, prospects and a case study. IEEE Access (2017)
14. About Immunization Information System (IIS)—CDC. Center for Disease Control and Prevention (2019). https://www.cdc.gov/vaccines/programs/iis/about.html
15. NPHCDA COVID-19 Website. Vaccination Registration (2021). https://nphcda.vaccination. gov.ng/
16. Egesi, T.: Nigeria immunization "app" makes a global impact. World Bank Blogs. https://blogs.worldbank.org/nasikiliza/nigeria-immunization-app-makes-a-global-impact. Accessed 2 Sept 2021
17. Nigeria Health Watch: Remind me: a tech solution to improve immunisation coverage in Nigeria. Medium. https://nigeriahealthwatch.medium.com/remind-me-a-tech-solution-to-improve-immunisation-coverage-in-nigeria-ebd1dbc56dbd. Accessed 7 Dec 2021

Remote at Court

Challenges and Solutions of Video Conferencing in the Judicial System

Carolin Wienrich$^{(\boxtimes)}$ ⓘ, Lennart Fries ⓘ, and Marc Erich Latoschik ⓘ

Julius Maximilians Universität Würzburg, Würzburg, Germany
carolin.wienrich@uni-wuerzburg.de
http://hci.uni-wuerzburg.de/

Abstract. This article targets one of the fundamental changes in the judicial system induced by the severe limitations due to the absence of face-to-face meetings: the application of video conferencing in court sessions, an application with special requirements in this critical domain. A semi-structured literature review that we conducted revealed a lack of human-centered approaches. Potentials and challenges, mainly focused on the needs of judges, were also identified. These challenges were then transformed into requirements for designs of video conferencing systems in the judicial context. We ultimately developed a low-fidelity prototype of a system that incorporates a novel combination of three use-case-specific features: a solution to manage fatigue, a solution to manage user participation, and cognitive aid based on artificial intelligence (AI). The aim of the last feature was to reduce cognitive load while improving the moderation quality of court session leaders. Through a heuristic evaluation by human-computer interaction (HCI) and domain experts, the benefits of the basic design ideas, as well as potential areas for improvement, were identified. This paper presents the first systematic analyses of the potentials and limitations of video conferencing in German court sessions. It brings the enormous challenges of a critical domain in society, as well as human-centered and value-sensitive digitalization and AI adoption, under the spotlight.

Keywords: EJustice · Video conferencing · AI cognitive aid · Human-centered AI · Value sensitive design

1 Introduction

Digitalization has become increasingly important in many areas of life. Its development gained much momentum during the COVID-19 pandemic, since industries, administrations, and civil services had to change quite rapidly and adapt

This research has been funded by the Bavarian Federal Ministry of Digitalisation in the project XR HUB Würzburg (project number A5-3822-2-16).

G. Salvendy and J. Wei (Eds.): HCII 2022, LNCS 13337, pp. 82–106, 2022.
https://doi.org/10.1007/978-3-031-05014-5_8

to the challenges posed by lockdowns and the absence of physical meetings. As a result, many have adopted video conferencing as a daily solution for necessary communications and collaborations. However, the adoption of video conferencing as a medium of remote communication and collaboration has different requirements depending on the specific use case. The present contribution analyses possibilities and challenges of video conferencing in court sessions and presents a prototype meeting the special requirements of a digital court session.

Through objective examination, while being fair to all parties in strict coherence to all laws, one finds challenges in the adoption of digitalization in the judicial system. Nevertheless, several countries have started to explore the usage of video conferencing in the judicial system. The United Kingdom (UK) was one of the earliest adopters of video conferencing in court, also publishing a set of useful guidelines as early as March 2020 [37]. According to the National Center for State Courts, Texas judges collectively held 1,800 virtual hearings in early 2020 [34]. In Germany, the Munich State Court had scheduled over 100 civil cases in the digital format by 2020 [36]. In February 2021, the Minister of Justice and Europe, Guido Wolf, announced that 1,200 judges in the German state of Baden-Württemberg would have access to the video conferencing software "Cisco Webex Meetings" [31].

However, adherence to democratic principles and constitutional rights are necessary for appropriate implementation of digital applications such as video conferencing. These principles and rights guarantee fair conditions for all involved parties and ensure unbiased judicial decision-making. Thus, in using video conferencing during court sessions, special measures must be taken to safeguard these principles and rights. One crucial right is the right to get judged by a lawful judge who is impartial and unbiased [39]. Further, every official court session participant (excluding uninvolved observers) has the right to be heard, which must be guaranteed and respected under any circumstances [8,35,39]. This, for example, also requires unobstructed access to social-attention signals. Typical screen-based video conferencing solutions impede particularly these signals. In addition, fatigue, participation, and direct assistance are important considerations for an appropriate design of human-computer interface at court.

It is essential to make justice accessible to all [1] and ensure equality for all involved parties [35]. Further, transparency of court sessions among the public is critical in light of the special requirements for court session leaders, that is, the judges, when using video conferencing [39,40]. Apart from this pioneering work, other researchers have already identified challenges regarding the moderation quality (e.g., observations on the distribution of the talking frequency of participants), the perception of participants (e.g., credibility), the workload (e.g., fatigue), and media competencies (e.g., the operation of the system) [8,11,40].

Overall, the following questions arise: (1) Can digital court sessions guarantee the described special principles and constitutional rights? and (2) Do digital court sessions affect the moderation quality, the perception, and the workload of judges? Both questions underline the sensitivity of the given use case, which we believe can be best tackled through a human-centered design with key methods to support digitalization processes [24]. A design approach with a focus on the user must include the recurrent feedback of actual end users in the process of research and development, in order to gain a holistic perspective of the proposed product and reap rewards from both the research experience and the experience of the end user. Such an approach can also lead to higher acceptance through the inclusion of the user in the design cycle [25, 26].

However, human-computer interaction (HCI) approaches are still rare in the judicial context. Only a few studies have focused on a user-centered transaction design (e.g., [21]) or on a user-friendly courtroom [20]. Further, a human-centered design has rarely been applied to accompany digitalization in the judicial context [20]. Many studies have addressed the digitalization of the judicial system in general. However, the literature lacks a systematic overview of these studies and connections to fields engaging in human-centered digitalization of courtrooms. Further, crucial requirements of a digitalized judicial system, such as court leaders' multifaceted responsibilities, are rarely addressed. Even though human-centered design processes can contribute to meeting these challenges, no study (to the authors' best knowledge) has been found to analyze and improve video conferencing in court sessions through user-centered design processes.

To bridge this gap, we conducted a semi-structured literature review summarizing the scientific literature on the use of video conferencing tools during court sessions (step 1). In this paper, first, we outline possibilities and challenges stemming from the literature review and discuss them, focusing mainly on the needs of judges. Then, we transfer the results of step 1 into human-centered design methods to gather ideas on how digital courts might be improved. Next, through a requirement analysis, the identified challenges are transferred into concrete demands for video conferencing design in the judicial context (step 2). Following this, as our main contribution to the research efforts in this domain, we introduce a low-fidelity prototype of a cognitive aid applying artificial intelligence (AI) to reduce the cognitive load and to improve the attention of the court session leader toward the needs of other trial members. Finally, we gather inputs for improving the low-fidelity prototype with a heuristic expert evaluation and another evaluation at a symposium with realistic end users (step 3).

2   Step1: Literature Review

The first step was conducting a semi-structured review of the existing literature. The goal of the review was to obtain an overview of the previous research into the digitalization of justice and the challenges associated with such an endeavor. The point of interest was the implications of virtual hearings for the judicial system and video conferencing on the participants, particularly the judge. However, a lack of scientific articles on the field of justice led to the inclusion of articles from other areas addressing moderating or leading participants in video conferences.

2.1   Method

The semi-structured review followed the *Prisma approach* [19], including four distinct phases as illustrated in Fig. 1. The research for this study was conducted through Google Scholar and the ACM Digital Library, with some articles being found through the references of studies identified as relevant for the review.

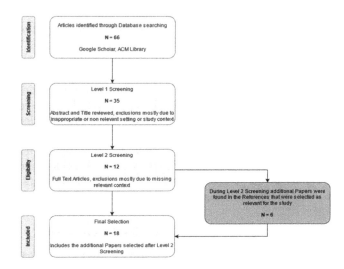

Fig. 1. Diagram of the scanning and selection process for relevant literature

In the first phase, we identified relevant papers through a search by looking at their titles (n = 66). The studies that were selected had to fit into one or more of three categories defined by the following criteria:

1. The articles provide insights about the adoption of e-justice in different countries before and during the pandemic.
2. The articles describe challenges in and possibilities for the use of video conferencing during a court session.
3. The articles include the rule of moderators in video conferencing.

To capture these categories, we searched for the following keywords, ignoring case sensitivity:

`"Video Conferencing Challenges" OR "Video Conferencing Moderating" OR "Video Conferencing Psychology" OR "Video Conferencing Justice" OR "E-Justice" OR "Justice Digitalization"`

When searching the Google Scholar database, we utilized the advanced search option with the specification to "find articles with at least one of the words" and selected the option for words to occur "anywhere in the article." In the ACM

Digital Library, we searched the ACM Full-Text Collection and selected the option to search "anywhere" within the article with the above keywords; we did not add any filters for the search. In both libraries, we delimited the time frame to only include articles published between 2017 and May 2021. There were two reasons for this delimitation to prefer contemporary research: (1) Except for results from a basic research, we believed, many technological developments might impede the straightforward transferability of older approaches and results to state-of-the-art solutions; and (2) Video conferencing experienced a significant upturn recently, and hence it seemed safe to assume that it would have generated a broader scientific reflection likewise.

The second step included abstract scanning. Most articles were excluded due to irrelevant contexts, for example, a paper detailing the steps to take in India to implement a fairer video conferencing solution (e.g. [30], which did not provide relevant insights into the points of interest. Thus, the number of relevant studies was reduced to 35. In the third step, we read the full text and decided that 12 out of the 35 articles were suitable for review. Then, we found six additional articles through the related works discussed and cited in these 12 papers, including one article published before 2017. Consequently, the final selection included 18 articles that we analyzed in greater detail. Our selection represents papers from a wide range of authors, preventing significant bias in our results.

2.2   Review Results Focusing on E-Justice in General

The discussion of insights starts with the results addressing e-justice and how different countries have adopted video conferencing tools to modernize their judicial systems.

E-justice refers to the use of information technology and remote communication to improve accessibility of the judicial system while simultaneously strengthening its foundations through improving cooperation between institutions and reducing the duration of procedures [38].

Both Rossner et al. [1] and Sourdin et al. [5] describe the reinvention of the judicial system as a long-time project that has been drastically accelerated as a result of the global pandemic COVID-19. In their paper, Sourdin et al. [5] describe five different courts of North America, three different courts of Asia, seven different courts of Oceania, two different courts of Africa, and four different courts of Europe which started using supporting technologies such as video conferencing to hold proceedings during the pandemic. While this list is not exhaustive, it helps paint a picture of how much COVID-19 has forcibly advanced the digitalization of the judicial system.

McIntyre et al. [2] frame the effort to devitalize a remarkable success in many countries, specifically Australia and the UK. They also mention that online dispute resolution had never been attempted in the UK until 2018 and that Australia only had pilot projects at that time. During the first lockdown, 85% of the English Business and Property Courts hearings were held virtually [32]]. As early as April 2020, the Federal Court of Australia had introduced guidelines to hold proceedings virtually [33].

There are mixed opinions about the future of the (digitalized) judicial system. Vovk [7], for example, describes the increasingly innovative and quick solutions that have made their way into justice during the last year. He shows that Ukraine was fairly quick to improvise and to use video conferencing during court sessions. On the other hand, Germany took a more conservative path and concentrated on establishing some solid groundwork before widely adopting the video conferencing technology at court. The paper finally notes that further regulations may be needed, for example, to guarantee the principle of open justice, but also that the digitalization of justice will continue to advance.

Burova et al. [6] outline a possible way to further legitimize e-justice in the Russian Federation. They highlight the importance of transparency, accessibility, and protection as guiding principles that have to be followed in e-justice to make it a viable alternative. The accessibility requirement is also mentioned by Rossner et al. [1], who focus on virtual courtrooms. Rowden [3] addresses another potential problem, particularly for judges. He discusses the possible erosion of authority due to the missing physical courtroom, highlighting another challenge in adopting virtual courts. Donoghue [4] warns that improper use of technology may limit participation, as well as access to justice, but they otherwise paint a positive picture of the possibilities that come with proper use, such as increasing the efficiency and effectiveness of justice.

Gorodovenko et al. [8] provide an overview of the rights that need to be fulfilled, including the right of access to justice dealt by competent judges, the right to be heard and to get practical help, the right to be considered innocent until proven guilty, and finally, the right to a fair trial free from bias, with transparent communication and an appropriate time window for the hearing. We address some of these points in the following section relating to the possibilities and challenges of video conferencing in the context of justice. Finally, they bring up a few challenges such as inadequate infrastructure, insufficient training, and lack of digital competencies, particularly for those responsible for the court session procedure, that is, the judges. The 2020 study of Sourdin et al. emphasizes the need to move toward a digital platform while ensuring that no human rights get violated [5].

The review of results related to e-justice in general shows that video conferencing has rapidly changed the use of digital technology in the judicial system. The following section scopes the possibilities and challenges that virtual court sessions face.

2.3 Review Results Focusing on Video Conferencing in Court Sessions

Rudnev and Pechegin [9] investigated the principle use of video conferencing technology to generally improve the overall judiciary process. The authors specifically point to the possibilities of such technology in terms of increased access to and simplification of court sessions. This view is shared by Hilgendorf [35], who also sees improved accessibility and the potential to increase fairness and impartiality through digital technology to support the judicial system. Additionally, both essays mention how video conferencing would help speed up the processes significantly and thus reduce the judicial system's long-term workload [9,35]. Grønbæk et al. [10] propose technological solutions to improve participants' attention during hybrid meetings.

In contrast, others identify problems, obstacles, and critical points to consider when using video conferencing at court. Rossner et al. [1] describe that many courts started to use video conferencing during the pandemic. They highlight the differences between the usage of third-party solutions such as Zoom and Microsoft Teams and the usage of individual solutions developed in-house, specifically pointing out data protection and safety concerns relating to third-party products.

Despite the potential advantages of solutions for attention management as proposed by *MirrorBlender* [10], current solutions only rarely include the sophisticated functions necessary to realize these advantages.

The potentially increased cognitive workload due to the adoption of video technology, that is, of video calls, was already investigated in 2008 by Ferran and Watts by [11]. They examined two determinants of information processing-argument quality (as central cue) and likeability (as peripheral cue)-and how cognitive load impacts these determinants. They conducted a study with 143 participants, comparing face-to-face meetings and video conferencing. Their results revealed some core insights. Firstly, cognitive load influenced the way information was processed. Second, likeability influenced information processing more under high cognitive-load conditions. In low cognitive-load conditions, argument quality impacted information processing stronger. Participants reported significantly lower cognitive loads during face-to-face meetings than they did in video conferencing conditions.

The authors mention that rich media, such as video conferencing, change the dynamics of communication in such a way that specific peripheral cues, including likeability, become more influential than in face-to-face situations. This poses a challenge: keeping the cognitive load manageable so as not to lean toward biased processing.

During the coronavirus pandemic, anyone who has used video technology to keep in touch or work has either heard of or experienced "Zoom fatigue." However, despite the ample speculations and anecdotal evidence, very little research has been conducted on this phenomenon. Recently, Fauville et al. [12] investigated the phenomenon, surveying 10,600 participants about their experiences of using video conferencing through an online questionnaire. The results revealed multiple relevant factors enhancing fatigue:

- **Mirror Anxiety** relates to being constantly able to see oneself and thus perceive oneself as an active participant. As a result, one's focus shifts toward one's own frame and to how others may see the actor. This outcome is usually stronger among women than among men.
- **Hyper Gaze** refers to the permanent eye contact with other participants which leads to physical anxiety. This is also described by Takac et al. in their

study [13] to propose a therapy for people with a public speaking phobia through utilizing exposure to virtual reality. Being constantly watched can lead to the development of fears and thus increase stress and fatigue during and after a meeting. This is one reason why Tomprou et al. propose that using the audio-only function may sometimes help improve the quality of conferencing, especially in terms of productivity [14]. They found that groups not focused on visual cues could increase their collective intelligence and synchronize their vocal cues much better than groups with visual cues. They use their results to question the utility of video support in general.

- In contrast, Ferran and Watts [11] as well as Fauville et al. [12] both found that the lack of non-verbal cues during video calls is a major contributing factor toward high fatigue.
- Additionally, fatigue seems to increase with frequency and burstiness, indicating to the value of short rests between meetings.
- According to Fauville et al., work contexts generally induce the highest fatigue [12]. Thus, it seems critical to reduce accumulation of this fatigue in sensitive work environments such as in the field of justice.

2.4   Review Results Focusing on Moderation in Video Conferences

In the last step of the literature review, we focused on the unique role of court session leaders, that is, judges. As mentioned earlier, the moderation quality, the perception of the participants, the judges' workload, and the media's competencies were identified as challenges for judges in digital courtrooms. Unfortunately, there were no studies specifically targeting the roles and responsibilities of court session leaders during virtual moderation. Hence, we included relevant studies from other fields which discussed the possibilities and challenges of virtual moderation.

El Ouardy and Schreiber [17] describe three problems stemming from virtual moderation. The first concerns physicality: Absence of the real environment may be unsettling for some users. The authors propose clearly structured and transparent communication to reduce these disadvantages. According to them, doing so should provide for holistic learning experiences and improve competencies.

The second problem concerns visibility. As mentioned before, constant awareness of oneself might have negative effects, substantiating the implications pointed out by Fauville et al. [12] and Takac et al. [13]. In addition, it might distract one's attention from other participants and their perceptions. A solution suggested for this problem involves changing the camera settings. Another suggestion provided is to regulate the display of one's own camera.

Finally, the authors point out the problem of physical separation. Participants cannot draw upon the full breadth and depth of their perceptions in virtual environments due to limitations in screen sizes and virtual fields of view. This may hinder discussion among participants and limit the communication of the moderators. They suggest letting participants talk about themselves or present their environments to make the interactions more real. They also discuss the potentials of augmented or virtual reality, which could offer an illusion of physicality.

Stang and Zhao [18] describe communication as a synergy of information, messaging, and comprehension. In their study on cross-cultural communication and collaboration, they found that it was especially essential for the non-native speakers to be included the discussion explicitly and have a clear way of communicating.

Sometimes, the native speakers would be too focused on explaining their perspectives or would use words that the non-native speakers did not understand. Context-specific language seemed to have been preferred by even the non-native speakers to communicate the basic ideas better.

Finally, the authors underline the importance of finding context-specific communication strategies among the participants before diving into the video conference discussion. This step, they argue, would improve comprehension and also help avoid exclusion, as well as minimize confusion among participants.

Kim et al. [15] show the utility of a bot moderating a chatroom. Their results include reaching an authentic consensus and equal involvement of all participants, indicating the benefit of using digital aids for moderation. It may be essential to note that this study was done with a sample of Korean participants. Transferability of the results to the more individualistic Western culture and other less technology-oriented cultures has not been established yet.

In a similar vein, Lee et al. [16] indicate that collaboration between a human moderator and a supporting bot can help enhance the quality of discussion. This synthesis would allow the inclusion of human expertise that is hard to replicate using an artificial system, while at the same time utilizing the latter's benefits.

2.5   Summary of Possibilities and Challenges

The review of the final 18 articles reveals valuable possibilities and challenges relating to e-justice and the usage of video conferencing in court sessions. Table 1 summarizes the challenges, and Table 2 summarizes the potentials we have identified.

Overall, prior research has shown some valuable benefits of adopting the video conferencing technology in different use cases. Most of these results seem promising also for justice, although there have been no proper studies in this area yet. However, the identified disadvantages might be particularly challenging when using video conferencing tools during court sessions.

For instance, a high cognitive load could impede the responsibilities of court session leaders, such as giving all trial members equal chances to speak. Nevertheless, the studies we have review were not conducted with justice in mind. Consequently, two main questions arise: (1) What can we learn from the identified challenges and possibilities for the design of video conferencing tools applied in court sessions? and (2) How can we support judges in fulfilling their multifaceted responsibilities when leading court trials?

Table 1. Summary of identified challenges from the review, the derived requirements, and proposed solutions.

	Challenges	Requirements	Proposal
Cognitive Load	Attention management	R1: Allow focusing on essential parts of the conference	Develop an AI recommender system to highlight the essential parts in real time
	Participation management	R2: Improve the participation of less vocal members; support the inclusion of all participants	Develop an AI recommender system to hint at whom to include more in real time
	Information processing management	R3: Increase reflective information processing; avoid biased information processing	Develop an AI recommender system to analyze arguments and hint at heuristic processing cues in real time
Fatigue	Mirror anxiety	R4: Reduce Mirror anxiety	Allow participants to manage the individual views and self-visibility
	Hyper gaze	R5: Reduce Hyper gaze	Allow participants to manage the subjective views of other participants
	Nonverbal cues	R6: Increase perceptibility of nonverbal cues	Provide systems that allow non-verbal communication such as eXtended Realities
	Accumulation of fatigue in work context	R7: Reduce the accumulation of fatigue in work contexts	Develop the best work-break balance through considering the specifics of virtual work
Moderation	Data safety	R8: Enable identification and data security	Develop systems that can operate without having unclear privacy laws
	Physicality	R9: Provide personalized avatars	Develop personalized avatars of high quality and possibilities for identification
	Visibility	R4: Reduce mirror anxiety	Explore potential solutions to manage self-visibility, e.g. fade out own view
	Perception	R1: Allow focusing on essential parts of the conference	Develop an AI recommender system to highlight the essential parts in real time
	Communication	R10: Encourage a holistic communication process	Provide innovative moderation tool
Justice	Transparency	R11: Provide transparent information	Explain how the technology works; make it easy and intuitive to use
	Accessibility	R12: Provide accessible technology for every person, especially vulnerable ones	Build a solid infrastructure; apply human-centered design processes; regard different target groups
	Protection of Rights	R13: Protect rights to be heard, to have fair proceedings, to have a competent judge and transparent communication	Provide low-cost infrastructure and a personalized, safe system
	Participation	R2: R2: Improve the participation of less vocal members; support the inclusion of all participants	Develop an AI recommender system to hint at whom to include more in real time

Table 2. Summary of identified possibilities from the review, the derived potentials, and solution proposals

Possibilities	Potentials	Proposals
Bot support Human Bot Collaboration	P1: Collaborate with cognitive aids to improve the conference quality	Develop an AI recommender system to support the judge/moderator in real time
Augmented & Virtual Reality	P2: Include beneficial parts of augmented reality and virtual reality technology	Use personalized avatars and extended reality to improve presence, nonverbal communication, and identification
Efficiency & Effectivity	P3: Improve the efficiency of meetings	Develop an AI recommender system to support the judge/moderator in real time
Relief	P4: Provide relief to the moderators	
Simplification	P5 Simplify the process for moderators and participants	

To address these questions, we transform the challenges into concrete requirements that could guide the design of digital aids supporting virtual court sessions and task fulfillment of court session leaders.

3   Step 2: Requirement Analyses and Connections to Human-Computer Interaction

In the following step, we incorporated the challenges and possibilities identified through the review into a human-centered design process. We classified the review results into four requirement categories: cognitive load, fatigue, moderation, and judicial specifics (see Tables 1 and 2).

The judicial specifics and moderation requirements were derived from our research insights detailed in Sects. 2.2 and 2.4, respectively. We decided to split cognitive load and fatigue into two separate categories due to their specific challenges, which we previously discussed in Sect. 2.3; the two are granular enough to not be summarized under the generic header of videoconferencing.

The requirements are continuously numerated and shortened to R in the following section.

3.1   Requirements to Reduce Cognitive Load

The literature review revealed lacking attention management during video conferences (e.g., [10]). Referring to the judicial context, R1 calls for judges to focus on the essential parts of the conference. Distractions from less important parts or due usability issues should be avoided. Further, attention should be distributed fairly among all court members.

Thus, R2 demands the involvement of less vocal members and the control of dominant vocal members. Supporting judges in including all participants could lead to increased fairness of proceedings. Ferran and Watts [11] showed that a high cognitive load leads to preferring likeability over argument quality during video conferences. However, reflective and central information processing is vital to guarantee fair perception and judgment by judges.

R3 stresses increasing reflective management to avoid biased processing of information.

3.2   Requirements to Reduce Video Conference Fatigue

The review revealed many factors increasing fatigue during video conferences [11–14]. R4-R7 scope these factors. R4 calls for the reduction of mirror anxiety and the management of self-visibility. R5 demands the reduction of hyper gaze effects and the management of others' visibility. R6 emphasizes increasing the perceptibility of nonverbal cues. Finally, R7 addresses the reduction of accumulated workload reported, particularly in work contexts [12].

3.3   Requirements to Improve Moderation Quality

Some of the following requirements can be seen as extensions of the requirements regarding workload and fatigue reduction (i.e., perception refers to R1, and visibility refers to R4).

Since court session leaders carry a special moderation responsibility, improvement of the moderation quality is addressed by R8-R10. R8 calls for unambiguous participants' identification and safe data processing.

R9 deals with increasing the sense of embodiment through the use of (photorealistic) avatars.

Finally, R10 scopes the communication process in general and demands fluent and ordered trial communication.

3.4   Requirements to Consider Judicial Specifics

For a successful application in the domain of justice, we need to adhere to some further requirements. First, it is essential to provide transparent information about the system's functioning (R11) and make it accessible for everyone, especially vulnerable people (R12).

R13 scopes the protection of citizens' rights during a court session. The right to be heard and have fair and quick proceedings under a competent judge has been considered the most relevant [8,35,39].

Finally, as we have already mentioned, improving participation plays a huge role in ensuring the fairness of proceedings (R2).

3.5   Potentials to Improve Video Conferencing During Trials

Besides challenges, the review results reveal promising possibilities of using digital tools in the judicial context. We derived three central potentials pointing to innovative concepts that might improve the quality of video conferencing systems during trials.

Based on the results of Kim et al. [15] and Lee et al. [16], cognitive aids bear promising features to improve conference quality (P1).

P2 refers to the beneficial aspects of augmented, virtual, and mixed realities. For example, an avatar might enhance one's sense of presence or one's feeling of embodied interaction with another human being.

In contrast to the results showing high cognitive load and fatigue during video conferencing, researchers regarding e-justice generally point to advantages stemming from more efficient processes through digitalization [4,5,35]. These advantages helped us identify the opportunity to provide additional support to participants for efficient court processes (P3).

Overall, through the requirement analysis, we transformed the identified challenges into eleven concrete demands for video conferencing design in the judicial context. In the final step, possible solutions are implemented and evaluated in a human-centered design cycle.

Since considering all requirements is beyond the scope of the present article, the pilot solution focuses on improving attention management, reducing fatigue, and increasing participation. The low-fidelity prototype contains unique video conference settings and a cognitive aid realized through AI.

4   Step 3: Low-Fidelity Prototype and Heuristic Evaluation of an Artificial-Intelligence-Based Cognitive Aid Improving Video Conferencing During Trials

4.1   Conceptional Basis of the Prototype

Our low-fidelity prototype is based on the benefits of cognitive aids in general. It pilots concepts of cognitive aids and settings to improve video conferencing overall. It specifically targets the identified requirements in the judicial context.

Cognitive aids are external representations supporting mental processes during complex or demanding tasks [22]. Typical examples are checklists, mnemonics, or sensors. [22] classify cognitive aids according to the underlying cognitive processes, such as attention, memory, perception, decision, and knowledge. They also describe how these must be designed to support the corresponding cognitive process.

While our initial literature review did not focus on cognitive aids, McLaughlin and Byrne [22] and Chapparo et al. [23] can be referred to for recent reviews on cognitive aids. We briefly highlight important aspects of cognitive aids here to provide a good understanding of our solution. In only one reviewed study was a type of cognitive aid introduced to increase discussion quality in video conferences.

Kim et al.[15] investigated the benefits of a moderation chatbot in a virtual group discussion. The participants discussed social problems that none of them was directly involved in. The bot was programmed to include the less vocal people in the debate through explicitly addressing them and asking them for their opinion. The study's results show that the bot improved the discussion structure through getting participants' independent thoughts and different perspectives. In addition, the bot helped reach an authentic depiction of the groups' consensus, increasing the group members' subjective satisfaction.

Another study investigated the benefits of options for unique settings. *MirrorBlender* allowed for dynamic repositioning and resizing of the video frames in a shared space [10]. The participants could also blend virtual frames on top of each other. This allowed them to accentuate one specific frame while overshadowing or hiding another to decide their current point of focus individually.

In addition, Grønbæk et al. [10] attempted to enable perspective taking in the sense of "what you see is what I see," intending to improve remote work and make the collaborators aware of the virtual people they were interacting with. Their study showed increases in the sense of embodiment, good attention toward deictic gestures, and an inclusive collaborative experience. Especially, the remote participants of the study were able to bring their attention to themselves through manipulating the translucency, scale, and position of their video in the shared space. Thus, the authors concluded that this kind of technology for hybrid meetings could increase participation.

These studies hint at the potentials of cognitive aids and unique settings to improve video conferencing experiences. Based on the European Commission for the Efficiency of Justice's (CEPEJ) groundwork, Hilgendorf [35] describes the use of cognitive aids, with a focus on AI, in justice as a technical revolution that should present a reflective evolution of the judicial system.

Nevertheless, while cognitive aids are pervasive in systems where safety is critical, such as medicine or aviation [23], and show first promising results for video conferences [15], no research (to the authors' best knowledge) addresses cognitive aids in video conferencing court sessions.

The analyses of requirements and potentials presented earlier provide many hints for design features of such a cognitive aid or other unique settings options. Thus, in designing our prototype, we utilized an AI-based cognitive aid to support the moderation quality. Besides, the unique settings provided by the video conferencing system should improve participation and fatigue management.

4.2   Introduction of the Prototype

The prototype provides two views: the view of the participants and the view of the moderator (i.e., the judge).

The participants get three options: they can request to speak, they can request a break, and they can choose their self-view. Figure 2 shows the basic functionalities of the participant view.

Slide "a" is the basic starting view with all the available functions when none is activated. Slide "b" shows the view after the participant has requested

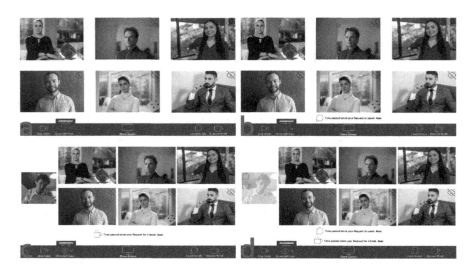

Fig. 2. Paradigmatic screens from a participant's point of view of the low fidelity prototype. Please see the text for the detailed explanation.

to talk. Slide "c" displays the screen with an active request for a break made by the participant. Finally, slide "d" shows the screen with both requests activated.

While in "a" and "b" the self-view is disabled, "c" and "d" show different self-view options; "c" shows the self-view with full opacity, whereas "d" depicts a self-view with lower opacity. The ability of participants to request to speak and request a break should help improve both their participation and attention management, respectively fulfilling R1 and R2, while the option to control their self-view might help reduce mirror anxiety (R4). In combination, the available functions should satisfy the need to protect special rights (R13) and help realize the potential for improving the efficiency of and simplifying the process (P3).

The moderator can view the requests of participants, can choose options for viewing themselves and others, and can additionally activate and deactivate an AI-based cognitive aid. Figure 3 shows the basic functionalities of the moderator view.

Slide "a" depicts the basic view, with the red-colored attention signs indicating participants' requests to speak or requests for a break. Slide "b" shows the same view with additional hints from the cognitive aid. These recommendations can help support participation management. For example, blue speech bubbles indicate that the corresponding participants should be involved in the discussion more frequently. Slide "c" displays the possibility to mute participants. Finally, slide "d" depicts the view when the cognitive aid is deactivated.

Again, in "a" and "b" the self-view is disabled, while "c" and "d" show different self-view options; "c" shows the self-view with full opacity, whereas "d" depicts the self-view with lower opacity. Similar to the participant view, this

Fig. 3. Paradigmatic screens from a moderator's point of view of the low fidelity prototype. Please see the text for the detailed explanation (Color figure online)

interface tries to improve attention management (R1) and participation (R2) through showing the speech and break requests from each participant.

Additionally, the display of the time passed since each request was made should enable the moderator to prioritize the participation order. The AI-based cognitive aid provides hints for the moderator based on an analysis of the speaking time of each participant, recommending whom to include more actively in the discussion through asking them to share their points of view (P1).

In the low-fidelity prototype, the AI was only implemented conceptually, meaning that the options were merely depicted by symbols without actual functionality. The moderators can also manage their own self-view to help reduce mirror anxiety (R4). The interface attempts to provide innovative moderation tools (R10), as well as protect special rights, through utilizing the cognitive aid to reach a more equal distribution of speaking time across the board (R13) while also improving the efficiency of the process and simplifying it (P3).

4.3 Heuristic Evaluation of the Prototype

Method. To evaluate the prototype, we conducted a heuristic evaluation with a total of three HCI experts (two female). We followed the established procedure [27], with slight adaptations according to our use case.

The experts first received basic information about the prototype's goals and were then instructed about their respective roles, starting with an evaluation from a participant's point of view. They then explored the prototype for 3 min to form an independent opinion about it.

After the exploration, they reported on the functionalities of the prototype. This process was followed by a structured discussion about the quality of interaction with the prototype, the settings options, and the AI-based cognitive aid. The question structure for the heuristic evaluation can be found in Appendix A.

Results from the Participant Perspective. The experts rated the display of time passed since any request as valuable and good. The option to manipulate the self-view through changing the opacity and/or turning off the personal camera view was encouraged as well.

The icons were well received by and understandable to the experts, although there were some criticisms about the choice of colors. One expert noted that blue icons might not be suitable for some backgrounds due to visibility problems.

All experts agreed that the proposed settings options would be used and should be retained. However, they also offered some recommendations.

When asked about the option to control other members' camera views along with one's self-view, they agreed that it could improve the experience. One expert mentioned that this functionality might be perfect for witnesses giving their testimony, due to a reduced observer effect, which relates to R5.

Another idea forwarded by an expert was to allow the participants to sort the windows of other conference attendees by relevance for themselves. They shared that doing so might improve attention toward the more critical people in the conference.

On being enquired about how the interaction with the AI could look from a participant's point of view, the experts unanimously agreed that the interaction should not be direct but more in the form of nudges. They suggested visualizations for speaking time to encourage participants to speak by themselves instead of being asked to speak.

Results from the Moderator Perspective. In terms of the moderator view, most functions were well received and deemed necessary by the experts. They focused mainly on the option of seeing the time passed since any attendee request and the time passed since the last break, which they felt was essential. One expert even suggested making this time always visible, regardless of whether the AI was on or off.

However, there were some problems with icon comprehension, and the blue speech bubbles visible in slide "b" of Fig. 3 were mistaken to indicate the members currently speaking. Additionally, the "Hide" and "Mute" buttons appearing on every camera panel were confusing. During an interaction, the two would behave similarly (e.g., muting the attendee or hiding their camera), but one icon was initially crossed out, and the other was not. One expert cited these as counterintuitive and confusing during the review phase.

Most of the discussion, however, was centered around AI functionality and control. The experts suggested thinning the design, since some buttons were so similar or ambiguous that they were almost redundant, such as the Stop AI and Stop Interaction buttons.

In addition, they agreed that the interaction should be nonintrusive. They pointed out that the AI should not be overloaded with unnecessary functions so as to not distract the moderator and not do more harm than good regarding their ability to concentrate on the essential parts of the conference.

One expert also encouraged enabling the AI to generate a post-conference report detailing all the requests and hints made during the meeting. They pointed out the possibilities that doing so might have for analyzing and improving remote proceedings.

4.4   Updated Prototype

The feedback from the heuristic evaluation was incorporated in the updated version of the prototype, which aimed to alleviate the inconsistencies and confusion associated with the initial low-fidelity prototype.

Fig. 4. Paradigmatic screens from a participant's point of view of the improved prototype. Please see the text for the detailed explanation. (Color figure online)

The functionality of the participants' screen view was drastically increased, with the options to sort by group and to show a diagram of the talking time added.

Additionally, a green outline was added to indicate the current speaker, eliminating the confusion identified during the heuristic evaluation about who was speaking. In the upper-right corner of the speaker's window, their current talking time is displayed.

Slide "a" depicts the base view showing all the buttons for the participant to express themselves to the moderator or adjust their view. Slide "b" shows the view of the participant who has faded the window of another conference attendee using a slider for opacity adjustment. Additionally, the participant gets to see their active request to talk.

Slide "c" shows a functionality unanimously recommended by the experts: the option of grouping participants by relevance. It also displays a small self-view window of the participant on the left side of the green group. We used color coding to distinguish between the moderators in our use case (i.e., judges) and the two opposing parties. Red would always be used for the party opposing the participant. Further, the view in slide "c" also shows notifications for both active requests of the participant-to talk and to take a break.

Finally, slide "d" shows the diagram displaying the talking duration of all conference attendees, which was suggested after the heuristic evaluation of the initial prototype. The diagram also shows the average talking time and highlights the talking time of the participant at the top.

Fig. 5. Paradigmatic screens from a moderator's point of view of the improved prototype. Please see the text for the detailed explanation. (Color figure online)

In terms of the moderator's view, the primary goal of the update was to simplify the functionality as requested by the evaluating experts.

Slide "a" shows the basic overview with a drastically simplified interface for control of the AI. According to the feedback, a continuous display of the time since the last break was added for a better overview of the conference flow. Additionally, requests made by participants are shown by red bubbles in the left-top corner of their respective windows.

The view in slide "b" shows that the AI is deactivated, made apparent by a pop-up notification signaling that the AI will not be able to interact with the participants It also has the mute function on display which can be used to forcibly moderate talking time. When a talking participant is muted, their window does not have the green outline anymore.

Slide "c" shows the small self-view window of the moderator and also the activated hints in blue speech bubbles; an active-mic icon signifies that the participant should be encouraged to talk, whereas a muted-mic icon indicates that they must be encouraged to take a break as they are too dominating.

These hints are generated by the cognitive aid and visually represented for the moderator to act upon them at their own discretion. As with the initial prototype, the AI was included only symbolically to indicate its intended function and use. The option to fade other participants' windows, as in the participant's view, was included also in the moderator's view.

Finally, the screen in slide "d" shows the option of kicking a participant from the session, which was added considering the feedback. Kicking out a participant will remove them from the live session until the moderator decides to let them back in by explicitly confirming the same through another prompt.

4.5   Evaluation by End Users at a Law Symposium

The improved prototype was presented at the "Mensch-Recht-Digitalisierung" symposium of the Higher Regional Court of Bamberg and the University of Wuerzburg. After the presentation, which also included an overview of the work done so far, the attendees of the symposium were given the opportunity to run a test of the prototype and report their opinions, as well as to provide further feedback for the next iteration, through unstructured interviews.

Being unstructured, the interviews had no guidelines [28]; rather, the attendees were allowed to explore the prototype on their own, and the interviewer initiated conversations and asked questions about what they were doing on the fly.

In total, four attendees took the time to test the prototype thoroughly and give their feedback. All of them reported that the prototype's functionality was understandable. They all approved of the newly added possibility to group the participants. Three of the four attendees also wished for an option to resize and relocate the windows of the participants in a way they saw fit. Two of them recommended including this function for the moderator's view too.

The ability to fade other participants' windows was deemed a useful function for the participants, but not so much for the moderator, since an overall view is vital for a well-organized session.

The diagram showing the distribution of the talking time as a way to encourage more participation was not unanimously received well. Some thought the diagram was too simplistic and not interactive enough. We received a suggestion to improve the display of and add the sorting feature to the diagram as well, so that one could see the participation of a particular group at a glance. Concurrent with the experts in the heuristic evaluation, one attendee shared that a direct prompt from the AI asking participants to speak would be intrusive and inappropriate. Another came up with an idea for the moderator's view: enabling the AI to present the moderator with an automatic list of bullet points of the most important statements shared by the participants.

5   Discussion

The digitalization of judicial systems gains increasingly in importance during the coronavirus pandemic. The present work focuses on the most fundamental change brought about by the phenomenon: the application of video conferencing in court sessions. The use of video conferencing for court sessions has special requirements adhering to democratic principles and constitutional rights.

In the present contribution, we addressed these requirements in three steps. The semi-structured literature review (step 1) resulted in a list of challenges and possibilities corresponding to the application of video conferencing in court sessions. However, the review also revealed a lack of research in the field of justice; in general, too, empirical results quantifying anecdotal reports are rare. For example, Fauville et al. [12] published the only study investigating the "Zoom fatigue" phenomenon. Other articles describe challenges in terms of the moderation quality in video conferences.

For example, El Ouary and Schreiber [17] share insights on problems associated with virtual moderation, but again, theirs is merely an opinion piece without any empirical data. Moreover, key HCI methods (e.g., target group and context analysis, iterative prototyping) to develop user-centered digital solutions have not been applied so far. In this regard, in the present work, the review results were analyzed to derive requirements focusing on court session leaders-judges. Based on this analysis, we introduced a low-fidelity prototype for a virtual court session with an AI-based cognitive aid and special settings options, aiming to improve moderation quality while reducing fatigue and cognitive load. A heuristic evaluation with HCI experts and domain experts underlined the goodness of the basic ideas and elicited broad recommendations for improvements to the prototype.

Some limitations restrict the contribution of the present paper. First, although during the evaluation the HCI experts hinted at some usability and user experiences problems, the target group might indicate different issues. Due to the contact restrictions in Germany, an evaluation with the target group could only be done with few domain experts (judges). Further, the pilot prototype addresses only some of the identified requirements, whereas the analysis revealed many potentials; in this regard, future studies can explore different possibilities to improve virtual court sessions. Finally, the low-fidelity prototype only simulates the functions.

The interaction experience and evaluation of the AI-based cognitive aid might be different for prototypes that are further developed. In this regard, a new HCI approach called eXtended AI [29] proposes using extended realities (e.g., virtual reality) to simulate digital interactions more realistically. Thus, future researchers might implement a virtual simulation of such prototypes to investigate their feasibility more vividly. A virtual simulation will also enable showing the demonstrator in a court session environment during remote user testing.

5.1   Conclusion

In this paper, we first analyzed the challenges and potentials of video conferencing in court sessions and derived requirements from an HCI perspective. Then, we addressed the requirements using a pilot prototype including an AI-based cognitive aid and unique settings options. Thus, we have shown one potential avenue to improve the modernization process of the judicial system in Germany. Furthermore, as video conferencing gains in importance in many contexts, the analyzed challenges and potentials are not limited to the field of justice; they could be transferred to a wide variety of fields, from public services to e-learning.

A   Appendix A: Evaluation Questions

Part 1: Participant

Introduction to the mindset of a participant in a virtual court session

- Context, Perspective...

Review

- What functions did the prototype have?
- What did you do/What could you do?

Discussion

Usage

- Could you imagine using any functions and why or why not?
- Request to speak, Request a break, Self View...

Self View

- What did you think of the possibility to manipulate your own video feed?
- What did you think about the small size of your own video feed?
- What kind of impact would this have on your ability to focus?

AI

- How would you imagine your interaction with the AI?
- What would be important for you in an interaction with the AI?
- How would you want the AI Interaction to look and feel?

Icons

- Were the icons understandable for you?

Misc.

- Any other things you want to say?

Part 2: Moderator

Introduction to the mindset of a moderator in a virtual court session

– Context, Perspective...

Review

– What functions did the prototype have?
– What did you do/What could you do?

Discussion

Usage

– Could you imagine using any functions and why or why not?
– Start/Stop AI, Stop/Activate Hints, Mute, Self View...

Self View

– What did you think of the possibility to manipulate your own video feed?
– What did you think about the small size of your own video feed?
– What kind of impact would this have on your ability to focus?

Interaction

– What did you think about the interaction with the AI?
– Is there anything that you feel is missing from the current AI design?
– Would you use the AI? Why/Why not?

Icons

– Were the Icons understandable for you?

Misc.

– Any other things you want to say?

References

1. Rossner, M., Tait, D., McCurdy, M.: Justice reimagined: challenges and opportunities with implementing virtual courts. In: Current Issues in Criminal Justice, vol 33, pp. 94–110, Taylor&Francis (2021)
2. McIntyre, J., Olijnyk, A., Pender, K.: Civil courts and COVID-19: challenges and opportunities in Australia. Altern. Law J. **45**, 195–201 (2020)
3. Rowden, E.: Distributed courts and legitimacy: what do we lose when we lose the courthouse? Law Cult. Hum. **14**, 263–281 (2018)

4. Donoghue, J.: The rise of digital justice: courtroom technology, public participation and access to justice. Modern Law Rev. **80**, 995–1025 (2017)
5. Sourdin, T., Li, B., McNamara, D.: Court innovations and access to justice in times of crisis. Health Pol. Technol. **9**, 447–453 (2020)
6. Burova, I., Volkova, M., Lenkovskaya, R.: E-justice in civil cases and economic disputes in the Russian Federation. JURÍDICAS CUC **17**, 629–648 (2021)
7. Vovk, O.: Rechtspflege per Videokonferenz: Von Gerichtsverhandlungen per Videokonferenz zum digitalen Gericht? Moderne Lösungen in Zeiten von Corona in Deutschland und der Ukraine. Recht Innovativ **4**, 51 (2020)
8. Gorodovenko, V., Bondar, O., Udovyka, L.: Justice in the COVID-19 era through the prism of judicial power. Ius Humani. Law J. **10**, 51–72 (2021)
9. Rudnev, V., Pechegin, D.: The impact of the leading digital technologies on criminal proceedings: a case of video conferencing. In: 6th International Conference on Social, Economic, and Academic Leadership (ICSEAL-6-2019), pp. 323–329, Atlantis Press (2020)
10. Grønbæk, J., Saatçi, B., Griggio, C., Klokmose, C.: MirrorBlender: supporting hybrid meetings with a malleable video-conferencing system. In: Proceedings of the 2021 CHI Conference on Human Factors in Computing Systems, pp. 1–13 (2021)
11. Ferran, C., Watts, S.: Videoconferencing in the field: a heuristic processing model. Manag. Sci. **54**, 1565–1578 (2008)
12. Fauville, G., Luo, M., Muller Queiroz, A., Bailenson, J., Hancock, J.: Nonverbal Mechanisms Predict Zoom Fatigue and Explain Why Women Experience Higher Levels than Men, Available at SSRN 3820035 (2021)
13. Takac, M., Collett, J., Blom, K., Conduit, R., Rehm, I., De Foe, A.: Public speaking anxiety decreases within repeated virtual reality training sessions. PLoS ONE **14**, e0216288 (2019)
14. Tomprou, M., Kim, Y., Chikersal, P., Woolley, A., Dabbish, L.: Speaking out of turn: how video conferencing reduces vocal synchrony and collective intelligence. PLoS ONE **16**, e0247655 (2021)
15. Kim, S., Eun, J., Seering, J., Lee, J.: Moderator chatbot for deliberative discussion: effects of discussion structure and discussant facilitation. Proc, ACM Hum.-Comput. Interac. **5**, 1–26 (2021)
16. Lee, S., Song, J., Ko, E., Park, S., Kim, J., Kim, J.: SolutionChat: real-time moderator support for chat-based structured discussion. In: Proceedings of the 2020 CHI Conference on Human Factors in Computing Systems, pp. 1–12 (2020)
17. El Ouardy, J., Schreiber, A.: Same same, but different - Koerperlichkeit und Moderation im virtuellen Raum. Interculture Journal: Online Zeitschrift fuer interkulturelle Studien **19**, 77–83 (2021)
18. Stang, A., Zhao, Q.: Gestaltung virtueller kollaborativer Teamarbeit am Beispiel des Planspiels Megacities. Konsequenzen für die Moderation aus deutsch-chinesischer Perspektive. In: interculture journal: Online Zeitschrift fuer interkulturelle Studien **19**, 27–43 (2020)
19. Moher, D., Liberati, A., Tetzlaff, J., Altman, D.G.: Bevorzugte Report Items für systematische Übersichten und Meta-Analysen: Das PRISMA-Statement. In: DMW-Deutsche Medizinische Wochenschrift, vol 136, Georg Thieme Verlag KG Stuttgart (2011)
20. Hagan, M.: A human-centered design approach to access to justice: generating new prototypes and hypotheses for interventions to make courts user-friendly. Ind. JL & Soc. Equal., vol 6, HeinOnline (2018)

21. Solarte-Vasquez, M., Hietanen-Kunwald, P.: Transaction design standards for the operationalisation of fairness and empowerment in proactive contracting. In: International & Comparative Law Review/Mezinárodní a Srovnávací Právní Revue, vol. 20 (2020)
22. McLaughlin, A., Byrne, V.: A fundamental cognitive taxonomy for cognition aids. Hum. Factors **62**, 865–873 (2020)
23. Chaparro, A., Keebler, J., Lazzara, E., Diamond, A.: Checklists: a review of their origins, benefits, and current uses as a cognitive aid in medicine. Ergon. Des. **27**, 21–26 (2019)
24. Beyer, H., Holtzblatt, K.: Contextual design. Interactions **6**, 32–42 (1999)
25. Damodaran, L.: User involvement in the systems design process-a practical guide for users. Beh. Inf. Technol. **15**, 363–377 (1996)
26. Maguire, M.: Methods to support human-centred design. Int. J. Hum.-Comput. Stud. **55**, 587–634 (2001)
27. Nielsen, J., Molich, R.: Heuristic evaluation of user interfaces. In: Proceedings of the SIGCHI Conference on Human Factors in Computing Systems, pp. 249–256 (1990)
28. Zhang, Y., Wildemuth, B.: Unstructured interviews. In: Applications of Social Research Methods to Questions in Information and Library Science, pp. 222–231. Libraries Unlimited Westport, CT (2009)
29. Wienrich, C., Latoschik, M.: eXtended artificial intelligence: new prospects of Human-AI interaction research. arXiv preprint arXiv:2103.15004 (2021)
30. Baladhikari, S.: Use of Technology in Access to Justice. University of North Bengal (2020)
31. Videoverhandlungen und Digitalisierungsschub für die Justiz. https://www.baden-wuerttemberg.de/de/service/presse/pressemitteilung/pid/videoverhandlungen-und-digitalisierungsschub-fuer-die-justiz/. Accessed 2 Aug 2021
32. The Future of Disputes: Are Virtual Hearings Here To Stay?. https://www.bakermckenzie.com/-/media/files/insight/publications/2021/01/future-of-disputes-campaign-brochure.pdf. Accessed 2 Aug 2021
33. Supreme Court of Victoria: VIRTUAL HEARINGS: Information for practitioners about virtual hearings in the Supreme Court. https://www.supremecourt.vic.gov.au/law-and-practice/virtual-hearings. Accessed 2 Aug 2021
34. State court judges embrace virtual hearings as part of the 'new normal'. https://www.ncsc.org/newsroom/public-health-emergency/newsletters/videoconferencing. Accessed 2 Aug 2021
35. Hilgendorf, E.: Die Schuld ist immer zweifellos? - Offene Fragen bei Tatsachenfeststellung und Beweis mit Hilfe intelligenter Maschinen. In: Beweis, pp. 229–252. Nomos Verlagsgesellschaft mbH & Co. KG (2019)
36. Immer mehr digital Gerichtsprozesse. https://www.sueddeutsche.de/bayern/justiz-muenchen-immer-mehr-digitale-gerichtsprozesse-dpa.urn-newsml-dpa-com-20090101-201215-99-698932. Accessed 2 Aug 2021
37. Manz, R., Spoenle, J.: Corona-Pandemie - Die Verhandlung per Videokonferenz nach 128a ZPO als Alternative zur Präsenzverhandlung
38. Libre Research Group: e-Justice. https://libreresearchgroup.org/en/a/e-justice. Accessed 17 Dec 2021
39. Kuch, D.: Recht auf den gesetzlichen Richter (Art. 101 Abs. 1 S. 2 GG). JURA-Juristische Ausbildung **42**, 228–238 (2020)
40. Glunz, B.: Psychologische Effekte beim gerichtlichen Einsatz von Videotechnik: eine empirische und rechtsvergleichende Untersuchung zum US-amerikanischen, australischen und deutschen Zivilprozess, Mohr Siebeck (2012)

Scene Design of Virtual Singing Bar Oriented to Metauniverse

Xin Zhou, Nuoya Fang, and Zhongwei Gu[✉]

Shanghai Dianji University, Shanghai, China
zhao_young9468@163.com, 1443407485@qq.com, zwgu@qq.com

Abstract. Karaoke is an important part of human music and entertainment nowadays. Facing the continuous development of Internet technology, the traditional offline KTV industry has been devastated by the impact of the global new crown epidemic, and the malpractice of online K-song platform development model is becoming more and more severe. In this paper, the advantages and disadvantages of online and offline karaoke service are studied, and the virtual reality technology is combined to develop the virtual karaoke bar system design based on the metauniverse. The scene design and function mapping of the system are given. In the following research, the system will be further studied, extended and applied.

Keywords: Metaverse · VR · Online karaoke

1 Introduction

Throughout history, music has been an important tool for human beings to reflect real life and emotional concepts. Whether in ancient times music can be used as a signal of hunting, a means of war and diplomacy in the Middle Ages, or a tool of entertainment and emotion of modern people, all reflect the indispensable position of music in human life. With the development of modern human material civilization life, people's entertainment life continues to flourish, music entertainment application scenes are also growing, and KTV is one of the important scenes.

With the development of Internet technology, online karaoke has been realized. Online karaoke software mainly focused on song recording has caused a huge impact on the offline KTV industry, meeting the needs of more users who are not limited to the scene and time of karaoke. And since 2019, Under the impact of the new coronavirus (COVID-19) epidemic on the global real economy, the traditional offline KTV industry is hard to escape, and people's demand for online entertainment, such as karaoke, is even stronger when their own movements are limited. In 2021, the first year of the metauniverse, the demand for virtual entertainment industry from both the industry and consumer point of view has greatly increased. At present, VR applications are mainly concentrated in the game industry, culture and education, etc. Starting from VR karaoke in emerging markets and people's expectation for the launch of online karaoke VR video content, this study plans to develop and design music entertainment scenes based on karaoke combined with virtual reality technology.

© The Author(s), under exclusive license to Springer Nature Switzerland AG 2022
G. Salvendy and J. Wei (Eds.): HCII 2022, LNCS 13337, pp. 107–116, 2022.
https://doi.org/10.1007/978-3-031-05014-5_9

The application system covers a variety of functions and scenes, which can meet people's needs for VR karaoke in many aspects. In addition to recording songs, users can also enjoy VR music video, VR shopping experience, "meta-universe" VR concert and online friends and other functions, so that users can enjoy high-quality virtual karaoke experience. In this way, while meeting the needs of current karaoke users, the innovation of enterprises and the development of VR industry have brought a good power.

2   Project Contexts

2.1 Metaverse

Domestic Background. On August 29, 2021, the media reported that Yiming Zhang would invest 1.5 billion DOLLARS (about 9.6 billion YUAN) to acquire "Pico", a MANUFACTURER of VR hardware and software [1]; On September 16, 2021, Tsinghua University released the first metauniverse report in the academic world: Research Report on the Development of the Metauniverse in 2020–2021 [2]. On November 11, 2021, the unveiling ceremony of China Mobile Communications Federation Meta-Cosmos Industry Committee (hereinafter referred to as "Meta-cosmos Industry Committee") was officially held [3]. On December 27, 2021, Baidu Create (AI Developer Conference) was held in Creator City APP. It is known that this is the first conference held in the meta-universe in China, which can accommodate 100,000 people interacting with the screen at the same time [4]. On December 30, 2021, Shanghai municipality issued the "14th Five-year Plan for the Development of Shanghai Electronic Information Industry", laying out the meta-universe [5].

Foreign Background. In March 2021, Roblox, "the first stock of 'meta-universe'", was officially listed on THE New York Stock Exchange. The share price rose from $45 to $70 on the day of listing, and the total market value is nearly $45 billion [6]. In April 2021, Epic Games, the world's leading 3D engine technology provider, completed a $1 billion financing with a post-investment valuation of $28.7 billion. The financing will be mainly used for the company's development and metauniverse-related development [7]. The rapper Travis Scott is valued at $28.7 billion globally by Epic Games. The company has announced that the funding will be used primarily for growth and development of the metauniverse, following Fortnite's virtual concert, which was watched by 27.7 million people. On October 28, Facebook officially changed its name to "Meta" (from Metaverse, meaning the metauniverse), which means that it has made a radical bet on the metauniverse [8]. In November 2021, The Seoul Municipal Government of South Korea recently released the Five-year Plan of Meta-cosmos Seoul, announcing that from next year, it would create a meta-cosmos administrative service ecology in all business areas of the municipal government, including economy, culture, tourism, education and letters and visits in three stages [9]. Late On Jan. 18, Microsoft (MSFT.O) said it would buy Activision Blizzard (ATVI.O) for nearly $70 billion in cash, making it the world's third-largest gaming company by revenue [10].

2021 is known as the first year of the Metaverse, a concept first described in Neil Stephenson's 1992 science fiction novel Avalanche: "Just put on your headphones and goggles, find a terminal, by entering another three-dimensional reality simulated by a computer. Everyone can have their own doppelganger in a virtual space parallel to the real world. The similar concept first appeared in China on November 27, 1990. Qian Xuesen mentioned in his letter to Wang Becoming an academician that "Virtual Reality" was translated as "Lingjing" in Chinese. RMB current understanding of the universe is not a generally accepted conclusion, this study combining previous [11, 12] point of view, and believe that the universe is a collection of Internet, virtual reality, chain blocks, and artificial intelligence and so on the underlying technology support, in the real world of human can use information and communication technology and intelligent equipment into a virtualized dressing society, This virtual society originated from the real world, gradually improved parallel to the real world, and eventually developed to a certain extent beyond the real world.

2.2 Virtual Singing Bar

Currently, successful VR music apps in the market include Rhythm Lightsaber, WAVE and Epic Games' Fortnite virtual music performance service, etc., while there are no successful VR karaoke apps.

3 Scene Design

See Fig. 1.

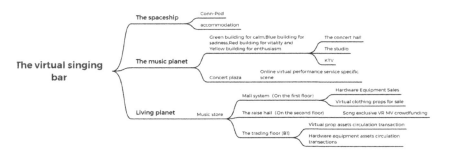

Fig. 1. Scene design of the virtual singing bar

3.1 The First Scene: The Main Page

Scene Picture. After entering the APP, the main interface is a spaceship model, in which the character is placed in the spaceship. The headphone with the head display plays the guiding voice "Welcome to the universe of play, we are about to start a new journey, please select the planet to which the spaceship will sail". At this time was the user interface is the spacecraft operation room control panel and the back of the windshield, look out through the windshield, is A dark color of the universe, the universe in the middle of two planets, respectively is A planet A planet (life), planet B planet (dc), users can handle button control central screen want to heading to the planet, And then the scene on the outside of the windshield changes, showing the dynamic effects of the spacecraft flying in space and showing the process of heading to the stars. In addition, there is a mechanical door behind the figure, and behind the door is the living cabin, which contains holographic communicator, record display table, wardrobe and mirror. The living cabin is the "my" part of the main carrying functions, corresponding to "message", "work", "character image" and other functions.

Process. Select the planet you need to enter through the spacecraft handle, and show the process of the spacecraft flying to the planet through the dynamic effect of the spacecraft moving and the vibration of the handle, so as to improve the user's experience.

The head display can capture the user's turning around, turning the head and other movements through the sensor to call up the page of the living cabin.

The Event

1. Avatar's travel to a virtual planet
2. The movement of virtual characters between spacecraft operation rooms
3. Virtual characters change virtual clothes, play music and communicate with their friends in the virtual world by hologram in the living cabin

Mode operation is mainly realized by external handle device operation.
Operation through the joystick on the handle to control the movement of the character, confirm the key to return.

Dynamic Effect. There is a dynamic effect of spaceship flight in the process of spaceship to the planet; When the user opens the door of the living room, there is a dynamic effect and sound of opening the mechanical door of the spaceship. The lights in the living quarters change from dim to bright; When your hologram a friend, the monitor displays an avatar of that friend.

3.2 Other Scenarios: "My Living Quarters"

Scene Picture. The user unbuckled his seat belt and descended from the pilot's seat of the spacecraft into the living quarters behind the cockpit. Users are free to decorate the capsule, such as setting up a phonograph TV to play songs or music videos they have recorded. Organize your closet to see what your avatar is wearing. Click on your computer to view your shopping history, friends list, etc. Music equipment display cabinet to display their own handle microphone and head display equipment. Later, you can invite friends to visit the living cabin and enjoy "listening together" and other functions.

Process. Users log in to the APP, put on the display, enter the "My" interface, and choose to view and edit related content.

The Event. View the user home page

Free scene design of user's living cabin

Way. The head motion capture is realized by wearing the display, and the hand motion capture is realized by infrared sensor.

Operation. Put on the title and enter the VR scene
More actions and functions are available on the gamepad

Experience. Review the recording work
The experience of dressing up your virtual character.

3.3 The Scend Scene: Music Planet

General Scene Screen. The user from the main interface using the spacecraft handle click into the "play planet", the spacecraft will enter the planet. Users arrive at the planet, exit through the ship's hatch, and land in the central square of the recording planet. The main colors of the four recording buildings are based on the combination of Thayer's emotional model and Eton's 12 color ring, expressing calm and sadness through low energy green and blue. High energy red and yellow to express vibrant, enthusiastic musical mood. Users freely choose to enter the building through the handle operation (Fig. 2).

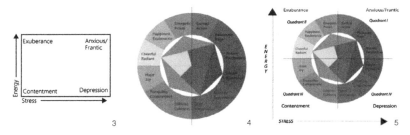

Fig. 2. The combination of Thayer's emotional model and Eton's 12 color ring

Other Scenarios: Karaoke Room. Scene Picture. Users can use the note conveyor belt to go to the solo room, choir room or concert hall. The basic structure of the solo studio is a recording studio structure. Users select sound songs through the virtual karaoke platform. Before recording, the central control screen will pop up the selected songs for special effects selection.

The basic structure of the chorus room adopts the physical KTV layout. When entering the chorus room, users can choose the mode by operating the central control screen through the handle, and create their own karaoke room or enter the fully open chorus room. After entering, you can communicate with chorus objects through virtual communicator, and finally complete chorus recording.

The basic structure of the concert hall adopts the structure of the theater. Users can make a reservation in advance before entering the concert hall. The system will push the arrangement of the guests of the concert hall to subscribers at the scheduled time, so that other users can sign up for the concert. After entering the concert hall, users operate the handle to select seats, and can adjust the volume and light freely after sitting. Users can choose to quit halfway or quit the venue after the performance.

Process. Click the APP icon to enter the home page of the application -- user login -- put on the headset, configure the microphone -- select the recording room -- select the song sound through the virtual song selection platform -- enter the VRmv experience -- complete the song selection, complete recording or re-recording/exit the mode at any time if the concert hall is finished or not.

The Event. User movement on the surface of the planet and inside the building
User's song recording
User's K song mode selection
Experience the VR mv
VR recording experience
Users enjoy the performance experience of virtual concerts

Way. Click the APP interface to select
Wearing head display, handheld microphone type handle operation
Wearing the head display to enter the recording mode, the handle to select the song recording platform volume, sound effects, microphone for singing.

Dynamic Effect. Dynamic music, for example, gives people the feeling of shaking and swaying
Sound 3D Surround
Representation of entities in VR MV

Experience. Achieve mv scene reproduction
To the user immersive, place yourself in the sense of reality

Scene: Concert
Scene Picture. After landing on the planet, users first arrive at one of the concert venues - the central square. The central part of the square will set up the music works of users of the platform or the concert arrangement information of users to be held on the suspended central control screen, including time, place and price, etc. Users can reserve the virtual concert venue in advance before the concert. The system will push the concert arrangement to subscribers at the scheduled time, so that other users can sign up for the concert. At that time, large or small concert venues will be allocated according to the number of participants.

The concert venue adopts the mode of performance stage + audience seats, mostly set in the square around the building. Singer users can choose the lighting and atmosphere of the concert in advance. The personal image of the singer user will be ten times larger than that of the audience during the performance. The character image will be gradually enlarged during the process from backstage to the stage through the Avenue of Fame, until the singer user reaches the stage and reaches the maximum size. In the auditorium, the audience can send voice support in real time, or wave the handle as a support stick during the concert. Whether the audience user can open the mic and sing together with the singer user can be operated by the singer user's handle.

Process. Users will need to make an appointment ahead of time, when opening concert appointment to choose the type of a good concert, lighting pattern, the theme of the concert and other relevant information, and then system robot will push for a particular user (including personality algorithms recommend the target users and the singer fan), it will also put the concert hall on the big screen. Count the size of the audience the day before the concert and assign the concert hall. In a concert, the singer comes to the front stage from backstage and can start the concert directly.

The Event

1. Singer users hold concerts online
2. Audience users participate in concerts and provide assistance

Way

The singer user sings through the handset's microphone.

Audience users can press the "Pick up" button on the back of the handle to grab and wave the virtual props they have purchased to participate in the concert interaction.

Operation

Experience the scene and lights of the concert by wearing a headset, and sing and help with a microphone.

Dynamic Effect

The singer plays a section of starlight channel from the background to the front stage, and the concert scene plays the lighting effect. The audience user can play the assisted dynamic effect by pressing the button.

3.4 Scenario 3: Living Planet

Scene Picture

In the main interface, the user controls the spacecraft to the "living planet" by manipulating the virtual central control screen through the handle. The spacecraft then enters the planet. The user can experience the acceleration of the spacecraft, accompanied by the roaring sound of the spacecraft engine in his hearing.

Upon arrival, users will see a variety of shopping mall buildings, crowdfunding hall display outside (refer to business district buildings), and users will feel the prosperity of the metauniverse world. Enter the crowdfunding hall from the gate on the first floor of the mall, and the large screen will display the weekly crowdfunding songs and display the virtual music video effects of the songs. You can choose to enter the second-hand trading market on the second floor or the system mall on the second floor by the handle operation and instant movement. In the future, the mall will continue to expand and develop the music tour city.

Users can experience a completely different style from the ultra-modern style of the whole meta-universe when entering the second-hand market on the negative floor, and fully appreciate the excitement of the market and the happiness of trading and social interaction. Users can choose shops and build their own shops according to their preferences, and "say hello" to virtual users of other users through the handle for second-hand trading and making friends.

After entering the system mall on the second floor, users can see endless display cabinets. Users can choose the products they are interested in through the handles, including the microphone handle independently developed by the company, head display and other products jointly signed by other merchants and brands (virtual dress, etc.). After the user selects, the product will be displayed to the user for viewing through a large screen VR, and the user can freely choose to buy.

Process

Users log in the APP to enter the home page -- wear the display -- select the virtual image -- enter the living planet -- select the mall with the handle -- conduct virtual VR transactions.

The Event

User's shop, second hand transactions
    User movement
    User voice communication

Way

Wearing the head display into VR, handle operation, use virtual image free trade display screen.

Operation

1. Users make shopping choices by using the handle, and instant logistics service will be provided upon placing orders
2. In the second-hand trading market, users use virtual images to trade and make friends
3. Voice communication is realized through microphone transmission when making friends and trading, and body interaction is realized through external device head display
4. Users can move freely on the living planet through the eight directions of the joystick (see the hardware microphone diagram for details)

Dynamic Effect

1. Dynamic effect of 3D large-screen display of commodities during crowdfunding
2. The action state and sound effect of the user's virtual character when moving
3. Voice and sound effects when making friends (3D surround, etc.)

Experience. Users' real shopping experience can enjoy a social atmosphere (Fig. 3).

Fig. 3. Functional mapping of the project system

The virtual singing bar project has four main functions, namely VR vision, karaoke function, social function and motion capture.

VR visual function is the core of this project. VR music video is the key to improve users' visual experience during karaoke, realize the leap from the traditional two-dimensional plane to three-dimensional, and make users more immersed, more enjoyable and better experience quality during karaoke.

Motion capture function, through the head display and external equipment to identify, capture and record the user's physiological movements, making the user's karaoke more playable; Richer interaction mechanisms; With the presentation of action, the content of VR music works can be further enriched.

Karaoke function is the central event of the project, and all other events revolve around karaoke. Karaoke song request, recording music post processing and production, and VR music video editing are the core of user content creation.

Social function, through the likes/rewards, transactions and greetings/voice chat/virtual contact, human-computer interaction, connect VR music world of all virtual characters, forming a virtual society.

The Research Conclusion. Based on the domestic and foreign research on the meta-universe and virtual singing bar, this paper summarizes and thinks about the existing literature, and puts forward the design of virtual singing bar system based on the meta-universe. The scene design and function map of the system are described. Whether from the current economic development situation or market demand, the application of virtual singing bar system based on the meta-universe is very extensive.

The construction of a virtual singing bar system based on the meta-universe can greatly meet people's demand for online karaoke VR video.

Through the construction of the virtual singing bar system based on the meta-universe, it can break the status quo of online karaoke platform being single and stereotyped, and bring application innovation.

The construction of virtual singing bar system based on the meta-universe can create new profit points and boost economic growth during the popular period of the meta-universe.

By constructing the virtual singing bar system based on the meta-universe, it makes up the gap in the previous field and creates a new research field, which provides a reference for future scholars.

References

1. Zhao, D., Liu, Z.: Tencent and Byte dance competes for the entrance ticket of the meta-universe. Chin. Entrepreneur **10**, 81 (2021)
2. Tsinghua University publishing: 2021 yuan the universe development research report (PDF attached) [EB/OL], 24 December 2021. https://www.sohu.com/a/511077648_453160. Accessed 07 Feb 2022
3. Yuancosmos Industry Committee of China Mobile Communication Federation formally established the universe [EB/OL], 11 November 2021. https://xw.qq.com/cmsid/20211112A02F1T00. Accessed 07 Feb 2022
4. Sa, Y.: Meeting on "Meta-universe" – 2021 Baidu AI developer conference held in meta-universe. China Convention Exhib. **24**, 36–37 (2021)
5. Shanghai issued the 14th Five-year Plan for the Development of Electronic Information Industry: The universe technology foresight layout yuan [EB/OL]. 04 January 2022. https://baijiahao.baidu.com/s?id=1720984838572142964&wfr=spider&for=pc. Accessed 07 Feb 2022
6. Yang, K.: The explosion of "meta-universe", what can be brought by the "meta-universe" outside the game. Fortune Times **10**, 20 (2021)
7. Metauniverse depth 163 pages report: metauniverse's future conjecture and investment opportunity analysis. [EB/OL]. (2021–11–03) [2022–02–07]. HTTP: / / https://new.qq.com/rain/a/20211103A039DU00
8. Shen, S., Shi, D.: Can Facebook's "face changing" metauniverse be redeemed? Bus. Sch. **12**, 51–54 (2021)
9. Yang, M.: Seoul will make yuan universe administrative service ecology. Econ. J.,24 November 2021 (004). https://doi.org/10.28425/n.cnki.NJJRB.2021.008064
10. Chen, Y., Wu, K.: China Bus. J. (B18), 24 January 2022
11. Pu, Q., Xiang, W.: Metauniverse and its influence and Reform on human society. J. Chongqing University (SOCIAL SCIENCES EDITION), 1–12. http://kns.cnki.net/kcms/detail/50.1023.C.20220129.1921.002.html. 07 Feb 2022
12. Shen, Y., Xiang, A.: Separate the mate universe from the science fiction and bubble regions. The global times30 November 2021 (015). https://doi.org/10.28378/n.cnki.nhqsb.2021.011247

User Experience and Adoption
of Mobile Communications

Technology Acceptance Before and After Covid Pandemic

Lee Yen Chaw[1]([✉]), Andrew Chu[1], Chee Ling Thong[2], and Mcxin Tee[3]

[1] UCSI Graduate Business School, UCSI University, Kuala Lumpur, Malaysia
chawly@ucsiuniversity.edu.my, andrewchu@live.com.my
[2] Institute of Computer Science and Digital Innovation, UCSI University, Kuala Lumpur, Malaysia
chloethong@ucsiuniversity.edu.my
[3] Faculty of Business, Communications and Law, INTI International University, Negeri Sembilan, Malaysia
mcxin.tee@newinti.edu.my

Abstract. The purpose of this study is to investigate factors that influence learners' intention towards accepting online learning tools before and after Covid pandemic in different learning environments. A total of 350 sample collected prior to Covid pandemic in Malaysia whereas 627 sample collected at post Covid pandemic in China. UTAUT model and TAM served as the frameworks whereas PLS-SEM was used for data analysis. The findings disclosed that both Performance Expectancy and Effort Expectancy have positive relationship with students' Behavioral Intention of accepting online learning tools in the Malaysia's study before Covid pandemic under the blended learning environment. However, the effect size ($f2$) of Performance Expectancy is small ($f2 = 0.020$), and Effort Expectancy has no effect ($f2 = 0.015$) in predicting Behavioral Intention in adopting online learning tools. While comparing to another similar study conducted in China after covid pandemic in the mobile learning environment, Performance Expectancy (perceived usefulness) has large effect size ($f2 = 0.403$), and Effort Expectancy (ease of use) has medium effect size ($f2 = 0.241$) on students' adoption of online learning technologies. By comparing results of the two studies, the effect size of Performance Expectancy increased from small to large effect, while Effort Expectancy increased from no effect to medium effect. This shows that the widespread of Covid pandemic has impacted the learning approaches in education institutions likewise the perception of students towards technology acceptance. Importance-performance matrix analysis was used as a post-hoc procedure to measure the importance and performance of the exogenous constructs for both studies.

Keyword: Technology acceptance · Adoption · Blended learning · Mobile learning · TAM · UTAUT · Pandemic

1 Introduction

With the advanced in the web technology, education institutions have taken the opportunity to opt for blended learning approach to enrich students' learning experience [1].

G. Salvendy and J. Wei (Eds.): HCII 2022, LNCS 13337, pp. 119–132, 2022.
https://doi.org/10.1007/978-3-031-05014-5_10

Blended learning integrates conventional classroom learning and online learning where learning and teaching is no longer confined to classroom when technologies open up new innovative ways [2]. This helps to overcome some limitations of face-to-face classroom learning where learning can still be continued at different time and space [3, 4]. Different definitions of blended learning have been used in the previous literatures. Past studies have shown that the applications of blended learning are increasing, yet its true potential has not been fully utilized to support learning process [5, 6]. Majority of the institutions of higher learnings (IHLs) used LMS as a complementary online learning tool to support teaching and learning in a blended learning environment. Furthermore, most of the physical classes were still be conducted prior to covid pandemic occurred. Students were not mandated to adopt full online learning by most IHLs particularly in developing countries. However, with the strike of highly contagious virus – covid 19 around the globe since early 2020 which resulted countries gone into lockdown. Students unexpectedly found themselves struggling to accommodate to a full online learning environment in which physical classroom was not made available to them in addition to not meeting their course-mates and instructors in person [7]. In spite of the fact that some students might have experience with a blended learning environment before, a complete online learning environment was deemed entirely new to many [7]. As technology continues to evolve, students learn not only through face-to-face, and computer mediated tools but also increasingly through mobile-learning or m-learning [10]. Hence, the objective of the study is to compare technology acceptance behaviour before and after covid pandemic happened in different countries with different learning environments among students in IHLs. According to [11], majority of the research on blended learning have been on individual country and rarely researched on a cross country comparison. Therefore, by having cross country comparison will enable individual countries to learn experience from another country. In response to the call by research scholars, two countries namely Malaysia and China were chosen as the target location of this study in view of these nations are belonged to developing nations with latter emerged as an international higher education hub particularly with rapid advancement in wireless technology in recent years. This study aims to address a research question: What are the differences in terms of factors affecting technology acceptance before and after pandemic happened among students when learning landscape has drastically changed? These insights can be very useful for IHLs and academic practitioners to better create the learning context to meet the needs of diverse students transit smoothly from one learning environment to another.

2   Literature Review

2.1   Theories in Technology Acceptance

According to the Technology Acceptance Model (TAM), an individual behavioral intention to use an information system or technology is decided by two important features namely perceived usefulness (PU) and perceived ease of use (PEOU) [8, 9]. PU can be explained as the degree of an individual believes that using an information system or technology will improve his or her job performance. PEOU refers to the degree of an individual believes that using an information system or technology will free him or her from hassle or with less inconveniences [12]. However, TAM has its weaknesses such as not being able to provide sufficient insight into individuals' perspective of novel systems and fail to consider the relationship between usage attitude and usage intention [10].

To address TAM limitations, the Unified Theory of Acceptance and Use of Technology (UTAUT) model was introduced in 2003 by Venkatesh and associates [14] which combined alternative views on user and innovation acceptance from eight established models/theories. The theory of UTAUT was validated by Venkatesh et al. [14] in a longitudinal study. Without doubt, it is considered a well-developed and updated technology acceptance model. Moreover, it is widely used in the education research [15–17] besides examining technology acceptance for organization settings.

UTAUT is capable of carries a 70% explanatory power in determining users' intention to use information technology [14, 18]. In this study, we adopted four major constructs from the original UTAUT Model: performance expectancy, effort expectancy, social influence, and facilitating conditions and also include moderators such as age and genders to assess students' intention to use online tools for learning in the Malaysia study [19].

It is interesting to note that there are some similarities between TAM and UTAUT models. Performance Expectancy in UTAUT model has quite similar meaning to the term perceived usefulness in TAM model, while Effort Expectancy in UTAUT model has similar meaning to the term perceived ease of use in TAM model [20]. Moreover, [21] reported that Performance Expectancy and Effort Expectancy are essentially Perceived Usefulness and Perceived Ease of Use in their paper. Mobile Technology Acceptance Model (MTAM) has been recommended by [22] in recent years as they argue that the model fit better for the mobile environment as compared to the previous technology acceptance models or theories. The features of Usefulness and Ease of Use has also been incorporated into the said model.

2.2 Technology Acceptance in Blended Learning Environment–Before Pandemic

Many research studies have reported on blended learning since it flourished for nearly two decades [23]. According to [11], blended learning involved a paradigm shift from instructor-centric to student-centric where students become active and interactive learners in the learning process. This means students will engage more responsibilities in their learning with the help of learning system provided by the universities. Explained by [1], blended learning basically refers to the mixture of conventional classroom learning and e-learning, where the approach for blended learning is"based on formal or informal, scheduled or self-paced physical class-based or virtual learning environment designed for students". Scholars have warned that by merely incorporating online features to replace classroom experience will not meet learners' need and such action may even lead to unexpected failure [12, 24]. Thus, it is important to examine factors that may impact technology acceptance among students in a blended learning environment. Technology acceptance is defined as "the willingness of an individual to adopt the use of technology for facilitating task performance based on the support it was designed to provide." [17]. [25] conducted a study on the continued usage intentions of a web-based learning management system in Tanzania using UTAUT model and the results showed that performance expectancy was a strong predictor. This indicates that learners with high performance expectancy is more likely to use online tools in the blended learning environment than learners with lower performance expectancy. In other words, learners are willing to adopt online technology because they perceived this will improve their learning performance. Similarly, effort expectancy also predicted continued usage intention of the online tools [25].

2.3 Technology Acceptance in Mobile Learning Environment – After Pandemic

Government around the globe have responded to the Covid pandemic crisis by issuing a public health order that include social distancing, isolation, and self-quarantine [17, 26]. In view of the health hazard situations, education institutions need to make drastic change by shifting conventional teaching and learning or even blended learning modes to full online almost overnight. Fortunately, technology allows education continues to operate even during the lockdown period. With the advancement in mobile technology, students can access learning material via mobile devices such as smart-phone and tablet. Mobile learning (m-learning) is a critical aspect of digital education, and so its acceptance and adoption generates great interest to stakeholders [10]. Nevertheless, recent studies [34, 35] have revealed that using mobile learning as one of the online learning platforms has not received high usage by students at IHLs. Thus, researchers have called to examine comprehensively the critical factors that may affect university students' acceptance of m-learning [10]. It is interesting to note that IHLs in China have introduced mandatory m-learning courses which provide an alternative way for students to learn without attending physical classes during covid pandemic [13]. It is not easy to explain the acceptance of m-learning from student's point of view when such practices are the only choice under the impact of covid pandemic [13]. The empirical studies conducted by [27] during the university closure as a result of COVID pandemic revealed that perceived usefulness becomes less vital features for students to decide to use the technology when limited choices were made available to them. The non-significant effect of perceived usefulness towards behavioural intention shows that resistance towards new technology may not be as important as it was before [27].

3   Research Methodology

For Malaysia study, hard copy questionnaires were distributed in classes of the three diploma programmes in one of the private universities in Malaysia in June 2019, before covid pandemic. Prior to distribution of the questionnaires, researcher had obtained permission from the principal of the University. The duration of the data collection was two weeks. The questionnaire consisted of two sections. Section A asked three demographic questions. Section B focusses on the UTAUT constructs – performance expectancy, effort expectancy, facilitating conditions, and social influence, which may have an influence on behavioural intention to use online learning tool. The items used to measure the constructs were derived from past studies to ensure content validity. We have refined the questionnaire to suit the context of the current study. Each statement used for Section B was presented on a five-point Likert scale question ranging from 1 ("strongly disagree") to 5 ("strongly agree").

For China study, it is based on the empirical study conducted by [13] during post pandemic. This study used an online self-administered questionnaire survey. Respondents are students from universities in China. Main constructs of TAM such as usefulness and ease of use were included in the questionnaire and measure using the seven-point Likert scale question ranging from 1 ("strongly disagree") to 7 ("strongly agree").

4   Data Analysis – Malaysia Study

4.1   Demographic Characteristics

Table 1 shows the demographic profile of respondents for the Malaysia study. A total of 350 responses were received from students. No missing data or outliers were found. In general, we received slightly more responses from female students (53.14%) than male students (46.86%). Most of the students were between 18–20 years old (89.43%), which covers the main age group of students who are pursuing Diploma studies in university.

Table 1. Demographic profile of respondents

Characteristics		Number	Percentage (%)
Gender	Male	164	46.86
	Female	186	53.14
	Total	**350**	**100**
Age	17	6	1.71
	18	87	24.86
	19	157	44.86
	20	69	19.71
	21	17	4.86
	22	8	2.29
	23	2	0.57
	24	2	0.57
	Others	2	0.57
	Total	**350**	**100**
Programme	Diploma in Business Administration	231	66.00
	Diploma in Information Technology	71	20.29
	Diploma in Hotel Management	48	13.71
	Total	**350**	**100**
Semester of study	Semester 1	126	36.00
	Semester 3	70	20.00
	Semester 4	118	33.71
	Semester 6	36	10.29
	Total	**350**	**100**

More than half of the students (66%) were studying Diploma in Business Administration programme. Subsequently, 56% of the students were in Year 1 study (semester 1 and 3), 44% of students were in Year 2 study (semesters 4 and 6).

4.2 Outer Measurement Model Analysis

The objective of measurement model evaluation is to examine reliability and validity of measurement instruments used in this research. After conducting the analysis, we decided to delete the items of FC4, SI1 and SI2 as the outer loadings are lower than 0.708 (FC4: 0.463; SI1: 0.578; SI2: 0.576). As mentioned by [28], not more than 20% of the items can be deleted until the satisfactory value of AVE has achieved. After deleted these 3 items, the result shows all constructs have met satisfactory level of CR result of higher than 0.7, and AVE result of higher than 0.5, based on threshold indicated by [28]. Next, most of the outer loadings are higher than 0.708, except PE2 (0.682) and FC3 (0.690). However, based on [28], loadings lower than 0.708 can be kept if the AVE result is higher than 0.5. Hence, we decided to keep these two items. Table 2 showed internal reliability of consistency and convergent validity have therefore been verified.

Table 2. Loadings, composite reliability and average variance extracted.

Latent construct	Items	Loadings	Composite Reliability (CR)	Average Variance Extracted (AVE)
Performance Expectancy (PE)	PE1	0.804	0.852	0.592
	PE2	0.682		
	PE3	0.834		
	PE4	0.747		
Effort Expectancy (EE)	EE1	0.700	0.832	0.554
	EE2	0.701		
	EE3	0.808		
	EE4	0.762		
Social Influence (SI)	SI3	0.808	0.847	0.735
	SI4	0.903		
Facilitating Conditions (FC)	FC1	0.834	0.844	0.646
	FC2	0.876		
	FC3	0.690		
Behavioral Intention (BI)	BI1	0.943	0.956	0.879
	BI2	0.930		
	BI3	0.939		

Discriminant validity of the model was evaluated through Fornell-Larcker criterion. Table 3 indicates that all constructs show sufficient discriminant validity as the square root of AVE is larger than the correlations for all reflective constructs [29]. Moreover, Hetero-Trait-Mono-Trait (HTMT) through 5000 subsamples of bootstrapping technique was used to check discriminant validity. As shown in Table 4, using a 95% confidence interval, the lower and upper confidence intervals do not include 1, it indicates every construct in the sample are statistically distinct. Hence, discriminant validity has been confirmed [28].

Table 3. Fornell-Larcker criterion

Latent Construct	BI	EE	FC	PE	SI
Behavioral Intention	**0.937**				
Effort Expectancy	0.465	**0.744**			
Facilitating Conditions	0.483	0.526	**0.804**		
Performance Expectancy	0.490	0.504	0.582	**0.769**	
Social Influence	0.572	0.510	0.458	0.519	**0.857**

Table 4. Hetero-Trait-Mono-Trait (HTMT)

Latent Construct	Original Sample (O)	Sample Mean (M)	Bias	5.00%	95.00%
PE -> BI	0.138	0.139	0.002	0.042	0.230
EE -> BI	0.123	0.128	0.005	0.029	0.212
SI -> BI	0.337	0.334	−0.003	0.237	0.434
FC -> BI	0.180	0.180	0.001	0.077	0.278

4.3 Inner Structural Model Analysis

In this research, collinearity issue is not a concern as all values are below the threshold of 3.3 [30] as shown in Table 5. Next, bootstrapping technique with 5000 subsamples at one-tailed 0.05 significance level was applied to assess hypothesized relationships to create T Statistics and p-value for each path coefficient. Table 6 presents all hypotheses suggested are positive and significant as P Values are <0.05, and all T Statistics are >1.645 [28].

Coefficient of determination, R^2 value of 0.431 is more than the threshold of 0.33 [31] which indicates a substantial model. Next, effect sizes, f^2 are assessed by following [32] guideline. As shown in Table 7, Performance Expectancy (0.020) and Facilitating Conditions (0.030) have small effect in producing R^2 for Behavioral Intention. Social Influence (0.139) has close to medium effect in producing R^2 for Behavioral Intention. However, Effort Expectancy (0.015) has no effect in producing R^2 for Behavioral Intention. Hence, Effort Expectancy has no substantial contribution to the construct and does not explain much variance in the target construct. Following, predictive relevance, Q^2

Table 5. Inner VIF values

	Behavioral Intention
Performance Expectancy	1.783
Effort Expectancy	1.639
Social Influence	1.570
Facilitating Conditions	1.725

Table 6. Results of structural model

PLS Path	Original sample (O)	Sample mean (M)	Standard deviation (STDEV)	T Statistics (IO/STDEVI)	P Values	Confidence interval		Remarks
						5.00%	95.00%	
PE -> BI	0.144	0.144	0.058	2.491	0.006	0.051	0.240	Supported
EE -> BI	0.119	0.126	0.054	2.205	0.014	0.032	0.209	Supported
SI -> BI	0.357	0.354	0.058	6.182	0.000	0.267	0.456	Supported
FC -> BI	0.173	0.175	0.061	2.848	0.002	0.074	0.273	Supported

Notes: Significant at 5% level, $p < 0.05$

of the model is assessed. If Q^2 value is larger than 0, it means the model has predictive relevance for dependent variable [30]. The Q^2 value of Behavioral Intention (0.352) is larger than 0, indicates the model has sufficient predictive relevance.

Table 7. Coefficient of determination, effect size and predictive relevance

	R^2	f^2	Q^2
Behavioral Intention	0.431		0.352
Performance Expectancy		0.020	
Effort Expectancy		0.015	
Social Influence		0.139	
Facilitating Conditions		0.030	

4.4   Importance and Performance Matrix Analysis

A post-hoc procedure was conducted using the Importance and Performance Matrix Analysis (IPMA) to gauge the importance and performance of independent variables namely Performance Expectancy, Effort Expectancy, Social Influence and Facilitating Conditions. Table 8 and Fig. 1 show the highest importance is Social Influence (0.440), followed by Facilitating Conditions (0.198), Performance Expectancy (0.177), and lastly Effort Expectancy (0.169). Besides, the highest performance is also Social Influence (80.86), followed by Effort Expectancy (78.02), Facilitating Conditions (70.58), and lastly Performance Expectancy (67.19).

Table 8. IPMA result

	Importance (Total Effect)	Performance (Index Values)
Performance Expectancy	0.177	67.19
Effort Expectancy	0.169	78.02
Social Influence	0.440	80.86
Facilitating Conditions	0.198	70.58

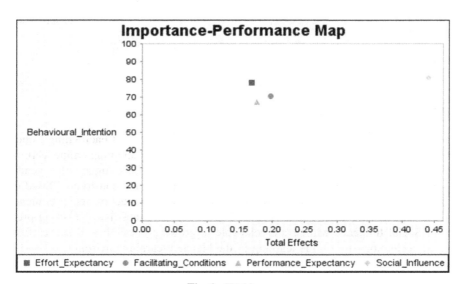

Fig. 1. IPMA map

4.5 Moderation Analysis

Product indicator approach was applied to carry out moderation analysis. Table 9 suggests that gender and experience do not moderate all the relationships among the constructs as the P Values and T Statistics cannot meet the threshold of P Values < 0.05, and T Statistics > 1.645 [28].

Table 9. Moderation analysis

Relationship	Original Sample (O)	Sample Mean (M)	Standard Deviation (STDEV)	T Statistics (|O/STDEV|)	P Values	Remarks
PE *Gender -> BI	−0.125	−0.128	0.124	1.012	0.156	Not supported
EE *Gender -> BI	−0.040	−0.055	0.139	0.287	0.387	Not supported
SI *Gender -> BI	−0.128	−0.128	0.117	1.089	0.138	Not supported
EE * Experience -> BI	−0.010	−0.022	0.076	0.127	0.449	Not supported
SI * Experience -> BI	0.064	0.017	0.084	0.762	0.223	Not supported
FC * Experience -> BI	0.040	0.015	0.064	0.628	0.265	Not supported

5 Discussion

Performance Expectancy, Effort Expectancy, Social Influence, and Facilitating Conditions have positive impact on students' behavioral intention in adopting online learning tools under the blended learning environment. However, results suggest that gender and experience do not moderate all the relationships among the constructs. Based on the results of IPMA, Behavioral Intention reveals that the construct of Social Influence has both highest performance and highest importance. It means that the strong presence of Social Influence will be a crucial role in growing possibility of successfully adopting technology for online learning in the blended learning environment. Hence, the universities should focus on Social Influence and looking for innovative approach to highlight the unique role of social factor and generate a collective adoption of behavior among students. Next, Facilitating Conditions is the second highest importance and third highest performance in the prediction of Behavioral Intention. It means that online learning will become more feasible once the required technological infrastructure becomes more available and effectual to students. Therefore, universities should provide adequate technical and infrastructural resources, such as availability to access the online learning tools within a reasonable response time [33], with the aim of supporting the technology adoption among students.

Performance Expectancy in UTAUT model is similar to the term perceived usefulness in TAM model, while Effort Expectancy in UTAUT model is similar to the term perceived ease of use in TAM model [20]. Based on the results obtained from Malaysia study, both Performance Expectancy and Effort Expectancy have shown positive relationship with students' Behavioral Intention of adopting online learning tools in blended learning environment. Nevertheless, the analysis results indicated that Performance Expectancy has small effect size ($f2 = 0.020$), and most surprisingly Effort Expectancy shows no effect ($f2 = 0.015$) in the prediction of Behavioral Intention of adopting online learning tools. It means strength of the relationship between Effort Expectancy and Behavioral Intention is extremely weak, indicates zero effect in predicting Behavioral Intention. Our study was conducted in Malaysia prior covid pandemic. While comparing to another similar study conducted in China after covid pandemic happened [13], Performance Expectancy (perceived usefulness) has large effect size ($f2 = 0.403$), and Effort Expectancy (ease of use) has medium effect size ($f2 = 0.241$) on students' adoption of using online learning technologies. By comparing results of the two studies which had been carried out prior and post covid pandemic, the effect size of Performance Expectancy has increased from small to large effect, while Effort Expectancy has increased from no effect to medium effect. It clearly shows that the mass spreading of covid pandemic has changed the landscape of learning method in IHLs. Moreover, the results of IPMA [13] indicates that perceived usefulness has the highest importance level and ease of use has the second highest importance level. Students strongly believe that adopting the technology innovations of online and mobile learning system can help them to achieve better learning performance. They form positive attitude towards online and mobile learning system, particularly have a stronger positive attitude after covid pandemic happened as technologies are perceived to save effort and time, deliver current and trustworthy information in their learning process.

6 Conclusion, Limitations and Future Research

Although Covid pandemic is a major disruptor for current education scenario, it has fastened the speed in implementing innovative solutions in IHLs worldwide. From the present studies, it can be said that students are positive towards accepting m-learning after experiencing sudden global health crisis as compared to before covid pandemic where full online learning played a limited role in education. Perceived usefulness and ease of use remain played a significant role in influencing technology acceptance among students in the post pandemic which deserves further attention by the academic practitioners and technology support team. We acknowledge the fact that this paper has limitations particularly the study about technology acceptance in the mobile environment with post Covid pandemic scenario where data analysis was solely based on the work of [13] and thus may not be fully comparative with the study done before Covid pandemic in Malaysia. Therefore, future work may consider by comparing the same learning environment in different countries or replicate the comparative studies with similar model. Additionally, it may be worth to explore the possible future learning technologies for IHLs when Covid pandemic eventually becomes endemic.

References

1. Siddiqui, S., Soomro, N.N., Thomas, M.: Blended learning source of satisfaction of psychological needs. Asian Assoc. Open Univ. J. **15**(1), 49–67 (2020). https://doi.org/10.1108/aaouj-11-2019-0054
2. Tang, C.M., Chaw, L.Y.: Digital literacy: A prerequisite for effective learning in a blended learning environment? Electron. J. e-Learning **14**(1), 54–65 (2016)
3. Tang, C.M., Chaw, L.Y.: Digital literacy and effective learning in a blended learning environment. In: Proceedings of the European Conference on e-Learning, ECEL, pp. 601–610 (2015)
4. Chaw, L.Y., Tang, C.M.: What makes learning management systems effective for learning? J. Educ. Technol. Syst. **47**(2), 152–169 (2018). https://doi.org/10.1177/0047239518795828
5. Gupta, J., Garg, K.: Reflections on blended learning in management education: a qualitative study with a push-pull Migration Perspective. FIIB Bus. Rev. (2021). https://doi.org/10.1177/23197145211013686
6. Garrison, D.R., Kanuka, H.: Blended learning: uncovering its transformative potential in higher education. Internet Higher Educ. **7**(2), 95–105 (2004). https://doi.org/10.1016/j.iheduc.2004.02.001
7. Tang, C.M., Chaw, L. Y.: Media and public opinion about online learning during the Covid pandemic: a content analysis of newspaper articles. In: 20th European Conference on e-Learning, Berlin, Germany (2021)
8. Davis, F.D.: Perceived usefulness, perceived ease of use, and user acceptance of information technology. MIS Q. Manage. Inf. Syst. **13**(3), 319–339 (1989). https://doi.org/10.2307/249008
9. Venkatesh, V., Davis, F.D.: Theoretical extension of the Technology Acceptance Model: four longitudinal field studies. Manage. Sci. **46**(2), 186–204 (2000). https://doi.org/10.1287/mnsc.46.2.186.11926
10. Chao, C.M.: Factors determining the behavioral intention to use mobile learning: an application and extension of the UTAUT model. Front. Psychol. **10**, 1–14 (2019). https://doi.org/10.3389/fpsyg.2019.01652
11. Poon, J.: A cross-country comparison on the use of blended learning in property education. Prop. Manag. **32**(2), 154–175 (2014). https://doi.org/10.1108/PM-04-2013-0026
12. Park, S.Y.: An analysis of the technology acceptance model in understanding university students' behavioral intention to use e-learning. Educ. Technol. Soc. **12**(3), 150–162 (2009)
13. Yuan, Y.P., Wei-Han Tan, G., Ooi, K.B., Lim, W.L.: Can COVID-19 pandemic influence experience response in mobile learning? In: Telematics and Informatics, vol. 64 (2021). https://doi.org/10.1016/j.tele.2021.101676
14. Venkatesh, V., Morris, M.G., Davis, G.B., Davis, F.D.: User acceptance of information technology: toward a unified view. MIS Q. Manag. Inf. Syst. **27**(3), 425–478 (2003). https://doi.org/10.2307/30036540
15. Birch, A., Irvine, V.: Preservice teachers' acceptance of ICT integration in the classroom: applying the UTAUT model. Educ. Media Int. **46**(4), 295–315 (2009). https://doi.org/10.1080/09523980903387506
16. McKeown, T., Anderson, M.: UTAUT: capturing differences in undergraduate versus postgraduate learning? Educ. Train. **58**(9), 945–965 (2016). https://doi.org/10.1108/ET-07-2015-0058

17. Raza, S.A., Qazi, W., Khan, K.A., Salam, J.: Social isolation and acceptance of the Learning Management System (LMS) in the time of COVID-19 pandemic: an expansion of the UTAUT model. J. Educ. Comput. Res. **59**(2), 183–208 (2021). https://doi.org/10.1177/073563312096 0421

18. Venkatesh, V., Thong, J.Y.L., Xu, X.: Consumer acceptance and use of information technology: extending the unified theory of acceptance and use of technology. MIS Q. **36**(1), 157–178 (2012). https://doi.org/10.2307/41410412

19. Williams, M.D., Rana, N.P., Dwivedi, Y.K.: The unified theory of acceptance and use of technology (UTAUT): a literature review. J. Enterp. Inf. Manag. **28**(3), 443–448 (2015). https://doi.org/10.1108/JEIM-09-2014-0088

20. Sair, S.A., Danish, R.Q.: Effect of performance expectancy and effort expectancy on the mobile commerce adoption intention through personal innovativeness among Pakistani consumers. Pakistan J. Commer. Soc. Sci. (PJCSS) **12**(2), 501–520 (2018)

21. Hew, J.J., Lee, V.H., Ooi, K.B., Wei, J.: What catalyses mobile apps usage intention: an empirical analysis. Ind. Manag. Data Syst. **115**(7), 1269–1291 (2015). https://doi.org/10.1108/IMDS-01-2015-0028

22. Ooi, K.B., Tan, G.W.H.: Mobile technology acceptance model: an investigation using mobile users to explore smartphone credit card. Expert Syst. Appl. **59**, 33–46 (2016). https://doi.org/10.1016/j.eswa.2016.04.015

23. Siraj, K.K., Al Maskari, A.: Student engagement in blended learning instructional design: an analytical study. Learn. Teach. Higher Educ. Gulf Perspect. **15**(2) (2019). https://doi.org/10.18538/lthe.v15.n2.283

24. Kilmurray, J.: E-learning: It's more than automation. The Technology Source archives (2003)

25. Lwoga, E.T., Komba, M.: Antecedents of continued usage intentions of web-based learning management system in Tanzania. Educ. Train. **57**(7), 738–756 (2015). https://doi.org/10.1108/ET-02-2014-0014

26. Anderson, R.M., Heesterbeek, H., Klinkenberg, D., Hollingsworth, T.D.: How will country-based mitigation measures influence the course of the COVID-19 epidemic? Lancet **395**(10228), 931–934 (2020). https://doi.org/10.1016/S0140-6736(20)30567-5

27. Mailizar, M., Burg, D., Maulina, S.: Examining university students' behavioural intention to use e-learning during the COVID-19 pandemic: an extended TAM model. Educ. Inf. Technol. **26**(6), 7057–7077 (2021). https://doi.org/10.1007/s10639-021-10557-5

28. Ramayah, T., Cheah, J., Chuah, F., Ting, H., Memon, M. A.: Partial least squares structural equation modeling (PLS-SEM) using smart PLS 3.0. In: An Updated Guide and Practical Guide to Statistical Analysis. Pearson, Kuala Lumpur, Malaysia (2018)

29. Fornell, C., Larcker, D. F.: Structural equation models with unobservable variables and measurement error: Algebra Stat. (1981)

30. Hair Jr., J.F., Sarstedt, M., Ringle, C.M., Gudergan, S.P.: Advanced Issues in Partial Least Squares Structural Equation Modeling. SAGE Publications (2017)

31. Chin, W.W.: The partial least squares approach for structural equation modeling. Modern Meth. Bus. Res. 295–336 (1998)

32. Cohen, J.: Appl. Psychol. Meas. **12**(4), 425–434 (1988)

33. Hossain, M.A., Hasan, M.I., Chan, C., Ahmed, J.U.: Predicting user acceptance and continuance behavior towards location-based services: the moderating effect of facilitating conditions on behavioral intention and actual use. Australasian J. Inf. Syst. **21** (2017)

34. Loh, X.-K., Lee, V.-H., Loh, X.M., Tan, G.W.-H., Ooi, K.B., Dwivedi, Y. K.: The dark side of mobile learning via social media: How bad can it get? Inf. Syst. Front. 0123456789 (2021). https://doi.org/10.1007/s10796-021-10202-z
35. Pikhart, M., Pikhart, M.: Human-computer interaction in foreign language learning human-computer interaction in foreign language learning applications: applied linguistics viewpoint of mobile learning applications: applied linguistics viewp. Procedia Comput. Sci. **184**, 92–98 (2021). https://doi.org/10.1016/j.procs.2021.03.123

What Drives Mobile Game Stickiness?
A Perspective from Uses and Gratifications
Theory

Maomao Chi[1][✉], Yunran Wang[2], and Haiyan Ma[1][✉]

[1] School of Economics and Management, China University of Geosciences, Wuhan, China
chimaomao@vip.163.com, 7893531@qq.com
[2] School of Information Management, Central China Normal University, Wuhan, China

Abstract. Despite the huge growth potential that has been predicted for mobile game continuous usage intention, little is known about what motives users to be sticky under the mobile game context. Drawing on the Uses and Gratifications theory (UGT), this study aims to investigate the influencing effects of players' characteristics and the mobile game structures on players' mobile game behavior (e.g. stickiness). After surveying 439 samples, the research model is tested with Partial Least Squares Structural Equation Modeling (PLS-SEM). The results indicate that both individual gratifications and mobile game presence positively affect users' stickiness. Furthermore, we find that leisure boredom of individual situations and integration of mobile game governance positively affect users' stickiness. The results provide further insights into the design and governance strategies of mobile games.

Keywords: Mobile games · Uses and gratifications theory · Stickiness

1 Introduction

Mobile devices such as smartphones, tablet computers, and other mobile Internet devices attract mass users for the convenience to access resources and engage in activities (e.g. to study, work, meet friends). With the popularity of mobile devices, mobile games have also rapidly gained an enormous share in the game industry. Compared to games on PC and console, the percentage of mobile game playing is steadily rising from 39.2% in 2015 to 75.1% in 2020, which implies that more and more players tend to play games on mobile devices (iResearch 2020). Although mobile games enjoy a prominent prospect, they still face the problem of low stickiness, which causes the loss of users. A report from GameAnalytics (2019) reveals that mobile games only hold a low user stickiness, even the best performing mobile game only has a retention rate of 4% to 6%.

Prior related studies seldom focus on how to attract users and increase their stickiness in the mobile game context. Stickiness has already been discussed in related fields, including three main contexts: e-commerce websites, social media and the online games industry. First, in the e-commerce context, past researches indicated that augmenting

G. Salvendy and J. Wei (Eds.): HCII 2022, LNCS 13337, pp. 133–149, 2022.
https://doi.org/10.1007/978-3-031-05014-5_11

e-commerce websites with social features will positively affect websites stickiness (Friedrich et al. 2019) Based on social theory, social identity theory, loyalty theory and customer engagement literature, Molinillo et al. (2020) explored that social support and community factors lead to customer loyalty and stickiness. Second, stickiness has also been examined in the field of social media, such as blogs (Lu and Lee 2010) and Youtube (Chiang and Hsiao 2015). Factors like the length of using time, content quality, enthusiasm could affect users' stickiness on the media (Xu et al. 2018). Finally, concerning researches on online games, stickiness has been extensively examined to investigate users' continuous use intention, and most of them are built on technology acceptance model (TAM) (Hsu and Lu 2004; Malaquias et al. 2018) and flow theory (Huang et al. 2017; Arı et al. 2020).

Based on the above discussion, we can summarize the research gap that past online game literature mainly developed their research models based on adoption behavior theories, such as TAM (Liu and Li 2011; Rafdinal et al. 2020). While technology acceptance factors (e.g. perceived usefulness, perceived ease of use) are of importance, users are also concerned about hedonic and utilitarian gratification that they can gain from playing mobile games. These gratification needs are more significant in the mobile game context (Ha et al. 2007).

Hence, this paper distinguished two dimensions of players' characteristics and the mobile game structures based on UGTs, and further explore their effects on players' stickiness. According to Uses and Gratifications theory (UGT) individual situation and gratification are derived from the user perspective. By satisfying users' needs, their behaviors to the game might be influenced. The mobile game structure perspective is considered from the incentives and governance. Developing the good quality game structure can influence users' in-game experience, which also have an impact on their stickiness. Past studies have applied UGT to examine the effect on user behavior in the game environment (Li et al. 2015; Chen et al. 2018; Wei and Lu 2014), however, most of them only adopted individual gratification perspective, scarcely considering the effect of mobile game mechanisms. We developed our extended research model by integrating both players' characteristics and the mobile game structures to better understand users' stickiness. Therefore, this study attempts to solve the following two research questions: *What factors influence players' stickiness? How do these factors affect players' stickiness?*

2   Theoretical Background

2.1   Mobile Game Adoption Behavior

Mobile games can be defined as video games played on mobile devices. When reviewing the literature on mobile games, we find that most of the relative research is based on adoption behavior theory. Previous researches are mainly built on Technology Acceptance Model (TAM) and Unified Theory of Acceptance and Use of Technology 2 (UTAUT2) to examine users' behavior intention.

In the context of mobile games, TAM is widely used to investigate players' attitudes and use intentions. Rafdinal et al. (2020) examined mobile game features and found that ease of use and usefulness can affect players' use intention and attitude. Lee and Quan

(2013) added user-related factors (e.g. self-efficacy, innovativeness, self-expressiveness) and service-related factors (e.g. visibility, incentives) to the TAM model to investigate users' intention. Meanwhile, several studies examined users' mobile game adoption behavior by using UTAUT2. Baabdullah (2020) extended UTAUT2 to investigate factors that affect the adoption of mobile social network games (M-SNGs) and found that attitude would have an impact on perceived fun and convenience, which further influence users' intention to play. By proposing a simplified UTAUT2 model in the mobile game context, it has also been proved that players' game adoption behavior was affected by habit and playing intention (Ramírez-Correa et al. 2019).

Based on the above summarizations, we find that existing researches explore users' use intention in the mobile game context, only a few investigate the stickiness behavior(Chen et al. 2018; Lee et al. 2018), and other critical factors beyond technology (e.g. hedonic and utilitarian gratification) related are limited explored.

2.2 Uses and Gratification Theory (UGT)

The uses and gratifications theory was originally developed to explore users' reactions to mass media in the 1940s. UGT has been utilized to explain the psychological needs of individuals that motivate their use of a particular medium. Despite being a theory to explain users' choices on traditional media (e.g. television, newspaper) (Rubin 1983; Berelson 1949), UGT has also been widely applied to examine different novel modern media forms, such as the Internet (Ko et al. 2005), social media (Smock et al. 2011), and mobile devices (Chen 2018; Kaur et al. 2020).With the rapid diffusion of mobile devices and digital games, many literatures were also increasingly adapting UGT to examine online games (Wu et al. 2010; Li et al. 2015) mobile games (Wei and Lu 2014; Hamari 2015; Hamari et al. 2019), esports (Weiss and Schiele 2013) and so on. Media scholars found that UGT provides a user-centered view (Leung and Wei 2000), that is, users seek satisfaction through the media. Those satisfactory needs are like entertainment, leisure, personal identity, social connection and so on (Cho et al. 2003). Therefore, UGT is particularly suitable to examine mobile game stickiness.

Weibull (1985) proposed a UGT model that depicted the process of media use. He suggested that we should not only consider media as a technical channel, but also need to pay attention to related policies, resources, and users. The individual and the media structure are components of the social structure because the whole society can be classified into two realities; one is that society is based on media and the other is that users can influence media (Weibull 1985). Weibull's model provides us with a view that we should take both mobile game users and the mobile game structure into our research model. Therefore, we can examine more thoroughly which factors will affect users' stickiness in mobile games based on UGT.

3 Research Model and Research Hypotheses

To explore influencing mechanisms on stickiness mobile game participants, we develop an extended theoretical framework based on UGT model. Figure 1 shows the proposed research model by incorporating individual characteristics, mobile game structure, stickiness.

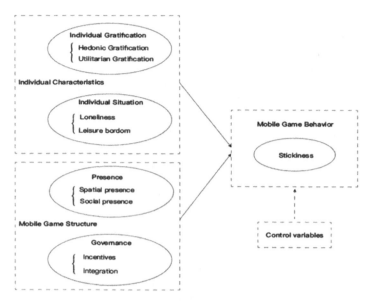

Fig. 1. Conceptual Model

3.1 Relationships Between Individual Gratification and Stickiness

Individual gratifications are relevant to the individual mobile game use experience and will further influence motivation and behavior on the mobile game use (Weibull 1985; Wu et al. 2010). From previous research, gratification can be mainly classified into hedonic gratification and utilitarian gratification (Wu et al. 2010; Li et al. 2015). Hedonic gratification is gained from hedonic consumption and it is the motivation of game-playing behavior. It is influenced by two main factors: imaginary and emotional response. These two factors help users escape from the real world and provide them with a fun experience (Su et al. 2016; Van der Heijden 2004). Utilitarian gratification is captured by utilitarian factors like achievement, self-presentation, and will further influence user behavior when playing the mobile game (Li et al. 2015; Gan and Li 2018). In the mobile game context, it usually refers to the gratification that players try to get achievements, such as status and skills in the game. Compared with hedonic gratification, utilitarian gratification is harder to obtain because the gaining process costs users more effort and time. Above all, gratification has already been used to investigate the original intention of mobile game playing (Ha et al. 2007).

H1: Hedonic gratification will positively influence stickiness in mobile games
H2: Utilitarian gratification will positively influence stickiness in mobile games

3.2 Relationships Between Individual Situation and Stickiness

Individual situation refers to personal characteristics and the environment surrounding, which will influence the behavior in the mobile game (Chen and Leung 2016; Wei and Lu

2014). Two factors that have been used to represent individual situation, loneliness and leisure boredom. Loneliness is an interpersonal deficit which is a lack of social interaction or closeness with others (Weiss 1973). Previous research suggested that people with loneliness are positively correlated with problematic internet use (Dong et al. 2021) and excessive gaming behavior (Ok 2021). (Leisure boredom is experienced when a person has too much time available with too few things to do (Hill and Perkins 1985). When people are at a high level of leisure boredom, they will have much more desire to have fun (Bryant and Zillmann 1984). Therefore, it has been proved that leisure boredom will cause many types of addiction, such as addiction to websites or games (Chen and Leung 2016).

H3: Loneliness will positively influence stickiness in mobile games
H4: Leisure boredom will positively influence stickiness in mobile games

3.3 Relationships Between Presence and Stickiness

Presence can be defined as a psychological state that a person is immersed in the mobile game with subjective consciousness (Weibel et al. 2008). Presence is the most significant character of mobile games, because it's central in shaping players' experience in the game, mainly divided into spatial presence and social presence (Ijsselsteijn et al. 2000; Tamborini and Skalski 2006). Spatial presence means a sense of being physically present in the virtual environment (IJsselsteijn et al. 2000), and it is a cognitive experience (Wirth et al. 2007). Generally, spatial presence can be understood as players immersing in the game and feeling that they are in a new world created by the game (Hilken et al. 2017). A strong spatial presence often provides users with an immersing environment, and such experience will enhance their stickiness (Wu et al. 2010; Li et al. 2015). Social presence refers to the psychological sense of physically interacting with others in the virtual world (Qiu and Benbasat 2005). Nowadays, many mobile games are equipped with various types of social functions to encourage players to share, be online, cooperate, etc. It is proved that social interaction is an important factor that motivates users to play games and helps to understand their continuous use intention (Wu et al. 2010).

H5: Spatial presence will positively influence stickiness in mobile games
H6: Social presence will positively influence stickiness in mobile games

3.4 Relationships Between Governance and Stickiness

Governance of the mobile game refers to mechanisms that game publishers construct and use to influence players (Wu et al. 2010; Scott 2013). Tiwana (2013) divided mobile games governance into three dimensions: autonomy, integration and incentives. Autonomy refers to the division of rights between platform owners and participants, which is not significant in the context of mobile games. Hence, we will not discuss it in our research. Incentives is a common approach to governance. It is a means for mobile game publishers to motivate players to continue playing the game, improving the utility of players and making their goals consistent with publishers. Incentives will foster players' loyalty, and lead to the behavior of continuous game use (Bhattacherjee 2001).

For instance, mobile games will reward players for daily check-in and activeness. This increases the players' game retention and exerts a positive impact on their stickiness. Integration is another important factor in platform governance guaranteed by control (Tiwana 2013). In the mobile game context, mobile game publishers try to govern the relationship between players and the platform through various controls (e.g. formal control, informal control). These controls could benefit the relationship between players and platforms, increasing players' interactions with games (e.g. set goals in advance to guide players, develop the virtual community).

H7: Incentives will positively influence stickiness in mobile games
H8: Integration will positively influence stickiness in mobile games

4 Methodology

4.1 Measurement Development

To access the research model, we prepare to take a cross-sectional survey to collect data. The items of the questionnaire are adapted from related literature to ensure validity. The survey items of Individual Gratifications are adapted from Li et al. (2015). The survey items of Loneliness are adapted from Russell (1996). The items of Leisure Boredom are adapted from Iso-Ahola and Weissinger (1990). The items of Presence are adapted from Wu et al. (2010). The items of Incentives are adapted from Bhattacherjee (2001). The survey items of Integration are adapted from Kirsch et al. (2002) and Koo (2009). Research constructs are measured using multiple items on a five-point Likert scale. Furthermore, to ensure consistency, the questionnaire was translated to Chinese and back-translated to English. The questionnaire is piloted among 60 mobile game players. Based on the result of a pilot study, the questionnaire was refined by respondents' feedback as well as sentences were rephrased and ambiguous questions were eliminated. The final measurements of the variables are shown in Appendix A.

4.2 Data Collection

This research surveyed various mobile games players to access the proposed model. Five types of mobile games were chosen (e.g. role-playing game, multiplayer online battle arena, shooter game, strategy, casual game), and each representative game selected (e.g. Genshin Impact, Glory of Kings, Game for Peace, Hearthstone, Happy Pop) was the most popular one in the Chinese mobile game market in 2020 (iResearch 2020).

The questionnaire was promoted online in China. Participants with mobile game using experience were encouraged to complete, and we also obtained their approval to use the data for study at the beginning of the questionnaire. The survey links were opened from April 4 to April 19, 2021, two weeks in total. A total of 536 questionnaires were collected and 439 were complete and valid. Respondents comprised 209 (48%) males and 230 (52%) females. Over half (54%) of respondents are between 20 and 24 years. The detailed information on demographics is listed in Table 1.

Table 1. Demographics of the sample.

Measure	Items	Frequency	Percentage
Gender	Male	209	48%
	Female	230	52%
Age (years)	Below 20	80	18%
	20–24	238	54%
	25–30	79	18%
	Above 30	42	10%
Education level	Secondary/high school	70	16%
	Junior college	78	18%
	College/university	267	61%
	Master/PhD	24	5%
Wage (CNY)	Below 1500	157	36%
	1500–3000	133	30%
	3000–5000	85	19%
	5000–10000	45	10%
	Above 10000	19	4%
Mobile game types	Role-playing game (RPG)	46	10%
	Multiplayer Online Battle Arena (MOBA)	131	30%
	Shooting game (STG)	63	14%
	Real-Time Strategy game (RTS)	76	17%
	Leisure game	94	21%
	Other	29	7%
Use time (hours per day)	Below 1	111	25%
	1–2	141	32%
	2–4	101	23%
	Above 4	86	20%
Payment in three months (CNY)	0	127	29%
	1–100	158	36%
	101–500	102	23%
	501–1000	38	9%
	Above 1000	14	3%

5 Data Analysis

5.1 Measurement Model

Following the two-step analysis procedure, reliability and convergence validity, and discriminant validity of the measurement model were assessed using SmartPLS 3.0. As illustrated in Table 2, all key constructs' Cronbach's alpha values and composite reliabilities (CR) are highly above 0.70 (Fornell and Larcker 1981), which shows the convergent validity is sufficient for our study. The average variance extracted (AVE) values of all variables are higher than the recommended threshold of 0.50. Table 3 shows the squared roots of the AVE of each construct, which are all exceeded the off-diagonal elements of the corresponding rows and columns. The item loading of each construct exceeds 0.70, whereas the cross-loadings of variables are lower than the main construct's loading, as well as the heterotrait-monotrait ratio of correlations (HTMT) for all variables are all below 0.85. Hence, our study has well-supported discriminant validity.

Table 2. Construct reliability and convergence validity analysis.

Construct	Items	Factor Loadings	T-values	Cronbach's Alpha	CR	AVE
Hedonic Gratification (HG)	HG1	0.728	20.749	0.824	0.882	0.653
	HG2	0.801	30.321			
	HG3	0.865	60.753			
	HG4	0.831	40.949			
Utilitarian Gratification (UG)	UG1	0.849	46.823	0.854	0.911	0.774
	UG2	0.893	77.733			
	UG3	0.897	74.681			
Loneliness (LS)	LS1	0.917	4.532	0.843	0.901	0.754
	LS2	0.842	3.250			
	LS3	0.845	3.430			
Leisure Boredom (LB)	LB1	0.893	67.367	0.889	0.931	0.818
	LB2	0.921	112.508			
	LB3	0.900	70.872			
Spatial Presence (SPP)	SPP1	0.882	66.571	0.859	0.913	0.779
	SPP2	0.870	52.442			
	SPP3	0.895	86.086			
Social Presence (SCP)	SCP1	0.895	80.486	0.864	0.916	0.785

(*continued*)

Table 2. (*continued*)

Construct	Items	Factor Loadings	T-values	Cronbach's Alpha	CR	AVE
	SCP2	0.882	65.560			
	SCP3	0.881	52.654			
Incentives (IC)	IC1	0.859	38.254	0.829	0.897	0.744
	IC2	0.870	53.402			
	IC3	0.859	39.231			
Integration (IT)	IT1	0.874	58.537	0.869	0.911	0.719
	IT2	0.858	49.815			
	IT3	0.850	46.628			
	IT4	0.808	34.495			
Stickiness (SN)	SN1	0.760	28.585	0.865	0.909	0.714
	SN2	0.883	73.770			
	SN3	0.884	79.256			
	SN4	0.848	62.533			

Table 3. Discriminant validity.

Construct	1	2	3	4	5	6	7	8	9	10	11	12	13	14
1. HG	**0.81**													
2. UG	0.48	**0.88**												
3. LS	−0.12	−0.1	**0.87**											
4. LB	0.31	0.31	0.15	**0.9**										
5. SPP	0.61	0.41	−0.01	0.3	**0.88**									
6. SCP	0.52	0.49	−0.09	0.32	0.48	**0.89**								
7. IC	0.4	0.38	−0.07	0.23	0.36	0.36	**0.86**							
8. IT	0.41	0.3	−0.18	0.26	0.38	0.42	0.42	**0.85**						
9. SN	0.5	0.44	−0.06	0.46	0.46	0.46	0.35	0.39	**0.85**					
10. Age	0.05	0.10	−0.07	0.13	0.01	0.09	0.05	0.02	0.08	**NA**				
11. Gender	0.01	−0.20	−0.09	0.13	−0.07	−0.05	−0.07	0.00	−0.03	−0.06	**NA**			
12. Education	−0.02	−0.08	−0.06	−0.04	−0.07	0.02	0.05	0.05	−0.09	0.29	0.09	**NA**		
13. Wage	0.05	0.20	0.13	−0.02	0.08	0.09	0.06	0.01	−0.01	0.51	−0.12	0.14	**NA**	
14. Type	−0.10	−0.07	−0.11	−0.01	−0.12	−0.14	−0.03	−0.15	−0.12	0.11	0.19	0.03	−0.07	**NA**

5.2 Structural Model

To eliminate the effect of irrelevant variables, this study adds demographic variables, including gender, age, education and wage. Game type is also included to investigate influences on stickiness. The result indicates that age ($\beta = 0.118$, t = 2.687), education ($\beta = -0.086$, t = 1.955) and wage ($\beta = -0.155$, t = 3.462) have significant impacts, while and game type ($\beta = -0.054$, t = 1.447) and gender ($\beta = 0.054$, t = 1.399) do not.

The structural equation modeling (SEM) technique is applied to examine the structural model, testing the effects among ten latent variables. Figure 2 presents the standardized path coefficients of constructs using the bootstrapping method, as well as displays the explained construct variances (R^2 value) for the conceptual model. Overall, the R^2 value for stickiness is 0.447, indicating that the research model has great predictive power.

As hypothesized, the paths from hedonic gratification ($\beta = 0.147$, t = 2.619), utilitarian gratification ($\beta = 0.159$, t = 3.078), leisure boredom ($\beta = 0.263$, t = 5.825), spatial presence ($\beta = 0.124$, t = 2.219), social presence ($\beta = 0.095$, t = 1.862) and integration ($\beta = 0.087$, t = 1.713) significantly and positively affect stickiness. These findings support hypotheses H1, H2, H4, H5, H6 and H8. Loneliness ($\beta = -0.045$, t = 1.069) and incentives ($\beta = 0.064$, t = 1.206) do not show an important influence on stickiness as shown by dotted lines. Thus, H3 and H7 are not supported.

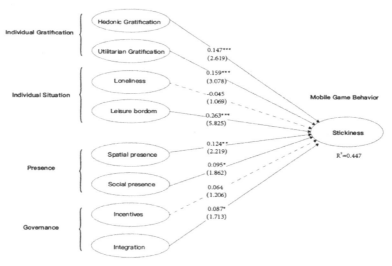

Note: *p<0.1, **p<0.05, ***p<0.01

Fig. 2. Results for the structural model.

6   Discussion and Conclusion

This study extends the UGT model to explore the factors that influence users' stickiness in the mobile game context. Several findings can be obtained from our analyses.

Firstly, in the aspect of individual characteristics, we find that the influence of individual gratification is higher than that of individual situation. On the one hand, gratification is a determinant of users' mobile game sticky behaviors (H1 is supported). The results highlight the importance of gratification in the UGT, which corresponds with prior research as well as our expectations. UGT has been widely applied to the online game context and found that users' gratification sought would significantly affect players' continuous motivation and stickiness (Wu et al. 2010; Li et al. 2015). Therefore, gratification is essential in both PC and mobile game playing. On the other hand, in the individual situation, only leisure boredom significantly affects the stickiness (H5 is supported; H4 is not supported). Consistent with the previous research, it was proved that high level of leisure boredom could significantly affect the intensity of mobile game use, while loneliness and self-control were not (Chen and Leung 2016).

Secondly, the results suggest that both presence and governance perform well in the mobile game structure. Presence consists of spatial presence and social presence has proved to be effective in influencing user stickiness in our research (H5 and H6 supported). Presence is fundamental to shaping users' experience, meeting the needs of immersion in mobile games (Tamborini and Skalski 2006). It has also been proved that presence will positively affect sticky behavior in the online game environment (Li et al. 2015). As for the mobile game governance, we also find that integration plays an important role in influencing users' stickiness (H8 is supported). Surprisingly, the impact of incentives (H7) on stickiness is not significant. This indicates that the construction of game mechanisms (e.g. virtual communities, pre-set goals) are of importance to mobile games to retain users. Compared with virtual currency, skins or equipment in games, players may care more about those well-set goals or efficient social channels that will shape a better experience. Another reason might be that the existing incentives are not attractive or effective enough to influence users' stickiness. For example, many mobile games are equipped with efficient reward systems, which in turn will lead to reward fatigue (Fischer 2020).

6.1 Implication for Researches

With the opportunity provided by the mobile game market, more and more developers are attracted to make innovations in the entertainment industry. Meanwhile, many academic studies have also noted the development of this phenomenon and made lots contributions to examining the behavior of users on the mobile game platform. However, few pieces of research consider from the perspective of the influence of users' characteristics and the mobile game structure. From a theoretical standpoint, this study makes three contributions to this area of inquiry.

Firstly, this study applies UGT to the mobile game context to examine users' stickiness. Compared with TAM and Flow theory (Malaquias et al. 2018; Su et al. 2016), UGT not only considers the impact of users themselves, but also examines the features of mobile games. Therefore, we can integrate more relevant factors to comprehensively investigate users' stickiness behavior by adopting UGT model. Notably, both of the individual characteristics and the mobile game structure perform well in our study.

Secondly, our research extends the UGT model and enriches the body of related studies. The role of users was often concerned and valued in previous UGT research (Li et al. 2015; Mi et al. 2021). However, our study also concerns the impact of the mobile game structure, and proves that the game structure is as essential as the individual characteristics in influencing user behavior. Besides, we add additional aspects (i.e. individual situation and governance) to each perspective of users and mobile games to investigate the influence to users' mobile game behavior. The significance of leisure boredom and integration suggest their feasibility of predicting stickiness in the mobile game environment.

Thirdly, while incentives received much attention in the platform-related literature (Jedari et al. 2017; Wang et al. 2020; Tiwana 2013), this study finds it is not significant in the mobile game context. Instead, our research notes that players prefer games that have well-constructed integration mechanisms, such as convenient communication channels, good goals setting, tutor relationships and so on. Games with the above mechanisms can integrate players and increase interactions with platforms, which will further influence players' stickiness. Therefore, the role of the integration should be noticed when investigating user behavior in the mobile game environment.

6.2 Implication for Practice

The results of this study provide mobile game developers and publishers with some insights to entice and retain users. Firstly, users' characteristics are of necessity to be considered. Our findings suggest that individual gratifications and individual situations have positive effects on users' stickiness. Therefore, when considering factors influencing the popularity and retention rate of a mobile game, publishers should also adopt a view from a user standpoint. By tracking user data, promoting online surveys and other methods, mobile game publishers could obtain and extract user characteristics, habits and so on. This may provide a guide for the further development and design of mobile games.

Secondly, this research provides some guidance for the governance practice of mobile game platforms. Through the result, we find that integration is more effective than incentives in increasing user stickiness in the mobile game context. Based on this discovery, we put forward two suggestions for mobile game publishers. On the one hand, they should adjust their incentive mechanisms to encourage users' continuous game use. On the other hand, mobile game publishers should exert more effort on integrating players as well as aligning their goals with the platform.

Appendix A. Constructs and items

Measurement Items	
Hedonic Gratification	**Items adapted from** Li et al. (2015)
HG1	It's exciting to play the mobile game
HG2	Playing the mobile game gives me a lot of pleasure
HG3	I play the mobile game because I can't do in real life

(continued)

(continued)

Measurement Items	
HG4	Mobile games allow me to pretend I am someone/somewhere else
HG5	I play mobile games when I feel frustrated
HG6	Playing mobile games is best way to block off the world around me
Utilitarian Gratification	**Items adapted from** Li et al. (2015)
UG1	I feel that it is important to beat others in the mobile game
UG2	I have more power than other players in the mobile game
UG3	I have items/equipment which are better than those of other players' in the mobile game
UG4	I play the mobile game, because I want other players in this game to perceive me as skilled
UG5	I play the mobile game, because I want other players in this game to perceive me as friendly
Loneliness	**Items adapted from Russell** (1996)
LS1	I feel lonely
LS2	I feel that I am no longer in tune with the people around me
LS3	I feel that there are no one I can talk to
Leisure Boredom	**Items adapted from** Iso-Ahola and Weissinger (1990)
LB1	For me, leisure time just drags on and on
LB2	Leisure time is boring
LB3	In my leisure time, I don't know what else to do
LB4	In my leisure time, I don't know what I want to do
LB5	Leisure time activities do not excite me
Spatial Presence	**Items adapted from** Wu et al. (2010)
SPP1	The mobile game comes to me and became part of my world
SPP2	The mobile game creates a new world for me, and the world disappears when I disconnect the mobile game
SPP3	The mobile game created an extension of my world, and part of my world disappeared when I disconnect the mobile game
SPP4	During the mobile game I feel like I am in the world the game created
Social Presence	**Items adapted from** Wu et al. (2010)
SCP1	When I see that other players are confused, I offer help
SCP2	I trust that other players in the mobile game will help me if I need it
SCP3	I feel connected to other players in the mobile game environment
SCP4	In my interactions with other players, I am able to show what kind of player/person I really am

(continued)

(*continued*)

Measurement Items	
SCP5	I feel like I am a member of a community during the game playing
Incentives	**Items adapted from** Bhattacherjee (2001)
IC1	I get rewards for my purchase in the mobile game, such as double the recharge
IC2	The mobile game offers incentives for my continued use, such as continuous sign-in rewards
IC3	Mobile games will reward me with virtual or physical objects (such as equipment, skins, game related products, etc.)
Integration	**Items adapted from** Kirsch et al. (2002) **and** Koo (2009)
IT1	The mobile game publishers expect me to follow a sequence of steps toward the accomplishment of specific goals (e.g. guiding players to establish mentoring and alliance relationships with other players in the game)
IT2	The mobile game publishers use pre-established targets (e.g. the degree of interaction with others in the game) as benchmarks for my performance evaluation
IT3	The mobile game publishers actively construct ways for players to communicate (e.g. communication channels in the game, the virtual community)
IT4	The mobile game publishers want me to understand the mobile game's goals, values and norms
Stickiness	**Items adapted from** Lin (2007)
SN1	I would stay a longer time on this mobile game than other games
SN2	I intend to prolong my stay on this mobile game
SN3	I would visit this mobile game as often as I can
SN4	I intend to open this mobile game every time I use the phone

References

Arı, E., Yılmaz, V., Elmastas Dikec, B.: An extensive structural model proposal to explain online gaming behaviors. Entertainment Comput. **34**, 100340 (2020)

Baabdullah, A.M.: Factors influencing adoption of mobile social network games (M-SNGs): the role of awareness. Inf. Syst. Front. **22**, 411–427 (2020)

Berelson, B.: What'missing the newspaper'means. Commun. Res. 1948–1949 111–129 (1949)

Bhattacherjee, A.: An empirical analysis of the antecedents of electronic commerce service continuance. Decis. Supp. Syst. **32**, 201–214 (2001)

Bryant, J., Zillmann, D.: Using television to alleviate boredom and stress: selective exposure as a function of induced excitational states. J. Broadcast. Electron. Media **28**, 1–20 (1984)

Chen, C., Leung, L.: Are you addicted to Candy Crush Saga? An exploratory study linking psychological factors to mobile social game addiction. Telematics Inf. **33**, 1155–1166 (2016)

Chen, C.-P.: Understanding mobile English-learning gaming adopters in the self-learning market: the uses and gratification expectancy model. Comput. Educ. **126**, 217–230 (2018)

Chen, C.-S., Lu, H.-P., Luor, T.: A new flow of Location Based Service mobile games: non-stickiness on Pokémon Go. Comput. Hum. Behav. **89**, 182–190 (2018)

Chiang, H.-S., Hsiao, K.-L.: YouTube stickiness: the needs, personal, and environmental perspective. Internet Res. **25**, 85–106 (2015)

Cho, J., De Zuniga, H.G., Rojas, H., et al.: Beyond access: the digital divide and Internet uses and gratifications. It Soc. **1**, 46–72 (2003)

Dong, H., Wang, M., Zheng, H., et al.: The functional connectivity between the prefrontal cortex and supplementary motor area moderates the relationship between internet gaming disorder and loneliness. Progress Neuro-Psychopharmacol. Biol. Psychiatry **108**, 110154 (2021)

Fischer, F. (2020). https://www.gamedeveloper.com/disciplines/reward-fatigue

Fornell, C., Larcker, D.F.: Evaluating structural equation models with unobservable variables and measurement error. J. Mark. Res. **18**, 39–50 (1981)

Friedrich, T., Schlauderer, S., Overhage, S.: The impact of social commerce feature richness on website stickiness through cognitive and affective factors: an experimental study. Electron. Commer. Res. Appl. **36**, 100861 (2019)

Gameanalytics (2019). https://gameanalytics.com/benchmarks/

Gan, C., Li, H.: Understanding the effects of gratifications on the continuance intention to use WeChat in China: a perspective on uses and gratifications. Comput. Hum. Behav. **78**, 306–315 (2018)

Ha, I., Yoon, Y., Choi, M.: Determinants of adoption of mobile games under mobile broadband wireless access environment. Inf. Manage. **44**, 276–286 (2007)

Hamari, J.: Why do people buy virtual goods? Attitude toward virtual good purchases versus game enjoyment. Int. J. Inf. Manage. **35**, 299–308 (2015)

Hamari, J., Malik, A., Koski, J., et al.: Uses and gratifications of pokémon go: why do people play mobile location-based augmented reality games? Int. J. Hum.-Comput. Interact. **35**, 804–819 (2019)

Hilken, T., de Ruyter, K., Chylinski, M., Mahr, D., Keeling, D.I.: Augmenting the eye of the beholder: exploring the strategic potential of augmented reality to enhance online service experiences. J. Acad. Mark. Sci. **45**(6), 884–905 (2017). https://doi.org/10.1007/s11747-017-0541-x

Hill, A.B., Perkins, R.E.: Towards a model of boredom. Br. J. Psychol. **76**, 235–240 (1985)

Hsu, C.-L., Lu, H.-P.: Why do people play on-line games? An extended TAM with social influences and flow experience. Inf. Manage. **41**, 853–868 (2004)

Huang, H.-C., Huang, L.-S., Chou, Y.-J., et al.: Influence of temperament and character on online gamer loyalty: perspectives from personality and flow theories. Comput. Hum. Behav. **70**, 398–406 (2017)

Ijsselsteijn, W.A., De Ridder, H., Freeman, J., et al.: Presence: concept, determinants, and measurement. In: Human Vision and Electronic Imaging V. International Society for Optics and Photonics, pp. 520–529 (2000)

Iresearch (2020). http://report.iresearch.cn/report_pdf.aspx?id=3679

Iso-Ahola, S.E., Weissinger, E.: Perceptions of boredom in leisure: conceptualization, reliability and validity of the leisure boredom scale. J. Leisure Res. **22**, 1–17 (1990)

Jedari, B., Liu, L., Qiu, T., et al.: A game-theoretic incentive scheme for social-aware routing in selfish mobile social networks. Future Gener. Comput. Syst. **70**, 178–190 (2017)

Kaur, P., Dhir, A., Chen, S., et al.: Why do people purchase virtual goods? A uses and gratification (U&G) theory perspective. Telematics Informat. **53** (2020)

Kirsch, L.J., Sambamurthy, V., Ko, D.-G., et al.: Controlling information systems development projects: the view from the client. Manage. Sci. **48**, 484–498 (2002)

Ko, H., Cho, C.-H., Roberts, M.S.: Internet uses and gratifications: a structural equation model of interactive advertising. J. Advertising **34**, 57–70 (2005)

Koo, D.-M.: The moderating role of locus of control on the links between experiential motives and intention to play online games. Comput. Hum. Behav. **25**, 466–474 (2009)

Lee, C.-H., Chiang, H.-S., Hsiao, K.-L.: What drives stickiness in location-based AR games? An examination of flow and satisfaction. Telematics Inform. **35**, 1958–1970 (2018)

Lee, S., Quan, C.-F.: Factors affecting Chinese ubiquitous game service usage intention. Int. J. Mob. Commun. **11**, 194–212 (2013)

Leung, L., Wei, R.: More than just talk on the move: uses and gratifications of the cellular phone. Journalism Mass Commun. Q. **77**, 308–320 (2000)

Li, H., Liu, Y., Xu, X., et al.: Modeling hedonic is continuance through the uses and gratifications theory: an empirical study in online games. Comput. Hum. Behav. **48**, 261–272 (2015)

Lin, J.C.-C.: Online stickiness: its antecedents and effect on purchasing intention. Behav. Inf. Technol. **26**, 507–516 (2007)

Liu, Y., Li, H.: Exploring the impact of use context on mobile hedonic services adoption: an empirical study on mobile gaming in China. Comput. Hum. Behav. **27**, 890–898 (2011)

Lu, H.P., Lee, M.R.: Demographic differences and the antecedents of blog stickiness. Online Inf. Rev. **34**, 21–38 (2010)

Malaquias, R.F., Malaquias, F.F.O., Hwang, Y.: Understanding technology acceptance features in learning through a serious game. Comput. Hum. Behav. **87**, 395–402 (2018)

Mi, L., Xu, T., Sun, Y., et al.: Playing Ant Forest to promote online green behavior: a new perspective on uses and gratifications. J. Environ. Manage. **278**, 111544 (2021)

Molinillo, S., Anaya-Sánchez, R., Liébana-Cabanillas, F.: Analyzing the effect of social support and community factors on customer engagement and its impact on loyalty behaviors toward social commerce websites. Comput. Hum. Behav. **108**, 105980 (2020)

Ok, C.: Extraversion, loneliness, and problematic game use: A longitudinal study. Personality Individ. Diff. **168**, 110290 (2021)

Qiu, L., Benbasat, I.: An investigation into the effects of text-to-speech voice and 3D avatars on the perception of presence and flow of live help in electronic commerce. ACM Trans. Comput.-Hum. Inter. (TOCHI) **12**, 329–355 (2005)

Rafdinal, W., Qisthi, A., Asrilsyak, S.: Mobile game adoption model: integrating technology acceptance model and game features. Sriwijaya Int. J. Dyn. Econ. Bus. **4**, 43–56 (2020)

Ramírez-Correa, P., Rondán-Cataluña, F.J., Arenas-Gaitán, J., et al.: Analysing the acceptation of online games in mobile devices: an application of UTAUT2. J. Retailing Consum. Serv. **50**, 85–93 (2019)

Rubin, A.M.: Television uses and gratifications: the interactions of viewing patterns and motivations. J. Broadcast. Electron. Media **27**, 37–51 (1983)

Russell, D.W.: UCLA loneliness scale (Version 3): reliability, validity, and factor structure. J. Pers. Assess. **66**, 20–40 (1996)

Scott W R. Institutions and organizations: ideas, interests, and identities. Sage publications (2013)

Smock, A.D., Ellison, N.B., Lampe, C., et al.: Facebook as a toolkit: a uses and gratification approach to unbundling feature use. Comput. Hum. Behav. **27**, 2322–2329 (2011)

Su, Y.-S., Chiang, W.-L., Lee, C.-T.J., et al.: The effect of flow experience on player loyalty in mobile game application. Comput. Hum. Behav. **63**, 240–248 (2016)

Tamborini, R., Skalski, P.: The role of presence in the experience of electronic games. Playing video games: Motives, responses, and consequences **1**, 225–240 (2006)

Tiwana, A.: Platform ecosystems: aligning architecture, governance, and strategy. Newnes (2013)

Van Der Heijden, H.: User acceptance of hedonic information systems. MIS Q. 695–704 (2004)

Wang, Y., Gao, Y., Li, Y., et al.: A worker-selection incentive mechanism for optimizing platform-centric mobile crowdsourcing systems. Comput. Networks **171**, 107144 (2020)

Wei, P.-S., Lu, H.-P.: Why do people play mobile social games? An examination of network externalities and of uses and gratifications. Internet Res. **24**, 313–331 (2014)

Weibel, D., Wissmath, B., Habegger, S., et al.: Playing online games against computer-vs. human-controlled opponents: Effects on presence, flow, and enjoyment. Comput. Hum. Behav. **24**, 2274–2291 (2008)

Weibull, L.: Structural factors in gratifications research. In: Rosengren, K.E., Wenner, L., Palmgreen, P. (eds.) Media Gratifications Research. Sage, London (1985)

Weiss, R.S.: Loneliness: The Experience of Emotional and Social Isolation. The MIT Press(1973)

Weiss, T., Schiele, S.: Virtual worlds in competitive contexts: analyzing eSports consumer needs. Electron. Mark. **23**(4), 307–316 (2013). https://doi.org/10.1007/s12525-013-0127-5

Wirth, W., Hartmann, T., Böcking, S., et al.: A process model of the formation of spatial presence experiences. Media Psychol. **9**, 493–525 (2007)

Wu, J.-H., Wang, S.-C., Tsai, H.-H.: Falling in love with online games: the uses and gratifications perspective. Comput. Hum. Behav. **26**, 1862–1871 (2010)

Xu, F., Qi, Y., Li, X.: What affects the user stickiness of the mainstream media websites in China? Electronic Commer. Res. Appl. **29**, 124–132 (2018)

Research on the Construction of the Quality Maturity Evaluation in the Product R&D Phase

Sun Lei, Zhongwei Gu, Youxiang Cui, and Haibo Tang[✉]

Department of Quality Management Engineering, Pudong District, Businness School, Shanghai Dianji University, No. 300 Shuihua Road, Lingang New City, Shanghai 201306, China
zwgu@qq.com

Abstract. With the popularization of the concept of comprehensive quality management in Chinese enterprises, more and more enterprises begin to realize that doing a good job in quality management needs to start from the source. The design and development stage is an important process for the formation and finalization of product quality, and the quality management work at this stage is crucial to determine the product quality level.

With digital mobile communication products as the research background, this paper summarizes the international methodology of product design and development process, such as ISO9001 international quality management system, advanced product quality planning (APQP), project management knowledge system (PMBOK), door diameter management system (SGS), integrated product development (IPD) and product lifecycle management (PLM), etc. Through a systematic summary and research on the quality management method of the above design and development process, the quality maturity evaluation index system is constructed. Help the product to carry out quantitative product development quality maturity evaluation in the concept definition stage, sample verification stage, pilot test confirmation stage, small batch climbing stage and mass production stage of the design and production process.

Through the product maturity evaluation system, the quality maturity status of the product design and development process can be easily measured, so that the project stakeholders can have clear objectives and risk management for each process of the product design and development. Easy solve the opacity of quality management and problem exposure lag in the design development process, so that the design quality is well prevented in advance.

Keyword: Design and development · Process quality · Management quality · Maturity product · Maturity evaluation

1 Research Background and Significance

Product quality is designed, not made, let alone tested. This sentence shows that the design and development is the most critical process of product quality formation. Once the design is completed, the inherent quality characteristics of the product are then determined (Fig. 1). It is a very important link for enterprises to ensure product quality

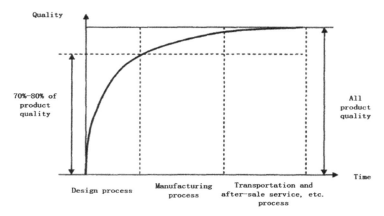

Fig. 1. Quality decision curve

to ensure the quality management of product development and design process and ensure the work quality and process quality of the design and development process.

However, the design and development process is a relatively closed process. Many often rely on the wisdom and ability of design and development engineers. Many enterprises also don't know how to effectively manage the design and development process? The most common ones can only be tested with similar samples to test the quality level of the design process. Obviously, this post-hoc management is also an uneconomical management method. How to make the design and development process activities more transparent? Through the collaboration across functional departments, to improve the efficiency of the product design and development process, and ensure the project delivery on schedule. At the same time, by reducing the cost and waste caused by a failure of success, improve the profit of the project and enhance the competitiveness of enterprise research and development.

2 Theoretical Research and Review

The authors track and study the quality management method of product design and development process internationally. For example, Chapter 8(8.3.1–8.3.6) (Fig. 2) of the International Standard ISO9001:2015 International Quality Management System (QMS) Standard (Fig. 3) has more detailed the planning, demand management and design and development management of the design and development process.

8.3 Design and development of products and services

8.3.1 General

8.3.2 Design and development planning

8.3.3 Design and development inputs

8.3.4 Design and development controls

8.3.5 Design and development outputs

8.3.6 Design and development changes

Fig. 2. ISO9001:2015 Chapter 8.3.1–8.3.6

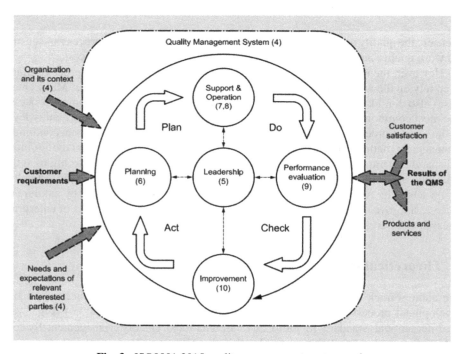

Fig. 3. ISO9001:2015 quality management system cycle

The advanced product quality planning (APQP) standard(Fig. 4) created by the automobile industry divides the product design and development process into five typical stages of management: concept and planning, product design and development, process design and development, product and process verification and confirmation and feedback, and evaluation and correction.

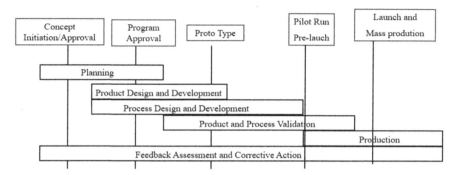

Fig. 4. APQP five phase process mapping

The International Project Management Association (PMI) has published the Project Management Knowledge System (PMBOK) (Fig. 5) and regards all products as project management, and carries out comprehensive management from different dimensions through 10 knowledge points of project management. At the same time, product design and development is regarded as a process. The process management method is adopted, and the standards of input and output through the door diameter management system (SGS) (Fig. 6) is set to standardize the achievement of product design and development process node (S G S).Integrated product development (Integrated Product Development), is a set of product development models and methods. The IPD idea comes from the Product and Life cycle Optimization Act (PACE: Product And Cycle-time Excellence).The integrated product development (IPD) method, guided by the framework of integrating many industry best practice elements, moves from the establishment of end-to-end process management to achieve the goal of shortening product time to launch, improving product profit, effectively conducting product development, and providing greater value to customers and shareholders. Product Life-Cycle Management (PLM), from the management of the entire life process of product scrapping. PLM is an advanced enterprise information idea, which makes people think about how to use the most effective way and means to increase income and reduce costs for enterprises in the fierce market competition.

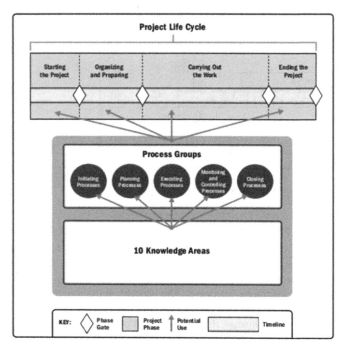

Fig. 5. Project life cycle flowchart of PMBOK

Fig. 6. Production stage-gate system chart

The management methods of the above product design and development process are summarized in Table 1 below.

Table 1. Product design and development management method summary

No	Product design and development management method	The characteristics of the method
1	ISO9001:2015 International Quality Management System (QMS)	Carry out management from demand management, input and output management, review, verification and confirmation means

(*continued*)

Table 1. (*continued*)

No	Product design and development management method	The characteristics of the method
2	Advance Product Quality Planning (APQP)	Five phases: Concepts and Planning, Product Design Development, Process Design Development, product and process verification and feedback, evaluation and correction
3	Project Management Knowledge System (PMBOK)	Ten complete knowledge points of project management
4	Door Trail Management System (SGS)	The targets for the input and output are specified
5	Integrated Product Development (Integrated Product Development)	Build a process management for the end-to-end full-lifecycle
6	Product Life-cycle Management (Product Life-Cycle Management, PLM)	Advanced enterprise information technology, digital management thought

Through the summary of the above product design and development process methods, we can clearly see that there are more mature methods that can be adopted. Based on the process management method proposed in ISO9001 standard, end-to-end process design and information and digital means for monitoring.

3 Construction of Evaluation Indicators

Combined with the rapid development of mobile communication products in China, the research results will be applied in the design and development process of mobile communication products. The stages of the development process based on mobile communication products are divided into concept definition stage, sample verification stage, pilot test confirmation stage, small batch climbing stage and mass production stage. Several defects occur after each development phase is tested. If only the number of defects is controlled, some very serious defects may not be solved in time, and the final project fails; in the next stage, there may still be many defects in the mass production stage; and if all defects must be improved to enter the next stage, there is no way to meet the time plan of the project. How can it not only ensure the quality of the product, but also maximize to meet the time requirements of the project. Communication Products (Maturity-Utilized System of Telecommunication, MUST),

3.1 MUST (Maturity-Utilized System of Telecommunication) Design

Maturity-Utilized System of Telecommunication evaluation system are consist of four parts: Maturity-Utilized System of Telecommunication evaluation system model (Fig. 7), matrix model, Score matrix definition and Maturity-Evaluation System of Telecommunication evaluation stage target. Maturity-Evaluation System of Telecommunication evaluation system are applied for every node of the whole design and development process, which involved all the test and checking results of design and development. The system can be intuitively and quantitatively reflects the current quality maturity level of project, and can be the decision-making basis of evaluating project whether can go into the next phase.

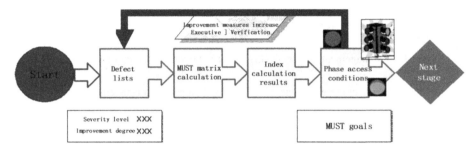

Fig. 7. Maturity-Utilized System of Telecommunication evaluation system model

When evaluating project stage maturity, the specific method to the maturity evaluation matrix is: the score of each defect is equal to its level of serious weight coefficient multiply defects of improvement weight coefficient, and then add together each defect scores, the result is the final score of the stage of maturity. See Table 2:

Table 2. Maturity-Evaluation System of Telecommunication evaluation matrix model

Evolution	Severity				
	A (20)	B (10)	C (5)	D (1)	Total
4	$X_{(A, 4)}$	$X_{(B, 4)}$	$X_{(C, 4)}$	$X_{(D, 4)}$	
3	$X_{(A, 3)}$	$X_{(B, 3)}$	$X_{(C, 3)}$	$X_{(D, 3)}$	
2	$X_{(A, 2)}$	$X_{(B, 2)}$	$X_{(C, 2)}$	$X_{(D, 2)}$	
1	$X_{(A, 1)}$	$X_{(B, 1)}$	$X_{(C, 1)}$	$X_{(D, 1)}$	
Total					
Maturity-Evaluation System of Telecommunication evaluation index	******				
Target Maturity-Evaluation System of Telecommunication evaluation stage	******				

The formula of Maturity-Evaluation System of Telecommunication as follows:

$$MUST\ index = \sum_{s=A}^{D} \sum_{e=1}^{4} s \times e \times X(s, e)$$

Among them:

s—— severity

e—— evolution

X(s, e)—— the number of defects for each rank

The following is a detail introduction for scoring definition of Maturity-Evaluation System of Telecommunication evaluation matrix model:

1. **Severity (s)**

    Severity can be divided into 4 levels, specific definition as follows:

    A Level(weight 20): These defects can lead to communication products can't reach the certification requirements(such as radio frequency (rf),EMC, safety, etc.)or other laws and regulations and other compulsory standards which did not meet the requirements.

    B Level(weight 10): Such defects will lead to customer refused or cause unable to production.

    C Level(weight 5): Such defects will not affect product main functions, but may not be accepted by some customers and lead to rejection, or will affect the production difficulty level. Even though other customer can accept it, the customers still are not satisfied, and then affecting the credibility of the brand.

    D Level(weight 1): Such defects are only minor flaws, which will not affect the product performance and production, the frequency of occurrence is very low, generally only can find in the internal professional test.

2. **Evolution (e)**

    Evolution can be divided into 4 levels, specific definition as follows:

    4 Level: Reasons for problems unknown--the root cause of the problem is not found or cannot be reproduce. However, it may also occur that find out the improvement method under the situation of not determining the root cause.

    3 Level: Unknown improvement methods--Improved method is not found or is not strong enough argument for improvement measures effectively (through calculation, evidence or manual model and simulation).

    2 Level: Unconfirmed improved method-Improvement method has been demonstrated but not yet confirmed by actual(Through tested or be approved).

    1 Level: Improvement method is not applied to the production--Method has been confirmed, but may be due to reasons such as need time to prepare improvement method has not been applied to production.

4 Conclusions

This paper discusses the concept of Maturity-Evaluation System of Telecommunication, and combine the product life cycle management theory with the product design and development. The Maturity-Evaluation System of Telecommunication classification definition is given, and established the management model of Maturity-Evaluation System of Telecommunication is built up. Finally it discusses the Maturity-Evaluation System of Telecommunication application in product design and development of quality management. Through research and application of Maturity-Evaluation System of

Telecommunication management strategy, product designers can intuitive to get detailed information of every stage in the process of product design and development to improve the efficiency of product design and development, shorten the product design and development cycle, and to help enterprises continuously improve product quality and their own core competitiveness in the product design process.

References

1. Jin, C., Sun L., Weng M.: Research and Development Quality Management. China Quality Inspection Press, 11 January 2013
2. Sun, L.: Quality Management Practical Complete Book, 1st edn. People's Post and Telecommunications Press, Beijing (2011)
3. (Japan) Jiu, M.: Quality Management for Design and Development, 1st edn. China Quality Inspection Publishing House, Beijing (2011)
4. Zhou, H.: Product Research and Development Management, 1st edn. Electronic Industry Publishing House, Beijing (2012)
5. Ma, L.: Quality Operations in Japan, 1st edn. China Economic Publishing House, Beijing (2009)
6. Guo, F., Jin, X.: Quality Management, 1st edn. Electronic Industry Publishing House, Beijing (2011)
7. (Japan) Masayaki, I.: On-Site Improvement, 1st edn. Machinery Industry Publishing House, Beijing (2010)
8. Hassan, A., Siadat, A., et al.: Conceptual process-an improvement approach using QFD, FMEA and ABC methods. Robot. Comput.-Integr. Manuf. **26**, 302–305 (2010)
9. Hubig, L., Lack, N., Mansmann, U.: Statistical process monitoring to improve quality assurance of inpatient care. BMC Health Serv. Res. **20**, 21–23 (2020)
10. Lubomir, B., Paul, J.: Applications of statistical process control in the management of unaccounted for gas. J. Natural Gas Sci. Eng. **76**, 103194–103196 (2020)
11. Baxter, R.B.: Enterprise risk management: the effect on internal control quality. Erasmus Sch. Econ. (6), 324–352 (2017)
12. Bolatan, G.I.S., Gozlu, S., Alpkan, L., Zaim, S.: The impact of technology transfer performance on total quality management and quality performance. Soc. Behav. Sci. (13), 73–86 (2018)
13. Battini, D., Faccio, M., Persona, A.: Design of an integrated quality assurance strategy in production systems. Int. J. Prod. Res. (5), 203–235 (2012)
14. Doyle, J., Ge, W., Mc Vay, S.: Determinants of weaknesses in internal control over financial reporting. J. Account. Econ. **44**(1), 193–223 (2007)
15. Edmondson, A.C., McManus, S.E.: Methodological fit in management field research. Acad. Manage. Rev. **32**(4), 1246–1264 (2007)
16. Ellal, A., Yerrarmilli, V.: Stronger risk controls, lower risk: evidence from US bank holding companies. J. Fin. **68**(5), 1757–1803 (2013)
17. Hloitash, R., Hoitash, U., Bedard, J.C.: Internal control quality and audi pricing underthe Sarbanes-Oxley Act Auditing. J. Pract. Theory **27**(1), 105–126 (2008)
18. Gordon, L.A., Loeb, M.P., Tseng, C.Y.: Enterprise risk management and firm performance: a coningency perspective. J. Account. Pub. Pol. **28**(4), 301–327 (2009)
19. Hlay, D.C., Knechel, W.R., Wong, N.: Audit fees: a met analysis of the effect of supply and demand atribules contenporary. Account. Res. **23**(1), 141–191 (2006)
20. Grace, M.F., Leverty, J.T., Phillips, R.D., Shimpi, P.: The value of investing inenterprise risk management. J. Risk Insur. **82**(2), 289–316 (2015)

21. Dyle, J., Ce, W., MeVay, S.: Dernian of weakneses n imemal cntw vefifinancial eparing. J. Acceuning Becunics, 210–235 (2000)
22. Krishnan, J.: Audit committee quality and intemal control: an empirical analysis. Account. Rev. **80**(2), 649–675 (2005)
23. Kumar, A., Stecke, K.E., Motwani, J.: A quality index-based methodology for improving competitiveness: analytical development and empirical validadon, pp. 26–30. University of Michigan Business School (2002)
24. Qimpro Standards Organization: International Quality Maturity model. Dipstic-ks, 4 (2002)
25. Yeung, A.C.L., Chan, L.Y., Lee, T.S.: An empirical taxonomy for quality management systems: a study of the Hong Kong electronics industry. J. Oper. Manage. **21**(1), 45–62 (2003)
26. Zhao, X., Yeung, C.L., Lee, T.S.: Quality management and organizational context inselected service industries of China. J. Oper. Manage. **22**, 575–587 (2004)
27. Ryu, K.-S., et al.: A data quality management maturity model. ETRI J. **4**(2), 191–204 (2006)
28. Ful-Chiang, W.: Optimization of correlated multiple quality characteristics using desirability function. Qual. Eng. **17**, 117–126 (2005)
29. Evans, J.R., Ford, M.W.: Value-driven quality. Q. Manage. J. **15**(4), 19–22 (2000)
30. Tang, C.-Z.: Developing a matrix to explore the relationship between partnering and total quality management in construction. J. Harbin Inst. Technol. **11**(4), 422–427 (2004)

How Arousing Benefits and Ethical Misgivings Affect AI-Based Dating App Adoption: The Roles of Perceived Autonomy and Perceived Risks

Zhuang Ma[1], Woon Kian Chong[2(✉)], and Linpei Song[3]

[1] International Business School,
Chongqing Technology and Business University, Chongqing 400067, China
Zhuang.Ma@ctbu.edu.cn
[2] S P Jain School of Global Management, Singapore 119579, Singapore
tristan.chong@spjain.org
[3] School of Business Administration, Gachon University, Seongnam-si 13120, Korea
songlinpei@gachon.ac.kr

Abstract. AI-based applications (apps) have presented tremendous ethical challenges such as AI biases and privacy breaches, leading to the issue of privacy paradox. The paradox is more salient for dating apps than ordinary shopping apps, as data breaches in dating apps could relate to users' close social circles such as families and colleagues, suggesting more serious ethical and even legal consequences. Given the limited attention to user' arousal-ethics paradox, we developed and empirically examined a conceptual framework regarding how the arousing benefits of dating apps, users' ethical misgivings, users' perceived autonomy and perceived risks collectively affect their adoption of dating apps. Survey data from 319 construction workers confirmed that arousing benefits are associated with users' perceived autonomy, which leads to dating apps adoption. In contrast, users' ethical misgivings, associated with perceived risks, are negatively related to dating app adoption. This study contributes to the interdisciplinary field of privacy paradox that involves big data, artificial intelligence, user experience, and ethics by examining ethical consumption and practical suggestions to AI-based dating app developers.

Keywords: Artificial Intelligence · Dating application · Perceived autonomy · Perceived risks

1 Introduction

Featured with volume, velocity, variety, and veracity, big data have provided great potential for firms to understand and capture consumer value [1]. Big data are often generated through sensor networks, social media, internet clicks, and mobile apps, and empowered with business values through artificial intelligence (AI) [2]. For instance, data mining techniques (e.g., link analysis & association rule learning) could identify high-value

G. Salvendy and J. Wei (Eds.): HCII 2022, LNCS 13337, pp. 160–170, 2022.
https://doi.org/10.1007/978-3-031-05014-5_13

customers and understand their patterns and preferences in using the functions of the mobile apps, allowing firms to offer personalized promotions to products and services [1]. The AI market was valued at $16.06 billion in 2017 and is expected to reach $190.61 billion by 2025. However, practitioners and researchers have warned that AI could be dangerous and render humans obsolete and useless [2]. In particular, mobile apps often require users' location, personal preferences, gender, age, interests, and other personal data to serve specific functions, allowing AI to access sensitive information about users [3, 4]. AI-based apps have presented tremendous ethical challenges such as AI biases and privacy breaches. In response, researchers have investigated 1) the ethics of digital governance [5] and 2) how app developing companies reveal processes of sensitive data deployment as an ethical re-sponge to consumer concerns [6], and 3) and consumer responses to AI-based apps that collect sensitive information [7].

Consumers hold mixed feelings about AI: enjoying the superior capabilities of AI-enabled services while worrying about the negative implications of privacy breaches; a phenomenon known as privacy paradox [8, 9]. One type of data-sensitive app has been dating apps, which support the search for romantic and sexual partners [6, 10]. Dating apps are most suitable to investigate the ethical concerns of paradox research as they involve intensive data generation, algorithmic processing, and cross-platform sharing of sensitive data [10]. According to Guardian's journalist Judith Duportail, dating apps can access users' gender, sexual orientation, location data, political affiliation, and religion, but also data about users' activity on social media platforms (e.g., information from Facebook and Instagram accounts & conversations with every match on the app) [11]. Compared to other data-sensitive apps such as financial and shopping apps, dating apps could, in the event of a privacy breach, result in more serious consequences to users. Known examples of such breaches include 'Ashley Madison data breach', where 60 Gb of detailed user data (including user data from Saudi Arabia, where adultery is subject to a death sentence) on this extramarital affair website were released. Given the limited attention on ethical implications of data-sensitive apps from a consumer perspective, this study examines consumers' trade-off decisions between the arousing benefits promised on dating apps and the ethical misgivings over the possibility of data breach. Users in the privacy paradox may also make adoption decisions based on their knowledge about how AI-based apps works [7]. Drawing on existing literature, we proposed and empirically examined a new conceptual framework to unravel how users' data related knowledge, i.e., perceived autonomy & perceived risks, affect users' adoption of dating apps, given the privacy paradox (i.e., arousing benefits & ethical misgivings).

The remainder of this paper is structured as follows. The next section summarizes the existing literature on dating apps introduces the key variables in the conceptual framework related to consumer adoption of those apps. Section 3 introduces the research design and samples used in this study. Section 4 presents the details of the results of the survey and data analysis. Section 5 discusses this paper and suggests the study's implications from different perspectives, limitations and directions for future research.

2 Literature Review

2.1 Dating Apps and Users' Privacy Paradox

The boom in dating apps has raised marketing interests and social concerns among practitioners and researchers [6, 12]. Indeed, the mobile apps allow users to connect with current loved-ones but also explore new ones while keeping the disconnected or geographically distant family members in touch. This is achieved through dating apps (e.g., Badoo, Momo, & Tinder) which generate location-based data (through GPS & postcodes), which after sophisticated calculative and ordering algorithms, could facilitate searching, photo sharing, texting, matching, and meeting among users [13, 14]. The registration and use of a dating app will trigger cross-platform connections where data related to the users' personal profile and preference information will be shared. Such data enable app developers to optimize and capitalize on user experience. However, cross-platform data sharing and integration have resulted in privacy concerns in the context of mobile dating apps.

According to Dinev and Hart [25], people develop different concepts of privacy according to their interpretations. In other words, if a certain behavior could bring about more positive outcomes (e.g., income & romance) than negative outcomes (e.g., exposure), mobile app users will disclose their personal information in exchange for the benefits, provided that their personal information can be used in ways that do not generate any negative consequences in the future [16]. For social media (e.g., dating app) users, such negative consequences can include social, psychological or informational threats 17 from familiar individuals and app developers [13]. For dating app users, those threats may come from familiar individuals (e.g., colleagues & neighbors) could be more embarrassing and intimidating than those from app developers that share user data to third-party platforms.

2.2 Arousing Benefits

Dating app developers have designed app interfaces in ways that could stimulate user attention, engagement, and consumption. Those interfaces could provide atmospheric cues that suggest arousing benefits. We define 'arousing benefits' as the aesthetics involved in a dating app and the displayed photos of its existing users, sensory descriptions of user information (e.g., height & weight) and the interactive chat links that create an interactive and exciting atmosphere. As users increasingly take dating apps as a kind of game, developers add functions that support social interaction, flirting, traveling, and meetups [18]. Moreover, dating apps allow users to find strangers in nearby locations, check their pictured profiles [19]. As users tend to post attractive photos of themselves to increase publicity, these photos create an arousing effect on those browsing their profiles. Previous studies [20, 21] on user experience have confirmed the positive impacts of arousing benefits on users' adoption of apps. However, those studies fail to consider the mediating mechanism in the relationship, especially given the issue of the privacy paradox, suggesting further investigation to explain users' adoption of dating apps.

2.3 Ethical Misgivings

Users may have legal and ethical misgivings when adopting dating apps. According to the revenue and usage statistics report (2022) of Tinder, a dating app with over 100 million subscribers worldwide, around 30% of subscribers were married. Put the legal perspectives aside; those married subscribers may bear ethical misgivings when using the app. Ethical misgivings in this study refer to app users' concerns that their behaviors (e.g., lying & cheating) are wrong and unfair to those around them (e.g., families & partners). Another group of dating app users could involve those who aim to make friends, travel, and seek actual relationships. However, the unethical reputation of certain dating apps as hook-up websites could also bring ethical misgivings to those people.

2.4 Perceived Autonomy

Perceived autonomy in this study refers to users' evaluation of the degree to which they have control over their sensitive data on dating apps. Dating apps increasingly include the gamification functions where users are allowed to determine the various functions (e.g., the show of location, age, income on profile, & removal of visiting history). Moreover, dating apps enable users to select other users based on different demographic features (e.g., age & height), thereby promoting their perceived autonomy. Users with knowledge about the kind of data kept in privacy and that disclosed to the public could willingly give up certain data to enjoy the arousing benefits.

Therefore, the following hypotheses can be developed:

H1: Arousing benefits are positively associated with users' perceived autonomy.
H2: Perceived autonomy is positively associated with users' adoption of dating apps. In contrast, some users may worry that even if the dating apps promise not to release their personal information, their data could still be breached by hackers and sold for money, as illustrated in the data leakage cases. As such, these users may demonstrate fears of being controlled. Such fears could be more salient when users are adopting new technologies such as dating apps [22]. As such, the following hypothesis could be predicted:
H3: Ethical misgivings are negatively associated with users' perceived autonomy.

2.5 Perceived Risks

While ethical misgivings describe an individual's moral judgement regarding wrong behaviors, perceived risks in this study refer to dating app users' perception and evaluation of the possible negative results from personal data disclosure. The known risks perceived by dating apps include fake men/women and sales of personal data, which, fueled by the reported cases of data breach and user exposure, could raise user concerns about their privacy. Perceived risks could also lead users to the conviction that they lose control of their privacy once logging into a dating app [23]. Moreover, users with ethical misgivings are more likely to associate dating app usage with the various risks. Given such discussion, the following hypotheses can be proposed:

H4: Ethical misgivings are negatively associated with perceived autonomy.

H5: Ethical misgivings are positively associated with perceived risks.
H6: Perceived risks are negatively associated with users' adoption of dating apps.

The above hypotheses constitute a theoretical framework (see Fig. 1), which was empirically tested.

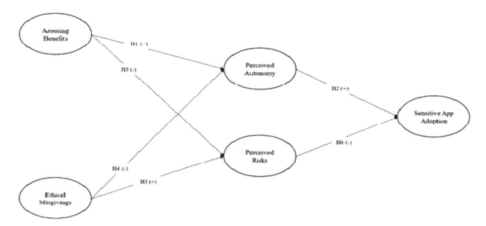

Fig. 1. Conceptual framework

3   Methods

3.1   Measures

1) Arousing benefits (AB)
   The scale for 'arousing benefits' was adapted from 'sensational seeking' in Harden & Tucker-Drob [24]. The three items include 'I enjoy the sensational benefits promised in this app', 'I enjoy new and exciting experiences with new people through this app', and 'Life without sensations in it could be too dull for me'. All items were rated on a 5-point Likert scale (1 = strongly disagree, 5 = strongly agree). The Cronbach alpha of this variable was 0.89.

2) Ethical misgivings (EM)
   The scale for 'ethical misgivings' was adapted from 'underreporting ethics' in Glenthorne and Kaplan [25]. The five items include 'When using this app, I will feel guilty', 'Using this app goes against my moral principles', 'I think it is morally wrong to use this app', 'I think it is unfair for my family/partner if I use this app', and 'I think it is dishonest to use this app'. All items were rated on a 7-point Likert scale (1 = strongly disagree, 7 = strongly agree). The Cronbach alpha of this variable was 0.91.

3) Perceived autonomy (PA)
   The scale for 'perceived autonomy' was adapted from 'perceived loss of autonomy' in Rauschnabel, He, and Ro [26]. The four items include 'When using this app, I

could maintain my control over the activities', 'When using this app, I could maintain my discretion over my decisions,' 'When using this app, I could maintain control over each step of various situations', and 'When using this app, I could decide what activities the developers can monitor.' All items were rated on a 5-point Likert scale (1 = strongly disagree, 5 = strongly agree). The Cronbach alpha of this variable was 0.90.

4) Perceived risks (PR)

The scale for 'perceived risks' was adapted from 'perceived risks' in Chopdar et al. [9]. The four items include 'I believe that this app could bring negative consequences to me', 'I believe that I should follow recommendations to reduce the risk of privacy breach', 'The risk of privacy breach is higher using this app than shopping apps', and 'I believe that the risk of privacy breach is high low when using this app frequently'. All items were rated on a 5-point Likert scale (1 = strongly disagree, 5 = strongly agree). The Cronbach alpha of this variable was 0.92.

5) Dating app adoption (DA)

The scale for 'dating app adoption' was adapted from 'branded app adoption' in Hsieh, Lee, and Tseng [20]. The three items include 'I intend to continue using this app rather than discontinue its use', 'I intend to increase my use of this app in the future', and 'If I could, I would like to continue my use of this app'. All items were rated on a 5-point Likert scale (1 = strongly disagree, 5 = strongly agree). The Cronbach alpha of this variable was 0.87.

6) Control variables

We controlled the variables that might give alternative explanations for the factors that affect user adoption of dating apps, including user age, gender, education, income, and relationship status which are used in related studies (e.g., Lutz & Ranzini, 2017) [27].

3.2 Sampling

The sample comprised 682 employees from two construction firms in Chongqing, China. With the help of the human resources department of each firm, we sent survey links to employee WeChat through a Wechat group. Those employees were selected because they often worked and lived at construction sites that were far from downtown areas and lacked entertainment facilities. We informed respondents that the survey was voluntary and that their names and responses would be kept confidential and used only for this study. To improve the response rate, we gave each respondent one bottle of soft drink (US $ 0.7). Among the 682 invited employees, 319 of them provided valid responses.

4 Results

4.1 Common Method Bias

To check the problem of common method bias, we conducted Harman's single-factor test. The analysis returned five factors with eigenvalues greater than 1, with the first factor explaining less than 40% [27] of the variance (39.41% of 78.48%). This suggested that there were no serious indications of common method variance.

4.2 Confirmatory Factor Analysis

To ensure the construct validity of the variables, we first undertook a series of confirmatory factor analyses (CFA) to evaluate the convergent and discriminant validities [28] of the five variables (i.e., arousing benefits (AE), ethical misgivings (EM), perceived autonomy (PA), perceived risks (PR), & dating app adoption (DA)), and then used Mplus 8.0 to analyze all hypotheses.

As is shown in Table 1, when the hypothesized model is compared with a series of competing models, the five-factor model indicates the best fit of all. The values on the fit indices showed that the five-factor CFA model provided a good fit for the data ($\chi 2$/DF = 1.129, CFI = .996, TLI = .995, RMSEA = .020, and SRMR = .031). This result offered a significant improvement in chi-square over a series of competing models.

Table 1. Confirmatory factor analysis of the models

Model	Description	$\chi 2$	DF	$\chi 2$/DF	CFI	TLI	RMSEA	SRMR
Hypothesized model	Five-factor model	160.25	142	1.129	.996	.995	.020	.031
Model 1	Four-factor model	878.194	146	6.015	.824	.794	.125	.109
Model 2	Three-factor model	1332.589	149	8.944	.715	.673	.158	.132
Model 3	Two-factor model	1934.701	151	12.813	.571	.514	.192	.125
Model 4	One-factor model	2341.353	152	15.404	.474	.408	.212	.140

Note: CFI = Comparative Fit Index, TLI = Tucker-Lewis Index, RMSEA = Root Mean Square Error of Approximation, SRMR = Standardized Root Mean Square Residual

4.3 Correlation, Reliability, and Discriminant Validity

Means, standard deviations, Cronbach's alpha and correlations of all variables used in this study are provided in Table 2. Table 2 shows that all Cronbach's alphas are higher than the suggested 0.70, thereby indicating a good reliability [29]. And we also examined the discriminant validity. The square roots of AVEs were higher than their correlation coefficients with other factors that strongly support the discriminant validity [30].

Table 2. Descriptive statistics, reliabilities, correlations, and discriminant validities.

	Mean	SD	Cronbach's Alpha	AB	EM	PA	PR	DA
AB	2.60	0.91	.89	.85				
EM	3.99	1.72	.91	−.42**	.81			
PA	3.61	1.01	.90	.35**	−.42**	.84		
PR	3.61	0.91	.92	−.41**	.43**	−.40**	.86	
DA	3.85	1.09	.87	.19**	−.21**	.42**	−.35**	.84

Notes: **, p < 0.01
AB, arousing benefits; EM, ethical misgivings; PA, perceived autonomy; PR, perceived risks; DA, dating app adoption. N = 319. Square roots of AVEs are on the diagonal.

4.4 Hypothesis Testing

According to Table 3, the result of the path analysis demonstrates that AB has a positive effect on PA ($\beta = .21$, p < 0.05), hypothesis 1 was supported; PA has a positive effect on DA ($\beta = .38$, p < 0.05), hypothesis 2 was supported; AB has a negative effect on PR ($\beta = −.31$, p < 0.05), hypothesis 3 was supported; EM has a negative effect on PA ($\beta = −.39$, p < 0.05), hypothesis 4 was supported; EM has a positive effect on PR ($\beta = .32$, p < 0.05), hypothesis 5 was supported; PR has a negative effect on DA ($\beta = −.25$, p < 0.05), hypothesis 6 was supported.

Table 3. Results of hypotheses testing

Path	STD.Estimate	STD.Est./S.E.	P-Value
AB-PA	.21	3.42	.00
EM-PA	−.39	−6.71	.00
AB-PR	−.31	−5.20	.00
EM-PR	.32	5.44	.00
PA-DA	.38	6.64	.00
PR-DA	−.25	−4.10	.00

Notes: AB, arousing benefits; EM, ethical misgivings; PA, perceived autonomy; PR, perceived risks; DA, dating app adoption.

5 Discussion

The rise of dating apps and the breaches of user data generate many problems regarding user interest and wellbeing. So far, dating app providers have mostly focused on designs and user experience, while researchers [13] increasingly raise alarms on the social concerns of user privacy on dating apps. We respond to such concerns by empirically testing how dating app users make trade-off decisions between the arousing benefits available on dating apps and their ethical misgivings. Our results suggest that the arousing contents from dating apps and users perceived autonomy lead to repeated dating app adoption. In contrast, users' ethical misgivings combined with perceived risks would discourage them from using dating apps.

5.1 Theoretical Implications

This paper contributes to the research in the interdisciplinary field of privacy paradox that involves big data, artificial intelligence, user experience, and ethics. Previous paradox-related studies investigate the ethics of firms and how consumers perceive privacy risks related to AI-based apps [8, 14]. In the unique context of dating app adoption, we advance knowledge on this topic by adopting a user perspective. In doing so, we answer the factors that guide dating app users' moral behaviors. Unlike mobile shopping apps [9], dating apps may present ethical concerns for some users, together with consequences that could be devastating to their families, career, and even lives. We further examined how dating app users perceive the degree of autonomy they have on the possible privacy disclosure, and they perceive the associated risks for doing so. Our discus-sion on users' ethical misgivings and perceived risks provides a good starting point for scholars to further explore AI ethics from a user perspective, the implications of such issues for all the stakeholders (e.g., users & their families).

5.2 Practical Implications, Limitations and Future Research

We suggest that AI-based dating app developers consider more stakeholders (e.g., users and their families) when designing the app interfaces. For instance, messages could be developed when collecting user demographic information (e.g., relationship status) to raise their concerns of ethical consumption, and remind them of the moral consequences of their behavior on dating apps. Now that AI-based dating apps could, at user permission, obtain data through other social media platforms (e.g., Facebook & Instagram), AI are likely to deduce the relationship status of users and identify fake information, dating app developers are encouraged to take the social responsibility to establish an ethical and healthy environment for users who can ethically benefit from these apps.

This study is also subject to limitations that suggest future research. First, we collected data from construction workers who often live separately with families, assuming that they are more likely to adopt dating apps than those living close to families and going home on a daily basis. Future research could include users of various careers in the study. Second, we used cross-sectional data, i.e., data collected at one point in time. Future research can collect data at different points in time through longitudinal methods. More-over, users are often unaware of the ethical misgivings and perceived autonomy/risks that guide their dating app adoption, so self-reported questionnaires are not sufficient to capture the moments and reasons why users feel that their specific behavior is ethically right or wrong. Future studies could adopt qualitative and observational methods for a finer picture of the topic.

References

1. Chen, Q., Zhang, M., Zhao, X.: Analysing customer behaviour in mobile app usage. Ind. Manag. Data Syst. **117**, 425–438 (2017)
2. Du, S., Xie, C.: Paradoxes of artificial intelligence in consumer markets: ethical challenges and opportunities. J. Bus. Res. **129**, 961–974 (2021)
3. Chong, W.K., Ma, Z.: The quality of user experiences for mobile recommendation systems: an end-user perspective. Ind. Manag. Data Syst. **121**, 1063–1081 (2021)
4. Pham, A., et al.: HideMyApp: Hiding the Presence of Sensitive Apps on Android (2019)
5. Rowe, F.: Contact tracing apps and values dilemmas: a privacy paradox in a neo-liberal world. Int. J. Inf. Manage. **55**, 102178 (2020)
6. Albury, K., Burgess, J., Light, B., Race, K., Wilken, R.: Data cultures of mobile dating and hook-up apps: emerging issues for critical social science research. Big Data Soc. **4**, 1–11 (2017)
7. Ryu, S., Park, Y.: How consumers cope with location-based advertising (LBA) and personal information disclosure: the mediating role of persuasion knowledge, perceived benefits and harms, and attitudes toward LBA. Comput. Hum. Behav. **112**, 106450 (2020)
8. Pentina, I., Zhang, L., Bata, H., Chen, Y.: Exploring privacy paradox in information-sensitive mobile app adoption: a cross-cultural comparison. Comput. Hum. Behav. **65**, 409–419 (2016)
9. Chopdar, P.K., Korfiatis, N., Sivakumar, V.J., Lytras, M.D.: Mobile shopping apps adoption and perceived risks: a cross-country perspective utilizing the Unified Theory of Acceptance and Use of Technology. Comput. Hum. Behav. **86**, 109–128 (2018)
10. Wilken, R., Burgess, J., Albury, K.: Dating apps and data markets: a political economy of communication approach. Dating Apps Data Markets: A Political, pp. 1–40 (2019)
11. Heilweil, B.R.: Tinder may not get you a date. It will get your data, pp. 1–9 (2022)
12. Marinos, S.: Tinder craze: a casual sex cesspool or a swipe right for true love? Her. Sun. (2014, online). Accessed 12 Dec 2021
13. Lutz, C., Ranzini, G.: Where dating meets data: investigating social and institutional privacy concerns on tinder. Soc. Media Soc. **3**, 1–12 (2017)
14. Ameen, N., Hosany, S., Paul, J.: The personalisation-privacy paradox: consumer interaction with smart technologies and shopping mall loyalty. Comput. Hum. Behav. **126**, 106976 (2022)
15. Dinev, T., Hart, P.: An extended privacy calculus model for e-commerce transactions. Inf. Syst. Res. **17**, 61–80 (2006)
16. Yang, S., Wang, K.: The influence of information sensitivity compensation on privacy concern and behavioral intention. ACM SIGMIS Database Adv. Inf. Syst. **40**, 38–51 (2009)
17. Dienlin, T., Trepte, S.: Is the privacy paradox a relic of the past? An in-depth analysis of privacy attitudes and privacy behaviors. Eur. J. Soc. Psychol. **45**, 285–297 (2015)
18. Timmermans, E., De Caluwé, E.: Development and validation of the Tinder Motives Scale (TMS). Comput. Hum. Behav. **70**, 341–350 (2017)
19. Blackwell, C., Birnholtz, J., Abbott, C.: Seeing and being seen: co-situation and impression formation using Grindr, a location-aware gay dating app. New media Soc. **17**, 1117–1136 (2015)
20. Hsieh, S.H., Lee, C.T., Tseng, T.H.: Branded app atmospherics: examining the effect of pleasure–arousal–dominance in brand relationship building. J. Retail. Consum. Serv. **60**, 102482 (2021)
21. Lee, Y.-K., Park, J.-H., Chung, N., Blakeney, A.: A unified perspective on the factors influencing usage intention toward mobile financial services. J. Bus. Res. **65**, 1590–1599 (2012)
22. Wünderlich, N.V., Wangenheim, F.V., Bitner, M.J.: High tech and high touch: a framework for understanding user attitudes and behaviors related to smart interactive services. J. Serv. Res. **16**, 3–20 (2013)

23. Connolly, R., Bannister, F.: Consumer trust in Internet shopping in Ireland: towards the development of a more effective trust measurement instrument. J. Inf. Technol. **22**, 102–118 (2007)
24. Harden, K.P., Tucker-Drob, E.M.: Individual differences in the development of sensation seeking and impulsivity during adolescence: further evidence for a dual systems model. Dev. Psychol. **47**, 739–746 (2011)
25. Blanthorne, C., Kaplan, S.: An egocentric model of the relations among the opportunity to underreport, social norms, ethical beliefs, and underreporting behavior. Account. Organ. Soc. **33**, 684–703 (2008)
26. Rauschnabel, P.A., He, J., Ro, Y.K.: Antecedents to the adoption of augmented reality smart glasses: a closer look at privacy risks. J. Bus. Res. **92**, 374–384 (2018)
27. Podsakoff, P.M., MacKenzie, S.B., Lee, J.Y., Podsakoff, N.P.: Common method biases in behavioral research: a critical review of the literature and recommended remedies. J. Appl. Psychol. **88**, 879–903 (2003)
28. Anderson, J.C., Gerbing, D.W.: Structural equation modeling in practice: a review and recommended two-step approach. Psychol. Bull. **103**, 411 (1988)
29. Hair, J.F.: Multivariate data analysis (2009)
30. Fornell, C., Larcker, D.F.: Evaluating structural equation models with unobservable variables and measurement error. J. Mark. Res. **18**, 39–50 (1981)

The Surprise of Underestimation: Analyzing the Effects and Predictors of the Accuracy of Estimated Smartphone Use

Catharina Muench$^{(\boxtimes)}$ (iD), Johanna Link, and Astrid Carolus (iD)

Julius-Maximilians University Wuerzburg, Oswald-Kuelpe-Weg 82, 97074 Wuerzburg, Germany
catharina.muench@uni-wuerzburg.de

Abstract. Smartphone usage had often been measured using self-reported time estimates. Due to the limitations of such self-reports (e.g., effects of social desirability or limited memory performance), this type of measurement had often been criticized. Users tended to overestimate or underestimate their screen time. The goal of the current study was to examine the accuracy of estimated screen time, identify predictors of this accuracy and explore the impact of accuracy feedback on users' well-being and their motivation to limit future smartphone use. In an online survey N = 153 participants (68.6% female) were asked about their well-being, mindfulness, motivation for future limitations of smartphone use and to estimate their smartphone screen time. Moreover, objective screen time was measured with the help of built-in applications: Digital Wellbeing (Android) and Screen Time (iOS). The analyses showed that significantly more subjects underestimated themselves than overestimated themselves. After being provided with feedback on the accuracy of their screen time estimations, participants reported their well-being and their motivation for smartphone limitation, again. Results showed that objective screen time, compulsive phone use and mindfulness did not predict the accuracy of screen time estimations. Feedback on estimation accuracy did not affect limitation motivation but (partially) well-being. The perceived impact of Covid-19 pandemic significantly affected both well-being and limitation motivation. The present paper interprets and relates the results to research in this area and derives implications for future research.

Keywords: Smartphones · Use estimation · Self-reports accuracy · Screen time measurements · Digital well-being · Mindfulness

1 Introduction

People use their smartphones frequently in their everyday lives [see 1]. Ohme et al. [2], for example, reported an average frequency of 70 smartphone uses per day and a daily usage time of more than four hours. With the growing popularity of the smartphone in recent years, its use and associated impact on people's lives have become popular research topics [see 3–5]. For example, Lee et al. [6] showed in a study that one minute of adolescents' daytime smartphone usage was associated with 0.12 min decrease in their

© The Author(s), under exclusive license to Springer Nature Switzerland AG 2022
G. Salvendy and J. Wei (Eds.): HCII 2022, LNCS 13337, pp. 171–190, 2022.
https://doi.org/10.1007/978-3-031-05014-5_14

total sleeping time the following night. Research also shows that an immediate change in one's usage behavior is not at all obvious: even if users are aware of the negative effects of excessive smartphone use, their usage duration will not decrease, and they will not ask for help to reduce it [7]. In this context, a few studies have begun to analyze measures of smartphone usage, which in most cases are users' estimation of their duration of usage [2, 8, 9]. However, research on users' estimated smartphone use and the consequences of an overestimation as well as an underestimation of its impact on their emotions and cognitions is still rare [see 9]. To address this research gap, the present paper aims for the analysis of (1) the accuracy of screen time assessments as well as its influencing factors and (2) users' well-being and motivation to limit smartphone use after they have been presented numbers of both their own estimation and their actual smartphone usage duration.

This paper begins with a summary of previous research on smartphone usage data as well as different measurement approaches studies have carried out. Then, an overview of the risks of problematic smartphone use and its consequences are presented, which lead over to possible interventions to maximize users' mindfulness and well-being. In line with previous research, we carry out an intervention aiming for an increase in users' awareness. More concrete, we present the participants with accuracy feedback regarding their self-estimated smartphone use compared to an objective screen time, we take from the smartphone settings. Furthermore, we analyze the impact of associated factors on participants' accuracy of their screen time estimation and its consequences regarding users' well-being and motivation to limit smartphone use in the future. As the study was conducted during the COVID-19 pandemic, we controlled for the impact of this specific time to allow a comparison with research conducted before the pandemic.

2 Theoretical Background and Hypotheses

2.1 A Subsection Sample

Accompanying their owners 24/7 led researchers to even call the smartphone a "digital companion" [10], which seems to be more to their owners than just a technical device. Current statistics show that smartphones take an integral part in our daily lives and are in permanent use, resulting in usage times from almost three [5] or five [1, 11] up to nine hours [12]. To assess usage times, most studies use self-reported data of the participants [see 5, 11], which is associated with methodological limitations [see 13–15]. To date, no consistent self-report measure for screen time is available [14]. Additionally, self-reporting is prone to social desirability biases [13], and people have difficulties in exactly recalling and assessing their behaviors, especially ones that occur very often [15]. Built-in applications (apps) such as iOS Screen Time [16] or Digital Wellbeing [17] offer a more objective alternative. First studies compared users' estimated screen time to automatically recorded analyses and found conflicting results regarding both overestimations and underestimations of screen time [see 2, 8, 9]. Schulz van Endert and Mohr [18], for example, reported that 71% of their participants overestimated their smartphone use. Comparing self-reports to iOS Screen Time data, Hodes and Thomas [8] also noticed an average overestimation. However, in other studies referring to the same iOS function, most of the sample underestimated one's own daily smartphone use

[2, 9]. For example, Felisoni und Godoi [19] observed a 48.5% higher objective vs. self-estimated screen time.

Summarizing, valid and reliable measurements of usage are a crucial challenge of current media effects research, which often investigate associations between (increased) usage times on the one hand and negative effects on the other. To gain valuable insights and to successfully replicate and compare studies, research needs valid and reliable instruments. Research so far, however, relies on very different measure approaches resulting in limited comparability.

Sewall et al. [9] complement the effects of non-accurate self-assessments and point out further factors which limit assessment accuracy: besides well-being, the user's actual screen time was found to influence the accuracy of estimated screen time assessments. Moreover, research shows that problematic smartphone use, also known as compulsive use [20] leads to deficient self-regulation and negative outcomes [21] and is probably associated with decreased users' self-awareness potentially affecting estimations of usage times [22]. Furthermore, mindfulness - a sub-dimension of self-compassion [23], which describes "the state of being attentive to and aware of what is taking place in the present" [24, p. 822] - has been shown to impact people's perception of time [see 25]. Consequently, mindfulness could also affect the accuracy of smartphone use estimates.

Although omnipresent in media research, only little research focuses on the analyses of estimation accuracy and potential factors causing biases in the estimates. Addressing this gap, our first research question asks:

RQ1: How accurate are self-reports of screen time and which factors influence the accuracy?

2.2   Impact of Smartphone Use on Users' Well-Being

Negative consequences of media and smartphone use is a major topic of current media research [4, 5]. While popular media tend to overemphasize the idea of addictive smartphone use [26], researchers prefer terms like compulsive or problematic smartphone use [9, 27, 28]. Problematic smartphone use is described as an uncontrolled and habitual use of the smartphone [29] with negative consequences for the user's life [26] in terms of both physical and psychological effects [5, 30] with a range from problems with neck muscles [30] to the loss of self-control [5, 19] as well as increased emotional instability [5].

One research focus is on the analysis of the impact of phone use on subjective well-being, which can be described as general happiness, that not only consists of constant positive affect, but also rare negative affect and cognitive evaluations [31, originally from 32]. Looking at previous research on the association between smartphone use and subjective well-being, studies show that especially problematic smartphone use is positively related to negative affect [see 33, 34]. One possible explanation for this relation is that people with greater negative affect use their smartphone as a means for compensation [33].

Despite the dominant perspective on negative consequences some work also show positive outcomes. In the same study, Horwood and Anglim [34] reveal that smartphone use for communication, like voice calls or SMS, is positively associated with positive affect, as well as negatively related with negative affect. "The positive experience of connecting directly with personally important others" might explain this association [34, p. 9]. Studies analyzing users' awareness regarding their smartphone usage behavior showed that intensive, compulsive smartphone use leads to an underestimation of smartphone use [35, 36] and is negatively associated with smartphone vigilance [22]. However, research showed that errors in the estimation of digital technology use is associated with users' well-being [9, 37]. We carefully consider our intervention as a technique to maximize users' self-awareness in terms of their smartphone usage behavior and ask the following second research question:

RQ2: How does underestimation of smartphone use influence users' well-being?

Since March 2020 the corona virus has been acknowledged as a worldwide pandemic that is still ongoing in 2022 [38]. This state of exception has shown to impact everyone's daily life by reducing well-being [39] and increasing peoples' anxiety [40]. Consequently, we analyzed the second research question controlling for the impact of the COVID-19 pandemic on participants' well-being.

2.3 The Impact of Interventions: Feedback on Inaccurate Estimations of Phone Use

Mindfulness techniques were shown to have an impact on emotion regulation processes [41]: more self-awareness leads to a more effective dealing with negative emotions and challenging situations [23]. In this context, mindfulness was positively associated with smartphone vigilance [25] as mindful users can recognize excessive (social) media behavior [42]. Previous research on smartphone usage and well-being showed that more mindful smartphone use leads to reduced usage [43] and increased well-being [see 44–46]. In this context, research refers to "digital well-being" to describe an optimal balance between the advantages and disadvantages of smartphone and technology use as a key factor of a healthy life in our digitized world [47, 48]. Studies analyzing users' digital well-being and mindfulness carry out different techniques as interventions, whereas "Digital detox" as an intervention to reduce negative effects of smartphone use and prevent problematic use has become a trend in recent years [46]. Accordingly, smartphone users "consciously decide to disconnect entirely from email, social media, news and the internet in general" [49, p. 361]. Apps that record and display screen time can also play an important role for reducing negative effects concerning smartphone use [46] and can support the improvement of digital self-awareness [50]. Additional features, such as limiting the usage time for certain apps [51] are common among so-called "Digital Detox apps" [46]. For example, the Digital Wellbeing for Android users and iOS's Screen Time allow a detailed collection of smartphone use data and provide graphical representations of several intervals of usage of certain apps [17, 52]. In addition, smartphone users can limit the utilization time of apps [17, 53], set up timeouts [16] and deactivate notification signals [17]. The use of such apps showed positive consequences in terms of screen time and problematic smartphone use [46, 51]. These results were explained with processes of self-regulation and mindfulness [46, 51], allowing users to compare their own behavior to inner standards. Referring to the idea of "cognitive dissonance", discrepancies between one's own behavior and one's standards might cause motivation to adjust one's behavior [54]. However, research on "cognitive dissonance" knows about the stability of behavior. Thus, it is not certain that people really change their usage behavior. To reduce cognitive dissonance, they can make use of several mechanisms: change their behavior, change the cognition (e.g., their standards), justify their behavior or ignore conflicting information [55]. Consequently, the effects of becoming aware of discrepancies between one's own estimations and actual measures can result in processes of self-regulation and mindfulness [46, 51]. However, following the predictions of "cognitive dissonance theory" the multiple outcomes of this mis-assessments are largely unexplored. To further explore the underlying mechanisms, the third research question asks:

RQ3: How does the awareness of underestimated usage time influence users' motivation to limit smartphone use?

Previous research showed that the COVID-19 pandemic affects smartphone use [see 8, 56, 57]. Hodes and Thomas [8] reported a significant increase in smartphone use during lockdown while Fernandes et al. [56] showed a rise in the use of social network sites and streaming services. A study by Ohme et al. [57] concentrated on smartphone use in the first week of the pandemic in Belgium and found that the objective screen time raised, on average, by about 28% or 45 min. The researchers described the smartphone as "key instruments that help citizens stay informed, in sync, and in touch with society during times of crisis" [57 p. 1]. Therefore, when analyzing RQ3, the impact of the COVID-19 pandemic on participants' smartphone usage behavior needs to be considered.

2.4 Hypotheses

To summarize research so far, smartphones are ubiquitous in peoples' lives and are frequently used every day [1, 2]. Research on the effect of this usage often relies on self-reports as a method to measure smartphone usage. However, studies showed that participants' ratings lack accuracy [2, 8, 9, 13–15]. Particularly, the average daily screen time was often underestimated [2, 9]. Thus, the first hypothesis (H1) postulates:

H1: Participants underestimate their smartphone use significantly more often than they overestimate it.

Research revealed that interindividual differences not only influence the way media and especially smartphones are used but also affect users' estimates of smartphone use [58, 59]. In this context, on the one hand, objective smartphone use [9, 35] and compulsive smartphone use were negatively associated with smartphone vigilance [22]. Moreover, intensive (compulsive) smartphone use was positively associated with habitualization [29] and negatively related to autonomy and self-control [34] leading to an underestimation of actual smartphone use [36]. Mindfulness was positively associated with smartphone vigilance [25] as mindful users could recognize excessive (social) media behavior [42]. Against this background, H2 assumes the combination of these predictors to significantly explain the variance of the accuracy of estimated smartphone use:

H2a: Objective smartphone use is a significant predictor of the accuracy of the estimated smartphone use.
H2b: Perceived compulsive smartphone use is a significant predictor of the accuracy of the estimated smartphone use.
H2c: Mindfulness is a significant predictor of the accuracy of the estimated smartphone use.

Previous studies showed discrepancies between the estimated and the objective screen time [2, 9]. Digital detox apps and screen time tracking can assist with getting aware of this discrepancy, because they enable a comparison between the estimation and objective screen time [16, 53] and improve digital self-awareness [50] or result in self-regulation processes and mindfulness [46, 51]. Reflecting on the discrepancy between a person's standard (here: estimated smartphone use) and its behavior (here: objective smartphone use) can evoke cognitive dissonance between people's self-image and their actual behavior [55]. Cognitive dissonance is experienced as psychological stress known to be associated with a decrease of positive emotions and an increase of negative. Consistently, research showed that errors in the estimation of digital technology use is associated with users' well-being [9, 37]. Moreover, public and academic discourse refers to intensive smartphone use as "problematic" and therefore as not desirable. Consequently, feedback on one's underestimation of smartphone use should result in less stressful cognitive dissonance than to learn that you are using the phone more intensively than you have thought and reported. As a result, the third hypotheses distinguish between underestimation and overestimation and postulate different reactions:

H3a: Feedback on one's underestimation results in less positive affect than feedback on one's overestimation.
H3b: Feedback on one's underestimation results in more positive affect than feedback on one's overestimation.

As people seek psychological consistency, perceived discrepancies or cognitive dissonances and resulting psychological stress lead to people's intention to reduce the cognitive dissonance [55]. Thus, the feedback on inconsistencies between the estimated and the actual screen time could function as a motivator to reduce one's screen time. Therefore, H4 postulates:

H4: Feedback on one's underestimation results in a higher motivation to reduce future smartphone use than feedback on one's overestimation.

Various studies showed an impact of the COVID-19 pandemic on people's well-being [see 39, 40] as well as smartphone use [8, 56], which is why the impact of the COVID-19 pandemic was considered as a covariate for H3a, H3b and H4.

3   Methods

3.1   Participants

153 German speaking participants (46 males, 105 females, 2 diverse) with an age range from 15 to 70 years (M = 26.88; SD = 9.92) took part in an online survey. A little more than half of the participants were users of Apple's smartphone with the iOS operating system (n = 86). The rest used a smartphone with the Android operating system (n = 67). On average, participants spend about 3.5 h a day (M = 209.53 min, SD = 102.95) using their phone. A total of 56 participants were already using digital detox apps.

3.2   Design and Procedure

In a causal-comparative designed study with two measurement times, participants were asked to answer an online questionnaire. At the beginning of the survey participants were welcomed and informed about the course of the study and agreed to the ethical guidelines of the German Psychological Association as well as their participation. Then, participants had to answer demographic questions before continuing with the scales for well-being (focus on state), mindfulness and compulsive smartphone use (pre-feedback measures). Next, they were asked to estimate their average daily smartphone use and assess their motivation for limiting their smartphone use. Afterwards, they were instructed to look up their objective screen time in terms of their average daily screen time of the last week. Depending on their smartphone operating system, they were guided via screenshots to the settings of their phones to report the precise amount of screen time (Fig. 1).

Fig. 1. Screenshot of how to look up the objective smartphone use for smartphones with an iOS operating system using iOS Screen Time

In the next step, participants received *accuracy feedback* on their estimation of smartphone use compared to the objective measure ("Your estimation: xx minutes, Your objective screen time: xx minutes"). In addition, they had to evaluate their accuracy of estimated smartphone use. By choosing the fitting statement, they stated whether they estimated their smartphone use correctly, overestimated, or underestimated it. Next, participants were again asked for their current well-being (focus on current state) and their motivation for limiting their smartphone use. Finally, participants indicated the extent to which the ongoing COVID-19 pandemic affected both their well-being and their smartphone use.

3.3 Measures

Following the procedure of the study, measures are presented in the order of their query. Thereby, we distinguish between measures, which are presented before (baseline measures) and after the feedback on the comparison of estimated with objective screen time.

Baseline Measures. Inspired by Sewall et al. [9] and Ohme et al. [2], *estimated smartphone use* was measured using self-reports. Participants were asked to answer the open question "On average, how many minutes per day do you use your smartphone?". Smartphone use was considered as every interaction with the smartphone - except for background activities such as listening to music as they are not tracked by the used apps [see 17, 52].

To indicate the *objective smartphone screen time*, the applications Digital Wellbeing (for Android users) and Screen Time (for iOS users) were used. In accordance with the methodological approach of Sewall et al. [9], participants were instructed to open these statistics in their settings to then type in the answer (in minutes per day) of the following question "According to the app, how much daily time did you spend with your smartphone last week on average?".

The accuracy of estimated smartphone use was calculated in three different ways:

(1) The *accuracy index* of estimated smartphone use was calculated following the analytical approaches of Ohme et al. [60] and Timotijevic et al. [61]: the difference between the estimated and objective smartphone use was divided by the objective smartphone use. As a result, a value ranging from 1 (100% overestimation) to −1 (100%, underestimation) indicates how much subjects overestimated or underestimated their own usage. To use the accuracy index for an overall comparison regarding participants' errors in their estimation for H2 we changed the minus signs from the underestimation values to positive signs to get an overall accuracy index with a value from 0 (complete accuracy between estimated smartphone use and objective screen time) to 1 (least accuracy with an under-/overestimation of 100%) for the dependent variable for H2.

(2) The *objective accuracy grouping* aimed for the differentiation of participants based on their accuracy of smartphone use estimation. It is based on (1) the percentual accuracy index and distinguishes three groups [61]: (A) "correct estimation" including participants with a maximum discrepancy of −10 or +10%), (B) "overestimation" with more than +10% deviation and (C) "underestimation" with a deviation of more than −10% (dependent variable for H1).

(3) The *perceived accuracy grouping* also aims for the differentiation of participants. After participants have been presented with the comparison of their estimated and objective screen time, they were instructed to assign themselves to one out of three groups: (A) "I spend more time on the smartphone than I estimated." (B) "I spend as much time on the smartphone as I estimated." or (C) "I spend less time on my smartphone than I estimated." (independent variable smartphone use estimation for H3 & H4).

Problematic smartphone use was measured using a German translation of the "Compulsive Usage of Mobile Phones Scale" [originally from 27, translated by 11]. By answering 13 items (i.e., "The first thing I do each morning is to check my mobile phone for missed calls or messages.") on a 7-point Likert scale (from 1 "not correct at all" to 7 "fully correct") subjects rated how much they agreed with the given statements. For analysis a mean score was determined. The scale had an internal consistency of $\alpha = .86$.

For measuring *mindfulness*, the German translation of the "Mindfulness Attention Awareness Scale" (MAAS) by Michalak et al. [62, originally from 24] with 15 items was used (i.e., "I do jobs or tasks automatically, without being aware of what I'm doing." or "I find myself preoccupied with the future or the past."). On a 6-point Likert scale (from 1 "almost never" to 6 "almost always") participants rated how often they currently experience the given situations. To avoid wrong answers due to a change in the orientation of the scale, the MAAS scale was reversed. For the analysis, answers were reversed again and a MAAS score for each subject was calculated ranging from 15 to 90. The internal consistency of the MAAS was $\alpha = .88$.

The study took place during the COVID-19 pandemic. To consider *the influence of the COVID-19 pandemic* on smartphone use and well-being two newly developed items were presented ("How much do you feel negatively influenced in your smartphone use behavior by the COVID-19 pandemic?" and "How much do you feel negatively influenced in your well-being by the COVID-19 pandemic?"). On a 5-point Likert scale (from 1 "not at all" to 5 "very much") subjects rated the perceived amount of influence of the COVID-19 pandemic.

Repeated Measures. *Well-being* was measured using the German translation of the "Scale of Positive and Negative Experience" (SPANE) by Berend and Vogt [63, originally from 64]. The scale consists of 12 statements (six items for negative experience and six items for positive experience, i.e.: "… I was angry", "… I was frightened" for negative experience or "(„… I had good feelings", "… I felt happy" for positive experience). Well-being was measured two times. First, subjects rated how often they experienced each condition in the past four weeks on a 5-point Likert scale (from 1 "never or rarely" to 5 "very often or always"). Second, and after they were provided with feedback on the accuracy of their smartphone use estimation (factor 2: feedback pre/post), subjects rated their agreement with each condition at this very moment, again on a 5-point Likert scale (from 1 "not at all" to 5 "totally"). Following Diener et al. [64], the item values of the positive and negative experience were indexed separately (Scale range 6 to 30). The internal consistency of the positive scale was $\alpha = .92$ (baseline) and $\alpha = .94$ (state after the intervention). The negative scale had an internal consistency of $\alpha = .84$ (baseline) and $\alpha = .90$ (after the intervention).

Motivation to limit smartphone use was measured by one item ("I am motivated to rethink and limit my smartphone use."), which was rated on a 5-point Likert scale (from "fully disagree" to "fully agree").

4   Results

4.1   Descriptive Analyses

The descriptive analysis of all measures is presented in Table 1. Subjects estimated an average smartphone screen time of $M = 180.84$ ($SD = 111.96$) minutes per day. Objective screen time measures resulted in $M = 209.53$ ($SD = 102.95$) daily minutes. Across all participants and based on the mean percentage accuracy index, participants underestimated themselves by an average of 13% ($M = -0.13, SD = .31$). Based on the objective accuracy grouping three groups were distinguished: (1) "correct estimation" (participants with a maximum discrepancy of -10 or $+10\%$), (2) "overestimation" (more than $+10\%$ deviation) and (3) "underestimation" (deviation of more than -10%).

Group (1) includes 23.5% of the total sample estimating themselves correctly. Their mean estimated screen time was $M = 215.50$ ($SD = 112.37$) minutes, compared to $M = 219.17$ ($SD = 111.65$) minutes objectively measured. Estimated and objective measures deviated by only 1.7% ($M = -0.02$, SD $= 0.05$).

Group (2) includes 17.7% of the participants. They overestimated their smartphone screen time with the estimated time ($M = 253.37$ min per day; $SD = 152.70$) being 37.0% ($SD = 0.21$) higher than their objective measure ($M = 182.90; SD = 104.94$).

Group (3) includes 58.8% of the subjects who underestimated themselves by more than 10% with an average estimate of $M = 145.22$ ($SD = 79.15$) minutes per day and an average objective result of $M = 213.66$ ($SD = 98.55$) minutes. Contrasting both measures, the estimated screen time was on average 32.2% less than the objective measure ($M = -0.32, SD = 0.17$).

Table 1. Descriptive analysis for all measures

Variable	M	SD
Estimated smartphone use min/day	180.84	111.96
Objective screen time min/day	209.53	102.95
Accuracy index of estimated smartphone use	$-.13$	.31
Problematic smartphone use	2.89	1.02
Motivation to limit smartphone use (pre feedback)	3.48	1.17

(*continued*)

Table 1. (*continued*)

Variable	M	SD
Motivation to limit smartphone use (post feedback)	3.47	1.20
Negative affect (pre feedback)	15.60	4.35
Negative affect (post feedback)	13.01	4.85
Positive affect (pre feedback)	21.64	3.96
Positive Affect (post feedback)	20.49	4.54
Mindfulness	61.40	11.55
Influence of COVID-19 pandemic on well-being	3.68	1.04
Influence of COVID-19 pandemic on smartphone use	3.22	1.38

4.2 Hypothesis Testing

A binomial test was used to inference statistically test hypothesis **H1** with the objective accuracy grouping, postulating that significantly more participants underestimated (group 3) their screen time than overestimated it (group 2). Based on the distinguished groups from 3.3.1 (and 4.1, descriptive analyses), we compared group 2 (overestimation) with group 3 (underestimation). The test for binomial distribution showed that significantly more participants underestimated themselves (50% more) than they overestimated themselves, $p < .001$. The proportion of underestimating participants was 77.0% and of overestimating participants was 23.0%.

To test hypotheses **H2a-c** a multiple linear regression was calculated to predict the accuracy index from objective screen time, perceived compulsive phone use and mindfulness. No significant regression equation was found ($F_{(3, 149)} = .11, p = .95$.), with an R^2 of .002. Objective smartphone use ($\beta = -.05, SE = .00, p = .59$), compulsive phone use ($\beta = .05, SE = .02, p = .65$) and mindfulness ($\beta = .01, SE = .002, p = .88$) were not significant predictors of the accuracy of estimated smartphone use.

Hypotheses **H3a-b** refers to participants' ratings after they had been provided with feedback on their accuracy of their time estimations. H3a-b assumed that underestimating participants reported significantly less positive affect (H3a) and significantly more negative affect (H3b), compared to overestimating or correctly estimating participants. A one-way repeated measures ANCOVA was conducted with two factors: (1) "smartphone use estimation" (factor levels: overestimation, correct estimation, underestimation) and (2) "accuracy feedback" (factor levels: pre, post), the dependent variables positive and negative affect. Participants' perceived impact of the COVID-19 pandemic was integrated as a covariate. A significant interaction was found (Fig. 2) between time and separation for negative affect ($F_{(2, 149)} = 4.28, p = .03, \eta^2 = .05$), but not for positive affect ($F_{(2, 149)} = 1.04, p = .36, \eta^2 = .01$).

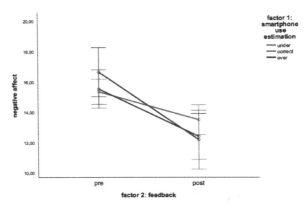

Fig. 2. Effects of accuracy of smartphone use estimation and feedback (pre/post) on negative affect (range from 6 to 30) controlling for COVID-19 well-being.

In contrast to our assumptions, pairwise comparisons showed that participants who underestimated themselves reported significantly less negative affect after the feedback than before - compared to participants who overestimated or estimated correctly (see Table 2). Consequently, Hypotheses 3a and 3b were rejected.

Table 2. Descriptives for the interaction of the independent variable x time for negative affect

Feedback	Estimation of smartphone use	M	SD
Pre	Under	15.31	4.59
	Correct	15.21	4.03
	Over	17.33	3.61
Post	Under	13.48	5.11
	Correct	12.21	4.07
	Over	12.58	4.98

Notes. The scale negative affect has a range from 6 to 30

Analyses of the intraindividual effects comparing measures before and after the accuracy feedback did not reveal a significant main effect of pre/post feedback neither for positive affect, $F_{(1,149)} = 1.53$, $p = .22$, $\eta^2 = .01$ nor for negative affect, $F_{(1,149)} = .14$, $p = .71$, $\eta^2 = .001$. Analyzing the interindividual effects of smartphone use estimation, no significant main effect was found neither for positive affect ($F_{(1,149)} = .11$, $p = .90$, $\eta^2 = .001$) nor negative affect ($F_{(1,149)} = .21$, $p = .81$, $\eta^2 = .003$). For both well-being measures the covariate influence of COVID-19 pandemic was significant with $p < .001$.

Hypothesis **H4** assumed that participants who had learnt that they underestimated their smartphone reported significantly higher motivation to limit their smartphone - compared to overestimated or correctly estimating participants. A one-way repeated measures ANCOVA was conducted with two factors: (1) smartphone use estimation using the perceived accuracy grouping measure (factor levels: overestimation, correct estimation, underestimation), (2) the accuracy feedback (factor levels: pre, post) and participants' perceived influence of the COVID-19 pandemic as a covariate. No significant interaction ($F_{(2, 149)} = 1.55$, $p = .22$, $\eta^2 = .02$) or main effects were found, so H4 was rejected. The perceived impact of the COVID-19 pandemic was a significant covariate, again ($p < .001$). However, descriptively, the data seem to confirm the assumption at least per tendency. After the accuracy feedback, participants who underestimated their smartphone usage reported a minimally higher motivation to limit their use whereas overestimating or correctly estimating participants reported a minimal decrease (Fig. 3).

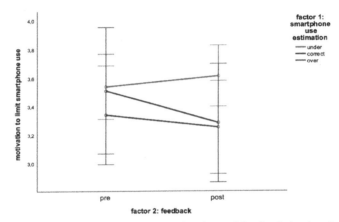

Fig. 3. Effects of accuracy of smartphone use estimation and feedback (pre/post) on motivation to limit smartphone use (range from 1 to 5) controlling for COVID-19 smartphone use.

5 Discussion

The study's aim was to analyze users' estimated smartphone use and compare it to the usage derived from the phone's settings. Furthermore, the study aimed for the analysis of the impact of feedback on the users' objective phone usage, on their emotions and their willingness to limit their smartphone use in the future. Descriptive statistics indicated an average estimated screen time of three hours but an objective amount of about 3.5 h. Regarding other studies, both the estimated and the objective screen time of the present sample were lower compared to other studies (see [1] with 5.05 h for objective screen time and 4.12 h for estimated use) or even only half as large [see 12]. Compared to research so far, the present study revealed rather small deviations between objective and estimated screen time [9, 13]. Consequently, we would interpret this finding as a first indicator of the validity of self-assessments of smartphone usage time. However, with about two third underestimating their usage by more than 10%, this study clearly confirmed the overall tendency of users to underrate the time they spend with their device resulting in the call for more fine-grained measures.

Regarding **hypothesis 1** (subjects significantly more often underestimate their smartphone use than overestimating it), the results of our study showed that participants underestimated their smartphone use more often. Thus, our results contributed to the heterogenous picture so far with research indicating overestimations of smartphone use [see 8, 18, 65] and studies showing underestimations [2, 9, 19]. Reasons for underestimating smartphone use were discussed by Hodes and Thomas [8] as habitual processes that could develop in relation to smartphone use and a loss of the sense of time associated with it [66]. Measurement and response format might also have an influence on the estimation of use [15]. A study by Sewall et al. [9], on the one hand, which used a similar methodological approach like the present study (by asking for estimated screen time using open response format as daily use in minutes), for example, also showed a strong tendency to screen time underestimation. Montag et al. [65], on the other hand, who asked about weekly screen time, found an overestimation of objective screen time. To account for the heterogeneity of results in the field and to increase comparability, future studies should follow the methodological approaches of previous studies very closely and should distinctly report their approaches. An alternative methodological approach to increase the reliability of the objective screen time measurement would be the controlled transcription of participants' smartphone log-data by asking for screenshots [2, 8].

Hypothesis 2 focused on the explanation of the variance of the accuracy index value of estimated smartphone use and assumed that the three predictors objective screen time, compulsive smartphone use and mindfulness would significantly contribute to the explanation. The results showed that none of the predictors was significant and contrasted previous research showing that intensive (and compulsive) smartphone use led to a worse accuracy in the estimation of smartphone use [9, 35, 36] and that higher mindfulness might lead to a better estimation of time and smartphone vigilance [25]. Further dispositional characteristics associated with smartphone use [e.g., self-control, 18, 67; the other subdimensions of self-compassion, 18] should be considered in future studies and added to the model to explain more variance in the accuracy index.

According to **hypothesis 3**, subjects underestimating their smartphone use reported a lower well-being (less positive affect and more negative affect) after they had received feedback on their objective usage- compared to subjects who overestimated their smartphone use. Results were partly in line with our assumptions as participants who underestimated their smartphone use reported more negative affect after the accuracy feedback than overestimating participants. Contrary to our assumptions and previous research, all three groups reported less negative affect after the accuracy feedback than before the feedback [9, 37]. One possible reason for participants' overall decrease in negative affect could be that their estimation, which on average deviated only half an hour from their objective use, might have exceeded their expectations. Perhaps, they feared greater deviations when confronted with the unexpected comparison of screen time indicators and were rather relieved. Against this argument stands the fact that more than one third of the participants already used digital detox apps, which probably impacted their smartphone use estimates. Future studies should further analyze how often and since when participants use digital well-being functions as a covariate to minimize confounding effects. However, the fact that the statistical analyses did not show significant results for positive affect points out the importance of a multifaceted conceptualization of well-being as the subdimensions of the SPANE scale showed different characteristics. Furthermore, future studies could analyze well-being not only using subjective self-assessments, but also physiological measurements to derive measures not influenced by social desirability. As expected, the impact of the COVID-19 pandemic on well-being was a significant covariate. Post-hoc analyses showed significant correlations between the COVID-19 pandemic and participants' well-being (positive affect$_{pre}$, $r = -.34$, $p = .001$; positive affect$_{post}$, $r = -.25$, $p = .002$; negative affect$_{pre}$, $r = .42$, $p = .001$; negative affect$_{post}$, $r = .21$, $p = .01$) complementing previous research that found negative effects of the pandemic on well-being [39, 40]. Future study should consider further confounding variables, which might impact the emotional experience [e.g., psychological vulnerability, 68, or resilience variables, 69].

Finally, **hypothesis 4** assumed that feedback on one's underestimation resulted in a higher motivation to reduce future smartphone use than feedback on one's overestimation. In contrast to our assumptions based on previous research showing that cognitive dissonances led to an intention to reduce the cognitive dissonance [55], our results showed no significant change in participant's motivation to limit their smartphone use after the accuracy feedback and no significant differences between the three estimation groups based on the perceived accuracy grouping. However, descriptive analyses showed a trend pointing in the assumed direction (see Fig. 3) as underestimating participants reported a higher motivation for change after the accuracy feedback than the other groups. Overestimating participants reported less motivation. As with previous studies [8, 57], the perceived impact of COVID-19 pandemic had a significant effect on subjects' motivation to limit smartphone use. Post-hoc analyses showed significant correlations between the COVID-19 pandemic and participants' motivation to limit smartphone use (motivation$_{pre}$, $r = .35$, $p = .001$; motivation$_{post}$, $r = .51$, $p = .001$) showing that the more participants perceived to be influenced by the pandemic in their smartphone usage behavior, the more they were motivated to limit their smartphone use. The smartphone appeared to play an important role in everyday life, especially in a pandemic, by providing access to e.g., communication with others, information, or news [57]. As a result, users were probably more attached to their devices with a more automatic and less mindful smartphone use leading to cognitive dissonances they were likely to reduce when confronted with it [55]. This study aimed to increase participants' mindfulness about their smartphone usage behavior; future studies could further analyze users' behavior in a long-term analysis for possible cognitive, emotional, and behavioral changes following a long-term mindfulness intervention. Future studies should also consider a more fine-grained analysis of phone use (e.g., use and motivation to limit certain functions or apps) and of participants' cognitions (e.g., regarding their amount of objective smartphone use and their evaluation of it). Further confounding variables might have impacted the results and need to be considered in future research [e.g., nomophobia, 70; FoMO and attachment, 71].

6   Conclusion

The current study aimed to analyze the accuracy of screen time assessments and its influencing factors as well as users' well-being and motivation to limit phone use in the future after receiving feedback regarding the accuracy of their smartphone use estimations. The results showed that more users underestimated than overestimated their smartphone usage and that the accuracy of estimation was not significantly influenced by the analyzed predictors (usage behavior: objective screen time, perceived compulsive phone usage; mindfulness). Consequently, this study leaves open questions about factors that explain the discrepancies between estimated and actual time. Interestingly, after being provided with feedback on the accuracy of their time estimations, participants reported less negative effect - independently of the type of feedback (under/correct/over) with underestimating participants reporting the highest levels of negative affect after the feedback. The intention to reduce one's smartphone use as one crucial aspect of digital well-being, was not significantly but at least descriptively affected by the accuracy feedback. When interpreting the results, the effects of the COVID-19 pandemic on the participants had to be considered as the perceived impact of the pandemic was shown to have significant effects on well-being and smartphone use. Across the different studies within the research area, these effects underline the importance of considering the effects of an ongoing worldwide pandemic. Moreover, this study points out the importance of the methodological considerations when it comes to time measurements in the context of media use. The most common way to rely on self-reports seems to be of limited reliability as people tend to underestimate their smartphone use. Utilizing built-in applications, which automatically measure screen time, seem to be a promising way to more reliable measurement results. In terms of the overall focus on digital well-being, utilizing these apps could be a promising way to supervise one's own behavior and to allow reflection, which might lead to more awareness (and probably happiness) after all.

References

1. Andrews, S., Ellis, D.A., Shaw, H., Piwek, L.: Beyond self-report: tools to compare estimated and real-world smartphone use. PLoS ONE **10**(10), e0139004 (2015). https://doi.org/10.1371/journal.pone.0139004
2. Ohme, J., Araujo, T., de Vreese, C.H., Piotrowski, J.T.: Mobile data donations: assessing self-report accuracy and sample biases with the iOS Screen Time function. Mob. Media Commun. **9**(2), 293–313 (2020). https://doi.org/10.1177/2050157920959106
3. Bian, M., Leung, L.: Linking loneliness, shyness, smartphone addiction symptoms, and patterns of smartphone use to social capital. Soc. Sci. Comput. Rev. **33**(1), 61–79 (2015). https://doi.org/10.1177/0894439314528779
4. Przybylski, A.K., Murayama, K., DeHaan, C.R., Gladwell, V.: Motivational, emotional, and behavioral correlates of fear of missing out. Comput. Hum. Behav. **29**(4), 1841–1848 (2013). https://doi.org/10.1016/j.chb.2013.02.014
5. Twenge, J.M., Campbell, W.K.: Associations between screen time and lower psychological well-being among children and adolescents: evidence from a population-based study. Prev. Med. Rep. **12**, 271–283 (2018). https://doi.org/10.1016/j.pmedr.2018.10.003
6. Lee, P.H., Tse, A.C.Y., Wu, C.S.T., Mak, Y.W., Lee, U.: Objectively-Measured Smartphone Usage, Sleep Quality, and Physical Activity Among Chinese Adolescents and Young Adults. Preprint, submitted in 21 May 2020. https://doi.org/10.21203/rs.3.rs-30312/v1

7. Kaysi, F., Yavuz, M., Aydemir, E.: Investigation of university students' smartphone usage levels and effects. Int. J. Technol. Educ. Sci. (IJTES) **5**(3), 411–426 (2021). https://doi.org/10.46328/ijtes.235
8. Hodes, L.N., Thomas, K.G.: Smartphone screen time: inaccuracy of self-reports and influence of psychological and contextual factors. Comput. Hum. Behav. **115**, 106616 (2021). https://doi.org/10.1016/j.chb.2020.106616
9. Sewall, C.J.R., Bear, T.M., Merranko, J., Rosen, D.: How psychosocial well-being and usage amount predict inaccuracies in retrospective estimates of digital technology use. Mob. Media Commun. **8**(3), 379–399 (2020). https://doi.org/10.1177/2050157920902830
10. Carolus, A., Binder, J.F., Muench, R., Schmidt, C., Schneider, F., Buglass, S.L.: Smartphones as digital companions: characterizing the relationship between users and their phones. New Media Soc. **21**(4), 914–938 (2018). https://doi.org/10.1177/1461444818817074
11. Muench, R., Muench, C.: me without my smartphone? never! predictors of willingness for smartphone separation and nomophobia. In: Stephanidis, C., Antona, M. (eds.) HCII 2020. CCIS, vol. 1226, pp. 217–223. Springer, Cham (2020). https://doi.org/10.1007/978-3-030-50732-9_29
12. Roberts, J., Yaya, L., Manolis, C.: The invisible addiction: cell-phone activities and addiction among male and female college students. J. Behav. Addict. **3**(4), 254–265 (2014). https://doi.org/10.1556/jba.3.2014.015
13. Boase, J., Ling, R.: Measuring mobile phone use: self-report versus log data. J. Comput.-Mediat. Commun. **18**(4), 508–519 (2013). https://doi.org/10.1111/jcc4.12021
14. Kaye, L.K., Orben, A., Ellis, D.A., Hunter, S.C., Houghton, S.: The Conceptual and Methodological Mayhem of "Screen Time." Int. J. Environ. Res. Public Health **17**(10), 3661 (2020). https://doi.org/10.3390/ijerph17103661
15. Schwarz, N., Oyserman, D.: Asking questions about behavior: cognition, communication, and questionnaire construction. Am. J. Eval. **22**(2), 127–160 (2001). https://doi.org/10.1016/S1098-2140(01)00133-3
16. Apple Inc. https://support.apple.com/de-de/guide/iphone/iphbfa595995/ios. Accessed 11 Feb 2022
17. Google LLC: Digital Wellbeing (Version 1.0.351358120). https://play.google.com/store/apps/details?id=com.google.android.apps.wellbeing. Accessed 11 Feb 2022
18. Schulz van Endert, T., Mohr, P.N.C.: Likes and impulsivity: investigating the relationship between actual smartphone use and delay discounting. PLoS ONE **15**(11), 1–15 (2020). https://doi.org/10.1371/journal.pone.0241383
19. Felisoni, D.D., Godoi, A.S.: Cell phone usage and academic performance: an experiment. Comput. Educ. **117**, 175–187 (2018). https://doi.org/10.1016/j.compedu.2017.10.006
20. James, D., Drennan, J.: Exploring addictive consumption of mobile phone technology. In: Australian and New Zealand Marketing Academy Conference, Perth, Australia (2005)
21. Caplan, S.E.: Theory and measurement of generalized problematic Internet use: a two-step approach. Comput. Hum. Behav. **26**(5), 1089–1097 (2010). https://doi.org/10.1016/j.chb.2010.03.012
22. Ochs, C., Sauer, J.: Curtailing smartphone use: a field experiment evaluating two interventions. Behav. Inf. Technol. 1–19 (2021). https://doi.org/10.1080/0144929X.2021.2007284
23. Neff, K.: Self-compassion: an alternative conceptualization of a healthy attitude toward oneself. Self Identity **2**(2), 84–101 (2003). https://doi.org/10.1080/15298860309032
24. Brown, K.W., Ryan, R.M.: The benefits of being present: mindfulness and its role in psychological well-being. J. Pers. Soc. Psychol. **84**(4), 822–848 (2003). https://doi.org/10.1037/0022-3514.84.4.822
25. Kramer, R.S.S., Weger, U.W., Sharma, D.: The effect of mindfulness meditation on time perception. Conscious. Cogn. Int. J. **22**(3), 846–852 (2013). https://doi.org/10.1016/j.concog.2013.05.008

26. Billieux, J.: Problematic use of the mobile phone: a literature review and a pathways model. Current Psychiatry Rev. **8**(4), 299–307 (2012). https://doi.org/10.2174/157340012803520522

27. Lee, Y.-K., Chang, C.-T., Lin, Y., Cheng, Z.-H.: The dark side of smartphone usage: psychological traits, compulsive behavior and technostress. Comput. Hum. Behav. **31**, 373–383 (2014). https://doi.org/10.1016/j.chb.2013.10.047

28. Mahapatra, S.: Smartphone addiction and associated consequences: role of loneliness and self-regulation. Behav. Inf. Technol. **38**(8), 833–844 (2019). https://doi.org/10.1080/0144929x. 2018.1560499

29. Tran, J.A., Yang, K.S., Davis, K., Hiniker, A.: Modeling the engagement-disengagement cycle of compulsive phone use. In: Proceedings of the 2019 CHI Conference on Human Factors in Computing Systems, pp. 1–14 (2019). https://doi.org/10.1145/3290605.3300542

30. Lee, H., Choi, Y.S., Lee, S., Shim, E.: Smart pose: mobile posture-aware system for lowering physical health risk of smartphone users. In: CHI EA 2013: CHI 2013 Extended Abstracts on Human Factors in Computing Systems, pp. 2257–2266. Association for Computing Machinery, New York (2013). https://doi.org/10.1145/2468356.2468747

31. Tov, W., Diener, E.: Subjective wellbeing. In: Keith, K.D. (eds.) The Encyclopedia of Cross-Cultural Psychology, pp. 1239–1245. Wiley (2013). https://doi.org/10.1002/9781118339893. wbeccp518

32. Diener, E., Emmons, R.A.: The independence of positive and negative affect. J. Pers. Soc. Psychol. **47**(5), 1105 (1984). https://doi.org/10.1037/0022-3514.47.5.1105

33. Wolniewicz, C.A., Tiamiyu, M.F., Weeks, J.W., Elhai, J.D.: Problematic smartphone use and relations with negative affect, fear of missing out, and fear of negative and positive evaluation. Psychiatry Res. **262**, 618–623 (2018). https://doi.org/10.1016/j.psychres.2017.09.058

34. Horwood, S., Anglim, J.: Problematic smartphone usage and subjective and psychological well-being. Comput. Hum. Behav. **97**, 44–50 (2019). https://doi.org/10.1016/j.chb.2019. 02.028

35. Vanden Abeele, M., Beullens, K., Roe, K.: Measuring mobile phone use: gender, age and real usage level in relation to the accuracy and validity of self-reported mobile phone use. Mob. Media Commun. **1**(2), 213–236 (2013). https://doi.org/10.1177/2050157913477095

36. Lin, Y.-H., et al.: Time distortion associated with smartphone addiction: identifying smartphone addiction via a mobile application (App). J. Psychiatr. Res. **65**, 139–145 (2015). https:// doi.org/10.1016/j.jpsychires.2015.04.003

37. Sewall, C., Rosen, D., Bear, T.M.: Examining the accuracy of estimated smartphone use: How well-being and usage level predict discrepancies between estimated and actual use. PsyArXiv (2019). https://doi.org/10.31234/osf.io/3sju4

38. WHO.   https://www.euro.who.int/de/health-topics/health-emergencies/coronavirus-covid-19/statements/statement-two-years-on,-we-could-be-entering-a-new-phase-in-the-pan demic-with-plausible-hope-for-stabilization,-yet-too-early-to-drop-our-guard.   Accessed 11 Feb 2022

39. Ohlbrecht, H., Anacker, J., Jellen, J., Lange, B., Weihrauch, S.: Zu den Auswirkungen der Corona-Pandemie auf das subjektive Wohlbefinden und die Alltagsbewältigung: Ergebnisse einer Online-Befragung. Otto-von-Guericke-Universität, Magdeburg (2020), https://www.soz.ovgu.de/isoz_media/Mikrosoziologie/Working+Paper-p-1536.pdf. Accessed 11 Feb 2022

40. Wang, C., et al.: Immediate psychological responses and associated factors during the initial stage of the 2019 coronavirus disease (COVID-19) epidemic among the general population in China. Int. J. Environ. Res. Public Health **17**(5), 1729 (2020). https://doi.org/10.3390/ije rph17051729

41. Taren, A.A., et al.: Mindfulness meditation training and executive control network resting state functional connectivity: a randomized controlled trial. Psychosom. Med. **79**(6), 674–683 (2017). https://doi.org/10.1097/PSY.0000000000000466

42. Schultz, P.P., Ryan, R.M.: The "why," "what," and "how" of healthy self-regulation: mindfulness and well-being from a self-determination theory perspective. In: Ostafin, B.D., Robinson, M.D., Meier, B.P. (eds.) Handbook of Mindfulness and Self-Regulation, pp. 81–94. Springer, New York (2015). https://doi.org/10.1007/978-1-4939-2263-5_7

43. Lan, Y., et al.: A pilot study of a group mindfulness-based cognitive-behavioral intervention for smartphone addiction among university students. J. Behav. Addict. **7**(4), 1171–1176 (2018). https://doi.org/10.1556/2006.7.2018.103

44. Economides, M., Martman, J., Bell, M.J., Sanderson, B.: Improvements in stress, affect, and irritability following brief use of a mindfulness-based smartphone app: a randomized controlled trial. Mindfulness **9**(5), 1584–1593 (2018). https://doi.org/10.1007/s12671-018-0905-4

45. Howells, A., Ivtzan, I., Eiroa-Orosa, F.J.: putting the 'app' in happiness: a randomised controlled trial of a smartphone-based mindfulness intervention to enhance wellbeing. J. Happiness Stud. **17**(1), 163–185 (2014). https://doi.org/10.1007/s10902-014-9589-1

46. Schmuck, D.: Does digital detox work? Exploring the role of digital detox applications for problematic smartphone use and well-being of young adults using multigroup analysis. Cyberpsychol. Behav. Soc. Netw. **23**(8), 526–532 (2020). https://doi.org/10.1089/cyber.2019.0578

47. Carolus, A., Augustin, Y., Breitenbach, S.: Power of self-compassion – an analysis of the mediated effect of unhealthy social media use on subjective well-being. In: Proceedings of the 12th Media Psychology Conference (2021)

48. Vanden Abeele, M.M.P.: Digital wellbeing as a dynamic construct. Commun. Theory **31**(4), 932–955 (2021). https://doi.org/10.1093/ct/qtaa024

49. Anrijs, S., et al.: MobileDNA: relating physiological stress measurements to smartphone usage to assess the effect of a digital detox. In: Stephanidis, C. (ed.) HCI International 2018 Posters' Extended Abstracts. HCI 2018. CCIS vol. 851, pp. 356–363. Springer, Cham (2018). https://doi.org/10.1007/978-3-319-92279-948

50. Zimmermann, L.: "Your screen-time app is keeping track": consumers are happy to monitor but unlikely to reduce smartphone usage. J. Assoc. Consumer Res. **6**(3), 377–382 (2021)

51. Ko, M., et al.: NUGU. a group-based intervention app for improving self-regulation of limiting smartphone use. In: CSCW 2015: Proceedings of the 18th ACM Conference on Computer Supported Cooperative Work & Social Computing, pp. 1235–1245 (2015). https://doi.org/10.1145/2675133.2675244

52. Apple. https://support.apple.com/de-de/HT208982#:%7E:text=Mit%20Bildschirmzeit%20kannst%20du%20auf,was%20genau%20du%20verwalten%20m%C3%B6chtest. Accessed 11 Feb 2022

53. Android. https://www.android.com/intl/de_de/digital-wellbeing/. Accessed 11 Feb 2022

54. Bandura, A.: Social cognitive theory of self-regulation. Organ. Behav. Hum. Decis. Process. **50**(2), 248–287 (1991). https://doi.org/10.1016/0749-5978(91)90022-L

55. Festinger, L.: A Theory of Cognitive Dissonance. Stanford University Press, California (1957)

56. Fernandes, B., Biwas, U.N., Tan-Mansukhani, R., Vallejo, A., Essau, C.A.: The impact of COVID-19 lockdown on the internet use and escapism in adolescents. Revista de Psicología Clínica con Niños y Adolescentes 7(3), 59–65 (2020). https://doi.org/10.21134/rpcna.2020.mon.2056

57. Ohme, J., Vanden Abeele, M.M.P., Van Gaeveren, K., Durnez, W., De Marez, L.: Staying informed and bridging "social distance": smartphone news use and mobile messaging behaviors of flemish adults during the first weeks of the COVID-19 pandemic. Socius: Sociolo. Res. Dyn. World **6**, 1–14 (2020b). https://doi.org/10.1177/2378023120950190

58. Kahn, A.S., Ratan, R., Williams, D.: Why we distort in self-report: predictors of self-report errors in video game play. J. Comput.-Mediat. Commun. **19**, 1010–1023 (2014). https://doi.org/10.1111/jcc4.12056

59. Kobayashi, T., Boase, J.: No such effect? The implications of measurement error in self-report measures of mobile communication use. Commun. Methods Meas. **6**(2), 126–143 (2012). https://doi.org/10.1080/19312458.2012.679243
60. Ohme, J., Araujo, T., de Vreese, C.H., Piotrowski, J.T.: Mobile data donations: assessing self-report accuracy and sample biases with the iOS Screen Time function. Mob. Media Commun. **9**(2), 293–313 (2021). https://doi.org/10.1177/2050157920959106
61. Timotijevic, L., Barnett, J., Shepherd, R., Senior, V.: Factors influencing self-report of mobile phone use: the role of response prompt, time reference and mobile phone use in recall. Appl. Cogn. Psychol. **23**(5), 664–683 (2009). https://doi.org/10.1002/acp.1496
62. Michalak, J., Heidenreich, T., Ströhle, G., Nachtigall, C.: Die deutsche version der mindful attention and awareness scale (MAAS) Psychometrische Befunde zu einem Achtsamkeits-fragebogen. Z. Klin. Psychol. Psychother. **37**(3), 200–208 (2008). https://doi.org/10.1026/1616-3443.37.3.200
63. Berend, B., Vogt, D.: German translation of the Scale of Positive and Negative Experience (SPANE). http://labs.psychology.illinois.edu/~ediener/Documents/SPANE_German.pdf. Accessed 11 Feb 2022
64. Diener, E., et al.: New measures of well-being. In: Diener, E. (ed.) Assessing Well-Being. Social Indicators Research Series, vol. 39, pp. 247–266. Springer, Dordrecht (2009). https://doi.org/10.1007/978-90-481-2354-4_12
65. Montag, C., et al.: Recorded behavior as a valuable resource for diagnostics in mobile phone addiction: evidence from psychoinformatics. Behav. Sci. **5**(4), 434–442 (2015). https://doi.org/10.3390/bs5040434
66. Fullwood, C., Quinn, S., Kaye, L.K., Redding, C.: My virtual friends: a qualitative analysis of the attitudes and experiences of Smartphone users: implications for Smartphone attachment. Comput. Hum. Behav. **75**, 347–355 (2017). https://doi.org/10.1016/j.chb.2017.05.029
67. Berger, S., Wyss, A.M., Knoch, D.: Low self-control capacity is associated with immediate responses to smartphone signals. Comput. Hum. Behav. **86**, 45–51 (2018). https://doi.org/10.1016/j.chb.2018.04.031
68. Satici, S.A.: Psychological vulnerability, resilience, and subjective well-being: the mediating role of hope. Personality Individ. Differ. **102**, 68–73 (2016). https://doi.org/10.1016/j.paid.2016.06.057
69. Yıldırım, M., Çelik, T.F.: social support, resilience and subjective well-being in college students. J. Posit. Sch. Psychol. **5**(2), 127–135 (2021). https://doi.org/10.47602/jpsp.v5i2.229
70. Yildiz-Durak, H.: Investigation of nomophobia and smartphone addiction predictors among adolescents in Turkey: demographic variables and academic performance. Soc. Sci. J. **56**(4), 492–517 (2019). https://doi.org/10.1016/j.soscij.2018.09.003
71. Parent, N., Dadgar, K., Xiao, B., Hesse, C., Shapka, J.D.: Social disconnection during COVID-19: The role of attachment, fear of missing out, and smartphone use. J. Res. Adolesc. **31**(3), 748–763 (2021). https://doi.org/10.1111/jora.12658

Users' Satisfaction of Personality Types Integration in HCI

Kasthuri Subaramaniam[1,2(✉)] and Sellappan Palaniappan[2]

[1] Institute of Computer Science and Digital Innovation, UCSI University, Kuala Lumpur, Malaysia
kasthurisuba@ucsiuniversity.edu.my
[2] School of Information Technology, Malaysia University of Science and Technology (MUST), Petaling Jaya, Malaysia

Abstract. Humans can interact via the user interfaces is an information system. Traditional student-centered learning software often has a similar user interface via which the student can engage with the software, and the information is provided in a consistently identical manner to all users, regardless of personality type or learning style. The effectiveness of applications relies on the end user's acceptance. This study investigates the viability of incorporating human personality types in user interface designs in order to have systems that are more usable by all personality types of people. The primary research question concerns whether a user interface designed for a given personality type provides for better learning engagement. This study uses the Myers-Briggs Type Indicator to classify students' personality types, then links these personality types to specific user interface features to see if a user interface tailored to their learning preferences improves learning. The general concept of this study is that the experimental group is given a set of user interfaces tailored to their personality types. In the control group, participants are provided with a general user interface. A semi-structured interview was conducted, and the promising results show that the engagement and acceptance of the designed user interfaces for the respective human personality groups.

Keywords: Satisfaction · Themes · MBTI · User interface

1 Introduction

The goal of this study was to establish the relationship of students' personality type preferences as determined by the Myers-Briggs Type Indicator (MBTI) personality test with their accomplishment and contentment in a mobile-based learning environment. The approach to this problem is based on the idea that when students are actively engaged and satisfied, they are more likely to learn more effectively. The research question is that there is a relationship between students' MBTI personality types, user interface designs and online educational achievement and satisfaction. The findings of this study can be used to make recommendations for effective user interface designs for mobile-based learning by incorporating personality profiles. This study investigated the relationship between students' MBTI personality type, performance and satisfaction judgements for students registered in mobile-based learning.

Therefore, the simplification of the overall research question for this study is "Learning is affected by personality type" [13]. The primary research question concerns whether a user interface designed for a given personality type provides for better learning.

2 Background

The goal of human-computer interaction engineering is to design a user interface that is simple, effective and engaging in a way that yields the desired outcome. This means that to obtain the desired output, the minimal input is required from the operator and with that, the computer minimizes undesired outputs to the human being [3, 7].

The interface is the system from the user's point of view for a modern application with a graphical user interface (GUI). The interface is what the user sees and interacts with; anything which cannot be recognised as a part of the interface is less important for the user, provided it works [9]. The mismatch between a user's expectations and available computer user-interface styles is one of the key difficulties concerning a user's interaction with computers [25]. In addition, the dependency of society on computer-based systems continues to grow, as the systems that embrace humans, machines, and engineered systems themselves become ever more complex [1].

Misuse of colours and design elements, too many widgets, excessive learning time, unnecessary information, visual clutter, physical constraints of the context, to name a few, all contribute to the bad designs of interfaces [2, 11, 17]. Ben Shneiderman [20] states in the foreword of his classic book on user interface design that:

"Frustration and anxiety are part of daily life for many users of computerized information systems. They struggle to learn command language or menu section systems that are supposed to help them do their job. Some people encounter such serious cases of computer shock, terminal terror, or network neurosis that they avoid using computerized systems." [20].

The concerns raised by Shneiderman [20] are valid. Graphic user interfaces, windows, icons, and mouse selections have addressed many of the most severe interface issues [21]. The most important implication of information system design is that if people are going to utilize it, the system must suit their demands [24]. Users will either refuse to use the system (if they have a choice) or utilize it as little as possible if the system does not meet their demands [16]. Even in a "Windows world", many have come across user interfaces that are difficult to learn, to use, to understand, and in some cases, many are completely annoyed [14]. However, we must accept that someone put time and effort into creating each of these interfaces, and it is unlikely that the designer did it on purpose.

There is a lack of understanding of the value of user interfaces in the field of computer science and the complexities of designing powerful ones that appeal to all types of people. Many software developers do not view interfaces as part of the system and, worse, the user is rarely seen as part of it [14]. If serious steps are not taken, this situation can result in systems that are complicated to use. The indicators include human factors such as age, gender, ethnic groups etc. as well as personality types. It is best hoped that successful interface design would emerge by taking all these variables into account and result in desirable software applications for all levels of users.

Thus, an effective graphical user interface plays a very important role in developing and designing a mobile app [23]. This design research will establish a practical design solution to apply the 'theoretical achievements' of the technology and students' responses into the 'practical design process'.

The essence of these variables needs to be understood on how they affect HCI to compensate for individual differences in the design process for user interfaces of a mobile app. This, therefore, justifies the research of individual differences in HCI. In short, this research examines several facets of user interface design with the incorporation of human personality types on mobile app learning applications for students. According to Cardinali [4], Sarsam and Al-Samarraie [19] and Lima and Benitti [10], user interface designs in a computer system plays a very important role to allow a system to function effectively.

Personality dimensions change individuals' aesthetics factors and that affects the preferences provided. For example, a user who is not pleased with the system may not produce work as required as they may be demotivated by the system itself. In other words, individuals prefer interfaces that have a better "look and feel" than others, and their aesthetic choice is closely linked to their personality [19]. Therefore, by designing an interface based on user preferences and psychological variables, we can expect increased user satisfaction as well as more efficient interaction [2, 5, 8, 19, 22].

3 Methodology

3.1 Interview Protocol

Creswell and Creswell [6] have suggested that the primary instrument of the sample for data collection, analysis, and interpretation is the researcher for qualitative research. The researcher has completed the data collection technique through recorded interviews and the use of open-ended questions [18]. Each session of the interview lasted about 45 min. The investigation consisted of an in-depth qualitative interview process. The open-ended questions were considered acceptable since one subject was the focus of the study [18]. The collected information will remain confidential and maintained in a safe location. After three years from the completion date of the investigation, all related transcripts obtained from the analysis will be destroyed accordingly. Due to the assurance from the researcher and the understanding of the study, the participant felt more at ease when answering questions on their background. The research tool used has allowed participants to honestly react with more information.

The handwritten notes, typed notes, and videos were recorded during the interview process shared by the students. Each of the participants was labelled with a code to ensure confidentiality. This was a completely anonymous study: no personal information was collected, and it is not possible to link data back to any individuals.

The interview protocol was clarified before the interview process to ensure participants understood the procedure. This protocol was standardized for all participants. An interview protocol was used as an instrumentation technique for the usability of the learning application. This kind of interview facilitates the systematic collection of detailed data and simplifies comparability among the personality types of students.

The questions in this interview session have helped answer the formulated secondary research questions. Questions such as impressions on their "personalized" interfaces, the likes and dislikes on the design, and their recommendations to further improve the designed interfaces were framed to the research problem. In other words, the overall research question, *"In an electronic learning platform, do students with different personality types learn and gauge better when using a user interface designed to their personality preference?"* supported with the secondary questions in accommodating users' with their needs of personalized user interface design were reflected by the responses from the inquiry.

The first question made the participant feel relaxed and the participants were asked to talk about their backgrounds and understanding of the research. It included the learning materials that they have used on a learning platform before. The second question moved to the core of the research issue. Questions 3, 4, and 5 were framed towards the research questions on the experience and improvement of the visual user interface in adapting diversified personality traits to the needs of users. Question 6 provided an opportunity for the participant to reflect on the answers to preceding inquiries, as well as to give any final comments that added to the investigation's relevance. In a semi-structured interview, open-ended questions are the best method for a qualitative investigation to collect rich and contextual data [18]. The six open-ended enquiry questions are as follows:

1. Please describe your background. How do you feel being a part of a participant in this study? Do you use any learning platforms for e-learning? Do you have any comments to make on the learning platforms that you have used before?
2. Do you think a "personalized user interface" learning platform will be a better option to be provided to students? In other words, should the opportunity be given to students to have an individualized visual user interface based on their personality type?
3. Do you know your personality type? How was your experience in using the personalised user interface a moment ago?
4. Did you enjoy learning using the personalised platform? Was the user interface design usable to your learning style?
5. Did you spend more time adapting to the features of the interface design? Would you spend more time on the learning materials, since now it accommodates to your liking?
6. How can the user interface(s) be improved if you have any suggestions? Any additional knowledge and experiences you might have to offer that can add value to the inquiry can be addressed here.

3.2 Data Collection

The researcher has used the main research question in performing the method of data collection. The research objective has been determined in exploring students with different personality types who learn and gauge better when using a user interface designed to their personality preference. The semi-structured and open-ended questions were the data collection method. This has provided reliable data for the qualitative method.

The focus of the semi-structured interviews was on participants of specific personality types for the personalized user interface design. The questions for the interview were created and included in the procedure for the interview. The form of the interview process indicated and documented the name, date and time of the interview and the intent of the qualitative investigation of the researcher [6]. The standardised protocol was applied throughout the data recording. The six questions of the interview were included in the interview procedure. A fair pause between each question has made it possible for respondents to collect ideas before answering [6, 18].

The first interview question was to establish relationships with participants followed by the remaining questions to address the research questions. The five interview questions consisted of the primary, probing, and follow-up questions. The probing questions were raised to address more clarification on the subject such as learning experience and gauging of learning materials. The last question aimed to encourage participants in giving suggestions to better improve the user interface designs. The method of the interview involved careful observation and encouraging participants to discuss additional common experiences important to the research issue. The researcher interviewed participants using the video recording method. All the participants agreed on the video-recorded interviews.

Interview schedules were set via phone calls and emails. Following initial contact with the participants, the researcher provided the participants with informed consent. The interview process followed the basic rules of the interview procedure. The researcher performed a pilot study by interviewing four individuals who fulfilled the study's selection criteria. The purpose of the pilot study is to assess the adequacy of the questions and to evaluate whether the research is feasible [12]. Majid et al. [12] argued that the reliability of the interview protocol and the data collection process could be acquired by a pilot study.

The following procedures were applied for each interview: (a) the establishment of a good relationship with the subject, (b) the introduction of study questions, goal, intent and limitations, (c) the execution and receipt of the informed consent form, (d) the use of the interview protocol, (e) the questioning technique used to elicit information and, if possible, to elaborate the question, and (f) thanking the participant for the time and effort with a small token of appreciation.

The choice of participants was made on a selection basis meaning the participants were comprised of three different groups of personality types. The audio-visual recordings were also useful for analyzing the usability of the user interfaces. Once the experiments and the interviews commenced (i.e. after the interfaces were designed), no re-adjustment of the user interfaces was made as that would have required additional students of a specific personality type to be found. However, these data do help in setting a direction for future work.

The collected data was securely maintained by the researcher in a protected location with a password. After three years, all documents will be disposed of accordingly which will include notes, interview transcripts and other materials related to the research [6].

4   Results and Findings

The interviews with the participants were conducted after the consent forms were acknowledged and signed. Participants were assigned labels such as S-1, S-2, S-3, etc. Table 1 displays the demography of each participant. The leading questions for this research study were inquired as provided in Sect. 3.1. The inquiry was about the students' learning and engagement in a learning platform that was designed based on their personality types. Follow-on questions were applied in the interviews as needed. Participants' responses are used to identify and categorise recommendations for improving the user interface for the different personality types of students in future. The objective of the study is to determine and understand that in an electronic learning platform, students with different personality types learn and gauge better when user interfaces are designed to their personality preference.

Table 1. Demographics of participants for the SUS instrument and interviews

Students	Group (experimental/control)	Age groups (15–18, 19–25, 26–30, 31–34)	Gender	Personality type
S-1	Experimental	19–25	F	ESTJ
S-2	Experimental	19–25	F	ESTJ
S-3	Experimental	26–30	M	ESTJ
S-4	Experimental	15–18	F	ESTJ
S-5	Experimental	19–25	M	ESTJ
S-6	Experimental	19–25	M	ISFJ
S-7	Experimental	26–30	M	ISFJ
S-8	Experimental	19–25	F	ISFJ
S-9	Experimental	15–18	M	ISFJ
S-10	Experimental	19–25	F	ISFJ
S-11	Experimental	31–34	M	INFJ
S-12	Experimental	19–25	F	INFJ
S-13	Experimental	19–25	M	INFJ
S-14	Experimental	26–30	F	INFJ
S-15	Experimental	19–25	F	INFJ
S-16	Control	26–30	F	Unknown
S-17	Control	19–25	F	Unknown
S-18	Control	19–25	M	Unknown
S-19	Control	31–34	M	Unknown
S-20	Control	19–25	M	Unknown

The open-ended and follow-up questions were employed for the recorded interviews. The data analysis in this part was collected from recorded video interviews. The interviews were conducted with 20 participants comprising of 5 participants each with ESTJ, ISFJ, INFJ and unknown types, respectively. The researcher ensured the effectiveness of standardized study which included the collection and storing of the consent forms safely from all participants. A semi-structured interview was used to collect information. In order to achieve data saturation, a qualitative query analysis was performed numerous times. The rules and regulations of the interview was explained to the interviewees prior to the interview sessions. The inquiry is about engagement and performing better when user interfaces are designed to their respective personality types. Each participant was allocated 45 min of the interview sessions. All the participants were told to share their true feelings and experiences in using the personalised user interface designed apps.

The questions in this interview session have helped answer the formulated secondary research questions. Questions such as impressions on their "personalized" interfaces, the likes and dislikes on the design, and their recommendations to further improve the designed interfaces were framed to the research problem. In other words, the overall research question, "In an electronic learning platform, do students with different personality types learn and gauge better when using a user interface designed to their personality preference?" supported with the secondary questions in accommodating users' with their needs of personalized user interface design were reflected by the responses from the investigation.

The first question made the participant feel relaxed and the participants were asked to talk about their backgrounds and understanding of the research. It included the learning materials that they have used on a learning platform before. The second question moved to the core of the research issue. Questions 3, 4, and 5 were framed towards the secondary research questions on the experience and improvement of the visual user interface in adapting diversified personality traits to the needs of users. Question 6 provided an opportunity for the participant to reflect on the answers to preceding questions and to share concluding thoughts which added value to the investigation. The use of open-ended questions in a semi-structured interview was the best method for a qualitative investigation to collect rich and contextual data [18]. The six detailed open-ended enquiry questions are described next.

The first interview question was about the background of participants. This was to establish rapport with them. Questions about the feeling of being a part of this study, learning platforms used, and the experience of using those platforms, if any, were inquired. The second question was based on the participant's opinion on whether the "personalized user interface" learning platform should be provided to students based on their personality types. The third question is about their personality types which follow the experience in using the personalised user interface app. The fourth question was about the acceptance of using the app and finding out whether the user interface design was usable to the participant's learning style. The fifth question was about spending the amount of time adapting to the features of the interface design since it accommodates the participant's liking. The last question of the interview session encouraged participants to provide extra information and experience that could help the exploratory inquiry. The six open-ended enquiry questions are categorised as themes and the findings are explained in the following sections.

Theme 1: Background and Experience. All participants interviewed were students from different higher learning institutions and the 20 participants interviewed agreed to be a part of the study. The demographics of the participants including their personality types are shared in Table 1. All participants have used some form of e-learning platform which is known as Learning Management System (LMS) from their institutions as their study materials were uploaded there. Participants S2, S3, S4, S7, S8, S9, S11, S12, S14, S17, S19, and S20 have indicated that these learning platforms need to be revamped as the information presented for their learning purpose is cluttered and does not give a sense of engagement. Moreover, participants S2, S3, S7, S11, S14, S19 and S20 added that the presentation of the materials was very "dull" and does not interest them to use those study materials. The term "dull" was used to refer to the visual cue elements. The participants S1, S5, S6, S10, S13, S15, S16, and S18 had some reservations about commenting on their learning platforms. Therefore, follow-on questions were inquired to make them more comfortable and questions about what they liked most on the learning platforms were asked. These participants mentioned that they were happy that there were such systems whereby students can engage and use materials that supported their studies at the higher learning institutions. However, they disclosed that the layout of the materials was not appealing for them to use.

Theme 2: Learning Platform and Interface Elements. Every participant unanimously agreed that a "personalized user interface" learning platform will be a better option. They preferred if their study materials were individualized based on their personality types for them to engage more and draw their interest to studying those materials uploaded by their respective instructors. The participants indicated that visual elements such as fonts, colours and layout are essential on the learning platform. With these elements incorporated, the participants would learn better, and they will be able to retain their study materials better.

Theme 3: Personality Types and Personalised User Interface App. Participants S1 to S15 were not aware of their personality types until they took the Jung Typology Test. Participants S1 to S15 fell under the experimental group as they were given the task to experience the use of the personalised user interface app based on their respective personality types. Participants S1–S5 of ESTJ, participants S6–S10 of ISFJ, and participants S11–S15 of INFJ indicated that the personalised user interface app had met beyond their expectations. Participants S16-S20 of the unknown personality types did not find uniqueness in the app as the app was just a regular app that they used. However, this control group unanimously argued that user interface elements could be improved in terms of colours, fonts, layout, and navigational aspects. According to participant S19, "I can still use the app, the design is nothing to fancy about and the app did not meet my expectation." Participant S20 indicated that the visual user interface elements should complement one another such as the dark background of the screen should go well with the icons and fonts.

Theme 4: Learning and Usability. All the participants in the experimental group enjoyed using the personalised mobile learning app. The participants found the personalised app usable, and they had a good time learning the specific topic with much ease. The app also stimulated their interest in that topic. In the control group, the participants did not find any difference from the regular apps. The app accommodated diversified users and not individualized needs. The expectation of participants, S-16, S17 and S20 quoted that simplicity in design is the best approach. They mentioned that they do not want the app to be complex but reiterated that simplicity of presentation is always the best but unfortunately, that has always not been the case!

Theme 5: Time Spent and Adaptation. Participants S1–S20 took some time looking into the features incorporated on the app as that was the first time they had been introduced to the personalised app. However, upon looking into the app, participants S1–S15 took an average of 2 min to get on with the app and they could use the app with ease. Meanwhile, participants S16–S20 took an average of 4 min and had a little difficulty adapting to the app. Representatives of each experimental group, S4, S6 and S11 participants quoted:

"…The layout matched my liking. I loved the colours used on the notes' pages. The colours used were not an eyesore and I would spend more time on the learning materials than I used to – and definitely with the materials that they have now, I can retain what I have studied in class!"

The control group participants S16 and S18 respectively quoted:

"…The app has no difference from the ones that I am currently using. Not much to say about the features as they are just the regular ones that I use every day. I would just download the materials or read them when the need arises."

Theme 6: Improvement and Suggestion. Sharing of real-life experiences and more profound insights influenced the question of improvement and suggestion positively. The analysis presented recommendations for individualizing visual user interfaces from participants. Three participants from each personality group. S3, S9, and S13 quoted:

"…Simplicity is what we are looking for. We want something to be very easy to understand and very easy to use. The layout of the materials should be presented logically apart from the colours and fonts used. Understandably, a lot of user interface designers use universal icons, which helps because that will avoid language barriers. We would prefer if user interface designers paid more attention to the different groups of people such as personality types to consider designing to our preferences. The functionality always comes first, and designers are trying to deliver that at the simplest way, but we hope that the specialized or the personalised interface designs can be catered to our needs."

Two participants S16 and S17 from the unknown personality type quoted:

"We are on one commonly designed platform so why the fuss of making the app to several different designs to accommodate diversified users. On the other hand, we strive for simplicity and making it universal will have everyone use the same app. But on the grounds of learning materials, it will be best that the adoption of personality types is investigated – this is to ensure that students learn best with the individualized designed app. However, the only factor would be the additional cost involved in the different designs."

5 Conclusions and Recommendations

Users who had interfaces that matched their personality type generally expressed satisfaction with their interfaces and claimed that they would use them for additional topics if they become available. Many participants in the experimental group suggested ways to improve the interfaces. Surprisingly, those suggestions were largely in the usability category. Participants in the control group, on the other hand, commented:

"...more colours required...," "...include mind-mapping and animations...," "...it's unclear..., it has to be step-by-step...," "...confusing...," and "...too abstract...."

Many of the participants were in total agreement with having a good strategy in designing user interfaces based on personality types. Based on the participants of S1–S20 quotations on diversified people:

"... users of today are different from users of yesterday or 10–20 years ago. Therefore, a strategy must be adopted to accommodate the user interface elements that include icon, images, drop-down menus, layout, space arrangement, and features in a personalized designed app."

Participants agree with utilizing a simple layout and appropriate features provided the elements of personality traits are incorporated. Simplicity is positively associated with perceived ease of use and the user's intent to use [15]. Participation of users through feedback, studies, and questionnaires will give vital information and a deeper understanding of users' preferences and functional features. Participants S2, S4, S7, S9, S11, S13, S14 and S15 quoted:

"... to develop a user-centred interface design, it will require a reverse-engineering strategy by starting from the end users' needs. Requirements need to be gathered such as personality types and user interface elements need to be sorted out from the end-users so that grouping can be done accordingly to the respective personality groups. In other words, it is almost like reverse engineering from the end-user and the tasks to be done."

The analysis revealed the requirements of a personalised mobile learning app. The analysis and recorded responses exposed the familiarity, real-life experience, and honest feelings of participants about the app. Overall, the participants highlighted the necessity for a personalized app as well as changes in the mindset of users and improvements in the user interface elements. Participants noted that a truly innovative approach must be incorporated in the development. Therefore, users' preferences, demands, technological competence, flexibility in users' controls, and accommodation of diverse user groups including the personality types need to be addressed. To produce enhanced apps, an increase in users' engagement is required before designing the apps. This is to ensure that the apps are simple, with high functionality and personalized to the different personality types of users.

The respondents in the study shared similar ideas on how user interface designers may produce products that are flexible in configuration based on user's preferences and needs to accommodate a wide range of users. Exclusive features and an easy-to-navigate interface are required for unique users. The results from the data analysis revealed the real-world experience of utilising the personalised mobile learning app. The simplicity and individualization of the app's user interface are the commonalities in enhancing the designs based on the participants' direct quotations. The outcomes of the study will lead to the development of assessment methodologies and procedures for better-designed user interfaces in the future.

References

1. Jalil, A.B., Kolandaisamy, R., Subaramaniam, K., Kolandaisamy, I., Khang, J.Q.G.: Designing a mobile application to improve user's productivity on computer-based productivity software. J. Adv. Res. Dyn. Control Syst. **12**(03), 226–236. (2020). https://doi.org/10.5373/JARDCS/V12SP3/20201257. Special Issue
2. Alves, T., Natálio, J., Henriques-Calado, J., Gama, S.: Incorporating personality in user interface design: a review. Pers. Individ. Differ. **155**, 109709 (2020)
3. Bennett, S., McRobb, S., Farmer, R.: Object-Oriented Systems Analysis and Design Using UML. McGraw Hill Higher Education, New York (2005)
4. Cardinali, R.: Productivity improvements through the use of graphic user interfaces. Industrial Management & Data Systems (1994)
5. Condenço, J., Gama, S., Gonçalves, D.: ColorCode: exploring social and psychological dimensions of color. MSc dissertation. Universidade de Lisboa - Instituto Superior Técnico, Lisbon (2018)
6. Creswell, J.W., Creswell, J.D.: Research Design: Qualitative, Quantitative, and Mixed Methods Approaches, 5th edn. Sage Publications, Thousand Oaks (2018)
7. Jylhä, H., Hamari, J.: Development of measurement instrument for visual qualities of graphical user interface elements (VISQUAL): a test in the context of mobile game icons. User Model. User-Adap. Inter. **30**(5), 949–982 (2020). https://doi.org/10.1007/s11257-020-09263-7
8. Kim, J., Lee, A., Ryu, H.: Personality and its effects on learning performance: design guidelines for an adaptive e-learning system based on a user model. Int. J. Ind. Ergon. **43**(5), 450–461 (2013)
9. Kirkpatrick, G.: Critical Technology: A Social Theory of Personal Computing. Routledge, New York (2017)
10. Lima, A.L.D.S., Benitti, F.B.V.: UsabilityZero: can a bad user experience teach well? Inform. Educ. **20**(1), 69–84 (2021)
11. Liu, Y., Zhang, Q.: Interface design aesthetics of interaction design. In: Marcus, A., Wang, W. (eds.) HCII 2019. LNCS, vol. 11583, pp. 279–290. Springer, Cham (2019). https://doi.org/10.1007/978-3-030-23570-3_21
12. Majid, M.A.A., Othman, M., Mohamad, S.F., Lim, S.A.H., Yusof, A.: Piloting for interviews in qualitative research: operationalization and lessons learnt. Int. J. Acad. Res. Bus. Soc. Sci. **7**(4), 1073–1080 (2017)

13. Myers, I.B., Myers, P.B.: Gifts Differing – Understanding Personality Type, pp. 139–147. Davies-Black Publishing, Palo Alto (1995)
14. Oulasvirta, A.: User interface design with combinatorial optimization. Computer **50**(1), 40–47 (2017)
15. Ozturk, A.B., Bilgihan, A., Nusair, K., Okumus, F.: What keeps the mobile hotel booking users loyal? Investigating the roles of self-efficacy, compatibility, perceived ease of use, and perceived convenience. Int. J. Inf. Manage. **36**(6), 1350–1359 (2016)
16. Pearlson, K.E., Saunders, C.S., Galletta, D.F.: Managing and Using Information Systems: A Strategic Approach. Wiley, New York (2019)
17. Reinecke, K., Bernstein, A.: Knowing what a user likes: a design science approach to interfaces that automatically adapt to culture. Mis Q. **37**, 427–453 (2013)
18. Rubin, H.J., Rubin, I.S.: Qualitative Interviewing: The Art of Hearing Data. Sage Publications, London (2011)
19. Sarsam, S.M., Al-Samarraie, H.: Towards incorporating personality into the design of an interface: a method for facilitating users' interaction with the display. User Model. User-Adap. Inter. **28**(1), 75–96 (2018). https://doi.org/10.1007/s11257-018-9201-1
20. Shneiderman, B.: Future directions for human-computer interaction. Int. J. Hum.-Comput. Interact. **2**(1), 73–90 (1990)
21. Shneiderman, B., Plaisant, C., Cohen, M., Jacobs, S., Elmqvist, N., Diakopoulos, N.: Designing the User Interface: Strategies for Effective Human-Computer Interaction. Pearson, London (2016)
22. Su, K.W., Chen, C.J., Shue, L.Y.: Implication of cognitive style in designing computer-based procedure interface. Hum. Fact. Ergon. Manuf. Serv. Ind. **23**(3), 230–242 (2013)
23. Subaramaniam, K., Ern-Rong, J.L., Palaniappan, S.: Interface designs with MBTI personality types. In: Proceedings of Mechanical Engineering Research Day, 2020, Melaka, Malaysia, 16 December 2020, pp. 178–179 (2020)
24. Subaramaniam, K., Ern-Rong, J.L., Palaniappan, S.: Interface design with personality types: an effective e-learning experience. Evergreen – Joint Journal of Novel Carbon Resources Sciences & Green Asian Strategy (2021)
25. Subaramaniam, K., Palaniappan, S.: Learners' perception on integration of human personality types on mobile learning platform. In: Salvendy, G., Wei, J. (eds.) HCII 2021. LNCS, vol. 12796, pp. 329–343. Springer, Cham (2021). https://doi.org/10.1007/978-3-030-77025-9_27

The Security and Privacy Protection Framework for Wearable Devices

Youxiang Cui[1], Zhongwei Gu[1(✉)], Lei Sun[1,2], Haibo Tang[1], and Lumeng Cui[2]

[1] Department of Quality Management Engineering, Business School, Shanghai Dianji University, No. 300 Shuihua Road, Pudong District, Lingang New City, Shanghai 201306, China
Cuiyouxiang@aliyun.com, 21390138@qq.com
[2] Integrated Management Center in Zhigou Town, Zhucheng 262202, Shandong, China

Abstract. Although wearable devices have high potential in the emerging scenarios, these scenarios face many security and privacy challenges. It is because of the inherent openness of wearable devices limitation of the network, terminal resource and the technology. This brings a lot of obstacles to design of security and privacy protection solutions in wearable device and network. However traditional security and privacy protection method do not fit in these emerging scenarios. Security and privacy issues have gradually become a huge challenge for emerging wearable device applications. Therefore, the design of application security and privacy protection scheme of wearable devices has been widely concerned and focused by academia and industry.

Keywords: Wearable device · Security and privacy protection · PII · ISO27701 · GDPR

1 Introduction

With the development of information technology, the development of wearable devices is also undergoing profound changes. The future wearable device is not only a communication media, but also supports various vertical industries, such as mobile payment, mobile social networking, smart transportation and smart medical treatment, so as to realize the in-depth integration of the physical world and information technology. Therefore, users' wearable devices carry a lot of privacy information, such as identity information, bank account information, medical and health information, location information and mobile track information, which makes users' demand for privacy protection in wearable devices more prominent.

This paper systematically studies the key technologies of user privacy protection in wearable devices by analyzing the threat of privacy disclosure faced by users' wearable devices. Through the above research, not only can effectively protect the user's personal privacy information, meet the needs of users in daily life, also product polar driving the wearable equipment industry and application service of health to flourish, to realize the grand strategy "Internet+", to protect personal privacy, had a profound influence on social harmony and stability.

G. Salvendy and J. Wei (Eds.): HCII 2022, LNCS 13337, pp. 203–210, 2022.
https://doi.org/10.1007/978-3-031-05014-5_16

2 Literature Review

Personal data, also known as personal information or personally identifiable information (PII) [1–3] is any information relating to an identifiable person.

Personal data is defined under the GDPR as "any information relating to an identified or identifiable natural person ('data subject'); an identifiable natural person is one who can be identified, directly or indirectly, in particular by reference to an identifier such as a name, an identification number, location data, an online identifier or to one or more factors specific to the physical, physiological, genetic, mental, economic, cultural or social identity of that natural person" [4, 5].

PII has become prevalent as information technology and the wearable devices have made it easier to collect PII leading to a profitable market in collecting and reselling PII. PII can also be exploited by criminals to cheat or steal the identity of a person, or to aid in the planning of criminal acts [6]. PII leakage becomes the main means of telecom fraud. As a response to these threats, many privacy policies specifically address the gathering of PII.

2.1 ISO/IEC 27701: Security Techniques—Extension to ISO/IEC 27001 and ISO/IEC 27002 for Privacy Information Management—Requirements and Guidelines

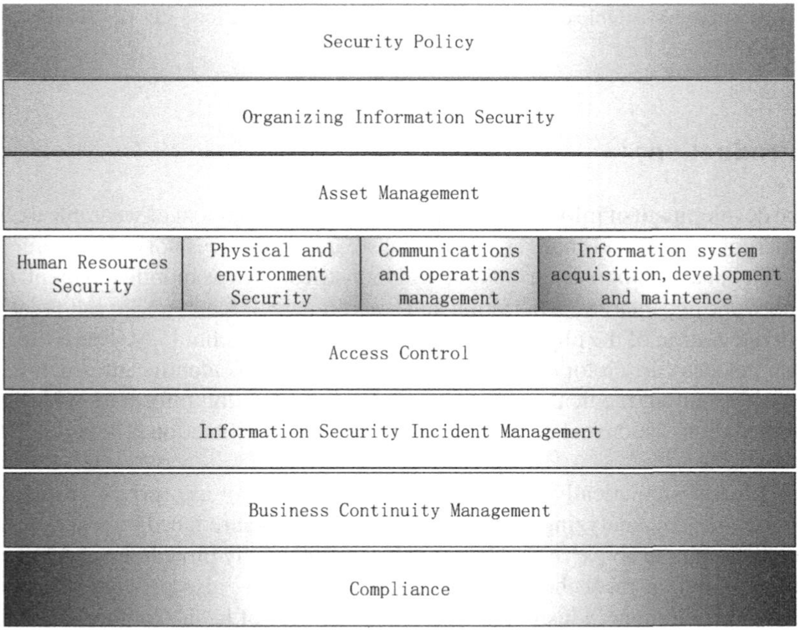

| Security Policy |
| Organizing Information Security |
| Asset Management |

| Human Resources Security | Physical and environment Security | Communications and operations management | Information system acquisition, development and maintence |

| Access Control |
| Information Security Incident Management |
| Business Continuity Management |
| Compliance |

Fig. 1. Framework of ISO27001

ISO/IEC 27001 is an international standard on how to manage information security, as shown in Fig. 1. ISO/IEC 27001 is widely known, providing requirements for an information security management system (ISMS), though there are more than a dozen standards in the ISO/IEC 27000 family. Using them enables organizations of any kind to manage the security of assets such as financial information, intellectual property, employee details or information entrusted by third parties.

ISO 27701 is a privacy extension to ISO/IEC 27001 that establishes additional requirements and provides guidance for the protection of privacy as potentially affected by various personal data processing. With a variety of privacy and security regulations increases, so do the calls for new ways for these two teams to collaborate, communicate more effectively, and use common tools. Technology is needed for the maintenance and continual improvement of a privacy information management system (PIMS) in accordance with ISO 27701, as shown in Fig. 2 (formerly known as "ISO 27552"), as well as the planning and implementation of global privacy laws and frameworks.

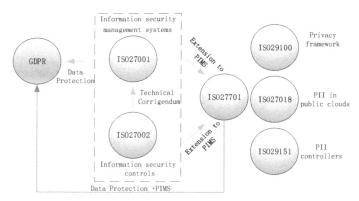

Fig. 2. Framework of ISO27001

2.2 General Data Protection Regulations (GDPR)

Under the GDPR, data controllers and processors must implement "appropriate technical and organizational measures" to protect and ensure the privacy of the personal data they process.

Since the implementation of the EU General Data Protection Regulation ("GDPR") and similar legislation on personal data protection, enterprises must now provide adequate protection for their customers' personal data. Many enterprises use automated personally identifiable information ("PII") scanning systems to process PII to ensure full compliance with the law. However, personal data saved in non-electronic form cannot be detected by these automated scanning systems, resulting in PII not being able to be accurately identified [4].

The information provided by the wearable device's users may include their private and confidential information. In light of the EU GDPR and the legislation on personal data protection, enterprises will be at risk of law violation if they do not have adequate information management infrastructure.

Principles relating to processing of personal data is shown in Fig. 3.

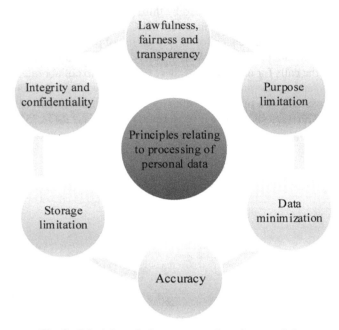

Fig. 3. Principles relating to processing of personal data

Personal data shall be:

1. Lawfulness, fairness and transparency: processed lawfully, fairly and in a transparent manner in relation to the data subject;
2. Purpose limitation: collected for specified, explicit and legitimate purposes and not further processed in a manner that is incompatible with those purposes; further processing for archiving purposes in the public interest, scientific or historical research purposes or statistical purposes shall, in accordance with Article 89(1), not be considered to be incompatible with the initial purposes;
3. Data minimization: adequate, relevant and limited to what is necessary in relation to the purposes for which they are processed;
4. Accuracy: accurate and, where necessary, kept up to date; every reasonable step must be taken to ensure that personal data that are inaccurate, having regard to the purposes for which they are processed, are erased or rectified without delay;
5. Storage limitation: kept in a form which permits identification of data subjects for no longer than is necessary for the purposes for which the personal data are processed; personal data may be stored for longer periods insofar as the personal data

will be processed solely for archiving purposes in the public interest, scientific or historical research purposes or statistical purposes in accordance with subject to implementation of the appropriate technical and organizational measures required by this Regulation in order to safeguard the rights and freedoms of the data subject;

6. Integrity and confidentiality: processed in a manner that ensures appropriate security of the personal data, including protection against unauthorized or unlawful processing and against accidental loss, destruction or damage, using appropriate technical or organizational measures.

3 Design of Security and Privacy Protection Framework of Wearable Devices

The possibilities and limits of wearable devices technology play an increasingly important role in our personal everyday lives and in our societies. The extent to which humans can enjoy their fundamental rights depends not only on legal and safety frameworks and social norms, but also on the features of the wearable devices' technology at their disposal. Recent discoveries of inappropriate use of personal data created by wearable devices have driven the public debate on data protection to an unprecedented level. It is necessary that the shaping and the use of wearable devices technology takes account of the need to respect the rights of individuals.

"Privacy by Design" and "Privacy by Default" have been frequently-discussed topics related to data protection. The principle "Privacy by Design" which is in the General Data Protection Regulation, that the current approach in the data protection guidelines, which requires persons responsible already to include definitions of the means for processing technical and organizational measures (TOM). TOMs must be taken already at the time of planning a processing system to protect data safety.

Many efforts in standardization have been ongoing to integrate privacy requirements in system design in different standardization organizations and initiatives [7]. The most popular methods are often take existing approaches to IT security risk management as a model to extend and modify them to privacy risk management such as the ISO has issued standards for a privacy framework (ISO/IEC 29100) and a privacy architecture (ISO IEC 29101) related to PII within an information and communication technology environment, as shown in Fig. 4. Their work includes the extension of the standards ISO/IEC 27001 and 27002 on management of information security to privacy management.

Design of security and privacy goals is more than IT security and based on six protection goals.

1. PII confidentiality: ensures the protection against unauthorized and unlawful processing.
2. PII integrity: ensures that data remain intact, complete, and up-to-date.
3. PII availability: ensures that the data are available and usable in the intended process.
4. PII unlinkability: ensures that data are processed and analysed only for the purpose for which they were collected.
5. PII intervenability: provides the possibility for the data subjects to exercise their rights

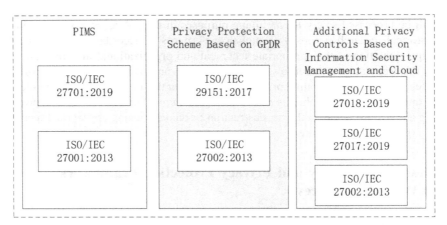

Fig. 4. Integrate privacy requirements in system design

6. PII transparency: is necessary for the monitoring and control of the data processing. Transparency ensures that data subjects and supervisory authorities can identify deficiencies and, if necessary, demand appropriate procedural changes.

4 Discussion and Conclusions

Rapid wearable devices technological developments and globalization have brought new challenges for the protection of personal data produced by wearable devices. The scale of the collection and sharing of personal wearable devices data has increased significantly. Technology allows both private companies and public authorities to make use of personal wearable devices data on an unprecedented scale in order to pursue their activities. there are significant risks to the protection of natural persons, in particular with regard to online activity.

Those developments and challenges require a strong and more coherent wearable devices data protection framework, backed by strong enforcement, given the importance of creating the trust that will allow the digital economy to develop across the market. Natural persons should have control of their own personal wearable devices data. Legal and practical certainty for natural persons, economic operators and public authorities should be enhanced.

In order to prevent creating a serious risk of circumvention, the protection of natural persons information should be technologically neutral and should not depend on the techniques used in wearable devices. The protection of natural persons should apply to the processing of personal wearable devices data by automated means, as well as to manual processing, if the personal data are contained or are intended to be contained in a filing system.

The protection of natural persons created by wearable devices with regard to the processing of personal data by competent authorities for the purposes of the prevention, investigation, detection or prosecution of criminal offences or the execution of criminal penalties, including the safeguarding against and the prevention of threats to public security and the free movement of such data, is the potentially urgent subject of a specific legal act in China.

Wearable devices data processing shall be lawful only if and to the extent that at least one of the following applies:

1. the wearable devices data subject has given consent to the processing of his or her personal data created by wearable devices for one or more specific purposes;
2. Wearable devices data processing is necessary for the performance of a contract to which the data subject is party or in order to take steps at the request of the data subject prior to entering into a contract;
3. Wearable devices data processing is necessary for compliance with a legal obligation to which the controller is subject;
4. Wearable devices data processing is necessary in order to protect the vital interests of the data subject or of another natural person;
5. Wearable devices data processing is necessary for the performance of a task carried out in the public interest or in the exercise of official authority vested in the controller;
6. Wearable devices data processing is necessary for the purposes of the legitimate interests pursued by the controller or by a third party, except where such interests are overridden by the interests or fundamental rights and freedoms of the data created by wearable devices data subject which require protection of personal data, in particular where the data subject is a child.

References

1. Management of Data Breaches Involving Sensitive Personal Information (SPI). Va.gov. Washington, DC: Department OF Veterans Affairs. 6 January 2012. Archived from the original on 26 May 2015. Accessed 25 May 2015
2. Stevens, G.: Data Security Breach Notification Laws (PDF), 10 April 2012. fas.org. Accessed 8 June 2017
3. Greene, S.S.: Security Program and Policies: Principles and Practices, p. 349. Pearson IT Certification, Indianapolis, IN, US (2014). ISBN 978-0-7897-5167-6. OCLC 897789345
4. Personal Data. General Data Protection Regulation (GDPR). Retrieved 23 October 2020
5. Personal Data. https://gdpr-info.eu/art-4-gdpr/
6. Nokhbeh, R.: A study of web privacy policies across industries. J. Inf. Priv. Secur. 13, 169–185 (2017)
7. See a list (non exhaustive) of privacy related standardization initiatives in IPEN wiki: https://ipen.trialog.com/wiki/Wiki_for_Privacy_Standards#Privacy_Standards
8. Jasmontaite, L., Kamara, I., Zanfir-Fortuna, G., Leucci, S.: Implementation of Data Protection by Design and by Default: Framing guiding principles into applicable rules. EDPL, vol. 4 (2018). forthcoming
9. Data protection authorities and their organisations (WP29, EDPB) will provide appropriate guidance on implementation of the GDPR provisions
10. Kranzberg, M.: Technology and history: "Kranzberg's Laws." Technol. Cult. 27(3), 544–560 (1986)
11. Rannenberg, K.: ISO/IEC standardization of identity management and privacy technologies. Datenschutz und Datensicherheit - DuD 35(1), 27–29 (2011). https://doi.org/10.1007/s11623-011-0008-z

12. Lee, S., Kim, J., Shon, T.: User privacy-enhanced security architecture for home area network of Smartgrid. Multimedia Tools Appl. **75**(20), 12749–12764 (2016). https://doi.org/10.1007/s11042-016-3252-2

13. Iversen, E.J., Vedel, T., Werle, R.: Standardization and the democratic design of information and communication technology. Knowl. Technol. Pol. **17**, 104–126 (2004). https://doi.org/10.1007/s12130-004-1027-y

14. Fal', O.M.: Standardization in information technology security. Cybern. Syst. Anal. **53**(1), 78–82 (2017). https://doi.org/10.1007/s10559-017-9908-8

15. see: https://www.rug.nl/research/research-data-management/data_protection-gdpr/data-protection-impact-assessment/protection-goals

16. see: https://www.iso.org/isoiec-27001-information-security.html

17. ISO/IEC 27001 International Information Security Standard published. bsigroup.com. BSI. Accessed 21 2020

The Integrated Model Based on Big Data for Wearable Service Quality Trust

Zhongwei Gu[1], Hongwei Ma[1(✉)], and Xiao Liu[2]

[1] Shanghai Dianji University, Pudong, Shanghai, China
Weihong1616@sina.com
[2] Xiamen University of Technology, Xiamen, Fujian, China
xliu@xmut.edu.cn

Abstract. The traditional trust adoption problem data comes from the question-naire survey. The accuracy and objectivity are not high, and the practical applica-tion value is limited. The output of the research is usually the subjective factors affecting trust, and the deep reasons for low user trust are not deeply explored. This study aims to propose a new set of consumer wearable service quality trust integration model based on big data, deeply integrate the two different research fields of big data mining and trust adoption, and quantitatively describe how wear-able service quality characteristics, privacy environment, business characteristics, personality characteristics and other factors affect consumers' trust and adoption of wearable services.

Keywords: Wearable services · Quality trust integration · Big data

1 Introduction

Previous studies on trust adoption mostly used literature research to collect influencing factors, questionnaire survey to collect empirical data, and structural equation to test the hypothesis of the model. Although these methods are mature, they often have unstable data quality, high subjectivity, insufficient quantitative analysis and research, and the conclusions are limited. It is because of these practical needs and confusion, that this paper studies the quality trust of wearable services based on big data technology.

Based on the analysis method of big data mining, this paper integrates the theoretical methods of big data science, consumer behavior and e-commerce, carries out interdis-ciplinary research, deeply integrates the two different research fields of big data mining and trust adoption, and quantitatively depicts the characteristics of Wearable service quality, privacy environment, business characteristics, personality characteristics and how these characteristics affect consumers' trust and adoption of wearable services. The research results can more comprehensively and truly understand consumers' concerns and demands, help enterprises overcome the bottleneck of wearable product research and development, eliminate the uncertain factors affecting consumers' trust, enhance the competitiveness of products and services, and better meet consumers' needs. It also helps to promote the healthy development of the intelligent wearable industry of the Internet of things in the era of big data, meet people's yearning for a better life of interconnected things, and provide reference for the government to improve relevant industrial policies. It has very important practical and theoretical significance.

2   Key Scientific Problems to Be Solved

This paper intends to solve the following key problems:

1. For model building, the key scientific problems is how to factor large data mining, it is using web crawler technology from social network, community BBS, literature, third-party source data such as database and study and so on, and then through the design of ETL data cleaning conversion, storage, calculation, design, modeling, association analysis, Several factors affecting the quality and trust of wearable services are obtained, and criteria for factor screening are established.
2. For empirical methods, the key scientific issue is how to establish a mapping relationship between big data acquisition indicators and scale measure items through the design of empirical big data acquisition indicators. And how to persuade consumers to participate in big data collection research, and develop software to collect relevant big data, after analysis and processing, transform and map into the measure value of variable measurement items in the model.
3. For cluster comparison, the key scientific issue is how to improve the clustering algorithm and establish an effective cluster model for wearable service consumers. Based on this cluster model, the target users can be clustered and grouped, and different user models can be empirically compared and analyzed.

3   Research Contents

The overall goal of this project is to quantitatively describe how factors such as wearable service quality characteristics, privacy environment, business characteristics and personality characteristics affect consumers' trust and adoption of wearable services based on big data technology. Specific sub-objectives include:

1. Explore the antecedent variables of trust in wearable services through factor big data mining.
2. Through the comprehensive trust model of wearable services, the relationship between model variables is comprehensively clarified.
3. Verify the comprehensive model of wearable services through empirical big data collection and processing and structural equation model, find the key factors affecting trust in wearable services and study the particularity of consumer behavior of wearable services.
4. Through user big data clustering, empirical comparative research is conducted on the influencing factors of user trust in different clusters, and the differences of influencing factors of trust in different clusters are found.

This paper mainly studies the following contents:

1. Construction of Wearable service quality sub model: from the perspective of service quality characteristics, through web crawler technology and factor big data mining, combined with literature research, collect factors affecting Wearable service quality, mine antecedent variables, identify Wearable service quality characteristics, and construct Wearable service quality sub model.
2. Construction of Wearable service quality trust integration model: Based on UTAUT2 (technology adoption and utilization integration theory) theoretical model, on the basis of e-commerce and mobile commerce trust model, the Wearable service quality sub model is integrated, and the Wearable service quality trust integration model is constructed by integrating privacy environment, business characteristics, personality characteristics and other factors [1].
3. Empirical research method design: according to the trust integration model of Wearable service quality, a comprehensive scale and measurement items are designed. Then, through the empirical big data collection index design, a mapping relationship is established between the big data collection index and the measurement items of the scale.
4. Empirical big data analysis: develop Wearable service application data collection software, formulate big data collection rules, collect big data of contracted users and process relevant big data.
5. Construction of user big data clustering model and algorithm improvement: by improving the clustering algorithm based on adaptive chaotic particle swarm optimization, combined with consumer characteristic big data, a wearable service consumer clustering model is established. According to this clustering model, the target users are clustered.
6. Empirical comparative study on grouped users: using SEM, this paper makes an empirical analysis on the integration model and different grouped user models, so as to find the key factors affecting Wearable Service trust, the particularity of Wearable service consumer behavior and the differences of influencing factors of different cluster trust, analyze the reasons and put forward countermeasures.

4   Research Method

Firstly, in the model construction stage, based on factor big data mining, web crawler technology, questionnaire survey, literature research and other methods, explore and collect some factors affecting the trust of wearable services; By analyzing the comprehensive factors affecting Wearable Service trust, this paper constructs a wearable service quality trust integration model. Secondly, in the model verification stage, through the empirical big data collection index design and mapping with the antecedent variable measure of Wearable Service trust, and then through the development of Wearable service application data collection software, collect the big data of contracted users and analyze and process the relevant big data. Finally, in the segment of clustering and comparison, the user big data mining, clustering and empirical comparative analysis based on consumer characteristics are carried out.

Specific research methods include:

1. Factor big data mining: Based on Python web crawler technology, from social networks, community forums, literature, third-party databases and research reports, through data collection, ETL data cleaning and conversion, storage design, computing design, mining modeling and association analysis, we get the factors that affect the trust of wearable services [1].
2. Empirical big data analysis: through the design of empirical big data collection indicators and mapping with the measurement items of antecedent variables of Wearable Service trust, and then through the development of Wearable service application data collection software, collect the big data of contracted users, analyze and process relevant big data, and convert it into questionnaire measurement value [2].
3. User big data mining: by improving the clustering algorithm based on adaptive chaotic particle swarm optimization and combined with consumer characteristic big data, a wearable service consumer clustering model is established. Cluster the target consumers according to the model [3, 4].
4. Model integration method: according to the factor big data mining results and literature research [5–7], starting from the characteristics of Wearable service quality, the sub model of Wearable service quality is constructed by exploring the antecedent variables of Wearable service quality. At the same time, based on the UTAUT2 theoretical model, on the basis of e-commerce and mobile commerce trust model, combined with the service quality sub model, this paper constructs a wearable service quality trust integration model.
5. The model verification method mainly adopts big data clustering, questionnaire survey, structural equation model and statistical analysis. According to the big data mining results of users, the target consumers are grouped. Then, using SEM structural equation, this paper makes an empirical analysis on different cluster users, so as to find various factors affecting Wearable Service trust, the particularity of Wearable service consumer behavior and the differences of influencing factors of different cluster trust, analyze the reasons and put forward countermeasures [8–10].

5   Construction of Integration Model

The integration model studied in this paper is shown in Fig. 1.

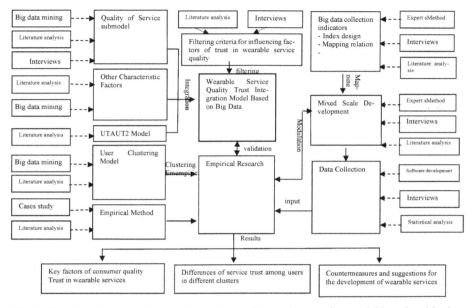

Fig. 1. Structure diagram of wearable service quality trust integration model based on big data

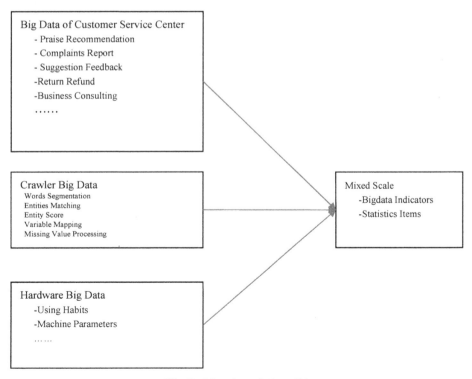

Fig. 2. Mapping relations [1]

The integration model is composed of sub-models:

1. Wearable service quality sub model: explore the antecedent variables of Wearable service quality sub model and build the model with the help of factor big data mining, literature analysis, research and interview. These antecedent variables may come from wearability (durability, comfort, aesthetics, endurance, size), functionality (health, sports, safety, payment, entertainment), personalization (differentiation, intelligence, customization), integration (connection, interaction, control), etc.

2. Collection of other characteristic factors: with the help of factor literature analysis and big data mining, the factors affecting consumers' trust in wearable services may come from business characteristics (business reputation, business scale), personality factors (privacy concerns, trust tendency, security concerns), environmental characteristics (structural guarantee, privacy policy), etc.

3. UTAUT2 model: technology adoption and utilization integration theory (UTAUT2) is an extension of UTAUT (eg.Unified Theory Of Acceptance And Use Of Technology). In the UTAUT model, there are four factors that play a decisive role in consumers' technology acceptance and use behavior, namely performance expectation, effort expectation, social impact and convenience. Based on the four factors, UTAUT2 adds three new factors: hedonic motivation, price value and habit. In the empirical research, it is proved that the new three factors play an important role in consumer trust and new technology adoption. As the latest technology adoption theory, UTAUT2 has strong conviction in explaining the new business system.

4. Screening criteria for influencing factors of Wearable Service Trust: after factor big data mining, literature analysis and model integration, there are many factors entering the integration model, so it is necessary to study a factor screening criteria. This part will screen candidate variables into the integration model on the basis of expert interviews and literature research.

5. Construction of Wearable service quality trust integration model: after screening, the Wearable service quality trust integration model is constructed from seven factors of UTAUT2 theoretical model, several factors of Wearable service quality sub model, environmental characteristics, business characteristics, personality characteristics and other factors.

6. Big data acquisition index design: the design of big data acquisition index should meet the technical feasibility and implementation feasibility. After a long period of big data collection, it is necessary to dynamically adjust the index value to meet the requirements of the measurement item mapping rules in the mixed scale.

7. Mixed scale development: not all questionnaire measurement items can be mapped by big data measurement indicators. A small number of items that cannot be mapped need to be collected by traditional questionnaire or wearable devices based questionnaire. Therefore, the final comprehensive scale mixes big data measurement items with questionnaire items.

8. Data collection: through the development of data collection software app and the solicitation of contracted users, the big data of key indicators in the use process of wearable services are collected, which are transformed into questionnaire measurement values after big data analysis and processing.

9. Construction of user clustering model: firstly, starting from the resource dimension and motivation dimension of VALSTM model, combined with demographic and psychological characteristics, this paper constructs a wearable service consumer clustering model. In order to obtain better clustering effect, the clustering algorithm based on adaptive chaotic particle swarm optimization effectively integrates the fuzzy mean clustering and the improved PSO algorithm, which avoids the defects of the original fuzzy mean clustering algorithm, such as weak self adaptability, easy to fall into local minimum and unsatisfactory clustering effect.

10. Traditional empirical method: structural equation model is a method to establish, estimate and test causality model. The model contains both observable explicit variables and potential variables that cannot be observed directly. Structural equation model can replace multiple regression, path analysis, factor analysis, covariance analysis and other methods to clearly analyze the role of single indicators on the whole and the relationship between single indicators. Through structural equation multi group analysis, we can understand whether the relationship of variables in different groups remains unchanged and whether the mean value of each factor is significantly different.

11. Empirical research: to do empirical analysis with the help of structural equation model, we must first prepare the data and collect the appropriate amount of sample data. It is generally believed that the maximum likelihood estimation (MLE) is suitable for estimating the structural equation when the number of samples is at least 100, then reliability analysis and validity analysis are carried out, and finally the fitting degree of the model is evaluated. After the transformation of big data acquisition index data, this paper meets the requirements of structural equation model. Therefore, the integration model and different cluster user models are empirically analyzed by using structural equation.

12. Research results: through the comprehensive research of this paper, we can find the key factors affecting the trust of wearable services, the particularity of consumer behavior of wearable services and the differences of influencing factors of trust in different clusters, analyze the reasons and put forward countermeasures.

Figure 2 shows how to map metrics based on big data into variables that the model can handle.

6   Discussion and Conclusion

Big data technology is different from traditional statistical methods. Big data studies massive "overall data" and is no longer confined to accurate statistical "small data". At the same time, big data analysis does not pursue causality like statistics, but focuses on correlation. It is a beneficial attempt to study the trust of wearable services based on big data thought, big data thought, big data technology and methods.

The specific features and innovations of this paper lie in the innovation of research methods and model integration, including the following aspects:

1. In terms of research perspectives and research methods, based on the perspective of big data, this topic adopts big data related technologies to expand the research

methodology of trust. In terms of specific big data application, it has successively adopted technologies such as factor big data mining, empirical big data collection and user big data clustering. Firstly, based on factor big data mining and web crawler technology, this paper explores and collects several factors affecting the trust of wearable services. Secondly, through the empirical big data collection index design, and mapping with the antecedent variable measure of Wearable Service trust, and then through the development of Wearable service application data collection software, collect the big data of contracted users and analyze and process the relevant big data. Finally, in the empirical part, the user big data mining and clustering based on consumer characteristics are also carried out.

2. In the aspect of model construction, starting from the characteristics of Wearable service quality, the sub model of Wearable service quality is constructed by exploring the antecedent variables of Wearable service quality. At the same time, based on the theoretical model of UTAUT2 (technology adoption and utilization integration theory), based on the trust model of e-commerce and mobile commerce, integrate the sub model of service quality and construct the trust integration model of Wearable service quality, which has more comprehensive research value of trust factors.

3. In the aspect of empirical analysis, by improving the clustering algorithm based on adaptive chaotic particle swarm optimization and combining the big data of consumer characteristics, a wearable service user clustering model is established. According to this clustering model, the target consumers are grouped. Then, using SEM structural equation, this paper makes an empirical analysis on different cluster users, so as to find various factors affecting Wearable Service trust, the particularity of Wearable service consumer behavior and the differences of influencing factors of different cluster trust, analyze the reasons and put forward countermeasures.

References

1. Gu, Z., Cui, Y., Tang, H., Liu, X.: Customer satisfaction evaluation method based on big data. In: Salvendy, G., Wei, J. (eds.) HCII 2021. LNCS, vol. 12796, pp. 19–26. Springer, Cham (2021). https://doi.org/10.1007/978-3-030-77025-9_3
2. Cheng, L., Cao, J., Gu, Z.: Design of customer satisfaction evaluation system based on big data. In: Salvendy, G., Wei, J. (eds.) HCII 2021. LNCS, vol. 12796, pp. 3–10. Springer, Cham (2021). https://doi.org/10.1007/978-3-030-77025-9_1
3. Hu, Q., Shen, J.: A cluster and process collaboration-aware method to achieve service substitution in cloud service processes. Sci. Programm. 2020(1), 1–12 (2020)
4. Gu, Z., Xu, F.: A novel firefly algorithm to solve the parameter self-tuning problem of PID controller. J. Syst. Manag. 026(001), 101–106 (2017)
5. Gu, Z., Xiong, H., Hu, W.: Empirical comparative study of wearable service trust based on user clustering. J. Organ. End User Comput. (JOEUC) 33(6), 1–16 (2021)
6. Gu, Z., Wei, J.: Empirical study on initial trust of wearable devices based on product characteristics. J. Comput. Inf. Syst. 61, 520–528 (2020)
7. Gu, Z., Wei, J.: Wearable services adoption study from a perspective of usability. In: Salvendy, G., Wei, J. (eds.) HCII 2020. LNCS, vol. 12216, pp. 16–22. Springer, Cham (2020). https://doi.org/10.1007/978-3-030-50350-5_2

8. Pahnila, S., Siponen, M., Zheng, X.: Integrating habit into UTAUT: the Chinese eBay case. Pac. Asia J. Assoc. Inf. Syst. **3**(2), 1–30 (2011)
9. Gu, Z., Wei, J., Xu, F.: An empirical study on factors influencing consumers' initial trust in wearable commerce. J. Comput. Inf. Syst. **56**(1), 79–85 (2016)
10. Schapp, S., Cornelius, R.: U-Commerce – Leading the New World of Payments, A Visa International and Accenture White Paper. http://www.corporate.visa.com/av/ucomm/u_whit epaper.pdf

Mobile Commerce and Advertising

The Effect of Influencer Persona on Consumer Decision-Making Towards Short-Form Video Ads—From the Angle of Narrative Persuasion

Haoyu Chen and Jifan Ren[✉]

Harbin Institute of Technology, Shenzhen 518055, China
renjifan@hit.edu.cn

Abstract. The growth of Internet and social media have substantially changed how customers engage, interact, and communicate with brands and marketers. Individuals with strong personal appeal and influence play a key role in facilitating greater brand outreach and better performance of online ads. Influencers convey similar or distinct persona to match different atmosphere of social media platforms and types of products and services that they intend to promote. Simultaneously, influencers constantly produce textual and visual narrations of their lives and experiences to enhance consumer trusts and foster consumer responses. However, little is known about the role of influencer personal image establishment on driving online consumer engagement. Besides, there are lack of researches that consider the consolidated effect of influencer persona and narratives during the persuasion process. Instagram, Facebook, Sina Weibo and Twitter have been the most examined social media platforms. However, short video-based social media platforms such as TikTok that embed distinct product and content structures still lack academic attention. In light of the significant role of influencers on consumer attitudes and behaviors, and as this research domain is still developing, a research from a new research perspective is needed. This study derives practical implications across various domains, such as social media marketing, digital advertising, and video advertisement in which identification of key factors of information propagators is essential. Taken together, the findings highlight the critical interplay of influencer persona, expressions of the posts and consumer psychological factors in driving consumer engagement and purchase intention, especially for short-form video-based ads.

Keywords: Influencer marketing · Social media marketing · Influencer persona

1 Introduction

Technological advancements such as Mobile applications, social media and Internet of Things (IOT) have led to new ways of information sharing, delivering and communication (Melumad et al. 2019; Peng et al. 2018). In particular, social media that provides online channels for high-speed information diffusing and users participating forms an increasingly important way for brands, advertisers and marketers to communicate with

G. Salvendy and J. Wei (Eds.): HCII 2022, LNCS 13337, pp. 223–234, 2022.
https://doi.org/10.1007/978-3-031-05014-5_18

their consumer segments. Firms have been incorporated social media for ongoing brand promotion and customer relationship management for years. Users have tendencies to blindly consume the content shared on social media (Shareef et al. 2020). Compared to the fact that consumers acted as passive recipients under firm marketing strategies in the past, they have stronger power to voice their choices towards brands recently. Social media even enables consumers to serve as promoters and participants for products, services and brands (Lamberton and Stephen 2016), which drastically changes the relationship among brands and consumers. The rapid adoption of internet and social media enables some individuals to attract mass audience and then become influencers with strong personal appeal and influence on others' attitudes and responses (Godey et al. 2016). The large follower groups support influencers due to their admirable social prestige, authenticity and position (Lin et al. 2018; Lou and Yuan 2019). Approximately 40% of followers purchased products and services after seeing influencer recommendations on social media such as Instagram or YouTube (Digital Marketing Institute 2019). It is beneficial to for firms to leverage the power of influencers for better outreach (Arora et al. 2019). Consequently, influencer marketing has become prevalent in firm marketing strategies.

With the prevalence of influencer marketing on social media, influencers keep producing textual and visual narrations of their personal image, lives and experience which appeal to followers and audience (De Veirman et al. 2017). Influencers' personal reviews of product accompanied by the expression of their daily lives and experiences make consumers consider their comments as authentic and relatable (Schouten et al. 2020). Similarly, Lou and Yuan (2019) stated that the informative contents generated by influencer and related values could enhance consumer trust. The disclosure of sponsorship and hashtag of influencers' posts helps consumers and viewers to identify the selling intent of influencers and advertisers. However, it does not necessarily result in a loss of consumer engagement with the posts (Lou et al. 2019), or negative attitudes towards influencers, related message or products. The rational explanation is that stories and narratives shared by influencers drive consumers to feel the emotions and experiences of influencers and bring followers to a positive state in which followers put aside their guard and skepticism (Feng et al. 2021). Moreover, influencers' persona and personal image that generated from influencers' narratives in personal or social context also present influential effect over their followers. Therefore, the cumulative impact of influencer's narratives of their personal image and persona is crucial in persuasion process and to foster positive consumer responses. An understanding of this phenomenon is needed to meet the interests of academic research and marketing practice.

Among studies in social media marketing and influencer marketing, mainstream social media platforms such as Instagram, Facebook, Sina Weibo and Twitter have been the most examined social media platforms (Vrontis et al. 2021). However, short video-based social media platforms such as TikTok that embed distinct product and content structures still lack academic attention. Moreover, there is little integrative assessment that considers the consolidated effect of narratives and persona shared by influencers which are prevalent for endorsement effectiveness. Specifically, little is known about how to approach influencers' short-from video ads aspects of persona establishment and narratives to optimally cultivate consumers' self-satisfaction and meet their psychological needs, and ultimately enhance their purchasing intention. Brands, marketers and advertisers receive little guidance on how different influencers persona and narratives will alter consumer responses. Therefore, towards this research direction, it is essential to provide an in-depth explanation into the role of influencers' narration and persona establishment in influencer marketing on social media.

To address the gap in the existing literature, an exploratory study of social media influencers' posts from views of the narrative strategies and persona-building is conducted. Specifically, this study will propose an approach to figure out the integrative effect between types of persona that are determined and shared by influencers and the narrative strategies adopted while delivering short-form video ads during consumer decision-making process. Given this purpose, this study raised the following research questions:

1. Will different types of influencers' persona and narratives result in different consumers responses?
2. If so, how responses differ in various scenarios and among customers of different age groups?
3. How narratives and persona shared by influencers exert impact on the psychological needs and engagement among the audience?

To answer each of these questions, the concept of transportation will be adopted to explain the cumulative effect of influencer persona and narrations in audience affective responses. The models will be also supplemented by variables such as empathy, parasocial interaction and consumers' self-satisfaction. The empirical evidence for this study will come from surveys and experiments.

This exploratory research provides theoretical and practical insights in two ways. Firstly, this study explores the cumulative role of narrative strategies adopted by influencers in their posts and persona that could alter audience's attitudes towards short-form video ads. Secondly, this study incorporates the concept of transportation to examine the relationship among influencers' posts and audience and explain audience responses from psychological perspective.

2 Literature Review

2.1 Social Media and Influencer Marketing

Recently, the prevalence of influencer marketing on social media and the growing influence of influencers on audience have attracted mass attention of various fields. Social media platforms and influencer marketing have become mainstays in the marketing channels that utilized by brands and advertisers. In addition to strong research interests in the field of business press, the growing adoption of influencer marketing and the soared number of influencers have also led to growing academic attention (Hughes et al. 2019). The idea of using opinion leaders and influencers to exert strong influence on consumers' decision-making has been lasted for many years. Early concepts could be traced back to the experiment conducted by Lazarsfeld, Berelson, and Gaudet in 1948. Their findings indicated that mass media has impact on audiences' behaviors and attitudes through the power of opinion leaders rather than directly influencing the audience (Lazarsfeld et al. 1948). That notion was further developed latter in 1995. Finding highlighted the mediating effect of influencers' personal comments and interpretation of information from mass media on consumers (Katz and Lazarsfeld 2017).

Extant studies from various research fields have been focused heavily on a wide range of influencers variables (e.g., attractiveness, expertise, credibility, influencer-product fit, content attributes, psychological-related influential factors) and consumer beneficial outcomes (e.g., consumer engagement, brand and product attitude, purchase intention and behavior) (Vrontis et al. 2021). In the context of implementing influencer marketing strategies, researchers commonly describe consumers' beneficial behaviors as positive attitude towards influencers, posts, brands and products, and purchase intention. As firms recognize the pivotal role of social media influencers during the product persuasion process, they have been launching mass influencer campaigns to promote services and products on social media platforms. This has been supported by many studies. For instance, Ge and Gretzel (2018) unveiled that influencer campaigns become important means to enhance marketing communications in social media and marketing field. 86% of brands and marketers incorporated influencer campaigns and services into their firm marketing strategies in 2018. The consolidated power of the influencers, their networks and their followers form and accelerate the dissemination of information and the co-creation of the brand value and image (Martínez-López et al. 2020). Since marketers increasingly favor and rely on influencer marketing for better brand outreach, it is expected that this trend will surge and shape the future of marketing field (Appel et al. 2019). With this trend, strategic insights on how to better capitalize on influencer marketing on social media are still needed with the aim to maximize the influential effect of influencers' and to increase the brand's influence to better promote products and services (Huang et al. 2014).

2.2 Influencer Persona

The definition of persona differs in various scenarios. For instance, the term of persona initially refers to costume masks in theatrical performance which then develops as the social roles, image or characters shared by performers (Bishop 2007). In addition, persona could be the roles from individuals' psychological perspective or the image and appearances being presented in the physical and social context. It can also be the role or character that matches performers on stage and dramas. Furthermore, persona stands for settings and image of fictitious characters in animations and games including personalities, facial and physical expressions, style and clothing, and even status of characters (Wang 2020). Similarly, in the context of social media, the characters that share persona or personal image are generally deemed to be virtual influencers. Specifically, persona of influencers includes the appearances, identities, images, lifestyle and even sense of value that set by influencers. It can be conveyed to the mass through words, behaviors, and narratives regarding their feelings, emotion, past experiences and lives created by influencers on social media platforms.

It is human nature to portray persona or image in positive lights in order to impress other individuals, and behave according to those persona and protagonists while interacting with others (Goffman, 2002). This explains the fact that social media influencers intentionally set better image and roles than what they actually are when interacting and engaging with followers to maintain their attractiveness (Wang 2020). In the context of positive persona, followers will consider influencers as trustworthy friends and then show higher tolerance towards the quality of influencers' posts and their behaviors (Wang 2020). Related impression and information generated from performers' behaviors and narratives is the persona of the performer (Jacobsen and Kristiansen 2014), which refers to the persona of influencers on social media platforms. Above all, in the context of social media, positive persona helps to shorten the distance and establish a sense of intimacy between influencers and audience which can further enhance endorsement effectiveness.

2.3 Influencer Narrative and Concept of Transportation

Researches in narration and persuasion have been lasted for many years. Altman and Taylor (1973) stated that sharing of personal feelings, stories, thoughts and experiences with others could engender positive relationships amongst individuals. Extant studies on narrative persuasion argue that influencer posts are typical examples of persuasive narratives which clearly present characters, story plots, storylines and outcomes to attract audience and followers (Feng et al. 2021; Escalas 2007). Social media influencers constantly create stories to maintain their popularity in followers and let audience mentally feel and show identity with influencers' idea, value and experiences and ultimately, accept influencers' product recommendation (Escalas 2007). Short-form video-based ads usually complete product persuasion and recommendation through protagonists' comments of goals, actions, experiences, comments or outcomes before and after the use of product. Hence, short-form video-based ads on social media could be considered as narrative ads or story advertising that are created by influencers to foster audience engagement and positive responses.

A crucial factor of short-form video-based ads, or narrative ads that drives the success of product recommendation and consumer engagement is empathy (Escalas 2007). Short-form ads engender positive consumer attitudes and responses through empathetic persuasion process. This is a psychological and mental process in which viewers of the video ads take on perspective of characters and then, imagine and perceive similar experiences of characters in the ads rather than physically using the products (Kim et al. 2017). As influencers usually form their image, persona and experiences from positive aspects, it is much easier for audience of ads to empathize influencers' experiences in positive manners through the empathetic process (Chang 2013). This then helps to generate positive affections and product attitudes, and consequently, foster beneficial consumers responses towards the ads.

In the same vein, the success of influencer marketing regarding narrative persuasion and empathetic process could be academically explained by the concept of transportation. This concept view-points that audience' attention, emotion, imagery, and affections are interrupted and stimulated by stories plots shared by presenters. Simultaneously, the audience empathizes and imaginatively project themselves into the relevant experiences and strong emotions of presenters while neglecting real-world matters such as time, social and physical sites, and real personal experiences (Chang 2013). Similarly, the concept of transportation and narrative persuasion literature was extended by Green (2004) who unveiled that empathetic audience which namely the transported individuals tend to show positive behaviors and attitudes towards narrative ads. The rational explanation is that the empathetic audience spontaneously shows sympathy and approves the idea and value of influencers in the ads while developing vicarious feelings. As such, the audience of short-form video-based ads are more likely to generate positive attitudes which could latter result in higher consumer engagement and increasing purchase intentions.

3 Methodology

3.1 Platform Selection

Traditional text and picture-based platforms such as Instagram, Facebook and Twitter are the most considered platforms, influencer campaigns on those platforms have been attracted plenty of attention from the field of business press and operation, and academic researches (Vrontis et al. 2021). On the contrary, short-form video-based social media platforms that embed distinct product and content structures still lack attentions from various domains. According to Hughes et al. (2019), the relationship between influencers' posts and follower's engagement on social media platforms varies with ads type and social media platforms. For example, high hedonic content paired with campaigns are vital for consumer engagement generated by blog posts which mainly structured with text and picture. However, influencers' posts with high hedonic value are better matched with trial campaigns on Facebook in which campaign giveaways play negative effect on consumers. Apart from that, although the most significant difference between those social media platforms is the content and structure that users can create and upload, short-form video-based social media platforms show several characters that differ from traditional mainstream social media platforms. Influencers and participants embed obvious persona and personal image on short-form video-based social media platforms (Wang 2020). Specifically, the establishment of personal image and persona on short-form video based social media platforms are much clearer and more successful. Audience and users might be more susceptible of influencers persona and narratives under this circumstance, which will further have implications over the effectiveness of influencer endorsement.

Besides, platforms such as TikTok and Kwai provide an atmosphere in which more users are encouraged to produce and upload content, especially the content with sense of entertainment. As such, these short-form video-based platforms unveil higher engagement rates comparing to other social media platforms and networks at all follower levels. For example, micro-influencers on TikTok generated an engagement rate of 17.96% while the figures for Instagram and YouTube are 3.86% and 1.63% respectively. As for figures of mega-influencers across different platforms, the engagement rates that generated by mega-influencers are 4.96% on TikTok, 1.21% on Instagram, and only 0.37% on YouTube (Influencer Marketing Hub 2022). Since engagement is an important factor that determines the effectiveness and perceived attractiveness of influencer messages (Jang et al. 2021), it is necessary to scrutinize the influencers characteristics that serve as antecedents of consumers' attitude towards short video ads. Since each short-video based social media platform has different atmospheres, audience and followers with various preferences are attracted and impacted by influencers with different persona and image. Therefore, it is important to examine the efficacy of influencer endorsement and their effect on consumers on short-from video platform which is hardly focused.

3.2 Influencer Selection

As for the data to examine the effect of influencers' persona and narratives on consumers, influencers will be mainly selected and categorized into three types to explore the integrated effect in different scenarios and that meet consumers' various needs. Influencers will be categorized as 1) fashion and beauty types in which influencers usually exert attractive appearance and actively seeking the latest trends and news; 2) pets, sports and travel types in which influencers always create their original content and shares their daily lives; 3) reviewer types in which influencers constantly provide personal comments regarding current and latest affairs, new products, and services. The psychological needs, personal experience and understanding of audience and viewers will vary according to the types of ads and products being promoted. The selection of influencers based on the classification above is excepted to better measure the effectiveness of product persuasion without any high biases.

3.3 Audience Selection

With the prevalence of influencer campaigns on social media platforms, consumers obtain mass opportunities and channels to interact and engage with people sharing real comments and reviews through social media channels. In this context, consumers in different generation tend to demand for more personalized and interactive service experiences wherein they are more connected and capable to communicate with brands and marketers. Although influencers' posts and messages could trigger audience purchase intentions, the power of influencers' persuasiveness varies from generation to generation depending on consumers' different needs and motivation. Each consumer segments and generation will differently be impacted by marketing messages, as consumers in different generation and age have distinct cognitive, affective, and conative needs and motivations. According to Lou and Yuan (2019), the power of users, algorithms, and platform conspired determines the success of influencer marketing.

Participants of surveys and questionnaires in this paper will be classified into three groups: 1) group 1 represents young adults who were born from 1992 to 2001; 2) group 2 refers to people who were born between 1981 and 1991; 3) group 3 consists of adults who were born before the year of 1981. The reason to label consumers and audience by age is that people with different age have different degrees of exposure to influences and narratives. This trend is more pronounced in young adults (Chang 2013). Related concepts were supported by other researchers. According to De Jans et al. (2018), influencer marketing is one of the most effective means to enhance brand loyalty in Millennials and for better performance of marketing communications and branding purposes. Young consumers are more likely to empathize influencers' feelings and experiences while viewing persona and narratives created by protagonists with similar age and background (de Graaf 2014; Chang 2013). Younger consumers' purchase inspirations and intentions are more likely to be stimulated and affected by social media influencers' posts (Interactive Advertising Bureau 2019; Lou and Yuan 2019), whereas general consumers from other generation tend to be more conservative and rational.

3.4 Method

To explore the effect of narration strategies and persona used by influencers, the big data approach is applied to answer three research questions. Three types of influencers and three groups of consumers will be analyzed. The NEO-FFI questionnaire is chosen to measure participants' attitudes and responses through a five-point Likert scale ranging from "strong approval" to "strong disapproval". In the context of social media and influencer marketing, simulation and regression models have been adopted to measure the impact of influencers while taking account of consumer engagement (Choi et al. 2016; Popescu et al. 2016). Hence, in this study, four linear regression models, which are OLS, KNN, SVM and Lasso Regression model, are modelled to measure influence of influencers with various persona and, structures and means of narratives, and to identify the optimal mix of impact features, for instance, positive persona and first-person narrative. In addition, consumers' psychological variables such as empathy, para-social interaction and consumers' self-satisfaction that may be affected during the narrative process are considered as features. Feature engineering will also be conducted in this study as the above models will measure the effect of influencers based on consumers responses on the influencers' posts from questionnaires. In order to detailly investigate the joint effect influencers' persona and narrative over consumers, this study establishes a 2 × 2 metrics to test the effect in various scenarios.

3.5 Discussion

Based on influencer marketing and narrative persuasion literature, we raised three research questions. As for the first research question, this paper examines the difference in consumer attitudes and responses when consumers are exposure to short-form video-based ads in which influencers share different type persona and narratives. The results are expected to suggest that positive persona and narratives from first-person perspective are more likely to generate empathic reactions and positive affections from audience and viewers of the narrative ads. In the second research question, various scenarios in which influencers embed different types of roles and persona are investigated. For instance, trend-seekers in fashion and beauty types, authorship in pets, sports and travel types, and commenters that provide conversations. Since audiences and viewers of short-form video-based ads present diverse demands and motivations in these scenarios, they will differently empathize and imaginatively project themselves into experiences of influencers. These will lead to different marketing effects and performance. Moreover, through considering the age of consumers, the results are expected to reveal that younger adults are more likely to be impacted by influencers who serve as trend seekers in fashion and beauty domains. The third research question focuses on consumers psychological aspects. The results are expected to indicate that empathy, para-social interaction and consumers' self-satisfaction are major variables that are impacted by influencers persona and narratives, which can then lead to higher consumer engagement and growing purchase intentions. Taken together, the results of experiment are in accordance with narrative persuasion researches that when audience empathize into the experiences of the characters, they may think from the protagonists' point of view (Chang 2013; Escalas 2007). Consequently, this empathic and narrative persuasion process can foster the success of product recommendation and better marketing performance.

3.6 Limitation and Future Research Direction

Data of this paper comes from surveys and questionnaires that consist of fictitious endorsers and stimulated senses. However, fictitious endorsers may lack the ability to possess characteristics of real influencers with whom followers physically engage with on social media platforms. For instance, fictitious endorsers do not share persona and interact with their followers in a consistent fashion. Hence, one limitation of this study is that using fictitious endorsers and simulated scenarios may not be capable to fully examine the cumulative impact of influencer's narratives of personal image and the persona on consumer decision-making and real responses. Furthermore, simulated scenarios such as surveys and questionnaires may fail to capture consumers' real and instant responses which could be considered as audience understanding and empathic reactions in context of influencers narrative persuasion. Previous studies have applied audience's clicks of "likes" to measure their positive feelings and affections towards posts and messages generated from social media platforms (Hong et al. 2017; Seo et al. 2018). Hence, further studies on this direction could employ the number of clicks and likes generated from influencers' posts to better examine users cumulated positive responses on social media platforms.

3.7 Contribution and Implications

In terms of the theoretical implications, although the role of narrative in marketing fields and the power of influencer campaigns have been explored extensively (Vrontis et al. 2021; Chang 2013; Escalas 2007), its cumulative effect in the context of influencer marketing and narrative has received little academic attention. This paper helps to expand boundaries of extant researches in social media influencer marketing and reveals important factors of influencers that positively affect consumers' attitude towards short video ads from a new research perspective.

From the angle of practical implications, the findings of this paper are expected to reveal that cumulative effect of positive persona and first-person narratives will positively alter customer attitudes towards the short-form video ads on short video social media platforms. Consumers and audience are expected to present higher engagement and positive product attitudes through the narrative persuasion and empathetic process while getting access to the narrative ads on short-form video-based social media platforms. These are key findings that brands, advertisers and marketers should consider, as influencer campaigns are becoming increasingly important in the current advertising marketing context. Taken together, these findings will further be utilized for the purpose of social media promotion, larger outreach and better performance of short video ads.

3.8 Conclusion

Recently, influencer marketing has become prevalent in firms' digital marketing strategies. Not only marketers and service providers, but also plenty of researchers tend to figure out the profound influence of influencers over their followers and potential consumers from multiple dimensions. Within this context, this exploratory research examined influencers' narrative strategies, and adopted the concept of transportation between influencers and their audience to explore the cumulative effect of narratives and influencer persona during persuasion process. Specifically, given the integrated effect of transportation among influencers and audience, influencers' persona and the first-person narratives of their experiences and lives, audience of short-from video ads tend to present positive responses towards influencers' personal images and their persuasions. Therefore, this study expands boundaries of extant researches in social media influencer marketing and digital advertising by shedding light on the cumulative role of influencer persona and narratives.

Acknowledgement. This work was supported by the Natural Science Foundation of China (grant number 71831005) and Shenzhen Humanities & Social Sciences Key Research Bases (grant number KP191001).

References

Altman, I., Taylor, D.A.: Social Penetration: The Development of Interpersonal Relationships. Holt, Rinehart & Winston, New York (1973)

Appel, G., Grewal, L., Hadi, R., Stephen, A.T.: The future of social media in marketing. J. Acad. Mark. Sci. **48**(1), 79–95 (2019). https://doi.org/10.1007/s11747-019-00695-1

Arora, A., Bansal, S., Kandpal, C., Aswani, R., Dwivedi, Y.: Measuring social media influencer index-insights from Facebook, Twitter and Instagram. J. Retail. Consum. Serv. **49**, 86–101 (2019)

Bishop, P.: Analytical Psychology and German Classical Aesthetics: Goethe, Schiller, and Jung, Volume 1: The Development of the Personality. Routledge, London (2007)

Chang, C.: Imagery fluency and narrative advertising effects. J. Advert. **42**(1), 54–68 (2013)

Choi, T.M., Chan, H.K., Yue, X.: Recent development in big data analytics for business operations and risk management. IEEE Trans. Cybernet. **47**(1), 81–92 (2016)

De Graaf, A.: The effectiveness of adaptation of the protagonist in narrative impact: similarity influences health beliefs through self-referencing. Hum. Commun. Res. **40**(1), 73–90 (2014)

De Jans, S., Cauberghe, V., Hudders, L.: How an advertising disclosure alerts young adolescents to sponsored vlogs: the moderating role of a peer-based advertising literacy intervention through an informational vlog. J. Advert. **47**(4), 309–325 (2018)

De Veirman, M., Cauberghe, V., Hudders, L.: Marketing through Instagram influencers: the impact of number of followers and product divergence on brand attitude. Int. J. Advert. **36**(5), 798–828 (2017)

Digital Marketing Institute: 20 Surprising Influencer Marketing Statistics (2019). https://digitalmarketinginstitute.com/blog/20-influencer-marketing-statistics-that-will-surprise-you. Accessed 8 Feb 2022

Escalas, J.E.: Self-referencing and persuasion: narrative transportation versus analytical elaboration. J. Consum. Res. **33**(4), 421–429 (2007)

Feng, Y., Chen, H., Kong, Q.: An expert with whom I can identify: the role of narratives in influencer marketing. Int. J. Advert. **40**(7), 972–993 (2021)

Ge, J., Gretzel, U.: Emoji rhetoric: a social media influencer perspective. J. Mark. Manag. **34**(15–16), 1272–1295 (2018)

Godey, B., et al.: Social media marketing efforts of luxury brands: influence on brand equity and consumer behavior. J. Bus. Res. **69**(12), 5833–5841 (2016)

Goffman, E.: The presentation of self in everyday life 1959. Garden City, NY, 259 (2002)

Green, M.C.: Transportation into narrative worlds: the role of prior knowledge and perceived realism. Discourse Process. **38**(2), 247–266 (2004)

Huang, J., Zhang, J., Li, Y., Lv, Z.: Business value of enterprise micro-blogging: empirical study from weibo.com in sina. J. Global Inf. Manage. (JGIM) **22**(3), 32–56 (2014)

Hughes, C., Swaminathan, V., Brooks, G.: Driving brand engagement through online social influencers: an empirical investigation of sponsored blogging campaigns. J. Mark. **83**(5), 78–96 (2019)

Hong, C., Chen, Z.F., Li, C.: "Liking" and being "liked": how are personality traits and demographics associated with giving and receiving "likes" on Facebook? Comput. Hum. Behav. **68**, 292–299 (2017)

Influencer Marketing Hub: TikTok Statistics (2022). https://influencermarketinghub.com/tiktok-stats/. Accessed 8 Feb 2022

Interactive Advertising Bureau: 2019 Influencer Marketing Report (2019a). https://www.iab.com/wp-content/uploads/2019/03/Rakuten-2019-Influencer-Marketing-Report-Rakuten-Marketing.pdf. Accessed 8 Feb 2022

Jacobsen, M.H., Kristiansen, S.: The Social Thought of Erving Goffman. Sage Publications, Thousand Oaks (2014)

Jang, W., Kim, J., Kim, S., Chun, J.W.: The role of engagement in travel influencer marketing: the perspectives of dual process theory and the source credibility model. Curr. Issue Tour. **24**(17), 2416–2420 (2021)

Katz, E., Lazarsfeld, P.F.: Personal Influence: The Part Played by People in the Flow of Mass Communications. Routledge, New York (2017)

Kim, E., Ratneshwar, S., Thorson, E.: Why narrative ads work: an integrated process explanation. J. Advert. **46**(2), 283–296 (2017)

Lamberton, C., Stephen, A.T.: A thematic exploration of digital, social media, and mobile marketing: research evolution from 2000 to 2015 and an agenda for future inquiry. J. Mark. **80**(6), 146–172 (2016). https://doi.org/10.1509/jm.15.0415

Lazarsfeld, P.F., Berelson, B., Gaudet, H.: The People's Choice: How the Voter Makes Up His Mind in a Presidential Campaign. Columbia University Press, New York (1948)

Lin, H.C., Bruning, P.F., Swarna, H.: Using online opinion leaders to promote the hedonic and utilitarian value of products and services. Bus. Horiz. **61**(3), 431–442 (2018). https://doi.org/10.1016/j.bushor.2018.01.010

Lou, C., Tan, S.S., Chen, X.: Investigating consumer engagement with influencer-vs. brand-promoted ads: the roles of source and disclosure. J. Interact. Advert. **19**(3), 169–186 (2019)

Lou, C., Yuan, S.: Influencer marketing: how message value and credibility affect consumer trust of branded content on social media. J. Interact. Advert. **19**(1), 58–73 (2019)

Martínez-López, F.J., Anaya-Sánchez, R., Fernández Giordano, M., Lopez-Lopez, D.: Behind influencer marketing: key marketing decisions and their effects on followers' responses. J. Mark. Manag. **36**(7–8), 579–607 (2020)

Melumad, S., Inman, J.J., Pham, M.T.: Selectively emotional: how smartphone use changes user-generated content. J. Mark. Res. **56**(2), 259–275 (2019). https://doi.org/10.1177/0022243718815429

Peng, J., Agarwal, A., Hosanagar, K., Iyengar, R.: Network overlap and content sharing on social media platforms. J. Mark. Res. **55**(4), 571–585 (2018)

Popescu, P.S., Mihaescu, M.C., Popescu, E., Mocanu, M.: Using ranking and multiple linear regression to explore the impact of social media engagement on student performance. In: 2016 IEEE 16th International Conference on Advanced Learning Technologies (ICALT), pp. 250–254. IEEE, July 2016

Schouten, A.P., Janssen, L., Verspaget, M.: Celebrity vs. Influencer endorsements in advertising: the role of identification, credibility, and Product-Endorser fit. Int. J. Advert. **39**(2), 258–281 (2020)

Seo, Y., Li, X., Choi, Y.K., Yoon, S.: Narrative transportation and paratextual features of social media in viral advertising. J. Advert. **47**(1), 83–95 (2018)

Shareef, M.A., Kapoor, K.K., Mukerji, B., Dwivedi, R., Dwivedi, Y.K.: Group behavior in social media: antecedents of initial trust formation. Comput. Hum. Behav. **105**, 106225 (2020)

Vrontis, D., Makrides, A., Christofi, M., Thrassou, A.: Social media influencer marketing: a systematic review, integrative framework and future research agenda. Int. J. Consum. Stud. **45**(4), 617–644 (2021)

Wang, A.: Influencer persona and audience engagement: an analysis of the user decision-making differences between traditional and short-video-based social media (Doctoral dissertation, Massachusetts Institute of Technology) (2020)

Yang, A., Kent, M.: Social media and organizational visibility: a sample of Fortune 500 corporations. Public Relat. Rev. **40**(3), 562–564 (2014)

Social Media Advertising and Consumer Purchase: A Literature Review

Tianxi Gao[✉]

Trinity College Dublin, Dublin, Ireland
tgao@tcd.ie

Abstract. This paper provides an overview of the literature on the use of social media advertising (SMA) and the key factors that affect the effectiveness of SMA. A total of 92 manuscripts published in top ranking journals in the last decade are reviewed. At the firm level, factors, such as brand's social role, time to post on social media platforms, frequency of social media posts, and genre of the posts, are found to affect consumer's purchasing decision and intention to share. At the individual consumer level, factors including demographic characteristics, general attitude toward online advertising, and privacy concerns are found to influence consumer's buying behaviors.

Keywords: Social media advertising · Social role · Consumer buying behaviors · Attitude toward advertising

1 Introduction

Mariam Webster Online (2004) defines social media as "forms of electronic communication (such as websites for social networking and microblogging) through which users create online communities to share information, ideas, personal messages, and other content (such as videos)." Social media platforms are a new popular carrier for companies to promote products and services. A recent survey indicates that three out of four advertisers had used social media and Internet for advertising and promotion, while over 60% of them had a specific plan to expand their budgets for social promotion and research on customer behaviors (Shaw 2018). Compared to traditional advertising and other types of digital marketing, social media advertising (SMA) is considered a faster and more cost-efficient way of approaching customers (Appel et al. 2019). With the prevelance of social media, consumers adapt new consumption habits such as seeking more information from social media platforms (Zhang et al. 2017). For instance, consumers share using experience on social media platforms, and new users take these coments as reference before making purchase decisions (Xu et al. 2010). Some of changes are due to constraint of time and location, and others are because of personal values and social influence (Bigne et al. 2005). As a result, many industries innovate to match changes in customers' lifestyles; for example, media companies offer digital version of newspapers, and they publish mobile applications where people can check news in a convinient way.

G. Salvendy and J. Wei (Eds.): HCII 2022, LNCS 13337, pp. 235–245, 2022.
https://doi.org/10.1007/978-3-031-05014-5_19

Similarly, traditional promotion has been replaced in many industries. Before, products such as cosmetics or clothing are most sold in retail stores. The promotion doesn't vary much especially to those, holding really strong brand loyalty. However, with the development of internet and social media, consumers' purchase behaviors will change quickly (Appel et al. 2019). Existing research has examined the differences between traditional marketing promotion and promotion through social media platforms. However, researches on consumers' goals when interacting with brand through social media are lacking (Naylor et al. 2012). In addition, social media platforms create a new opportunity that consumers are able to exchange information before making any purchase decision in a relatively short amount of time (Liu and Lopez 2014). According to de Vries et al. (2017), while traditional promotion is still effective today, firm-to-consumer social messages and impressions generate the similar effectiveness, and the trend is shifting from traditional advertising to social media advertising. However, research on the effects of other touch points and their interactions with e-shopping and social media sites is scarce (Lim et al. 2014). Given the scant research into social media advertising and especially its impact on consumer behaviors, this paper conducts a review of the literature on social media advertising. The purpose of this paper is to unravel the thereotical foundations for social media advertising as well as factors that influence consumer behaviors when exposed to social media advertising.

2   The Literature Review Procedure

When approaching to literatures, this study perfomed a keyword-search strategy on top journals that are ranked as ABS 3 and above. Besides the area of marketing, this study also included journals from the area of information systems (IS) since the IS literature also include studies on social media advertsing and social media marketing in general. The keywords used were "social advertising/advertisement", "social media advertising/advertisement", "social media platform", and "online advertising/advertisement". The search covered all the relevant literatures available on these top journals in the time period of 2010 to 2021. Only papers written in English were considered, and the search was conducted with Google Scholar and search engine within each journal. In the results, an initial sample contained 420 manuscripts with the key words that appeared in these papers. Then, advanced search was applied by selecting keywords as exact phrase. Manuscripts that contains such keywords above in the title and abstract are selected, and then each manuscript was carefully reviewed to make sure the content is highly relevant. At the end, 92 manuscripts were eventually reviewed. The distribution of these papers in the target journals is listed in Table 1.

The papers included in the literature review were content-analyzed in Excel, and 92 articles were categorized and their key findings were summarized. The researchers extracted key elements from these 92 articles and formed an Excel spreadsheet. These elements included year of publishment, published journal, main theory mentioned, context of research, data collection method, key variables of the study, key findings, and future research directions.

In general, the existing research has examined the use of social media as a tool of advertising, the involvement of social media platforms from both consumer and firm

Table 1. Summary of literatures

Journals	ABS ranking	Number of papers selected
Journal of Consumer Psychology	4*	5
Journal of Consumer Research	4*	3
Journal of Marketing	4*	19
Journal of Marketing Research	4*	11
Journal of Academy of Marketing Science	4*	5
Marketing Science	4*	3
International Journal of Research in Marketing	4	6
Journal of Retailing	4	2
European Journal of Marketing	3	4
Industrial Marketing Management	3	1
International Marketing Review	3	1
Journal of Advertising	3	10
Journal of Advertising Research	3	2
Journal of Interactive Marketing	3	3
Journal of International Marketing	3	2
Journal of Public Policy and Marketing	3	1
Marketing Letters	3	2
Marketing Theory	3	1
Psychology and Marketing	3	6
Quantitative Marketing and Economics	3	1
Decision Support Systems	3	2
International Journal of Electronic Commerce	3	1
Internet Research	3	1

perspectives, and the interactions between firms and consumers. The firm level perspectives include (a) social roles of brand (Huang et al. 2013; Li et al. 2020a, b; Summers et al. 2016); (b) characteristics of the post contents in social media platforms (Kanuri et al. 2018; Pancer et al. 2018; Xu et al. 2010); and (c) time and scheduling of the posts (Anderl et al. 2016; Kanuri et al. 2018). The essensial determinants of consumers' purchase behaviors include (a) consumer characteristics (Dahl et al. 2012; Xu et al. 2010); (b) consumers' attitudes toward online advertising and social media advertising (Li et al. 2012; Peng et al. 2018; Trusov et al. 2010); and (c) privacy concern (Kumar et al. 2016a; Tucker 2013).

3 Theoritical Positioning

First, we reviewed the theories used to study social media advertising to better understand its theoretical positioning. Table 2 below shows details about theories used. These theories are categorized around studies at the firm level, studies at the consumer level, and studies on the outcomes of SMA. Some studies (n = 12) did not refer to a specific theory, and several studies (n = 3) proposed new perspectives to examine online advertising and its relative consumer impacts. The most cited theories are Social Impact Theory (Zhang et al. 2014; Naylor et al. 2012; Colicev et al. 2018; Trusov et al. 2010; Li et al. 2012), Social Role Theory (Chen et al. 2017; Li et al. 2020a, b; Huang et al. 2013), Motivation Theory (Kumar et al. 2016a, b; de Vries et al. 2012; Kim et al. 2019) and Game Theory (Hartmann 2010; Zubcsek and Sarvary 2011). The Motivation Theory is used to explain consumer's purchasing behaviors, and the rest of three theories are used to explain firm's promotion strategy and the logic behind their targeting through social media channels. For instance, several papers introduced new concepts that derived from the Social Impact Theory, and some intergrated Social Role Theory with social network analysis technique (Li et al. 2012; Zhang et al. 2014). Some paper uses the Game Theory to explaine their findings where people make different decisions based on their opportunity cost (Zubcsek and Sarvary 2011).

Three studies proposed new theories that are associated with online advertising and consumer behaviors. One implies that engagement constructs are causally related to consumers' active and passive use of a mobile location-based social network (Pagani and Malacarne 2017). It notes that people are more interested in reading other comments or collecting information when other people around them experience a deeper sense of community (Pagani and Malacarne 2017). A new behavioral theory was also proposed to understand how the attributes of ads could affect consumer's buying intention (Fossen and Schweidel 2019). In addition, Borah et al. (2020) highlight that the use of humor in online advertising can create higher firm value. These theories are helpful in explaining how people react to social media advertising when different elements are involved such as location, tones of ads, and devices that consumers use (Nolan and Varey 2014).

4 Social Media Platforms

Most of the current studies have examined popular social media platforms such as Facebook, Twitter, Instagram, YouTube, LinkedIn, Snapchat, and Google + (Voorveld et al. 2018). Different social media platforms have different advantages. The most commonly used channels were ranked as social networks, microblogs, and microsites, blogs, and video sharing respectively, and the least favourable channels were virtual worlds, social games, and wikis (Ashley and Tuten 2014). Among those social media platforms, Facebook, Google +, and LinkedIn socred highest on the dimensions topicality, and Facebook outplays all platforms on social interaction (Minton et al. 2012). Instagram also ranked top on dimensions of topicality and pastime; while YouTube and Snapchat are the most popular platforms on the entertainment dimension (Voorveld et al. 2018).

Firms are using social media platforms as one of their promotion startegies, and research shows that advertising on multiple platforms is a more effective approach compared with the use of a single platform only (Snyder and Garcia-Garcia 2016). Most firms

Table 2. Overview of theories of social media advertising

Firm level	Consumer level	Outcomes
Audience Value Maximization Algorithm	Achievement Attribution Theory	Hierarchy of Effect Theory
Game Theory	Appraisal Theory	Reciprocity
Implicit Theory	Balance Theory	Self-efficacy Theory
Psychological Ownership Theory	Behavioral Reasoning Theory	Simultaneous-move games
Psychological Reactance Theory	Construal Level Theory	Theory of Reasoned Action
Rhetorical Theory	Hedonic Adaptation Theory	
Social Impact Theory	Just-world Theory	
Self-perception Theory	Mental Accounting	
Self-regulation Theory	Motivation Theory	
Social Role Theory	Self-signaling Theory	
Time Allocation Theory		

use a combination of traditional advertsing (Television advertising and newspaper) and social media advertising, but in general, brands that heavily rely on social media platforms earn higher brand awareness and have more followers (Ashley and Tuten 2014). Cross-platform advertising creates the highest ROI for a brand, and the ROI is maximized when messages are customized to each individual (Snyder and Garcia-Garcia 2016).

5   Firm Level

Firms use social media as platforms to display advertising, and existing literatures have examined some key factors that influence the interaction between firms and consumers. Consumers have different attitudes when firms are building different brand images on social media platforms. The contents of advertising plays a big role regarding consumers' reactions. Time and frequency of advertising displayed also affect consumers' purchasing decisions. This section describes the key findings about how fimrs are involved with social media on three categories.

Role of Brand.   When brands are positioning, they label themselves with various tags or focus (Summers et al. 2016). Firms usually build such culture and goals in their mission statement. Some research has studied the impact of company's social roles when they are deemed as "leaders", "friends", and "challengers". Consumers view products with greater market shares as "leaders" and products with lower shares as "challengers" (Li et al. 2020a, b). For instance, in automobile industry, cars using gaoline are the leaders because they take the biggest share from the market, and motocycles are challengers

(Borah et al. 2016). Any sort of e-bike and electronic cars are considered as "friend" because firms are creating images such as environment friendly and new energy. The way how brand displays advertising can create different consequence based on a brand's social role. For a brand that represents themselves as a friend to its customers, consumers tend to rate positively when its advertising is displayed horizontally and near to the image of customers (Bronner and de Hoog 2014). For "leaders", however, people rate positively when ads are located above and far from image of customers (Huang et al. 2013). In addition, studies have found that consumers react differently when brands are making comparisons. For instance, consumers are found to respond more favorably to "leader vs. challenger comaprsion", where the "leader" product is making comparison to "challenger" products to show its dominant advantage, and they respond less favorbaly to "challenger vs. leader comparison", where a "challenger" product looks for comparison against a "leader" (Li et al. 2020a, b).

Contents and Posts on Social Media Platforms. When firms post on social media channels, people evaluate the content and context and show their attitudes toward the posts by "liking", "sharing", "following", "reposting", "commenting", and/or "tagging". In general, simple posts are liked more when contents are longer, and people comment more when such posts are easy to read (Pancer et al. 2018). While liking, tagging, and sharing are the most common social media behaviors, liking and following a brand have the lowest consumer effort on engagement behaviors (John et al. 2017). Commenting and mentioning a friend in comments are more socially motivated (Pentina et al. 2018). In addition, people are more engaged when there are personal ties between senders and potential receivers (Trusov et al. 2010). However, such "influence of narrative transportation is negatively moderated by advertising disclosure that elicits persuasion knowledge" (Seo et al. 2018, pp. 1), and the negative impact of persuasion knowledge can be reduced when the ads received a high number of "likes" and "sharings".

Time and Scheduling. A majority of studies has been devoted to understanding consumer's activities and time schedules on checking social media. It is important to know when to post and how frequently to post on social media channels. As a result, previous studies have explored that consumers react differently when seeing the same content on different time periods of the day. For instance, Kanuri et al. (2018) find that posting content in the afternoon receives fewer link clicks than doing so in the morning. Post contents with positive emotions receive higher link clicks, and contents with negative emotions generate fewer link clicks in the afternoon than in the morning. Moreover, Anderl et al. (2016) suggest that consumer activities in the past can also influence their current purchase probability. In other words, consumers' past purchase can play a significant role in affecting their repeated purchase. And usually they would be more likely to share or comment when they see posts about their purchased products on social media platforms (Toker-Yildiz et al. 2017). Therefore, firms should occasionally make posts about their existing products to increase product recall and secure brand loyalty.

6   Consumer Level

Existing literature has explored factors that affect consumer's behaviors when using social media. Consumers' knowledge and level of confidence are highly involved with their social meida activities (Errmann et al. 2019). Consumers' general attitude toward advertising would differently affect their decision making when seeing the same ads. Privacy concern is also a key elements that easily draws consumers' attentions. This section provides detailed findings about the interaction between consumer and social media.

Consumer Characteristics

Self-esteem & Personal Knowledge. Consumer's self-esteem is found to play a significant role when they are required to evaluate a product or a brand (Wu et al. 2020). Consumer with low self-esteem would evaluate a product negatively when they receive suggestions from a referent, while people with high self-esteem are less likely to be influenced by other peoples' purchasing behaviors (Dahl et al. 2012). The research suggests that people with low self-esteem are more sensitive when they receive and exchange comparison information, and they tend to question their own judgement. In contrast, people with high self-esteem would evaluate products and brands equivalently regardless of the amount of competing information they receive and whom they receive such information from. In addition, people who don't have knowledge about the products would use referent as a guidance, and they would evaluate brands and products more positively when such referent comes from well-known sources such as popular magazine or celebrities. Consumers who have knowledge about the products or have personal experience with the products would use media as a tool to share user experience and evaluate brands and products (Xu et al. 2010).

Types of Users. Leaders in social media can be defined as influencers whose posting would largely draws other users' attentions or reactions such as "liking" and "commenting" (Hughes et al. 2019). Leaders are more active, and they usually make decisions independently (Appel et al. 2019). Leaders are more engaged on social media platforms, and they are the ones who usually make original posts. Followers can be identified as people who have lower amount of engagement on social media platforms, and their main activities are liking, sharing, and sometimes commenting. A good way to identify leaders on social media platforms is to look at one's number of subscribers, post frequency, and the number of likes, sharings, and comments on each original post (Wang et al. 2019). Leaders are influential when suggesting products because consumers see them as more persuasive than firm representatives (Huang et al. 2020). Therefore, an influential user leaving the platform could negatively affect firm's revenue because his/her followers are more likely to be affected by this influential user when they make purchase decisions (Trusov et al. 2010). It is an effective approach for firms to target users who have large numbers of common followers when they release a new product or service (Peng et al. 2018). Consumers may not care about what product or service that a firm advertises, but they care more about where they receive the information (Li et al. 2012). For instance, when consumers are surfing on the internet, products that are shared many times by other consumers are more likely to gain their attention. consumers assume that these are good products because many consumers make evaluation based on their personal experience (Appel et al. 2019).

Attitude Towards Social Media Advertising. Several studies have demonstrated that consumers' attitude toward general advertising and consumers' attitude toward social media are one of the key variables that would affect consumer's purchase decision. For instance, consumers tend to have more positive attitude toward ads when they see more ambient media that surprises them; therefore it increases consumer's intention to buy (Hutter and Hoffmann 2014). Consumer's attitude toward social media advertising has a positive effect on both message interaction behavior and social interaction behavior (Johnston et al. 2018). When online advertising is credible and trustworthy to consumers, they tend to have positive attitude toward online advertising, and therefore higher purchase intention (Errmann et al. 2019). When consumers think online advertising undermines their culture and social values, they will have negative attitude toward social media advertising (Wang and Sun 2010). As suggested by Li and colleagues, people will not be annoyed by advertisements shared by their friends, but they will be when advertisements are sent automatically by the platform (Li et al. 2012). Consumers are concerned with how advertisement approach to them because they do not want to be manipulated by big data even though it sometimes make their purchasing experience easier and more convenient (Deuze 2016).

Privacy Concern. Retailers such as Amazon analyze consumers' buying behaviors by using consumers' search history data and their previous purchase information to predict their interests. Other social media platforms collect consumer's word choice of posts and analyze what they may want to see. advertisers then use big data to deliver personalized advertising. It raises increasing privacy concerns where people feel their devices are spying on them (Tucker 2013). Personal engagement can significantly influence active usage especially when consumers are now concerned about privacy issues (Pagani and Malacarne 2017). Studies have consistently suggested that customers with greater privacy concerns are less likely to participate in firms' social media sites (Kumar et al. 2016a, B). Privacy issues can hurt both social media platforms and brands when an unethical behavior is exposed. Such privacy emergency creates unnecessary reputation risks for firms that use social media platform to display ads and collect consumers' information. Since social media advertising is a new channel comparing with television advertising and newspaper advertising, privacy policies are not generally understood. Research on government policy and interaction between social media's regional effects and consumer's bargaining power is scarce (Tucker 2013).

7 Conclusion

This paper has reviewed over 90 manuscripts that are published in top ranking journals in the past decade. This paper offers an overview of what has been mostly studied regarding social media advertising. Current research from top journals has generally examined the performance implications of social media advertising on consumer-related factors and firm-related factors. The variables affecting the performance and evaluation of advertising from both senders' and receivers' perspectives include firm's realeasing time and frequency, genre of the advertising, firm's social roles, conusmer's attitude toward online advertising, privacy concern, and consumer's characteristics and knowledge. Desipte the research progress, this paper also identifies revenue for future research. As the existing literatures focus on social media promotions on Facebook and other popular platforms, it is worth further investigation on the social media platforms other than Facebook, Twitter, Instagram, YouTube, LinkedIn, Snapchat, and Google +. It is challenging to indentify the same user who uses both Facebook and Twitter; therefore, cross platform effect is an area worth to dig deeper into. Future research should also investigate the frequency of advertisement displayed in social media platform how it influences consumers' intention to buy and rebuy. It is also worthwhile to investigate how the characteristics of advertisement such as length of advertisement, display (portrait vs. landscape) can influence consumers' attitudes toward the ads.

References

Anderl, E., Schumann, J.H., Kunz, W.: Helping firms reduce complexity in multichannel online data: a new taxonomy-based approach for customer journeys. J. Retail. **92**(2), 185–203 (2016)

Appel, G., Grewal, L., Hadi, R., Stephen, A.T.: The future of social media in marketing. J. Acad. Mark. Sci. **48**(1), 79–95 (2019). https://doi.org/10.1007/s11747-019-00695-1

Ashley, C., Tuten, T.: Creative strategies in social media marketing: an exploratory study of branded social content and consumer engagement. Psychol. Mark. **32**(1), 15–27 (2014)

Bigne, E. et al.: The impact of internet user shopping patterns and demographics on consumer mobile buying behaviour. J. Electron. Commer. Res. **6**(3), 193–209 (2005)

Borah, A., Tellis, G.J.: Halo (spillover) effects in social media: do product recalls of one brand hurt or help rival brands? J. Mark. Res. **53**(2), 143–160 (2016)

Borah, A., et al.: Improvised marketing interventions in social media. J. Mark. **84**(2), 69–91 (2020)

Bronner, F., de Hoog, R.: Social Media and consumer choice. Int. J. Mark. Res. **56**(1), 51–71 (2014)

Chen, X., Van Der Lans, R., Phan, T.Q.: Uncovering the importance of relationship characteristics in social networks: implications for seeding strategies. J. Mark. Res. **54**(2), 187–201 (2017)

Colicev, A., et al.: Improving consumer mindset metrics and shareholder value through social media: the different roles of owned and earned media. J. Mark. **82**(1), 37–56 (2018)

Dahl, D.W., Argo, J.J., Morales, A.C.: Social information in the retail environment: the importance of consumption alignment, referent identity, and self-esteem. J. Consum. Res. **38**(5), 860–871 (2012)

de Vries, L., Gensler, S., Leeflang, P.S.H.: Popularity of brand posts on brand fan pages: an investigation of the effects of social media marketing. J. Interact. Mark. **26**(2), 83–91 (2012)

de Vries, L., Gensler, S., Leeflang, P.S.H.: Effects of traditional advertising and social messages on brand-building metrics and customer acquisition. J. Mark. **81**(5), 1–15 (2017)

Deuze, M.: Living in media and the future of advertising. J. Advert. **45**(3), 326–333 (2016)

Errmann, A., et al.: Divergent effects of friend recommendations on disclosed social media advertising in the United States and Korea. J. Advert. **48**(5), 495–511 (2019)

Fossen, B.L., Schweidel, D.A.: Social TV, advertising, and sales: are social shows good for advertisers? Mark. Sci. **38**(2), 274–295 (2019)

Hartmann, W.R.: Demand estimation with social interactions and the implications for targeted marketing. Mark. Sci. **29**(4), 585–601 (2010)

Huang, S., et al.: Social advertising effectiveness across products: a large-scale field experiment. Mark. Sci. **39**(6), 1142–1165 (2020)

Huang, X.(I.), Li, X., Zhang, M.: "Seeing" the social roles of brands: how physical positioning influences brand evaluation. J. Consum. Psychol. **23**(4), 509–514 (2013)

Hughes, C., Swaminathan, V., Brooks, G.: Driving brand engagement through online social influencers: an empirical investigation of sponsored blogging campaigns. J. Mark. **83**(5), 78–96 (2019)

Hutter, K., Hoffmann, S.: Surprise, surprise. Ambient media as promotion tool for retailers. J. Retail. **90**(1), 93–110 (2014)

John, L.K., et al.: Does "liking" lead to loving? The impact of joining a brand's social network on marketing outcomes. J. Mark. Res. **54**(1), 144–155 (2017)

Johnston, W.J., et al.: Behavioral implications of international social media advertising: an investigation of intervening and contingency factors. J. Int. Mark. **26**(2), 43–61 (2018)

Kanuri, V.K., Chen, Y., Sridhar, S.(H.): Scheduling content on social media: theory, evidence, and application. J. Mark. **82**(6), 89–108 (2018)

Kim, M.-Y., Moon, S., Iacobucci, D.: The influence of global brand distribution on brand popularity on social media. J. Int. Mark. **27**(4), 22–38 (2019)

Kumar, A., et al.: From social to sale: the effects of firm-generated content in social media on customer behavior. J. Mark. **80**(1), 7–25 (2016a)

Kumar, V., Choi, J.W.B., Greene, M.: Synergistic effects of social media and traditional marketing on brand sales: capturing the time-varying effects. J. Acad. Mark. Sci. **45**(2), 268–288 (2016b)

Li, X., et al.: The challenge of being a challenger: social dominance orientation shapes the impact of "challenger vs. leader" comparisons. J. Consum. Psychol. **31**(1), 55–71 (2020a)

Li, X., Wang, C., Zhang, Y.: The dilemma of social commerce. Internet Res. **30**(3), 1059–1080 (2020b)

Li, Y.-M., Lee, Y.-L., Lien, N.-J.: Online social advertising via influential endorsers. Int. J. Electron. Commer. **16**(3), 119–154 (2012)

Lim, J.-S., Al-Aali, A., Heinrichs, J.H.: Impact of satisfaction with e-retailers' touch points on purchase behavior: the moderating effect of search and experience product type. Mark. Lett. **26**(2), 225–235 (2014)

Liu, Y., Lopez, R.A.: The impact of social media conversations on consumer brand choices. Mark. Lett. **27**(1), 1–13 (2014)

Minton, E., et al.: Sustainable marketing and social media. J. Advert. **41**(4), 69–84 (2012)

Naylor, R.W., Lamberton, C.P., West, P.M.: Beyond the "like" button: the impact of mere virtual presence on brand evaluations and purchase intentions in social media settings. J. Mark. **76**(6), 105–120 (2012)

Nolan, T., Varey, R.J.: Re-cognising the interactive space. Mark. Theory **14**(4), 431–450 (2014)

Pagani, M., Malacarne, G.: Experiential engagement and active vs. passive behavior in mobile location-based social networks: The moderating role of privacy. J. Interact. Mark. **37**, 133–148 (2017)

Pancer, E., et al.: How readability shapes social media engagement. J. Consum. Psychol. **29**(2), 262–270 (2018)

Peng, J., et al.: Network overlap and content sharing on social media platforms. J. Mark. Res. **55**(4), 571–585 (2018)

Pentina, I., Guilloux, V., Micu, A.C.: Exploring social media engagement behaviors in the context of luxury brands. J. Advert. **47**(1), 55–69 (2018)

Seo, Y., et al.: Narrative transportation and paratextual features of social media in viral advertising. J. Advert. **47**(1), 83–95 (2018)

Shaw, A.: Council post: How social media can move your business forward. Forbes (2018). https://www.forbes.com/sites/forbescommunicationscouncil/2018/05/11/how-social-media-can-move-your-business-forward/?sh=551618cb4cf2. Accessed 4 Dec 2021

Snyder, J., Garcia-Garcia, M.: Advertising across platforms: conditions for multimedia campaigns: a method for determining optimal media investment and creative strategies across platforms. J. Advert. Res. **56**(4), 352–367 (2016)

"Social media." Merriam-Webster.com Dictionary. Merriam-Webster. https://www.merriam-webster.com/dictionary/social%20media. Accessed 8 Feb 2022

Summers, C.A., Smith, R.W., Reczek, R.W.: An audience of one: behaviorally targeted ads as implied social labels. J. Consum. Res. **43**(1), 156–178 (2016)

Toker-Yildiz, K., et al.: Social Interactions and monetary incentives in driving consumer repeat behavior. J. Mark. Res. **54**(3), 364–380 (2017)

Trusov, M., Bodapati, A.V., Bucklin, R.E.: Determining influential users in internet Social networks. J. Mark. Res. **47**(4), 643–658 (2010)

Tucker, C.E.: Social networks, personalized advertising, and privacy controls. J. Mark. Res. **51**(5), 546–562 (2013)

Voorveld, H.A., et al.: Engagement with social media and social media advertising: the differentiating role of platform type. J. Advert. **47**(1), 38–54 (2018)

Wang, Q., et al.: What makes online content viral? The contingent effects of hubusers versus non–hub users on social media platforms. J. Acad. Mark. Sci. **47**(6), 1005–1026 (2019)

Wang, Y., Sun, S.: Examining the role of beliefs and attitudes in online advertising. Int. Mark. Rev. **27**(1), 87–107 (2010)

Wu, C.W., Guaita Martínez, J.M., Martín Martín, J.M.: An analysis of social media marketing strategy and performance in the context of fashion brands: the case of Taiwan. Psychol. Mark. **37**(9), 1185–1193 (2020)

Xu, A.J., Wyer, R.S.: Puffery in advertisements: the effects of media context, communication norms, and consumer knowledge. J. Consum. Res. **37**(2), 329–343 (2010)

Zhang, X., et al.: An examination of social influence on shopper behavior using video tracking data. J. Mark. **78**(5), 24–41 (2014)

Zhang, Y., et al.: Online shopping and social media: friends or foes? J. Mark. **81**(6), 24–41 (2017)

Zubcsek, P.P., Sarvary, M.: Advertising to a social network. Quant. Mark. Econ. **9**(1), 71–107 (2011)

The Synergistic Effect of Sales Discount and Mobile Advertising: How KOL Influence Online Education Community Purchases

Jiao Ge[✉] and Jinyu Guo

Harbin Institute of Technology (Shenzhen), Shenzhen, People's Republic of China
jiaoge@hit.edu.cn

Abstract. Understanding the marketing mixed strategy with internet Key Opinion Leader (KOL) marketing in online brand community has remained a challenge for both academics and practitioners. Previous studies have explored different characteristics of KOL and their impact on customer purchase attentions. Contributing to this stream of the literature, our study explores the direct effect of KOL activeness and influence characteristics on customer online education real purchases as well as the mediating effect of sales discount and mobile advertising on such effect. Using real online education community individual transaction data collected from May to the end of August 2019 with the sample size of 29070 transactions. Our study shows that both high degree of activeness and influence level of KOL has a direct effect on online user's real purchase amounts and purchase times. And such effect can be mediated through sales discount and mobile advertising. The results have great implications to guide firms in terms of their marketing strategies in maximizing the return on investment in sales discount, mobile advertising and KOL marketing.

Keywords: Online key opinion leader · Online brand community · Sales discount · Mobile advertising · Education purchases

1 Introduction

Online Brand Community refers to the Online Community in which enterprises or Brand parties participate and play a leading role. Online brand community can be also regarded as a virtual interactive network established by enterprises to maintain long-term relationships with consumers of specific brands. According to the Report on China's Internet Development Trend, The number of Internet users in China reached 1.08 billion in February 2020, with diverse and inclusive needs. The success of online brand communities is inseparable from users' positive contributions, such as sharing their consumption experience, discussing usage issues, and commenting on newly launched products (Shen et al. 2018).

Demiray (2019) showed that the interaction between consumers and brands becomes more dynamic and powerful through online brand communities. Social media supports online brand communities and community members by actively join in content creation

G. Salvendy and J. Wei (Eds.): HCII 2022, LNCS 13337, pp. 246–255, 2022.
https://doi.org/10.1007/978-3-031-05014-5_20

(Kamboj and Rahman 2017). If enterprises can help community members reducing the cost of information acquisition through brand community, users' willingness to participate in community communication can be improved, and users' trust and even satisfaction to the community can be increased. Homburg et al. (2015) studied how consumers react to the company's active participation in consumer-to-consumer interaction in firm's online community. Luo et al. (2016) suggested that effective interaction can promote the harmony of online brand communities and improve the quality of community relations. All these previous studies on online brand communities either the analysis of the mechanism of online brands or the studies of user behavior of online brand communities. However, the research of online brand communities on users' purchasing behavior needs to be supplemented, especially how online opinion leaders influence users' actual purchasing behavior through online brand communities.

The Key Opinion Leader (KOL) is an intermediary of information dissemination and an active person in transmitting information (Lazarsfield 1944). Rogers (1995) defined key opinion leader as "the degree to which an individual can influence other individuals' attitudes or public behaviors in a desired way with relative times". Opinion leaders are often at the center of a network that includes connected users of information. Three major factors that determine opinion leaders' influence are the elaboration of values of network, professional knowledge and technology, and the nature of social network. Subsequent studies have found that the common characteristics of KOLs include education level, moral image, social reputation (Mancuso 1969) and participation level in product activities (Corey 1971).

With the development of Internet technology and the promotion of online shopping, network KOLs have become the focus of people's research, mainly studying how to identify KOLs and what kind of influence they will have. Liu et al. (2020) studied the different influences of the interaction, authority and activity of KOL characteristics on online communities based on social capital theory. Hughes et al. (2019) found that the influence of KOL blog publishing on consumers' online engagement depends on the characteristics of bloggers and article content, while the type of social media platform and the intention of competing product advertising further mitigated this effect. Therefore, the studies of KOLs characteristics not only include activeness and influences, but also extended to include self-plasticity, uniqueness and product participation level. However, how network KOLs influence online customers' actual purchasing behavior remains to be further studied.

Therefore, this paper intends to solve two research questions: (1) in online brand communities, how do the characteristics of online KOLs influence the actual purchasing behavior of users, and what are the specific impacts? (2) What role do corporate promotional activities in online brand communities, such as price promotion and mobile advertising, play in the effect of online KOLs on online customers' real purchasing behaviors? To solve these questions, hypotheses with literature reviews were first developed. Empirical methodology then is explained with data and model explanations. Econometric models are estimated and results are presented and discussed to the end.

2 Literature Review and Hypotheses

Para-social Interaction Theory was first used to define the relationship between the audience and performers (Horton and Wohl 1956), which was considered to be an illusion of intimacy compared to real interpersonal relationships. Trough internet, multiple fans can form an online community, and members share similar values, beliefs and interests with bloggers (Nambisan and Watt 2011). Welbourne and Grant (2015) believed that due to the quasi-social interaction established by unique speakers, YouTube channels with one speaker are more popular and influential than channels with multiple speakers. Celebrities who connect more with the audience are more persuasive (McCormick 2016). Liu et al. (2020) studied that with the increase of opinion leader activities, activities promote unilateral introduction of knowledge, declaration of common goals and elimination of members' perceived uncertainty, which can eventually be transformed into people's actual behaviors for the sustainable development of online communities. Based on this quasi-social interaction theory, the one-way information transmission between network KOLs and users builds a quasi-social interaction relationship between them. In this relationship, different characteristics of network KOLs will have different influences on users. Therefore, we propose:

H1: online education community KOLs with different characteristics have different influence on consumer purchases.

The activity degree of network Key Opinion Leaders (KOLs) refers to the enthusiasm of network opinion leaders in social media (Li et al. 2013). When KOLs are in a high degree of activity, they are more active online and potentially generate more contents. Which implies sending more information to users online. Swani et al. (2013) pointed out that users can confirm the information published by network KOLs on social media by browsing number, while the number of "likes" indicates that users have positive feelings about the content published by network opinion leaders. Li et al. (2013) took the network opinion leaders of Weibo platform as the research object, and measured the user activity through the number of original Weibo posts, forwarded Weibo posts and comments, reflecting the initiative of user nodes in communication. According to Shen et al. (2018), online KOLs have positive impacts on users' purchase intention. Therefore, the research hypothesis associated with KOLs activity is proposed as follows:

H1a: KOLs with high degree of activity increases consumers' online purchases.

The influence of network KOLs refers to the influence of network opinion leaders on users' purchasing through social media (Li et al. 2013). Previous studies expressed the influence of network opinion leaders qualitatively based on their approval, support and trust from users, or measured the influence of network opinion leaders simply by the number of fans or supports. Jiang et al. (2011) studied that the number of followers on Twitter is weakly correlated with user influence. Li et al. (2013) measures the influence of online opinion leaders by the coverage degree and reading degree of their published texts. They used the number of retweets to measure the value of a microblog and the number of comments to measure the popularity of a microblog when evaluating the user nodes in the microblog network, both of which represent user influence. Generally speaking, the greater the influence of network opinion leaders is, the more attractive it is to users. Therefore, the research hypothesis associated with KOLs influence is proposed as follows:

H1b: KOLs with high degree of influence increases consumers' online purchases.

Promotion includes advertising, personal sales, public relations and various forms of promotional activities (Kim and Lee 2017). In this research, promotions in online brand communities are the discounts that users get when they buy products. Wu et al. (2015) showed that companies with emphasis on the promotion of customer between the depth of the community participation significantly increase the purchase times, moreover, among preventive clients, the impact of deep engagement is quite different. Meire et al. (2019) investigated the role of corporate social media interaction plans centering on customer experience interaction events in influencing customers' emotions in digital interaction, and suggested that marketers can influence customer interaction performance and the mood of digital interaction, and that informational content generated by marketers (rather than emotional content) can enhance customer emotion for adverse event outcomes. Cai et al. (2016), based on the theory of purchase value, proved that providing low discounts for non-essential purchases would reduce perceived transaction value and consumers' purchase tendency by using the second scan panel data set (6 different product categories) and 5 experiments (actual purchase). However, this effect reverses when the purchase is large or necessary. Guha et al. (2018) studied the relationship between discount depth and purchase intention and concluded that sales induced by price promotion depends largely on the depth of the discount. Humna and Celeste (2018) showed that loyal customers switch brands according to positive situations such as promotional activities. In this study, promotional offers are the benefits that users get through online brand communities. Shoham et al. (2008) believed that the relationship between KOLs and audiences is actually one of replication and promotion. Therefore, the hypotheses of research on promotional offers in online brand communities are as follows:

H2: sales discount posted in online community by KOLs mediates the effect of KOLs on customer purchases.

Mobile advertising in this paper refers to the advertising in the form of products published by enterprises through online brand communities. This kind of mobile advertising from the online brand community can also represent the ability of the online brand community to spread marketing. Goldfarb and Tucker (2011) believed that mobile advertising can replace offline advertising and promote consumers' purchase intention. Swani et al. (2013) pointed out that consumer social interaction in advertising is a proxy for consumer engagement and the effectiveness of advertising messages. Because enterprises have a variety of marketing means, they tend to promote their brands and products more widely in the form of mobile advertising. Therefore, online brand communities tend to push as many online advertisements as possible to further attract users in online brand communities, increase users' purchasing intention and enhance their purchasing behavior. This paper hopes to verify whether mobile advertising has a significant impact on users' purchasing behavior by analyzing their purchasing behavior records. In this study, enterprises publish online advertisements and some promotional offers in online brand communities through online opinion leaders. Therefore, they can match online opinion leaders by tracking users' promotional offer sources, and then verify the influence of online advertisements published by online opinion leaders on actual purchasing behaviors. Therefore, research assumptions about mobile advertising in online brand communities are as follows:

H3: brand mobile advertising in online education community mediates the interrelationships between KOL characteristics and customer purchases.

3 Methodology

3.1 Data

This study selects Penguin Tutoring, an online education platform operated by Tencent, as the research object. Based on the development and sales data of the platform and online brand communities, we collect user transaction data for K1 to K12 education. The data collection period is from May 1, 2019 to August 31, 2019. The characteristics of network KOLs and corresponding user transaction data are recorded by internal work of enterprises and manually sorted. The most relevant 14 network KOLs are identified according to the matching period from May to August. The method of screening user transaction records is to screen out all transaction records of all users through transaction user IDS guided by network KOLs every day. The account information of these 14 network opinion leaders and the product participation of account management personnel are obtained (i.e., Follow teachers to live class and cooperate with teachers and students to interact with each other), daily transaction user information and transaction amount guided by online KOLs. The daily number of all kinds of posts, views and likes of these 14 KOLs from May to August are also collected on the online education platform. Final sample size used in this research is 29070 transaction level data from May 1, 2019 to August 31, 2019 for all 14 KOLs.

Dependent Variable. The online education community users' actual purchases, including the purchase amount and purchase times are used as dependent variables. The purchase amount is the description of a single transaction at a certain time node, and the purchase times is the description of repeated purchase behaviors of users in chronological order. LnPurchasePikt represents the logarithm in RMB, of the purchase amount of the transaction numbered i that occurred at time t for the kth KOL. Same goes to the purchase numbers, PurchaseNikt, in units of one purchase.

Independent Variables. The independent variables of the model include the degree of activity and the degree of influence of network KOLs. Activityikt represents the Activity of the network KOLs, and Impactikt represents the influence of the network KOLs. Past studies use AHP method to process the number of original ideas, reposts, comments, comments, reposts and fans representing network opinion leaders, so as to obtain indicators of activity, influence and authority. Liu et al. (2020) authoritatively measured the characteristics of opinion leaders by the number of fans, followers and mutual followers. In this research, since Tencent Penguin Tutoring is taken as the research object, the characteristic data of Impactikt of network KOLs consists of the number of posts, views and comments. Therefore, Impactikt is obtained from the actual amount of consumption guided by network KOLs. Since the influence of network KOLs does not change by day, the actual amount of purchase guided by network KOLs is calculated based on the transaction time and the total amount within one week before and after the transaction, to reasonably represent the influence of network opinion leaders before and after the trading day.

Mediating Variables. Promotion of online brand community (Promotion$_{ikt}$) and mobile advertising of online education community (Onlinead$_{ikt}$) are two mediating variables. Promotion$_{ikt}$ is defined as product original price minus the price paid by users, then divided by product original price. Onlinead$_{ikt}$ is coded as 0, 1 respectively to indicate whether the transaction is an online advertisement published by enterprises or not with 0 means no and 1 means yes.

Controls Variables. User Return (Return$_{ikt}$) and network KOL gender (Female$_{ikt}$) are two control variables. The user's return or exchange record is one of the characteristics of the user's purchase behavior reflecting the user's purchase habit which might have impacts on customer's purchase behaviors. Therefore, the user with the return or exchange behavior is recorded as 1, and the user without the return or exchange record is recorded as 0 for Return$_{ikt}$. Female$_{ikt}$ is representing gender of one of the characteristics of network KOL, which marked as 1 and male is marked as 0.

3.2 Model

The econometric panel models that used to test the proposed hypotheses are listed below as model 3-1, 3-2 and 3-3.

$$Y_{ikt} = \beta_0 + \beta_1 * Activity_{ikt} + \beta_2 * Impact_{ikt} + \beta_3 * Promotion_{ikt} + \beta_4 * Onlinead_{ikt} + \mu_i^{id} * \beta_5$$
$$+ \mu_{k*}^{kol} \beta_6 + Controls_{ikt} * \beta_7 + \varepsilon_{ikt}^Y \tag{3-1}$$

$$Promotion_{ikt} = \alpha_0 + \alpha_1 * Activity_{ikt} + \alpha_2 * Impact_{ikt} + \mu_i^{id} * \alpha_3 + \mu_{k*}^{kol} \alpha_4 + Controls_{ikt} * \alpha_5 + \varepsilon_{ikt}^P \tag{3-2}$$

$$Onlinead_{ikt} = \gamma_0 + \gamma_1 * Activity_{ikt} + \gamma_2 * Impact_{ikt} + \mu_i^{id} * \gamma_3 + \mu_{k*}^{kol} \gamma_4 + Controls_{ikt} * \gamma_5 + \varepsilon_{ikt}^A \tag{3-3}$$

Where Y_{ikt} is a 2 * ikt vector of dependent variables which include $PurchaseP_{ikt}$ and $PurchaseN_{ikt}$. i indicates individual customers from 1 to n. k represents KOLs from 1 to k. t is the purchasing time. Both $Activity_{ikt}$ and $Impact_{ikt}$ are independent variables representing KOL's characteristics. $Promotion_{ikt}$ and $Onlinead_{ikt}$ are mediating variables representing sales discount and mobile advertising, respectively. μ^{id} and μ^{kol} are n * n and k * n vectors of the fixed effects for individual customer and KOL, respectively. $Controls_{ikt}$ is a 2 * ikt vector of control variables which include $Return_{ikt}$ and $Female_{ikt}$. β_0 to β_4, α_0 to α_2, γ_0 to γ_2 are estimated parameters. β_5, α_3, and γ_3 are the parameter of n * 1 and n * 1 vector. $\varepsilon^Y{}_{ikt}$, $\varepsilon^P{}_{ikt}$, and $\varepsilon^A{}_{ikt}$ are residuals where each follows normal distribution with mean zero and constant variance.

4 Data Analysis and Results

In this research, fixed effects panel model is applied to control for differences between individual customers and individual KOLs. We ran the Hausman test to decide whether a fixed- or random-effects model would be the right choice. The Hausman test suggested that a fixed-effects model is preferable. Table 1 reports the fixed-effects model results. When purchase times (*Purchasen*) is used as the dependent variable in the model, Poisson regression with maximum likelihood estimation is applied for this count number

Table 1. Estimation results

Variables	Model 3-1 (LnPurchaseP)	Model 3-1 (PurchaseN)	Model 3-2 (Promotion)	Model 3-2 (Onlinead)
Control variables				
Return	−0.059 (0.046)	0.049***(0.002)	0.031**(0.011)	0.017(0.015)
Female	−0.346 (0.632)	−1.247***(0.063)	−0.014(0.156)	−0.427**(0.200)
Independent variables				
Activity	0.310***(0.067)	0.245***(0.008)	−0.088***(0.016)	0.084***(0.021)
Impact	0.911***(0.062)	−0.581***(0.006)	−0.040**(0.015)	−0.136***(0.019)
Promotion	−0.424***(0.024)	−0.523***(0.004)		
Onlinead	−2.744***(0.019)	0.334***(0.003)		
Individual fixed effects	Controlled	Controlled	Controlled	Controlled
KOL fixed effects	Controlled	Controlled	Controlled	Controlled
Constant	3.892***(0.445)	3.443***(0.003)	0.046(0.110)	0.459**(0.141)
Number of observations	29070	29070	29070	29070
R-squared	0.545	0.587 (Pseudo R2)	0.232	0.196
F	34.05	65083.30 (LR)	8.60	6.95
Prob > F	0.000	0.000 (Prob > Chi2)	0.000	0.000

***: $p < .01$; **: $p < .05$; *: $p < .10$; standardized errors in parentheses

dependent variable model. Linear panel models are applied to other dependent variable models.

As shown in the results of Model 3-1 in Table 1, network KOLs' activity level has a significant positive impact on user purchase amount ($\beta = 0.310$, $p < 0.001$) and user purchase times ($\beta = 0.245$, $p < 0.001$), supporting *H1a*. The influence level of network KOLs has a significant positive impact on users' purchase amount ($\beta = 0.911$, $p < 0.001$), and a significant negative effect on users' cumulative times of purchase ($\beta = -0.581$, $p < 0.001$), partly supporting *H1b*.

In terms of the mediating effect of sales discount, as the results shown in Model 3-1 in Table 1, Sales discount has a significant negative effect on both purchase amount ($\beta = -0.424$, $p < 0.001$) and purchase times ($\beta = -0.523$, $p < 0.001$). In addition, the results of Model 3-2 and Model 3-3 in Table 1 show that online KOLs' activity level ($\beta = -0.088$, $p < 0.001$) and influence level ($\beta = -0.040$, $p < 0.05$) have significant effects on sales discount promoted by KOLs. Therefore, the mediating role of sales discount between the effect of activity level and influence level of network KOLs on customers' online community purchase amount and purchase times is verified, supporting *H2*.

In terms of the mediating effect of mobile advertising, as shown in Model 3-1 in Table 1, Mobile advertising has a significant negative effect on purchase amount ($\beta = -2.744$, p < 0.001) but a significant positive effect on purchase times ($\beta = 0.334$, p < 0.001). In addition, the results of Model 3-2 and Model 3-3 in Table 1 show that both KOL activity level ($\beta = 0.084$, p < 0.001) and influence level ($\beta = -0.136$, p < 0.001) have significant effects on mobile advertising. Therefore, the mediating role of mobile advertising for the effect of both KOL activity level and influence level on the amounts of users' online education community purchase and the times of users' purchase has been verified, supporting *H3*.

5 Discussion

The characteristics of network opinion leaders are measured by activeness and influence. Data regression results show that both the activity and influence characteristic of network KOLs have significant positive impacts on consumers online education community purchasing behaviors. This is consistent with previous research results on the identification of network opinion leader characteristics Li et al. (2013). Therefore, for the network KOLs in the online brand community, maintaining a high degree of activity and actively expanding their influence are the most effective methods to guide the increase of users' purchasing behavior and promote the increase of users' purchasing amount.

The estimation results also showed that both sales discount and mobile advertising that distributed by KOLs in the online education community are playing the mediating role in the relationship between the characteristics of KOL activeness and influence and consumers' online education purchase amounts and also purchase times. Our results are consistent with the previous research for KOLs. Guha et al. (2018) suggested that promotional offers have a positive impact on consumers' purchase intention. Wu et al. (2015) believed that in-depth community participation increases the times of user purchases. Camacho et al. (2019) showed that higher engagement intensity leads to higher creative quality and better business performance. Goldfarb and Tucker (2011) believed that mobile advertising will increase users' purchase intention. However, we not only extend the current KOL research to online brand community of education industry with real transactional data, but also found the mediating role of sales discount and mobile advertising for the KOL impacts on consumers' purchase behaviors.

Therefore, the marketing strategies that we suggest for enterprise online community marketing with KOLs are: (1) at the beginning of building online brand community, attention should be paid to the form and scope of topic communication of online brand community from the perspective of community model, so as to help and encourage KOLs to increase their activeness and influence in online brand community. (2) using as much as incentives to encourage KOLs to actively participate in online community topic discussions and brand activities, and to pay attention to maintaining customer group relations, and to maintain their influence on user groups. (3) In the operation process of online brand communities, instead of sending the sale promotion or sending mobile advertising likes directly by the company to online users, issuing sales discountal coupons or mobile advertising links through online KOLs can generally increase users' purchasing behavior, which is conducive to improving brand owners' sales.

Acknowledgement. The research is funded by the National Natural Science Foundation of China (Grant number: 71831005).

References

Cai, F., Bagchi, R., Gauri, D.K.: Boomerang effects of low price discounts: how low price discounts affect purchase propensity. J. Consum. Res. **42**(5), 804–816 (2016)

Camacho, N., Nam, H., Kannan, P.K., Stremersch, S.: Tournaments to crowdsource innovation: the role of moderator feedback and participation intensity. J. Mark. **83**(2), 138–157 (2019)

Corey, L.G.: People who claim to be opinion leaders: identifying their characteristics by self-report. J. Mark. **35**(4), 48–53 (1971)

Demiray, B.: Exploring the impact of brand community identification on Facebook: firm-directed and self-directed drivers. J. Bus. Res. **96**, 115–124 (2019)

Goldfarb, A., Tucker, C.: Online display advertising: targeting and obtrusiveness. Mark. Sci. **30**(3), 389–404 (2011)

Guha, A., Biswas, A., Grewal, D., Verma, S., Banerjee, S., Nordfalt, J.: Reframing the discount as a comparison against the sale price: does it make the discount more attractive? J. Mark. Res. **55**(3), 339–351 (2018)

Homburg, C., Ehm, L., Artz, M.: Measuring and managing consumer sentiment in an online community environment. J. Mark. Res. **52**(5), 629–641 (2015)

Horton, D., Wohl, R.R.: Mass communication and para-social interaction: observations on intimacy at a distance. Psychiatry Interpersonal Biol. Process. **19**(3), 215–229 (1956)

Hughes, C., Swaminathan, V., Brooks, G.: Driving brand engagement through online social influencers: an empirical investigation of sponsored blogging campaigns. J. Mark. **83**(5), 78–96 (2019)

Humna, H., Celeste, R.: Evaluating the impact of promotional activities on brand loyalty. J. Mark. Logist. **8**(1), 63–87 (2018)

Jiang, L., Yu, M., Zhou, M.: Target—dependent Twitter sentiment classification. In: C1 Proceedings of Annual Meeting of the Association for Computational Linguistics, pp. 151–160. Association for Computational Linguistics, Oregon, USA (2011)

Kamboj, S., Rahman, Z.: Understanding customer participation in online brand communities: literature review and future research agenda. J. Cetacean Res. Manag. **20**(3), 306–334 (2017)

Kim, S.H., Lee, S.A.: Promoting customers' involvement with service brands: evidence from coffee shop customers. J. Serv. Mark. **31**(7), 733–744 (2017)

Lazarsfeld, P.F.: The Election is over. Public Opin. Q. **8**(3), 317–330 (1944)

Li, Y.Y., Ma, S.Q., Zhang, Y.H., Huang, R., Kinshuk: An improved mix framework for opinion leader identification in online learning communities. Knowl.-Based Syst. **43**, 43–51 (2013)

Liu, Y., Gu, Z.L., Ko, T.H., Liu, J.: Identifying key opinion leaders in social media via modality-consistent harmonized discriminant embedding. IEEE Trans. Cybern. **50**(2), 717–728 (2020)

Luo, N., Zhang, M., Hu, M.: How community interactions contribute to harmonious community relationships and customers' identification in online brand community. Int. J. Inf. Manag. **36**(5), 673–685 (2016)

Mancuso, J.R.: Why not create opinion leaders for new product introductions? J. Mark. **33**(3), 20–25 (1969)

McCormick, K.: Redefining the celebrity: 'self-made' versus 'manufactured' celebrity endorsers' impact on consumers' attitudes and purchase intentions. Fashion Style Popular Cult. **3**(3), 339–356 (2016)

Meire, M., Hewett, K., Ballings, M., Kumar, V., Van Den Poel, D.: The role of marketer-generated content in customer engagement marketing. J. Mark. **83**(6), 21–42 (2019)

Nambisan, P., Watt, J.H.: Managing customer experiences in online product communities. J. Bus. Res. **64**(8), 889–895 (2011)

Rogers, E.M.: Diffusion of Innovations. The Free Press, New York (1995)

Shen, X., Li, Y., Sun, Y., et al.: Person-environment fit, commitment, and customer contribution in online brand community: a nonlinear model. J. Bus. Res. **85**, 117–126 (2018)

Shoham, A., Ruvio, A., Davidow, M.: (Un)ethical consumer behavior: Robin Hoods or plain hoods? J. Consum. Mark. **25**(4–5), 200–210 (2008)

Swani, K., Weinberger, M., Gulas, C.: The impact of violent humor on advertising success: a gender perspective. J. Advert. **42**(4), 308–319 (2013)

Welbourne, D.J., Grant, W.J.: Science communication on YouTube: factors that affect channel and video popularity. Public Underst. Sci. **25**(6), 706–718 (2015)

Wu, J., Huang, L., Zhao, J.L.: The deeper, the better? Effect of online brand community activity on customer purchase frequency. Inf. Manag. **52**(7), 813–823 (2015)

Do We Need to Push Harder When Social Commerce Crosses Borders: A Cross-cultural Empirical Research

Shangui Hu, Fengle Ji[✉], and Jiankai Wang[✉]

Anhui University of Technology, Ma'anshan, People's Republic of China
stanley@ahut.edu.cn, JFL13608928535@163.com, onairwang@163.com

Abstract. When social media facilitates social commerce to cross borders, international customers encounter unexpected challenges due to cultural novelties. How environmental factors influence customers' trust and their engagement in cross-cultural social commerce operations remains under-investigated because social media usage does not necessarily generate customers' engagement in social commerce. Based on the S-O-R paradigm, a large scale of 2058 samples from 135 countries were surveyed to examine the proposed research model. The regression analysis results explicate the mechanism whereby two dimensions of social media usage, informational and socializing, exert impacts on customers' trust toward social commerce and final engagement. Further, cultural distance has been identified as a deterring environmental factor negatively influencing customers' engagement in cross-cultural social commerce environment. Both theoretical and practical implications are also discussed.

Keywords: Social commerce · Trust · Engagement · Cross-cultural environment

1 Introduction

The advancement of information technology transforms traditional electronic commerce into an evolved form which enables users to leverage on interaction function of various social media platforms to share posted information and make communications before their purchase behaviors (Wang and Zhang 2012; Liu et al. 2020). The new form of electronic commerce, conceptualized as social commerce, effectively converges social media platforms and Web 2.0 technologies (Hajli and Sims 2015). As a result, the new business paradigm from a seller-oriented to customer-oriented model has led to a tremendous growth of trade volume (Tuncer 2021). The vast benefits brought by the successful transformation have encouraged business executives to take every possible measure to attract potential customers and seek customers' engagement in social commerce (Osatuyi et al. 2020). As such, numerous studies have been conducted about the determinants of customers' engagement in social commerce, such as social media usage (Wang and Herrando 2019; Mikalef et al. 2017; Osatuyi et al. 2020). However, inconsistent findings have been reached pertaining to how social media usage facilitates the operation process of social commerce and thereby enhancing customers' engagement (Zhang et al. 2017; Tuncer 2021). Given that the importance of social media platforms and inclusive research findings about the roles of social media usage in social commerce operations, there is an urgent need to further examine whether and how social media usage enhances users' positive psychological changes and further engagement behaviors.

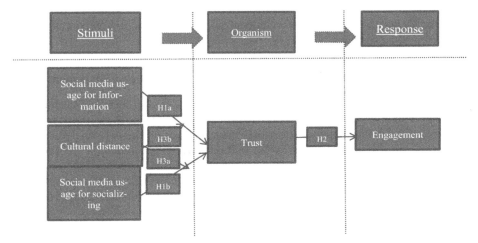

Fig. 1. Proposed research model

2   Conceptual Framework and Hypothesis Development

2.1   Social Media Usage and Trust Toward Social Commerce Websites

In social commerce, socializing motivation of social media usage demonstrates to be an effective conduit to obtain more knowledge about products' information provided on social commerce websites and the content embedded (Zhang and Benyoucef 2016). Accordingly, increased social connections through social media usage facilitate customers or potential customers to establish and maintain robust interpersonal relationships with other customers. Interactions through social media enable customers to seek accurate suggestions and comments about contents' credibility on social commerce websites (Hajli et al. 2017). Further, socializing through social media usage reduces users' concerns about the information quality of social commerce websites, which mainly refers to service, accuracy, usefulness, relevance and sufficiency of the information and knowledge about social commerce website itself and the contents embedded (Wu et al. 2015; Shawky et al. 2020). Thus we hypothesize that:

H1a: Social media usage for socializing purpose increases customers' trust toward social commerce websites.

Research has also identified that informational support helps customers make reasonable evaluation on social commerce websites and products information embedded in the websites (Wang et al. 2020; Yan et al. 2016). In complex international business environment, in order to relieve potential risks and uncertainties generated by information symmetry such as transaction risks, privacy disclosure and information fraud, customers prefer to rely on social media to seek and confirm accurate information to relieve their worries (Hu et al. 2021; Soroya et al. 2021). To attain informational support, customers will use social media to search for accurate information to ensure the authenticity of information released by social commerce websites.

Based on the above statement, we hypothesize that:

H1b: Social media usage for informational purpose increases customers' trust toward social commerce websites.

2.2 Trust Toward Social Commerce Websites and customer's Engagement

When potential customers have established trust attitude toward social commerce websites, they demonstrate more willingness to interact with those who share similar interests and preferences in the community to satisfy their gratification need of social interaction (Shen et al. 2019; Chang and Chen 2008). In this regard, social commerce websites provide such an important platform with resources and information pertaining to reviews, livechat, suggestions and recommendations (Busalim et al. 2021). Based on sufficient informational support and emotional support from community members realized through social interaction, potential customers and customers will demonstrate more engagement in social commerce (Cheung et al. 2015; De Vries and Carlson 2014; Wang et al. 2020). Based on the above statement, we logically hypothesize that:

H2: Customers' trust increases their engagement in social commerce.

2.3 Moderating Role of Cultural Distance

Notwithstanding potential customers can be facilitated with sufficient information through social media, the existence of cultural distance objectively prevents customers from capturing, comprehending or even misunderstanding the attained information sufficiently. And this attenuates the information quality acquired from social media usage. Previous research indicates that information quality demonstrates significant effects on customers' trust toward social commerce (Chen et al. 2015). Based on above statement, we logically hypothesize that:

H3a: Cultural distance attenuates the effects of informational social media usage on customers' trust toward social commerce.

Cultural distance indicates to exert deterring effects on establishment of social connections and effectiveness of communications between people from different cultural backgrounds (Galchenko and van de Vijver 2007; Hu et al. 2020). Likewise, cultural distance brings more obstacles to potential customers to comprehend website design philosophy and products' culture embedded when they communicate with other members through social media usage. Thus trust building or transfer is unlikely to take place when potential customers base their intention to socialize through social media usage within such an entity (Qin and De-Juan-Vigaray 2021). Based on the above statement, we logically hypothesize:

H3b: Cultural distance attenuates the effects of socializing social media usage on customers' trust toward social commerce.

3 Research Methodology

In order to examine the proposed hypothesis, the study has conducted a survey with assistance from more than 40 public universities in China. The questionnaires were delivered to international students with designated links through one of the largest survey platform named Wenjuanxing (www.wjx.cn). And the final total of 2058 questionnaires was collected back from students of 135 countries.

To measure the construct of social media usage, a six-item scale was used, which was adapted from Hughes et al. (2012). And we adopted a five-item scale from Busalim et al. (2021) to measure customer engagement. Further, drawing on Shin's (2013) measure of trust on social commerce websites, a three-item scale was used to capture customers' perceived trust. Another six-item scale was adopted from Chen et al. (2010) to measure the construct of cultural distance.

4 Analysis and Results

4.1 Reliability and Validity

Table 1. Measurement of constructs

Constructs	Dimensions	Items	Loadings	CR	AVE	Cronbach alphas
SMU	Socializing	3	0.853–0.885	0.766	0.908	0.843
	Information	3	0.791–0.873	0.869	0.689	0.763
TSC		5	0.86–0.915	0.946	0.777	0.927
ESC		5	0.874–0.92	0.956	0.814	0.943
CD		6	0.747–0.886	0.928	0.680	0.906

Notes: SMU, social media usage; TSC, trust toward social commerce websites; ESC, engagement in social commerce; CD, cultural distance

4.2 Hypothesis Testing

The results of the data analysis showed that all hypotheses were validated. Moreover, results indicated that cultural distance negatively moderates the relationships between two dimensions of social media usage and trust toward social commerce websites (Fig. 3 and 4).

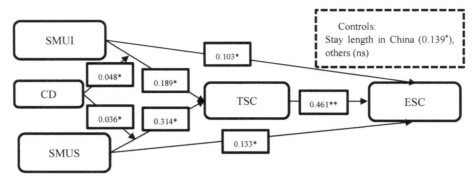

Fig. 2. Results of the hypothesized model

Table 2. Results of the mediating effect

Mediating effect	Estimate	SE	P	BC 99% CI	
				Lower	Upper
SMUI-TSC-ESC	0.087	0.013	0.000	0.051	0.121
SMUS-TSC-ESC	0.145	0.015	0.000	0.110	0.186

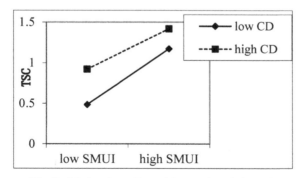

Fig. 3. Moderating effect of CD on the relationship

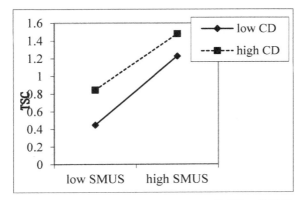

Fig. 4. Moderating effect of CD on the relationship between SMUI and TSC between SMUS and TSC

5 Discussion

The current study partially unveils the mechanism whereby social media usage, driven by different value perspectives, generates the formation of customers' trust toward social commerce, thereby influencing their engagement in social commerce. In general, the current study makes several important contributions both theoretically and practically.

The study first extends the S-O-R to the cross-cultural social commerce environment. What's more, the current study considers both positive environmental stimuli (social media usage) and negative one (cultural distance) as a necessary supplement to extant literature mainly focusing on singular cultural business background and positive environmental stimuli. Moreover, this study explicates that customers' usage of social media is driven by different value perspectives and motivates customers' trust toward social commerce, thereby facilitating their engagement in social commerce. As such, customers' trust is re-examined in the current study and demonstrates to be an effective conduit to transfer the positive effects of informational and socializing social media usage on the formation of customers' engagement in cross-cultural social commerce. In addition, this study makes a difference by identifying that cultural distance mitigates the positive effects of social media usage on customers' trust and their engagement in social commerce. This finding contributes to researching social commerce conducted internationally with rapidly increasing number of global customers.

In spite of theoretical spotlights, the study also makes contributions to social commerce practices. In light of the significance of social media to enable successful operations of social commerce by generating potential customers' internal trust and then enhancing their engagement in social commerce, more real efforts should be made on building up social media platforms by practitioners. Besides, the study has also confirmed that trust is an effective conduit to build up customers' engagement in cross-cultural business environment. Considering that trust is a critical element in social commerce and it has direct positive associations with customers' engagement, anchors should work out more effective measures to achieve and maintain customers' trust. Last but not the least, when social commerce continues to be international, customers from different countries with unique cultural backgrounds should be targeted differently.

6 Limitations

Despite of contributions mentioned, the current study also has limitations which should be addressed by future efforts. First, customer's engagement has been regarded as multidimensional including cognitive, affective, and behavioral dimensions (Hollebeek et al. 2014). In the current study, we only examined customers' engagement as a whole construct. Second, every country essentially differentiates itself from others in many cultural aspects. The current study focuses on the cross-cultural social commerce in China. International customers' social media usage, trust toward social commerce websites and engagement are pertaining to the Chinese business environment. Third, in light of complexity of cross-cultural social commerce, more environmental elements that may influence customers' trust and their engagement behaviors should be explored. Fourth, the self-reported data might be another limitation.

Acknowledgement. The research was financially supported by 2019' National Education Sciences Planning Project of China (BBA190019), Anhui Provincial Natural Science Foundation (1908085MG238), Anhui Provincial Teaching Reforming Project (2020jyxm0206), and Anhui University of Technology Research Project (2020syzm01). We very much appreciate insightful comments and suggestions from the anonymous reviewers and experts.

References:

Busalim, A.H., Ghabban, F., Hussin, A.R.C.: Customer engagement behaviour on social commerce platforms: an empirical study. Technol. Soc. **64**, 101437 (2021)

Chang, H.H., Chen, S.W.: The impact of online store environment cues on purchase intention: trust and perceived risk as a mediator. Online Inf. Rev. **32**(6), 818–841 (2008)

Chen, G., Kirkman, B.L., Kim, K., Farh, C.I.C., Tangirala, S.: When does cross-cultural motivation enhance expatriate effectiveness? A multilevel investigation of the moderating roles of subsidiary support and cultural distance. Acad. Manag. J. **53**(5), 1110–1130 (2010)

Chen, J.V., Yen, D.C., Pornpriphet, W., Widjaja, A.E.: E-commerce web site loyalty: a cross cultural comparison. Inf. Syst. Front. **17**, 1283–1299 (2015)

Cheung, C.M.K., Shen, X.-L., Lee, Z.W.Y., Chan, T.K.H.: Promoting sales of online games through customer engagement. Electron. Commer. Res. Appl. **14**(4), 241–250 (2015)

De Vries, N., Carlson, J.: Examining the drivers and brand performance implications of customer engagement with brands in the social media environment. J. Brand Manag. **21**(6), 1–21 (2014)

Galchenko, I., van de Vijver, F.J.R.: The role of perceived cultural distance in the acculturation of exchange students in Russia. Int. J. Intercult. Relat. **31**(2), 181–197 (2007)

Hajli, N., Sims, J.: Social commerce: the transfer of power from sellers to buyers. Technol. Forecast. Soc. Change **94**, 350–358 (2015)

Hajli, N., Sims, J., Zadeh, A.H., Richard, M.-O.: A social commerce investigation of the role of trust in a social networking site on purchase intentions. J. Bus. Res. **71**, 133–141 (2017)

Hollebeek, L.D., Glynn, M.S., Brodie, R.J.: Consumer brand engagement in social media: conceptualization, scale development and validation. J. Interact. Mark. **28**(2), 149–165 (2014)

Hu, S., Hu, L., Wu, J., Wang, G.: Social media usage and international expatriate's creativity: an empirical research in cross-cultural context. Hum. Syst. Manag. **40**, 197–209 (2021)

Hu, S., Liu, H., Zhang, S., Wang, G.: Proactive personality and cross-cultural adjustment: roles of social media usage and cultural intelligence. Int. J. Intercult. Relat. **74**, 42–57 (2020)

Hughes, D.J., Rowe, M., Batey, M., Andrew, L.: A tale of two sites: Twitter vs. Facebook and the personality predictors of social media usage. Comput. Hum. Behav. **28**, 561–569 (2012)

Liu, Y., Zhao, H., Wei, Z., Pavel, S.: Interpreting and predicting social commerce intention based on knowledge graph analysis. Electron. Commer. Res. **20**(1), 197–222 (2020). https://doi.org/10.1007/s10660-019-09392-1

Mikalef, P., Giannakos, M.N., Pappas, I.O.: Designing social commerce platforms based on consumers' intentions. Behav. Inf. Technol. **36**(12), 1308–1327 (2017)

Qin, L., De-Juan-Vigaray, M.D.: Social commerce: is interpersonal trust formation similar between U.S.A. and Spain? J. Retail. Consum. Serv. **62**, 102642 (2021)

Osatuyi, B., Qin, H., Osatuyi, T., Turel, O.: When it comes to Satisfaction … It depends: an empirical examination of social commerce users. Comput. Hum. Behav. **111**, 106413 (2020)

Shawky, S., Kubacki, K., Dietrich, T., Weaven, S.: A dynamic framework for managing customer engagement on social media. J. Bus. Res. **121**, 567–577 (2020)

Shen, X.L., Li, Y., Sun, Y., Chen, Z., Wang, F.: Understanding the role of technology attractiveness in promoting social commerce engagement: moderating effect of personal interest. Inf. Manag. **56**(2), 294–305 (2019)

Shin, D.-H.: User experience in social commerce: in friends we trust. Behav. Inf. Technol. **32**(1), 52–67 (2013)

Soroya, S.H., Farooq, A., Mahmood, K., Isaho, J., Zara, S.: From information seeking to information avoidance: understanding the health information behavior during a global health crisis. Inf. Process. Manag. **58**, 102440 (2021)

Tuncer, I.: The relationship between IT affordance, flow experience, trust, and social commerce intention: an exploration using the S-O-R paradigm. Technol. Soc. **65**, 101567 (2021)

Wang, C., Zhang, P.: The evolution of social commerce: the people, management, technology, and information dimensions. Commun. Assoc. Inf. Syst. **31**, 105–127 (2012)

Wang, Y., Herrando, C.: Does privacy assurance on social commerce sites matter to millennials? Int. J. Inf. Manag. **44**, 164–177 (2019)

Wang, Y., Wang, J., Yao, T., Li, M., Wang, X.: How does social support promote consumers' engagement in the social commerce community? The mediating effect of consumer involvement. Inf. Process. Manag. **57**, 102272 (2020)

Wu, Y.C.J., Shen, J.P., Chang, C.L.: Electronic service quality of Facebook social commerce and collaborative learning. Comput. Hum. Behav. **51**, 1395–1402 (2015)

Yan, Z., Wang, T., Chen, Y., Zhang, H.: Knowledge sharing in online health communities: a social exchange theory perspective. Inf. Manag. **53**(3), 643–653 (2016)

Zhang, K.Z.K., Benyoucef, M.: Consumer behavior in social commerce: a literature review. Decis. Support Syst. **86**, 95–108 (2016)

Zhang, M., Hu, M., Guo, L., Liu, W.: Understanding relationships among customer experience, engagement, and word-of-mouth intention on online brand communities. Internet Res. **27**(4), 839–857 (2017)

Dynamic Effects of Seller Competition on Platform Product Abundance from Short-Term and Long-Term Perspective

Qi Liu[1] ⓘ, Zhen Zhu[1(✉)] ⓘ, and Jian Mou[2] ⓘ

[1] School of Economics and Management, China University of Geosciences,
Hubei 430074, China
zhuzhen@cug.edu.cn
[2] School of Business, Pusan National University, Busandaehak-ro 63beon-gil, Geumjeong-gu,
Busan 46241, Republic of Korea

Abstract. Previous studies argued that seller competition has both stimulating and crowding-out effects on products on the platform. These two seemingly contradictory views were rarely examined from time series analysis. Considering the characteristics of network effects over time, the dynamic effect of seller competition and product abundance is decomposed based on the time effect from the short-term and long-term perspective. By collecting detailed information on travel products from Ctrip.com, the panel vector autoregression model is specified to empirically test the hypotheses. The results show that seller competition has a positive effect on product abundance in the short time (one-period lagged). Seller competition does not affect product abundance in the long time (twenty-period lagged) as the two countervailing network effects (i.e., positive and negative network effects) cancel each other out. Our study provides empirical evidence for the dynamic nature of network effects over time. Moreover, our findings offer crucial managerial implications for platforms and sellers to choose effective competitive strategies.

Keywords: E-commerce platform · Network effect · Seller competition · Product abundance · Short-term and Long-term effects · Panel vector autoregression

1 Introduction

E-commerce platforms play an important role in promoting economic growth with the rapid development of Internet technology [1]. In 2019, the transaction volume of e-commerce platforms was 34.81 trillion Yuan in China, an increase of 6.7% from 2018[1]. A large number of business practices show that the high transaction volume is attributed to the abundance of products on the e-commerce platform. Abundant products serve the diverse needs of consumers, which in turn attracts more sellers [2]. Product abundance refers to the scale of tradable products on platforms [3].

---

[1] From 2020 Yearly China E-commerce Report.

© The Author(s), under exclusive license to Springer Nature Switzerland AG 2022
G. Salvendy and J. Wei (Eds.): HCII 2022, LNCS 13337, pp. 264–273, 2022.
https://doi.org/10.1007/978-3-031-05014-5_22

Product abundance depends on the supply of sellers, who face intense competition while entering markets to provide products [4]. However, previous research is equivocal about the effect of seller competition on product abundance on platforms. On the one hand, some studies have confirmed the positive effect of seller competition on product abundance, and they regard seller competition as a signal of consumer demand [1, 4]. On the other hand, some scholars argue that seller competition has a negative effect on product abundance. They suggest that seller competition crowds out products on the market because it is regarded as a signal of competitive pressure [5, 6].

Although the above two views have enhanced our understanding of the effect of seller competition on product abundance, many studies are limited to one perspective. However, sellers pay different attention to the two signals shown by seller competition at different stages of enterprise development [7]. Combined with the diversified strategic targets of sellers in different development stages and the asymmetry of network effect on the platform in time and magnitude, it is crucial to examine the time effect of seller competition on product abundance [7, 8]. Our research question is as follows, what is the relationship between product competition and product abundance on an e-commerce platform from short-term and long-term perspectives?

2 Theoretical Backgrounds and Research Hypotheses

2.1 Network Effects

Network effects refer to the value of a participant depending on the number of other participants that he or she can interact with on the platform [2]. Network effects can be categorized as either cross-side network effects (CNEs) or same-side network effects (SNEs) [9]. CNEs refer to the utility of participants on one side of a platform depending on the size of participants on the other side [8]. SNEs are defined as how characteristics of participants on one side of a platform affect participants on the same side [9]. Overall, network effects can be both positive as well as negative [10]. Positive network effects mean that the platform becomes more valuable as more users join, while negative network effects are the opposite.

The presence of network effects has been studied in the previous literature [11]. More recently, a nascent stream of literature has started to focus on the dynamic of network effect in time and the asymmetry in magnitude [2, 8]. For instance, Chu and Manchanda [8] quantified CNEs and SNEs. They find that the CNEs are asymmetric in magnitude and investigate the nature of CNEs over time. Similarly, Song et al. [2] empirically examined how the CNEs are temporally asymmetric on software platforms. They find that an increase in the installed base of the user-side results in long-term growth on the application side, but the reverse effect is primarily short-term.

Although previous studies have examined how the existence of network effects might impact the seller competition effect in the market [4, 11], most of these studies adopted a static perspective, ignoring the dynamics of network effects over time.

2.2 Seller Competition

There are two streams of research on the understanding of seller competition. One stream of research confirms that seller competition expands the abundance of products because they regard seller competition as a signal of market demand [4, 12]. Since sellers are uncertain about the number of consumers on the platform, they could infer that there are many consumers in the market from the behavior of sellers competing fiercely in the market [4]. Therefore, a market with intense competition among sellers attracts more sellers to offer products [1]. The second stream of research argues that seller competition crowds out products on the market, and seller competition is suggested as a signal of competitive pressure [5, 6]. Fierce competition reduces the profitability of the product because sellers tend to adopt low-price strategies when facing competition, resulting in sellers choosing to withdraw from the current market [6].

Sellers focus on different strategic targets as the market develops, resulting in different attention to signals shown by competition and the time effect of seller competition. In the short term, sellers will be attracted to the market with a large number of consumers because sellers focus on the profitability of products. However, over time, sellers will consider how to survive under competitive pressure and the company's sustainable strategy. Therefore, the short-term and long-term perspective on the effect of seller competition on product abundance is presented.

Short-Term Effect of Seller Competition on Supply Abundance. The concepts of short-term and long-term effects are defined in the marketing literature [2]. Extending these two concepts to e-commerce platforms, we define the short-term effect as an immediate response of product abundance to seller competition. Similarly, the long-term effect refers to the persistent response of product abundance to seller competition. The short-term and long-term effects are not mutually exclusive.

In the short term, the sellers focus on the profitability of the product, which depends on the consumer demand for the product [6]. Considering the positive cross-side network effect between sellers and consumers, we expect product abundance to expand as seller competition intensifies. Because the intense seller competition implies a high demand for the product [11, 13]. Seller competition can attract more consumers to purchase by increasing product diversity and lowering product prices. Likewise, more consumers imply that the market is valuable, thus indirectly enhancing sellers' determination to participate in the market [9]. In addition, compared with the "comfortable" market environment, competition pressure can enhance sellers' entrepreneurship and improve sellers' innovation awareness [14]. Thus, we propose our first hypothesis.

H1: In the short term, seller competition has a positive effect on product abundance on an e-commerce platform.

Long-Term Effects of Product Competition on Supply Abundance. In contrast, over time, sellers on e-commerce platforms focus on how to survive in a fiercely competitive market instead of profit-driven. Sellers pay more attention to the seller's same-side network effect to avoid being pushed out of the market by competitors.

Negative same-side network effects appear when sellers compete with each other to interact with consumers [11]. For instance, the expected profits of sellers decrease with the entry of competitors, and sellers compete for the attention of consumers. The number of consumers stimulates sellers to enter while ignoring the competitors that have already existed in the platform, resulting in the phenomenon of "supply exceeds demand" and the risk of vicious competition. As a result, some sellers may withdraw from the highly competitive market [5]. Therefore, when facing intense competitive pressure in the long term, sellers may adjust their strategies and choose to withdraw from the current market to lessen the competitive pressure [12], thus reducing the product abundance in the market. Hence, we propose the following hypothesis.

H2: In the long term, seller competition has a negative effect on product abundance on an e-commerce platform.

3   Research Design

3.1   Data Collection

We tested our hypotheses by using a half-monthly longitudinal dataset on Ctrip.com, the largest tourism e-commerce platform in China, from July 1, 2017 to October 1, 2019 (55 periods). We collect the data from the tourism e-commerce platform mainly because the characteristics of tourism products having a departure city and destination are helpful to clarify the competitive boundary of the market. We select six main departure cities (i.e. Shanghai, Beijing, Guangzhou, Shenzhen, Chengdu, and Wuhan), and eight popular international destinations (e.g. United States, Europe, Japan, etc.). Therefore, 48 (6 * 8) market segments are chosen by the combination of departure city and destination. We collect the travel product data from the above 48 market segments on Ctrip.com. We regularly collected data on the 1st and 15th of each month and crawled data for 55 periods. The line chart of the total number of travel products in each period is shown in Fig. 1.

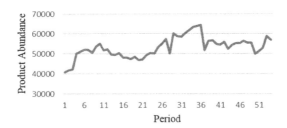

Fig. 1. Line chart of the total number of travel products in each period

3.2   Measurement of Variables

The seller competition in the market is measured by the Hirschman-Herfindahl index (HHI) [15]. HHI refers to the sum of the square of the percentage of each company's market share in a market. This measurement is more comprehensive by considering the number of companies and the degree of the company's participation.

$$HHI = \sum_{i=1}^{N}(X_i/X)^2 = \sum_{i=1}^{N} S_i^2 \tag{1}$$

where X is the total sales in the market, X_i is the sales of seller i, S_i denotes the market share of seller i, N is the total number of sellers in the market. In particular, there is a negative correlation between HHI and the intensity of seller competition in the market. To interpret the results more intuitive, Competition = 1-HHI.

Product abundance is measured by the number of tradable travel products in each market segment. Most previous work on product abundance mainly focuses on the importance of product boundary and diversity on the platform [3]. In this paper, product abundance is defined as the scale of tradable products provided by sellers.

We also added two control variables to the model. The first one is word-of-mouth (WOM), which is quantified by the average rating values of tourism products in the market segment [16]. In addition, We control for seasonal effects by using a set of three seasonal dummy variables (SEA = [Summer, Autumn, Winter]) in the model.

3.3 Descriptive Statistics

The descriptive statistics and correlation matrix for all variables are shown in Table 1. The results show that there is a quite difference between the values of the dependent and independent variables. To reduce the impact of the difference in the data distribution on regressive results, we take the natural log of all variables except the dummy variables when establishing the model.

Table 1. Descriptive statistics and correlation analysis

Variable	Mean (S.D)	Max/ Min	1	2	3	4	5	6
1. Abundance	1078.30 (523.86)	2467.00/ 103.00	1					
2. Competition	0. 65 (0.24)	0.99/ 0.08	0.37*	1				
3. WOM	1.17 (0.33)	2.47/ 0.29	− 0.22*	0.12*	1			
4. Summer	0.28 (0.45)	1.00/ 0.00	− 0.03	-0.03	− 0.01	1		
5. Autumn	0.28 (0.45)	1.00/ 0.00	− 0.03	0.03	− 0.15*	− 0.38*	1	
6. Winter	0.22 (0.42)	1.00/ 0.00	0.08*	− 0.02	− 0.01	− 0.33*	− 0.33*	1

Notes: * $p < 0.05$

4 Hypothesis Testing and Results

4.1 Model Specification and Estimation

The panel vector autoregression (PVAR) model is established in our empirical analysis to test our hypotheses. PVAR model allows us to capture the interdependence and dynamic interaction between variables [2, 17], which helps to quantify the short-term and long-term effects in the hypothesis.

The procedure of the PVAR method includes four steps [2, 17]. First, the Granger causality test is conducted to determine the appropriateness of using PVAR, and the test results show that there is bidirectional causality between product abundance and seller competition (Table 2). Second, the stationarity of time series data is tested based on the panel unit-root test, and we find that all variables are stationary (Table 3). Third, we determine the optimal lag length of the model using information criteria and choose a two-period lag (AIC = 12.4172). Finally, we derive orthogonalizing impulse response functions (IRFs) and calculate elasticities between the key variables to test hypotheses[1]. IRFs describe the response of one variable to an exogenous shock to another variable while keeping all other shocks at zero. In addition, To address the heteroscedasticity issue suggested by the White test ($\chi 2 = 318.52$; $p = 0.000$), we use a robust standard error in estimating the PVAR model[15]. Moreover, the PVRA system satisfies stability conditions.

Table 2. Granger causality test results

Equation/Excluded	chi^2	p-value
Abundance/ Competition	71.387	0.000
Competition/ Abundance	35.811	0.000

Table 3. Panel unit root test results

Variable	LLC test	IPS test	Fisher-PP test	Conclusion
Abundance	− 7.449(0.000)	− 5.837(0.000)	4.283(0.000)	Stationary
Competition	− 20.216(0.000)	− 27.673(0.000)	97.677(0.000)	Stationary
WOM	− 9.301(0.000)	− 11.588(0.000)	14.489(0.000)	Stationary

A two-variable PVAR model is specified to capture the dynamic effect of competition on abundance, and all control variables are considered as exogenous in the model.

Therefore, the PVAR specification is given:

$$
\begin{bmatrix} Abundance_t \\ Competition_t \end{bmatrix} = \begin{bmatrix} C_{Abundance} \\ C_{Competition} \end{bmatrix} + \sum_{j=1}^{J} \begin{bmatrix} \emptyset_{11}^{j} \emptyset_{12}^{j} \\ \emptyset_{21}^{j} \emptyset_{22}^{j} \end{bmatrix} \begin{bmatrix} Abundance_{t-j} \\ Competition_{t-j} \end{bmatrix}
$$
$$
+ \sum_{j=1}^{J} \begin{bmatrix} \tau_{11}^{j} \tau_{12}^{j} \tau_{13}^{j} \tau_{14}^{j} \\ \tau_{21}^{j} \tau_{22}^{j} \tau_{23}^{j} \tau_{24}^{j} \end{bmatrix} \begin{bmatrix} WOM_{t-j} \\ Summer_{t-j} \\ Autumn_{t-j} \\ Winter_{t-j} \end{bmatrix} + \begin{bmatrix} \varepsilon_{Abundance,t} \\ \varepsilon_{Competition,t} \end{bmatrix} \qquad (2)
$$

where t refers to periods, J represents the lag order of the model, where J equals the two-period lag, C is an intercept, ε is a white-noise disturbance and it is a normal distribution with $N(0, \Sigma)$, and $(C, \emptyset, \tau)$ are the parameters to be estimated.

4.2 Hypothesis Testing

To test the short-term and long-term effects of seller competition in hypotheses, we derive impulse response functions (IRFs). The short-term effects are assessed by examining whether the one-period lagged changes of the response of product abundance to a shock in seller competition are significant [2]. We tracked the 20-period[2] lagged changes to assess the long-term effects because the value of the impulse response function usually stabilizes after such a long time [2, 15]. Based on the results of IRFs, we can calculate the elasticity of seller competition to product abundance. Elasticity analysis refers to the percentage change of one variable caused by a 1% change in another variable. The elasticities are presented in Table 4.

Table 4. The elasticity of seller competition to product abundance

	Short-term					Long-term
	One-period lagged	Two-period lagged	Four-period lagged	Ten-period lagged	Nineteen-periods lagged	Twenty-periods lagged
Competition → Abundance	0.081***	0.222***	0.297***	− 0.006	0.002	0.003
	(0.005)	(0.009)	(0.014)	(0.014)	(0.007)	(0.007)

Notes: * p < 0.1, ** p < 0.05, *** p < 0.01. Standard errors are included in parentheses

As shown in Table 4, seller competition has a positive and significant short-term effect on product abundance (elasticity is 0.081, p < 0.001). Therefore, H1 is supported. What is more, we found that the elasticity of product abundance to seller competition is not consistent over time. The elasticity is positive and increases in magnitude over time in the first four periods, then decreases in magnitude over time between the fifth and tenth periods. Finally, the elasticity is not significant after ten periods.

---

[2] The empirical results also show that the IRF value tends to be stable in the 20th period.

The long-term effects of seller competition on product abundance are not significant (elasticity is 0.003, p = 0.718, see the last column of Table 4). Thus, H2 is not supported, which suggests that in the long term, seller competition has no effect on product abundance rather than negative effects. A potential explanation is that there are both positive cross-side network effects and negative same-side network effects among sellers on e-commerce platforms, and the two countervailing effects cancel each other [11]. Our results are illustrated in Fig. 2, which shows impulse response functions and illustrates short-term and long-term effects.

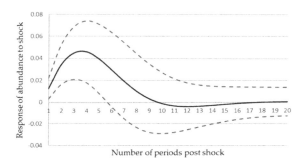

Fig. 2. Impulse response functions results of seller competition to product abundance

4.3 Robustness Check

We verify the robustness of our results in two ways. First, we split the original data into two samples according to whether the departure city of travel products is a first-tier city, and re-estimate the PVAR model. Second, we verify our results by expanding the sample. We collect additional data on outbound travel products from Nanjing to the 15 popular destinations mentioned above. We rerun the PVAR models using additional data and our findings remain robust.

5 Discussion and Contribution

5.1 Main Results and Theoretical Contributions

In this paper, both the short-term and long-term effects of seller competition on product abundance are empirically investigated by using more than 3,300,000 outbound tour packaged products from Ctrip.com. The results showed that seller competition immediately triggers a significant expansion of product abundance in the short-term time. Then the positive effect of seller competition on product abundance increases in magnitude over time in the first four-period lagged (approximately two months). The long-term effects of seller competition on product abundance are zero, implying that seller competition does not consistently stimulate an increase in product abundance. Moreover, we conduct additional analyses to verify the robustness of our results.

Our study offers two important theoretical implications to the extant literature. First, the evidence on the time effect of seller competition enriches the research based on network effects. Most previous studies adopted a static perspective to investigate how the existence of network effects impacts the seller competition effect [5, 11], ignoring the dynamics of network effects over time. The results of the study show that there is a significant difference between the short-term and long-term effects of seller competition on product abundance. Our study enriches the empirical evidence about network effects changing over time. Second, we extend the research of seller competition by considering the different strategic targets of sellers, which was less noticed in previous studies. In this paper, we distinguish two strategic targets for sellers, namely profit driven and sustainable development driven. Different strategic targets of sellers explain why sellers focus on different signals exhibited by competition.

5.2   Practical Implications

Beyond the theoretical contributions, our results have implications for platforms and sellers. First, it is crucial for platforms to adopt appropriate strategies to stimulate the growth of product scale. Our research suggests that e-commerce platforms can expand the scale of products by strengthening the intensity of seller competition in the short term. For example, the platform may incentivize more sellers to compete by relaxing the entry threshold. However, in the long term, platform owners may consider stimulating sellers to seek new markets through platform governance. Second, for sellers, our results provide a strategic design for product entry. When sellers are profit-oriented, they should provide more products to enter the intensely competitive market, which implies diversified consumer demand. When sellers are driven by the sustainable development strategy, sellers may consider entering an emerging market with less fierce competition to capture customers ahead of rival firms.

5.3   Limitations and Future Research

Our research has two limitations. First, this article does not examine whether the relationship between seller competition and product abundance has changed at different stages of platform development because we do not have data from Ctrip's inception. Second, our research object is a specific tourism e-commerce platform. Future research may consider generalizing the insights on the effect of seller competition on product abundance by examining other e-commerce platforms.

Acknowledgments. This research was supported by the National Natural Science Foundation of China under Grant 71672183.

References

1. Li, X.L., Ren, X.Y., Zheng, X.: Managerial tactics for sellers' competition and performance of the e-commerce platform: implication from the dynamic analysis of VAR model. Nankai Bus. Rev. **17**(5), 73–82 (2014). https://doi.org/10.3969/j.issn.1008-3448.2014.05.009

2. Song, P.J., Xue, L., Rai, A., Zhang, C.: The ecosystem of software platform: a study of asymmetric cross-side network effects and platform governance. MIS Q. **42**(1), 121–142 (2018). https://doi.org/10.25300/misq/2018/13737

3. Boudreau, K.J.: Let a thousand flowers bloom? an early look at large numbers of software app developers and patterns of innovation. Organ. Sci. **23**(5), 1409–1427 (2012). https://doi.org/10.1287/orsc.1110.0678

4. Tucker, C.E., Zhang, J.J.: Growing two-sided networks by advertising the user base: a field experiment. Mark. Sci. **29**(5), 805–814 (2010). https://doi.org/10.1287/mksc.1100.0560

5. Simonsohn, U.: Ebay's crowded evenings: competition neglect in market entry decisions. Manage. Sci. **56**(7), 1060–1073 (2010). https://doi.org/10.1287/mnsc.1100.1180

6. Wen, W., Zhu, F.: Threat of platform-owner entry and complementor responses: evidence from the mobile app market. Strateg. Manag. J. **40**(9), 1336–1367 (2019). https://doi.org/10.1002/smj.3031

7. Gong, X.L.: Analysis on the choice of financial management objectives of enterprises at various stages of development. J. Huangshi Inst. Technol. (Hum. Soc. Sci.) **29**(01), 12–15 (2012). https://doi.org/10.3969/j.SSN.1671-7422.2012.01.003

8. Chu, J.H., Manchanda, P.: Quantifying cross and direct network effects in online consumer-to-consumer platforms. Mark. Sci. **35**(6), 870–893 (2016). https://doi.org/10.1287/mksc.2016.0976

9. McIntyre, D.P., Srinivasan, A.: Networks, platforms, and strategy: emerging views and next steps. Strateg. Manag. J. **38**(1), 141–160 (2017). https://doi.org/10.1002/smj.2596

10. Thies, F., Wessel, M., Benlian, A.: Network effects on crowdfunding platforms: exploring the implications of relaxing input control. Inf. Syst. J. **28**(6), 1239–1262 (2018). https://doi.org/10.1111/isj.12194

11. Belleflamme, P., Peitz, M.: Managing competition on a two-sided platform. J. Econ. Manag. Strategy **28**(1), 5–22 (2019). https://doi.org/10.1111/jems.12311

12. Zhu, F., Liu, Q.H.: Competing with complementors: an empirical look at amazon. Com. Strat. Manag. J. **39**(10), 2618–2642 (2018). https://doi.org/10.1002/smj.2932

13. Cennamo, C., Santalo, J.: Platform competition: strategic trade-offs in platform markets. Strateg. Manag. J. **34**(11), 1331–1350 (2013). https://doi.org/10.1002/smj.2066

14. Turner, S.F., Mitchell, W., Bettis, R.A.: Responding to rivals and complements: how market concentration shapes generational product innovation strategy. Organ. Sci. **21**(4), 854–872 (2010). https://doi.org/10.1287/orsc.1090.0486

15. Li, Q., Wang, Q.S., Song, P.J.: The effects of agency selling on reselling on hybrid retail platforms. Int. J. Electron. Commer. **23**(4), 524–556 (2019). https://doi.org/10.1080/10864415.2019.1655209

16. Rosario, A.B., Sotgiu, F., De Valck, K., Bijmolt, T.H.A.: The effect of electronic word of mouth on sales: a meta-analytic review of platform, product, and metric factors. J. Mark. Res. **53**(3), 297–318 (2016). https://doi.org/10.1509/jmr.14.0380

17. Love, I., Zicchino, L.: Financial development and dynamic investment behavior: Evidence from panel var. Q. Rev. Econ. Finan. **46**(2), 190–210 (2006). https://doi.org/10.1016/j.qref.2005.11.007

What's the Role of Mega-influencers in Live Streaming E-commerce—A Natural Experiment

Honglong Wang, Guoxin Li, and Shaohui Wu[✉]

School of Management, Harbin Institute of Technology, Harbin, China
20b910034@stu.hit.edu.cn, {liguoxin,wushaohui}@hit.edu.cn

Abstract. Live streaming e-commerce is becoming prevalent and its new business model attracts much attention from the marketing and information systems fields. In this paper, we examine the relationships between influencers and the role of mega-influencers on the live streaming e-commerce platform. Based on a large-scale dataset and a natural experiment, we explore how influencers' performance is affected and how the audiences' visits and purchases change for other influencers when mega influencers leave the platform. We find that there exist two significant effects from mega influencers, including a signaling effect and a drainage effect. When mega influencers left the live streaming platform, the audiences' visits for other influencers significantly decrease, suggesting that there exists a significant drainage effect on audiences' visits from mega influencers. There is a significant number of audiences' visits coming from mega influencers to other influencers. When mega influencers leave from the platform, the sales for other influencers also significantly decrease with the controlled audiences' visits, showing a significant signaling effect from mega influencers. Our paper illustrates that the treatment effects of mega influencers continuously affected other influencers. Based on a causal forest approach, we show that there exist heterogeneously treatment effects across influencers. The influencers with a large number of followers are affected more than the influencers with a small number of followers.

Keywords: Live streaming · Mega-influencer · Hierarchical distribution · Natural experiment

1 Introduction

In recent years, with the development of the mobile internet and the pandemic background, people are more likely to watch live streaming shows and buy products from influencers. In Mckinsey's report, China's live streaming e-commerce would reach \$171 billion in 2020, with a 280% increase from 2017[1]. In another report from Statista, the live streaming e-commerce was forecast to generate 11 billion U.S. dollars in online sales in the United States in 2021 and the e-commerce revenue created from live streaming

---

[1] https://www.mckinsey.com/business-functions/mckinsey-digital/our-insights/its-showtime-how-live-commerce-is-transforming-the-shopping-experience.

© The Author(s), under exclusive license to Springer Nature Switzerland AG 2022
G. Salvendy and J. Wei (Eds.): HCII 2022, LNCS 13337, pp. 274–285, 2022.
https://doi.org/10.1007/978-3-031-05014-5_23

was expected to increase threefold, reaching 35 billion dollars by 2024[2]. By the year 2020, in China, the number of live influencers has reached 1.23 million and the number of live streaming viewers has reached 388 million, accounting for 40% of the total internet users. Nearly two-thirds of live streaming users have purchased after watching live streaming. Live streaming e-commerce is becoming an important business for both firms and internet users[3].

As a new business model which integrates social, entertainment, and shopping functions, live streaming e-commerce attracts a large number of influencers and audiences. Audiences can watch live streaming shows and buy products directly from the influencers. A typical phenomenon for live streaming commerce fields is that there exists a long-tail pattern for influencers, i.e., several mega influencers on a live streaming platform may have a super large number of followers while the number of followers for most of the influencers are relatively small. Mega influencers are important for live streaming platforms since they can attract a huge number of visits and sales. For instance, the mega influencer Viya in Taobao Live has more than 86 million followers. There could be more than 82 billion RMB gross merchandise volumes and 1.73 million new followers during one of her 14-h live streaming shows[4]. Based on the background of the huge number of visits and sales for mega influencers, a natural question is that what is the impact of mega influencers on other influencers? Whether there exists a significant impact from mega influencers on other influencers? And what's the role of mega influencers for the platform? Answering these questions is important to theoretically understand the relationships between mega influencers and other influencers, which could systematically illustrate the circumstance environment in the emerging live streaming field. These questions are also important for the live streaming platform since they can take direct and personalized strategies to manage their influencers.

The main contributions of this paper are as follows. First, unlike existing research on live streaming commerce, which largely focuses on viewers' or influencers' specific factors, we illustrate the relationships between influencers. Based on a rich dataset and a natural experiment, we show that influencers can be significantly affected by mega influencers. In this paper, we theoretically illustrate that there could be two different effects from mega influencers, including the drainage effect and signal effect. Second, we explore how mega influencers' effects change over time and show that mega influencers could continuously affect other influencers. The treatment effects are significant in both the short and long terms. Last but not least, based on the causal forest approach, we examine the heterogeneous treatment effect across influencers. We show that not all influencers are treated equally. The influencers with a larger number of followers are affected more than those with a smaller number of followers. These findings are important to theoretically understand the ecosystems of influencers in live steaming e-commerce. Our findings also have important managerial implications for the live streaming platforms to manage their influencers with heterogeneous strategies.

---

[2] https://www.statista.com/statistics/1276120/livestream-e-commerce-sales-united-states.

[3] https://m.thepaper.cn/baijiahao_15268431.

[4] https://cdmana.com/2021/11/20211105033902496n.html.

2   Related Literature

The emerging live streaming commerce has attracted much attention from different perspectives. First, some scholars examined what factors would affect viewers' engagement and sales performance from the influencers' perspective [12, 13, 15, 17, 19]. Li 2018 illustrates that influencers' characteristics and the self-presentation of unique images can attract followers and form their identities and personal brands [12]. Lin et al. (2021) showed that influencers' emotions have a different impact on their viewers' engagement and payments [13]. Luo et al. (2021) explored how product sales in live streaming shows can be affected by influencers' persuasiveness of linguistic styles. Based on Hovland's persuasion model and text analysis, they show that influencers' linguistic persuasive types in live streaming shows could be classified into five types, which lead to different sales performances [15]. Park and Lin (2020) explored the relationships between influencers and the products in their live streaming shows [17]. They illustrate that the factors including the congruence between the celebrity and the product, congruence between the live content and the product, and the congruence between the self and the product significantly affect consumers' purchase intention. Wongkitrungrueng et al. 2020 discussed how to promote sales and customer engagement during live streaming from the perspective of sellers' strategy [19]. They provided a framework for understanding relationship mechanisms in live streaming e-commerce by identifying four sales approaches (transaction, persuasion, content, and relationship) and twelve strategies.

Second, consumers' engagement and purchase behaviors are also attracted much attention from the viewers' perspective [5, 6, 9, 11, 14]. Lu et al. 2021 how viewers' tip behavior can be affected by the viewer size in live streaming shows [14]. They illustrate a positive relationship between viewer size and average tip per viewer. Based on a uses and gratifications framework, Cai and Wohn 2019 identifies four motivations and three scenarios for individuals' live streaming watching behaviors [6]. Haimson et al. 2017 studied what makes consumers' live events engaging and show that immersion, immediacy, interaction, and sociality were important to the engagement of watching live events [9]. Hu et al. 2017 illustrate that individuals' personal experience and co-experience could significantly affect the broadcaster identification and group identification, which then have a significant impact on individuals' continuous live streaming watching intentions [11]. Cai et al. 2018 explore the relationship between hedonic and utilitarian motivations and shopping intention [5]. They find that individuals' hedonic motivation is positively related to celebrity-based intention and utilitarian motivation is positively related to product-based intention.

Different from prior studies, this paper first examines the relationships between influencers. We illustrate that the mage influencers' impacts include both signaling effect and drainage effect. Our empirical results show that these two effects last for a relatively long time and could be heterogeneous across different levels of influencers. These findings are important to theoretically understand the role of mega influencers and bring to light the influencer ecosystems in the live streaming field.

3 Data and Descriptive Analysis

The empirical work in this study is based on a rich dataset from one of the top Chinese live streaming e-commerce platforms, Kuaishou. Like other platforms in the live streaming field, there exist hierarchical and long-tail distributions for influencers. There could be significant differences in the number of followers between mega influencers and other influencers.

Our dataset includes the top 670 influencers' data from the Kuaishou Platform between Oct 1, 2020, and Jan 31, 2021. The influencers' ID, gender, and number of followers are recorded in our dataset. The information about the cumulative number of visits, sales, the starting time, and the ending time for each live streaming show is also recorded. In our paper, the live streaming data is aggregated to analyze the overall pattern. Specifically, we aggregate influencers' live streaming show data into biweekly level data. The detailed statistics of this dataset are shown in Table 1.

Table 1. Data descriptive statistics

	Mean	SD	Min	Max
Biweekly sales	13.02	2.84	2.30	22.18
Biweekly followers' visits	10.32	1.67	6.91	15.01
Biweekly number of shows	6.88	5.93	1	48
Biweekly show time	10.55	1.24	4.72	13.43
Average number of followers	13.05	0.65	8.70	17.41
Gender	0.48	0.50	0	1

Notes. The items of biweekly sales, biweekly viewers' visits, biweekly showtime, the average number of followers are log-transformed

During our time window, the mega influencer was banned from Kuaishou since Nov 2020, because the abrupt scandal. This exogenous shock provides us with an ideal natural experimental setting to explore the relationships between influencers in live streaming e-commerce. To estimate the treatment more clearly, we collect data from another live streaming e-commerce platform as the control group. In the control group, we have the influencers' platform ID, gender, and the number of followers. We also have information about the cumulative number of visits, sales, the starting time, and the ending time for each live streaming show.

4 Econometric Models

4.1 Main Effects Using Difference in Differences

In our econometric models, we adopted the difference in differences model to examine the treatment effect on other influencers with two-way fixed effects, which is wildly used in natural experimental settings [2, 7, 8, 10, 16, 18]. Our DID with two-way fixed effects effectively addressed the empirical challenge wherein the treated and control groups had some pretreatment systematic differences because it compared the challenges in the outcomes between these two groups after explicitly accounting for the pretreatment systematic difference. In this paper, we examine two variables of influencers' behavior in live streaming commerce: (1) visits from followers (Model 1) and (2) sales (Model 2) from influencers in a fortnight. Specifically, the model for estimating the main effect on visits and sales is specified as follows:

$$y_{it} = \alpha_0 + \alpha_1 * Treatment_i \times Post_t + X_{it} + c_i + d_t + \varepsilon_{it}, \tag{1}$$

where y_{it} is the total sales or the total viewers'visits for influencer i in fortnight t. $Treatment_i$ equals 1 for the treated group (influencers in the Kuaishou platform) and 0 for the control group. $After_t$ is a time indicator that equals 1 for the period after treatment and 0 otherwise. ε_{it} is the standard error clustered at the influencer level to account for within-group serial correlation, and X_{it} include the control variables.

Our identification strategy must satisfy the common (parallel) trend assumption in the DID approach [2]. A different pre-treatment trend would lead to the invalidation of the DID estimation because it would introduce bias. Following Card and Krueger (2000), we check the common trend assumption first by plotting the data from multiple periods [7]. Our results provide clear visual evidence of a common underlying trend between the treatment group and the control group.

4.2 Short-Term Versus Long-Term Effect

Having a deep understanding of the duration of the treatment could have important impacts on live streaming firms' decisions and management for influencers. To explore the impact of treatment during different periods, we first divide the time after treatment into two periods: short-term period after treatment and long-term period after treatment. Specifically, we classify the time within the first two fortnights after treatment as the short-term period while the time more than two fortnights after the treatment is the long-term period. To explore the dynamic patterns in different periods, we estimate the treatment effect on visits and sales in short-term and long-term periods specifically following Model 3 (Visits) and Model 4 (Sales).

$$y_{it} = \alpha_0 + \alpha_1 * Treatment_i \times Short_t + \alpha_2 * Treatment_i \times Long_t + X_{it} + c_i + d_t + \varepsilon_{it} \tag{2}$$

where y_{it} is the audiences' total purchases or the total visits for influencer i in fortnight t. Dummy variable $Treatment_i$ equals 1 for the treated group (influencers in the Kuaishou platform) and 0 for the control group. Dummy variable $Short_t$ is a time indicator that equals 1 for the time within the first two fortnights after treatment and 0 otherwise. Dummy variable $Long_t$ is a time indicator that equals 1 for the time after the first two fortnights and 0 otherwise. ε_{it} is the standard error clustered at the influencer level to account for within-group serial correlation, and X_{it} is a vector of control variables for influencer i in fortnight t. In Model 3 and Model 4, the interaction terms α_1 and α_2 capture the impacts of treatment on audiences' visits and purchases respectively in the short-term and long-term respectively.

4.3 Heterogeneity in Treatment Effect Across Influencers Hierarchy

The difference-in-difference regression model in our previous section does not capture potential treatment effect heterogeneity across difference influencers. The treatment effect of the mega influencer' leaving may have significant impacts on some influencers but insignificant impacts on others. In this section, we employ a causal forest approach to analyze the heterogeneous treatment effects. The detailed causal forest approach used in our paper is shown as follows.

To describe the causal forest approach, we denote by X_i the characteristics of influencer i, and by W_i a treatment dummy that equals 1 if she is in the treatment group and 0 otherwise. Following the potential outcomes framework [1], we denote by $Y_i^{(1)}$ and $Y_i^{(0)}$ the potential outcomes that influencer i would have experience with and without the treatment respectively. We define the effect of the mega influencer for influencer i as $\beta_i = Y_i^{(1)} - Y_i^{(0)}$. We have $\beta_i \neq \beta_j, \exists i \neq j$, if the effect is heterogeneous and $\beta_i = \beta_j, \forall i \neq j$, if the effect is homogeneous. The fundamental problem of causal inference is that we do not observe both potential outcomes and for a given influencer. Instead, we observe only the realized outcome $Y_i = W_i Y_i^{(1)} + (1 - W_i) Y_i^{(0)}$, so we cannot compute the individual-level treatment effect β_i. From the previous study [3], to address this fundamental problem, a common approach is to temporarily ignore individual-level treatment effects and focus on conditional average treatment effects. For a given value of influencer characteristics x, the objective could be translated to estimate the treatment effect $\beta(x) = E\left[Y_i^{(1)} - Y_i^{(0)} | X_i = x\right]$.

5 Empirical Results

5.1 Results for Main Effects

We first explore the impact of treatment on other audiences' visits. The results are shown in the left column of Table 2. We find that the coefficient of -0.2486 is negative and significant, showing that viewers' visits for other influencers' significantly decrease. This result suggests that there exists a significant drainage effect of mega influencers in viewers' visits, i.e., there are a significant number of visits for other influencers are coming from mega influencers. When mega influencers leave the platform, a significant number of viewers lose their interest in the platform and decide not to watch other influencers' live streaming shows. As a result, we find that viewers' visits for other influencers significantly decrease after the treatment. Meanwhile, we also find that live streaming show time and frequency play important role in influencers' visits. Specifically, our estimated results show that there would be more followers' visits from longer show time as well as more show frequency.

We also explore how other influencers' sales change after the treatment. In Table 2, when we controlled for both influencers' fixed effects and time-fixed effects, we find that the estimates of other influencers' sales are also negative and significant. It means that, with controlled viewers' visits, other influencers' sales still significantly decreased. This result suggests a signaling effect of mega influencers in live streaming commerce. The banning of mega influencers shows a bad signal from the platform and viewers begin to

Table 2. Average treatment effect

Variables	Model 1	Model 2
	(DV = Visits)	(DV = Sales)
Post × Treatment	−0.2486 (0.0289)***	−0.3527 (0.0423)***
Time length	−0.6370 (0.0365)***	−0.9393 (0.0529)***
Show frequency	−0.4153 (0.0466)***	−0.6347 (0.0553)***
Cumulative visits	−	−0.7292 (0.0264)***
Individual fixed effect	Yes	Yes
Time fixed effect	Yes	Yes
Number of observations	9,479	9,475
Adjusted R-squared	0.4807	0.4696

Notes. Robust standard errors are in parentheses. Outcome is log-transformed. Significance levels: *p < 0.1, **p < 0.05, ***p < 0.01. Coefficients for the intercepts are omitted due to brevity

decrease their trust in the platform. As a result, when viewers are still watching the live streaming shows, they show smaller interest on purchase. Therefore, we find that other influencers' sales significantly decrease when viewers' visits are controlled. In the right column of Table 2, we also find that live streaming show time, frequency, and followers' visits play important role in influencers' sales.

5.2   Results for Effects Between Short-Term and Long-Term

Following Model 3 and Model 4, we explore whether there exists a continuous impact of treatment on visits and sales. As we discussed before, we divide the time after treatment into two periods: short-term and long-term periods, and then estimate the treatment effects in both short-term and long-term periods. The results for estimated results of the treatment effect on influencers' visits and sales are shown in Table 3.

Table 3. Short-term versus long-term treatment effect

Parameters	Model 3	Model 4
	(DV = Visits)	(DV = Sales)
Short × Treatment	−0.0873 (0.0288)***	−0.0843 (0.0449)***
Long × Treatment	−0.3857 (0.0352)***	−0.5916 (0.0518)***
Time length	0.6498 (0.0369)***	0.9760 (0.0533)***
Show frequency	0.4018 (0.0469)***	−0.6478 (0.0552)***
Audiences' visits	−	0.6956 (0.0266)***

(continued)

Table 3. (*continued*)

Parameters	Model 3	Model 4
Individual fixed effect	Yes	Yes
Time fixed effect	Yes	Yes
Number of observations	9,479	9,479
Adjusted R-Squared	0.4878	0.4785

Notes. Robust standard errors are clustered by influencers in parentheses. The outcome is log-transformed. Significance levels: *p < 0.1, **p < 0.05, ***p < 0.01

In Table 3, the coefficients of Short × Treatment and Long × Treatment are −0.0873 and −0.3857 respectively. They are both negative and significant, showing that there exist continuously significant impacts on viewers' visits. Furthermore, we find that the impact on visits is larger in the long-term than short-term and there are smaller visits in the long run. We also find a similar pattern in Model 4. The coefficients of Short × Treatment and Long × Treatment are −0.0843 and −0.5916 respectively, showing that the treatment continuously affects influencers' sales. Meanwhile, the treatment impact on sales is also larger in the long-term than short-term and there are small sales in the long term.

5.3 Results for Effects Cross Influencer Hierarchy

We first illustrate the heterogeneous treatment of viewers' visits to influencers in Fig. 1. In Fig. 1, the horizontal axis indicates the estimated treatment effects across all influencers and the vertical axis indicates the number of influencers. The histogram in white shows the distribution of the effects across all influencers. From the spread of this histogram, we see a wide variation of the treatment effect with the smallest and largest values equal to −0.4590 and −0.0879, respectively. The average effect across all influencers is − 0.2484, which is consistent with findings in our DID model.

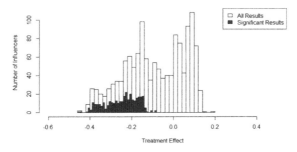

Fig. 1. Heterogeneous treatment effects on audiences' visits

As noted in the previous study [4], this approach can provide insights about the strength of heterogeneity, because the subgroups thus defined rely on using out-of-bag predictions and do not directly depend on the outcomes or treatment themselves. Similar to previous studies [3, 19], we further categorize influencers into different subgroups. Specifically, we divide all influencers into one of five categories based on the number of followers with equal size. Meanwhile, we also divide all influencers into one of two categories based on their genders. As the result, all influencers are categorized into one of the ten subgroups. We calculate the average treatment effect on visits for the ten subgroups respectively. Figure 2 illustrates the specific heterogeneous subgroup treatments analysis.

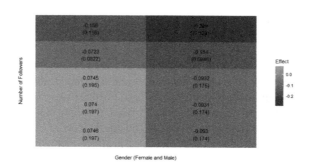

Fig. 2. The heterogeneous treatment effect on visits with different dimensions

In Fig. 2, the left and right columns represent the effects on female and male gender influencers respectively. The bottom row represents the treatment effect on influencers with the smallest number of followers in our dataset. The higher rows denote there is a larger number of followers for the influencers. In Fig. 2, we find that the treatments on visits are significant mainly for influencers with a large number of followers while the impacts on influencers with a small number of followers are limited. A possible explanation is that the viewers for influencers with a small number of followers are relatively more loyal than the viewers for the influencers with a large number of followers. As a result, with the left of the mega influencer, there is a significant number of viewers who are also leaving the platform. Among those leaving viewers, the percentages of viewers for influencers with a small number of followers are relatively small, which could explain the significant decrease in viewers' visits mainly for the influencer with a large number of followers. Meanwhile, we do not find the significant heterogeneous impacts of viewers' visits across male and female influencers, suggesting that gender does not play a significant moderating role in the treatment effect.

Similar to the previous analysis, we illustrate the heterogeneous treatment of sales with a causal forest approach as follows. Specifically, Fig. 3 shows the significant heterogeneous treatment effects across influencers.

In Fig. 3, the horizontal axis indicates the estimated treatment effects of sales across all influencers and the vertical axis indicates the number of influencers. The histogram in white shows the distribution of the effects across all influencers. From the spread of this histogram, we see a wide variation of the treatment effect with the smallest and largest values equal to −0.9805 and 0.5175, respectively. The average effect across all influencers is −0.5445, which is consistent with our findings in our DID model. One

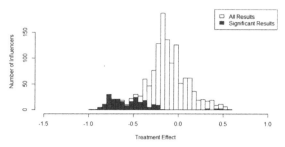

Fig. 3. The heterogeneous treatment effect on sales across influencers

interesting finding is that there exist some influencers who have significant increases in sales after the treatment. This result also illustrates the significant heterogeneous treatment effect on sales across influencers. The histogram in blue shows the distribution of the effects that are significantly different from zero at the 10% significance level. From Fig. 3, we see that most effects are significantly negative from zero at the 10% significance level.

Similar to the previous discussion, we further categorize influencers into ten subgroups to examine the heterogeneous treatment effects on sales. We calculate the average treatment effect on purchases for the ten subgroups respectively. Figure 4 illustrates the specific heterogeneous subgroup treatments analysis.

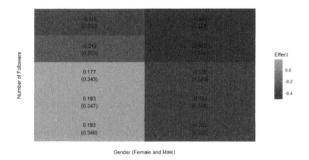

Fig. 4. The heterogeneous treatment effect on sales with different dimensions

In Fig. 4, the left and right columns represent the effects on female and male gender influencers respectively. The bottom row represents the treatment effect on influencers with the smallest number of followers in our dataset. The higher rows denote there is a larger number of followers for the influencers. In Fig. 4, we find that the treatments on visits are significant mainly for influencers with a large number of followers while the impacts on influencers with a small number of followers are limited. Consistent with previous discussions, we explain that the viewers for influencers with a small number of followers are relatively more loyal than the viewers for the influencers with a large number of followers. As a result, with the left of the mega influencer, there is a significant number of viewers who are also leaving the platform. Among those leaving viewers, the percentages of viewers for influencers with a small number of followers are relatively small, which could explain the significant decrease in viewers' visits mainly for the influencer with a large number of followers.

6 Conclusions

Live streaming is becoming prevalent in our daily lives. More and more internet users tend to watch live streaming shows and buy products from influencers. Based on a natural experiment and a unique dataset, this paper takes the first step towards understanding the relationships between mega influencers and other influencers in the live streaming e-commerce setting. Our econometric and causal inference analysis theoretically provides many important findings. First, we illustrate the significant signaling effect and drainage effect from mega influencers on other influencers. With mega influencers' leaving, the viewers' visits and sales for other influencers significantly decrease. Second, our paper shows that mega influencers' treatment effects last for a relatively long time. The viewers' visits and purchases for other influencers significantly decrease in both the short term and long term. Finally, we find that the treatment effects of mega influencers are heterogeneous across influencers. The influencers with a large number of followers are more affected than the influencers with a smaller number of influencers. The findings in our paper have important managerial implications for live streaming platforms to manage their influencers and take personalized management strategies.

Acknowledgments. The research was financially supported by the National Natural Science Foundation of China under grant [number 71831005 & 71771063].

References

1. Abadie, A.: Semiparametric difference-in-differences estimators. Rev. Econ. Stud. **72**(1), 1–19 (2005)
2. Angrist, J.D., Pischke, J.S.: Mostly Harmless Econometrics: An Empiricist's Companion. Princeton University Press, Princeton (2008)
3. Athey, S., Tibshirani, J., Wager, S.: Generalized random forests. Ann. Stat. **47**(2), 1148–1178 (2019)
4. Athey, S., Wager, S.: Estimating treatment effects with causal forests: an application. Observational Stud. **5**(2), 37–51 (2019)
5. Cai, J., Wohn, D.Y., Mittal, A., Sureshbabu, D.: Utilitarian and hedonic motivations for live streaming shopping. In: Proceedings of the 2018 ACM International Conference on Interactive Experiences for TV and Online Video, pp. 81–88 (2018)
6. Cai, J., Wohn, D.Y.: Live streaming commerce: uses and gratifications approach to understanding consumers' motivations. In: Proceedings of the 52nd Hawaii International Conference on System Sciences (2019)
7. Card, D., Krueger, A.B.: Minimum wages and employment: a case study of the fast-food industry in New Jersey and Pennsylvania: reply. Am. Econ. Rev. **90**(5), 1397–1420 (2000)
8. Chevalier, J.A., Mayzlin, D.: The effect of word of mouth on sales: online book reviews. J. Mark. Res. **43**(3), 345–354 (2006)

9. Haimson, O.L., Tang, J.C.: What makes live events engaging on Facebook Live, Periscope, and Snapchat. In: Proceedings of the 2017 CHI Conference on Human Factors in Computing Systems, pp. 48–60 (2017)
10. Hwang, M., Park, S.: The impact of walmart supercenter conversion on consumer shopping behavior. Manag. Sci. **62**(3), 817–828 (2016)
11. Hu, M., Zhang, M., Wang, Y.: Why do audiences choose to keep watching on live video streaming platforms? An explanation of dual identification framework. Comput. Hum. Behav. **75**, 594–606 (2017)
12. Li, R.: The secret of internet celebrities: a qualitative study of online opinion leaders on Weibo. In: Proceedings of the 2018 Hawaii International Conference on System Sciences, pp. 533–542 (2018)
13. Lin, Y., Yao, D., Chen, X.: Happiness begets money: emotion and engagement in live streaming. J. Mark. Res. **58**(3), 417–438 (2021)
14. Lu, S., Yao, D., Chen, X., Grewal, R.: Do larger audiences generate greater revenues under pay what you want? Evidence from a live streaming platform. Mark. Sci. **40**(5), 964–984 (2021)
15. Luo, H., Cheng, S., Zhou, W., Yu, S., Lin, X.: A study on the impact of linguistic persuasive styles on the sales volume of live streaming products in social E-commerce environment. Mathematics **9**(13), 1576 (2021)
16. Narang, U., Shankar, V.: Mobile app introduction and online and offline purchases and product returns. Mark. Sci. **38**(5), 756–772 (2019)
17. Park, H.J., Lin, L.M.: The effects of match-ups on the consumer attitudes toward internet celebrities and their live streaming contents in the context of product endorsement. J. Retail. Consum. Serv. **52**, 101934 (2020)
18. Proserpio, D., Zervas, G.: Online reputation management: estimating the impact of management responses on consumer reviews. Mark. Sci. **36**(5), 645–665 (2017)
19. Wongkitrungrueng, A., Dehouche, N., Assarut, N.: Live streaming commerce from the sellers' perspective: implications for online relationship marketing. J. Mark. Manag. **36**(5–6), 488–518 (2020)

Consumers' Intention to Buy Agricultural Products via Livestreaming Platforms in Southern China

Ping Xu[1], Bing Zhu[2]($\boxtimes$) (ID), and Ke Wang[3]

[1] Department of Educational Psychology, School of Leisure Sports and Management, Guangzhou Sport University, Guangzhou 510500, Guangdong, China
xupprivate@hotmail.com
[2] Department of Marketing, Assumption University, Bangkok 10210, Thailand
bingzhu@msme.au.edu
[3] School of Economics and Management, Henan Institute of Science and Technology, Henan 453003, China

Abstract. The emergence of livestreaming commerce has become more prevalent especially during the pandemic period. This present study attempts to reveal Chinese consumers purchase intention for agricultural products via livestreaming platforms. For this purpose, the Theory of Planned Behavior is applied to reveal the influence of Chinese consumers' subjective norm, attitudes, s and perceived planning behaviors on their purchase intentions when buying agricultural products through livestreaming platforms. The researchers designed an online survey from January to April 2020 in China. Convenient sampling was applied to collect 517 questionnaires from the respondents who have no experience in buying agricultural products from livestreaming platforms. After data cleaning, 400 sets of questionnaires were valid to use. Structural Equation Model was applied to analyze the relationship among the variables. The findings indicated that the path from subjective norm ($\beta = .554$, $p < .001$), attitude ($\beta = .314$, $p < .001$) and perceived behavioral control ($\beta = .139$, $p < .05$) significantly affect consumers' intention to buy agricultural products from livestreaming platforms.

Keywords: Theory of planned behavior · Agriculture food · E-Commerce livestreaming platform

1 Introduction

The outbreak of COVID-19 in 2019 has had an unimaginable impact on business activities. Restrictions on social distancing and the imposition of pandemic control measures have accelerated the dramatic growth of e-commerce. According to the recent data from China Internet Network Information Center [14], online shoppers' number has reached 0.812 trillion by June 2021, which recorded an increase of 29.65 million since December 2020. This number of online shopping users covers 80.3% of the total internet users, and as an effect, Chinese online retail sales has reached 6,113.3 billion yuan, increasing 23.2% than last year (p. 41–42) [14]. The ever-increasing e-commerce cannot be achieved without profound internet penetration. As of June of 2021, Chinese internet users' number has reached 1,011 million with internet penetration rate 71.6% [14]. The popularity of the internet and the mature development of e-commerce have successfully incubated the livestreaming platforms.

Livestreaming becomes trendy globally, through which users can broadcast any activities they like to share such as eating, exercising, singing, dancing, etc. [29]. Livestreaming refers to a "broadcast video streaming service with synchronization and cross-mode (video, text, and image) interactivity provided by network-based platforms and mobile applications" [15]. Throughout the livestreaming platform, "users ("live broadcasters", or *Zhubo* in Chinese) have generated content types ("vertical") for onscreen performances, which include social eating, karaoke singing, games, painting and cooking" [15, 40, 41]. The emergence of livestreaming platforms has not only greatly promoted the rapid growth of social media entertainment in China [15], but sales through such platforms have also sprung up.

According to the statistics from iiMedia Consulting, in 2019, the total scale of Chinese livestreaming has reached 433.8 billion yuan [30] and its market value has already amounted to around 1.2379 trillion Yuan in 2020 [35]. In 2020, Chinese livestreaming users' number has reached 265 million [14] and the users who placed orders on livestreaming e-commerce accounted for 66.2% of the users who watched the livestreaming e-commerce, that is, nearly two-thirds of the users made a purchase after watching the livestreaming e-commerce [30]. Thus, it is not questionable that livestreaming has become a major shopping channel for online shoppers in China [35]. Currently, Taobao, Douyin and Kuaishou are the top three livestreaming platforms with monthly active users of 69.9 million, 46.9 million and 26.8 million, respectively [42]. The promising scenario of livestreaming commerce has brought a way out for many businesses such as the sale of agricultural products especially in underdeveloped regions. Under this situation, "agricultural products + live broadcast of goods" is rapidly emerging through which agricultural products with local characteristics have also begun to be sold through livestreaming platforms. While many high-quality agricultural products have a way out, live broadcasting has also become a channel for farmers in underdeveloped areas to get rid of poverty and increase their income.

With the continuous expansion of the agricultural product livestreaming market and the enhancement of the economy and consumption power of consumer groups, merchants and farmers can utilize livestreaming platforms to understand consumers' willingness to purchase agricultural products, thereby capturing consumption trends of agricultural products. In this context, studying consumer behavior for livestreaming sales becomes vital. This will not only enrich the empirical research on consumer online buying behavior, but also provide insights for related parties such as live broadcast platforms, local governments and farmers who wish to join the e-commerce bandwagon. In addition, as a new trend of e-commerce, livestreaming commerce has also led scholars to study consumer behavior related to this practice. However, the empirical findings are still insufficient. For this reason, this study employed profound Theory of Planned Behavior (TPB) model to reveal how Chinese consumers respond to shopping via livestreaming platforms. In particular, we try to understand the extent to which perceived behavioral control, subjective norm and attitude, affect individual consumer's intention to buy agricultural products via livestreaming platform. The structure of this study is arranged as follows. First, literature review is provided in part 2, and the research design is explained in part 3. The discussion and conclusion are provided in part 4 followed by implications in part 5.

2 Literature Review

As a classic attitude-behavior relationship theory in social psychology, American psychologist Ajzen [1] developed TPB theory in 1985 based on Rational Behavior Theory. The TPB believes that an personal authentic behavior is determined by behavioral intention [1], which is comprehensively influenced by the three variables of perceived behavioral control, subjective norms and attitude [1]. Attitude indicates the personal evaluation of a specific behavior, while subjective norm indicates social influences might trigger or hinder individual's engagement in a particular behavior [2]. Perceived behavioral control refers to a personal self-perception on one's own ability to control corresponding opportunities and resources to perform a behavior [32]. More importantly, intention is understood as "indications of how hard people are willing to try and of how much of an effort they are planning to exert in order to perform the behavior" [2]. The TPB has been widely examined by scholars in different fields and its popularity increases the explanatory power and predictive power in education [22], management [13], marketing [16, 49] and tourism [37, 38], etc. Especially with the popularization of e-commerce, the TPB model has aroused the interest of mainstream scholars including Arora and Sahney [6], Cheah [11] and Han [26]. For example, Boobalan [9] explored altruistic motives' influence on purchasing organic food based on TPB model, in which attitudes to organic food are the main factor in the American groups, and subjective norms play a major role in the Indian groups in purchasing and consuming organic food. Tang [45] applied TPB model to study online shopping intentions and behaviors, in which website trust and online shopping attitudes play a significant role in establishing online shopping intentions and actual behaviors.

2.1 Behavioral Intention (BI)

Behavioral intention indicates an individual presents his or her readiness to perform a behavior [3, 18]. This implies that a stronger intention tends to result in an actual behavior [2]. In the context of consumer behavior, purchase intention implies consumers' intentional willingness [33] to buy a particular product. Purchase intention has been widely studied by various scholars, which include Wagner, Borell, Sarah & Modenesi [47], Wang, Lee Wu & Liu [48] Escobar-Rodríguez & Bonsón -Fernández [17]. Accordingly, in this present study, behavioral intention measures the degree of which individual consumer is trying to purchase agricultural products via livestreaming platforms.

2.2 Perceived Behavioral Control (PBC), Subjective Norm (SN) and Attitude (ATT)

PBC implies individual consumer's perception about the difficult degree of taking a specific action [3, 31]. The key is how well an individual is able to control "time, money, skills, opportunities, abilities, resources or policies" etc. [32]. PBC has been found to affect directly on behavioral intention by various studies including Ajzen [2], Lin Wang, Wang and Lee [33], Liao and Fang [32] and Liu, Shi and Amin [34], etc. For instance, Gupta [23] established a green purchase behavior model among Indian consumers based on TPB, in which perceived behavioral control variable significantly influence Indian consumers' green buying behaviors. Rang and Soyoung [39] investigated Korean consumers' purchasing well-being food intention based on TPB theory. Their results showed that PBC has the strongest effect on Korean consumers behavioral intention to purchase. In this study, PBC refers to a consumer's perception on buying agricultural products' ease or difficulty via livestreaming platforms. In other words, consumers might think that they have control over the knowledge, resources, opportunities, which will trigger their intention to engage in livestreaming commerce [33]. Accordingly, the hypothesis one is formulated:

H1: PBC significantly affects consumer's intention to buy agricultural product via livestreaming platform.

Subjective norms refer to consumer's judgments of certain behaviors in order to cater to the habits of the entire society or their own groups [5]. According to Ajzen [2], subjective norms are reflected in such a manner that if one is performing a particular behavior, he or she will be influenced by those people whom he or she thinks are important to his or her life. In view of this, subjective norms signify that reference groups (e.g., parents, relatives, friends, colleagues, etc.) can guide specific behavioral intentions [32]. Tu and Hu [46] identified the factors that affect consumers' willingness to accept clothing rentals and they found that subjective norms facilitate interpersonal relationship as consumers pay more attention to friends' information sources when making decisions. In addition, in the study of Chen, Liang, Liao and Kuo [12], findings indicated that subjective norms play a key role on hedonic and utilitarian values. In this present study, subjective norms indicate that references groups who consumers think are important to their lives will likely influence consumers' intention to buy agricultural products via livestreaming platforms. Correspondingly, the hypothesis two is developed:

H2: Subjective norm significantly affect consumer's intention to buy agricultural product via livestreaming platform.

Attitude refers to the affirmative or negative regard an individual holds towards something; the degree to which he or she approves the behavior under consideration [4]. Hee [27] defined attitude as the social pressure that an individual perceives when making a decision on whether to perform a certain behavior or not, and these pressures usually come from family members and relatives, friends and colleagues, which largely affect his favorableness or disagreement towards the attitude object [2]. Zhang and Liu [50] explored why consumers try to use eco-friendly intelligent home services by applying TPB, and the results confirmed the significant and positive effects of attitude on consumers' intention to use eco-friendly intelligent home services. Tan, Ooi and Goh [44] examined the determinants of consumers' purchase intention for high efficiency and energy saving household appliances in Malaysia and the findings showed that consumers' more-favorable attitudes toward high efficiency and energy saving household appliances. Also PBC significantly influence their purchase intention as well. Spence, Stancu, Elliott and Dean [43] also explored consumer purchase intentions towards traceable beef steak and minced beef. The findings revealed that attitude was the main determinant, SN was the second determinant, and PBC was the third determinant of intention to purchase the above mentioned traceable products. In this present study, attitude refers to consumers' preference towards buying agricultural products via livestreaming platforms, which is expected to positively influence their intention to eventually buy agricultural products sold via livestreaming platforms. Thus, the hypothesis three is developed:

H3: Attitude towards buying agricultural product via livestreaming platform significantly affect consumer's intention to buy agricultural product via livestreaming platform.

3   Research Design

Firstly, the questionnaire was developed based on a standardized TPB questionnaire proposed by Ajzen [2]. Secondly, the researchers conducted a pilot test by inviting 30 respondents to assess if the questionnaires could be well-understood and it is free from technical errors. The online survey was conducted between January to April 2020 in China after reliability of questionnaires was confirmed. Convenient sampling was applied to collect 517 questionnaires from the respondents who have no experience of buying agricultural products from livestreaming platform. After data cleaning, 400 questionnaires were considered to be valid to use. SEM was applied to analyze the variables' relationship [8] based on AMOs 26.

4   Research Findings

4.1   Respondents' Demographic Information

Mainly, the respondents are female (61.3%) aged between 21–30-year old (39%) with a monthly salary of 2,500 Chinese Yuan to 4,000 Chinese Yuan (44%), and in which, 64.3% of them hold bachelor's degree. More interestingly, 35.8% of the respondents intend to buy fresh fruits and 31.5% of them prefer to buy fresh vegetables from livestreaming platforms.

4.2   Convergent Validity and Discriminant Validity

The convergent validity results showed in Table 1 (Appendix 1) includes the factor loading (λ), reliability, composite reliability and AVE. As shown in Table 1, all factor loading indices (λ) surpassed 0.5. In terms of reliability, Cronbach's α ranged from 0.827–0.860, which were higher than the suggested threshold of 0.7 [36]. With regard to AVE, the values varied from 0.546 to 0.664, which were higher above 0.5 (recommended value), and the values of composite reliability surpassed a recommended value of 0.7 [25]. In conclusion, the results of convergent validity test in this study were confirmed. As for discriminant validity: Table 2 (Appendix 2) presents the discriminant validity test results. As the AVE square root were bigger than the inter-construct correlation [19], the discriminant validity in this study is confirmed.

4.3 SEM Results

The SEM was applied to obtain more "precious specification of hypothesis and operationalizations of constructs" (Bagozzi & Yi, 2012, p. 12) [7]. Seven model-fit indices including χ2/df, RMSEA, GFI, AGFI, NFI, TLI and CFI were employed to evaluate the goodness of fit for SEM (Byrne, 2016) [10]. χ2/df = 1.217, GFI = 0.969, AGFI = 0.954, RMSEA = 0.023, TLI = 0.992, NFI = 0.96 and CFI = 0.994, which meet the requirements suggested by Byrne [10], Hair, Bush & Ortinau [24], Hu & Bentler [29], Gefen Straub & Boudreau [20]. Thus, a good fit for the structural equation model is assured.

In addition, path analysis of hypothesized model was presented in Fig. 1. The path from PBC (β = .139, p < .05), SN (β = .554, p < .001), and ATT (β = .314, p < .001) significantly affect consumers' intention to buy agricultural products from livestreaming platform. Hence, all the hypotheses are supported.

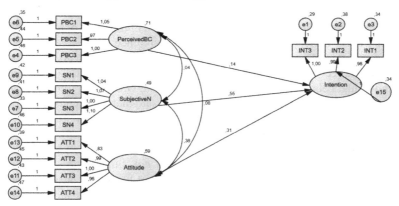

Fig. 1. Path analysis of hypothesized model.

5 Discussion and Conclusion

Based on TPB, this paper analyzed the factors that influence consumers' purchase intentions from the perspective of livestreaming platforms. According to the model, four variables of PBC, SN, ATT and intention are identified, and the research model and hypotheses were established. The results confirmed that PBC, SN and ATT positively and significantly influence consumers' intention to buy agricultural products via livestreaming platforms, in which SN presented the strongest influence followed by ATT and PBC.

With regard to the positive role of perceived behavioral control, it signified that when the respondents feel that shopping via livestreaming is easy, or when they have sufficient resources, their purchase intention to buy agricultural products tends to be higher; otherwise, they will hesitate to engage in livestreaming commerce. For example, when product information (such as price, product origin, volume, weight, delivery and payment method) is unclear or the product itself is not visually well presented by farmers or internet celebrities, consumers will hesitate to make purchasing decisions. When the livestreaming platforms provide a better user experience such as 7-day no-reason return policy (policy), sufficient supply (product availability), appropriate promotional discounts (monetary incentives), on-time delivery (time matter) etc., these kinds of facilitating factors will promote consumers' purchase intention. In general, the more perceived facilitation factors, the easier it is to promote livestreaming buying intention through the livestreaming platform, and vice versa. Ghaderi, Hatamifar and Ghahramani [21] identified smartphone's APP as one of facilitating factors to provide local tourism better traveling experience in Iran. The findings indicated that tourists' PBC plays an important role on their travel intentions.

When the subjective norm plays the most important role in influencing consumer's buying intention, it means that in the process of buying agricultural products, respondents feel the influence of the reference groups such as their relatives or friends, who know the products or channels well. This is also in line with a collectivistic nature of Chinese society in which individual behaviors are greatly influenced or restricted by their surrounding environment. For example, when the reference groups recommended that buying agricultural products from livestreaming platform is worth to do, the respondents tend to take this recommendation into account. Due to the influence of the subjective norms, individual behavioral responses will unknowingly conform to or refer to group norms or the opinions of important groups. It can be said that when consumers purchase products on livestreaming platforms, generally they will feel social pressure from their reference groups, explaining that the impact of the reference group on consumers is still great. In the context of livestreaming shopping, it is important for an individual to feel if others support his or her shopping experience or not. In addition to being affected by subjective norms, some behaviors are also affected by the social setting in which the individual is currently involved. By and large, subjective norms shows a significant impact on buying agricultural products intentions from livestreaming platforms. Jain [31] identified the moderating influence of SN on purchase intions of luxury goods. The findings revealed that SN was positively related to purchase intentions of luxury goods. In addition, SN was found to moderate between luxury purchase intentions and attitude.

When clients wants to purchase agricultural products via livestreaming platforms, they feel positive and optimistic towards the platforms, thus their purchase intention becomes strong. When the livestreaming platform has active and smooth interaction with users and makes use of professional and lively presenters to explain the products, consumer's attitude towards shopping on the livestreaming platform will become positive. Thus, this positiveness likely provokes a strong intention to buy thereby resulting in an actual buying behavior. Thus, in order to form a positive consumer attitude, a good control on product quality and service quality and a training on visual presentation are encouraged. In addition, appropriate promotions and advocacy should be in the consideration among online merchants and farmers.

6   Implications

This present study has provided implications from different perspectives. From the theoretical perspective, the application of TPB model enriches the existing studies of TPB especially in the context of livestreaming commerce. Also, the findings portray the contemporary scenario in which Chinese consumers respond to livestreaming commerce, which could serve as a reference for those researchers who are interested in conducting livestreaming-related study.

From the managerial perspective, as Chinese consumers present a high level of intention to buy agricultural products via livestreaming platforms, the market opportunities are promising when consumers convert their intention to buy to actual buying behavior. Thus, how to trigger consumer's willingness to buy becomes critical. Hence, livestreaming platforms should try to enhance consumer willingness to purchase through a series of practices such as making the buying process easier, providing detailed information, incentivizing and motivating users to gain better electronic word-of-mouth etc. In addition, with regard to the decline in purchasing power during the pandemic, industry authorities might reduce the production cost of agricultural products by providing policy and technical support to agriculture (enterprises) in order to reduce the final price of products in the market. More importantly, local governments, online merchants and farmers (enterprises) of agricultural products can use the current popular webcasting methods to promote relevant knowledge of agricultural products, expand the scope of influence and let the consumers know more about nutrition and palatability of agricultural products in a subtle way. Consequently, consumers will be generating more positive attitude towards buying agricultural products via livestreaming channels.

From societal perspective, through the livestreaming platforms, farmers on the one hand can increase their income by selling their local agricultural products in the e-commerce industry chain; on the other hand, the emergence of the livestreaming platforms has also largely cultivated the e-commerce skills of farmers and related personnel, thereby driving surrounding people to use the internet for their business activities. This will not only promote inclusive benefits in less-developing regions, but also achieve further equalization of regional consumption [14]. Ultimately, the gap in economic development and consumption levels between city and countrysides, economically developed areas and economically underdeveloped regions, will be narrowed to a certain extent.

Funding Acknowledgement. This work has received funding from Guangdong Provincial Education Department of China. It is a part of 2021 Guangdong Province Key Scientific Research Platform and Project "Research on the Economic Effects of Vocational Education Innovation Supply in Guangdong-Hong Kong-Macao Greater Bay Area Based on the Rural Revitalization Strategy" (2021ZDZX4070).

Appendix 1

Table 1. Convergent validity.

Construct	Factor loading	Reliability	Composite reliability	AVE
Intention		.860	0.764	0.664
INT1	.785			
INT2	.832			
INT3	.814			
Perceived behaviour control		.838	0.838	0.634
PBC1	.875			
PBC2	.863			
PBC3	.858			
Subjective Norm		.842	0.843	0.574
SN1	.753			
SN2	.807			
SN3	.726			
SN4	.751			
Attitude		.827	0.828	0.546
ATT1	.735			
ATT2	.803			
ATT3	.781			
ATT4	.702			

Appendix 2

Table 2. Fornell-Larcker criterion.

	ATT	INT	PBC	SN
ATT	0.811			
INT	0.531	0.884		
PBC	0.106	0.180	0.869	
CN	0.586	0.574	0.062	0.824

References

1. Ajzen, I.: From intentions to actions: a theory of planned behavior. In: Kuhl, J., Bechmann, J. (eds.) Action Control: from Cognition to Behavior, pp. 11–39. Springer-Verlag, New York, NY. (1985)
2. Ajzen, I.: The theory of planned behavior. Organ. Behav. Hum. Decis. Process. **50**(2), 179–211 (1991)
3. Ajzen, I.: Perceived behavioral control, self-efficacy, locus of control and the theory of planned behavior. J. Appl. Soc. Psychol. **32**(4), 665–683 (2002). https://doi.org/10.1111/j.1559-1816.2002.tb00236.x
4. Ajzen, I., Driver, B.L.: Application of the theory of planned behavior to leisure choice. J. Leis. Res. **24**, 207–224 (1992). https://doi.org/10.1080/00222216.1992.11969889
5. Ajzen, I., Fishbein, M.: Understanding Attitudes and Predicting Social Behavior. Englewood Cliff: Prentice – Hall (1980)
6. Arora, S., Sahney, S.: Consumer's webrooming conduct: an explanation using the theory of planned behavior. Asia Pac. J. Mark. Logist. **30**(4), 1040–1063 (2018). https://doi.org/10.1108/APJML-08-2017-0185
7. Bagozzi, P.R., Yi, Y.: Specification, evaluation, and interpretation of structural equation models. J. Acad. Mark. Sci. **40**, 8–24 (2012)
8. Beran, N.T., Violato, C.: Structural equation modeling in medical research: a primer. BMC. Res. Notes **3**(1), 267 (2010)
9. Boobalan, K., Nawaz, N., Harindranath, R.M., Gajenderan, V.: Influence of altruistic motives on organic food purchase: theory of planned behavior. Sustainability **13**, 6023 (2021). https://doi.org/10.3390/su13116023
10. Byrne, M.B.: Structural Equation Modeling with Amos: Basic Concepts, Applications, and Programming. Routledge, New York (2016)
11. Cheah, I., Phau, I., Liang, J.: Factors influencing consumers' attitudes and purchase intentions of e-deals. Mark. Intell. Plan. **33**(5), 763–783 (2015). https://doi.org/10.1108/MIP-05-2014-0081
12. Chen, H.-S., Liang, C.-H., Liao, S.-Y., Kuo, H.-Y.: Consumer attitudes and purchase intentions toward food delivery platform services. Sustainability (2020). https://doi.org/10.3390/su1223 10177
13. Chidchanok, A., Sylvia, S., John, K. M. K., Mokbul, M.A.: Local participation in community forest management using theory of planned behaviour: evidence from Udon Thani Province, Thailand. Euro. J. Dev. Res. **32**(1), 1–27 (2019). https://doi.org/10.1057/s41287-019-00219-1
14. CNNIC. The 48th statistical report on China's Internet development status (2021). https://n2.sinaimg.cn/finance/a2d36afe/20210827/FuJian1.pdf
15. Cunningham, S., Craig, D., Lv, J.: China's livestreaming industry: platforms, politics, and precarity. Int. J. Cult. Stud. **22**(6), 719–736 (2019)
16. Emanuel, A.S., Mccully, N., Gallagher, K.M., et al.: Theory of planned behavior explains gender difference in fruit and vegetable consumption. Appetite **3**, 693–697 (2012)
17. Escobar-Rodríguez, T., Bonsón-Fernández, R.: Analysing online purchase intention in Spain: fashion e-commerce. IseB **15**(3), 599–622 (2016). https://doi.org/10.1007/s10257-016-0319-6
18. Fishbein, M., Ajzen, I.: The influence of attitudes on behavior. In: Albarracín, D., Johnson, B.T., Zanna, M.P. (eds.) The Handbook of Attitudes, pp. 173–221. Lawrence Erlbaum Associates Publishers (2005)
19. Fornell, C., Larcker, D.F.: Structural equation models with unobservable variables and measurement error: algebra and statistics. J. Mark. Res. **18**(3), 328–338 (1981)

20. Gefen, D., Straub, D.W., Boudreau, M.-C.: Structural equation modeling and regression guidelines for research practice. Commun. Assoc. Inf. Syst. **4**(7), 2–77 (2000)
21. Ghaderi, Z., Hatamifar, P., Ghahramani, L.: How smartphones enhance local tourism experiences? Asia Pacific J. Tourism Res. **24**(8), 778–788 (2019). https://doi.org/10.1080/109 41665.2019.1630456[21]
22. Greeni, M., Khanh, L.K.: Investigating the relationship between educational support and entrepreneurial intention in Vietnam: the mediating role of entrepreneurial self-efficacy in the theory of planned behavior. Int. J. Manag. Educ. (2021). https://doi.org/10.1016/j.ijme.2021. 100553
23. Gupta, A.K.: Framing a model for green buying behavior of Indian consumers: from the lenses of the theory of planned behavior. J. Clean. Prod. (2021). https://doi.org/10.1016/j.jcl epro.2021.126487
24. Hair, F.J., Bush, P.R., Ortinau, J.D.: Marketing Research: in a Digital Information Environment. McGraw-Hill Education, New York (2009)
25. Hair, J.F., Black, W.C., Babin, B.J., Anderson, R.E., Tatham, R.L.: Multivariate Data Analysis Pearson Education Limited. Upper Saddle River, New Jersey (2009)
26. Han, B., Kim, M., Lee, J.: Exploring consumer attitudes and purchasing intentions of cross-border online shopping in Korea. J. Korea Trade **22**(2), 86–104 (2018). https://doi.org/10. 1108/JKT-10-2017-0093
27. Hee, S.P.: Relationships among attitudes and subjective norm: testing the theory of reasoned action across cultures. Commun. Stud. **51**(2), 162–175 (2000)
28. Hou, F.F., Guang, Z.Z., Li, B.Y., Chong, L.Y.A.: Factors influencing people's continuous watching intention and consumption intention in live streaming: evidence from China. Internet Res. **30**(1), 141–163 (2020)
29. Hu, L.T., Bentler, P.M.: Cutoff criteria for fit indexes in covariance structure analysis: conventional criteria versus new alternatives. Struct. Equ. Model. **6**(1), 1–55 (1999)
30. IiMedia Consulting. 2021 China live E-commerce industry research report. https://m.thepaper. cn/baijiahao_14475733
31. Jain, S.: Assessing the moderating effect of subjective norm on luxury purchase intention: a study of Gen Y consumers in India. Int. J. Retail Distrib. Manag. (2020). https://doi.org/10. 1108/ijrdm-02-2019-0042
32. Liao, W.-L., Fang, C.-Y.: Applying an extended theory of planned behavior for sustaining a landscape restaurant. Sustainability **11**, 5100 (2019). https://doi.org/10.3390/su11185100
33. Lin, G.-Y., Wang, Y.-S., Wang, Y.-M., Lee, M.-L.: What drives people's intention toward live stream broadcasting. Online Inf. Rev. **45**(7), 1268–1289 (2021)
34. Liu, Y., Shi, H., Li, Y., Amin, A.: Factors influencing Chinese residents' post-pandemic outbound travel intentions: an extended theory of planned behavior model based on the perception of COVID-19. Tourism Rev. **76**(4), 871–891 (2021). https://doi.org/10.1108/TR-09-2020-0458
35. Ma, Y.H.: Market value of live commerce in China 2018–2023 (2021). https://www.statista. com/statistics/1127635/china-market-size-of-live-commerce/
36. Nunnally, J.C., Bernstein, I.H.: Psychometric Theory. McGraw-Hill, New York (1994)
37. Quintal, V.A., Lee, J.A., Soutar, G.N.: Risk, uncertainty and the theory of planned behavior-a tourism example. Tour. Manage. **6**, 797–805 (2010)
38. Quintal, V.A., Thomas, B., Phau, I.: Incorporating the winescape into the theory of planned behavior examining new world wineries. Tour. Manage. **46**, 596–609 (2015)
39. Rang, L.H., Soyoung, A.: Intention to purchase wellbeing food among Korean consumers: an application of the theory of planned behavior. Food Qual. Prefer. (2021). https://doi.org/ 10.1016/j.foodqual.2020.104101
40. Recktenwald, D.: Toward a transcription and analysis of live streaming on twitch. J. Pragmat. **115**, 68–81 (2017). https://doi.org/10.1016/j.pragma.2017.01.013

41. Recktenwald, D., Du, Y.: Lagging behind twitch or on its own path: pressures and perks on domestic online live streaming in China. In: Proceedings of 3rd Annual Chinese DIGRA Conference, Providence University, Taichung, City, Taiwan, 1–2 July 2016 (2016).

42. Shiqu. The evaluation report of 20 livestreaming platforms: Which platform is better? Woshipm, April 2020. http://www.woshipm.com/it/3753544.html

43. Spence, M., Stancu, V., Elliott, C.T., Dean, M.: Exploring consumer purchase intentions towards traceable minced beef and beef steak using the theory of planned behavior. Food Control (2018). https://doi.org/10.1016/j.foodcont.2018.03.035

44. Tan, C.-S., Ooi, H.-Y., Goh, Y.-N.: A moral extension of the theory of planned behavior to predict consumers' purchase intention for energy-efficient household appliances in Malaysia. Energy Policy **107**, 459–471 (2017). https://doi.org/10.1016/j.enpol.2017.05.027

45. Tang, H., et al.: Factors affecting E-shopping behaviour: application of theory of planned behaviour. Behav. Neurol. (2021). https://doi.org/10.1155/2021/1664377

46. Tu, J.-C., Hu, C.-L.: A study on the factors affecting consumers' willingness to accept clothing rentals. Sustainability (2018). https://doi.org/10.3390/su10114139

47. Wagner, M.E. Borell, A.D.V. Sarah, L. and Modenesi, A.D.: Influences on the intention to buy organic food in an emerging market. Mark. Intell. Plan. (2017). https://doi.org/10.1108/mip-04-2017-0067

48. Wang, C.-Y., Lee, H.-C., Wu, L.-W., Liu, C.-C.: Quality dimensions in online communities influence purchase intentions. Manag. Decis. **55**(9), 1984–1998 (2017). https://doi.org/10.1108/MD-11-2016-0822

49. Yazdanpanah, M., Forouzani, M.: Application of the theory of planned behavior to predict Iranian students' intention to purchase organic food. J. Clean. Prod. **16**, 342–352 (2015)

50. Zhang, W.-Q., Liu, L.-L.: Unearthing consumers' intention to adopt eco-friendly smart home services: an extended version of the theory of planned behavior model. J. Environ. Planning Manage. (2021). https://doi.org/10.1080/09640568.2021.1880379

Virtual Influencers: The Effects of Controlling Entity, Appearance Realism and Product Type on Advertising Effect

Liangbo Zhang and Jifan Ren[✉]

School of Economics and Management, Harbin Institute of Technology Shenzhen, Shenzhen, China
renjifan@hit.edu.cn

Abstract. Virtual character technology is developing rapidly and is replacing human participation in social division of labor in many fields, such as online education, human customer service, marketing activities, etc. Among them, virtual influencer marketing has gradually become a popular phenomenon, and has been widely adopted among major social media platforms such as Instagram, Facebook, and TikTok. However, due to some long-standing user biases towards computer services, especially compared to human service providers, it is widely believed that computer service providers are lack of ability. As a type of computer product, virtual influencers are highly anthropomorphic in terms of appearance, voice, identity, interaction, etc. Among them, the realistic appearance is an important feature of virtual influencers, which may be an important factor affecting users' perception of their abilities, which in turn affect the advertising effectiveness. On the other hand, the controlling entity of virtual influencer is generally human or computer, that is, virtual influencer's behavior is generally manipulated by human or computer. Past studies suggest that the controlling entity are also an important factor affecting user attitudes.

Does appearance realism affect virtual influencer perception? What can we do to improve user attitudes towards virtual influencer advertisements? Is there an interaction effect between the virtual influencer's appearance realism level and the type of controlling entity? Or, how does the virtual influencer's level of appearance realism and the type of controlling entity match make the advertisement attitude better? We intend to conduct a 2 (appearance realism: high/low) × 2 (controlling entity type: computer/human) between-group experiments. The expected result are: tunder a high level of appearance realism, the effect of computer controlling entity is better than that of human-controlling entity. The reason is that high-level appearance realism improves the user's ability to perceive virtual idols. The ability expectations of virtual influencers reduce perceived ability and thus advertisement attitude. We will further examine the moderating effect of product types. For search products, the effect of using computer controlling entity for virtual idols with a high-level appearance realism is enhanced, the advertisement attitude should be stronger; for experience products, human entity should perform better in advertising regardless high or low appearance realism.

Keywords: Social media marketing · Virtual influencers · Appearance realism · Controlling entity · Advertisement attitude attitudes

G. Salvendy and J. Wei (Eds.): HCII 2022, LNCS 13337, pp. 298–305, 2022.
https://doi.org/10.1007/978-3-031-05014-5_25

1   Introduction

In recent years, with the rapid development of virtual vision technology and the maturity of the business environment, a large number of virtual influencers have emerged on social media platforms. Virtual influencer is a kind of virtual character or avatar, which has been defined as a person with an anthropomorphic appearance, created by a human or AI-enabled digital agents (Miao F et al. 2022). Similar to human social media influencers, virtual influencers are active in social media. They usually have a large number of fans, actively partner with global brands, act as brand ambassadors for products and services, and participate new product launches. For example, Miquela, the first digitally generated virtual influencer, was named one of the 25 most influential people on the internet by Time magazine in 2018, despite the fact that she is not human at all (Robinson B 2020). Until February 2022, she has more than 3 million followers on Instagram, and has made considerable advertising profits through advertising cooperation with brands, including Chanel, Calvin Klein and other top fashion brands.

There are many advantages with virtual influencers for marketing campaigns, most notably brand safety, since the media presence of virtual influencers is carefully crafted by the creator, there is little chance of accidental scandals (Thomas and Fowler 2021). On the contrary, while human brand ambassadors have a greater chance to involve negative events such as scandals. Second, virtual influencers can be easily used across virtual environments, making them recognizable everywhere, whether on an Instagram post or in a video game. Another advantage of the AI-enabled agent is that it could avoid potential problems caused by human emotions, and can provide 24-h uninterrupted and efficient customer service, saving labor costs and becoming an important strategic asset of the company (Thomaz et al. 2020; Lv X et al. 2021). For example, the use of virtual anchors for marketing live broadcasts at night has emerged in live broadcast platforms in China. Given the fast development of artificial intelligence and machine learning technologies, AI customer service can satisfy many different consumer needs, and AI agent is more patient and stable than human service providers. However, virtual influencer marketing still faces many challenges. First, people are biased towards AI customer service communication and problem-solving abilities, and are reluctant to waste time telling AI agnet their needs (Luo et al. 2019). To this end, companies are trying to make it imitating human speech as much as possible to "chat" with consumers (Adiwardana et al. 2020). This makes it difficult for consumers to correctly distinguish whether the conversational partner is a human or an AI (Candello et al. 2017). In terms of vision, the current technology has been able to synthesize virtual human images that are almost indistinguishable from real people. For example, the visual images of famous virtual influencers such as Imma and Miquela are very similar to those of human beings, which means that the visual aspect has reached a high level of realism. Of course, there are plenty of popular virtual influencers of low realism such as Hatsune Miku, Noonoouri, etc.

As an emerging AI technology service product, virtual influencers face the same challenges as other AI services. For example, the disclosure of AI identities would reduce humanized perception (Hendriks et al. 2020), user-AI collaboration efficiency (Ishowo Oloko et al. 2019), willingness to communicate (Luo 2019), and satisfaction (Shi et al. 2020). As a highly anthropomorphic AI service, one of the biggest features of virtual influencers is their visual human-likeness. Is it possible for the high visual similarity to make up for the stereotype of lack of service capabilities and improve the advertising effect? There are currently many virtual influencers of high and low realism in appearance on social media platforms, and they gain the attention of a large number of fans. However, different visual effects may lead to varying marketing outcomes in different conditions. Whether for the designers and operators of virtual influencers or potential brand partners, the choice of virtual influencers and the way presenting them need more research attention. Current virtual influencers may be controlled by real people or AI, known as controlling agents (Miao F, et al. 2022). With the introduction of relevant laws, the government began to require service providers to disclose the non-human identities of AI customer service agents (Alex 2020). We argue that matching different controlling entities with different levels of appearance realism may have different effects in interactive advertising endorsed by virtual influencers. The advertising effects of virtual influencers may also be different under different product types. For example, as a technical product, virtual people may be less likely to endorse experience products that rely on experience than search-based products that rely on data search.

Therefore, our research question was: Does the appearance realism of virtual influencers have an effect on perceptual abilities? Which controlling entity can bring better advertising effect? Is it affected by product type? Specifically, the human-like appearance of virtual idols is a significant indicator of external vision. For example, some virtual idols are almost visually indistinguishable from real people, while some virtual idols have a cartoon-like appearance. Secondly, since virtual idols are anthropomorphic products synthesized by technology, the controlling entity is generally controlled by real people or algorithms, and the behavior of virtual people is controlled by real people or algorithms. Under different levels of appearance authenticity, does the type of controlling entity have an impact on the advertising effect? In addition, the products endorsed by virtual idols can be divided into search and experience products. Will different product types have an impact on the level of appearance authenticity and the interaction of controlling entity types?

As virtual influencers are a relatively new phenomenon, research is still in its infancy. Recent research argues that AI influencers can generate positive brand benefits similar to those generated by human celebrity endorsers (Thomas V. L. and Fowler K. 2021). The research on how virtual influencers visually enhance the advertising effect and its mechanism is still very limited. Particularly, few studies have explored the influence of different controlling entitys and product types on the advertising effect of virtual influencers under different levels of appearance realism.

The market potential of virtual idols with goods is huge. They have varying degrees of human-likeness and different characteristics. Research on this topic contributes to our understanding of the path towards better marketing effect of using virtual idols. Another contribution of this study is improving consumers' acceptance of AI technology and providing insights in areas such as human-computer interaction. This paper is organized by the following structure: hypotheses are proposed based on marketing practice and existing research, and the research hypotheses are verified by experiment design. The research assumptions and expected research methods are described below.

2   Literature Review

2.1   Virtual Influencer

With the improvement of existing technologies and the emergence of new technologies, artificial intelligence technology will bring about major changes in marketing strategies (Davenport et al. 2020). In recent years, advances in digital technology have enabled the development of more complex virtual characters, often presented in three-dimensional form, with anthropomorphic appearances, unique personalities, identity backgrounds, behavioral patterns, and social lives (Ahn, et al. 2012; Bendoni and Danielian 2019). Five core technologies are key to synthesizing virtual characters: natural language processing, image recognition, speech recognition, problem solving, and machine learning (Kietzmann, et al. 2018). Compared with AI customer service and other virtual service providers, virtual influencers in social media are currently the virtual characters with a large amount of followers. They can stay young and alive for long period of time, and they can easily engage in activities such as brand marketing across platforms, but also they are far less likely to be involved in scandals than human influencers. As a result, a large number of top brands have started to use virtual influencers for marketing. In terms of the role of digital technology in marketing, Liu (2019) found that Twitter social bots are significantly effective in spreading word of mouth and have been effective in influencing brand virality. Virtual influencers can also improve users' attitudes towards products in marketing activities, and gain considerable profits for brands.

Previous studies have shown that visual cue is one of the factors that enhance the humanization of digital chat agents. For example, human-like appearance can effectively improve users' attitudes and behavioral intentions toward AI services (Go and Sundar 2019). Perhaps the most effective way to make digital service providers more human is through the visual adoption of personas over time. Since some impressions formed by visual cues are unconscious (Lee and Oh 2015), this kind of character appearance may bring some positive feelings to users and further form cognitive evaluations. Human-like visual cues may trigger humanized perception (Sundar 2008). In this way, when users perceive digital service providers as human beings to some extent, interaction intentions and behaviors will arise (Kim and Sundar 2012). Treating a digital service provider as human means that it may be viewed as having human-like capabilities. The current visual technology can make virtual characters visually almost indistinguishable from real people. For example, the virtual human creation software provided by MetHuman Creator (a free digital human creation site) can design virtual characters with a highly realistic appearance, even including Freckles, blood vessel distribution, iris and other details. Research has shown that the more anthropomorphic an avatar is, the more believable and capable it appears to be (Westerman, et al. 2015). We believe that the a high level of appearance realism may also lead higher perceived ability, even unconsciously. In advertisements involving virtual influencers, perceived ability elicited by high levels of appearance realism may in turn enhance positive user attitudes toward products. Therefore, we propose proposition P1 and P2:

P1: Compared with low-level appearance realism, high-level appearance realism can better improve virtual human perceived ability.

P2: Perceived ability promoted by high level of appearance realism promotes advertising attitudes.

2.2 Controlling Entity

A virtual influencer can be highly similar in appearance to a real person, and its behavior is usually controlled by a computer or a human. Is it needed to inform users who controls virtual influencers? As more and more technologies make it difficult for users to identify whether they are real people or computers (Candello et al. 2017), more and more organizations around the world, including the European Union and parts of the United States, seek to protect users' rights and interests, and are legally and ethically demanding Enterprises have put forward requirements for disclosing computer identities. Therefore in the future, when using computer customer service to provide services to users, it will become an inevitable trend for enterprises to disclose the computer identities of service providers in the future (European Commission 2018; Alex 2020). In the process of the virtual influencers interacting with the user, the user should be informed whether the object interacting with him is a human or a computer. That is, she should be informed whether the identity of the controlling entity is a human or a computer.

Compared with computers, avatars induce more social presence and stronger social influence when using human controlling entity (Fox et al. 2015). However, human controlling entities are not always performing better than computer controlling entities. Because related research has found that people experience negative perceptions when they recognize that they are interacting with humans rather than computer-controlled virtual characters due to unmet social expectations and reduced perceived automation (Kim, et al. 2016; Yokotani, et al. 2018). If a high level of appearance realism enhances the user's perception of the virtual influencer's ability, and if the user has been told that one is interacting with a computer at the time (i.e. the controlling entity is the computer), then this is in line with the user's expectations on the capacity of virtual influencers, which may improve the perceived ability. On the contrary, if the user knows that the controlling entity is a human, the perception of the virtual influencer's ability may be reduced. Therefore, we propose research proposition P3 and P4:

P3: Compared with the human controlling entity, when the controlling entity is a computer, the perceived ability strengthened by high appearance realism is enhanced;

P4: Compared with the computer controlling entity, when the controlling entity is a human, the perceived ability strengthened by high appearance realism is weakened.

2.3 Search and Experience Products

A large number of previous studies divided online product types into two types: search and experience products, and have examined the moderating effect of product type based on this typology (Zhang et al. 2014). If the product attributes can be identified before purchase, the product is a search-type product; if the product attributes cannot be learnt before purchase and use, and must be personally experienced, then the product is classified as an experience product (Klein 1998). Search products are generally easy to be evaluated objectively and easily compared, while evaluation and comparison of experience products are more subjective and difficult (Huang 2009). Compared with offline shopping, online platforms cannot directly judge product quality through contact and other methods, so there is a significant difference in online purchase intentions of these two types of products (Schmid et al. 2018). In online advertisements endorsed by network influencers, consumers need to rely more on other people's evaluation and use experience to make judgments about experience products. However, virtual influencers cannot provide consumers with the real experience of using products. Therefore, for experience products that rely on experiencial evaluation, the ability to perceive virtual influencers has a lower effect on advertisement attitudes. Compared with experience products, consumers usually evaluate products based on the relevant data of search-based products. These data can be quickly obtained through AI technology, so the perceived capability of virtual humans is consistent with consumers' needs for search-based products. In this case, perceived capability should have a stronger effect on advertisement attitude. Therefore, we propose following proposition P5 and P6:

P5: Under the type of search product, the effect of perceived ability on advertisement attitude is enhanced;

P6: Under the type of experience product, the effect of perceived ability on advertisement attitude is weakened.

3   Conceptual Model

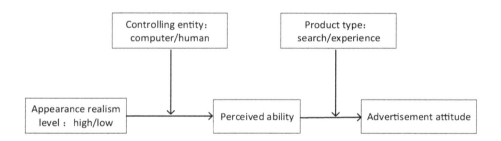

3.1   Method

We will design 4 studies to test the above propositions, 2 of which will use online experiments and the other 2 will use offline experiments. Among them, the purpose of experiment 1 is to test whether the level of appearance realism has an impact on the perception ability and the difference in the effect of different levels of appearance realism. The experiment will design 2 groups of experimental materials, and the participants will be randomly divided into 2 groups. The purpose of Experiment 2 was to examine whether controlling entity type had a moderating effect on the effect of appearance realism levels on perception. 2 (appearance realism: high/low) × 2 (control entity type: computer/human) between-group experiments will be employed. The experimental purpose of Experiment 3 was to examine the moderating effect of product type on the influence of perception ability on advertisement attitude, using 2 (appearance realism: high/low) × 2 (control entity type: computer/human) × 2 (product type: search type /experiential) experiment. The purpose of experiment 4 is to test the main effect again, and add real influencers as a control group to re-verify and supplement the conclusions drawn from the above experiments. 2 (appearance realism: high/low/human) × 2 (control entity) will be used. Type: computer/human) × 2 (product type: search/experience) between-group experiment. Finally, we will continue to improve and optimize the above content and experimental design in the following research.

Acknowledgement. This work was supported by the Natural Science Foundation of China (grant number 71831005) and Shenzhen Humanities & Social Sciences Key Research Bases (grant number KP191001).

References

Robinson, B.: Towards an ontology and ethics of virtual influencers. Australasian J. Inf. Syst. **24** (2020)

Thomas, V.L., Fowler, K.: Close encounters of the AI kind: use of AI influencers as Brand endorsers. J. Advert. **50**(1), 11–25 (2021)

Miao, F., Kozlenkova, I.V., Wang, H., et al.: An emerging theory of avatar marketing. J. Mark. **86**(1), 67–90 (2022)

European Commission, Mitteilung der Kommission an das Europäische Parlament, den Rat, den Europäischen Wirtschafts- und Sozialausschuss und den Ausschuss der Regionen, Brussels (2018)

Thomaz, F., Salge, C., Karahanna, E., et al.: Learning from the dark web: leveraging conversational agents in the era of hyper-privacy to enhance marketing. J. Acad. Mark. Sci. **48**(1), 43–63 (2020)

Lv, X., Liu, Y., Luo, J., et al.: Does a cute artificial intelligence assistant soften the blow? the impact of cuteness on customer tolerance of assistant service failure. Ann. Tour. Res. **87**, 103–114 (2021)

Luo, X., Tong, S., Fang, Z., et al.: Front. Mach. Hum. The impact of artificial intelligence chatbot disclosure on customer purchases. Mark. Sci. **38**(6), 937–947 (2019)

Adiwardana, D., et al.: Towards a Human-like Open-Domain Chatbot. Google Research (2020)

Candello, H., Pinhanez, C., Figueiredo, F.: Typefaces and the perception of humanness in natural language chatbots. In: Proceedings of the 2017 chi Conference on Human Factors in Computing Systems, pp. 3476–3487 (2017)

Alex, C.: Engler. Why AI systems should disclose that they're not human? Fast company (2020). https://www.fastcompany.com/90458448/why-ai-systems-should-disclose-that-theyre-not-human

Zhang, K.Z.K., Cheung, C.M.K., Lee, M.K.O.: Examining the moderating effect of inconsistent reviews and its gender differences on consumers' online shopping decision. Int. J. Inf. Manage. **34**(2), 89–98 (2014)

Klein, L.R.: Evaluating the potential of interactive media through a new lens: search versus experience goods. J. Bus. Res. **41**(3), 195–203 (1998)

Schmid, B., Axhausen, K.W.: In-store or online shopping of search and experience goods: a hybrid choice approach. J. Choice Model. **31**, 156–180 (2019)

Huang, P., Lurie, N.H., Mitra, S.: Searching for experience on the web: an empirical examination of consumer behavior for search and experience goods. J. Mark. **73**(2), 55–69 (2009)

Hendriks, F., Ou, C.X.J., Amiri, A.K., et al.: The power of computer-mediated communication theories in explaining the effect of chatbot introduction on user experience. Interaction **12**, 15 (2020)

Ishowo-Oloko, F., Bonnefon, J.F., Soroye, Z., et al.: Behavioural evidence for a transparency–efficiency tradeoff in human–machine cooperation. Nat. Mach. Intell. **1**(11), 517–521 (2019)

Shi, W., Wang, X., Oh, Y.J., et al.: Effects of persuasive dialogues: testing bot identities and inquiry strategies. In: Proceedings of the 2020 CHI Conference on Human Factors in Computing Systems, pp. 1–13 (2020)

Kietzmann, J., Paschen, J., Treen, E.: Artificial intelligence in advertising: How marketers can leverage artificial intelligence along the consumer journey. J. Advert. Res. **58**(3), 263–267 (2018)

Ahn, S.J., Fox, J., Bailenson, J.N.: uAvatars,ˆ in Leadership in Science and Technology: A Reference Handbook, William Sims Bainbridge, ed. Thousand Oaks, CA: Sage Publications, pp. 695–702 (2012)

Davenport, T., Guha, A., Grewal, D., et al.: How artificial intelligence will change the future of marketing. J. Acad. Mark. Sci. **48**(1), 24–42 (2020)

Bendoni, W., Danielian, F.: The future of influencer marketing in the digital age of virtual influencers. In: 2019 Global Fashion Management Conference at Paris, pp. 604–607 (2019)

Liu, X.: A big data approach to examining social bots on Twitter. J. Serv. Mark. (2019)

Go, E., Sundar, S.S.: Humanizing chatbots: The effects of visual, identity and conversational cues on humanness perceptions. Comput. Hum. Behav. **97**, 304–316 (2019)

Lee, E.J., Oh, S.Y.: Effects of visual cues on social perceptions and self-categorization in computer-mediated communication. Handb. Psychol. Commun. Technol. 115–136 (2015)

Sundar, S.S.: The MAIN model: a heuristic approach to understanding technology effects on credibility, pp. 72–100. MacArthur Foundation Digital Media and Learning Initiative, Cambridge, MA (2008)

Westerman, D., Tamborini, R., Bowman, N.D.: The effects of static avatars on impression formation across different contexts on social networking sites. Comput. Hum. Behav. **53**, 111–117 (2015)

Fox, J., Ahn, S.J., Janssen, J.H., et al.: Avatars versus agents: a meta-analysis quantifying the effect of agency on social influence. Human-Comput. Interact. **30**(5), 401–432 (2015)

Kim, K.M., Hong, J.H., Cho, S.B.: A semantic Bayesian network approach to retrieving information with intelligent conversational agents. Inf. Process. Manage. **43**(1), 225–236 (2007)

Yokotani, K., Takagi, G., Wakashima, K.: Advantages of virtual agents over clinical psychologists during comprehensive mental health interviews using a mixed methods design. Comput. Hum. Behav. **85**, 135–145 (2018)

Kim, Y., Sundar, S.S.: Anthropomorphism of computers: is it mindful or mindless? Comput. Hum. Behav. **28**(1), 241–250 (2012)

Mobile Interactions with Agents

Privacy of AI-Based Voice Assistants: Understanding the Users' Perspective

A Purposive Review and a Roadmap for Elevating Research on Privacy from a User-Oriented Perspective

Yannik Augustin$^{(\boxtimes)}$, Astrid Carolus , and Carolin Wienrich

Julius-Maximilians-Universität Würzburg, Würzburg, Germany
yannik.augustin@uni-wuerzburg.de

Abstract. Intelligent voice assistants (IVA) are on the rise: They are implemented into new smart mobile and stationary devices such as smartphones, smart watches, tablets, cars, and smart speakers. Being surrounded by always-on microphones, however, can be perceived as a threat to one's privacy since audio recordings are saved in the cloud and processed for e.g., marketing purposes. However, only a minority of users adapts their user behavior such as self-disclosure according to their privacy concerns. Research has attempted to find answers for this paradoxical outcome through concepts such as the privacy calculus or the privacy cynicism. Moreover, literature revealed that a large group of users lacks privacy awareness and privacy literacy preventing them from engaging in privacy-preserving behavior. Since previous studies in the scope of IVAs focused primarily on interviews or cross-sectional studies testing models predicting user behavior, desiderata for elevating future research are presented. This leads to a more user-centric approach incorporating e.g., a motivational-affective perspective and investigation of causalities.

Keywords: Privacy · Intelligent voice assistants · Voice-based AI

1 Introduction

Operating digital devices via the most obvious of all forms of communication brings a lot of convenience for users of intelligent voice assistants (IVA). While driving, messages can be sent, or route guidance can be activated without visual or haptic distraction. On the smartphone, texts can be entered without the arduous operation of virtual keyboards, and at home, voice assistants make it possible to save reminders or perform search queries without having to reach for the phone. These advantages are reflected in the steadily increasing user numbers of services such as Alexa (Amazon), Google Assistant (Alphabet), and Siri (Apple) (*Business* Wire 2020). In addition, these intelligent assistants have become truly mobile since they are implemented into a wide range of devices such as smartphones, smart speakers, smart watches, car systems, PCs, and headphones making them a constant companion for their users.

G. Salvendy and J. Wei (Eds.): HCII 2022, LNCS 13337, pp. 309–321, 2022.
https://doi.org/10.1007/978-3-031-05014-5_26

However, IVA technology is overshadowed by widespread skepticism - after all, the use of voice-based AI systems with their permanently activated microphones connected to the internet goes hand in hand with a significant impairment of one's own privacy and data security (Easwara Moorthy and Vu 2014). These perceived risks lead certain potential users to refrain from usage and some users to reduce or even stop using these devices or a few of their functions (O'Brien and Sohail 2020). On the contrary, and although both popular and scientific media address privacy concerns frequently, it seems to be still questionable to what extent privacy is really a pressing issue for end users. An analysis of consumer reviews about voice assistants in online forums, for example, showed that privacy and security were mentioned in only two percent of the texts examined (Fruchter and Liccardi 2018). Contradictory findings such as this that users do not adapt their behavior to their privacy concerns led to the postulation of the frequently cited privacy paradox (Barnes 2006). Recent studies have attempted to clarify or even refute the paradox (Dienlin and Trepte 2015) offering various explanations regarding the discrepancies between user thoughts and behavior.

Due to their novelty, IVAs have only been researched for quite a short time. Nevertheless, researchers from the fields of computer science (Pridmore et al. (2019); Zeng et al. 2017), human-computer interaction (Easwara Moorthy and Vu 2014; Pal et al. 2020), communication science (Buteau and Lee 2021; Lutz and Newlands 2021), and e-commerce (Balakrishnan et al. 2021) have shown particular interest. However, they often used heterogenous or in some cases unclear privacy concepts or aimed at behavioral predictions using simplified models such as the technology acceptance model (Davis 1989). Less consideration has been given to a more detailed analysis of the psychological or social processes in the context of human being interacting with voice-based technology. Consequently, our goal is to compile from the existing literature which theoretical concepts such as informational privacy are relevant in the IVA context and which privacy risks users actually face. Further, we want to answer what privacy concerns users have and to what extent these affect precautionary or avoidance behaviors. Moreover, we bring together theoretical constructs that attempt to explain the question of why voice assistants are used despite existing privacy and security risks, and which cognitive mechanisms are involved. Finally, the review and the analysis of the status quo leads over to the derivation and highlighting of research desiderata and initial ideas to address them in form of a road map. In sum, the present paper helps to broaden the existing perspective on privacy by focusing more on the human user of the technology and therefore on cognitive, emotional, and social processes within the user-device interaction.

To achieve the beforementioned goal, this nonsystematic review will look at selected papers in the domain of privacy and voice assistants across various scientific disciplines. This comprehensive compilation of previous results is needed to obtain a holistic picture of privacy-related concerns and their impact on users to derive desiderata elevating research in this important topic from a psychological perspective.

2   Privacy – No Explanation Needed?

As was evident from the review of publications in the topic area of privacy, some papers completely omitted definitions of the concepts investigated, e.g., privacy or cited various definitions that differed significantly from one another which makes it difficult to get a valid overview of the theoretical concepts of the research area. Rather, the impression arose that privacy for instance, is considered a generally understandable construct that does not require a detailed definition. From a general perspective, privacy is defined as a person's withdrawal from the public using psychological or physical barriers (Westin 1967). According to that, an individual is free to be in seclusion or not, to share personal information or not or to be anonymous or identifiable (Westin 1967). When it comes to a more concise definition, researchers have not agreed to one unified approach yet (Buchanan et al. 2007). Since privacy is a complex construct, there are definitions featuring multiple dimensions such as informational privacy, which states that individuals themselves influence the extent to which personal information is disclosed to others and physical privacy which encompasses e.g., the freedom of surveillance (Burgoon et al. 1989).

In the following, two more complex concepts are presented.

The first approach, the communication privacy management, proposes three strategies to control privacy (Petronio 2010). Privacy disclosure (1) describes the quality and quantity others are allowed to know, boundary linkage (2) refers to the entities that have access to the information, whereas boundary control (3) explains the extent of control someone has over the information after it has been leaked (Petronio 2010). Privacy disclosure is the most significant dimension through which users of IVAs can exert influence. Boundary linkage and control, on the other hand, may be relevant when selecting an IVA system, but they hardly play a role in everyday use, because this is the responsibility of the service providers.

A more recent concept is the privacy process model (Dienlin 2014) postulating that individuals perceive their current privacy context and evaluate it according to their privacy needs. Possible discrepancies between the current and the desired state yield in adapted behavior such as self-disclosure (Dienlin 2014). However, research revealed that, for instance, IVA technology is used although individuals perceive privacy concerns, and thus, should adapt their behavior. Therefore, it should be considered what potential risks users of IVAs are exposed to, to what extent concerns are manifested and to what degree behavior is adapted accordingly, or what cognitive mechanisms underlie them, in order to also be able to understand how behavior that is contradictory to attitudes arises.

3 Privacy Risks and Concerns with IVAs

It is not exclusive to IVA technology to feature risks regarding information and data privacy. However, the always-on nature of these services and their absence of a typical user interface make it especially difficult for many users to understand which of their information is processed and hence, potentially at risk. On the one hand, research has identified a taxonomy of privacy issues in the realm of IVA technology (Pal et al. 2020). On the other hand, research found security vulnerabilities affecting users' privacy in voice assistants – primarily when embodied in smart speakers (Alepis and Patsakis 2017).

With reference to the taxonomy of Pal and colleagues (2020), there are four main domains of privacy in the context of IVAs, namely contextual, bystander, data sharing, and environmental privacy. Regarding (1) contextual and partly (2) bystander privacy, one problem is the lack of authentication with voice assistants. This makes it possible for people within auditory and speaking range to activate the system and to obtain personal data (Pal et al. 2020). This is particularly significant when sensitive data such as calendars, e-mails, or instant messengers are connected to the IVA system, because unlike smartphones, voice assistants are not protected against unauthorized access via passcode or fingerprint, for example (Courtney 2017). Another privacy issue comes with the fact that IVAs are always listening. Just one vocal expression of the so-called "wake word" or anything phonetically similar initiates a voice recording of a potentially sensitive conversation which then immediately is sent to the service provider's cloud (Edu et al. 2021). In addition, it already happened that such voice recordings were transmitted to smart speakers of people in the contact list (Warren 2018). (3) Data sharing is considered to be another problem for personal data since it remains relatively unclear to users who has access to their valuable data in the end (Pal et al. 2020). Of equal ambiguity and concern are aspects of the (4) environmental privacy resembling the extent to which service providers might use the data for profiling and whether government authorities might use the data for their own purposes (Pal, Arpnikanondt, Razzaque et al. 2020).

Moreover, research reported AI learning in terms of algorithms IVAs refer to being manipulated by false data exposure and third-party skills to be possible vectors for attacks making it possible to hack smart speaker devices or to retrieve personal data (Edu et al. 2021; Kumar et al. 2019).

4   Focusing on the User's Perspective on Privacy Concerns

The presence of threats to one's privacy should be reflected in IVA users' concerns, which then manifest themselves in protective behaviors. Research has shown that privacy risks do not solely predict the intention to adopt IVA technology, but it is mediated through privacy concerns (Vimalkumar et al. 2021). Hence, it is necessary to examine if risks induce privacy concerns in users.

According to prospect theory (Kahneman and Tversky 1979), individuals would have to behave in such a way that they try to avoid risks rather than strive to make profits. However, current research does not provide this direct conclusion in the realm of IVA as results do not draw a clear picture (Lau et al. 2018; Zeng et al. 2017).

4.1   Effects of Privacy Concerns on User Behavior

In general, research only found little evidence that supports the hypothesis claiming that privacy concerns would yield in privacy-preserving behavior. According to Pradhan et al. (2018) a third of their participants stated to refuse to use some IVA functions due to privacy concerns or to shut down the smart speaker in several situations. According to another study, some smartphone users adapt their IVA usage to the context; when in public or if the task or topic was perceived as private, participants would claim to hesitate to use an IVA system (Easwara Moorthy and Vu 2014). In contrast, privacy concerns yield in a decreased acceptance of technology with biometrical sensors (Miltgen et al. 2013). Consequently, a few users seem to adapt their privacy behavior to their privacy needs although the majority does not. One factor influencing data disclosure seems to be digital literacy, because on the one hand, capable users show more avoidance behavior than less-literate ones and, for example, consciously weigh conversation topics close to IVAs or make more technical adjustments (Dienlin and Metzger 2016; Liao et al. 2019; Zeng et al. 2017). On the other hand, digital literacy refers to decreased privacy concerns (Liao et al. 2019). Furthermore, there is an effect of usage since users of smartphone or smart speaker IVAs indicated to have less privacy concerns than non-users (Liao et al. 2019).

4.2 Lack of Awareness

In order to engage in privacy-preserving behavior, individuals must have sufficient awareness of the risks described above, which, according to research findings, is not always the case. The previously mentioned result that the majority of voice assistant users have no privacy concerns was supported in a direct user survey (Lau et al. 2018). Most users reported to not have any privacy concerns which they reasoned in different ways. For example, some users doubted their transmitted data would be stored extensively, as this would require disproportionately large storage resources. Others argued with the low relevance of their own person or stated that they would not have to hide anything. These statements reflect a low level of awareness of both the importance of privacy and the technical processes involved, which is partly based on incorrect assumptions and a lack of knowledge. In addition, there are users overestimating their knowledge about the topic, and hence, underestimating the extent of aggregated data they are sharing with companies (Conti and Sobiesk 2007). The prementioned shortcomings of users are particularly problematic since voice assistants affect not only one's own privacy, but also that of bystanders (Pal et al. 2020).

Moreover, research revealed that interindividual differences such as age, gender and socioeconomic status, which have been shown to be predictors of technology acceptance, usage and skills (Robinson et al. 2015) are also relevant for the context of privacy. For example, elderly people view data processing and sharing more skeptically than younger ones (Bonilla and Martin-Hammond 2020). In contrast, younger generations grew up using digital media permanently. They are used to sharing data with various companies and the public posting personal data on social media platforms, for example (Courtney 2017). Then again, other research found young adults to have privacy awareness and to show protective behavior (Hargittai and Marwick 2016).

5 Explanatory Approaches for Solving the Privacy Paradox

The privacy paradox originated in research on social networking sites when studies showed that doubts about posting private information online were not reflected in reduced social media use (Barnes 2006). The privacy paradox was then frequently discussed and contradictory results were found. For example, skeptical users would actually publish fewer posts on social networking sites than uncritical users (Dienlin and Metzger 2016). However, studies in this area are hard to compare because they often refer to different definitions or dimensions of privacy. According to Dienlin and Metzger (2016), discrepancies between attitudes and behavior can be explained by investigating privacy as the multidimensional approach that it is. This includes additional measures like self-withdrawal and self-efficacy. For instance, lurkers protect their privacy from other people because they disclose less data about themselves, at least in (partial) public. Nevertheless, providers and other tracking services also collect valuable data during passive use of social media. This in turn leads the arc to the use of IVAs. Here, users do not primarily fear the publication of personal data, but rather the generation of complex personality and behavior models by manufacturers and providers (Pal et al. 2020).

In research, IVAs are often investigated in the form of smart speakers, because these devices are quite a novelty and thus of particular interest for e.g., economic purposes. This is reflected in various studies, which oftentimes aim to predict user attitudes, user intention or behavior in regards of, for instance, adoption rates. Therefore, theoretical models such as the TAM are applied which, indeed, deliver an insight into relevant factors that affect user behavior. For instance, Buteau and Lee (2021) found privacy risks and perceived safety to influence user attitude – besides technological aspects such as perceived usefulness and social factors. In principle, the paradox could be explained by such results because, after all, it has been found that human behavior is not only influenced by concerns about privacy. However, this falls short because in this way questions of causality, but on the other hand also of the underlying cognitive mechanisms, remained unanswered. Therefore, some of the most popular and promising approaches for clarifying the privacy paradox are explained and discussed in the following.

5.1 Privacy Calculus

Probably the most deployed approach to explaining the privacy paradox is the so-called privacy calculus (Laufer and Wolfe 1977). According to that framework, users compare the potential benefits of a technology with its risks in a utilitarian evaluation (Lee et al. 2013). Consequently, IVAs are used when their benefits appear to outweigh concerns about privacy intrusions. Benefits are, for example, positive outcomes such as convenience through personalized services or hands-free interaction with technology, social rewards, or enjoyment (Smith et al. 2011). In the scope of IVA technology, risks mainly refer to privacy-related problems such as unintentional disclosure or dissemination of personal information (Malhotra et al. 2004; Pal et al. 2020). In fact, it has been shown that users are willing to disclose personal data on condition that they receive personalized services in return (Lee et al. 2013).

The privacy calculus has also been examined in the context of IVAs with approving outcomes (Pal et al. 2020). In a dual factor approach it was shown that perceived benefits are a significant predictor for personal information disclosure and usage intention in a step further, and perceived risks negatively predicted personal information disclosure. However, users valued benefits more than perceived risks (Pal et al. 2020).

Furthermore, the concept of consciously evaluating advantages and disadvantages is not entirely new, as it is in line with rational decision making (Simon 1979). This theoretical approach was also applied in the context of factors that promote or inhibit IVA adoption; for example, with the result that perceived benefits may reduce resistance to IVAs (Balakrishnan et al. 2021). Interestingly, this effect was found only in men, which reveals the question of why women's rejection of IVAs is not significantly reduced by perceived benefits. In addition, research in the field of social network sites found similar effects regarding the moderating role of gender (Sun et al. 2015). According to Sun and colleagues (2015), women tend to focus on hedonic benefits, whereas men put more value towards utilitarian benefits. Regarding the balance between risks and benefits, females seem to primarily focus on risks whereas it is benefits for males. Another moderating factor seems to be culture as uncertainty avoidance was found to influence risk perception (Krasnova et al. 2012).

Overall, the privacy calculus is not free of criticism. On the one hand, the approach is not suitable for insights and understanding the processes of the mental models during the calculus. On the other hand, most privacy calculus models focused on negative or critical behavior like self-disclosure whereas protective measures such as self-withdrawal were disregarded (Dienlin and Metzger 2016). Moreover, studies focus primarily on IVA users. However, within the framework of the cognitive dissonance theory (Festinger 1962), people using the systems might perceive fewer risks than non-users or might overestimate benefits and underestimate risks due to the avoidance of cognitive dissonance. Moreover, the evaluation postulated in the privacy calculus requires users to have a certain level of understanding and awareness of possible risks. As a significant portion of users are not aware of these risks, it is unlikely that these users are capable of making an elaborate decision.

5.2 Trust

To avoid performing a dedicated risk-benefit analysis for each new interaction with an interaction partner, individuals develop either trust or distrust (Harrison McKnight et al. 2002). Regarding user attitudes toward intelligent voice assistants, one study indicates that users tend to trust corporations and governments, which is why they do not fear potential data misuse (Zeng et al. 2017). Additionally, according to a user survey, trust in major technology companies such as Microsoft, Google, and Amazon is relatively high with more than half of the participants claiming to have at least reasonable trust in those companies (Conti and Sobiesk 2007). Since all successful IVA systems are developed by these very businesses, and perceived trust can reduce perceived risk of data disclosure (Pal et al. 2020), users' missing privacy concerns or protective behavior could be partially explained by this fact. Additionally, trust in the service provider and the technology were found to be significant predictors for IVA adoption (Vimalkumar et al. 2021). However, other studies show that users will share personal data even if they have little trust in a corporation (Young and Quan-Haase 2013).

5.3 From Privacy Cynicism to Privacy Apathy and Privacy Fatigue

A newer, well-received approach aiming to solve the privacy paradox by incorporating previous concepts and solving some remaining questions, is the so-called privacy cynicism (Hoffmann et al. 2016). It will occur if users have privacy awareness and distrust a service, they would like to use but are not able to apply and satisfy their own privacy needs. The resulting state of helplessness is said to make users cynic (Hoffmann et al. 2016). Regarding this approach, cynicism acts as a coping strategy to avoid cognitive dissonance to be able to use voice assistants, even though this usage is perceived as risky and privacy adaptation seems to be beyond one's competences. Cognitive dissonance refers to a state of psychological stress the individual experiences when engaging in behavior that is opposing to one's own attitudes, e.g., as a consequence of using IVA systems although the risks are salient. Although cynicism is the result of a certain powerlessness, this does not mean that affected users would not continue to try to protect their privacy (Turow et al. 2015).

The so-called privacy apathy is a kind of intensification of the privacy cynicism approach. It postulates that individuals abandon all efforts and lose interest in the topic of privacy because they feel completely powerless to have control over the own information (Hargittai and Marwick 2016). Thus, this approach can be referred to that of post-privacy, according to which protection of one's own privacy is no longer possible due to technological progress (Hagendorff 2019).

A more comprehensive approach is privacy fatigue which incorporates cynicism and emotional exhaustion (Choi et al. 2018). According to an online survey study, privacy fatigue appears to influence privacy-protective behavior even more than concerns do. Consequently, a mixture of great complexity of the topic, the feeling of powerlessness and cognitive dissonance due to usage besides concerns could be overwhelming for users inducing a fatigue state (Choi et al. 2018).

6   Desiderata and Call for Future Research

The current literature review has worked out that research on privacy in the context of voice-based assistive systems has made substantial progress in the last few years. Based on findings of research on other contexts such as social media engagement, for example, the literature review reveals a growing body of literature on this topic. However, it also reveals fundamental desiderate in terms of (1) a theoretical framework aiming for the integration of the different conceptual approaches and (2) methodological advancements in terms of both measuring approaches and instruments as well as (3) more elaborate qualitative and especially quantitative empirical analyses to result in a more consolidated state of knowledge.

(1)   Call for a holistic approach in IVA privacy.

Previous research regarding privacy and voice assistants revealed single findings which are based on different definitions of privacy and its sub-dimensions, and different concepts elaborated in varying depths referring to various frames of reference. Consequently, it is necessary to create a consistent understanding of the underlying concepts of privacy. This requires a deeper understanding of the psychological processes within the human uses interacting with technology. If studies so far discuss mental processes at all, they are mostly limited to cognitive processes. However, the rather rational perspective on human beings and their interactions with technologies do not adequately represent the human being. Research on so-called media equation going back to the 1990s has shown that a technological device can be more to their human user than mere equipment. With their concept of media equation, Reeves and Nass (1996) assumed that people involuntarily and unconsciously tend to treat media entities, media devices and persons appearing in media content (fictional and real characters) as if they were real people. For example, empirical studies showed that social norms originally applying to human-human interactions also apply in the context of media and technology (Reeves and Nass 1996). Early research on desktop computers and more recent research on e.g., smartphones (Carolus, Muench, et al. 2019) and also on IVA (Carolus et al. 2021) have shown that technology triggers social reactions in the human user. Resulting behavioral patterns are similar to behavioral patterns of human-human interactions. Moreover, Carolus and her colleagues provided empirical evidence that users of smartphones seem to feel like they were in a social relationship with their device (Carolus, Binder, et al. 2019).

As a result, this paper argues to broaden the perspective on IVA privacy to include a more holistic consideration of the human being interacting with the system. Consequently, the paper encourages to a more profound discussion and explanation of the multiple levels of analysis the human users bring with them. Besides cognitive processes, future research needs to consider emotional-motivational and behavioral processes involved.

(2) Call for New Measures of IVA Privacy

Research on IVA privacy would benefit from methodological refinement. Reviewing the current state of research also results in methodological limitations. One of them arises from the lack of unity regarding the concepts being applied which resulted in divergent operationalizations and difficulties in comparing outcomes of other studies. For instance, some researchers introduced privacy risks and concerns as synonymous terms disregarding results that outlined conceptual differences. Another limitation of some studies is their relatively small sample sizes.

In regards of measurement, it seems not sufficient to use privacy scales coming from other domains without adaption for IVA systems since interaction with voice-based technologies encompass privacy risks that are different from that of social networking sites, for instance (Pal et al. 2020). Consequently, future research should focus on the development of domain-specific measures, such as questionnaires, knowledge tests or analyses of behavioral data.

(3) Call for quantitative-empirical experimental studies.

The current literature review has worked out that research on privacy in the context of voice-based assistive systems requires further development of empirical analyses. Most research conducted in that scope were qualitative-empirical studies like interviews or quantitative-empirical cross-sectional studies. Across the different studies presented, there is a fundamental demand for quantitative-empirical experimental study designs testing assumptions and hypotheses deducted from e.g., qualitative interviews. Furthermore, long-term studies analyzing users' behavior over time are promising approaches for future studies. In that way, factors such as privacy concerns could be manipulated investigating the causal effects of different characteristic attributes. For that purpose, suitable questionnaires adapted for IVAs are still needed (see paragraph before).

Summarizing the state of research presented in this paper, specific research areas emerge that should be addressed in future studies. Future research could further investigate emotional aspects of privacy in the IVA scope, for instance, users' well-being which could be impaired by cognitive dissonance or any of the follow-up conditions like privacy cynicism or apathy. Additionally, effects of anthropomorphism could be researched as too much realism of technological systems is said to induce aversive feelings in humans (e.g., uncanny valley; for an overview see: Mori et al. 2012).

With respect to gender differences in the effect of perceived usefulness on reduced use inhibition, it is important to examine the underlying reasons such as gender stereotypes affecting the different gender's attitudes and usage behaviors in the context of IVAs. Besides gender further interindividual differences such as age and also different cultural backgrounds should be analyzed in terms of potential moderating effects.

Finally, successful implementation of technology and usage of systems demands literacy to ensure that user actions are effective and mindful while avoiding risks. Research has shown that digital literacy decreases privacy concerns but leave unanswered the question of whether this is due to well-adjusted privacy-protective behavior or user's biased self-perception and overconfidence. In addition, self-efficacy was found to decrease privacy concerns (Easwara Moorthy and Vu 2014), highlighting the relevance to explore a holistic model of AI literacy for voice-based systems.

7 Conclusion

This paper has shown that intelligent voice assistants are on the rise. Besides the increasingly popular home assistants such as Amazon Alexa or Google Assistant, IVAs are implemented into further mobile and stationary devices such as smartphones, smart watches, tablet and smart home equipment or cars. The awareness of always-on microphones, however, can be perceived as a privacy threat. While one might assume that being aware of these risks results in corresponding behavior, research has shown that only a minority of users who are concerned about their privacy adapts their behavior in terms of reducing self-disclosure. In recent years, growing research efforts have tried to find explanations for this paradoxical outcome. First, studies revealed that a large group of users is simply not aware of the problem or has no strategies to handle it. Arguing from a societal perspective, educational campaigns should address these issues to raise privacy awareness and to develop privacy literacy to enable users to engage in privacy-preserving behavior. Second, referring to results from the analyses of e.g., social networking sites, studies on IVA presented a wealth of concepts ranging from the privacy calculus or privacy cynicism to privacy fatigue, for example. Arguing from a scientific perspective, future studies need to address research desiderata stemming from the dominance of qualitative studies or cross-sectional studies. Experimental testing of models predicting user behavior is a promising approach for future research. In sum, the present paper argues for a more user-centric approach that meets the complexity of the psychology of human users in terms of cognitive, motivational-affective, and behavioral processes involved.

References

Alepis, E., Patsakis, C.: Monkey says, monkey does: security and privacy on voice assistants. IEEE Access **5**, 17841–17851 (2017). https://doi.org/10.1109/access.2017.2747626

Balakrishnan, J., Dwivedi, Y.K., Hughes, L., Boy, F.: Enablers and inhibitors of ai-powered voice assistants: a dual-factor approach by integrating the status quo bias and technology acceptance model. Inf. Syst. Front. , 1–22 (2021). https://doi.org/10.1007/s10796-021-10203-y

Barnes, S.B.: A privacy paradox: social networking in the United States. First Mon. **11**(9), 5 (2006). https://doi.org/10.5210/fm.v11i9.1394

Bonilla, K., Martin-Hammond, A.: Older Adults' Perceptions of Intelligent Voice Assistant Privacy, Transparency, and Online Privacy Guidelines (2020)

Buchanan, T., Paine, C., Joinson, A.N., Reips, U.-D.: Development of measures of online privacy concern and protection for use on the Internet. J. Am. Soc. Inform. Sci. Technol. **58**(2), 157–165 (2007). https://doi.org/10.1002/asi.20459

Burgoon, J.K., Parrott, R., Le Poire, B.A., Kelley, D.L., Walther, J.B., Perry, D.: Maintaining and restoring privacy through communication in different types of relationships. J. Soc. Pers. Relat. **6**(2), 131–158 (1989)

Business Wire (2020). https://www.businesswire.com/news/home/20200427005609/en/Juniper-Research-Number-Voice-Assistant-Devices-Overtake

Buteau, E., Lee, J.: Hey Alexa, why do we use voice assistants? the driving factors of voice assistant technology use. Commun. Res. Rep. **38**(5), 336–345 (2021)

Carolus, A., Binder, J.F., Muench, R., Schmidt, C., Schneider, F., Buglass, S.L.: Smartphones as digital companions: characterizing the relationship between users and their phones. New Media Soc. **21**(4), 914–938 (2019)

Carolus, A., Muench, R., Schmidt, C., Schneider, F.: Impertinent mobiles-effects of politeness and impoliteness in human-smartphone interaction. Comput. Hum. Behav. **93**, 290–300 (2019)

Carolus, A., Wienrich, C., Toerke, A., Friedel, T., Schwietering, C.: 'Alexa, I feel for you!'-observers' empathetic reactions towards a conversational agent. Front. Comput. Sci. **3**, 46 (2021)

Choi, H., Park, J., Jung, Y.: The role of privacy fatigue in online privacy behavior. Comput. Hum. Behav. **81**, 42–51 (2018)

Conti, G., Sobiesk, E.: An honest man has nothing to fear: user perceptions on web-based information disclosure. In: Proceedings of the 3rd symposium on Usable privacy and security, Pittsburgh, Pennsylvania, USA (2007). https://doi.org/10.1145/1280680.1280695

Courtney, M.: Careless talk costs privacy [digital assistants]. Eng. Technol. **12**(10), 50–53 (2017). https://doi.org/10.1049/et.2017.1005

Davis, F.D.: Perceived usefulness, perceived ease of use, and user acceptance of information technology. MIS Q. 319–340 (1989)

Dienlin, T.: The privacy process model. Medien und Privatheit, 105–122 (2014)

Dienlin, T., Metzger, M.J.: An extended privacy calculus model for SNSS: analyzing self-disclosure and self-withdrawal in a representative U.S. sample. J. Comput.-Mediated Commun. **21**(5), 368–383 (2016). https://doi.org/10.1111/jcc4.12163

Dienlin, T., Trepte, S.: Is the privacy paradox a relic of the past? an in-depth analysis of privacy attitudes and privacy behaviors. Eur. J. Soc. Psychol. **45**(3), 285–297 (2015). https://doi.org/10.1002/ejsp.2049

Easwara Moorthy, A., Vu, K.-P.L.: Privacy concerns for use of voice activated personal assistant in the public space. Int. J. Hum. Comput. Interact. **31**(4), 307–335 (2014). https://doi.org/10.1080/10447318.2014.986642

Edu, J.S., Such, J.M., Suarez-Tangil, G.: Smart home personal assistants. ACM Comput. Surv. **53**(6), 1–36 (2021). https://doi.org/10.1145/3412383

Festinger, L.: A Theory of Cognitive Dissonance, vol. 2. Stanford University Press (1962)

Fruchter, N., Liccardi, I.: (2018, 2018/4//). Consumer attitudes towards privacy and security in home assistants. In: Conference on Human Factors in Computing Systems – Proceedings (2018)

Hagendorff, T.: Post-Privacy oder der Verlust der Informationskontrolle. In: Behrendt, H., Loh, W., Matzner, T., Misselhorn, C. (eds.) Privatsphäre 4.0, pp. 91–106. J.B. Metzler, Stuttgart (2019). https://doi.org/10.1007/978-3-476-04860-8_6

Hargittai, E., Marwick, A.: What can I really do? explaining the privacy paradox with online apathy. Int. J. Commun. **10**, 21 (2016)

Harrison McKnight, D., Choudhury, V., Kacmar, C.: The impact of initial consumer trust on intentions to transact with a web site: a trust building model. J. Strateg. Inf. Syst. **11**(3–4), 297–323 (2002). https://doi.org/10.1016/s0963-8687(02)00020-3

Hoffmann, C. P., Lutz, C., Ranzini, G.: Privacy cynicism: a new approach to the privacy paradox. cyberpsychology: J. Psychosoc. Res. Cyberspace, **10**(4) (2016). https://doi.org/10.5817/cp2016-4-7

Kahneman, D., Tversky, A.: prospect theory: an analysis of decision under risk. Econometrica **47**(2), 263–292 (1979). https://doi.org/10.1142/9789814417358_0006

Krasnova, H., Veltri, N.F., Günther, O.: Self-disclosure and privacy calculus on social networking sites: the role of culture. Bus. Inf. Syst. Eng. **4**(3), 127–135 (2012). https://doi.org/10.1007/s12599-012-0216-6

Kumar, D., et al.: Emerging threats in Internet of Things voice services. IEEE Secur. Priv. **17**(4), 18–24 (2019). https://doi.org/10.1109/msec.2019.2910013

Lau, J., Zimmerman, B., Schaub, F.: Alexa, Are you listening? In: Proceedings of the ACM on Human-Computer Interaction, 2(CSCW), pp. 1–31. (2018) https://doi.org/10.1145/3274371

Laufer, R.S., Wolfe, M.: Privacy as a concept and a social issue: a multidimensional developmental theory. J. Soc. Issues **33**(3), 22–42 (1977). https://doi.org/10.1111/j.1540-4560.1977.tb01880.x

Lee, H., Park, H., Kim, J.: Why do people share their context information on social network services? a qualitative study and an experimental study on users' behavior of balancing perceived benefit and risk. Int. J. Hum Comput Stud. **71**(9), 862–877 (2013). https://doi.org/10.1016/j.ijhcs.2013.01.005

Liao, Y., Vitak, J., Kumar, P., Zimmer, M., Kritikos, K.: Understanding the role of privacy and trust in intelligent personal assistant adoption. In: Taylor, N.G., Christian-Lamb, C., Martin, M.H., Nardi, B. (eds.) iConference 2019. LNCS, vol. 11420, pp. 102–113. Springer, Cham (2019). https://doi.org/10.1007/978-3-030-15742-5_9

Lutz, C., Newlands, G.: Privacy and smart speakers: a multi-dimensional approach. Information Society **37**(3), 147–162 (2021). https://doi.org/10.1080/01972243.2021.1897914/SUPPL_FILE/UTIS_A_1897914_SM1205.DOCX

Malhotra, N.K., Kim, S.S., Agarwal, J.: Internet users' information privacy concerns (IUIPC): the construct, the scale, and a causal model. Inf. Syst. Res. **15**(4), 336–355 (2004). https://doi.org/10.1287/isre.1040.0032

Miltgen, C.L., Popovič, A., Oliveira, T.: Determinants of end-user acceptance of biometrics: integrating the "Big 3" of technology acceptance with privacy context. Decis. Support Syst. **56**, 103–114 (2013)

Mori, M., MacDorman, K.F., Kageki, N.: The uncanny valley [from the field]. IEEE Robot. Autom. Mag. **19**(2), 98–100 (2012)

O'Brien, N., Sohail, M.: Infrequent use of AI-enabled personal assistants through the lens of cognitive dissonance theory. In: Stephanidis, C., Antona, M., Ntoa, S. (eds.) HCII 2020. CCIS, vol. 1293, pp. 342–350. Springer, Cham (2020). https://doi.org/10.1007/978-3-030-60700-5_44

Pal, D., Arpnikanondt, C., Razzaque, M.A.: Personal information disclosure via voice assistants: the personalization–privacy paradox. SN Comput. Sci. **1**(5), 1–17 (2020). https://doi.org/10.1007/s42979-020-00287-9

Pal, D., Arpnikanondt, C., Razzaque, M.A., Funilkul, S.: To trust or not-trust: privacy issues with voice assistants. IT Prof. **22**(5), 46–53 (2020). https://doi.org/10.1109/mitp.2019.2958914

Petronio, S.: Communication privacy management theory: what do we know about family privacy regulation? J. Fam. Theory Rev. **2**(3), 175–196 (2010). https://doi.org/10.1111/j.1756-2589.2010.00052.x

Pradhan, A., Mehta, K., Findlater, L.: Accessibility came by accident use of voice-controlled intelligent personal assistants by people with disabilities. In: Proceedings of the 2018 CHI Conference on Human Factors in Computing Systems, pp. 1-13 (2018)

Pridmore, J., Zimmer, M., Vitak, J., Mols, A., Trottier, D.: Intelligent personal assistants and the intercultural negotiations of dataveillance in platformed households. epublications.marquette.edu (2019). https://epublications.marquette.edu/comp_fac/33/

Reeves, B., Nass, C.: The media equation: how people treat computers, television, and new media like real people. Cambridge, UK **10**, 236605 (1996)

Robinson, L., et al.: Digital inequalities and why they matter. Inf. Commun. Soc. **18**(5), 569–582 (2015). https://doi.org/10.1080/1369118x.2015.1012532

Simon, H.A.: Rational decision making in business organizations. Am. Econ. Rev. **69**(4), 493–513 (1979). https://doi.org/10.2307/1808698

Smith, D., Xu.: Information privacy research: an interdisciplinary review. MIS Q. **35**(4), 989–1015 (2011). https://doi.org/10.2307/41409970

Sun, Y., Wang, N., Shen, X.-L., Zhang, J. X.: Location information disclosure in location-based social network services: privacy calculus, benefit structure, and gender differences. Comput. Hum. Behav. **52**, 278–292 (2015). https://doi.org/10.1016/j.chb.2015.06.006

Turow, J., Hennessy, M., Draper, N.: The tradeoff fallacy: how marketers are misrepresenting American consumers and opening them up to exploitation. Available at SSRN 2820060 (2015)

Vimalkumar, M., Sharma, S.K., Singh, J.B., Dwivedi, Y.K.: 'Okay google, what about my privacy?': user's privacy perceptions and acceptance of voice based digital assistants. Comput. Hum. Behav. **120**, 106763 (2021). https://doi.org/10.1016/j.chb.2021.106763

Warren, T.: Amazon explains how Alexa recorded a private conversation and sent it to another user (2018). https://www.theverge.com/2018/5/24/17391898/amazon-alexa-private-conversation-recording-explanation

Westin, A.F.: Privacy and Freedom. Atheneum (1967)

Young, A.L., Quan-Haase, A.: Privacy protection strategies on facebook. Inf. Commun. Soc. **16**(4), 479–500 (2013). https://doi.org/10.1080/1369118x.2013.777757

Zeng, E., Mare, S., Roesner, F.: End user security and privacy concerns with smart homes. In: Thirteenth Symposium on Usable Privacy and Security (SOUPS 2017), pp. 65–80 (2017)

Episodic and Semantic Memory for Interactions with Voice-Based Conversational Agents: Developing an Integrative Model of Technology Engagement and Cognitive Elaboration

Jens F. Binder[✉]

Nottingham Trent University, Nottingham NG1 4FQ, UK
jens.binder@ntu.ac.uk

Abstract. An integrative perspective is developed on memory performance in the context of voice-based conversational agents (VCAs). Memory, as an outcome of human-technology interaction, matters where technology is designed to enhance knowledge and to function as a cognitive support tool and aide. To date, this has meant focusing on the evaluation of specialist applications such as assistive and educational technologies. The increased use of VCAs in everyday life, in the form of smart speakers or as assistants for mobile phones, however, makes effects on memory more relevant to a large user base. Adding VCAs to multi-functional devices such as smartphones increases their potential to be taken as digital companions and to make interactions with them more meaningful. This has implications for different types of memory, semantic and episodic/autobiographical. Since memory is not stable, but malleable and context-dependent, its performance is likely to be influenced by the wide range of social cues that VCAs can convey. Further, VCAs can be expected to contribute to conversational engagement, the general state of involvement in a conversational setting, which in turn influences cognitive outcomes.

Keywords: Conversational agent · Digital companion · Conversational engagement · Memory

1 Introduction

This work aims to build an integrative perspective on memory performance in the context of voice-based technology, in particular of voice-based conversational agents (VCAs) where user voice is the only means of operation and human-like speech is the main output directed at a user.

Memory encompasses the encoding, storing and retrieval of information and as such it is arguably involved in any complex human behavior. The question pursued here concerns user memory performance as an outcome of human-technology interaction, in contrast to retrieving information from user memory during interaction. Put differently, performance refers to how much, and what sort of, information is remembered after an

G. Salvendy and J. Wei (Eds.): HCII 2022, LNCS 13337, pp. 322–334, 2022.
https://doi.org/10.1007/978-3-031-05014-5_27

interactive technology has been queried. This matters in situations where technology is designed to enhance knowledge, to educate and to function as a cognitive support tool and aide. Investigating memory performance in such contexts has a long-standing tradition in HCI, for example, when evaluating the outcomes of engaging with online learning environments [1]. However, these traditional concerns about memory have shown little resemblance to the quality of human-technology interaction that can be achieved by voice-based services, although an integration of voice-based interaction is now within easy reach for many day-to-day applications.

Voice and speech can be generated with increasingly human-like qualities. In many situations, this means that the outcomes of human-technology interaction will resemble more and more the outcomes of a conversation with a human interaction partner. The interaction becomes more complex, richer in social cues and more natural in terms of conversational structure and norms [2]. These changes should be most pronounced in the case of technologies that are fully speech-based, i.e., they are voice-operated and use speech as the sole output. These technologies are referred to here as voice-based conversational agents (VCAs). Other forms of voice-based technologies may combine auditory input and output with text and visual display, e.g., by reading back text input, or by turning user voice into text.

1.1 VCAs in the Context of Media Equation and Digital Companionship

While it is possible to interact with a VCA on static computers or laptops, the two main modes of use at present, arguably, involve smart speakers and mobile phones [3, 4]. Both technologies have been shown to be subject to personification on the user's side [5, 6], and the user-technology relationship in the case of smartphones has been likened to one of digital companionship [7].

The concept of digital companionship is based on media equation theory [8] which states that the medium for information processing, the computer system, gets equated with a human interaction partner [8, 9]. The reasons for this are seen to be based in our human evolution: our ability to communicate has evolved with other human, or at least animate, conversation partners. As a result, we are looking out for social cues during complex interactions, and we respond to such cues in a way that presupposes another human, not inanimate technology. Smartphones have been shown to hold a special place in users' networks of relevant social actors and technological devices, and they are easily perceived to be part of a more meaningful relationship [7, 10] involving the user. Similarly, interactive digital systems that make more use of social cues have been shown to be more persuasive, i.e., to bring about higher levels of user compliance with system requests [2, 11].

VCAs represent one more functionality that narrows the gap between human-human and human-technology interaction. What is more, they easily add to the companion nature of those technologies that are either always with us and close to us (smartphones), or occupy a space in our personal living environment (smart speakers). So far, the effects of VCAs have been discussed mostly in terms of user acceptance and general quality of interaction [3–5]. An investigation of memory will help to further our understanding when it comes to cognitive effects, which can be objectively measured, and the question of deeper psychological changes brought about by technology. While memory has always been important as a performance indicator for some technologies, VCAs and digital companions imply that memory for an interaction episode with technology can now become relevant to the user for personal, self-related reasons. This development will be outlined in the next sections.

2   Memory and Novel Forms of Human-Computer Interaction

2.1   Novel Research Questions Arising from Socially Complex Technology

Memory, it is argued, can be expected to be sensitive to the social cues that are included in generated speech, but the determining processes and factors are likely to differ depending on the type of memory that is under investigation.

The memory system in humans is complex and multi-faceted. The focus here is firstly on declarative memory – information that is in principle accessible by the individual through a conscious effort, and is represented by knowledge in a format that can be communicated. A crucial distinction within declarative memory is the one between semantic and episodic memory [12]. Not only do these refer to different types of knowledge, to a certain extent they can be seen as two separate systems affected by different processes.

Semantic memory consists of general, factual knowledge [13, 14]. In its simplest form, this can include dictionary-type definitions (knowing what things or concepts refer to) as much as shopping lists (knowing what items constitute the list) and exam revision material (knowing which statements constitute relevant knowledge).

In the context of human-technology interaction, investigating performance in relation to semantic memory does not pose particular challenges. Clearly defined recall or recognition tasks can be employed to assess whether information encountered during interaction has been retained by the user. Traditionally, a driving research question has been in which format knowledge should be organized and displayed by technology. In the context of VCAs, however, novel questions arise which are concerned with the ways in which social cues contained in speech allow for attention to be focused on, or diverted from, a knowledge task.

Episodic memory refers to personal experiences, to events and situations that unfold in a temporal sequence, remembered from a first-person perspective [15, 16]. Where the emphasis is most strongly on personal life events, episodic memory is also referred to as autobiographical memory [17].

In contrast to semantic memory, autobiographical memory is more clearly of a long-term nature, carries self-relevance and is retrieved in a process of active construction that draws dynamically on a knowledge base. While not all content of episodic memory may conform to these parameters, episodic and autobiographical memory are used interchangeably here, in the interest of simplicity. The dynamics involved in the construal of autobiographical memory are often due to the social context in which memories are retrieved.

Traditionally, there has been little reason to rank interactions with technology as life episodes of any longer-lasting relevance. In consequence, models of autobiographical memory have not been applied to the outcomes of such episodes. The advent of realistic speech generation, however, combined with natural language processing capabilities and algorithmically enhanced interaction, means that interacting with VCAs bears increased resemblance to human-human communication and genuine conversational settings. As such, interaction episodes become sufficiently socially enriched and complex to warrant their investigation from the viewpoint of autobiographical experience. As with semantic memory, the consideration of VCAs gives rise to novel questions that address the meaningfulness of human-technology interaction and its effects on human cognition.

2.2 Effects of Digital Technology on Memory

As outlined in the previous section, VCAs necessitate a rephrasing of established research questions. In the following, a brief overview is provided over different approaches to memory in HCI-related research. This overview, while not claiming to be exhaustive, demonstrates that an understanding of the malleability of memory is essential in order to address the cognitive consequences of interacting with VCAs.

Memory as a Performance Measure of Digital Technology. Memory performance has been studied in those domains where it is an outcome variable of immediate interest because the technology is supposed to provide support for it and other cognitive functioning. In educational settings, studies on online learning and training have investigated learner memory in the form of knowledge tests and other standard assessments of information retention and information accessibility. General findings in the field are by no means conclusive, in particular when the scaling up and wider implementation of digital learning environments are evaluated [1].

Specific interactive features and functionalities within such learning environments in the form of learning assistants have been shown to improve memory [18]. However, memory enhancement can still fluctuate across studies and environments, even for highly specific functions, and may be down to particular design features and wider context. Consider, for example, findings that ascribe a positive memory effect to instructor visibility in instructional videos [19] compared to those that do not [20].

A particular feature of learning systems that is closely related to VCAs are chatbots. These text-based conversational agents have been found to be particularly suitable for self-directed learning since they provide individualized support and feedback on learning progress in a flexible manner. These claims have been supported by a variety of studies showing positive effects on memory, for example in the context of IT university studies [21], foreign language learning [22] and general knowledge [23]. While these findings can be expected to transfer easily to VCAs, any additional effects due to the social cues contained in human-like generated speech and the context of a more life-like conversation remain to be tested.

Another area where technology-supported memory has received particular attention concerns assistive technologies for specific populations with cognitive impairments or disabilities that affect learning and retention [24]. This is where voice-based functionality is given added relevance since the engagement with technology itself is often limited in such populations [25].

Non-interactive forms of voice-based features are used in assistive technologies in the form of text-to-speech tools, and these have been shown to improve reading comprehension in the case of reading disabilities [26]. VCAs have been proposed where users can be expected to benefit the most from human-like interactions as in the case of dementia [27]. However, a rigorous assessment of the effects on memory is at present not available.

Changing the Organization and Accessibility of Knowledge in Memory. Next to studies that have evaluated the effectiveness of specific features and functionalities, other work has investigated the more pervasive effects on memory that may come from extended interaction with digital technology. This work is concerned not so much with memory performance, as a criterion of success, but with the organization and accessibility of knowledge in memory. Sparrow, Liu, and Wegner [28] found that being faced with a knowledge gap in a difficult quiz activated the concept of Google as a search engine in participants. Their interpretation was that Google search had become part of a transactive memory system with users and was accessed routinely to supply information that was not retrievable from the user's knowledge base. Sparrow and Chatman [29] go on to outline how the investment and distribution patterns of human cognitive resources may change in the face of ubiquitously available online information.

In a similar vein, Storm and Stone [30] demonstrated how the act of saving information digitally freed up cognitive capacity for the learning and remembering of new information. This off-loading of memory again suggests that digital systems can be used as external memory stores – not external to a central computational device, but external to the human memory system [31].

The concepts of off-loading and transactive memory concern first and foremost semantic memory. Far less is known about effects on autobiographical memory, its structure and the ways in which episodes are constructed from memory. Some researchers have argued that technologies that help us in the charting of everyday life and recording of personal information, namely social media, can stimulate autobiographical memory through reminiscence. This is a process of repeated rehearsal of past events, often directed at social relationships and joint experiences [32]. To the extent that social media can showcase specific pieces of personal information, they can also shape and guide reminiscence, for example by drawing attention to past friends [33].

There is at present a marked absence of research to outline the effects of VCAs on autobiographical memory. Reminiscence through social media is still reminiscence regarding the interaction with other humans. Carrying further the concept of digital companionship, however, requires to consider reminiscence regarding the interaction with VCAs. Similarly, transactional memory has been discussed in the context of passive technologies such as search engines, not in relation to highly interactive agents.

In sum, then, memory research in the context of HCI offers some insights into effects on both semantic and episodic memory that may translate to VCAs, but more theoretical elaboration is needed to fully assess the potential that VCAs carry. In the following, therefore, more consideration will be given to the malleability of memory performance and its general dependency on environmental conditions.

2.3 Context-Dependent Memory

Psychological models that imply malleable and context-dependent memory performance illustrate what factors in a more naturalistic human-VCA interaction are likely to affect memory. Memory has been shown to depend on social cues during the encoding and retrieval process. Socially motivated information processing, transactive memory and theories of a dynamic autobiographical memory system are the three main frameworks that allow for addressing the novel research questions associated with VCAs. As stated previously, these questions concern the ways in which social cues steer attention (for semantic memory) and the ways in which we respond to meaningful and socially significant interactions with technology (for episodic memory).

Regarding socially motivated information processing, a fundamental factor concerns animacy. Animacy refers at first to the perceived nature of the stimulus to be remembered (animate, in the sense of alive). Research has consistently shown that animate stimuli improve memory performance [34]. Animacy further affects language comprehension and the organization of knowledge in memory [35]. These effects are explained by the richer, more detailed encoding that is possible with animate stimuli [36] and the increased allocation of attentional resources to animate versus inanimate stimuli [37]. To be clear, research on animacy and memory has addressed the animate nature of the stimulus, but not of the medium. Still, it can be speculated that a more life-like, animate source of information, as constituted by VCAs, has similar effects.

Further forms of socially motivated information processing concern self-relevance and social categorization in the context of ingroup and outgroup membership. Intergroup settings provide strong drivers for selective attention and selective memory, and this extends to all information that can to some extent be associated with such settings. For example, better memory has been demonstrated for positive behaviors in ingroup members as compared to outgroup members [38]. These biases are explained in terms of ingroup favoritism, to preserve a positive ingroup identity [39]. Beyond favoritism, however, research has also shown that there is a general increase in memory performance for information relevant to the ingroup, rather than the outgroup, because ingroup matters command more attentional resources [40]. Transferring these findings to the domain of technology, VCAs are suited to the signaling of social group membership through a range of linguistic markers, and carry the potential to activate an awareness of ingroups and outgroups.

Transactive memory systems [41, 42] have already been used to explain how users turn to the Internet automatically to fill in knowledge gaps [28]. VCAs, however, can be a far more active component in transactive memory. They have the potential to take on different social roles and to simulate closeness and rapport to the extent that dynamics can be expected as they have been documented in human dyads and teams. Memory performance has been shown to be affected by the social characteristics of a team such as social closeness, familiarity and gender [43, 44]. It is worth noting that socially positive characteristics do not necessarily lead to better performance. Being teamed up with friends is more likely to reduce an individual's memory performance [43, 44]. This can be explained by an adaptive process that is at the core of the transactional memory system. An individual's information processing is based on assumptions about the knowledge structure of others in the system, and as such, efforts may be reduced when in the presence of reliable partners [45].

A much deeper-running level of self-relevance than discussed so far is at play when human-technology interaction turns into meaningful social experiences and becomes part of the knowledge base that underlies autobiographical memory. The functions and drivers associated with this type of memory are complex and go beyond those associated with semantic memory. Autobiographical memory refers to, as stated previously, personal experiences stored long-term but retrieved in an active and dynamic process [46–48]. In this perspective, autobiographical memory draws on a self-memory system, a more stable, long-term storage, but the assembly of episodic building blocks is not always the same and depends on goals of the working self, i.e., on the current psychological state of the individual [47].

While VCA-based interactions may show suitable complexity in order to be included in an autobiographical memory system, they also need to display sufficient levels of personal relevance. How can the meaningfulness of such interactions be determined? This may well depend on the extent to which VCA-based interactions can fulfil the various functions that have been ascribed to autobiographical memory. These functions have been labelled as "self", "social" and "directive" [49–51].

Self-based functions are those that provide a sense of coherence, identity and continuity. Remembering the past, as a sequence of actions, developments and events involving the self, helps to achieve this. Social functions refer to the maintenance of intimacy, to social bonding and to the upkeep of relationships. Reminiscence, recall of joint activities, instances of support and positive social exchanges all cater to the social needs of the individual. Directive functions provide guidance and orientation in the present, they support decision-making and goal formation. This functional account illustrates how strongly the current psychological needs of the individual determine what gets remembered and how. It also helps to identify how exactly VCAs could become part of this memory system.

In terms of self-based and social functions, VCAs are unlikely to be able to fully compete with human interaction partners. They have neither the durability nor the level of intimacy that come with the friends that really matter. However, echoing again digital companionship, VCAs can emulate weaker forms of human-human interaction and may be able to address self-based and social functions much more than less interactive technologies. In terms of directive functions, past interactions with VCAs may well constitute relevant informative experiences that provide guidance in the present. Psychologically meaningful interactions could result when the VCA meets urgent support needs (e.g., calling for help in emergency), when the VCA plays an instrumental role within a wider social context (e.g., communicating with friends, being used for a joint activity), or when the VCA enhances an episode of personal relevance (e.g., keeping a holiday organized).

In sum, the memory processes discussed allow for a theoretically informed identification of those characteristics that will make interactions with VCAs more or less memorable. Naturalness of voice, familiarity or resemblance with specific others, signaling ingroup membership, conveying impressions of competence and reliability are some of the factors that come with VCAs and that have been shown to affect human (semantic) memory. In addition, the potential for a socially meaningful interaction experience, a genuine conversational setting, is likely to extend effects on semantic memory to episodic memory. This depends on the capacity of VCAs to fulfil one or more functions that are typically ascribed to autobiographical memory (self-based, social, directive). The theoretical and methodological challenges that come with this extension are addressed next.

3   Conversational Engagement and VCAs

Any effects of VCAs on human memory are of particular interest where they are "unique", i.e., occur over and above those of comparable technologies such as text-based chatbots. Such unique effects can come from multiple sources. First of all, there are aspects of language and the illusion of natural speech. This includes all paraverbal signals associated with language: cadence, flow, timbre, rhythm, speed, prosody etc. Paraverbal signals can be expected, first of all, to affect perceptions of animacy. Then there are aspects of familiarity and speaker identity. Is the voice characteristic and conducive towards creating a virtual identity? Is the voice modelled on genuine, recognizable humans like the self or close others? Does the voice suggest any particular societal group or stratum? These aspects will trigger effects associated with social cognition and transactive memory.

In addition, beyond the technical aspects of speech generation, there is the question of how VCAs are integrated in devices to form a new, consistent whole that acts as conversation partner. A smart speaker does not explicitly offer any functionality other than voice-based interaction. The device is merely the embodiment of a VCA, typically with a fixed spatial location. Mobile phones seem to be on the other end of the spectrum. Mobile phones are normally smartphones, devices optimized for screen-oriented, handheld use, inviting haptic interaction and online connectivity, next to the original function of being a telephone. Yet, in terms of providing VCAs an environment in which they can take on character and meaning, mobile phones offer great potential.

Bringing this multitude of factors back to systematic research on memory performance poses a serious challenge. One avenue for further research is to isolate factors and subject them to experiment-based scrutiny. To date, this approach has been used to derive a robust hypothesis and method for studying the effects of voice on semantic memory [52], but more work in this area is needed to build a reliable empirical support base.

A second avenue consists in defining and capturing more inclusive concepts from conversational analysis that help to predict what happens as the overall quality of the interaction changes. Conversational engagement is proposed here as such a concept which has been developed specifically in the context of computer-mediated communication [53, 54].

Conversational engagement refers to the general state of activation and readiness to respond in conversational settings. Engagement is an indicator for immersion in the situation, the amount of cognitive resources and attention devoted to the conversation, and the general degree of social involvement.

Engagement has been conceptualized as a multi-dimensional construct encompassing wider bodily movement, gesturing, facial expression, but also paraverbal and verbal signals [54]. Its operationalization in research is likewise multi-dimensional, ranging from real-time motion capture to in-depth content analysis of recorded conversations.

Crucially, engagement has been related to cognitive conversational outcomes, and increases in engagement have been shown to lead to increased memory for conversational content [53]. Recall of content here did not happen as in the recall of pre-defined pieces of information, but in a wider sense as the recall of any aspect of the interaction that has left some longer-lasting impression on conversation partners. This suggests that engagement is a suitable concept for investigating effects on autobiographical, and not just semantic, memory.

In sum, conversational engagement offers a sufficiently complex concept to capture (a) the various ways in which VCAs can enhance and enrich human-technology interaction and (b) the various cognitive outcomes and different types of memory affected by such enhancement. The approach presented here seems to be particularly suitable where technology is already multi-functional and rich in affordances. It may be therefore that VCAs and mobile phones form the best area of application, as compared to smart speakers. Importantly, conversational engagement is not only a particular theoretical approach, but implies a clear set of methods and measures. While engagement has been previously applied to computer-mediated human-human settings, the transition to human-technology settings can be achieved seamlessly by adapting existing methodology [53].

4   Conclusions and Implications

In conclusion, VCAs present another milestone on the ongoing journey of technology towards becoming a complex conversation partner. A core outcome of conversational settings concerns memory, in the form of factual knowledge, but also in the form of stored personal experiences. VCAs add to the potential meaningfulness of human-technology interaction, and their cognitive effects should be assessed by both semantic and episodic memory performance. A summary of concepts and processes discussed in the present work is presented in Fig. 1.

Studies that have highlighted the context-dependency of memory can be utilized to identify a range of factors that fall under the social cues that VCAs can convey: animacy, familiarity, group membership and identity, team roles in transactive memory systems can all be signaled effectively through generated speech. In addition, models of autobiographical memory help to identify conditions under which human-technology interaction will acquire increased meaning and significance, namely when self-based, social and directive functions of memory are addressed by the technology. The theoretical integration presented here therefore allows for the derivation of testable hypotheses for further empirical study.

In addition, the effects of VCAs can also be addressed by recent work on conversational engagement, a broad construct that situates the link between VCA and memory outcomes in a wider framework of the effectiveness of conversational settings. This approach lends itself to further research since it specifies not only variables that influence engagement, but also a methodology to capture engagement and its outcomes.

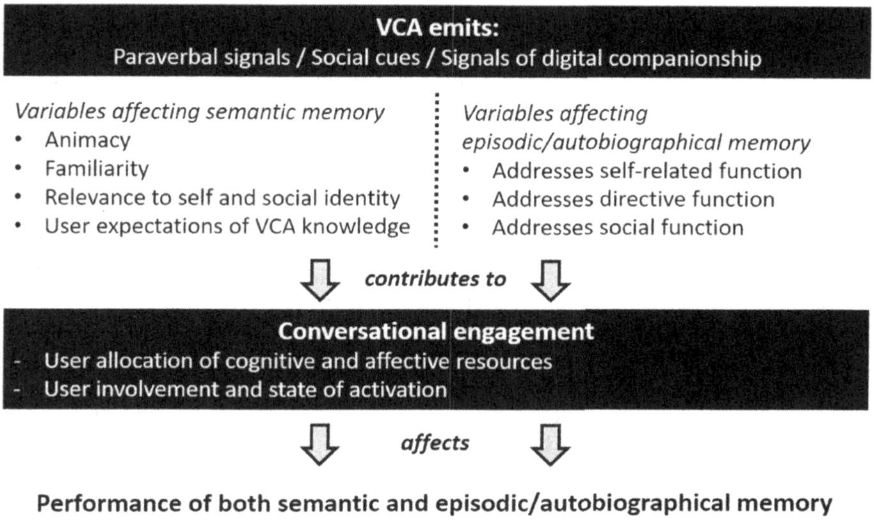

Fig. 1. Summative presentation of concepts and processes that integrate VCA characteristics, memory processes, and conversational engagement.

Next to the implications for research, the present investigation of memory is also intended to benefit developers and service providers as well as users. The increased use of VCAs in everyday life, in the form of smart speakers or as assistants for mobile phones, makes effects on memory more relevant to a large user base. Developers should consider how different aspects of generated speech affect human cognition and leave enough room for a flexible customization of speech output. Further, the choice of default settings for generated speech should also be informed by the likely effects on user memory. Service providers need to make conscious decisions as to the social role they envisage their products to play, and what users should be expected to "take away" from interacting with VCAs. Users, then, are best empowered by an awareness of the effects of VCA engagement, beyond mere appeal of the interaction. This will help them to choose system settings, contexts for use, and interaction goals in a more self-determined way. As technology becomes a conversational partner, such an awareness will maintain necessary levels of digital literacy and competence.

References

1. Davis, D., Chen, G., Hauff, C., Houben, G.J.: Activating learning at scale: a review of innovations in online learning strategies. Comput. Educ. **125**, 327–344 (2018)
2. Feine, J., Gnewuch, U., Morana, S., Maedche, A.: A taxonomy of social cues for conversational agents. Int. J. Hum. Comput. Stud. **132**, 138–161 (2019)
3. Miner, A.S., Milstein, A., Schueller, S., Hegde, R., Mangurian, C., Linos, E.: Smartphone-based conversational agents and responses to questions about mental health, interpersonal violence, and physical health. JAMA Intern. Med. **176**(5), 619–625 (2016)

4. Lovato, S. B., Piper, A. M., Wartella, E. A.: Hey Google, do unicorns exist? Conversational agents as a path to answers to children's questions. In: Proceedings of the 18th ACM International Conference on Interaction Design and Children, pp. 301–313. ACM, New York (2019)
5. Pradhan, A., Findlater, L., Lazar, A.: "Phantom Friend" or "Just a Box with Information" personification and ontological categorization of smart speaker-based voice assistants by older adults. In: Proceedings of the ACM on Human-Computer Interaction, CSCW vol. 3, pp. 1–21. ACM, New York (2019)
6. Fullwood, C., Quinn, S., Kaye, L.K., Redding, C.: My virtual friend: a qualitative analysis of the attitudes and experiences of Smartphone users: implications for Smartphone attachment. Comput. Hum. Behav. **75**, 347–355 (2017)
7. Carolus, A., Binder, J.F., Muench, R., Schmidt, C., Schneider, F., Buglass, S.L.: Smartphones as digital companions: characterizing the relationship between users and their phones. New Media Soc. **21**(4), 914–938 (2019). https://doi.org/10.1177/1461444818817074
8. Nass, C., Steuer, J., Tauber, E.R.: Computers are social actors. In: Proceedings of the SIGCHI Conference on Human Factors in Computing Systems, pp. 72–78. ACM, New York (1994)
9. Reeves, B., Nass, C.: The Media Equation: How People Treat Computers, Television, and New Media Like Real People and Places. CSLI Publications, Stanford (1996)
10. Carolus, A., Muench, R., Schmidt, C., Schneider, F.: Impertinent mobiles - effects of politeness and impoliteness in human-smartphone interaction. Comput. Hum. Behav. **93**, 290–300 (2019)
11. Fogg, B.J.: Persuasive Technology: Using Computers to Change What We Think and Do. Morgan Kaufmann, San Francisco, San Francisco (2003)
12. Knowlton, B.J., Squire, L.R.: Remembering and knowing: two different expressions of declarative memory. J. Exp. Psychol. Learn. Mem. Cogn. **21**(3), 699–710 (1995)
13. Kumar, A.A.: Semantic memory: a review of methods, models, and current challenges. Psychon. Bull. Rev. **28**(1), 40–80 (2020). https://doi.org/10.3758/s13423-020-01792-x
14. Yee, E., Chrysikou, E.G., Thompson-Schill, S. L.: Semantic memory. In: K. N. Ochsner, S. M. Kosslyn (eds.) The Oxford handbook of cognitive neuroscience, Vol. 1. Core topics, pp. 353–374. Oxford University Press: Oxford (2014)
15. Baddeley, A., Aggleton, J.P., Conway, M.A.: Episodic memory: New directions in research. Oxford University Press, Oxford (2002)
16. Baddeley, A.: The concept of episodic memory. Philosoph. Trans. Roy. Soc. London Ser. B: Biol. Sci. **356**(1413), 1345–1350 (2001)
17. Conway, M.A., Rubin, D.C.: The structure of autobiographical memory. In: Collins, A., Gathercole, S., Conway, M, Morris, P. (eds.) Theories of Memory, pp. 103–137. Lawrence Erlbaum Associates, Mahwah (1993)
18. Gargrish, S., Kaur, D.P., Mantri, A., Singh, G., Sharma, B.: Measuring effectiveness of augmented reality-based geometry learning assistant on memory retention abilities of the students in 3D geometry. Comput. Appl. Eng. Educ. **29**(6), 1811–1824 (2021)
19. Wang, J., Antonenko, P.D.: Instructor presence in instructional video: effects on visual attention, recall, and perceived learning. Comput. Hum. Behav. **71**, 79–89 (2017)
20. Kizilcec, R.F., Papadopoulos, K., Sritanyaratana, L.: Showing face in video instruction: effects on information retention, visual attention, and affect. In: Proceedings of the SIGCHI Conference on Human Factors in Computing Systems, pp. 2095–2102. ACM, New York (2014)
21. Abbasi, S., Kazi, H.: Measuring effectiveness of learning chatbot systems on student's learning outcome and memory retention. Asian J. Appl. Sci. Eng. **3**(2), 251–260 (2014)
22. Chen, H.L., Vicki Widarso, G., Sutrisno, H.: A chatbot for learning Chinese: learning achievement and technology acceptance. J. Educ. Comput. Res. **58**(6), 1161–1189 (2020)

23. Ruan, S., et al.: Quizbot: a dialogue-based adaptive learning system for factual knowledge. In: Proceedings of the 2019 CHI Conference on Human Factors in Computing Systems, pp. 1–13. ACM, New York (2019)

24. Dewar, B.K., Kopelman, M., Kapur, N., Wilson, B.A.: Assistive technology for memory. In: O'Neill, B., Gillespie, A. (eds.) Assistive Technology for Cognition: A Handbook for Clinicians and Developers, pp. 31–46. Routledge, Milton Park (2014)

25. Sharma, F.R., Wasson, S.G.: Speech recognition and synthesis tool: assistive technology for physically disabled persons. Int. J. Comput. Sci. Telecommun. **3**(4), 86–91 (2012)

26. Wood, S.G., Moxley, J.H., Tighe, E.L., Wagner, R.K.: Does use of text-to-speech and related read-aloud tools improve reading comprehension for students with reading disabilities? A meta-analysis? J. Learn. Disabil. **51**(1), 73–84 (2018)

27. Nakatani, S., Saiki, S., Nakamura, M., Yasuda, K.: Generating personalized virtual agent in speech dialogue system for people with dementia. In: Duffy, V.G. (ed.) DHM 2018. LNCS, vol. 10917, pp. 326–337. Springer, Cham (2018). https://doi.org/10.1007/978-3-319-91397-1_27

28. Sparrow, B., Liu, J., Wegner, D.M.: Google effects on memory: cognitive consequences of having information at our fingertips. Science **333**(6043), 776–778 (2011)

29. Sparrow, B., Chatman, L.: Social cognition in the Internet age: Same as it ever was? Psychol. Inq. **24**(4), 273–292 (2013)

30. Storm, B.C., Stone, S.M.: Saving-enhanced memory: the benefits of saving on the learning and remembering of new information. Psychol. Sci. **26**(2), 182–188 (2015)

31. Storm, B. C., & Soares, J. S. (2021). Memory in the digital age. Handbook of human memory: Foundations and applications

32. Peesapati, S.T., Schwanda, V., Schultz, J., Lepage, M., Jeong, S.Y., Cosley, D.: Pensieve: supporting everyday reminiscence. In: Proceedings of the SIGCHI Conference on Human Factors in Computing Systems, pp. 2027–2036. ACM, New York (2010)

33. Blok, M., Kok, A.A., De Boer, A.H.: "On Facebook I Met Old Friends again": the use of ICTs in the Process of Reminiscence among Older Adults. Gerontechnology **20**(2), 1–12 (2021)

34. VanArsdall, J.E., Nairne, J.S., Pandeirada, J.N., Blunt, J.R.: Adaptive memory: animacy processing produces mnemonic advantages. Exp. Psychol. **60**, 172–178 (2013)

35. Nairne, J.S., VanArsdall, J.E., Cogdill, M.: Remembering the living: episodic memory is tuned to animacy. Curr. Dir. Psychol. Sci. **26**(1), 22–27 (2017)

36. Meinhardt, M.J., Bell, R., Buchner, A., Röer, J.P.: Adaptive memory: is the animacy effect on memory due to richness of encoding? J. Exp. Psychol. Learn. Mem. Cogn. **46**(3), 416–426 (2020)

37. Leding, J.K.: Adaptive memory: animacy, threat, and attention in free recall. Mem. Cognit. **47**(3), 383–394 (2018). https://doi.org/10.3758/s13421-018-0873-x

38. Howard, J.W., Rothbart, M.: Social categorization and memory for in-group and out-group behavior. J. Pers. Soc. Psychol. **38**(2), 301–310 (1980)

39. Hogg, M.A., Abrams, D., Otten, S., Hinkle, S.: The social identity perspective: intergroup relations, self-conception, and small groups. Small Group Res. **35**(3), 246–276 (2004)

40. Van Bavel, J.J., Cunningham, W.A.: A social identity approach to person memory: group membership, collective identification, and social role shape attention and memory. Pers. Soc. Psychol. Bull. **38**(12), 1566–1578 (2012)

41. Wegner, D.M.: Transactive memory: a contemporary analysis of the group mind. In: Mullen, B., Goethals, G. (eds.) Theories of Group Behavior, pp. 185–208. Springer, New York (1987). https://doi.org/10.1007/978-1-4612-4634-3_9

42. Wegner, D.M., Erber, R., Raymond, P.: Transactive memory in close relationships. J. Pers. Soc. Psychol. **61**(6), 923–929 (1991)

43. Andersson, J.: Net effect of memory collaboration: how is collaboration affected by factors such as friendship, gender and age? Scand. J. Psychol. **42**(4), 367–375 (2001)

44. Andersson, J., Ronnberg, J.: Cued memory collaboration: effects of friendship and type of retrieval cue. Eur. J. Cogn. Psychol. **9**(3), 273–287 (1997)
45. Marion, S.B., Thorley, C.: A meta-analytic review of collaborative inhibition and postcollaborative memory: testing the predictions of the retrieval strategy disruption hypothesis. Psychol. Bull. **142**(11), 1141–1164 (2016)
46. Conway, M., Bekerian, D.: Organization in autobiographical memory. Mem. Cognit. **15**, 119–132 (1987)
47. Conway, M.A., Pleydell-Pearce, C.W.: The construction of autobiographical memories in the self-memory system. Psychol. Rev. **107**(2), 261–288 (2000)
48. Conway, M., Singer, J., Tagini, A.: The self and autobiographical memory: correspondence and coherence. Soc. Cogn. **22**, 491–529 (2004)
49. Bluck, S., Alea, N., Habermas, T., Rubin, D.C.: A tale of three functions: the self–reported uses of autobiographical memory. Soc. Cogn. **23**(1), 91–117 (2005)
50. Alea, N., Bluck, S.: I'll keep you in mind: the intimacy function of autobiographical memory. Appl. Cogn. Psychol. **21**(8), 1091–1111 (2007)
51. Bluck, S., Alea, N., Demiray, B.: You get what you need: the psychosocial functions of remembering. In: Mace, J. (ed.) The act of Remembering: Toward an Understanding of How We Recall the Past, pp. 284–307. Wiley-Blackwell, Hoboken (2010)
52. Binder, J. F., Bowen, R.: Memory performance and text-to-speech functionality. In: 1st AI-Debate Workshop, pp. 35–38. Otto von Guericke University, Magdeburg (2021). https://doi.org/10.25673/38479
53. Binder, J.F., Cebula, K., Metwally, S., Vernon, M., Atkin, C., Mitra, S.: Conversational engagement and mobile technology use. Comput. Hum. Behav. **99**, 66–75 (2019). https://doi.org/10.1016/j.chb.2019.05.016
54. Binder, J.F.: Establishing conversational engagement and exerting influence: the role of body movement in mediated communication. Manuscript submitted for publication (under review)

Design of WeChat Guide System in Exhibition Venues

Xiao Liu[1](✉), Kaixi Ke[2], Yuan Gao[1], Pengcheng Huang[1], and Xia Wang[3]

[1] Xiamen University of Technology, Xiamen, Fujian, China
xiaoanneliu@163.com
[2] Qihang Social Work Service Center, Jinjiang, Fujian, China
[3] Ningbo University of Technology, Ningbo, Zhejiang, China

Abstract. WeChat guide system is widely applied for events and activities in exhibition venues. This paper firstly defines WeChat guide system in exhibition venues. Then, two surveys concerning Xiamen International Conference and Exhibition Center are conducted with the methods of interview and questionnaire in order to explore the current situation of guide service in exhibition venues. Based on the elements of user experience and the survey results, product positioning, feasibility evaluation, users' demand and key technologies of WeChat guide system are analyzed. In the designing process, we focus on system visual design and system framework design (i.e., User Interface and Admin Zone) for WeChat guide system, taking Xiamen International Conference and Exhibition Center as the example. The design of WeChat guide system in exhibition venues contributes to promoting efficient operation and intelligent management in Smart MICE industry.

Keywords: Guide system · WeChat · Exhibition venues · Design · The Elements of User Experience

1 Introduction

Smart MICE is a new concept and phenomenon with the combination of information and communication technologies, which shows the upgrade and transformation of MICE [1, 2]. Theoretical and practical studies on Smart MICE have achieved more and more attention from researchers and practitioners for the industry, such as technological applications in conference centers [3, 4] and exhibitions [5–8], exhibition system designs [9, 10], or the attitudes towards technologies in the industry of conferences [11] and exhibitions [12]. Compared with previous research which focused on virtual or smart exhibition system design, this paper is aimed at designing a WeChat guide system in the environment of exhibition venues, so as to promote intelligent applications in Smart MICE.

2 Concept and Theoretical Model

2.1 WeChat Guide System in Exhibition Venues

Guide system is a comprehensive system which is composed of signs, navigation signboards, electronic devices, etc. It provides tourists with interpretation, guidance and other service functions and plays the role of positioning, guidance, recognition and regulation [13]. Employing such forms as text labels, broadcasting voice equipment, intelligent equipment and professional staff, the guide system is now commonly applied for the application of guide system in scenic spots, museums, art galleries, archives and libraries, mainly based on manual- or audio-guide. Exhibition venues are large architectural complexes that provide the main buildings and auxiliary functions for conferences and exhibitions, including both hardware and software [14]. According to their usage, scale, content, nature and function, exhibition venues can be specifically divided into different categories [15].

WeChat is a popular free social application which was launched by Tencent in 2011. It provides instant messaging services for smart terminal devices, characterized by instantaneity, superb performance, strong relational socialization, and decentralization [16]. WeChat Official Platform, also referred to as WeChat Official Accounts, includes Service Account, Subscription Account and Mini Program. The Service Account is an official service platform that provides business service and user management capabilities for enterprises and organizations. The Subscription Account disseminates information for media and individuals. The Mini Program is an easy program by scanning or searching, without any downloading or installation. This paper aims to design a WeChat guide system in the form of Service Account, taking Xiamen International Conference and Exhibition Center (hereinafter referred to as XICEC) as the example. Based on the abovementioned, WeChat guide system in this paper is an intelligent service platform which provides information, sign guidance, position identification and public surveillance for visitors in conference, exhibition and event venues.

2.2 The Elements of User Experience

User experience is referred to as the behaviors, reactions and feelings which are triggered in the process of product use by customers, and can be divided into five-level elements, including strategy, scope, structure, skeleton and surface [17], as shown in Fig. 1.

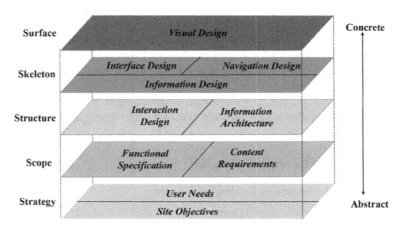

Fig. 1. The elements of user experience (Source: http://www.jjg.net/eleme [17])

WeChat guide system in exhibition venues is designed from the concrete to the abstract. According to the Elements of User Experience [17], user needs are externally-derived goals for the site which are identified through user research, while site objectives are business, creative or other internally derived goals for the site in the strategy level. Functional specifications are the feature sets for detailed functional descriptions that the site must include. Content requirements are the definitions of content elements required in the site. Both of functional specifications and content requirements aim to meet user needs in the scope level. In this paper, product positioning, feasibility evaluation, users' demand analysis of this system will be carried out based on the results of interview survey and questionnaire survey, corresponding to the strategy level and the scope level. In the structure level, interaction design is the development of application flows to facilitate user tasks, defining how the user interacts with site functionality. Information architecture is the structural design of the information space to propel intuitive access to content. In the skeleton level, interface design is the design of interface elements to promote the users' interaction with functionality. Navigation design is the design of interface elements to push the users' movement through the information architecture. Information design is concerning with the presentation of information to facilitate the users' understanding. Visual design is graphic treatment of interface elements and visual treatment of text, graphic page elements and navigational components in the surface level. In our paper, key technology analysis will be conducted. Moreover, visual design and framework design of WeChat guide system, including information architecture and module content design will proceed in the level of structure, skeleton and surface.

3   Current Situation Survey of Guide Service in XICEC

3.1   Methodology

The current situation of guide service in XICEC is investigated by means of interview survey and questionnaire survey. We selected three professionals as interviewees and took their advice on the questionnaire of pilot study. Then, we revised the questionnaire and collected data for the current situation of guide service in XICEC. Statistical analysis was conducted for subsequent WeChat guide system design as references.

3.2   Interview Outline and Questionnaire

Taking the research purpose into consideration, the interview outline of this study consists of nine questions. In the process of interviews, more related and open questions are provided according to the actual conditions, as the outline served as a subsidiary.

The final questionnaire includes three types of items, which are the current situation of visitors' behaviors and preferences (i.e., frequency, information access, reasons for visiting, pre-exhibition, on-site and post-exhibition behaviors, etc.), the current situation of guide service in XICEC (i.e., forms and evaluation of used guide service, suggestions for improvement, service function demand, etc.), and demographics (i.e., age, education background and occupation). Due to space limitation of this paper, the interview outline, questionnaire and data in this study are available on request from the corresponding author.

3.3 Findings of the Survey

According to the interviews from three experts, it is found that: (1) WeChat guide system in exhibition venues should be a mobile client-based application system that customers can actively access information. (2) It is crucial to define users for this system. The system should provide information for different users (such as organizers, exhibitors and professional visitors), in which they can classify, identify and search. (3) Key technologies in WeChat guide system design include computer network, wireless communication, LBS, object-oriented programming, positioning and navigation, etc. (4) The interface design should be user-friendly and convenient, and the functions in the system should be classified in detail as well. All of these proposals are accepted and followed in the process of WeChat guide system design.

Questionnaire data were collected anonymously from January 15 to February 23, 2017 by Wenjuanxing Platform, focusing on people who have visited XICEC before. A total of 400 questionnaires were distributed and 375 questionnaires were returned, among which, 371 were complete and usable for further analysis, with the valid response rate of 92.75%.

The majority of the respondents were within the age range of 31–40 years old group (36.93%), mostly with bachelor's degree (64.15%). In terms of occupations, the respondents were engaged in administration and logistics (16.44%), sales (14.56%) and marketing and public relations (12.13%), respectively. Table 1 shows demographic characteristics of the respondents.

Table 1. Social-demographic information of the questionnaire sample (N = 371)

Variable	Options	n	%
Age	≤30	162	43.67%
	31–40	137	36.93%
	41–50	62	16.71%
	51–60	9	2.43%
	≥60	1	0.27%
Educational background	Junior college and below	104	28.03%
	Undergraduate	238	64.15%
	Graduate	29	7.82%
Occupation	Administration & logistics	61	16.44%
	Sales	54	14.56%
	Marketing and public relations	45	12.13%
	Finance and audit	44	11.86%
	Customer service	42	11.32%
	Production	41	11.05%
	Human resources	35	9.43%
	Full-time student	21	5.66%
	Others	28	7.55%

Table 2 shows the results of descriptive analysis of visitors' behaviors and preference in XICEC. Most of the respondents have visited XICEC for 1–3 times (43.13%) and 4–6 times (40.97%) per year. They made preparation by WeChat or Weibo official account of XICEC and exhibitions (72.24%) or consulting others (62.53%) before the exhibition. The main reason for their visiting an exhibition is to obtain industry-related information (53.64%). Most of them took photos (62.52%) and searched for information by mobile devices (69.27%) during the exhibition. They were willing to make further communication with exhibitors (75.2%) after the exhibition. Respondents enjoyed the forms of exhibition in graphic interpretation (48.52%), physical display (39.08%), video interpretation (36.12%), audio interpretation (31.81%), virtual reality (31.54%), scene reconstruction (27.76%) and interactive multimedia (12.13%). The existing problems in XICEC are inadequate exhibits' information (76.82%), insufficient publicity for supporting activities (64.69%) and crowded exhibition environment (44.2%). More information can be found in Table 2.

Table 2. Descriptive analysis results of visitors' behaviors and preferences in XICEC (N = 371)

Variable	Options	n	%
Average times of visiting exhibitions per year	1–3 times	160	43.13%
	4–6 times	152	40.97%
	7–9 times	48	12.94%
	>9 times	11	2.96%
Access to information before the exhibition (Multiple choices)	WeChat or Weibo official account of XICEC and exhibitions	268	72.24%
	Consulting others	232	62.53%
	websites of XICEC and exhibitions	170	45.82%
	Visiting the exhibitions without preparation	52	14.02%
	Others	5	1.35%
Reasons for visiting exhibitions (Multiple choices)	To obtain industry-related information	199	53.64%
	Interest in supporting activities	153	41.24%
	Interest in exhibits	133	35.85%
	Accompanied visits	122	32.88%
	To enrich the spare time	114	30.73%
	Free tickets	69	18.6%
	Others	3	0.81%
Visiting behaviors (Multiple choices)	Taking photos	232	62.53%
	Appreciating the exhibits	174	46.9%
	Taking part in booth activities	169	45.55%

(continued)

Table 2. (*continued*)

Variable	Options	n	%
	Recording information	122	32.88%
	Taking part in supporting activities	88	23.72%
	Others	3	0.81%
Ways to learn about the exhibits (Multiple choices)	Searching for information by mobile devices	257	69.27%
	Browsing information by brochure	193	52.02%
	Consulting exhibitors	180	48.52%
	Bringing confusions home for further inquiry	118	31.81%
	Others	3	0.81%
Post-exhibition behaviors (Multiple choices)	Further communication with exhibitors	279	75.2%
	Sharing photos onto social media	243	65.5%
	Purchasing intended products	173	46.63%
	Others	7	1.89%
Forms of exhibition & interpretation (Multiple choices)	Graphic interpretation	180	48.52%
	Physical display	145	39.08%
	Video interpretation	134	36.12%
	Audio interpretation	118	31.81%
	Virtual reality	117	31.54%
	Scene reconstruction	103	27.76%
	Interactive multimedia	45	12.13%
	Others	2	0.54%
Existing problems in XICEC (Multiple choices)	Inadequate exhibit information	285	76.82%
	Insufficient publicity for supporting activities	240	64.69%
	Crowded exhibition environment	164	44.2%
	Others	4	1.08

Table 3 reveals current situation of guide service in XICEC. Most of the respondents have used the service in booth layout (71.43%), navigation signs (53.37%) and staff consultation (51.75%). 70.35% of the respondents made evaluations of "extremely good" and "good" for guide service in XICEC. With regard to the demand of service improvement, they showed strong preference for the extension of interpretation forms (60.38%), the provision of self-guidance mobile service (45.82%) and personalized guidance service (40.16%). 56.44% of the respondents felt "very satisfied" or "satisfied" with guide and navigation service in "iConvention" of XICEC. During the exhibition, 50.43% of the respondents used "iConvention" service for 1–3 h. They showed the service function demand for WeChat guide system mainly concerning tour guide tips (47.17%), audio interpretation (36.39%), navigation (32.88%) and exhibits index (32.08%). More details can be found in Table 3.

Table 3. Current situation of guide service in XICEC (N = 371)

Variable	Options	n	%
Used guide service (Multiple choices)	Booth layout	265	71.43%
	Navigation signs	198	53.37%
	Staff consultation	192	51.75%
	Map navigation in WeChat official account	110	29.65%
	Others	2	0.54%
Evaluation of used guide service	Extremely good	89	23.99%
	Good	172	46.36%
	General	81	21.83%
	Bad	26	7.01%
	Extremely bad	3	0.81%
Service improvement demand (Multiple choices)	To extend the forms of interpretation	224	60.38%
	To provide self-guidance mobile service	170	45.82%
	To provide personalized Guidance service	149	40.16%
	To add more exhibits information	129	34.77%
	To provide interactive community online service	127	34.23%
	Others	2	0.54%
Follow and subscribe "iConvention"	Yes	348	94.07%
	No	23	5.93%
Map navigation function usage in "iConvention"	Yes	288	77.65%
	No	83	22.35%
Visitor satisfaction with guide and navigation in "iConvention"	Very satisfied	36	9.74%
	Satisfied	173	46.7%
	General	99	26.65%
	Dissatisfied	48	12.89%
	Very dissatisfied	15	4.01%

(continued)

Table 3. (*continued*)

Variable	Options	n	%
"iConvention" service time for visitors	<1 h	88	23.78%
	1–3 h	187	50.43%
	4–6 h	78	20.92%
	>6 h	18	4.87%
Service function demand for WeChat guide system (Multiple choices)	Tour guide tips	175	47.17%
	Audio interpretation	135	36.39%
	Navigation	122	32.88%
	Exhibits index	119	32.08%
	Exhibition news	111	29.92%
	Supporting activity application	73	19.68%
	Exhibition-related games	62	16.71%
	Route recommendation	53	14.29%
	Venue map	49	13.21%
	Souvenir online store	15	4.04
	Interactive community	14	3.77
	Volunteer application	12	3.23
	Others	2	0.54

4 Evaluation and Analysis of WeChat Guide System

4.1 Product Positioning Analysis

According to the survey results above, WeChat guide system in exhibition venues is a mobile client-based WeChat official account application system, which provides information and services such as show-and-tell, booth guide and getting help for organizers, exhibitors and professional audiences. It is designed with diversified functions, detailed classification, user-friendly interface and easy operation.

4.2 Feasibility Evaluation

First, it is unnecessary for audiences to download independent App, for WeChat guide system can be found by searching the keyword in WeChat. Second, based on the original version of "iConvention" official account, we will design, adjust and supplement the functions of current WeChat Guide system to save cost in development. Third, the performance of DHTML (Dynamic HTML) technology and interface calling technology are relatively mature and stable, and easy to master and control. Fourth, there are a great number of open-source codes available in the network forum for us to design this system. Moreover, as the most influential conference and exhibition center in Fujian Province,

XICEC owns fixed brand activities, including China International Fair for Investment and Trade (CIFIT), China Xiamen International Stone Exhibition, China Xiamen International Buddhist Items & Crafts Fair, China Xiamen International Tea Industry Fair, Cross-Strait (Xiamen) Cultural Industry Expo, etc. Therefore, it is feasible to design and develop XICEC WeChat guide system.

4.3 Users' Demand Analysis

According to aforementioned survey results, the primary demand of visitors is to obtain industry-related information, while others are to observe exhibits and participate in post-conference and post-exhibition activities. Respondents are hopeful about the functions of exhibition tips, voice explanation, indoor navigation, exhibits index, route recommendation, interactive games, etc. Therefore, users' demands of WeChat guide system in exhibition venues are categorized into basic demand, expectation demand, and excitement demand, according to the priority.

In the respect of basic demand, there are three sub-systems, including Information Release System, Event Registration System and Graphic Navigation System. Information Release System is a service platform to release information about the exhibition halls, exhibitions, exhibitors, exhibits and exhibition guide to the public. Event Registration System is oriented toward users' publishing information and registering online. Based on the content and nature of exhibits, Graphic Navigation System is developed for users to select exhibition halls and booths, and click on the exhibit information list to get more detailed information.

In the respect of the expectation demand, there are five sections, which are Audio Guide System, Route Guide System, Interactive Community System, Volunteer Registration System, and E-commerce System. (1) Audio Guide System provides real-person automatic human-voice guide service. Visitors can observe the exhibits while listening to the guide after selecting and confirming the exhibits by clicking. (2) Route Guide System is endowed with two functions, which are Indoor Map and Route Recommendation in the venues. Visitors can check the details of the exhibition hall and the panorama of the site through the scale zooming of the Indoor Map. Route Recommendation includes Popular Routes and Customized Routes. Visitors' comments and likes will generate the data and information of popular routes and update them in real time. Visitors can also customize their unique routes based on their needs. (3) Interactive Community System is composed of Visitor Information Release, Q&A and Sharing. Visitors can release texts, pictures, emojis and videos for content creation and information dissemination, making their communication more convenient in real time and satisfy their social needs. (4) Volunteer Registration System provides the information about the theme, time and location of activities, consultation and registration, volunteer hours and service certificate application. (5) E-commerce System offers services such as Shop Recruitment, Online Order, Payment and Express Transportation.

In the respect of excitement demand, there are In-pavilion Navigation and Exhibition-related Games. The former comprises quick location and booth search, while the latter helps visitors to kill their spare time and relax themselves.

4.4 Key Technology Analysis

Taking the design ideas for reference [18], this paper proposes to design a WeChat guide system, which employs HTML, CSS, JavaScript as key technologies, Bootstrap as the front-end framework, Browser/Server (B/S) as the architecture, Linux as the operating system, PHP 5.3 as the programing language, Sublime Text 3 as the code editor, Apache HTTP server as the web server, MySQL database as the data storage and management database. There are predefined functions in the interface development of the WeChat Guide System to reduce developers' workload. In the interface call, the login account interface is designed for one-key associated binding with QQ account and Weibo account based on account authentication.

5 Design Process of WeChat Guide System

5.1 System Visual Design

Current product design mainly follows flat design, which is widely used in digital product design. It is characterized by concise interface layout, simple diagrams and elements, and clear design scheme. The design of WeChat Guide System in XICEC also follows the idea of flat aesthetics and the principles of simplification, clarity and integrality. It is designed with pure color and gradient color with a certain amount of animation effects and video elements, so as to achieve a vivid and independent presentation of the product.

5.2 System Framework Design

WeChat guide system in XICEC follows the design principles of WeChat Official Accounts. In order to reduce users' interference, the homepage of this system involves three custom menu options with no more than four layers in the system architecture. Each function module is clear and independent, so that there is no overlap. WeChat guide system of XICEC is composed of WeChat user interface and Web admin zone. Three custom menu options on the home page of this system include iMICE, iService and iWonder, which meet the basic demand, expectation demand, and excitement demand, respectively. Targeted customers include organizers, exhibitors and audiences. Venue staff and system administrators are users of Web admin zone to accomplish daily management, maintenance and data statistics.

Firstly, there are four paths from the home page to the secondary page of "iMICE", which are Home → i MICE → Exhibition Preview, Home → iMICE → Convention Preview, Home → iMICE → Tour Guide, and Home → iMICE → Route Recommendation. Moreover, there are four paths from the second-level page to the third-level page of "iMICE", including Tour Guide & Navigation → Guide to the Exhibition, Tour Guide & Navigation → Exhibition Map, Route Recommendation → Guide to the Exhibition, and Route Recommendation → Exhibition Map.

Secondly, the four paths from the home page to the second-level page of "iService" are as follows, i.e., Home → iService → My Order, Home → iService → Exhibition Equipment Service, Home → iService → Network Service, and Home → iService → Peripheral Service.

Thirdly, there are five paths from the home page to the second-level page of "iWonder", which are Home → iWonder → Exhibition Information, Home → iWonder → iActivities, Home → iWonder → iCommunity, Home → iWonder → Interactive Games, and Home → iWonder → Souvenir Online Store. Furthermore, there are two paths from the second-level page to the second-level page of "iWonder", i.e., Souvenir Online Store → Exhibition Information and Souvenir Online Store → iActivities. There are three paths from the second-level page to the third-level page of "iWonder", i.e., iCommunity → Interactive Community, iCommunity → Q&A Community, and iCommunity → Shared Community.

Fourth, there are four paths from Web Admin Zone to its second-level, i.e., Web Admin Zone → Account Management, Web Admin Zone → Function Management, Web Admin Zone → Data Statistics, and Web Admin Zone → Settings.

The information architecture and module contents of WeChat guide system in XICEC are shown in Fig. 2.

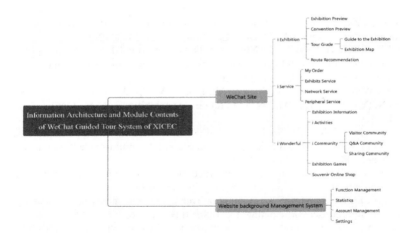

Fig. 2. Information Architecture and Module Contents of WeChat Guide System in XICEC

6 Conclusions

This paper defines WeChat guide system in exhibition venues firstly. Based on survey results of current situation for guide service in XICEC, visitors' behaviors and preference, existing problems in XICEC, and service function demand for WeChat guide system are investigated. Taking the elements of User Experience as theoretical model, WeChat guide system is designed according to product positioning, feasibility, users' demands, key technologies, visual design and framework design. The application of this WeChat guide system will promote the development of Smart MICE informatization, and the intelligent operation of conference & exhibition centers in China. Future research can focus on the application and expansion of relevant theories, such as intelligence, Internet of things and big data in Smart MICE, in order to achieve "smartness" in the real sense.

Fundings. This work was supported by the National Social Science Fund of China under No. 16CGL021.

References

1. Liu, X.: A conceptual framework for smart MICE ecosystem in China. In: Proceeding of the 2017 Euro-Asia Conference on Environment and CSR: Tourism, Society and Education Session (Part I), pp. 1–10 (2017)
2. Liu, X., Seevers, R., Gu, Z.-W., Yang, X.-H.: Smart MICE: definitions, foundations and development. In: Proceeding of 7th International Conference on Information Science and Control Engineering (ICISCE), pp. 1307–1311 (2020)
3. Fenich, G.G., Scott-Halsell, S., Ogbeide, G.-C., Hashimoto, K.: What the millennial generation from around the world prefers in their meetings, conventions, and events. J. Conv. Event Tour. **15**, 236–241 (2014)
4. Anderson, T.: 21st Century conventions: what's new? Alaska Bus. Monthly **31**(4), 98–100 (2015)
5. Ciurea, C., Zamfiroiu, A.A., Grosu, A.: Implementing mobile virtual exhibition to increase cultural heritage visibility. Informatica Economică **18**(2), 24–30 (2014)
6. Lee, J.-Y. Kim, Y-H. Yoon, Y.: An NFC-based O2O service model in exhibition-space. In: Proceeding of the 18th Annual International Conference on Electronic Commerce: e-Commerce in Smart connected World, pp. 1–8 (2016)
7. Liu, X., Wen, Z-H., Song, S., Song, L-M., Lin, H.-Y.: Speckle-reduced green and yellow-green Nd:YVO4(YAG)/PPMgLN lasers for cinema exhibition industry. Optik (243), 167427 (2021)
8. Liu, X., Zeng, X-T., Shi, W.-J., Bao, S.-F., Yu, T., Lin, H.-Y.: Application of a Novel Nd:YAG/PPMgLN laser module speckle-suppressed by multi-mode fibers in exhibition environment. Photonics **9**(1), 46 (2022)
9. Su, C.J., Yen, B.P.C., Zhang, X.: An internet based virtual exhibition system: conceptual design and infrastructure. Comput. Ind. Eng. **35**, 615–618 (1998)
10. Lim, J.H., Lee, E.S., Kim, S.K.: A study on web augmented reality based smart exhibition system design for user participating. Int. J. Smart Home **5**, 65–76 (2011)
11. Kim, D.-Y., Park, O.: A study on American meeting planners' attitudes toward and adoption of technology in the workplace. Tourism Hospitality Res. **9**, 209–223 (2009)
12. Koo, C., Chung, N., Ham, J.: Assessing the user resistance to recommender systems in exhibition. Sustainability **9**(11), 1–16 (2017)
13. Gao, T.-Y.: Design and Implementation of Guide Service System Based on Mobile Devices. Zhejiang University of Technology (2015)
14. Lin, D.-F.: MICE Venue Operation and Management. Chongqing University Press (2014)
15. Zheng, J-Y.: MICE Venue Operation and Management. Shanghai People's Publishing House (2006)
16. Li, D.: Features and application trends of WeChat. Pub. Commun. Sci. Technol. **22**, 46–58 (2013)
17. Garrett, J.J.: The Elements of User Experience. Peachpit Press (2002)
18. Qian, C.: Design of WeChat Museum Guide System for China Block Printing Museum and Yangzhou Museum Based on User Experience Theory. Yangzhou University (2013)

Music-Guided Imagination and Digital Voice Assistant – Study Design and First Results on the Application of Voice Assistants for Music-Guided Stress Reduction

Ingo Siegert[1]([✉]), Matthias Busch[1], Susanne Metzner[2], Florian Junne[3], and Julia Krüger[3]

[1] Mobile Dialog Systems, Otto von Guericke University Magdeburg, Magdeburg, Germany
ingo.siegert@ovgu.de
[2] Music Therapy, Faculty of Philosophy and Social Sciences, Leopold Mozart Centre, University Augsburg, Augsburg, Germany
[3] Department of Psychosomatic Medicine and Psychotherapy, Otto von Guericke University Magdeburg, Magdeburg, Germany

Abstract. In order to relax in everyday life, people use music from a sound carrier. The choice of music is made intuitively and according to one's musical preference. In a therapeutic context, these processes are professionally guided. In so-called receptive music therapy, the patient and therapist listen to music together.

The psychological processes triggered by this (e.g. imaginations, memories) are worked through in therapeutic conversation. But professional music therapy is not always feasible, as getting an appointment could take some time, the need for receptive music therapy is urgent at the time the treatment is not available, etc. Furthermore, voice assistants are increasingly dominating everyday life and represent an easy way to perform various tasks with minimal effort. The areas of application for voice assistants are diverse and range from answering simple information questions to processing complex topics and controlling various tasks.

Given these considerations of the wide availability and ease of use, a pilot study was designed to combine the effective approaches of music therapy with modern voice assistants. The study entails one interaction with an Alexa Skill allowing a music-imaginative journey in an interactive manner, and a control condition without interactive parts using a CD.

21 participants took part in the study, of which first analyses are presented in the paper. Especially results regarding the analyses of the user experience (AttrakDiff and meCUE) as well as a discussion of the subjective participants' reflections on the interaction regarding the limitations of commercial voice assistants are presented

Keywords: Voice assistant · Music therapy · User experience

© The Author(s), under exclusive license to Springer Nature Switzerland AG 2022
G. Salvendy and J. Wei (Eds.): HCII 2022, LNCS 13337, pp. 347–362, 2022.
https://doi.org/10.1007/978-3-031-05014-5_29

1   Introduction

Virtual Voice Assistants (vVAs) are increasingly being integrated in everyday life and represent an easy way to perform various tasks with minimal effort. This development has led to a rapidly growing user base for commercial voice assistants [9]. It is not limited to the US market, as another study showed that in 2019 60% of all Germans have already used voice assistants [22].

The application for voice assistants reaches through different areas. Users employ their voice assistants mostly for voice search, setting up an alarm clock and reminders, controlling other devices, or listening to music [20]. Especially the last use case is commonly applied [14].

One of the main purposes of listening to music in everyday life, is to enhance good mood and to relax. Hereby, the choice of music is made intuitively and according to one's musical preference.

Meanwhile, in medical contexts, music is offered to patients by hospital staff to regulate anxiety and stress. In the field of professional music therapy, several methods have been developed in order to promote physical and mental health or to alleviate illness-related suffering. The bio-psycho-social processes that are set in motion by making or listening to music are reflected and worked through in therapeutic conversations. Self-exploration, -regulation and -efficacy are among the most important goals of music therapy [1,8].

The Short Music Journey (SMJ) [5] is a music therapy technique, in which the patient listens to music in a relaxed posture and is encouraged by the therapist to be aware of inner images, associations and memories, which are reflected afterwards. It is a supportive technique used to develop mindfulness, regulate emotions and strengthen inner resources.

To stimulate these self-regulatory abilities in between therapy sessions, recommendations for listening to music at home are sometimes given in music therapy as well as in other psychotherapeutic treatment approaches. Because vVAs are increasingly taking on various functions in people's everyday lives anyway, the question arises as to whether assisted music listening can improve self-regulation between sessions especially in low frequent therapies.

To test the combination of SMJ and vVA in a first step, a 'Music Time-Out' (MTO) for healthy subjects to enhance well-being was designed and evaluated in a pilot study. We investigated the extent to which current commercial voice assistants can be used, including music and interactive parts to explore users' individual experiences during the application. Furthermore, first insights on the users' acceptance of such an application by exploring the user experience should be gained.

2   Background

2.1   Use of Smart Speakers for Relaxation Purposes

Smart speakers enable, through a constant internet connection and microphones, permanent access to vVAs of various manufacturers. Voice App (VAp) is an application for vVAs that allows external developers to deliver additional features to vVA users. On the Alexa platform, these VAp are also called 'Alexa Skills'.

A variety of VAps offer a mediation or relaxation feature for users of vVAs. For example, the German 'Techniker Krankenkasse', has published the VAp "TK Smart Relax"[1] for Alexa and Google Assistant [11]. It includes various exercises and relaxation formats, utilizes a professional speaker especially recorded for the Alexa skill. Furthermore, the app offers the option of personalizing the skill's functionalities for recurring usage. Regarding the interaction, it has to be mentioned that in this voice app, like for many others, the speech input is just needed for the navigation through the menu. It is not intended to have a dialog between the system and the user during the exercises themself.

2.2   User Experience of Speech-based Dialog Systems

People like to use technical systems if they enjoy the usage and/or evaluate them as useful to achieve their goals.

The so-called user experience is defined as "a momentary, primarily evaluative feeling (good-bad) while interacting with a product or service' which is 'a consequence of users' internal state (e.g. predispositions, expectations, needs, motivation, mood), the characteristics of the designed system (e.g. complexity, purpose, usability, functionality), and the context within which the interaction occurs (e.g. organizational/social setting, meaningfulness of the activity, voluntariness of use)" [3] as cited in [6, p. 4]).

In [13] user experience is understood in a holistic way. It is described as a consequence of users' conscious and unconscious individual ascription of even human-like mental states towards the system they interact with (anthropomorphization). This theoretical perspective was empirically underlined by a qualitative study on the interaction of users with a speech-based dialog system pretending to be able to individually support in everyday life [12].

In a qualitative analysis of user interviews ideal types of users were characterized by experiential patterns of the interaction and typical ascriptions towards the system. It supported the importance of subjective user experiences in interactions with speech-based systems on the acceptance of the system.

A very prominent example of a quite simple interaction model with a huge impact on the perceived quality of the interaction is 'ELIZA'. The chatbot 'ELIZA' [24] has attracted a lot of attention as it illustrates this effect of 'anthropomorphism' very well. In this context, 'ELIZA' simulates 'therapy' conversations in which it responds to user statements in a rule-based manner and usually simply converts the user's statements to kind of open questions that are returned and e.g. results in system statements such as 'Can you tell more about <noun-from-the-user's-statement>?'.

This leads to users evaluating the interaction with 'ELIZA' as positive because they felt understood by the system [4]. Moreover, this effect occurs even when users know that they are interacting with a technical system. The

---

[1] https://www.amazon.de/Die-Techniker-TK-Smart-Relax/dp/B074QM4KKQ.

mirroring of one's own statements and the resulting feeling of 'being understood' played a greater role for the users than having new perspectives opened up by the (technical) dialog partner.

3   Research Questions

The aim of the study is to find out in a first step whether healthy subjects would accept an SMJ in combination with a speech assistant for everyday use and which advantages and disadvantages arise to an interactive SMJ that is presented by an vVA. The overall goal, which cannot be answered by this study, is to contribute to technology-assisted music therapy.

For this purpose, the following research questions are raised:

– How do healthy participants experience an interactive music-guided imagination through a state-of-the-art speech assistant in comparison to non-interactive media? (*interaction-experience related question*)
– How can a music-guided imagination be mapped by state-of-the-art speech assistants? (*Technology-related question*)

4   Methods

To answer the research questions, the 'Alexa Skill' Music Time-Out (Alexa-MTO) was developed and an experiment was designed to evaluate the interaction of the users with the VAp. The study entails one interaction with the Alexa-MTO allowing a music-imagination in an interactive manner, using the vVA 'Alexa', and a control condition without interactive parts using a CD. The research questions will be answered by analyzing different quantitative and qualitative self-reports on the user experience of both, the VAp Alexa-MTO and the CD condition CD Music Time-Out (CD-MTO).

4.1   Intervention 'Music Time-Out' (MTO)

SMJ as Design Basis: As mentioned in Sect. 1 the method of SMJ [5] serves as a pattern for the design of the Voice App (VAp) "Music Time Out" (MTO). In SMJ, at first, patient and therapist explore the mood and problems the patient actually deals with. The therapist selects a piece of music that appears adequate for an imagination in relation to the patient's initial state. After a relaxation introduction the therapist invites the patient to follow the music and be aware of inner images, associations, feelings and memories, which arise. After the imagination the therapist supports the patient in self-exploring his feelings and images in a therapeutic conversation.

Experimental Condition: For the experimental condition, the VAp 'MTO' was developed. The dialog follows the scheme presented in Fig. 1: Alexa welcomes the user and asks for his/her actual mood ('Adressing Mood'). Afterwards, Alexa presents three pieces of music by playing the first few seconds of each and the user selects one of them.

Alexa gives instructions for relaxing and the following imagination ("Atmen Sie dreimal tief ein, und geräuschvoll wieder aus. <break time="2s"/> Und lassen Sie jedes Mal etwas mehr los") and the music starts.

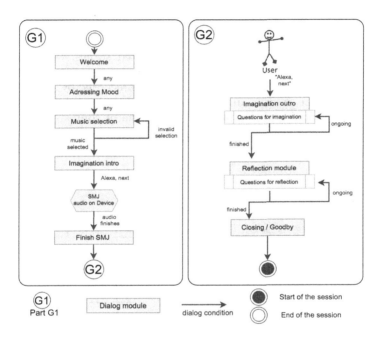

Fig. 1. Overview of the dialog modules. The Alexa Skill MTO will lead the user through a music-guided imagination

After the music Alexa instructs the user to slowly fade out the imaginations and come back into the here and now by the use of an awareness exercise ('Imagination outro'). Afterwards Alexa asks a few open questions to invite the user to reflect on his/her imagination ("Wenn Sie nun wieder ganz im Hier und Jetzt angekommen sind, <break time= "2s"/>spüren Sie bitte nach <break time="3s"/>Wie geht es Ihnen jetzt?") ('Reflection module'). Since the aim of the VAp was not to simulate a therapy session, the vVA did not reflect or analyse the experiences and thoughts the user reported on.

MTO uses the Alexa Skill Kit (ASK) to create an Alexa skill. The Alexa-MTO uses open questions in the dialog modules 'Addressing Mood' , 'Imagination outro' and 'Reflection module'.

It is designed in such a way that the user can answer the open questions as freely as possible. A subsequent analysis of the user's statements is only possible to a limited extent due to the structure of the ASK Framework. No transcription is sent from the Alexa service to the backend. Therefore, it was decided that Alexa-MTO will consider every intent except the 'Help-Intent' and 'Stop-Intent' as a valid answer to the 'open' questions as it is not feasible to capture every possible answer of the users in a specialized intent.

Control Condition: In order to assess the effects of the voice assistant's inter-activity, an audio CD imitating a commercially available relaxation CD is used as a control condition. For this purpose, the participant receives three CDs in advance, each containing a piece of music and provided with different cover images. The CD covers show relaxation-associated scenes, the impression of which enables the participants to select one CD each for the experiment. The instructions for the imagination on the CD were prerecorded by a female speaker. The structure of the session and the texts correspond to the contents of the modules 'Imagination' and 'Farewell'. For the sake of comparability, the voice recordings are as similar as possible to those of the experimental condition, both in terms of pause length and wording.

4.2   Course of Study

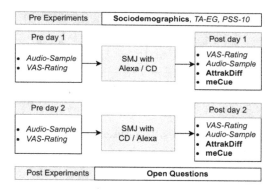

Fig. 2. Overview of procedure of both experiment days, parts in *italic* are collected but not evaluated in the current paper.

The MTO interactions are conducted on two consecutive days, which are randomized regarding the order of the conditions (Alexa-MTO or CD-MTO). In the test condition Alexa-MTO, the participant conducts a music-imaginative journey in an interactive manner. In the control condition CD-MTO the participant undergoes the same treatment, but without interaction. Figure 2 provides an overview of the procedure for both days of the experiment. The study took about 60 min per day.

On the first day of the survey, the participants were informed about the purpose of the study and about the data to be collected. The participants agreed to participate by means of a written consent form.

4.3   Recording Setup and Participant Selection

The recordings took place at the Institute of Information and Communication Engineering, University Magdeburg. They were conducted in a living-room-like surrounding in which they should make themselves "as comfortable as possible". This setting aimed to enable the participant to get into a natural communication atmosphere (in contrast to the distraction of laboratory surroundings). To conduct high-quality recordings, of the participants' voices, a headset (Sennheiser Chat 3) was used. The data is stored as uncompressed WAV with 44.1 kHz and 16bit.

4.4   Inclusion Criteria

The following inclusion criteria, German native speakers between 16 and 35, and the following exclusion criteria, hearing impairment, and significant speech impediments were established for participants. The recruitment was mainly carried out through university channels

4.5   Questionnaires

Sociodemographic Information, Experience in the Use of Voice Assistants, and Affinity to Technology. At the beginning of the experiment (day 1), various questionnaires are used to collect contextual information from the participants. For the collection of socio-demographic information as well as previous experience in the use of voice assistants, a self-developed questionnaire is used [21]. To get insights into the affinity for technology, TA-EG is used [7].

Stress Level. Furthermore, at the beginning of the experiment (day 1) PSS-10 is used to capture the perceived stress in the past four week [19]. To capture the influence of the SMJ on the assessment of the perceived stress, participants are asked to indicate the current stress level shortly before and shortly after the SMJ experiment (day 1 and day 2) in form of a Visual Analogue Scale (VAS) employing the Stressbarometer based on [15] and by answering a short questions "How do you feel" and "What are your name initials, the study course and the city you study in" which is recorded for later acoustic analysis.

The analysis of the stress measurements are part of our future work and will not be presented in this paper

User Experience

AttakDiff. After the experiment, participants are asked to indicate their experience of the usage of both SMJ conditions using AttrakDiff [2] and meCue [17, sec. 3.6.3.2] (day 1 and day 2). The questionnaire 'AttrakDiff' is used to evaluate the user experience of interactive systems [2]. The 'AttrakDiff' questionnaire is based on the assessment through semantic differentials, which allow statements about the different dimensions, Pragmatic Quality (PQ), Hedonic Quality - Identity (HQ-I), Hedonic Quality - Stimulation (HQ-S), and Attractiveness (ATT).

For each dimension, specific attributes in form of a semantic differential are given. The respondent answers using a 5-point scale. In the evaluation, the value '1' in each case stands for the tendency towards the negative characteristic, '3' for a neutral attitude of the respondent, and '5' for the tendency towards the positive extreme.

meCUE. The 'meCUE' questionnaire captures the participants' judgments about the emotional experience and the usage consequences of the users[17]. Module 3 describes positive emotions (pEm) and negative emotions (nEm) that arise during the use of the product. Module 4 depicts the users' product loyalty (PLoy) and intention of use (UInt). Finally, Module 5 asks for the overall evaluation of the product. This overall rating corresponds to the semantic differential between 'perceived as bad' 'perceived as good'. All other modules of the 'meCUE' questionnaire use a 7-point Likert scale.

Open Questions. At the end of the second interaction (day 2), a questionnaire with open-ended, narrative-stimulating questions is used to ask the participants about their experiences with the MTO after experiencing both conditions (Alexa-MTO and CD-MTO). The questionnaire asks both how participants were able to engage with the music-guided imagination and how they felt about the interaction with the Alexa-MTO. Participants were encouraged to share their impressions and thoughts in free-text responses. The focus of the questions is on the assessment of the 'Alexa' skill, which aspects were perceived positively and which negatively. Finally, the participants were asked for feedback for improvements to the voice app. The participants provided their assessments based on the following questions:

- **General impression** The participant should first state the first impression about the experiment MTO, and in particular with the general impression of the experimental condition Alexa-MTO.
- **Impression of the vVA** The next questions deals with the general impression of Alexa as a dialogue partner for the MTO, as well as the positive and negative feelings triggered during the interaction with Alexa.
- **Instructions of the vVA** These questions ask how participants were able to engage with Alexa's instructions with a focus on what was helpful and what was perceived as a hindrance in doing so.
- **Differences between CD-MTO and Alexa-MTO** Then, it is asked about the perceived differences between the experimental and control condition.

- **Favorite condition** Afterwards, it is asked which experimental condition (CD-MTO or Alexa-MTO) the participant would choose and why.
- **Feedback** The last question asks for improvement suggestions from the participant for the further development of the VAp MTO.

Within this paper, only a frequency analysis (counting of arguments across all participants) of the responses concerning technical aspects of the interaction with the VAp, positive characteristics of the MTO as well as a comparison judgment of the two conditions is conducted.

5 Results

5.1 Sample Description

The study involved 21 participants, 9 female and 12 male ones, the age ranges from 19 to 36 years (24.67 ± 4.51 y), because of recruiting difficulties we included one participant aged 36. The participants have at least a technical college entrance qualification. Furthermore, a wide variety of study courses, including Computer Science and Engineering but also Psychology, Medicine, Social Sciences, and Humanities.

Regarding the questions about the participants' previous vVA experience, it became apparent that all of them already had known 'Alexa' before the experiment, but only 38% had previous experience with Alexa, while only 24% stated that they had neither previous experience with 'Alexa' nor with any other assistant. Frequently mentioned reasons for using vVA were a simple control of e.g. music players or the basic presence of assistants on certain devices. Lack of access or need for use were given as reasons for non-use. Some also stated that they tended to avoid vSAs due to the fear of being tapped.

5.2 MeCue

Figure 3 represents the results of modules 3, 4, and 5 of the 'meCUE' questionnaire. Regarding Module 3 the participants do not associate any positive emotions with the interaction of the two conditions, but also no negative emotions. The perception of the dimension nEm is even rather negated. The differences between the conditions Alexa-MTO and the CD-MTO are neither significant for pEm nor nEm. For Module 4, the evaluation shows that participants would rather not prefer the use of any of both conditions, and they also do not feel connected to the conditions. Again, the differences that emerge between the two conditions are not significant.

The general judgement on the interaction with Alexa-MTO and the session with the CD-MTO is slightly positive, but as before, no significant difference can be found between the two conditions.

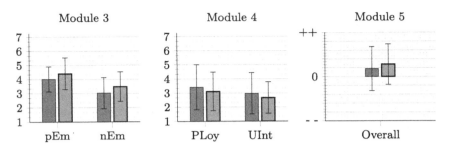

Fig. 3. Evaluation of the meCUE questionnaire regarding the two conditions Alexa-MTO (∎∎) and CD-MTO (∎∎).

5.3 AttrakDiff

The overall evaluation of the 'AttrakDiff' questionnaire indicates a neutral to a slightly positive attitude of the participants regarding both conditions, see Fig. 4. Only regarding HQ-S, the control condition is below the neutral value 3. We could furthermore identify a highly significant difference for the dimension HQ-S ($t(21) = 5.18$, $p = 0.00004581$).

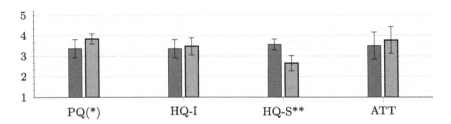

Fig. 4. Evaluation of the AttrakDiff questionnaire regarding the two conditions Alexa-MTO (∎∎) and CD-MTO (∎∎). Stars indicate (a tendency towards) significant differences.

Regarding PQ there is a tendency towards a significance difference between the two conditions ($t(21) = -2.811$, $p = 0.010780815$). Regarding the pragmatic quality, the individual semantic word pairs are depicted in Fig. 5. It is noticeable that especially the assessment for the pair 'technical-human' shows a clear difference between the two conditions. The participants perceive the vVA Alexa-MTO as 'technical', while the CD-MTO seems more 'human' ($t(21) = -4.26$, $p = 0.000379468$).

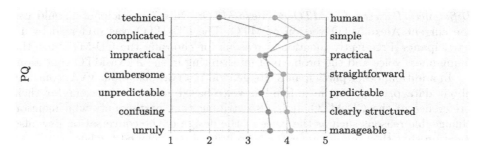

Fig. 5. Results of the semantic word pairs for PQ of the AttrakDiff questionnaire for Alexa (—•—) and CD (—•—).

5.4 Answers to Open Questions

Experienced Limitations Within the Interaction with Alexa: 19 participants (90%) made direct or indirect comments about "talking in-between" or interruptions by Alexa (e.g. "Alexa does not let me finish"), and described this as disruptive or hindering regarding "relaxation".

Another common criticism (14 participants) of the VAp MTO, is the rather technical voice, especially its pronunciation and intonation. In comparison to the human voice of the CD condition, the standard female voice of Alexa used for MTO is described as "computer voice" or "robotic". Some participants mention the quality as a "deficiency", others feel very disturbed by the voice.

Furthermore, 8 participants reported perceiving the dialog as too rigid and impersonal, focussing on the lack of reciprocity when Alexa does not respond to what is said, rather Alexa repeats the questions or does not recognize the user's statements. Especially in the combination with Alexa interrupting the user, some participants reported that they are strongly prevented from stress reduction.

Positive Characteristics: One third of the participants (8) state that they felt involved by communicating with the vVA. In addition, some add that they felt well guided through the interaction, which is described as structured and understandable and felt supported in reducing stress.

It is also mentioned that the operation via Voice User Interface (VUI) is simple and allows quick access to the MTO. Four participants reported that interacting with Alexa-MTO made the MTO feel more personal and "emphatic" than the CD-MTO control condition ("[I felt] better picked up by Alexa").

Others rated the interaction with Alexa as overall calming. In addition, the pauses in the dialogue made some participants feel self-determined in influencing the MTO; they perceived Alexa respected their need for time to come back from relaxation. In addition, 6 participants mentioned that the understandable instructions of the vVA helped them to relax with the MTO. Finally, it is positively mentioned by 7 participants that the VAp gave a good idea of the music piece through the interactive selection of the music.

Differences Between CD-MTO vs Alexa-MTO: Only 7 participants would use the current Alexa-MTO version of MTO. The CD-MTO was preferred by 14 participants. Frequently mentioned reasons for choosing the CD-MTO are the 'humanness'voice and the problem of interrupting in the Alexa-MTO condition.

In addition, other participants cite general reservations about vVA, concerns about data privacy, or the unfamiliar voice-based control as reasons for their preference of the CD-MTO. It is also striking that participants who mention changeable reasons such as the voice or the design of the conversation flow also mention that they might prefer the VAp if it were developed further.

In contrast, the most common *arguments for preferring Alexa-MTO* is that voice control is fundamentally easier and requires less preparation, that the interaction allows them to influence the session (music selection), and speaking with the vVA is perceived by them as more 'human' or 'active'.

6   Discussion and Conclusion

This paper presents the experimental setup and methods as well as initial results of a study on music-guided imagination, especially an adaptation of the method SMJ, by using a commercial voice assistants. 21 healthy participants answered questions regarding their user experience in an interactive SMJ compared to a control condition with linear CD.

6.1   How Do Healthy Participants Experience an Interactive Music-Guided Imagination Through a State-of-the-art Speech Assistant in Comparison to Non-interactive Media? (*interaction-Experience Related Questions*)

The two quantitative measurements of the user experience revealed only slight differences between Alexa-MTO and CD-MTO. Alexa is rated rather neutral, slightly positive in meCUE - Overall Assessment (see Fig. 3), as well as in the dimension Attractiveness (ATT) of AttrakDiff (see Fig. 4). Thus, it can be assumed, that in this study Alexa is experienced as "good" as a common CD for stress reduction. However, AttrakDiff allows a more detailed picture: The participants perceive the 'Alexa' condition as more stimulating and interesting than the CD condition (HQ-S). However, the pragmatic quality of Alexa-MTO is rated lower than that of the CD-MTO, indicating that the Alexa-MTO is perceived as less user-friendly or sociable for use in everyday life and lacks efficient support.

It is meaningful that the participants perceive Alexa as 'technical', while the CD seems more 'human'. This rating seems a bit odd at first glance, but is underlined by the subjective reports on Alexa's limitations.

Previous theories [18] and empirical studies show [12, besides others], that users tend to experience a technical system as a kind of social counterpart, when it sends out social cues like especially speech-based interaction. Alexa-MTO is not only speech-based, it furthermore asks open questions regarding "human topics" like emotions. Consequently, the users tend to expect higher communicative abilities, especially reciprocity and an understanding about turn taking routines. The disappointment of these expectations seem to weigh heavily and influence the overall ascription of a technical nature of Alexa.

6.2 How Can a Music-Guided Imagination Be Mapped by State-of-the-art Speech Assistants? (*Technology-Related Question*)

Although the presented results highlight limitations of the current state of the art speech assistants, they also indicate benefits of using an interactive music-guided imagination provided by a vVA for users. *Positive aspects* are, that the users made use of the opportunity to respond to the open questions that are designed to support the self-reflection. Furthermore, they felt to be able to control when the imagination should continue. However, *negative aspects* are, that the users expect more engagement from the dialog partner or at least a conversation oriented on the basic principles of interpersonal conversation (e.g. reciprocity). Due to the mentioned limitations a state-of-the-art speech assistant can not fulfil these expectations of the users adequately.

In the following we will discuss the limitations of state-of-the-art speech assistants reported by our sample:

1. The main limitation for using vVA like Alexa is the problem to integrate open questions into the design of the dialog. From a music-therapy perspective these questions should give the user the opportunity to express his situation and feelings.

   From a technical perspective it can be noticed that the use of open questions overwhelms the current capabilities of the Alexa system. A pause for thought from the user is understood by the system as the conclusion of the user's *dialog turn* [10]. This interruption of the vVA can be attributed to difficulties with the Automatic Speech Recognition (ASR) of the Alexa Service. The speech recognition models of the system were mainly trained with short voice commands, to serve as a voice-based interface for the users.

   Due to the limited possibilities to influence components of the speech processing pipeline of the Alexa Service as an external developer, it is not possible to solve these problems within the actual VAp. For the NLU component of the vAP the developer has to predefine topics Alexa should react to as intents, which is barely impossible for open questions used in the MTO.

   Some users experience this behaviour as a short time span to give answers to the system. This indicates that during the corresponding interaction, the user's statement was not acoustically understood by Alexa. At the moment, in case of acoustical problems, Alexa waits 8 s after a system response for a user's response, if the system cannot perceive an utterance within that period, a prompt of the last system response is played automatically

2. Also the strict division of the dialog in distinct dialog turns, that do not overlap, can be seen as a limitation for using currently available vVA systems

in this use case. If the system would offer external developers the opportunity to react to interruptions by the user, the VAp could notice that the user was not finished to answer the previous question. The VAp MTO would then apologize to the user that it interrupted the answer to the open question. This behaviour could help to fulfil the expectations users have when interacting with a vVA.

3. Since the Alexa Skill Kit (ASK) and the Alexa service only passe the analysis of the Natural Language Understanding (NLU) component without any textual transcription to the skill, it is not possible to further analyze the user statements for an improved conversational flow. Based on transcription, the MTO could have fulfilled the request of some users for a better understanding of the relaxation state.

4. Although, the *voice output* of Alexa is state-of-the-art, and also SSML-Tags[23] were used in the responses to slow down Alexa's voice and extend pauses to create a voice impression similar to a therapist. It could be a solution to also use pre-recorded instructions for the VAp, but we may lose then the flexibility to react to the user input, even if this also poses problems at the moment.

6.3   Limitations

Results are limited according to the small sample size. Additionally there are no adequate instruments for comparing user experience between interactive (Alexa) and non-interactive (CD) products. Thus, we had to fall back on instruments for interactive ones in order to make a quantitative comparison of Alexa-MTO and CD-MTO (meCUE, AttrakDiff), which may have led to biased results. Furthermore, a systematic in-depth analysis of the qualitative data from the open questions would have helped in further interpretating our results. Currently, our working group is starting a qualitative content analysis [16] of these data. Besides, the analysis of data regarding the stress regulation effect of MTO (PSS-10, VAS-rating, audio sample) will be another next step. This will allow an additional relevant perspective on the evaluation of MTO.

6.4   Implications for Future Research and Development

Despite lots of limitations our study shows that users are willing to use voice assistants for self-regulation support. Their criticisms can be traced back to technological problems rather than to an absent in a general acceptance. However, we want to emphasize, that our study is namely a step towards the exploration of users acceptance conditions of vVA in the field of (music) therapy, but it does not allow any conclusion on its effectiveness in therapeutic contexts.

The main technological challenge in the use of vVA Platforms like Alexa for music therapy contexts is the avoidance of unwanted interruptions because of misinterpretations of users needs in the dialog flow (turn taking, pauses). Therefore, alternative dialogs designs that enable users to express their situation without relying on open questions could be a first step . Furthermore, accessing the transcriptions of the user utterances may offer an opportunity to follow up on the answers of the user.

Future work should focus on a personalization of dialogs and applications. The initial results of the open questions indicate different user types characterized by typical patterns of experiences during the interaction with Alexa. As previous studies showed [12] the description of such types could allow a personalized dialog design for skills like 'Music Time-Out' (MTO) to respond adequately to users needs. Furthermore, in our study users expressed the wish that the vVA adapts to their preferences to influence how many questions should be asked and what music should be suggested by the system.

References

1. Agres, K.R., et al.: Music, computing, and health: a roadmap for the current and future roles of music technology for health care and well-being. Music Sci. **4** (2021). https://doi.org/10.1177/2059204321997709
2. Hassenzahl, M., Burmester, M., Koller, F.: AttrakDiff: ein Fragebogen zur Messung wahrgenommener hedonischer und pragmatischer Qualität. In: Szwillus, G., Ziegler, J. (eds.) Mensch & Computer 2003, Berichte des German Chapter of the ACM, vol. 57, pp. 187–196. Vieweg+Teubner, Wiesbaden, Germany (2003)
3. Hassenzahl, M., Tractinsky, N.: User experience - a research agenda. Behav. Inf. Technol. **25**(2), 91–97 (2006). https://doi.org/10.1080/01449290500330331
4. Hofstadter, D.R.: Fluid Concepts and Creative Analogies: Computer Models of the Fundamental Mechanisms of Thought, chap. Epilogue. Basic Books, The Ineradicable Eliza Effect and Its Dangers (1996)
5. Kaestele, G., Müller, D.: Kurze Musik-Reisen (KMR): Ein Tor Zur Innenwelt. Guided Imagery and Music-Koncepte und Klinische Anwendungen, pp. 108–125 (2013)
6. Karapanos, E.: User Experience Over Time, pp. 57–83. Springer, Berlin Heidelberg (2013). https://doi.org/10.1007/978-3-642-31000-3_4
7. Karrer, K., Glaser, C., Clemens, C., Bruder, C.: Technikaffinität erfassen - der Fragebogen TA-EG, vol. 8. VDI-Verl (2009)
8. Kasseler, K.: Thesen der Kasseler Konferenz. Musikther. Umsch. **19**, 232–235 (1998)
9. Kinsella, B.: Nearly 90 Million U.S. Adults Have Smart Speakers, Adoption Now Exceeds One-Third of Consumers. voicebot.ai, April 2020, https://perma.cc/336P-2C77. Accessed 28 April 2020
10. Kisser, L., Siegert, I.: Erroneous reactions of voice assistants "in the wild" - first analyses. In: Elektronische Sprachsignalverarbeitung 2022. Tagungsband der 33. Konferenz. Studientexte zur Sprachkommunikation, TUDpress, Sonderborg, Denmark (2022)
11. Krankenkasse, T.: TK smart relax: meditation & entspannung mit alexa (2021), https://www.tk.de/techniker/magazin/digitale-gesundheit/apps/alexa-tk-smart-relax-2009254
12. Krüger, J.: Subjektives Nutzererleben in der Mensch-Computer-Interaktion: Beziehungsrelevante Zuschreibungen gegenüber Companion-Systemen am Beispiel eines Individualisierungsdialogs. Verlag Barbara Budrich (2018)

13. Krüger, J., Wahl, M., Frommer, J.: Users' relational ascriptions in user-companion interaction. In: Kurosu, M. (ed.) HCI 2016. LNCS, vol. 9733, pp. 128–137. Springer, Cham (2016). https://doi.org/10.1007/978-3-319-39513-5_12
14. Kunst, A.: Beliebte Funktionen Virtueller Assistenten in Deutschland 2019, December 2019, https://de.statista.com/prognosen/984112/umfrage-in-deutschland-zu-regelmaessig-genutzten-funktionen-virtueller-assistenten
15. Lesage, F., Berjot, S., Deschamps, F.: Clinical stress assessment using a visual analogue scale. Occup. Med. **62**(8), 600–605 (2012). https://doi.org/10.1093/occmed/kqs140
16. Mayring, P.: Qualitative Content Analysis: Theoretical Foundation, Basic Procedures and Software Solution. SSOAR, Klagenfurt (2014)
17. Minge, M.: Nutzererleben messen mit dem meCUE 2.0 - Ein Tool für alle Fälle? In: Dachselt, R., Weber, G. (eds.) Mensch und Computer 2018 - Workshopband. GI, Bonn (2018). https://doi.org/10.18420/muc2018-ws16-0485
18. Reeves, B., Nass, C.: The media equation: how people treat computers, television, and new media like real people. Cambridge, UK **10**, 236605 (1996)
19. Schneider, E.E., Schönfelder, S., Domke-Wolf, M., Wessa, M.: Measuring stress in clinical and nonclinical subjects using a German adaptation of the perceived stress scale. Int. J. Clin. Health Psychol. **20**(2), 173–181 (2020). https://doi.org/10.1016/j.ijchp.2020.03.004
20. Serpil Tas, R.A.: Nutzung von sprachassistenten in deutschland. In: Sprachassistenten - Anwendungen, Implikationen, Entwicklungen : ITG-Workshop : Magdeburg, p. 39 (2020)
21. Siegert, I., Busch, M., Krüger, J.: Does users' system evaluation influence speech behavior in HCI?-first insights from the engineering and psychological perspective. Studientexte zur Sprachkommunikation: Elektronische Sprachsignalverarbeitung **2020**, 241–248 (2020)
22. Splendid Research GmbH: Studie: Digitale sprachassistenten und smart speaker, January 2019, https://www.splendid-research.com/de/studie-digitale-sprachassistenten.html
23. Taylor, P., Isard, A.: SSML: a speech synthesis markup language. Speech Commun. **21**(1–2), 123–133 (1997)
24. Weizenbaum, J.: Eliza-a computer program for the study of natural language communication between man and machine. Commun. ACM **9**(1), 36–45 (1966)

Effects of the Surroundings in Human-Robot Interaction: Stereotypical Perception of Robots and Its Anthropomorphism

Carolin Straßmann[1](✉) , Sabrina C. Eimler[1] , Linda Kololli[2],
Alexander Arntz[1] , Katharina van de Sand[1], and Annika Rietz[1]

[1] Institute of Computer Science and Research Institute of Positive Computing,
Hochschule Ruhr West University of Applied Sciences, Bottrop, Germany
{carolin.strassmann,sabrina.eimler,alexander.arntz}@hs-ruhrwest.de
{katharina.van-de-sand,annika.rietz}@stud.hs-ruhrwest.de
[2] Ruhr University Bochum, Bochum, Germany
linda.kololli@ruhr-uni-bochum.de
https://www.hochschule-ruhr-west.de/

Abstract. Stereotypes and scripts guide human perception and expectations in everyday life. Research has found that a robot's appearance influences the perceived fit in different application domains (e.g. industrial or social) and that the role a robot is presented in predicts its perceived personality. However, it is unclear how the surroundings as such can elicit a halo effect leading to stereotypical perceptions. This paper presents the results of an experimental study in which 206 participants saw 8 cartoon pictures of the robot Pepper in different application domains in a within-subjects online study. Results indicate that the environment a robot is placed in has an effect on the users' evaluation of the robot's warmth, competence, status in society, competition, anthropomorphism, and morality. As the first impression has an effect on users' expectations and evaluation of the robot and the interaction with it, the effect of the application scenarios has to be considered carefully.

Keywords: Social robots · Stereotypes · Stereotype Content Model · Application scenario · Halo effect · Media Equation

1 Introduction

In today's daily life, robots are used in more and more application fields. Previous studies have shown that users, based on the appearance of a robot, suggested different contexts of their application [16]. These contexts include domestic scenarios, such as healthcare or personal assistance, and public scenarios, such as business or public assistance, or even scenarios that include both, domestic and public aspects such as security, research, and education [16]. However, not only the robot

G. Salvendy and J. Wei (Eds.): HCII 2022, LNCS 13337, pp. 363–377, 2022.
https://doi.org/10.1007/978-3-031-05014-5_30

and its appearance determine application fields that are considered suitable, but also the application field in and of itself affects the confidence in robots to execute a task [25]. Moreover, different expectations about the personality and behavior of humanoid robots arise depending on the role or task they are used in [15]. Comparing a cleaning robot with a tour guide robot, [15] found that the robot's task influenced the perception of its personality and the user's compliance with the robot. These findings suggest that the associated stereotypes of the robot's task might be reflected in the expectations and perception of the executing robot. So far no study has investigated the influence of the mere application environment a robot is presented in. Thus, the present study investigates the influence of the application scenario settings on the perception and evaluation of robots.

2   Prior Work

It lies in the nature of stereotypes as perceptual biases that the same trait or behavior is evaluated differently and often guided by socially shared expectations and suggested traits (e.g. [9]). Descriptive stereotypes (how someone or something is) and prescriptive stereotypes (how someone or something should be) guide perception processes in interpersonal settings - especially when it comes to social roles. This is also the case in human-robot interaction.

Studies based on the Media Equation Theory [23] demonstrate that humans mindlessly [18] apply this kind of stereotypical perceptions onto computers and virtual entities like robots. [18] substantiates these findings with the social cues (e.g. voice, human-like communication pattern, human-like appearance) of technological devices since these cues trigger social responses like stereotypes in the interaction. In line with this, different studies found that stereotypes (e.g. with regard to perceived gender) are applied to computers [19], virtual agents [21] or robots [11].

As described above, the appearance of a robot guides the users' expectation in which application domain it should be applied [16]. In line with these findings, [24] found that the degree of a robot's anthropomorphism influences the assumed application domain (lower anthropomorphism is associated with industrial domains and robots with higher anthropomorphism are seen in social domains). Hence, the social cues of the appearance of a robot (e.g. its anthropomorphism) affect the stereotypical perception and this leads to an association with a potential application domain [16,24]. For instance, higher anthropomorphism might evoke feelings of care, trust, warmth, or trustworthiness, which stereotypically is associated with social domains. In turn, the role a robot is presented in (within a specific application domain), affects the (stereotypical) perception of its personality and the user's compliance with it [15]. Therefore, it can be assumed that the stereotypes connected to the role (e.g. higher extroversion of a museum's guide) affect the personality attributed to the robot. In this work, we investigate this kind of stereotypical perception in more detail. We assume that the application setting as such evokes similar stereotypes and leads to a halo effect [3], meaning that the global evaluation of a person or entity affects the evaluation of individual attributes

[20]. A halo effect was already found for the robot's appearance [27], showing that humans conclude personality traits of the robot from how its looks.

Moreover, the social context in which a robot is presented (a robot is presented either with another robot or with a human) has a halo effect on the evaluation of the robot's skills [8]. Another study demonstrated that robot touch can trigger a global perception, which - as a halo effect - evokes specific stereotypical perceptions of liking or capability [28]. Based on these findings, we assume that the robot's application scenarios (e.g. private home or hospital) triggers a global (stereotypical) perception, which users transfer onto the individual perception of the robot. More specifically, we rely on the stereotypical perception described in the Stereotype Content Model [10] as relevant perception dimensions. With the Stereotype Content Model [10], it has been suggested that there are two fundamental dimensions along which humans evaluate each other, namely warmth and competence. Additionally, it measures feelings of being in competition about social or financial resources as well as the attributed status of the social group a person that is to be evaluated belongs to allocate different members of social groups to four quadrants. This model has also been applied in Social Robots research, focusing on group interaction [22] and on the evaluation of different robots without a focus on the surroundings [17]. Also, it has been applied in other technological fields, such as in the evaluation of chatbots and conversational agents [26]. Accordingly, we investigate the following research question:

RQ1: How does the application scenario influence the users' perception of the robot?

3 Methods

In order to examine the presented research question, an online experiment with a within-subject design was used. Participants filled in a questionnaire set up in soscisurvey (www.soscisurvey.de), and evaluated eight pictures that presented the robot Pepper (www.softbankrobotics.com) in different settings.

3.1 Sample

A total of 206 participants completed the online questionnaire. 94 of them were female, 110 male and 2 did not disclose their gender identity. The average age was 23 ($M = 23.43$, $SD = 5.33$). All participants had a higher educational background. The sample was rather young, well-educated, and showed a rather high technological affinity ($M = 3.63$, $SD = 0.75$) with the Likert scale ranging from 1 (low affinity) to 5 (high affinity). Participants received course credits for their participation.

3.2 Material

The material that was to be evaluated by the participants consisted of cartoon pictures showing the humanoid robot Pepper in a variety of different settings.

The pictures were presented to the participants in randomized order. The scenarios included a private home, supermarket, train station, courtroom, library, hospital, kindergarten, and a workshop (see Fig. 1 for details). Pepper is present in all scenarios at the same position in the environment. A short description (e.g. "Below is an illustration of a robot working in a *private household*. Imagine that you enter *the private household* and meet the robot there. Please evaluate this robot with the help of the following questions.") and a supplementing cartoon picture (see Fig. 1) are used to present the different application fields to the participant. By using cartoons instead of real photographs, confounding factors such as different coloring, brightness, mood or perspectives should be excluded from the stimulus material. In doing this, potential effects should be narrowed down to the influence of the setting as such that might trigger implicit expectations and stereotypes.

3.3 Measures

To assess participants' attributions to the robot, constructs from the Stereotype Content Model were used [12,13]. As an integrated model bringing together several results from stereotype research, it suggests warmth and competence as two basic and distinct dimensions along which assessments are made. Additionally, status and feelings of competition are part of the model as complementing factors. The original items from [10] were adapted and overall a smaller number of items was used due to the repeated measures in the within-subject experimental design. Warmth was measured with 5 items ("warmhearted, benevolent, sincere, tolerant and likable") and had an overall good internal consistency ($\alpha > .853$). The 5 items "independent, intelligent, competitive, competent, and confident" have been used to measure competence, which showed overall an acceptable internal consistency ($\alpha > .689$). Participants rated the status they attributed to the robot via 2 items ("The robot shown has a high status in society." and "The robot shown contributes to the economic success."), which had a questionable to acceptable internal consistency ($\alpha > .464$). Another 2 items ("The robot shown takes jobs away from people in this field of work." and "The power of the robot shown decreases the power of the people working in this field.") were used to measure the feeling of competition the robot evoked in the participants. The internal consistency of this scale was acceptable ($\alpha > .689$). All scales were rated on a 5-pointed Likert scale ranging from 1 = "does not apply at all" to 5 = "fully applies". In addition, participants were asked to rate the robot's anthropomorphism with 4 semantic differential items ("Fake - Authentic", "Like a machine - Like a human", "Has no consciousness - Has a consciousness", "Artificial - Realistic") originating from the Godspeed subscale "Anthropomorphism" [5]. Its internal consistency was rather good ($\alpha > .755$). The semantic differential had 5 evaluation points. Moreover, 2 items ("The robot behaves according to moral rules." and "The robot avoids behavior that has unpleasant consequences.") from [4] were used to measure morality attributed to the robot. Participants rated these items on a 5-pointed Likert scale (1 = "do not agree at all" to 5 = "completely agree"). The internal consistency was overall acceptable ($\alpha > .618$). The exact

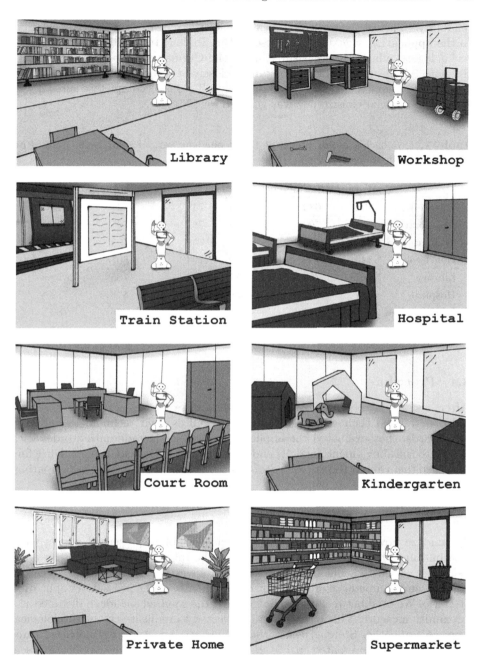

Fig. 1. Stimulus scenarios used in the experimental online study.

reliability values of the presented measures for the repeated measures in relation to the application scenarios are presented in Table 1. In addition, participants' technological affinity was measured using the German version of the ATI scale [14] with 9 items (e.g. "I like to look more closely at technical systems."). Again, a 5-pointed Likert scale (1 = "do not agree at all" to 5 = "completely agree") was used. The internal consistency was good ($\alpha = .897$).

Table 1. Cronbach's alpha values of the dependent variables for each application scenario (within-subject factor).

	Warmth	Competence	Status	Competition	Anthropo	Morality
Private home	.894	.689	.464	.741	.826	.697
Supermarket	.853	.790	.532	.787	.765	.642
Train station	.867	.766	.535	.758	.793	.659
Court room	.843	.799	.559	.794	.807	.643
Library	.867	.763	.577	.689	.755	.618
Hospital	.887	.762	.536	.766	.818	.712
Kindergarten	.904	.747	.680	.808	.866	.786
Workshop	.866	.757	.575	.757	.768	.620

3.4 Procedure

After a short introduction text, participants gave informed consent and provided details on their socio-demography as well as their technological affinity. Afterwards, they evaluated the application scenarios in randomized order with regard to the above-mentioned dependent variables. In the end, a short debriefing informed them about the research goal and thanked participants for participating.

4 Results

To analyze how a specific setting in which a robot is presented affects what attributions a human observer makes about the robot's traits, two cluster analyses were conducted. The first cluster analysis investigated clusters for perceived warmth and competence of the robot in dependence of the presented application scenario. We used between-group linkage and the squared euclidean distance as a proximity measure. This procedure was selected to replicate the methodological approach of earlier Stereotype Content Model studies. Analyses indicated three clusters that are presented in Fig. 2: Cluster 1 consists of the application scenario kindergarten. Cluster 2 contains the private home, supermarket, library, hospital, train station, and workshop. The courtroom builds Cluster 3.

To investigate the resulting cluster more deeply, ANOVAs and multiple comparisons with Bonferroni correction were used. Significant differences between

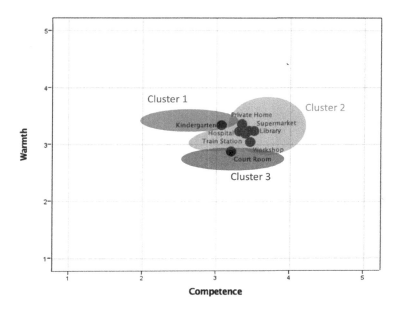

Fig. 2. Cluster analysis for warmth and competence.

the clusters are observable for warmth ($F(2, 1645) = 12.89$, $p < .001$, $n^2 = .563$) and competence ($F(2, 1645) = 17.91$, $p < .001$, $n^2 = .021$). Cluster 1 and 2 are associated with higher warmth than Cluster 3. In contrast, Cluster 2 evokes higher competence attribution than Cluster 1 and 3. See Table 2 for means and values of the pairwise comparisons.

Table 2. Comparison of the cluster data for perceived warmth and competence.

	Cluster 1		Cluster 2		Cluster 3		Bonferroni comparison		
	N = 206		N = 1236		N = 206		p-values		
	M	SD	M	SD	M	SD	1&2	2&3	1&3
Warmth	3.34	1.09	3.22	0.99	2.88	0.96	0.31	<.001	<.001
Competence	3.07	0.85	3.41	0.82	3.20	0.91	<.001	.003	.350

A second cluster analysis, using the same methodological procedure, investigated the clustering of the presented application scenarios with regard to status and competition (see Fig. 3). Again, three clusters were found: Cluster 4 contains the scenarios hospital, supermarket and train station. Cluster 5 includes a workshop and a library. And the scenarios private home, courtroom, and kindergarten build Cluster 6.

Using ANOVA and post-hoc comparison of the three clusters we investigated the differences between the clusters with regard to the attributed levels of status

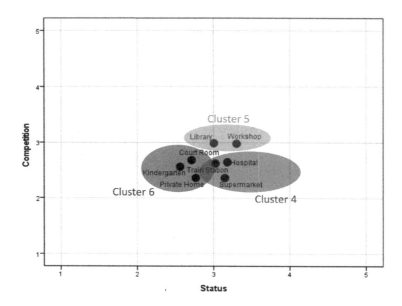

Fig. 3. Cluster analysis for status and competition.

and competition. Table 3 presents the associated values (means and p-values). Cluster 4 and 5 evoked higher perceptions of status than Cluster 6. In addition, scenarios in Cluster 5 were connected with higher competition than those in Cluster 4 and 6.

Table 3. Comparison of the cluster data for perceived status and competition.

	Cluster 4		Cluster 5		Cluster 6		Bonferroni comparison		
	N = 618		N = 412		N = 618		p-values		
	M	SD	M	SD	M	SD	4&5	5&6	4&6
Status	3.12	0.99	3.15	0.98	2.68	1.05	1.00	<.001	<.001
Competition	2.55	1.17	2.98	1.12	2.54	1.24	<.001	<.001	1.00

Furthermore, two repeated measures ANOVAs (with Greenhouse-Geisser correction) were used to analyze the differences in attributed anthropomorphism and morality between the presented scenarios.

The analysis revealed a significant difference between the application scenarios and the attributed level of anthropomorphism ($F(5.40, 1106.92) = 5.87$, $p < .001$, $n^2 = .028$). See Fig. 4 for the pairwise comparisons. The robot in the private home environment ($M = 2.31$, $SD = 0.98$) evoked more anthropomorphism than the kindergarten ($M = 2.12$, $SD = 1.03$), workshop ($M = 2.13$, $SD = 0.87$) and court room ($M = 2.00$, $SD = 0.89$) surrounding. Moreover, a robot in a court room elicited less anthropomorphism than the supermarket ($M = 2.24$, $SD = 0.89$), train station ($M = 2.21$, $SD = 0.94$), library ($M = 2.24$, $SD = 0.91$) and hospital ($M = 2.20$, $SD = 0.96$).

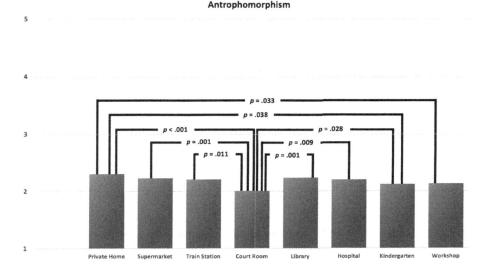

Fig. 4. Means and pairwise comparison of anthropomorphism attributed to the robot.

The second repeated measures ANOVA with Greenhouse-Geisser correction indicated a significant difference between the application scenarios regarding the morality attributed to the robot ($F(4.78, 979.70) = 2.80$, $p = .018$, $n^2 = .013$). See Fig. 5 for the pairwise comparisons. Solely, a robot in the private home setting ($M = 3.47$, $SD = 1.12$) evoked higher morality attributions than the workshop environment ($M = 3.24$, $SD = 1.06$).

5 Discussion

In a within-subject design online experiment, we investigated the influence of a robot's application setting on the users' perception and evaluation of the presented robot. Eight different scenarios have been compared using cartoon pictures of the humanoid robot Pepper in one of the following settings: library, workshop, train station, hospital, court room, kindergarten, private home and, supermarket. Prior work demonstrated effects of the role in which a robot was introduced [15], its appearance [28] as well as the social context [8] on the evaluation of the robot's personality. Accordingly, outer factors can predict the users' expectations and rating of robots, since they transfer their perception of a global factor on the individual perception of the robot as social entity. Therefore, we

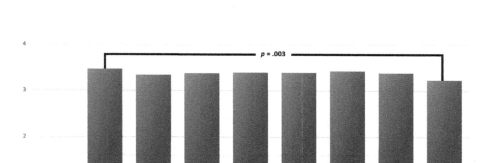

Fig. 5. Means and results of the pairwise comparison of the level of morality attributed to the robot.

assumed a halo effect [3, 20] of the setting a robots appears in: Users perceive the setting and associate specific stereotypes, feelings and expectations with it. More specific, we refer to the Stereotype Content Model [10] and investigated how the application scenario triggers stereotypical perceptions of warmth, competence, status in society and feelings of competition regarding the robot. Results of two exploratory cluster analyses demonstrated that the setting has an influence on users' attributions of warmth, competence, status, and competition to the robot.

Three clusters have been identified (see Fig. 2) differing in attributed warmth and competence, again demonstrating that the setting affects the evaluation of a robot. The pattern partly matches overall stereotypes of human society with regard to the job environment (e.g. kindergarten elicits more warmth than court room, while court room, in contrast, lead to higher levels of attributed competence to the robot). However, between multiple application scenarios, no differences with regard to warmth and competence were found. The application scenarios of Cluster 2 have a stronger service-orientation in common (private home, hospital, train station, supermarket, library and workshop). These service orientations seems to lead to a high attribution of both, warmth and competence.

The second cluster analysis revealed a different cluster solution for status and competition evaluations (see Fig. 3). The cluster (Cluster 5) with the highest status and competition evaluations includes the scenarios workshop and library. Both are application scenarios that are often discussed in the media and in which robots have already been placed in. We assume that participants' perception is also strongly correlated with the acceptance and expectations to embedded robots in the presented settings. As they might have heard from robots in these scenarios more often (e.g. in the media), they accept and expect them more to be placed in these settings. This might enhance the feeling that robots are valuable for society potentially causing attributions of higher status. In contrast, as the value of robots is high, users might also fear to be replaced, causing higher levels of competition feelings. Nevertheless, the evaluation of status goes against prior assumptions, since these settings do not reflect the work environments that will lead to higher attribution of status for human jobs. Here, work environments like the hospital or a court room are work environments associated with a high status attribution. This might indicate that status attributions to robots are made along other lines. Users seem to rate the robot's status, in the sense of its social status and economic success, higher in application scenarios, where they expect and accept the presence of robots more. However, we have not measured both factors within this study.

In addition, we found differences in the evaluation of the robot's anthropomorphism, and morality in relation to the presented application scenario. Overall, a robot embedded in a private home is attributed the highest levels of anthropomorphism and morality. Prior research found that robots with lower levels of anthropomorphism were preferred for industrial domains, while robots with higher anthropomorphism were preferred in social settings [24]. Our results showed that the private home setting was found to lead to higher levels of perceived anthropomorphism of the robot than the kindergarten and court room setting. While the workshop evaluation matches the assumption stated by prior research [24], this does not explain the differences between the social settings private home and kindergarten. Hence, the robot's appearance and anthropomorphism triggers preferences regarding the application scenario [16,24], but the application scenario itself seems to predict the perceived anthropomorphism in a slightly different way.

5.1 Limitations and Future Work

Needless to say, the present research has some shortcomings, which should be addressed in the future. The Pepper robot itself has to be mentioned as further limitation. It was a humanoid robot, that is often used and that has a high media coverage. Thus, users might already have some perceptions and prior attitude towards the robot. Unfortunately, it has not been measured whether participants were familiar with the robot or not. Additionally, we did not measure the perceived gender of the robot, although this has been found to affect the perception of warmth and competence [11].

It could be hypothesized that attributions are influenced by the acceptance of the robot in specific roles and settings and that this, in return, affects the evaluation measured in this study. However, acceptance has not been measured in this study. Future studies should investigate this in relation to the stereotypical perception of robots.

Moreover, this study was merely an observation study, which used cartoon pictures of the robot in different application scenarios accompanied by a short sentence mentioning the location (e.g. supermarket) and indicating that the robot is working there. Further details on the specific functionality, role or tasks the robot has to fulfill have intentionally not been given to test the effect of the environment. However, it can be assumed that the task the robot executes impacts how it is perceived [15]. Since there is a variety in what the robot could do or be used for in the different scenarios this might have led to different associations among the participants. Some might have imagined the robot in the court room to be an usher while others might have imagined the role of a decision-making member of the court. Accordingly, future studies should investigate the present findings in a real human-robot interaction to observe the interplay with the robot's behavior and position or task. The experimental design might also have an effect on the results. We used a within-subject design. Hence, participants evaluated the same robot in different scenarios and might have transferred their perception from one scenario to the other. We counterbalanced this effect using a randomized order of the stimuli. Nevertheless, usually stereotypical perceptions are related to specific individuals and it might have been difficult for participants to disengage from their first impression of the robot in line with a primacy effect.

Moreover, the convenience sample, which was rather young and well educated with a high technology affinity, is a further limitation. Future studies should replicate the findings with a more diverse sample, since it is important for the design of robots used in public spaces that we are aware what expectations people have and what kind of attributions are made.

In addition, the effect sizes are rather small and thus the effects might disappear in actual human-robot interactions when other factors (e.g. the robots nonverbal behavior or executed task) are considered by the users.

The next step is to investigate the presented findings in an actual interaction of users with the robot. Here, virtual reality (VR) could help to investigate the effects in a very controlled way (similar to the cartoon pictures). In lab or field studies, this would be difficult, since multiple confounding factors of the surrounding could affect the results. However, these factors could be controlled in a virtual setting, while an interaction with the robot is possible. Such VR-settings have already been used in the past and are an established methodological approach [1,2].

6   Conclusion

The present research highlights the effect of a human-robot interaction's setting on the perception and evaluation of the robot. Practitioners wanting to deploy robots, e.g. in public places, should be aware of the setting's effect on the human's perception, since it can have an impact on the collaboration or interaction between human and robot. For instance, co-workers in a workshop might feel higher competition with the robot and might therefore be more afraid to collaborate. In contrast, settings that elicit higher levels of competence attributed to the robot can trigger false expectations that the robot cannot meet. Such kind of expectation violation [7] could lead to a rejection of the robot and an overall poorer interaction quality. However, while the first impression in social interactions is important, the behavior during a longer interaction period can revise the first impression [6]. Accordingly, future research has to investigate the impact of the findings within actual human-robot interactions.

Acknowledgments. The presented work was partly supported by the Institute of Positive Computing (322-8.03.04-127491) funded by the Federal Ministry of Education and Research Germany. The authors thank all participants, as well as colleagues for their support: Elias Kyewski, Pasquale Hinrichs, Anna-Marie Schweizer, Lara Oldach, Noémi Tschiesche, Uwe Handmann. Presentation of this work is funded by the initiative for quality improvement in teaching of the Institute of Computer Science.

References

1. Arntz, A., Eimler, S.C., Hoppe, H.U.: Augmenting the human-robot communication channel in shared task environments. In: Nolte, A., Alvarez, C., Hishiyama, R., Chounta, I.-A., Rodríguez-Triana, M.J., Inoue, T. (eds.) CollabTech 2020. LNCS, vol. 12324, pp. 20–34. Springer, Cham (2020). https://doi.org/10.1007/978-3-030-58157-2_2

2. Arntz, A., Eimler, S.C., Hoppe, H.U.: A virtual sandbox approach to studying the effect of augmented communication on human-robot collaboration. Front. Robot. AI **8** (2021)

3. Asch, S.E.: Forming impressions of personality. Psychol. Sci. Publ. Interest **41**(3), 258–290 (1946)

4. Banks, J.: A perceived moral agency scale: development and validation of a metric for humans and social machines. Comput. Hum. Behav. **90**, 363–371 (2019). https://doi.org/10.1016/j.chb.2018.08.028

5. Bartneck, C., Croft, E., Kulic, D.: Measuring the anthropomorphism, animacy, likeability, perceived intelligence and perceived safety of robots. In: Proceedings of the Metrics for Human-Robot Interaction Workshop at the 3rd International Conference on Human-Robot Interaction (HRI 2008), pp. 37–44. IEEE (2008)

6. Bergmann, K., Eyssel, F., Kopp, S.: A second chance to make a first impression? How appearance and nonverbal behavior affect perceived warmth and competence of virtual agents over time. In: Nakano, Y., Neff, M., Paiva, A., Walker, M. (eds.) IVA 2012. LNCS (LNAI), vol. 7502, pp. 126–138. Springer, Heidelberg (2012). https://doi.org/10.1007/978-3-642-33197-8_13

7. Burgoon, J.K.: Interpersonal expectations, expectancy violations, and emotional communication. J. Lang. Soc. Psychol. **12**(1–2), 30–48 (1993)

8. Butler, R., Pruitt, Z., Wiese, E.: The effect of social context on the mind perception of robots. In: Proceedings of the Human Factors and Ergonomics Society Annual Meeting, vol. 63, pp. 230–234. SAGE Publications, Los Angeles (2019)

9. Eagly, A.H., Karau, S.J.: Role congruity theory of prejudice toward female leaders. Psychol. Rev. **109**(3), 573–598 (2002). https://doi.org/10.1037//0033-295x.109.3.573

10. Eckes, T.: Paternalistic and envious gender stereotypes: testing predictions from the stereotype content model. Sex Roles **47**(3), 99–114 (2002). https://doi.org/10.1023/A:1021020920715

11. Eyssel, F., Hegel, F.: (S)he's got the look: gender stereotyping of robots. J. Appl. Soc. Psychol. **42**(9), 2213–2230 (2012). https://doi.org/10.1111/j.1559-1816.2012.00937.x

12. Fiske, S.T., Cuddy, A.J., Glick, P.: Universal dimensions of social cognition: warmth and competence. Trends Cogn. Sci. **11**(2), 77–83 (2007). https://doi.org/10.1016/j.tics.2006.11.005

13. Fiske, S.T., Cuddy, A.J., Glick, P., Xu, J.: A model of (often mixed) stereotype content: competence and warmth respectively follow from perceived status and competition. J. Pers. Soc. Psychol. **82**(6), 878–902 (2002). https://doi.org/10.1037//0022-3514.82.6.878

14. Franke, T., Attig, C., Wessel, D.: A personal resource for technology interaction: development and validation of the affinity for technology interaction (ATI) scale. Int. J. Hum.-Comput. Interact. **35**(6), 456–467 (2019). https://doi.org/10.1080/10447318.2018.1456150

15. Joosse, M., Lohse, M., Pérez, J.G., Evers, V.: What you do is who you are: the role of task context in perceived social robot personality. In: Proceedings of the 2013 IEEE International Conference on Robotics and Automation, pp. 2134–2139. IEEE (2013)

16. Lohse, M., Hegel, F., Wrede, B.: Domestic applications for social robots: an online survey on the influence of appearance and capabilities. J. Phys. Agents **2**(2), 21–32 (2008). https://doi.org/10.14198/JoPha.2008.2.2.04

17. Mieczkowski, H., Liu, S.X., Hancock, J., Reeves, B.: Helping not hurting: applying the stereotype content model and bias map to social robotics. In: Proceedings of the 14th ACM/IEEE International Conference on Human-Robot Interaction (HRI), pp. 222–229. IEEE (2019). https://doi.org/10.1109/HRI.2019.8673307

18. Nass, C., Moon, Y.: Machines and mindlessness: social responses to computers. J. Soc. Issues **56**(1), 81–103 (2000). https://doi.org/10.1111/0022-4537.00153

19. Nass, C., Steuer, J., Tauber, E.R.: Computers are social actors. In: Proceedings of the SIGCHI Conference on Human Factors in Computing Systems, pp. 72–78 (1994)

20. Nisbett, R.E., Wilson, T.D.: The halo effect: evidence for unconscious alteration of judgments. J. Pers. Soc. Psychol. **35**(4), 250–256 (1977). https://doi.org/10.1037/0022-3514.35.4.250

21. Nowak, K.L., Fox, J.: Avatars and computer-mediated communication: a review of the definitions, uses, and effects of digital representations. Rev. Commun. Res. **6**, 30–53 (2018). https://doi.org/10.12840/issn.2255-4165.2018.06.01.015

22. Oliveira, R., Arriaga, P., Correia, F., Paiva, A.: The stereotype content model applied to human-robot interactions in groups. In: Proceedings of the 14th ACM/IEEE International Conference on Human-Robot Interaction, pp. 123–132. IEEE (2020)

23. Reeves, B., Nass, C.: The Media Equation: How People Treat Computers, Television, and New Media like Real People and Places. Cambridge University Press, Cambridge (1996)

24. Roesler, E., Naendrup-Poell, L., Manzey, D., Onnasch, L.: Why context matters: the influence of application domain on preferred degree of anthropomorphism and gender attribution in human-robot interaction. Int. J. Soc. Robot. 1–12 (2022). https://doi.org/10.1007/s12369-021-00860-z

25. Savela, N., Turja, T., Oksanen, A.: Social acceptance of robots in different occupational fields: a systematic literature review. Int. J. Soc. Robot. **10**(4), 493–502 (2017). https://doi.org/10.1007/s12369-017-0452-5

26. Seiler, R., Schär, A.: Chatbots, conversational interfaces, and the stereotype content model. In: Proceedings of the 54th Hawaii International Conference on System Sciences, pp. 1860–1867 (2021)

27. Syrdal, D.S., Dautenhahn, K., Woods, S.N., Walters, M.L., Koay, K.L.: Looking good? Appearance preferences and robot personality inferences at zero acquaintance. In: AAAI Spring Symposium: Multidisciplinary Collaboration for Socially Assistive Robotics, vol. 86, pp. 230–234. American Association for Artificial Intelligence (2007)
28. Yamashita, Y., Ishihara, H., Ikeda, T., Asada, M.: Investigation of causal relationship between touch sensations of robots and personality impressions by path analysis. Int. J. Soc. Robot. **11**(1), 141–150 (2018). https://doi.org/10.1007/s12369-018-0483-6

Speech-Based Virtual Assistant for Treatment of Alzheimer Disease Patient Using Virtual Reality Environment (VRE)

Tebepah Tariuge[✉]

Department of Computer Science, Ignatius Ajuru University of Education, Port Harcourt,
Nigeria
tariuget.tt@gmail.com

Abstract. One of the major diseases that affect the elderly is the Alzheimer disease (AD) which is characterized by partial or complete loss of memory. Early detection and early treatment could help in managing the Alzheimer disease on potential patients. This paper introduces a virtual reality assistant (VRA) into a virtual environment. The VRA gives commands to the user through a wearable immersive virtual reality Google. The patients are made to complete varying levels of tasks of which a deviation from the normal results of the task was an indicator of a potential sufferer of the AD. The VR used Natural Language in Artificial Intelligence for communicating, the tasks were designed with Unity Game Engine and VR cardboard Google was used. The result obtained showed that patients found the Virtual Reality Assistant in the simulation helpful.

Keywords: Virtual Reality Assistant (VRA) · Natural Language · Alzheimer disease · Google glasses · Virtual Reality Environment (VRE)

1 Introduction

A survey conducted by Harvard School of Public Health and Alzheimer's Europe consortium on Alzheimer disease (AD) stated that Dementia of the AD type is a major cause of health concern of Adult [1]. In the world as at 2015, a report recorded almost 46.8 million people worldwide were living with Dementia, and this number will most likely escalate to 131.5 million in 2050 [2]. A MEDLINE search of epidemiologic studies was conducted using Dementia and AD as key words. Out of 522 articles seen 41 was selected for review. 2 articles out of the 41 was recorded incidence in Nigeria one of which was in Zaria [3]. Which means data on the occurrence of Alzheimer in Nigeria is limited making the magnitude of problem unknown in Nigeria in as much as it has Public Health implication. The reason for these might be inadequate tools for assessing AD, which means the society might be ignorant of the occurrences of AD leaving our over 60 years Adults vulnerable to the disease with no option of early treatment. A secondary problem springs forth from the use of modern technology for the treatment of patients with AD. Patient over 60 years find it difficult and awkward to use simulations

G. Salvendy and J. Wei (Eds.): HCII 2022, LNCS 13337, pp. 378–387, 2022.
https://doi.org/10.1007/978-3-031-05014-5_31

as part of their treatment therapy. Very few researches have been reported to provide examples of user experience (UX) in a virtual world for AD patients [4]. This Speech-Based Assistant Virtual Simulation (SBAVS) is built to catch the attention of medical practitioners to see the need for detecting AD early and the importance of making AD patients relaxed during therapies and treatments.

1.1 Statement of Problem

The transition from one phase of technology to another phase of technology in the world is not easy for the people caught between both phases. Destructive technologies intervention has also worsen the ease of adaptability to new ways of doing things by the elderly. Technology has caught up with medical treatment and diagnosis as well as observed in telemedicine. Bearing this in mind, creating an easy user experience can help the elderly operate gargets that comes with the modern technology.

The aim of this study is to explore the use of a speech-based virtual assistant for the treatment of patient with Alzheimer disease using Virtual Reality Environment. The specific objectives of the study include to:

I.   design an Avatar with Natural Language ability in unity game engine
II. implement the virtual world using cardboard paper and the android phone

2   Related Works

Kumar et al. [5] wrote an article on Virtual Assistance using Artificial Intelligent (AI). Their research was about a service available to mobile phone user to help in organizing the user's activities. Their research was based on a hybrid of speech recognition technology, mobile technology and the internet. Although their proposed Virtual person assistance (VPA) improved time usage and gave a common platform for communication for contacts schedules and messages, their algorithm was very complex. The implication of this complex algorithm was excessive time needed to tidy up a task.

Buck et al. [6] attempted to address the issue that came with the rigidity of Siri and Google Now when users interact with them in their paper: Natural Language, Mixed-initiatives Personal Assistance. They did a study on a mixed-interactive user supports that used a dialog-based system which was dependent on natural language. They used the bag-of words model alongside the k-nearest-neighbour in their research. Although they were able to address the interactive rigidity that came with Siri and Google Now, their system was not fully adaptable to the cyber learning environment.

Artificial intelligence and Different methods enhanced with human features has been used to create interaction between humans and the computers. Aditya et al. [7] argued that, the AI component of the design was not given limited hardware control which they tackled in their paper titled "Virtual Personal Assistance". They used raspberry pi 3, a microphone and speaker as their hardware component and python for their scripting. Although their VPA could control hardware given to it, however, their VPA was deficient in self learning.

Liu et al. [8] in their research paper titled: "Augmented reality powers a cognitive assistant for the blind" created a wearable interactive system that could communicate with the blind through voice commands. Their experiment reinforced varying perspectives of visual cognition. Although the blind experimental were able avoid obstacles during movement, understand scenes, being able to create and remember spatial memories, they had issues in localization and tracking issues in narrow passages that was painted white.

Garzotto et al. [9] in their research paper titled: "Hololearn: Learning through mixed reality for people with Cognitive Disorder (CD)" developed a Microsoft dependent application called HoloLearn that helped people with cognitive disability. The subjects were made to use Mixed Reality (MR) application called a Microsoft HoloLens to help people improve independence in everyday life. A virtual assistant was introduced in the experiment to enhance the experimental experiences. Although their experiment was likeable by the CD participants, it was unable to completely help participants with severe CD.

In a research conducted by [4], a mixed Reality device which can be mounted on the head was created for Alzheimer Disease (AD). The name of this system is called a MemHolo. The AD volunteers for the experiments were immersed in a virtual world where they were introduced to holographic objects. The aim of the experiment was to accomplish cognitive tasks to enhance memory recollection of the AD patient. Although their work was the first to use HoloLens for AD patients, however, there experiment was limited to patients with early onset of AD. More so, the experiment was carried out on few persons with a short follow-up time.

A research conducted by [10] was centered on using Wearable Immersive Virtual Reality (WIVR) as a help tool for children suffering from a disorder called: Neurodevelopmental Disorder (NDD). They claimed that there was little or no technology existing that addressed NDD on children. Their work was on findings on how Wildcard could enhance attention skills of the patient. Their objects were highlighted as follows: collecting the key requirements, assessing iterative prototypes and performing an empirical study evaluation. Unity game engine was used to create the visual theme for the VR environment which was based on 2 story books used for therapy on children with NDD. Their study was limited to only children who participated in the experiment. In addition, their experiment could not tell the relevance of the skill acquired by the children to real life situations.

Vona et al. [11] introduced a speech-based virtual assistance called HoloLens in a mixed reality (MR) application to help patients with Cognitive disabilities (CD). The help rendered to CD patients was to learn less tedious daily routines and become self reliant. They discussed on how their speech based-virtual assistance was created and carried out their experiment on 15 volunteers. While their results showed that the presence of the speech based-virtual assistance in MR improved the volunteer's ability to perform optimally in the MR tasks.

Bozgeyikli et al. [12] did a survey on target intervention on autism spectrum disorder (ASD) using Virtual reality (VR). They discussed on the importance of VR intervention on patients with ASD, the difficulty ASD patients have in using VR for training purposes. They developed design guidelines in their article that worked better with children with

ASD. Using a systematic review, they were able to carry out a comparative study of the effects of VR on children with ASD. On the flip side, their guidelines were obtained from observation from interested parties which is less accurate from experimental studies.

2.1 Virtual Reality Assistant (VRA)

Virtual Reality Assistance features on mobile devices as Siri on I Phone and Google assistant on android phone. The VRA was built into these mobile to help humans in organizing and performing predictable tasks. Integrating speech recognition in the VRA is a relatively new technology [5]. VRA communication with Humans have evolved from monotonous mode of operation to a more dynamic way of communication [6]. A handful number of researchers have proposed papers on how to make Robot and human communication as effective as possible. VRA come in different forms; as a human avatar or a robot. In today's banking, human VRA in the form of Avatars are used to help customers open accounts or perform other predictable tasks (Fig. 1).

Fig. 1. Minion as the Virtual Reality Assistance in a garbage collection game (Source: [9])

Virtual Reality Environment (VRE). Virtual reality (VR) is defined as the creation of a pretend prowess which is an emulation of actual life scenarios [14]. Its aim is to hone an encompassing, sensual semblance of being present in another environment by using gargets and computer softwares [13]. The features of VR include: interactivity and presence. Interactivity deals with the way and manner a users can manipulate the VR environment in actual life. Presence is the illusion that comes with been in an environment that is different from the users present location.

To experience a virtual world, users usually wear a head mountable device where they are immersed in a virtual world. Hololens is an example of a mountable device that has been used in professional training, cinemas, education, and tourism [4]. It is owned by Microsoft. As at 2018, the Hololens cost 3000 USD [8]. SBAVS will be using a cardboard VR Google because it is easy to create. A current android phone with OS 4.1 or above is able to split the simulation into two views, 1 for the left eye and the other for the right eye. With a Biconvex lens attached to the Cardboard VR Google, the user is able to experience the illusion of a virtual world (Figs. 2 and 3).

Fig. 2. Cardboard VR Google (Source: Google's VR dreams are dead: Google Cardboard is no longer for sale I Ars Technica)

Fig. 3. Cardboard VR Google (Source: DODOcase Google Cardboard Virtual Reality Kit with NFC Tag (mobilefun.com))

SBAVS as a Tool for Early Detection of Alzheimer Disease. Variant of SBAVS has been used in industries to solve problems but the use of this technology in the vicinity of mental health is largely unexplored [4]. SBAVS has found its usefulness in the treatment of children with cognitive disability. The use of SBAVS has had a positive impact on patients introduced to it as a therapy. Studies have also shown that patients loved the SBAVS treatment better when a virtual assistant featured [9]. In addition, another study had a result that showed that blind patients that experimented with SBAVS were able to localized virtual voices that originated from their Hololens [8].

K-Mismatching. The basic principle of the K-mismatch problem is to find out if two sequences of fragments are isomorphic. If a pattern and an incoming stream of text are brought together, how much texts can one fine in the pattern? Two sequences of numbers are isomorphic if their sequences are identical: 4,1,2,3–63,12,23,42; Gawrychowski and Starikovskaya [14] claimed that these two numbers are essentially the same because they have their smallest number in the second position and their largest numbers in the first position. This instance is a nearly perfect situation, so an order preserving pattern was used instead where there is an input of a text length n and pattern length m: (t_1,

$t_2 \ldots t_n$) and $(p_1, p_2 \ldots p_m)$ and the output is: find if these two lengths are isomorphic (t_i, $t_{i+1} \ldots t_{i+m-1}$) $\sim (p_1, p_2 \ldots p_m)$ such that the length p_m is isomorphic 'i' to the pattern. Another case study could be finding an almost ordered Isomorphic to the pattern [14]. This simply means, modifying the two sequences to get them to be isomorphic. It could be by removing a character or modifying a character which is determined by a factor 'k': $(a_1 a_2 \ldots, a_m)$ $k/ \sim (b_1, b_2 \ldots b_m)$, choose up to k indices $i_1 < i_2 < k$, remove the numbers at the corresponding position from both sequence to make them isomorphic. Clifford et al. [15] used the hamming distance to established patterns between 2 or more sequences. The hamming distance is the number of mismatch between two stings. In K-mismatched, the pattern is already given and the string character comes in a character at a time. The hamming distance between the character and the pattern is calculated.

3   Materials and Methods

3.1   Analysis of the Existing System

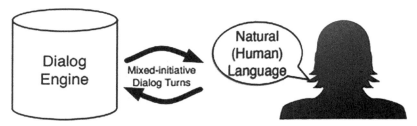

Fig. 4. Existing System Architecture of participant relationship in a human-computer dialog (Source: [6])

Figure 4 shows a system that communicates with a human. The dialogue engine is a hybrid of Natural Language Programming (NLP) and a mixed initiative dialogue toolkit based. The dialogue engine has the ability to understand and communicate with humans flexibly. The mixed-initiative dialog means that the system is able to reason and take initiatives like humans making the conversation sound real. NLP is an outshoot of Artificial intelligence that deals with the interaction of computers and humans. NLP programmes the mobile system in a manner that the programme can process data from natural language. The speech is broken down into segments in the process called segmentation. The broken down speech is further broken down into its constituent words in the process called tokenizing. Each word after tokenization is called a token. The next phase involves removing non-essential words like prepositions or stop words. At this point, the Virtual assistance is taught the human words that have been processed by grouping words in their tenses as one word; basically, by removing prefixes and suffixes from the same word in different form. This process is called stemming. The VRA is further taught based words and where they stem out from, this process is called Lemmatization. Finally, the VRA is taught the parts of speech and the parts of speech are used to tag the processed words.

The mixed-initiative dialog uses a bag-of-words model for another dialog channel. In particular, every sentence is parsed in the conversation into the matching vector features representing the frequencies of each meaningful word. Like NLP part of the model, words like: 'a', 'an,' and 'the' are removed from the conversation. Each bag-of-word feature vector is then normalized to $\ell 2$ norm. Next, is a mapping of unexpected utterance to a response which comes as a dialogue prompt.

Proposed SBAVS. In Fig. 5, the human is made to wear a headset that immerses him/her into a virtual environment. The user is able to communicate with a system which is called the dialog engine. The proposed system is a modification of the existing system. Simple instruction by humans to the system is very adequate so, a simple NLP integrated into the system will suffice. The mixed-initiative dialog system will be discarded from SBAVS. The NLP will be immersed into a virtual world environment. The humans will be able to interact with a virtual assistant using NLP. Implementing a speech-based virtual assistance in a virtual environment will improve patients experience during for example: eye test. When a patient is relaxed during therapy or test, the results obtained tend to be more accurate.

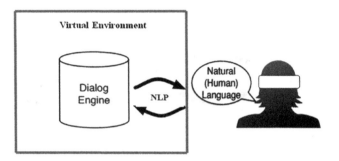

Fig. 5. Proposed speech-based virtual assistance simulation architecture

The SBAVS system was created in two stages. The requirements for the first stage were: Unity Game Engine (a software framework used in creating 3 Dimensional world by developers), Autodesk Maya, software and Photoshop. The virtual Assistant was created in Autodesk Maya and imported into Unity Game engine. The NLP was implemented on the virtual assistant. The end result was a simple 3D simulation for Personal Computer. When the simulation was launched on the PC, the user saw an avatar giving instructions and asking direct questions on how to navigate around the simulation.

The requirements for the second stage are: An android phone with Operating System 4.3 and a Google cardboard 2.0 or Google VR SDK for Unity. The Google VR SDK is available for free on the internet. The SDK was imported into the project in Unity by going through unity menu, Assets/import package/Shooters. Changing the simulation into VR was done through GoogleVR/Prefabs (a dialog box in Unity that allows you to change into parameters that supports VR). When Unity was restarted, the expected VR was experienced. When the user mounted the headset, they were able to communicate with the Virtual assistant on how to commence the simulation.

Machine learning in Natural Language Processing (MLNLP) was used for the interaction between the virtual assistant Interpreter (VAI) and the human. NLP programmed the VAI in a manner that the programmed could process data from natural language. A token is added to the word spoken by the human this process is called tokenization and the word is called a token. Prefixes and suffixes are removed from the word through a process called stemming. VRA is further taught based words and where they stem out from, this process is called Lemmatization. The word is matched to its exact corresponding word using K-mismatch (Fig. 6).

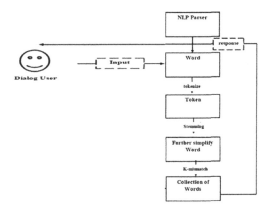

Fig. 6. Proposed architectural design of Natural Language processing units

4   Results and Discussions

The Task. When the user starts the simulation, stars appear at random on the screen. The player is expected to shoot these stars without moving their neck. The farther away the stars are from the lateral view, the more points the player makes if the stars are hit. All points are scored as the users hit a star. The scores are updated on the screen; the initial controls for the shooting are keys on the keyboard. Patients with AD were unable to see and shoot up to twenty four stars in sixty (60) seconds. The result was worst when the stars were out of the virtual field of the user (Fig. 7).

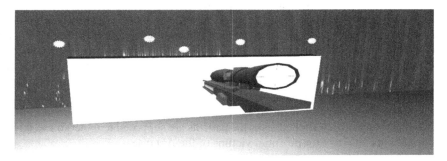

Fig. 7. Shoot at the stars to get points

Figure 8 shows the first menu the user sees in their virtual world in the simulation. The avatar VR assistant renders help to the user by asking how she could help. The user response was on how to start the simulation? The VR assistant respond is in Fig. 8

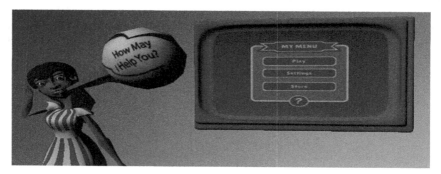

Fig. 8. SBAVS menu

Users: How do I start the simulation? (Fig. 9)

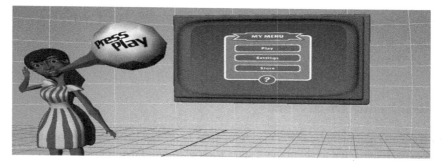

Fig. 9. SBAVS menu

5   Conclusion and Recommendations

In this study, a virtual Assistance was introduced into a simulation that is meant to detect Alzheimer Disease on aging people. The elderly finds it uncomfortable to use modern devices because of the advancement of technology in recent times. The VRA used NLP for communication with the human users. Her task was to make it easier for users of the system to understand and perform the simulation task at ease. The VRA was designed in Autodesk Maya and exported into the Unity game engine world. The NLP was programmed into her to make her understand simple questions from the users. This study only focused on implementing a VRA in a simulated VR environment. Further study will explore on the detailed tasks the patients are supposed to undergo and on how the simulation could test for potential victims of the AD disease.

References

1. Blendon, R., Georges, J., Seymour, M.: International survey highlights great public desire to seek early diagnosis of Alzheimer's. AAIC Poster (2011). https://www.hsph.harvard.edu/news/press-releases/alzheimers-international-survey/
2. Prince, M., Comas-Herrera, A., Knapp, M., Guerchet, M., Karagiannidou, M.: World Alzheimer Report 2016 Improving healthcare for people living with dementia. Coverage, Quality and costs now and in the future. Alzheimer's Disease International (2016)
3. Olayinka, O.O., Mbuyi, N.N.: Epidemiology of dementia among the elderly in sub-saharan Africa. Int. J. Alzheimers. Dis. **2014** (2014). https://doi.org/10.1155/2014/195750
4. Aruanno, B., Garzotto, F.: MemHolo: mixed reality experiences for subjects with Alzheimer's disease. Multimedia Tools Appl. **78**(10), 13517–13537 (2019). https://doi.org/10.1007/s11042-018-7089-8
5. Kumar, C.R.: Virtual assistant using artificial intelligence and Python. J. Emerg. Technol. Innov. Res. **7**(3), 1116–1119 (2020). www.jetir.org. ISSN-2349-5162
6. Buck, J.W., Perugini, S., Nguyen, T.V.: Natural language, mixed-initiative personal assistant agents. In: ACM International Conference Proceeding Series, no. 1 (2018). https://doi.org/10.1145/3164541.3164609
7. Aditya, K., Biswadeep, G., Kedar, S., Sundar, S.: Virtual personal assistance. IOP Conf. Ser. Mater. Sci. Eng. **263**(5), 0–5 (2017). https://doi.org/10.1088/1757-899X/263/5/052022
8. Liu, Y., Stiles, N.R., Meister, M.: Augmented reality powers a cognitive assistant for the blind. Elife **7**, 1–17 (2018). https://doi.org/10.7554/eLife.37841
9. Garzotto, F., Torelli, E., Vona, F., Aruanno, B.: HoloLearn: learning through mixed reality for people with cognitive disability. In: Proceedings - 2018 IEEE International Conference on Artificial Intelligence and Virtual Reality, AIVR 2018, pp. 189–190 (2019). https://doi.org/10.1109/AIVR.2018.00042
10. Garzotto, F., Gelsomini, M., Occhiuto, D., Matarazzo, V., Messina, N.: Wearable immersive virtual reality for children with disability: a case study Franca Garzotto work in progress/late breaking. In: IDC, pp. 478–483 (2017). https://doi.org/10.1145/3078072.3084312
11. Vona, F., Torelli, E., Beccaluva, E., Garzotto, F.: Exploring the potential of speech-based virtual assistants in mixed reality applications for people with cognitive disabilities. In: ACM International Conference Proceeding Series (2020). https://doi.org/10.1145/3399715.3399845
12. Bozgeyikli, L., Raij, A., Katkoori, S., Alqasemi, R.: A survey on virtual reality for individuals with autism spectrum disorder: design considerations. IEEE Trans. Learn. Technol. **11**(2), 133–151 (2018). https://doi.org/10.1109/TLT.2017.2739747
13. Radianti, J., Majchrzak, T.A., Fromm, J., Wohlgenannt, I.: A systematic review of immersive virtual reality applications for higher education: design elements, lessons learned, and research agenda. Comput. Educ. **147**, 103778 (2020). https://doi.org/10.1016/j.compedu.2019.103778
14. Gawrychowski, P., Starikovskaya, T.: Streaming dictionary matching with mismatches. In: Leibniz International Proceedings in Informatics. LIPIcs, vol. 128, no. 21, pp. 1–15 (2019). https://doi.org/10.4230/LIPIcs.CPM.2019.21
15. Clifford, R., Kociumaka, T., Porat, E.: The streaming k-mismatch problem. In: Proceedings of the Thirtieth Annual ACM-SIAM Symposium on Discrete Algorithms, pp. 1106–1125. Society for Industrial and Applied Mathematics, Philadelphia, PA (2019)

Emerging Mobile Technologies

Performance Evaluation of Self-adaptive Rectenna for RF Energy Harvesting Applications

Eman M. Abdelhady[1]([✉]) and Osama M. Dardeer[2]

[1] Modern Academy for Engineering and Technology, Cairo, Egypt
eng_emanabdelhady@yahoo.com
[2] Microstrip Department, Electronics Research Institute, Nozha, Cairo, Egypt

Abstract. This article presents a self-adaptive rectenna for RF energy harvesting applications. The receiving antenna is a slotted rectangular patch antenna with partial ground plane for operating at 2.45 GHz (IEEE 802.11 b&g). The amount of received power by the antenna depends mainly on the type of harvesting, either ambient or dedicated RF energy harvesting situation. As a consequence, a rectifier circuit is designed with two input parallel paths in order to have the ability to operate at both low and high input power levels. The automatic power distribution scenario is utilized in order to maintain high radio frequency-direct current (RF-DC) power conversion efficiency (PCE) over a wide range of RF input power. The complete rectenna is simulated taking into account the mismatch in both antenna and rectifier sections. The PCE of the proposed rectenna is kept above 50% over 30 dBm of RF input power (from −6.3 dBm to 23.7 dBm).

Keywords: Omnidirectional antenna · Power Conversion Efficiency (PCE) · Automatic power distribution · Self-adaptive rectenna · RF energy harvesting

1 Introduction

The available RF energy in the surroundings will be wasted if it is not decoded and captured by a suitable receiver [1]. The two main classifications in this field are ambient and dedicated RF energy harvesting. The available energy sources in the public places, restaurants, shopping centers, and so on can represent ambient RF energy harvesting scenarios at which the harvested power is low. On the other case, when a dedicated RF source is used this is considered dedicated RF energy harvesting scenario at which the harvested power is high. Different advantages can be exploited using suitable rectenna designs to capture the available RF energy depending on the destined application.

Different rectenna designs have been reported in [2–5] for RF energy harvesting applications. Some of these designs are self-adaptive and some are not adaptive. Both circularly and dual linearly polarized 2 × 2 antenna arrays are utilized in [2] for RF energy harvesting IoT system. In [3], the rectenna adopts a rectifier configuration at which two shunt diodes are used between the blocking capacitor and the series diode in order to maintain adaptive impedance tuning and adaptive power flow. A reconfigurable rectenna with an adaptive matching stub is proposed in [4] at which a depletion-mode field-effect transistor (FET) is installed and used as a switch. The performance of a self-adaptive rectifier is evaluated in [5], but the antenna design and effect are not taken into consideration.

In this paper, the performance of a self-adaptive rectenna is investigated. An omnidirectional antenna is adopted as the receiving antenna. The advantages and methods for designing both linear and circular omnidirectional antennas are stated in [6–9]. The mismatch in both the antenna and rectifier sections are taken into consideration in this paper. Automatic power distribution is adopted by using two input paths for the rectifier section. The PCE and input reflection coefficient (S11) are calculated for a wide range of RF input power adopting different rectifier topologies in the adaptive rectifier paths. The paper is organized as follows. Section 2 describes the design of the proposed receiving antenna. The design of the rectifying circuit is explained in Sect. 3. Section 4 is devoted to results of the proposed self-adaptive rectenna. The paper is concluded in Sect. 5.

2 Receiving Antenna Design

The geometry of the proposed rectangular slotted patch antenna with partial ground plane is illustrated in Fig. 1. The antenna is designed on an FR4 substrate with a dielectric constant of 4.3, thickness (h) of 1.6 mm, and loss tangent of 0.025. The antenna is fed by a microstrip feeding line at the center of the structure. The microstrip line has a 50 ohms characteristic impedance with a width W_f. The size of the antenna is 27 × 34.3 ×

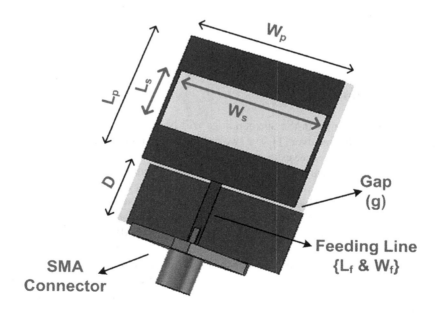

Perspective View

Fig. 1. Geometry of the proposed rectangular slotted patch antenna.

1.6 mm^3. A simple rectangular patch antenna is designed, then a rectangular slot is etched from this patch to present the main resonating mode for the proposed antenna. The slot dimensions are half-wavelength resonator at 2.45 GHz resonant frequency. In order to provide omnidirctional radiation pattern a partial ground plane is adopted as shown in Fig. 1. The other dimensions of the antenna are listed in Table 1.

Table 1. Dimensions of the proposed antenna (Unit: mm).

L_f	9	L_p	18
W_f	2.4	W_p	34.3
D	8.6	L_s	8
g	0.4	W_s	32.7

Extensive simulation trials have been carried out in order to reach the matching and omnidirectional pattern charcterisrics for the the proposed slotted patch antenna. The partial ground plane dimensions as well as the gap between the ground and the patch are the main factors which greatly affect the antenna results. The dimensions of the proposed antenna are optimized using the Particle Swarm Optimization (PSO) in the CST simulator. The proposed antenna has been investigated using two different simulators for better validation. The compared S11 characteristic of the proposed antenna is displayed in Fig. 2. The reflection coefficients are obtained by using two simulation software packages; Computer Simulation Technology Microwave Studio (CST MS) and High Frequency Structure Simulator (HFSS) for better validation to the design and theory. It is illustrated from Fig. 2 that the achieved frequency band (for |S11| < − 10 dB) is 2.33–2.55 GHz (with bandwidth of 220 MHz) for the 2.45 GHz ISM and WiFi frequency band.

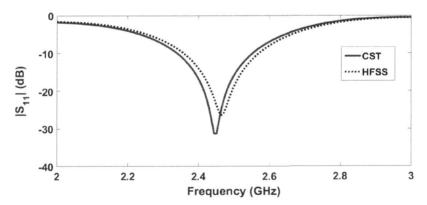

Fig. 2. Reflection coefficient of the proposed antenna.

In order to clearly demonstrate the antenna operation, the surface current distribution is monitored and portrayed in Fig. 3. Note that the current is mainly concentrated at the rectangular slot edges at 2.45 GHz with maximum at the sides and minimum at the center which proves that the slot acts as a half-wavelength resonator. The designed antenna radiation patterns are examined by numerical simulations. The 3-D radiation pattern is shown in Fig. 4(a). In addition, 2-simulation results for both the XZ-pane and YZ-plane radiation characteristics are illustrated in Fig. 4(b) and (c). The antenna radiates in almost all directions except the Y-axis direction which is termed an omnidirectional radiation pattern. The antenna gain variation is illustrated in Fig. 5. At 2.45 GHz, the achieved gain, directivity, and radiation efficiency are 3.34 dBi, 4.027 dBi, and 85.46%, respectively. It is worthy to note that the antenna is suitable for RF energy harvesting applications since it can collect signals from various directions simultaneously, when it is used as the receiving antenna in a rectenna structure.

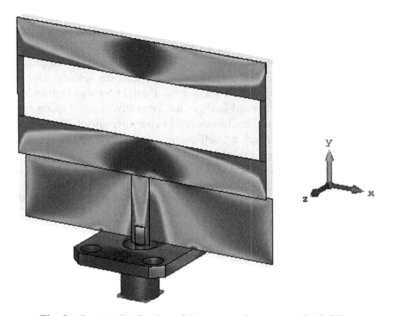

Fig. 3. Current distribution of the proposed antenna at 2.45 GHz.

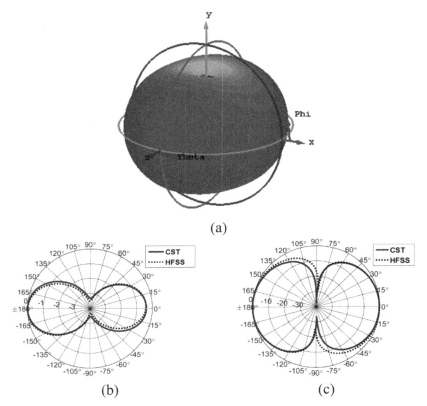

Fig. 4. 3D and 2D radiation patterns of the proposed antenna at 2.45 GHz; (a) 3D, (b) XZ-palne, and (c) YZ-plane.

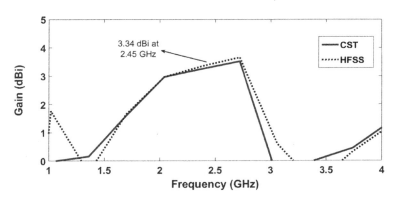

Fig. 5. Gain of the proposed slotted patch antenna.

3 Rectifying Circuit Design

The performance of RF harvester depends on many parameters such as RF-DC power conversion efficiency (PCE) of rectifier stage, the sensitivity of harvester, operation distance, and output power. The most challengeable target in designing is to enhance (PCE), which measures the ratio between harvester DC output power measured on the load terminals (P_{out}) and harvested power by the antenna (P_{in}) [10].

Improving the PCE maximum point value at a specific RF input power is one method to enhance PCE. The other method by keeping an acceptable PCE value over a wide range of RF input power which is more vital for RF harvesting applications. In diode rectifiers, the diode saturation point restricts PCE to be extended over a wide range of input power.

The adaptive rectifier design was started by Eman et al. in [5] to extend the dynamic range with PCE over 50%. It uses different diode topologies and packages to exploit their effect difference on the PCE curve. The design depends on an automatic power distribution method to route the input power automatically between two paths. The first path has a shunt diode rectifier cell with high efficiency in low input power levels. The second path uses three voltage doubler rectifier cells connected parallel to operate efficiently in high input power levels. The design is simulated adopting power source with 50 Ω internal resistance instead of connecting actual antenna, this paper evaluates the adaptive rectenna design by connecting the designed antenna proposed in Sect. 2 as illustrated in Fig. 6.

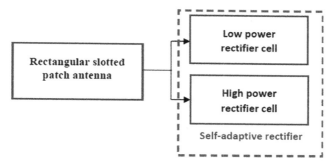

Fig. 6. The overall proposed rectenna adopting slotted patch antenna and self-adaptive rectifier.

4 Rectenna System Performance

This part introduces the simulation results of the overall rectenna using the Advanced Design System (ADS) software. The proposed slotted patch antenna is imported to ADS and connected to the adaptive rectifier input instead of the power source. The simulated S11 characteristics of overall rectenna are shown in Fig. 7. The S11 indicates rectenna input reflection coefficient without using an actual antenna, while S11$_{rectenna}$ indicates rectifier input reflection coefficient with using the proposed antenna, a slight difference is observed but the input reflection coefficient kept below −10 dB over more than 40 dBm of RF input power.

PCE in Fig. 8 shows a stable performance when the proposed slotted patch antenna is connected to the adaptive rectifier. The overall rectenna PCE is kept above 50% over 30 dBm of RF input power (from −6.3 dBm to 23.7 dBm). The achieved performance in case of using the proposed antenna makes the adaptive rectenna design a promising technique for RF energy harvesting applications.

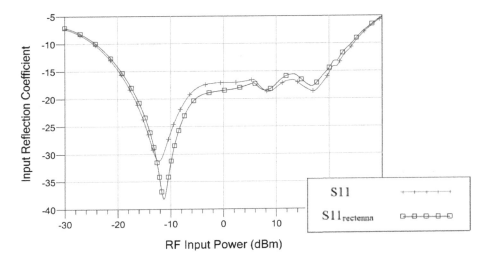

Fig. 7. Reflection coefficient characteristics of single rectifier compared with overall self–adaptive rectenna.

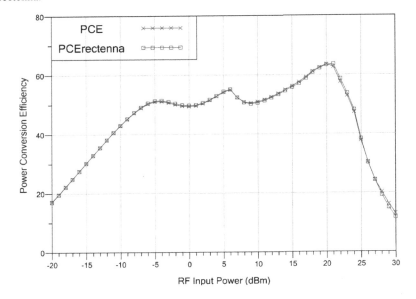

Fig. 8. Power conversion efficiency of single rectifier compared with overall self–adaptive rectenna.

5   Conclusion

This article presented a self-adaptive rectenna for RF energy harvesting applications. A slotted rectangular patch antenna with partial ground plane was used as the receiving antenna. The achieved frequency band (for $|S_{11}| < -10$ dB) was 2.33–2.55 GHz (with bandwidth of 220 MHz) for the 2.45 GHz band. An omnidirectional pattern was achieved with gain, directivity, and radiation efficiency were 3.34 dBi, 4.027 dBi, and 85.46%, respectively. Two input paths were adopted in the rectifier circuit to operate at both low and high input power levels to represent self-adaptive rectenna. The overall rectenna performance was evaluated considering the mismatch in both antenna and rectifier sections. The rectifier topologies adopted in this rectenna are the shunt diode model to deal with low RF input power, and voltage doubler topology to deal with high RF input power. The PCE is kept above 50% over 30 dBm variation in the rectifier dynamic range.

References

1. Dardeer, O.M., Elsadek, H.A., Abdallah, E.A., Elhennawy, H.M.: 2×2 circularly polarized antenna array with equal phases for RF energy harvesting in IoT system. IEEE Wirel. Power Transfer Conf. (WPTC) **2019**, 604–607 (2019). https://doi.org/10.1109/WPTC45513.2019.9055536
2. Eltresy, N.A., et al.: RF energy harvesting IoT system for museum ambience control with deep learning. Sens. J. **19**(20), 1–25 (2019)
3. Alja'afreh, S.S., Song, C., Huang, Y., Xing, L., Xu, Q.: A dual-port, dual-polarized and wideband slot rectenna for ambient RF energy harvesting. In: 2020 14th European Conference on Antennas and Propagation (EuCAP) 2020, pp. 1–5 (2020). https://doi.org/10.23919/EuCAP48036.2020.9135441
4. Lu, P., Huang, K.M., Yang, Y., Cheng, F., Wu, L.: Frequency-reconfigurable rectenna with an adaptive matching stub for microwave power transmission. IEEE Antennas Wirel. Propag. Lett. **18**(5), 956–960 (2019). https://doi.org/10.1109/LAWP.2019.2906671
5. Abdelhady, E.M., Abdelkader, H.M., Al-Awamry, A.A.: Self-adaptive rectenna with high efficiency over a wide dynamic range for RF energy harvesting applications. J. Commun. **16**(2), 67–75 (2021)
6. Cai, X., Sarabandi, K.: Broadband omni-directional circularly polarized antenna based on vertically and horizontally polarized elements. IEEE Int. Sympos. Antennas Propag. (APSURSI) **2016**, 1793–1794 (2016). https://doi.org/10.1109/APS.2016.7696603
7. Yektakhah, B., Sarabandi, K.: A wideband circularly polarized omnidirectional antenna based on excitation of two orthogonal circular TE_{21} modes. IEEE Trans. Antennas Propag. **65**(8), 3877–3888 (2017). https://doi.org/10.1109/TAP.2017.2714019
8. Zeng, H., An, J., Yu, Z., Wang, S.: Implementation method for circularly polarized omnidirectional antenna. Proced. Comput. Sci. **154**, 477–480 (2019)
9. Gu, H., Ge, L., Zhang, J.: A dual-band dual-polarized omnidirectional antenna. Front. Phys. **8**, 1–5 (2020)
10. Tran, L.-G., Cha, H.-K., Park, W.-T.: RF power harvesting: a review on designing methodologies and applications monitoring. Micro Nano Syst. Lett. **5**, 14 (2017)

Principles and Application of Mobile Cloud Computing in Payments and Health Care Solution

Barituka Barthy Murphy and Bunakiye R. Japheth[✉]

Department of Computer Science, Niger Delta University, Wilberforce Island Bayelsa State, Amassoma, Nigeria
{tukamurphy,bunakiye.japheth}@ndu.edu.ng

Abstract. In an attempt to curtail and prevent the spread of Covid-19 infection, social distancing has been adopted globally as a precautionary measure. Statistics shows that 75% of appointments most especially in the health sector are being handled by telephone since the outbreak of the Covid-19 pandemic. Currently most patients access health care services in real time from any part of the World through the use of Mobile devices. With an exponential growth of mobile applications and cloud computing the concept of mobile cloud computing is becoming a future platform for different forms of services for smartphones hence the challenges of low battery life, storage space, mobility, scalability, bandwidth, protection and privacy on mobile devices has being improved by combining mobile devices and cloud computing which rely on wireless networks to create a new concept and infrastructure called Mobile Cloud Computing (MCC). The introduction of Mobile cloud computing (MCC) has been identified as a promising approach to enhance healthcare services, with the advent of cloud computing, computing as a utility has become a reality thus a patient only pays for what he uses. This paper, presents a systematic review on the concept of cloud computing in mobile Environment; Mobile Payments and Mobile Healthcare Solutions in various healthcare applications, it describes the principles, challenges and opportunity this concept proffers to the health sector to determine how it can be harnessed is also discussed.

Keywords: Cloud computing · Mobile cloud computing · Mobile Health · Mobile payment · Security and privacy

1 Introduction

The COVID-19 pandemic is spreading rapidly and widely throughout the world, and as a result of its contagious nature the demand for online services has grown tremendously. There has been an up surge in the demand for online services most especially in the health sector where medical personnel are obliged to convert their day to day activities electronically and online. Research conducted by the American Medical Association found that most physicians saw an enormous advantage in using mobile device during the pandemic period. Consequently, the introduction of mobile technology in the

G. Salvendy and J. Wei (Eds.): HCII 2022, LNCS 13337, pp. 399–407, 2022.
https://doi.org/10.1007/978-3-031-05014-5_33

health sector had improved previously slow-growing areas in the health sector such as telemedicine and Ehealth. The health sector generates significant amounts of data daily, hence democratizing and securing access to this information is important therefore MCC in the health sector offers mobile healthcare delivery access to resources such as Electronic Health Record (EHR) and others medical services that are available on demand through computing infrastructure, applications and share, transmit, and process these data efficiently to be delivered to users as a service wherever and whenever it is needed on the clouds rather than the old traditional standalone application on local servers. Mobile cloud computing (MCC) has been identified as a promising approach to enhance healthcare services, with the advent of cloud computing, computing as a utility has become a reality thus one only pays for what he uses. In mobile cloud computing the cloud performs the heavy lifting of computing-intensive tasks and stores huge amounts of data.

This implies that data storage and processing are taken to a remote cloud outside of mobile devices hence mobile cloud computing (MCC) is known as an auspicious concept that presents a platform that provides better quality and rich computational resources. Mobile cloud computing in medical application will minimize the limitations of traditional medical treatment such as medical errors, security, privacy and small physical storage. The health sector generates significant amounts of data daily, democratizing and securing access to this information is important hence MCC in the health sector offers mobile healthcare delivery access to resources such as Electronic Health Record (EHR) and others medical services that are available on demand through computing infrastructure, applications and share, transmit, and process these data efficiently to be delivered to users as a service wherever and whenever it is needed on the clouds rather than the old traditional standalone application on local servers. Other advantages include Real-time automated analytics based on artificial intelligence routines and machine learning algorithms and promoted cooperation.

Although the concept of mobile cloud computing in the health sector seems so promising there are several factors such as loss of data governance, poor safety standards, user distrust of provided security issues include data bottlenecks, resource constraints, unpredictable performance, data locks and critical bugs in large-scale distributed cloud systems that affects MCC performance and may result in a catastrophic consequences in healthcare. The rest of the paper is presented as follows. Section 2 presents mobile cloud computing and healthcare Sect. 3 highlights the principles of mobile cloud computing Sect. 4 presents mobile cloud computing Architecture Sect. 5 highlights the opportunity and challenges of mobile cloud computing. Section 6 concludes this paper.

2   Mobile Cloud Computing and Healthcare

Cloud computing enables access to information stored from any location at any time, that can be used by any individual or organizations to increase productivity performance and drastically reduce cost [5]. NIST (National Institute of Standards and Technology, USA) defined Cloud computing as "a concept that enables a convenient, ubiquitous and provides computing resources through a network and server' [6]. Mobile Cloud Computing is the integration of cloud computing and mobile devices and harnessing the unlimited services offered by the cloud through mobile devices [7]. This implies that in

MCC capital cost and management is reduced as a result of network-connected resources shared to maximize their utilization. MCC healthcare applications can be classified into Imaging Information Applications, Biosignal and Telemonitoring Processing and Electronic Health Record.

A. ELECTRONIC HEALTH RECORD (EHR). An Electronic Health Record (EHR) is used electronically to collect and manage patient's health information by hospitals. This information includes patient's allegeries, vital sign, medication and patient's medical history. [2] reported on Electronic health record and its adoption by MCC and today various applications have been designed to use e-Health data. [3] focused on the integration of MCC and e-healthcare records and how these records can be secured in the MCC environment.

[4] were concerned by the limitations of wearable devices in MCC and suggested that an offline ciphertexts be generated when accessing polices and data.

[4] raised the issue of security in the cloud most especially in a case were voluminous data are stored by the cloud and stated their fears about cloud security issues in Personal Health Record (PHR) access. [4] presented an encryption-based paring method that could improve protection and accessibility of the user. [5] studied Electronic Medical Record (EMR) and its implementation in the cloud and highlighted the need for the integration of several data into a single platform and provides a similar accessible user interface.

B. Medical Imaging Storage Technologies. Picture Archiving and Communication System (PACS) is a medical imaging technology tool used to transmit and store images and relevant clinical report digitally in a secured manner. As a result of the growth of digital medical images throughout the healthcare sector the need for data analysis of images is very important [6]. [7] designed adaptive-self approach which offers a high-resolution medical image transmitted and retrieved in a reliable way over a network.

[8] presented a mobile cloud medical image administration system, which offer patients and physicians accessibility to medical data.[9] proposed a secured MCC infrastructure for the storage and transmission of data [10] develop an MCC storage system which can effectively manage medical images and health records of patients.

C. Biosignal Processing and Telemonitoring. Bioprocessing processing and Medical telemonitoring provides a platform that enhances the growth of health care services and reduces medical costs. [11] went on to say that bioprocessing creates an enabling environment for healthcare services no matter the distance this implies that it processes, collects, analyses and uses the information collected. [16] highlighted an MCC ECG telemonitoring technique adopted for children with mental disorder. [14] designed an MCC system that enable medical personnel such as doctors, nurses and to interact effectively in healthcare service provision. [15] designed an MCC that provides emergency through local medical personnel to patients. [13] proposed MCC healthcare system to analysze and capture real time biomedical signals (such as Blood pressure and ECG) from users located in different locations. [17] opined that MCC overcomes the limitations associated with the use of mobile devices such as CPU power and memory size in performing task which involves lots of time and energy thereby enhancing the benefits and capabilities of mobile devices. [18] highlighted another benefit of MCC by using multimedia applications as an example. Mobile cloud computing resolves the challenges of mobile devices by storing large multimedia files on the cloud that can be available to mobile users whenever a request is made hence resulting in a better performance. MCC enable patients to be monitored in real time from any part of the world and at any time.

Medical telemonitoring can be referred to the process of collecting biosignals from the human body, information gotten from this process can be used in monitoring and providing a better clinical diagnosis [22]. [19] presented an Electrocardiogram (ECG) measurement system which was created based on a mobile cloud infrastructure, to efficiently report health issues for elderly people. [20] proposed a mobile cloud vital sign detection system which stored and extracted user data, characteristics and history for each individual user under different circumstances, however when there is an emergency an alert would be reported. MCC have also been adopted and utilized for different kind of diseases and diagnosis [22]. Many researchers have said that medical telemonitoring improves healthcare efficiency and reduces medical costs [15].

3   Principles of Mobile Computing

MCC Mobile cloud computing combines mobile computing, cloud computing, and mobile Internet into one solution. It can be defined as the availability of cloud computing services in a mobile setting. It combines the benefits of all three technologies and is thus referred to as mobile cloud computing. Mobile cloud computing is a novel computing model in which data processing and storage are relocated from mobile devices to powerful and centralized cloud computing platform which can be accessible on mobile devices via wireless connections and web browsers.

This is similar to cloud computing, but the client side has been enhanced to make it mobile-friendly, but the core concept remains the same MCC can be split into cloud computing and mobile computing. Mobile user sends a request to the cloud via a web browser or desktop application, and the cloud's infrastructural managerial component allocates resources to the request and lunch a connection, while mobile cloud computing's monitoring and calculating functions are implemented to ensure QoS until the connection is established.

4   Mobile Cloud Computing Architecture

Mobile healthcare (m-healthcare) was developed to provide easy accessibility to mobile healthcare users to the resources such as (e.g. patient electronic health records) and provide a variety of distributed services. MCC is applied to healthcare to limits the errors such as small storage, medical errors and security of the traditional medical applications [23]. Mobile Cloud Computing is seen as "an infrastructure where data is been processed and stored outside of the mobile device" [24].

In [25] MCC is seen as a new model for mobile applications: "which is moved to a powerful and centralized computing platform in the cloud" (Fig. 1).

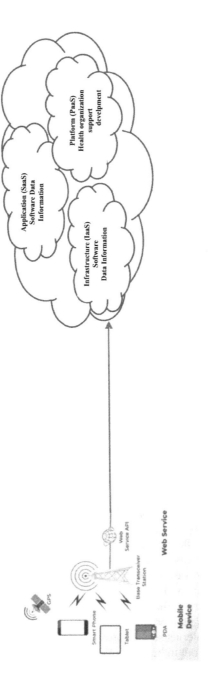

Fig. 1. Mobile cloud computing architecture

5 Opportunities and Challenges of Mobile Cloud Computing in Health Care

Mobile Cloud Computing require huge amounts of communication and computational resources which involves access to necessary health information anywhere and at any time hence the need for networked healthcare [15]. Although Mobile Cloud Computing offers great benefits, there are still some limitations such as data storage on the cloud, and protection of user's privacy from unauthorized access and from malicious attacks [27].

- Collaboration

Collaboration entails sharing of data. MCC has made data sharing much simpler and easier to achieve. MCC enable medical records to be remotely shared securely with important healthcare providers such as doctors and pharmacists from any location in the world real time. MCC also offers a platform for conferencing and updates on patient current health situations making MCC an ideal partner for healthcare personnel.

- Cost

MCC offers a platform through which services are paid for on the go. This implies that a patient only pays for the services they use.

5.1 Security Challenges of Mobile Cloud Computing in Health Care

MCC guarantees security because cloud service providers such as Azure and AWS used several protection n techniques such as customer-controlled encryption, network fireball and take precautionary measures to adhere with privacy regulations such as GDPR and HIPAA []. MCC has the capacity to raise alarm when there is a malicious activity. However, Covid- 19 and social distancing has generated voluminous amount of data most especially in the health sector where most people with little or no idea about information security issues prefer making consultation or working from home rather than going to the hospital. As shown in Fig. 2, the Security challenges of MCC-based healthcare applications could be categorized into Application, Data privacy, Internet Service Provider, CCE and Personal devices.

The use of MCC for data collection during the pandemic has been very phenomenal in curbing the deadly coronavirus disease and also discovering a medication that can eradicate the disease, however, vast majority of patients would rather prefer consulting from home which has led so many into to using their personal devices to transfer and also access data from the Internet, these methods may not be secured enough because data can be copied or hacked in the process.

The demand by users on Internet service providers (ISPs) as a result of the pandemic has been huge and has turned out to be a major challenge for Internet service providers (ISPs). [31] reported that the use of the internet in some European countries was up to 50%. As traffic reached a peak of 30% most ISPs in the UK had to relax data limit on

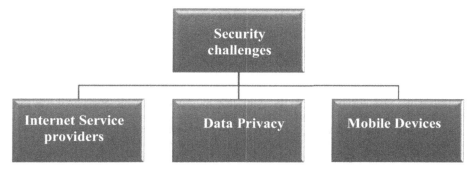

Fig. 2. Types of mobile cloud computing challenges in the health care

some of their internet platform in order to accommodate millions of Britons learning or working from home which resulted in ISPs downsizing on the quality of streaming device a typical example is the case of Netflix an online media platform famous for entertainment and streaming movies, prior to the Covid-19 era aired their videos using high definition because of the downsizing most Netflix videos were played in standard who had to air their video in standard [32].

5.2 Application Challenges

The issue of social distancing made learning or working from home inevitable however this challenge led to evolutional social media application that enable people from various location and at any time communicate as if they were together. [31] highlighted the need for a remote collaboration tools which enable a collective group of people working together without being physically together. virtual meetings and virtual work have become the best way to work and interact from home a typical example of work apps are Zoom, Ding talk and WeChat Work [32]. As a result of the rapid growth of work application it has been a major target for hackers as most of these applications has be hacked and pirated due to the security faults in the application. In January 2020, America's Zoom jumped from No. 180 to No. 28 at the end of February 2020 in terms of installs and downloads [32].

5.3 Personal Devices

Majority of those working from home barely understand the security issues surrounding the use of personal devices. Personal devices such as laptops, tablet and personal which hasn't been in use for a while might require an antivirus or an update for the operating system before it could be used on line. Cybercriminals have malicious software that tablets unsecured mobile devices to and gain access to vital information on these devices [32].

6   Conclusion

The application of cloud computing in healthcare seems promising as it offers flexibility, scalability, cutting down medical cost as computing as a utility has become a reality allowing a patients pay for what he uses and empowers global collaboration in the health sector which in turn can positively impact the health care in numerous way.

References

1. Olabiyisi, O.S., Fagbola, T.M., Babatunde, R.S.: An Exploratory Study of Cloud and Ubiquitous Computing Systems
2. Lo'ai, A.T., Mehmood, R., Benkhlifa, E., Song, H.: Mobile cloud computing model and big data analysis for healthcare applications. IEEE Access **4**, 6171–6180 (2016)
3. Liu, C.-H., Lin, F.-Q., Chen, C.-S., Chen, T.-S.: Design of secure access control scheme for personal health record-based cloud healthcare service. Secur. Commun. Netw. **8**(7), 1332–1346 (2015)
4. Lomotey, R.K., Nilson, J., Mulder, K., Wittmeier, K., Schachter, C., Deters, R.: Mobile medical data synchronization on cloud-powered middleware platform. IEEE Trans. Services Comput. **9**(5), 757–770 (2016)
5. Estuar, M.R., et al.: eHealth TABLET: a developing country perspective in managing the development and deployment of a mobile-cloud electronic medical record for local government units. In: Proc. IEEE 15th Int. Conf. Mobile Data Manage., vol. 1, pp. 313–316, July 2014
6. Somasundaram, M., Gitanjali, S., Govardhani, T., Priya, G.L., Sivakumar, R.:Medical image data management system in mobile cloud computing environment. In: Proc. Int. Conf. Signal, Image Process. Appl. (ICSIPA). KualaLumpur, Malaysia: Academic, pp. 11–15 (2011)
7. http://csrc.nist.gov/publications/nistpubs/800-145/SP800-145
8. Stantchev, V., Barnawi, A., Ghulam, S., Schubert, J., Tamm, G.: Smart items, fog and cloud computing as enablers of servitization in healthcare. Sensors Transducers **185**(2), 121 (2015)
9. Teng, C.-C., Green, C., Johnson, R., Jones, P., Treasure, C.: Mobile ultrasound with DICOM and cloud connectivity. In: Proceedings IEEE-EMBS Int. Conf. Biomed. Health Informat., Jan. 2012, pp. 667–670
10. Doukas, C., Pliakas, T., Maglogiannis, I.: Mobile healthcare information management utilizing cloud computing and Android OS. In: Proceedings of Annual International Conference IEEE Eng. Med. Biol., pp. 1037–1040, August/September 2010
11. Penzel, T., Kesper, K., Becker, H.F.: Biosignal monitoring and recording. In: Zieliński, K., Duplaga, M., Ingram, D. (eds.) Information Technology Solutions for Healthcare. Health Informatics. Springer, London (2006). https://doi.org/10.1007/1-84628-141-5_13
12. Abawajy, J.H., Hassan, M.M.: 'Federated Internet of Things and cloud computing pervasive patient health monitoring system.' IEEE Commun. Mag. **55**(1), 48–53 (Jan. 2017)
13. Džaferović, E., Vrtagić, S., Bandić, L., Kevric, J., Subasi, A., Qaisar, S.M.: Cloud-based mobile platform for EEG signal analysis. In: Proceedings of 5th Int Conf. Electron. Devices, Syst. Appl. (ICEDSA), pp. 1–4, December 2016
14. Jemal, H., Kechaou, Z., Ayed, M.B., Alimi, A.M.: Cloud computing and mobile devices based system for healthcare application. In: Proceedings of IEEE International Symposium Technology Soc. (ISTAS), pp. 1–5, November 2015
15. Venkatesan, C., Karthigaikumar, P., Satheeskumaran, S.: 'Mobile cloud computing for ECG telemonitoring and real-time coronary heart disease risk detection.' Biomed. Signal Process. Control **44**, 138–145 (2018)
16. Pusey, S.S., Camargo, J.E., Díaz, G.M.: Mobile cloud computing as an alternative for monitoring child mental disorders. In: Proceedings of International Conference Smart Health, 2016, pp. 31–42 (2016)

17. Doukas, C., Pliakas, T., Maglogiannis, I.: Mobile healthcare information management unitizing cloud computing and android OS. In: Annual International Conference of the IEEE on Engineering in Medicine and Biology Society (EMBC), pp. 1037–1040 (2010)

18. Varshney, U.: Pervasive healthcare and wireless health monitoring. J. Mob. Netw. Appl. **12**(2–3), 113–127 (2007)

19. Fong, E.-M., Chung, W.-Y.: Mobile cloud-computing-based health care service by noncontact ECG monitoring. Sensors **13**(12), 16451–16473 (2013)

20. Sung, W.-T., Chen, J.-H., Chang, K.-W.: Mobile physiological measurement platform with cloud and analysis functions implemented via IPSO. IEEE Sensors J. **14**(1), 111–123 (2014)

21. Cardellini, V., et al.: A game-theoretic approach to computation offloading in mobile cloud computing. Math. Program. **157**(2), 421–449 (2016)

22. Karaca, Y., Moonis, M., Zhang, Y.-D., Gezgez, C.: 'Mobile cloud computing based stroke healthcare system.' Int. J. Inf. Manage. **45**, 250–261 (2019)

23. Kopec, D., Kabir, M.H., Reinharth, D., Rothschild, O., Castiglione, J.A.: Human errors in medical practice: systematic classification and reduction with automated information systems. J. Med. Syst. **27**(4), 297–313 (200)

24. Ali, M.: Green cloud on the horizon. In: Proceedings of the 1st International Conference on Cloud Computing (CloudCom), Manila, pp. 451–459 (2009)

25. White Paper: Mobile Cloud Computing Solution Brief. AEPONA (2010)

26. Aceto, L., Morichetta, A., Tiezzi, F.: Decision support for mobile cloud computing applications via model checking. In: Proceedings of 3rd IEEE International Conference Mobile Cloud Computing, Services, Enginerring (MobileCloud), pp. 199–204, March 2015

27. Lisa, B.A.: Hospital uses cloud computing to improve patient care and reduce costs. http://www.microsofteu/cloudcomputing/casestudies/hospitalusescloudcomputingtoimprovepati entcareandredu cecosts.aspx. Accessed 19 Feb 2022

28. Jemal, H., Zied, K., Mounir Ben, A.: "An enhanced healthcare system in mobile cloud computing environment" in Vietnam. J. Comput. Sci. **3**, 267–277 (2016)

29. Daily Mail Online, British broadband and mobile internet providers see a surge in data usage, February 2022. https://www.dailymail.co.uk/sciencetech/article-8130709/Britishbroadband-mobile-internet-providers-surge-data-usage.html

30. Independent, Coronavirus: vodafone, O2 and other networks struggle amid huge surge in traffic, February 2022. https://www.independent.co.uk/life-style/gadgetsand-tech/news/corona virus-vodafone-o2-talktalk-down-outage-dataa9411286.html

31. Zainal, N.Z., Hussin, H., Nazri, M.N.M.: Big data initiatives by governments–issues and challenges: a review. In: Proceedings of the 6th International Conference on Information and Communication Technology for the Muslim World, 2016, pp. 304–309 (2016)

32. Neowin, Malicious coronavirus tracking app for Android locks users out of their device, April 2020. https://www.neowin.net/news/maliciouscoronavirus-tracking-appfor-and roid-locks-users-out-of-their-device

A Mixed Reality-Based Framework for Blended Learning Environment

Javid Iqbal[1]([✉]), Su Mon Chit[1], and Jia Hou Chin[2]

[1] Institute of Computer Science and Digital Innovation (ICSDI), UCSI University, Kuala Lumpur, Malaysia
javid@ucsiuniversity.edu.my
[2] Institute of Actuarial Science and Data Analytics (IASDA), UCSI University, Kuala Lumpur, Malaysia

Abstract. The process of bridging the gap between reality and virtual data has been possible through exponential technologies such as Mixed Reality (MR), Augmented Reality (AR) and Virtual Reality (VR). MR has so far proffered numerous advantages ranging from communication, navigation, medical aid, data modelling, visualization, and education to remote accessibility across diverse platforms. This paper proposes a systematic framework for knowledge acquisition and synthesis through MR based constructivism learning theory. The methodology uses a bottom-up approach and is based upon the Dryfus modelling. The existing drawbacks of poor learning retention, interactive knowledge acquisition and synthesis are addressed based upon MR technology. The framework provides the basis for embedding MR technology into analyzing and enabling human practical knowledge, as well as extending the scope for knowledge acquisition to rediscover the learning process in educational environments. Furthermore, existing MR based solutions for learning theories are reviewed. The validation of the proposed framework is carried out using technology acceptance model. The real-time knowledge acquisition device embedded with MR technology is explored and enhanced to demonstrate the accuracy and efficacy of the proposed framework.

Keywords: Technology based learning · Blended learning · Mixed reality

1 Introduction

In view of Facebook metaverse transformation, the expectation of high usage traffic for exponential technologies like VR, AR and MR is bound to touch new heights in the next decades. These immersive technologies will embed and integrate IoT, cloud, edge, and fog computing to provide diverse applications and cross-platform end user products.

Therefore, a unified and systematic framework model should be considered as the primary research focus to address the existing research gaps and avoid conflicting issues. Hence, the aim of this study is to propose an MR-based framework for blended learning environment. Furthermore, the COVID-19 pandemic has created havoc across the globe, where all the countries are focusing on the availability of resources to mitigate and manage the consequences of the pandemic. Novel solutions should be made available to users who want to focus on controlling and communicating access remotely. These solutions will enable the remote access across diverse environments via a systematic approach involving the immersive technology of MR without the need for physical presence of people and eliminating the necessity for highly touched surfaces.

2   Overview of MR, VR and AR

A clear understanding of the effects of novel solutions to overcome the consequences of the pandemic is to be focused upon currently. Hence, many researchers are working on the discovery of new solutions in the fields of health care, remote learning, economics, and national security that have been affected by the pandemic. Among these solutions is a possible technology that will replace the direct involvement of people and to enable remote learning through MR based applications and devices. Both the AR and MR technologies have the ability of remote controlling and accessing from distant places using virtual interfaces. The VR technology enables partial or full immersion of users in a complete artificial digital environment. The AR technology arguments, or in other words, overlays virtual objects on the real-world environment. AR is basically real world enhanced with digital objects, whereas VR is fully immersion into the virtual digital environment. On the other hand, the MR technology does not only arguments virtual objects onto real-world environment, but also anchors and allows user to interact with those objects, thus enabling both real world and virtual environment interactions. The virtuality continuum taxonomy has been depicted in Fig. 1. The figure depicts the three exponential technologies and their related interactions to achieve the respective virtual worlds. The structure of the paper further comprises of Sect. 3 that describes the background study, which is then followed by framework insights description in Sect. 4 and conclusion in Sect. 5.

3   Background Study

3.1   Technology Driven Learning

The MR technology allows one to fetch real world bottle, play a virtual video game, connect to someone at a remote place virtually, smack a video game character with real world objects and communicate with the virtual objects across the virtual space. These technologies are taking up a much faster pace of development, which makes the differences between AR, VR and MR seems to be sleek and puzzling. The post pandemic scenario has changed the lives of millions of people across different countries in the world. It has made remote access, remote learning, and communication as one of the necessities to survive the collateral damage done by COVID-19. Although there is an emergence of such immersive technologies pre-COVID-19, but the implementation of these technologies in real time and the utilization across diverse platforms has started to boom rapidly only at post-COVID-19, with the purpose of getting back to normalcy while maintaining health safety protocols. VR is the most widely known technology. It provides either fully or partially immersive experience, which enables the users to enter a virtual environment. The VR headgear device allows the users to navigate digital worlds that comprising of images and audio, as well as manipulating the virtual objects using markers that are connected to a centralized console or computer. This methodology has enabled learning in a blended environment which is far more interesting. This unique learning experience can lead to greater learning retention rate. There are many research in the literature about VR based techniques and methods in the education sector. On the other hand, AR imposes digitally generated content onto the real-world environment. One of the major successes of AR technology implementations is the Pokémon Go game that kept the netizens intrigued by its popularity and excitement for distinctive digital world interaction. This technology keeps the real-world environment as the medium but embeds it with digital attributes structuring enhanced layers of insights, complementing the real environment. The educational field has witnessed several research contributions ranging from medical assistance to virtual classrooms and virtual educators for expertising in artistic skills. MR integrates both real world and digital elements together.

3.2 MR in Education Sector

In MR, there is anchoring, interaction and manipulation of both virtual and real-world entities and environments, with the aid of sophisticated futuristic sensing and imaging techniques. One can immerse into the surrounding world, while interacting with virtual world through wearable MR based headset. It enhances the virtual digitally manipulative environment with simultaneous focus on both real and virtual worlds, dissipating between respective concepts, thereby escalating the gaming and remote access experience to a whole new level. With the advancement in multimedia, 3D graphics, and digitalization, there are research about MR technology for surgery and patient education related applications [1]. In education sector, MR has been applied to understand the complex and inaccessible phenomena through the intriguing visualization attributes. For example, for the study of the tangibility of the organ relationships in human body, explanation about planned surgical procedures using virtual renditions of computerized holography was proposed [1]. MR has been manifested to enhance students' understanding of spatial space and holographic structure, leading to increased rate of conceptual learning retention. MR has the capability of providing learning space, affording a safe distributive digital training environment [2]. The efficiency of MR in enhancing the visualization and communication skills with respect to the aspect of construction has improved over the decades to the extend in which it is proven to be equally effective, if not more, as compared to traditional learning processes.

Blended learning is an innovation in education sector in the revolutionary era of digitalization. It is an ideal model for learning experiences using the AR, VR and MR technologies. Nowadays, educators and students are embracing the new norms of virtual training and the issues that crops up with it [3]. These avenues need to be explored and tested to enhance and improvise educational experiences for all users. The taxonomy for blended learning components with respect to the reality technologies has been depicted in Fig. 2. The usability, engagement, and effectiveness of therapeutic rehabilitation in 3D immersive digital environments increases with the game mechanism, graphical user interface and design metrics [4]. The visualization retreating technologies such as MR,

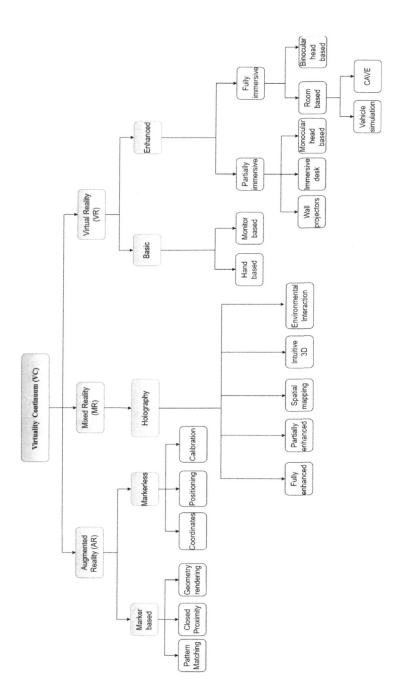

Fig. 1. Virtuality continuum-based taxonomy for digital world interactions.

VR, AR, and virtual stereomicroscopy provides improvised training methods and surgical workflow techniques for surgeons and medical students [5]. MR holds promising future by providing virtual improvisations to the imaginative vision, enabling a fully immersive environment for the user to have inherent communication with the anchored or superimposed digital information.

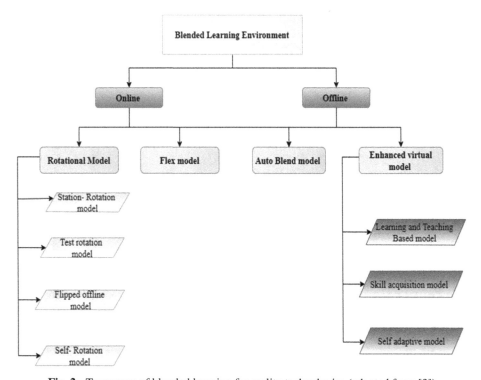

Fig. 2. Taxonomy of blended learning for reality technologies (adapted from [3])

3.3   Advantages of MR Over AR and VR

The technology of MR imparts content mastery, efficient communication, problem solving, self-directed training, critical analysis, and practical thinking in comparison to AR and VR [6]. It is essential to not only to examine whether the AR systems satisfy the real focus of education, but the systems should also be able to virtually supplement the learning process [7]. Furthermore, AR needs to undergo a more robust investigation for healthcare purposes as the subjective measures of medical procedural parameters are very limited or absent. The previous research contributions have provided many solutions to develop AR and VR applications based on cloud-based platforms [11, 18]. However, those solutions lack of a generalized and integrated model to tailor with the diverse nature of reality technologies. The MR technology is a promising direction for user interaction with data and it provides a rich experience when compared to AR and VR [8]. The research contribution in [9] presents the glasswork traditional craft in the form of MR installation enacting the gestures of a glass master holding a tool and getting rated on the accuracy and performance based on audiovisual feedback. The preliminary validation results have shown higher acceptance rate and improvised user interest for MR in comparison to AR or VR.

MR based immersive and interactive holograms influenced the users to have positive and effective learning experience. The presence and controlling of holograms with the sensory movement of touch, audio and visual improvised the learning flow of the students. Therefore, it was found that there was a direct correlation between immersive learning, highly calibrated information, with inclusion of skillful learning environment and flow of learning [10, 11]. Human activity tracking and recognition based on sensors have been widely employed due to the increasing utilization of sensing technologies, wearable devices, higher security, and privacy such as MR, in comparison to the visual based user movement recognition such as AR and VR [12].

With the advancements in the MR technology, the renditions between the representation of data on screens or other surfaces across the platform spaces become increasingly attention seeking and requires research focus. An overview of different data visualization states in MR followed by the facilitation of common visualization task has been explored in [13]. One of the challenges for those who learn arts using virtual environment is the lack of physical instruments, such as piano, during the training sessions, where there is a necessity to strike a balance between understanding theoretical concepts and practical knowledge acquisition. This can be well achieved using MR in comparison to AR or VR [14–16]. The MR immersive learning environments in assisting researchers and developers to consider improvised learning outcome, design principles and enhanced learning flow were discussed in [17]. The future research directions should focus on devising innovative MR based methods to explore the MR technology for increasing the quality of education and improvising the learning retention rate [19, 20].

4 Systematic Framework for MR Based Blended Learning Environment

The proposed framework followed a bottom-up approach based on Dreyfus skill acquisition model [21] and constructivism learning theory [22]. It forms the basis for embedding MR technology into enabling and improvising human practical knowledge to rediscover the learning process as depicted in Fig. 3.

The framework comprises of holographic data developed using unity engine, which is then communicated using HoloLens. This engine comprises of objects, MR toolkit, and web services (cloud/fog/computing architecture). The objects in the blended learning environment depicts the digital representation of the attributes and sensing technologies (visual and audio). Each object consists of classes that define functionality and workflow of the learning environment. The platforms in which the concept of blended learning are applied include virtual classrooms, learning/training studios, in-house practice areas along with intraprocedural parameters so that the framework works across diverse applications. The devices include Microsoft HoloLens, MR based headset, image markers

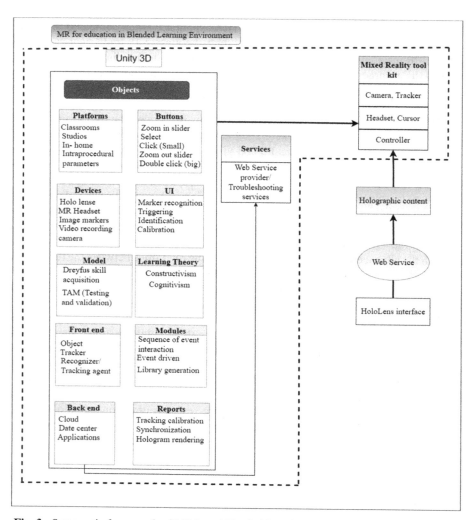

Fig. 3. Systematic framework of MR based blended learning environment (adapted from [2])

for movement rendition, cameras for recording audio and video output. The front end is the target object (user), tracker, recognizer or the tracking agent that can communicate with the holographic interface and allow for further interactions. The backend components are the centralized data center that perform the data processing and cloud-based applications that connect the device with web-based services. The buttons on the interface are utilized for the management, communication, and control of the holographic content through either the slider button or the click selection button based on the type of action being invoked. The user interface is designed and developed for the process of marker recognition, triggering of actions, identification of events and calibration of data for the information being fetched from the command center. The work modules of the framework consist of algorithms and C# programs for event sequence, interaction between objects, event driven procedural parameters and library generating functions. The report object provides data about the tracking calibration between the target object and holographic interface, synchronization between the events and information about hologram rendition.

The Microsoft HoloLens only allows and enables for the activation of objects through sensory gestures such as click or double click. To access the blended learning environment, the Holographic content needs to be activated in the HoloLens interface followed by connecting to the learning environment through the web services.

5 Conclusion and Future Work

The need for timely, efficient, and effective remote learning in the post COVID-19 times, has resulted in the rapid growth rate of MR technology adoption. The sensing and wearable technology assisted blended learning environment framework proposed in this paper is aimed to be developed, implemented, tested, and validated for user perception and acceptance rate as future work. The framework presented in this paper extends the scope of knowledge acquisition to reach new heights in remote learning process in blended environments.

The visually enhancing and interactive methodology for blended learning environment of MR-based training in the constructivism learning theory has been explored in this paper. With the advancement in the MR technology as well as the essence of skilful training, education will depend on the training tools and learning environment, in addition to the type of learning theories that are employed. The future of MR in the field of education and training has been envisioned to solve many existing technical challenges, but more importantly, it should also focus on creating a world-wide interest and excitement for MR based training thereby leading towards a revolutionary impact on the overall remote learning education platform.

Acknowledgement. This research is funded by UCSI University Research Excellence and Innovation Grant (REIG-ICSDI-2021/024).

References

1. Anton, E., Schuir, J., Teuteberg, F.: The force of habit: examining the status quo bias for using mixed reality in patient education. In: Proceedings of the 55th Hawaii International Conference on System Science, pp. 4248–4257 (2022)
2. Ogunseiju, O.O., Akanmu, A.A., Bairaktarova, D.: Mixed reality-based environment for learning sensing technology applications in construction. J. Inf. Technol. Constr. **26**(March), 863–885 (2021)
3. Kovalenko, V.V., Marienko, M.V., Sukhikh, A.S.: Use of augmented and virtual reality tools in a general secondary education institution in the context of blended learning. Inf. Technol. Learn. Tools **86**(6), 70–86 (2021)
4. Belinskiy, A.: Usability study mixed reality for upper body limb rehabilitation usability study mixed reality for upper body limb rehabilitation author , January (2022)

5. Torabinia, M., Caprio, A., Fenster, T.B., Mosadegh, B.: Single evaluation of use of a mixed reality headset for intra-procedural image-guidance during a mock laparoscopic myomectomy on an ex-vivo fibroid model. Appl. Sci. **12**, 2 (2022)

6. Southgate, E., Grant, S., Ostrowski, S., Norwood, A., Williams, M., Tafazoli, D.: School students creating a virtual reality learning resource for children (2022)

7. Brunzini, A., Papetti, A., Messi, D., Germani, M.: A comprehensive method to design and assess mixed reality simulations. Virt. Real. 0123456789 (2022). https://doi.org/10.1007/s10 055-022-00632-8

8. Elawady, M., Sarhan, A., Alshewimy, M.A.M.: Toward a mixed reality domain model for time-Sensitive applications using IoE infrastructure and edge computing (MRIoEF), no. 0123456789. Springer, US (2022). https://doi.org/10.1007/s11227-022-04307-8

9. Carre, A.L., et al.: Mixed-reality demonstration and training of glassblowing. Heritage **5**(1), 103–128 (2022)

10. John, B., Kurian, J.C., Fitzgerald, R., Goh, D.H.L.: Students' Learning Experience in a Mixed Reality Environment: Drivers and Barriers. Communications of the Association for Information Systems, pp. 556-581 (2022)

11. Kolovou, M.: In search of assessment shifts in embodied learning science research: a review. J. Sci. Educ. Technol. 0123456789 (2022). https://doi.org/10.1007/s10956-021-09952-x

12. Xia, S., Chu, L., Pei, L., Zhang, Z., Yu, W., Qiu, R.C.: Learning disentangled representation for mixed- reality human activity recognition with a single IMU sensor. IEEE Trans. Instrum. Meas. **70**(Mi), 1–14 (2021)

13. Lee, B., Jenny, B., Dwyer, T.: A Design Space for Data Visualisation Transformations Between 2D And 3D In Mixed-Reality Environments, vol. 1, no. 1. Association for Computing Machinery (2022)

14. Molero, D., Schez-Sobrino, S., Vallejo, D., Glez-Morcillo, C., Albusac, J.: A novel approach to learning music and piano based on mixed reality and gamification. Multimed. Tools Appl. **80**(1), 165–186 (2020). https://doi.org/10.1007/s11042-020-09678-9

15. Widiyanti, D.E., Asmoro, K., Shin, S.Y., Member, S.: HoloGCS : Mixed Reality-based Ground Control Station for Unmanned Aerial Vehicle, pp. 0–12 (2022)

16. Iqbal, J., Sidhu, M.S., Nasional, U.T.: A system framework for computer vision and AR based dance learning technology. Aust. J. Basic Appl. Sci. **9**(19), 27–34 (2015)

17. Aguayo, C., Eames, C., Cochrane, T.: A framework for mixed reality free-choice, self-determined learning. Res. Learn. Technol. **28**(1063519), 1–19 (2020)

18. Chen, C.J.: Theoretical bases for using virtual reality in education. Themes Sci. Technol. Educ. **2**(Special Issue) 71–90 (2009)

19. Kommetter, C., Ebner, M.: "A pedagogical framework for mixed reality in classrooms based on a literature review", EdMedia + Innov. Learn. **2019**(July), 901–911 (2019)

20. Elliott, J.B., Gardner, M., Alrashidi, M.: Towards a framework for the design of mixed reality immersive education spaces. In: Proceedings of the 2nd Eur. immersive Initiat. summit, Paris, Fr., no. November, pp. 63–76 (2012)

21. Iqbal, J., Sidhu, M.S.: Acceptance of dance training system based on augmented reality and technology acceptance model (TAM). Virt. Real. 0123456789 (2021). https://doi.org/10.1007/s10055-021-00529-y

22. Iqbal, J., Sidhu, M.S.: A taxonomic overview and pilot study for evaluation of augmented reality based posture matching technique using technology acceptance model. Procedia Comput. Sci. **163**, 345–351 (2019)

Expanding Rural Community Networks Through Partnerships with Key Actors

Ignacio Prieto-Egido[1]([✉]) [iD], Javier Simó-Reigadas[1] [iD], Eva Castro-Barbero[1] [iD], and River Quispe Tacas[2] [iD]

[1] Rey Juan Carlos University, 28942 Madrid, Spain
ignacio.prieto@urjc.es
[2] Pontifical Catholic University of Peru, Lima, Peru

Abstract. The infrastructures deployed by classical telecommunications operators are appropriate and cost-effective for urban-oriented business models, but rural areas with very low population density require alternatives both in terms of the technology used and in business models. New generation networks become more and more dense and heterogeneous, increasing the gap as operators cannot spend the required CAPEX and OPEX in sparsely populated areas where the revenues will certainly be very low.

At the same time, an increasing number of communities worldwide provide themselves networking solutions, which is becoming a global alternative movement called "community networks". However, rural areas are challenging because of the technical difficulties of getting connected to the world and the scarcity of technical skills, among other reasons. Other stakeholders such as municipalities or regional governments are also relevant actors but cannot provide a solution by themselves.

Partnerships between different actors for deploying rural connectivity could be the answer, taking advantage somehow of the "shared infrastructure model" proposed in IETF RFC7962. This paper analyses the relationship between different stakeholders and the main elements to consider when deploying mobile communications services in isolated and sparsely populated regions. The analysis uses a case study from the Napo River Network in Peru and compares it with other experiences such as Zenzeleni Networks in South Africa or Rizhomatica in Mexico.

Keywords: Rural communications · Community networks · Shared telecommunications infrastructures · Collaborative networking model

1 Introduction

Many rural communities in developing countries do not have access to communications services, unlike urban areas where these services have rapidly grown. This connectivity gap is mainly due to the high complexity and cost of classical telecommunications infrastructures and the urban-oriented business models of traditional operators, suited for dense

G. Salvendy and J. Wei (Eds.): HCII 2022, LNCS 13337, pp. 417–435, 2022.
https://doi.org/10.1007/978-3-031-05014-5_35

human concentrations but neither appropriate nor cost-effective in regions characterized by isolation, low population density, and scarcity of many critical resources.

In the last two decades, many communities have developed their own networking solutions in urban areas (and rarely in rural areas) [1], generating a global alternative movement of community networks that relies on a wide range of accessible technologies. Most of them use wireless mesh networks with some extra elements such as open mobile base stations or complementary high-capacity optical fiber links. However, in rural areas, the challenge remains very complex because of the high number of disconnected communities, the low population density, the scarcity of people with technical skills, the diversity of contexts, and the limited support from public institutions, among other reasons. In rare cases, governmental institutions have assumed the challenge to deploy and maintain rural telecommunications infrastructures to bear e-Health, e-Learning, or e-Government strategical services, but sustainability results are not always promising [2, 3].

As the complexity and cost of new generation telecommunications technologies grow, it is more and more difficult for a single stakeholder to take the whole responsibility of designing, deploying, and operating greenfield rural telecommunications infrastructures. In this sense, some authors propose to foster partnerships between different actors involved in deploying rural connectivity [4]. Due to the extreme difficulties that the rural contexts present for each stakeholder separately, ideas such as the 'shared infrastructure model' proposed in IETF RFC7962 [5] and complex partnerships as in the Napo case [6] suggest that those rural telecommunications infrastructures require the participation of many of them allied to make them feasible and sustainable. However, there are historical difficulties for partnerships involving private, public, and third sector entities that cannot be neglected.

This paper analyses the relationship between different stakeholders and the main elements to consider when deploying mobile communications services in isolated and sparsely populated regions. A simple analytic framework is proposed and then used to examine three different cases that permit to examine how partnerships have been built in a variety of scenarios and what the contributions of the different stakeholders have been. The impact of those contributions on the integral sustainability of the project is also regarded. Even though the results obtained may suggest certain partnerships, pushing those actors to cooperate respecting and trusting each other may be challenging in many cases. Those difficulties are out of the scope of this paper which only aims at suggesting processes that may be worth exploring.

The rest of the paper starts with a methodology section, continues with the analysis of elements required for rural telecommunications projects, and then the three cases proposed are examined and compared. After that, we will reflect on how each model addresses the different dimensions of integral sustainability. Finally, conclusions are extracted.

2 Methodology

The first step will be a systematic identification of all critical elements commonly required for the construction, operation, and maintenance of a rural telecommunications infrastructure.

Secondly, three different cases will be studied to analyze what actors participated substantially in deploying, operating, and maintaining a rural telecommunication network and their contributions. The three cases are the Napo project in the Peruvian Amazon Rainforest, Zenzeleni Networks in South Africa, and Rizhomatica in Mexico. These cases have been chosen because they are successful experiences very different among them in their specific objectives, geographical context, actors involved, and technology used. The authors have had easy access to accurate information about at least the first two cases.

Thirdly, considering that integral sustainability has different dimensions (technological, economic, institutional, cultural, and political), an estimation will be proposed on how those contributions impact on integral sustainability.

Finally, the cases will be examined, looking for differences and coincidences in the partnerships that have been established to provide all the necessary elements in deploying and maintaining mobile communications services in those projects. Relevant information on how these contributions impact sustainability will be studied in a separate analysis to highlight possible (dis)advantages for a given actor to contribute with a particular element. The methodology used to analyze the impact on sustainability is similar to a previous work explicitly focused on that aspect for the Napo project [6].

3   Elements Required for Rural Telecommunications Projects

Rural telecommunications infrastructures are complex systems. Many of the elements needed for the successful deployment and operation of these networks are intangible, and those may be critical. Accepting this, this paper focuses on fundamental elements in the tangible side.

Rural telecommunications networks usually extend on large areas to eventually reach sparse small towns or villages where access to the network happens in hotspots through base stations of any access technology (3G, 4G, 5G, WiFi,…). Although the ideal case for this kind of network would provide people ubiquitous access over the territory, real cost-effective networks only ensure coverage on populated areas and their surroundings. Rural telecommunications networks often have two different segments: (1) a transport network, typically a wireless mesh network, interconnecting human settlements among them and with a POP (*Point of Presence*) of a globally connected larger network, and (2) access networks deployed in the human settlements and using the transport network as backhaul. AAA (*Authentication, Authorization,* and *Accounting*) access network functions may require systems installed in data centers placed either close to the POP or even in the carrier's network. Although a particular network may differ from this basic scheme, this is assumed to be general enough, and it is represented in Fig. 1.

Assuming this basic architectural model, Table 1 disaggregates the main elements that will be seen separately when reviewing what contributions are needed in a collaborative rural telecommunications infrastructure. Obviously, many important details are not in this table, but it is comprehensive enough for an initial discussion about who can contribute with tangible assets required for a future rural telecommunications project.

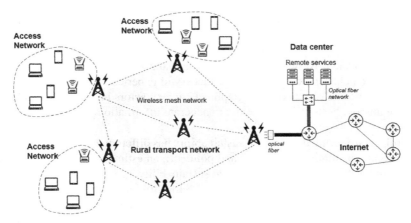

Fig. 1. Rural telecommunications network architecture representing a general scheme in which most existing networks may fit. (Note: icons from Icon Fonts, CC BY 3.0).

4   Case Studies

4.1   The Napo Network in Peru

The Napo network is a linear rural telecommunications network deployed along the Peruvian stretch of the Napo River from Iquitos up to the Ecuadorian border.

The network presently connects to global networks in a POP placed in Iquitos and extends 450 km to the North along the river using 17 enchained WiLD (WiFi over Long Distances) point-to-point wireless links ranging from 19 to 55 km long each. As the Amazon rainforest is very flat and with many tall trees, very high supporting structures

Table 1. Basic network elements for each network segment. Except for services, the difference is made in elements contributing to CAPEX (capital expenditure) or OPEX (operations expenditure).

Segment	CAPEX	OPEX
Transport network	- Communications equipment - Wired infrastructures - Civil work (supporting structures and canalizations) - Design & deployment	- Spectrum licensing - Carrier's POP - Maintenance - Operation & management - Powering
Access network	- Access points / base stations - AAA equipment - Civil work (supporting structures and canalizations)	- Spectrum licensing - Accounting and billing - Maintenance - Operation & management - Powering
Services	- Telephony service - Internet access service - Technical support to end-users - Vertical services (e-Health, e-Learning, etc.)	

(as much as 92 m) were deployed to ensure line of sight, the last 14 of them being placed in human settlements along the river.

The initial purpose for this infrastructure was the interconnection of the public health facilities in villages with the Iquitos hospital for telemedicine. Additionally, a parallel network was added on the same supporting structures in 2013 for backhauling a 3G access network deployed in eight of those villages [2] and providing voice and data services.

Context and History. Before the deployment of the Napo network in 2006–2007, there was no access to communications services in the area from Iquitos to the Ecuadorian border. The population density in the region is extremely low, but there are many small villages ranging from a few hundred inhabitants to a bit over 3000. Most people work in agriculture and farming, many of the villages have a health post, and a few have a bigger health center and a primary school.

In that context, the EHAS Foundation and the GTR (Rural Telecommunications Group) of the Pontifical Catholic University of Peru identified the need for a telemedicine network that they designed, deployed, and put into operation in 2007, funded by the Global Fund. The property of this infrastructure was transferred to the regional government of Loreto, as well as the responsibility for managing and maintaining it. Nevertheless, the GTR kept improving and supporting the network for many years.

Between 2013 and 2016, the TUCAN3G research project allowed the network upgrade with newer equipment and augmented capacity as well as the addition of the 3G access network. Nowadays, 8 villages have 3G services (voice and data) with Huawei micro-BS. In the meantime, the Peruvian government approved laws for creating and regulating a new type of wholesale entity called RMIO (Rural Mobile Infrastructure Operator). Hence, the consortium developing this project included Telefónica del Peru as MNO (Mobile Network Operator) and Mayu as SRO (Small Rural Operator, general category in which the Peruvian RMIO may be included). The introduction of the SRO in the equation had some positive collateral effects, as previously the regional government was finding it difficult to carry on with the telemedicine network maintenance, and the new deal included the assumption of this task by Mayu in exchange for the permission for using the supporting infrastructures for the backhaul of the mobile access network. The promising results of the TUCAN3G project attracted the interest of the Development Bank of Latin America (CAF), which invested money for extending and improving the network [3, 7].

Stakeholders. Although more detailed information may be found in [6], the following basic information makes it easier to understand how the different actors participate in this project.

- EHAS: non-profit organization (NGO) registered in Spain and Peru, aiming at improving the living conditions in rural developing regions through telemedicine networks and services. EHAS led the international project EHAS-@ALIS in which the Napo telemedicine network was designed and deployed in 2006–2007. After that, EHAS kept monitoring the network evolution and collaborating with GTR-PUCP in upgrading and improving the network and telemedicine services.

- GTR-PUCP: research & development group in the Pontifical Catholic University in Peru, sited in Lima. Since 1999, GTR has been working on designing, deploying, and improving telecommunications networks in isolated regions of Peru. Many of these projects were done in collaboration with EHAS. Engineers working in GTR are experts in designing, deploying, and monitoring rural radiocommunications infrastructures and are also experienced in cooperation with regional governments, operators, and local associations.
- The regional government of Loreto: since the inception of the Napo network, the regional government was supposed to receive the ownership of the infrastructure and carry on with the operation and maintenance for telemedicine purposes. The assumption of full responsibility in network operation and maintenance was challenging for this public institution for many reasons, and many efforts were made to reach an acceptable grade of service. The final solution was to transfer the responsibility for the network maintenance to Mayu.
- Mayu: as the Peruvian government officially regulated SRO with the RMIO regulation in 2015, Mayu became the first RMIO in Peru and accepted the management of the rural infrastructure of the Napo network. Mayu uses the infrastructure owned by the regional government of Loreto, installs additional equipment for the mobile communications services, including base stations, powering equipment, and other systems, and operates the regional mobile network. They also maintain the whole network, including parts that may only affect telemedicine. They connect the rural infrastructure to Telefónica's POP in Iquitos, where all the traffic (voice and data) is exchanged with Telefónica.
- Telefónica del Peru: country-wide MNO. They doubted whether to enter to provide mobile telephony service in an area as complicated as the Napo river basin because Peruvian regulations prevent it from abandoning the service in an area once it has begun to be provided. The TUCAN3G project explored and proposed a technical solution and a business model that allowed them to provide 3G services in several villages. Telefónica conditioned the choice of Huawei micro-BS so that they could provide AAA with the network controller they already had. They exchange user traffic in Iquitos and share management & operation with the SRO.
- Communities: more than 20.000 people in 14 villages are active or potential users of the Napo network. Users were interviewed prior to the design and deployment of the network to know their needs and expectations. They have also been considered later in evaluations. In addition, communities in this project are users and consumers but have never been active actors co-owning the network.

Analysis of Contributions. In the following, the actor(s) contributing to each element is/are identified:

Transport Network:

- Communications equipment – wireless links using Mikrotik IEEE 802.11ac equipment. All were installed and initially configured by EHAS and GTR-PUCP. The current responsible for the network operation (Mayu) manifests preference for carrier-class systems they use in other networks for the sake of robustness, so this might change in the next future. The link that connects with the city of Iquitos is already implemented with Carrier-class equipment and in a licensed band to avoid interference problems.

- Frequencies for wireless communication – unlicensed spectrum in the 5 GHz band. EIRP limitations in Peru exist but are less restrictive for rural areas.
- Wired infrastructures – none.
- Civil work (towers, canalizations, supports on buildings, etc.) - towers up to 92 m high with electrical protection were deployed by GTR-PUCP and EHAS and are currently maintained by Mayu.
- Interconnection point to global networks/backbone - In Iquitos, provided by Telefónica del Peru for both voice and data traffic.
- Network design & deployment – Made by GTR-PUCP and EHAS initially for telemedicine, extended and improved later for mobile communications by the same actors.
- Network maintenance – Initially a responsibility of the regional government, Mayu currently assumes this responsibility.
- Network operation & management- Initially, GTR-PUCP was in charge; currently, Mayu assumes this responsibility.
- Powering – Solar photovoltaic systems designed, installed, and initially maintained by GTR-PUCP. In the last years, Mayu has carried on with maintenance.

Access Network:

- Access points/base stations – 3G Huawei micro-BS deployed and maintained by Mayu.
- Frequencies for wireless communication – licensed.
- AAA equipment - Telefónica's Huawei controller hosted in their core network.
- Civil work (towers, canalizations, supports on buildings, etc.) - towers up to 92 m high with electrical protection were deployed by GTR-PUCP and EHAS and are currently maintained by Mayu. Same as for the transport network.
- Accounting and billing – Telefónica manages 3G service under the same conditions country-wide. Prepaid services or other commercial strategies do not differ from other regions in Peru, and Telefónica's users may use the service in the Napo network or elsewhere under the same conditions.
- Network maintenance – Mayu has a management system that may trigger alarms, and local collaborators on the field are skilled in identifying and solve simple problems. Technicians with a higher level of expertise work on the access network remotely and travel on the field when needed.
- Network operation & management – skilled staff from Telefónica and Mayu perform this task remotely with other rural networks in the country.
- Powering – adapted to the local resources. Some systems are powered with electricity service available, though most systems are powered using electrical photovoltaic systems. Initially installed by GTR-PUCP, Mayu is currently in charge.

Services:

- Telephony service - Telefónica provides the service.
- Internet access service - Telefónica provides the service.
- Technical support to end-users - It does not exist locally. Telefónica provides remotely as anywhere else in the country.
- Vertical services (e-Health, e-Learning, etc.). EHAS, GTR-PUCP, and the regional government of Loreto collaborate for providing eHealth services.

4.2 The Zenzeleni Network in South Africa

The Zenzeleni network is a community network promoted back in 2011 by the community of Mankosi and researchers from UWC (University of the Western Cape) to provide local connectivity and Internet access in a rural area in South Africa [8]. The first stage was intensive in research & development activities aiming at developing the network and services while ensuring that communities were always principal stakeholders on top of the decision-making structure. In that first stage, researchers from the UWC strongly supported the project as a whole and participated in network design and deployment, training of local technicians, and many other activities helping to guide and consolidate the process. In a second stage, Zenzeleni NPC was created as a non-profit structure for managing and scaling the project. Since 2017, the project is working autonomously managed by NPC as a second-layer structure serving communities that are organized in cooperatives.

Although the project initially focused on OTT (on the top) telephony services and the charge of phones with solar systems, it has evolved modulated by the needs and resources identified over the years. On the one hand, users are more generally demanding data access, showing less interest in OTT voice services. On the other hand, there is interest in providing telephony services using 3GPP technologies, which would be a much more efficient solution among other advantages, but this possibility for the moment has been blocked by MNOs owning spectrum.

The network enables users with WiFi clients such as smartphones or other portable devices to connect to any of the almost 80 hotspots throughout Zithulele and Mankosi to access the Internet or any local services of the network. Those hotspots are interconnected with the Internet through a POP available in a public university in Mthatha. The connection between Mthatha and the villages uses a wireless mesh transport network using WiLD systems. A cooperative fully manages the local access network in each village, and another organization, Zenzeleni NPC, oversees the transport network. Users can purchase Zenzeleni data vouchers that are sold directly by cooperative members. Although the telephony services were a target since the very first stage of the project, the current situation is that the interest in telephony is marginal, and the service offered is mainly Internet access.

Context and History. The project's genesis happened in 2012 in Mankosi, a rural community in one of the most disadvantaged areas of South Africa. The community, always leading the process but accompanied and encouraged by researchers from UWC, started working to deploy and maintain its own community network. Initially, the project aimed at providing cheaper voice services for the community because regular services from an MNO were unaffordable.

Three years later, the project was exhibiting extraordinary good results in some aspects and had also succeeded in obtaining recognition for telecommunications operation from the authorities. Paradoxically, the killer service seemed to be the access to the Internet, including social networks that, for example, permitted voice calls on some VoIP platforms or voice messages. The phone calls did not seem that successful, so the project focused on data.

As the model was successful, it evolved to a more complex two-layer structure to ease scalability. Communities (Zithulele and Mankosi) organized themselves in cooperatives. They assumed the deployment, operation, and maintenance of hotspots for public access networks, and Zenzeleni NPC assumed the rural transport network, serving the community hotspots and other services such as local businesses, NGOs, hospitals, and a school. Interconnection to global networks was possible thanks to an agreement with Easttel, a wholesale carrier with a point of presence in Mthatha, to which the transport network is connected.

There is interest in obtaining the right to use spectrum for mobile services because that would permit deploying base stations with larger coverage, but the service is provided through many WiFi hotspots in each village with very limited coverage.

Stakeholders

- Communities: very active and with a protagonist role in the project since the first steps. Organized in cooperatives, Zithulele and Mankosi manage and maintain their own local access networks presently composed of WiFi hotspots.
- UWC: their researchers strongly supported the design of the process, technical training, technical and business model decisions. Since 2017, Zenzeleni's two-layer structure in fully autonomous. UWC keeps two seats in the the the board of trustees, where also other external supporting institutions such as APC (Association for Progressive Communications) and Ellipse have a seat.
- Zenzeleni NPC: it is the non-profit organization that runs the transport network, supports the cooperatives, and connects to the point of presence of a long-haul optical fiber network run by Easttel. Zenzeleni NPC can develop this activity for those cooperatives and others thanks to the license exemption obtained from the Independent Communications Authority of South Africa (ICASA).
- Easttel: wholesale connectivity provider with a point of presence in the university campus in Mthatha, a city that is 60 km away from the villages. It is a private company offering their services for this project with very good conditions.

Analysis of Contributions. In the following, the actor(s) contributing to each element is/are identified:

Transport Network:

- Communications equipment – mostly Ubiquiti and Mikrotik wireless systems. Operated by Zenzeleni NPC.
- Frequencies for wireless communication – unlicensed spectrum in the 5 GHz band, though there is interest to obtain a license for spectrum in the 6–7 GHz for the arrival to Mthatha, where interferences may create problems.
- Wired infrastructures – none.
- Civil work (canalizationsand supporting structures) - Zenzeleni owns a few towers not taller than 15 m and uses masts, natural elevations and buildings as much as possible.
- Interconnection point to global networks/backbone - provided by Easttel in Mthatha for data traffic.
- Network design & deployment – initially communities with UWC researchers. New modifications of the network are now the responsibility of Zenzeleni NPC.
- Network maintenance – Zenzeleni NPC.
- Network operation & management- Zenzeleni NPC.
- Powering – Solar photovoltaic systems and/or batteries designed, installed, and initially maintained by members of the communities trained by UWC researchers, together with them. Now the responsibility of Zenzeleni NPC.

Access Network:

- Access points/base stations – Ubiquiti WiFi access points in hotspots, operated and maintained by the cooperatives. Interest for 4G base stations that the cooperatives could operate in the future.
- Frequencies for wireless communication – unlicensed. Interest in 4G licensed spectrum.
- AAA equipment – Data access managed by Zenzeleni NPC. Datacenter in Mthatha.
- Civil work (towers, canalizations, supports on buildings, etc.) - masts and support prepared by the cooperatives and collaborators taking advantage of buildings in the villages and geographical elevations.
- Accounting and billing – Vouchers are sold by cooperativists, captive portal, and other tools managed by Zenzeleni NPC.
- Network maintenance – The cooperatives take care of the access network elements, eventually with some support from Zenzeleni NPC.
- Network operation & management – low needs due to the simple access technology used. The cooperatives operate the access network, eventually with some support from Zenzeleni NPC. Cooperativists were initially trained by UWC.
- Powering – photovoltaic systems and batteries installed and maintained by the cooperativists, who were initially trained by UWC.

Services:

- Telephony service – Initially with VoIP clients in smartphones and connecting the network to a VoIP operator through the data network. This service has become marginal.

- Internet access service – Easttel offers it in the urban point of presence, Zenzeleni provides transport to the villages and the cooperatives distribute to users.
- Technical support to end-users – The cooperatives provide technical support to users, and they are supported by Zenzeleni NPC.
- Vertical services (e-Health, e-Learning, etc.). A school and a hospital are clients and use the network, as well as other private clients and a telecenter. Online services emerge progressively in the local domain as several actors use the network to provide them.

4.3 Rhizomatica in Mexico

The goal of Rhizomatica is to help people and communities build their own networks by creating and promoting open-source technology [9–11]. Moreover, Rhizomatica develops governance strategies to make those networks sustainable. In that line, Rhizomatica helped to create in Mexico a regional telecommunications cooperative community called *Telecomunicaciones Indígenas Comunitarias Asociación Civil* (TIC-AC). TIC-AC is a civil association of Indigenous and rural communities seeking to build, manage and operate their own communication networks.

Under this model, organized communities become owners and are responsible for operating and managing their local cellular network infrastructure. For its part, TIC-AC authorizes the community to use a frequency granted by the Federal Telecommunications Institute (IFT) to operate its local cellular network for 15 years. Together with TIC-AC, the community acquires, operates, and manages its network by installing a base station and the necessary equipment for its administration. They rely on Internet Service Providers to connect the village with the global networks. In addition, TIC-AC works agreements with Internet providers and facilitates technical support for the network.

Context and History. Rhizomatica began in 2009 as a "quest to make alternative telecommunication infrastructures possible for people around the world facing oppressive regimes, the threat of natural disaster, or the reality of living in a place deemed too poor or isolated to connect" [10]. As part of this goal, Rhizomatica helped create TIC-AC, which began providing cellular services in 2013 in Talea de Castro, Oaxaca. TIC-AC started using a private network scheme and a spectrum segment acquired for free for non-profit use.

In 2016 the Federal Telecommunications Institute of Mexico (FTI) created the first telecommunication service license for social indigenous use. Thanks to this decision (Decision 73/2016), community networks can use a part of the licensed spectrum to provide mobile services in the states of Oaxaca, Chiapas, Veracruz, Guerrero, and Puebla.

Nowadays, the network has expanded to 19 communities in two Mexican states and provides service to more than 3000 users. It offers unlimited local calls and messages and long-distance calls to all of Mexico and the world at very affordable rates.

Stakeholders

- Communities: they are the owners and the operators of the local cellular network infrastructure. In general, these communities have nearly complete autonomy regarding their government systems and concerning the management of their resources such as land, which is considered a common good.
- TIC-AC: is a telecommunications cooperative that encompasses the communities with mobile networks and provides a platform for resource and profit-sharing, interconnection with existing telecommunications infrastructure (telephone and Internet), technical capacity building and maintenance. TIC-AC has a governance structure in which the communities operate jointly.
- Small wireless Internet Service Providers (ISPs): they are connected to a network backbone (optical fiber) of a public telecommunications network. They may be license holders or registered resellers operating independently before implementing the community network.

Analysis of Contributions. In the following, the actor(s) contributing to each element is/are identified:

Transport Network.

- Communications equipment – WiFi equipment operated by the regional ISP.
- Frequencies for wireless communication – unlicensed spectrum in the 5 GHz band, though there is interest to obtain a license for spectrum in the 10 GHz to avoid interferences problems.
- Wired infrastructures – none.
- Civil work (towers, canalizations, supports on buildings, etc.) – installed or rented by the ISP.
- Interconnection point to global networks/backbone – provided by the ISP at market prices.
- Network design & deployment – ISP's responsibility.
- Network maintenance – ISP.
- Network operation & management- ISP.
- Powering – Solar photovoltaic systems and/or batteries designed, installed, and maintained by the ISP.

Access Network.

- Access points/base stations – open-source equipment based on OpenBTS owned by the community and supported by TIC-AC.
- Frequencies for wireless communication – licensed and granted by the Decision 73/2016 of the Federal Telecommunications Institute of Mexico (FTI).
- AAA equipment – open-source equipment based on OpenBSC owned by the community and supported by TIC-AC.

- Civil work (towers, canalizations, supports on buildings, etc.) - masts and support prepared by the communities taking advantage of buildings in the villages and geographical elevations.
- Accounting and billing – Each community defines its own rates and is responsible for collection.
- Network maintenance – The communities take care of the access network elements, eventually with some support from TIC-AC.
- Network operation & management – The communities operate the access network, eventually with TIC-AC support.
- Powering – the community must provide power through an electrical grid with UPS systems or through photovoltaic systems.

Services.

- Telephony service – National and international calls are made through a Voice over Internet Protocol (VoIP) service that is provided by a small operator and connects to the global telephone network. Local calls are unlimited.
- Internet access service – the ISP contracts at the urban point of presence and transports to the villages. Then the communities distribute to users.
- Technical support to end-users – The cooperatives provide the service supported by TIC-AC.
- Vertical services (e-Health, e-Learning, etc.). It is not documented.

4.4 Summary and Comparison of the Cases

In this subsection, the information explained in the previous one will be summarized in tables that permit the comparison of the three cases easily.

The following Table 2 shows the comparison between the three cases in terms of the transport network. In addition to indicating the stakeholders in charge of providing each network element, the table categorizes the main characteristics of the solution they offer. For example, in the case of equipment, the cost (high, medium, low), the complexity of use, and efficiency are classified. It is also highlighted whether services are provided locally or remotely and whether they require specialized personnel or not. As none of the cases deploys wired infrastructures in the transport network, that element is not included.

Let us take together the rows in Table 2 related to equipment, spectrum, and powering. Apparently, the three cases are very similar regarding the communications equipment used and spectrum use. Most transport network equipment is low-cost outdoor broadband wireless systems working in unlicensed bands. However, the three cases detect the need for carrier-class equipment operating in licensed bands for the links arriving to a city, where the gateway connected to a POP is usually placed. The slight difference in this is because the SRO in the Napo case uses that equipment and frequencies, while the transport network operators in the other two cases, for the moment, do not have access to licensed spectrum for this. Also, the SRO in Napo users more costly powering systems, more requiring in CAPEX but also more robust. All this increases the technical sustainability for the transport network in the Napo case, related to the others.

Looking at the rows related to civil work, maintenance and network operation and management, there are also some interesting differences. The supporting structures in a wireless mesh network are a dominant component in the CAPEX transport network. For the Napo network and Zenzeleni, they could deploy the transport network because they could get funding from donors or development agencies. For public institutions and collaborating actors such as universities or NGOs, obtaining funds for CAPEX is possible and introduces more flexibility for the network operation and maintenance, which are components of OPEX. In the three cases, we see many differences. Rhizomatica outsources all the three elements to ISPs, Napo outsources the OPEX elements (the regional government owns the CAPEX element and shares it), and Zenzeleni retains all the three in their own institution created by and for the communities. This variety of approaches suggests that this is very context specific. The message seems to be "look around and see what actor can get or invest the funds to build the supporting infrastructures, then identify who can better operate and maintain the network or build the institution for doing it". Another evidence is that the approach depends very much on the grade of community involvement. The projects that need to outsource any of these elements or all of them have somehow a weak point in the long-term institutional sustainability.

Table 2. Comparison of the three cases for the Transport Network.

Element	Napo	Rhizomatica	Zenzeleni
Equipment	**Mayu**: low-cost, easy to use, efficient	**ISP**: low-cost, easy to use, efficient	**NPC**: low-cost, easy to use, efficient
Frequencies for wireless communications	**Mayu**: not-licensed and licensed	**ISP**: not-licensed	**NPC**: not-licensed
Civil work	**PI**: Provide shared infrastructures	**ISP**: Install or rent	**NPC**: Partially funded by donations
Maintenance	**Mayu**: Locally, autonomous, medium-expertise	**ISP**: Locally, autonomous, medium-expertise	**NPC**: Locally, autonomous, medium-expertise
Network Operation & Management	**Mayu**: Remote, autonomous, high-expertise	**ISP**: Locally, autonomous, medium-expertise	**NPC**: Locally, autonomous, medium-expertise
Network design and deployment	**Mayu & EHAS & PUCP**	**ISP & TIC-AC**	**UWC & NPC**
Powering	**Mayu**: medium-cost, complex, robust, autonomous	**ISP**: low-cost, easy-to-use, local grid & autonomous	**NPC**: low-cost, easy-to-use, local grid & autonomous
Interconnection point to global networks	**TdP**: Voice and data, Market-cost	**ISP**: data, VoIP, market-cost	**Easttel**: data, low-cost

Finally, the three cases have interconnection points of different natures for traffic exchange with global networks. Rhizomatica and Zenzeleni deal with wholesale providers that provide Internet access. A first clue in this is that one can offer data services with that and even voice services because there are OTT VoIP providers that can perform as gateways to the phone network. Napo adopted a very different approach, involving an MNO (Telefónica del Perú) that provides the interconnexion point and the services to end users. The first ensures more freedom, the second makes things simpler and robust. In the second, the service is available when one leaves the rural network and goes anywhere else in the country. Communities that can organize themselves and build strong structures with technical skill probably will find advantages in the first model. It is also true that experiences in which an MNO and a community have a deal for cooperating in a frame of mutual trust and respect are rare, if any. The first model seems to be stronger in institutional sustainability, while the second makes the transport network more economically sustainable, as one does not pay for the traffic exchanged in the POP, on the contrary, the traffic is "sold" by the SRO to the MNO. The situation of the price or interconnexion rising cannot happen.

Table 3 continues the previous analysis for the access network. Looking at the access points used, powering, AAA systems, and frequencies, the three cases would like to use similar technologies, but the different actors operating the access network have different access to spectrum and carrier-class base stations and power systems. In case an operator owning 3G/4G spectrum licenses is in the project (Napo case), the use of carrier-class base stations can be taken for granted, and the network controller may be hosted in its core network, which is a traditional and robust solution. Suppose national regulations foresee a mechanism for a community or a non-profit organization to use that spectrum when it is not exploited in a region (Rhizomatica case). In that case, existing open-source access systems enable the project to use that kind of solution. If one has neither the cooperation of an MNO nor a favorable regulation (Zenzeleni case), only something like WiFi hotspots is available, a midway alternative that works but lacks efficiency and has several drawbacks related to reduced coverage and compatible terminals. From the first to the third case, the technical sustainability drops.

As in the transport network, supporting structures are dominant CAPEX components with a high entry barrier. In two cases, the communities provide them; in the other one (Napo) the regional public institutions have them and share them. Any case is valid and has advantages and drawbacks in terms of sustainability.

Aspects related to billing and technical support are also different depending on the role of communities. In the Napo case, communities are passive consumers of services, and providers bill and support users from the distance with null adaptation to any conditions and circumstances. In the other cases both accounting & billing and technical support are closer and better suited to the communities. That increases cultural and economic sustainability, as prices are naturally lower, and benefits are reinvested in the community.

Table 3. Comparison of the three cases for the Access Network.

Element	Napo	Rhizomatica	Zenzeleni
Access Points	**Mayu**: Carrier-class RAN, high-cost, medium-coverage, high-efficiency	**Community**: open-source RAN, medium-cost, medium-coverage, high-efficiency	**Community**: Wi-Fi, low-cost, low-coverage, low-efficiency
AAA Equipment	**TdP**: remote location, high-cost, shared	**Community**: local point, easy-to-use, dedicated	**Community**: local point, easy-to-use, dedicated
Towers or buildings	**PI**: Provide shared infrastructures	**Community**: Locally provided	**Community**: Locally provided
Accounting & Billing	**TdP**: remote location, country-wide policy	**Community & TIC-AC**: Locally, coordinated, local policy	**NPC & Community**: Locally, coordinated, local policy
Maintenance	**Mayu**: Locally, autonomous, medium-expertise	**Community**: Locally, coordinated, low-expertise	**Community**: Locally, coordinated, low-expertise
	EHAS & PUCP: technical support	**TIC-AC**: medium-expertise	**NPC**: medium-expertise
Operation & Management	**TdP & Mayu**: Remote, Coordinated, high-expertise	**Community**: Locally, coordinated, low-expertise	**Community**: Locally, coordinated, low-expertise
		TIC-AC: medium-expertise	**NPC**: medium-expertise
Powering	**Mayu**: medium-cost, complex, robust, autonomous	**TIC-AC**: low-cost, low-complexity, local grid & UPS	**Community**: low-cost, low-complexity, local grid & UPS
Frequencies	**Mayu**: licensed	**TIC-AC**: licensed	**Community**: not-licensed
Technical Support	**TdP**: remote location, country-wide policy	**Community**: Locally provided, local policy	**Community**: Locally provided, local policy

Finally, the other OPEX elements depend on the community's involvement and strength. Managing and maintaining an access network requires some technical expertise and local availability. Either there is an SRO filling this role professionally or a separate institution must be created (as is the case for Rhizomatica and Zenzeleni) with a minimum of technical staff and management staff. The second increases the cultural and institutional sustainability but is obviously more challenging to achieve.

The previous analysis can also be extended to the services offered in each scenario, which are compared in Table 4. When an MNO is involved, the service tariffs are usually homogeneous country-wide and will probably be less affordable. Moreover, the cost structure will not make the service profitable in low-income communities. When an SRO intervenes, service prices do not change, but the SRO can adapt its cost structure to rural settings and make the service profitable where it was not for the MNO.

Table 4. Comparison of the three cases for the Services.

Element	Napo	Rhizomatica	Zenzeleni
Voice call service	**TdP**: Usual phone calls with standard rates	**Community**: low-cost rates through VoIP services	**Community**: not provided
Internet access service	**TdP**: Conventional mobile access with standard rates	**Community**: low-cost rates	**Community**: low-cost rates
Vertical services	**EHAS & PUCP & PI**: Collaborative eHealth services	-	**Clients**: may offer local services

On the other hand, communities and non-profit organizations only aim to cover costs and can use alternative strategies to reduce costs and set low local tariffs. For example, locally managing and maintaining the network has already been mentioned. But they can also offer VoIP services to avoid dependence on the MNO.

Moreover, involving other institutions such as NGOs or universities can extend the available services and contribute to the model sustainability. In Napo, EHAS and PUCP take advantage of Mayu's bandwidth to strengthen the services of all the health facilities in the network through e-Health tools. To this end, they have developed an alliance with the Regional Government and Mayu. Mayu provides bandwidth to the Regional Government's health facilities in exchange for access to the latter's communications towers. In this way, sharing resources reduces costs for all parties involved.

5   Conclusions

This article contributes to identifying critical aspects to be considered in the deployment of communication services in isolated rural areas in a sustainable manner. It analyzes three successful cases that apply different approaches: from the proposal of community networks to the SRO (Small Rural Operator) model.

The main difference with other analysis is that this one performs a comparative analysis of three cases that follow very different models and still finds common lessons, and considers separately three segments: transport network, access network, and services. Although the actors participating in each case are different, some common critical issues can be identified in all cases: negotiation of interconnection with global networks; access to licensed frequencies for the access network; community participation in the process, and the involvement of public institutions. The analysis also reveals some interesting trends. An example is the interest in having licensed spectrum both for the transport network and the access network. Probably a sign of the maturity of the community networks movement, projects want the best solutions and creatively look for them. Regulators may learn from cases such as the Mexican one and find ways to liberate spectrum for the use of communities and non-profit organizations that want to provide services where nobody is doing so. Another trend is the creation of structures specialized in rural transport networks. They can come from communities and collaborating partners such as universities and NGOs with high engagement and determination. However, governments and regulators may also learn from the Peruvian case that created the RMIO/SRO figure.

When the above analysis includes considerations of integral sustainability, it is observed that involving different actors makes it easier for them to focus on specific aspects of sustainability. Cooperatives or local authorities strongly impact cultural and political sustainability but have less bargaining power than public institutions and wholesale telecommunication businesses. Also, the transport network management can be complex for a community, and involving ISPs, SROs, or other actors that bring communities together offers relevant advantages. In this sense, the figure of the SRO is playing an essential role in the case of Napo, although the sustainability of this model could be strengthened if local authorities or community cooperatives were more clearly incorporated.

The analysis also shows that, although there are various technologies to cover the needs of the access and transport network, wireless links continue to be the preferred solution for transport, and cellular technologies are more efficient and appropriate for the access network. This finding reinforces the importance of research into open-source technologies for both types of networks and the relevance of political advocacy to ensure that there are alternatives for access to mobile frequencies such as that opened by Rhizomatica in Mexico or offered by the SRO in Peru.

This analysis will be extended in future works by incorporating more examples of community networks that use different approaches and harvesting more accurate information about the cases. It also remains for future work to explore the role of MNOs in extending rural coverage and whether SROs can be a linking element between MNOs and community networks.

References

1. Braem, B., et al.: A case for research with and on community networks. In: ACM SIGCOMM Computer Communications Review, vol. 43(3), pp. 68–73 (2013)
2. Pittaluga, L.: Rivoir, A.: One laptop per child and bridging the digital divide: the case of plan CEIBAL in Uruguay. Inf. Technol. Int. Dev. **8**(4), 145–159 (2012)
3. Martinez-Fernandez., A., et al.: The TUCAN3G project: wireless technologies for isolated rural communities in developing countries based on 3G small cell deployments. IEEE Commun. Mag. **54**(7), 36–43 (2016)
4. Saldana, A., et al.: Alternative networks: toward global access to the internet for all. IEEE Commun. Mag. **55**(9), 187–193 (2017)
5. Saldana, J., et al: Alternative Network Deployments Taxonomy characterization technologies and architectures. IETF 7962 (2016)
6. Prieto-Egido, I., Simó-Reigadas, J., Martínez-Fernández, A.: Interdisciplinary alliances to deploy telemedicine services in isolated communities: the napo project case. Sustain. **10**, 2288 (2018)
7. Prieto-Egido, I., et al.: Small rural operators techno-economic analysis to bring mobile services to isolated communities: the case of Peru Amazon rainforest. Telecommun. Policy 44(10), 102039 (2020)

8. Rey-Moreno, C., et al: Experiences, challenges and lessons from rolling out a rural WiFi mesh network. In: Proceedings of the Symposium on Computing for Development, pp. 1–10. ACM, Bangalore (2013)

9. Magallanes-Blanco, C., Rodriguez-Medina, L.: Give Me a Mobile and I Will Raise a Community. Commun. Inf. Technol. Ann. (Stud. Media Commun.) **12**, 315–343 (2016)

10. Belli, L.: Community networks: The Internet by the people, for the people. Fundação Getulio Vargas Law School and Internet Society, Brasil (2017)

11. Rhizomatica Homepage. https://www.rhizomatica.org/. Accessed 10 Feb 2022

10 GHz Compact Shunt-Diode Rectifier Circuit Using Thin Film Ag/AZO Schottky Barrier Diode for Energy Harvesting Applications

Dalia Sadek[1]([envelope]) [ORCID], Abdelhalim Zekry[1] [ORCID], Heba Shawkey[2] [ORCID], and Somaya Kayed[3] [ORCID]

[1] Faculty of Engineering, Ain Shams University, Cairo, Egypt
Dalia.Sadek@Fa-hists.edu.eg
[2] Electronics Research Institute (ERI), Giza, Egypt
heba_shawkey@eri.sci.eg
[3] Obour High Institute for Engineering and Technology, 31 Elasmalia – Desert Road, Cairo, Egypt
dr.somayaismail@ohie.edu.eg

Abstract. A single layer microstrip diode rectifier circuit with a flexible thin film schottky diode is proposed. A compact half wave rectifier with a shunt-diode configuration is designed and implemented using off-shelf SMS-7630 low barrier Schottky diode tuned for a centre frequency of 10 GHz and fabricated one using 0.81 mm Rogers (RO4003c) substrate. The rectifier circuit with the commercial diode has a maximum conversion efficiency of 41% with 300 Ω load resistance. Al-doped-ZnO (AZO) semiconductor nanoparticle ink is used to fabricate a flexible thin film Schottky diode (TFSD). The proposed TFSD device consists of 3 layers, Ag/AZO/Cu and fabricated by deposition of a thin film of nanoparticle-ink AZO on a flexible copper tape substrate then applying an Ag electrode on the AZO to obtain the Schottky barrier diode with an active area of 1 mm^2. Measurements shows that the 280 nm thickness device has the maximum forward current density up to 0.28 A/cm^2 at 2 V. Also the measurements show that proposed rectifier has a maximum conversion efficiency 35% with 300 Ω load resistance which is smaller than that of the commercial diode because of the commercial diode is more conductive than the proposed thin film schottky diode. The overall size of the two rectifiers is 13.3 $\times$ 8.2 mm^2. The rectifier is simulated using an electromagnetic simulator with good agreement for both simulation and measurements.

Keywords: Energy harvesting · Rectifiers · Schottky diodes · Thin film schottky diode (TFSD) · Aluminum-doped zinc oxide (AZO) · Schottky contacts

1 Introduction

The use of wireless energy transfers as an alternative to traditional power sources embedded inside a building is greatly increasing. The development of high-efficiency rectenna as a critical component in converting RF power to dc power is increasing dramatically [1]. Earlier art designs function best at high input power, such as larger than 0 dBm, in the

G. Salvendy and J. Wei (Eds.): HCII 2022, LNCS 13337, pp. 436–445, 2022.
https://doi.org/10.1007/978-3-031-05014-5_36

frequency range 10 GHz or less [2–4]. In [2] Zbitou et al. built hybrid micro-wave sensitive rectenna with 65% efficiency for 20 dBm power input. Falkenstein et al. [3] designed a rec tenna with a 54% efficiency with a power density of 200 μW/cm2 or a power input of 9.54 dBm (assuming rectenna geometric area of 45 cm^2). Finally, Feifei Tan et al. created a rectifier [4] with a measured conversion efficiency of 72% and a length of 10 cm operating at 10 GHz with an input power of 87 mW. (19.4 dBm). Besides traditional rectenna implementation techniques, hybrid electronics systems enable the integration of electronic devices fabricated by different technologies driven by manufacturing considerations: sheets providing different functionality and different materials and devices. As the Schottky barrier diode (SBD) presents the main component in different electronics applications due to its use in semiconductor devices such as micro-wave photo detectors, transistors, solar cells, gas sensors, lasers, LEDs, and Nano-generators. Lintu et al. [5] constructed Au Schottky diodes on an RF sputtered ZnO thin film placed on an n-Silicon substrate and investigated their electrical properties using I-V and C-V measurements. With a rectifying ratio of 93, the I-V characteristics reveal the diode's rectifying nature. In [6] Alasghar et al. designed a 150 nm thickness, (AZO) thin film using the reactive DC-magnetron sputtering method in oxygen/argon gases. The temperature-dependent resistivity and the electrical behavior of the AZO/Au structure are compared. As a result, we were able to determine that Au contact is an appropriate electrode for thermoelectric devices, gas sensors, and dye-sensitized solar cells. Different literature fabricated thin film Schottky diode (TFSD) but they did not produce a complete circuit. The main idea of the paper is to compare the performance of the TFSD with the commercial diode in the rectenna circuits. For fair comparison, both diodes are set on the same substrate with the same layout. The main idea of the paper is to compare the off-shelf component with a thin film LAB-synthesis of the Schottky diode to be used in other applications. For fair comparison, both diodes are set on the same substrate with the same transmission lines structure (commercial copper on Rogers substrate) so that the effect of transmission lines is not considered in the comparison. This work presents a construction of a 10 GHz rectifier circuit for wireless power transmission with 2 different implementations for Schottky diode, off-shelf SMS-7630 and thin film Schottky diode implemented using nanoparticle ink AZO p-type semiconductor with a copper tap substrate and silver electrode. This paper is organized as follows: Sect. 2 introduces the shunt rectifier with an off-shelf Schottky diode. Section 3 presents the shunt rectifier with manufactured thin film Schottky diode. Section 4 depicts the results of the two rectifiers. Finally, Sect. 5 concludes the work.

2 Shunt RF Rectifier Circuit Architecture Using Off-Shelf Schottky Diode

The single shunt diode topology was chosen for the rectifier circuit. It is described fully in [7] and here we give an outline of it for the sake of completeness of the subject. The RF to DC conversion efficiency of the rectifier circuit is optimized at a given input power using a nonlinear optimization technique based on harmonic balance simulation and optimization goals (The optimization goal maximized the V_{dc} output voltage to maximize the conversion efficiency). A basic rectifier block design is shown in Fig. 1

with three primary sections: impedance matching for optimal power transfer between the antenna and the diode, a DC pass filter, and then a DC load. The diode selection and the impedance matching network are the two most important parts of a rectifier [8]. The rectifying device is the SMS-7630 low barrier schottky diode. The diode has a junction potential of 0.34 V and a break down voltage of 2 V. Because of its lower junction potential, the diode proved efficient for low-power operation [9]. Because a rectifier is a non-linear device, its input impedance is a function of input power, load, and frequency. In order to properly create the matching network, the non-linear impedance of the rectifier circuit was investigated. The shunt rectifier was tested using an electromagnetic simulator.

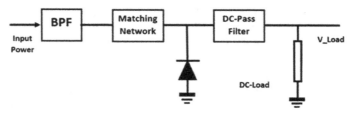

Fig. 1. General rectifier block diagram.

Using lumped LC components or microstrip lines, an impedance matching network (IMN) can be created in two methods. Lumped components become lossy at frequencies over 1 GHz, and the insertion loss of the matching network becomes significant, decreasing the rectifier's overall efficiency. A transmission line-based IMN was employed to avoid these lumped component losses [10]. The (IMN) is divided into two pieces. The first is a transmission line-based impedance transformer that was meant to match the real input impedance to 50 ohms in the desired band. (TL1) $\sim$ 1/8 λ0 (λ0 represents the wavelength at 10 GHz). Butterfly stub is the second one. Inserting stubs matched the imaginary input impedance (butterfly used to minimize the size of the rectifier). In ADS, the entire network was optimized to match the rectifier at the band for changing power levels. The rectifying circuit is built and tested, as illustrated in Fig. 2(a). Figure 2(b) shows the layout of the designed microwave rectifying circuit.

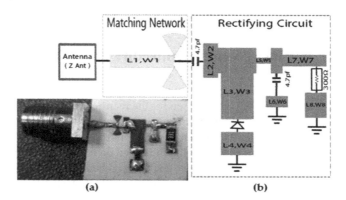

Fig. 2. (a) Photograph of the fabricated shunt rectifier (b) The shunt rectifier layout.

The suggested rectifying circuit is constructed on a Rogers (RO4003c) substrate with a relative dielectric constant of 3.38, a thickness of 0.81 mm, and a tan σ of 0.0026. Table 1 shows the geometric dimensions of the rectifying circuit represented in Fig. 2(b). The VNA (ROHDE&SCHWARZ ZVA6) is shown in Fig. 3(a) and is used to measure the return loss. Figure 3(b) depicts the measured data as well as the simulated |S11| of the rectifying circuit. It is well matched at 10 GHz with a simulated minimum |S11| of − 14 dB.

Table 1. Dimensions of the shunt rectifying circuit.

Geometrical parameters (mm)																
L1	W1	L2	W2	L3	W3	L4	W4	L5	W5	L6	W6	L7	W7	L8	W7
4	0.8	1	3	4	2.2	2	2.2	1	0.5	1	1.5	3	1	1.55	2.2

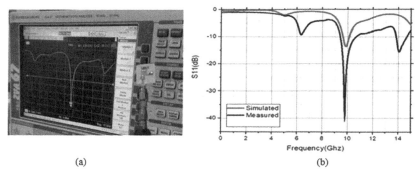

(a)   (b)

Fig. 3. (a) The measurement of S11 parameter using the VNA ROHDE&SCHWARZ ZVA6. (b) Comparison between simulation and measured reflection coefficient versus frequency.

The discrepancy between simulation and measurement is caused by various parameters, which are parasitic parameters in the PCB and Schottky diode at high frequencies, which can cause higher parasitic impedance and higher error [11].

3   Ag/AZO/Cu Thin Film Schottky Diode

The AZO Schottky diode device shown in Fig. 4 consists of 3 layers; a commercial copper tape as the flexible substrate, a thin film of p-type semiconductor nanoparticle-ink AZO (sigma Aldrich 807729 with 2.5 wt. %, of AZO in the solution and viscosity of 2.2 cP) and a silver measuring electrode. The active area of the structure (semiconductor) is 1 mm^2. The device is implemented in 280 nm thickness for the AZO.

3.1   TFSD Device Fabrication

The AZO layer was deposited on the copper tape by spin coating of Aluminum-doped zinc oxide nanoparticle ink. The spin coating is applied at 2000 rpm several times, heating the thin film on a hot plate at 80 °C and repeating the process several times. Finally, silver conductive paste is applied on the AZO surface and treated to 150 °C to obtain an Ag electrode.

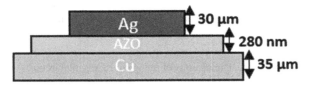

Fig. 4. Proposed thin film schottky diode device structure.

3.2   Rectifier Circuit Architecture Using Thin Film Schottky

The proposed TFSD is used to implement a complete shunt rectifier circuit similar to the commercial rectifier in Sect. 2 and the fabricated rectifier is depicted in Fig. 5(a). The measured S11 parameter of the rectifier circuit is shown in Fig. 5(b). There is an appreciable deviation at the 10 GHz frequency side of the S11 curve. This is due to the matching circuit, additional parasitic capacitance in the experimental device, in addition to the effects of the connectors at these higher frequencies. There are also fabrication tolerances to consider [12].

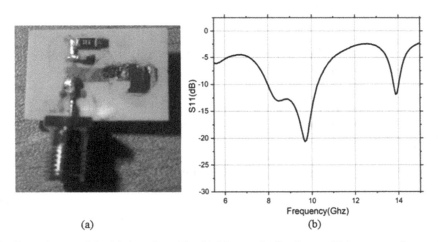

(a)   (b)

Fig. 5. (a) Image of the fabricated rectifier (b) Measured reflection coefficient versus frequency.

3.3 TFSD DC Current- Voltage (I-V) Measurement

The DC I-V properties for TFSD is examined using a Keithley Semiconductor Characterization System model 4200. The typical I–V characteristic curve of AZO Schottky diode is depicted in Fig. 6.

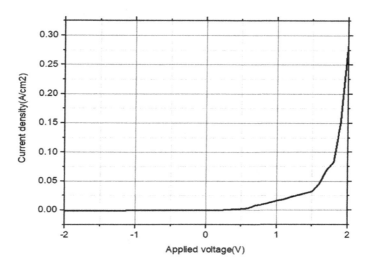

Fig. 6. I-V characteristics of the AZO Schottky diode.

The current–voltage (I–V) characteristics of the fabricated AZO thin film Schottky diode is measured in the voltage range between − 2 to 2 V at AZO thickness (280 nm). The current varies linearly at low voltage, whereas, with increasing applied voltage, the effective width of the barrier becomes narrower and the current increases exponentially, which indicates Schottky nature [13]. The I–V characteristics indicate a nonlinear rectifying behavior with a forward current density up to 0.28 A/cm^2 at 2 V.

4 Rectifier Circuits Measurements

The measurement setup is shown in Fig. 7(a) and Fig. 7(b). An Anritsu MG3697C RF/Microwave signal generator is used to send a microwave signal which connects to the rectifier at the proposed frequency of 10 GHz. Then a voltmeter is connected with the rectifier under test (RUT) to measure the DC output voltage for both rectifiers. As a result, the suggested rectifier's RF-DC conversion efficiency (η) is expressed as:

$$\eta = \frac{V_{DC}^2}{P_{in}R_L} \times 100\%$$

where VDC is the voltage across the resistive load RL, Pin is the RF input power.

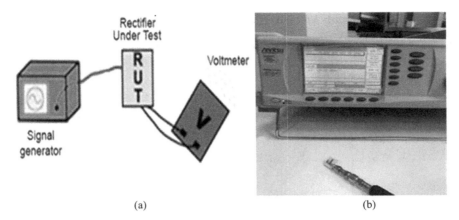

(a)   (b)

Fig. 7. (a) Rectifier measurement setup (b) Photo of the measurement setup.

4.1 Measurement Results for Rectifier with Off-Shelf Schottky Diode

The rectifier is tested over different input power levels. The simulated and measured DC output voltage and conversion efficiency versus the input power for the rectifier are displayed in Fig. 8(a) and (b) respectively. The performance was measured by sweeping the input power (Pin) from −10 dBm to 10 dBm at 300 Ω of load resistance. The simulation results were plotted with red markers and the measurement results were illustrated by black markers. The DC output can provide the maximum efficiency of 41%, 0.51 V output voltage at 7 dBm of input power.

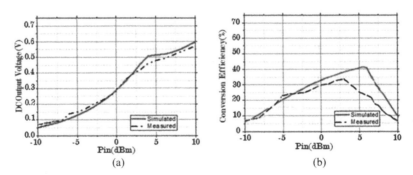

(a)   (b)

Fig. 8. (a) Measured and simulated performance of the proposed rectifier with off - shelf diode versus continuous wave input power at 10 GHz, (a) DC voltage and (b) conversion efficiency.

Figure 8 shows there is a peak value of the conversion efficiency at a specific input power Pin. There is also a large discrepancy between the simulation results and the measured ones, which can be attributed to the model of the rectifier diode in addition to the fabrication tolerances of the geometrical features. However, the difference in DC output voltage between the measured and simulated results is much less pronounced.

Table 2 shows the performance comparison between the proposed rectifier and others previously reported in the literature within the same frequency range. The rectifier in [4] has more efficiency than the proposed rectifier but with more power input needed and more size area. The proposed rectifier has more efficiency (34%) compared to [14] at the same power input, 0 dBm.

Table 2. RF-to-dc conversion efficiency vs power input & frequency.

Reference	Max efficiency	Power input (dBm)	Frequency (GHz)
[4]	72%	19.4	10
[14]	25%	0	10
This work	41%	7	10

4.2 Measurement Results for Rectifier with Thin Film Schottky Diode

The conversion efficiency of the rectifier is measured with respect to the rectifier load at the range of −10 dBm to 10 dBm of input power. The optimal load resistance is around 300Ω for 0 dBm input power at the frequency of 10 GHz. Figure 9(a) and (b) depict the measured DC output voltage and conversion efficiency values respectively. As a result, at 0 dBm of input power, the maximum conversion efficiency of 35% is achieved. As can be observed in Fig. 9, conversion efficiency increases until the input power approaches 0dBm, beyond which it rapidly drops. The conversion efficiency reaches 20% between −10 dBm and −2.5 dBm input power. At a frequency of 10 GHz for all input power levels, the shunt rectifier with off-shelf schottky diode has a greater conversion efficiency and DC voltage than a shunt diode rectifier with thin film diode, as seen in Figs. 8 and 9.

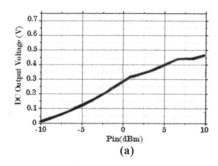
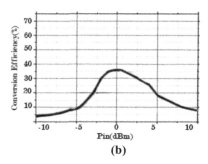

(a)   (b)

Fig. 9. Measured performance of the proposed rectifier with thin film diode versus continuous wave input power at 10 GHz, (a) DC voltage and (b) conversion efficiency.

This is attributed to the better conductive behavior of the commercial diodes than the proposed TFSD diodes at the same forward bias voltage. But it looks promising as, in spite of much less conduction current at the same forward DC voltage, its RF power harvesting parameters are close to a commercial diode. With the advancement of nanotechnology and polymer science, there is a growing interest in the research and development of both efficient and low-cost semiconductor thin film materials [15].

5 Conclusions

Rectifiers with a single shunt diode using off-shelf schottky and also the same design as the rectifier but replacing the off-shelf schottky with flexible thin film schottky configurations are successfully developed and analyzed in this study. A stub matching network is used for impedance matching between the antenna and rectifier sections. The proposed fabricated Schottky diode has a lower performance parameter than the commercial Schottky diode because it is less conductive than the commercial one. However, in spite of much less conduction current at the same forward DC voltage, its RF power harvesting parameters are close to the commercial diode. This is really an amazing result that needs more investigations in coming papers.

References

1. Christopher, R.V., Gregory, D.D.: Harvesting wireless power: survey of energy-harvester conversion efficiency in far-field; wireless power transfer systems. IEEE Microwave Magaz. **15**, 108–120 (2014)
2. Sadek, D., Shawkey, H., Zekry, A.: Multiband triple L-Arms patch antenna with diamond slot ground for 5G applications. ACES J. **36**(3), March 2021
3. Erez, F., Michael, R., Zoya, P.: Low-power wireless power delivery. IEEE Trans. Microwave 2012. Theory Techn. **60**(7), 2277–2286 (2012)
4. Feifei, T., Changjun, L.: Theoretical and experimental development of a high-conversion-efficiency rectifier at X-band. Int. J. Microw. Wirel. Technol. **9**, 985–994 (2016)
5. Lintu, R., Periasamy, C., Vinett, S.: Electrical characterization of Au/ZnO thinfilm Schottky diode on silicon substrate. Perspectives Sci. Direct **8**, 66–68 (2016)
6. Aliasghar, S., Laya, D.: Experimental and theoretical investigations on temperature and voltage dependence of an Au/AZO thin-film Schottky diode. International Nano Letters (2019)
7. Sadek, D., Zekry, A., Shawkey, H.A.: Compact and high efficiency rectenna for wireless power harvesting applications. Int. J. Antennas Propagation **2021**, 8 (2021)
8. Shabnam, L., Ajay, B.G., Ke, W.: A high-efficiency 24 GHz rectenna development towards millimeter-wave energy harvesting and wireless power transmission. IEEE Trans. Microwave. Theory Tech. **61**(12), 3358–3366 (2014)
9. Mutee, U., Rehman, Waleed, A., Wasif, T.K.: High Efficient Dual band 2.45/5.58 rectifier for RF energy harvesting applications in ISM band. In: Proceedings of Asia Pacific Microwave conference, IEEE (2017)
10. Mutee, U.R., Waleed, A., Muhammed, I.Q., Wasif, T.K.: A highly efficient tri band (GSM1800, WiFi2400 and WiFi5000) rectifier for various radio frequency harvesting applications. In: Progress in Electromagnetics Research Symposium Journal. (PIERS — FALL), Singapore, pp. 19–22 (2017)

11. Ekkaphol, K., Yan, Z., Ekachai, L.: A dual-band rectifier for RF energy harvesting systems. In: 11th International Conference on Electrical Engineering/Electronics, Thailand. IEEE (2014)
12. Karthikeya, G.S., Abegaonkar, M.P., Koul, S.K.: Low cost high gain triple band mmwave Sierpinski antenna loaded with uniplanar EBG for 5G Applications. In: IEEE International Conference on Antenna Innovations & Modern Technologies for Ground, Aircraft and Satellite Applications (2017)
13. Tsiarapas, C., Girginoudi, D., Georgoulas, N.: Electrical characteristics of Pd Schottky contacts on ZnO films. Mater. Sci. Semiconductor Process **17**, 199–206 (2014)
14. Eric, K., Rodenbeck, C.T., Taylor, B., Zoya, P.: Power-combined rectenna array for X-band wireless power transfer. In: MTT-S International Microwave Symposium. IEEE (2020)
15. Orkut, S.: Technological Background and Properties of Thin Film Semiconductors, Century Surface Science, April 2020

A Comparative Study of Navigation API ETA Accuracy for Shuttle Bus Tracking

Gan Shu Qian[1], Ammar Ashraf Bin Narul Akhla[1], Chee Ling Thong[1], Abdul Samad Shibghatullah[1(✉)], Su Mon Chit[1], Lee Yen Chaw[2], and Chiw Yi Lee[3]

[1] Institute of Computer Science and Digital Innovation, UCSI University, Kuala Lumpur, Malaysia
abdulsamad@ucsiuniversity.edu.my
[2] UCSI Graduate Business School, UCSI University, Kuala Lumpur, Malaysia
[3] UCSI College, Kuala Lumpur, Malaysia

Abstract. This study compares three selected navigation applications which are Google Maps, Waze and HERE WeGo, through the study of each application's Application Programming Interface (API). The study is focusing on the aspect of Estimated Time of Arrival (ETA) accuracy, in an attempt to determine which API are suitable to be integrated and implemented in the development of a shuttle bus application. To date, there are currently lacking studies that discuss or compare the implementation of API in the development of shuttle bus tracking and ETA application. This study focuses on finding which API is the best suitable for such development from an ETA perspective, using the navigation application where the APIs were implemented or based on as a tool of testing. An experiment was conducted in a city in Kuala Lumpur, Malaysia, by collecting the ETA of the navigation applications from multiple points while riding a scheduled shuttle bus. The ETA will be compared with actual arrival time (ATA) using RMSE, MAE and PE metric. Comparison results showed Google Maps app provides the most consistent ETA prediction accuracy in a conservative manner and is the most suitable to be incorporated into a simple bus tracking and ETA app. The significant contribution of this study is to provide a result of comparison of the ETA accuracy through selected navigation applications and comparison of their navigation API.

Keywords: Estimated time of arrival · Navigation applications · Google maps · Waze · HERE WeGo · Application Programming Interface

1 Introduction

Bus transportations services is one example of public transportations that serves as a mode of transportation in urban environments that includes metropolitan, city and campus areas. Taking a public shuttle bus as an example, factors such as frequency of bus services, safety, travel time, weather conditions, number of passengers and service information has a potential to influence the people's decision in selecting the bus as their transportation mode (Hiroi et al. 2019; Noor et al. 2020; Borhan et al. 2019). Commuters highly appreciate real-time information such as ETA, as these can help to

G. Salvendy and J. Wei (Eds.): HCII 2022, LNCS 13337, pp. 446–461, 2022.
https://doi.org/10.1007/978-3-031-05014-5_37

plan their journey to their respective destinations (Yue et al. 2017). ETA is an aspect that has been beneficial to all users, either for self-owned vehicles or public transportations users.

Aligning with the growth of technology, various applications have been developed for the purpose of bus tracking, as well as ETA estimation in order to improve the trust and perception of users towards public transportation. Several literatures and studies have discussed regarding the development of applications for such service. (Kadam et al. 2018; Sangkhapan et al. 2020; Tan et al. 2016; Sriram et al. 2017), are amongst the works done in the attempt to create an effective bus tracking app. Kadam et al. (2018) proposes a system to track public buses using GPS and IR sensors, and uses the Euclidean Distance formula to calculate an ETA. Sangkhapan et al. (2020) proposed Smart Bus Management System Architecture Using Mesh App and Service Architecture using 3 main modules: smart IoT stack, smart GPS tracking system, and smart bus management system (SBMS) to support multiple hardware settings. Tan and Wong (2016) proposed a campus bus tracking system using WiFi proximity technique which means, the location of the bus will only be known if it is inside the campus, the ETA calculator will be based on the distance between the Wireless Access Points and the GPS information. Sriram et al. (2017) uses Artificial Neural Networks (ANN) to calculate the ETA for public commute using the data collected by the hardware mounted on the bus through MQTT (Message Queuing Telemetry Transport) protocol. Yue et al. (2017), Thong et al. (2019), and Chit et al. (2017) are examples of studies proposing a bus tracking app in the Kuala Lumpur region. While Yue et al. (2017) only focus on preliminary study on development of the bus tracking application, Thong et al. (2019), and Chit et al. (2017) have already developed a bus tracking application. However, there is a lack of literature and studies that discusses or implements the Application Programming Interface (API), developed by various organizations such as Google, Waze and others in the development of applications for bus tracking and ETA service.

Other than developing the application which provides such functionality by implementing the developer's mechanism and algorithm, incorporating a reliable API is also an option. API has the benefit of providing automation making completion of the task faster with less human effort, allowing customization and personalization service for the end users, great integration with users' system and equality in data update when new data update is available (Bauer et al. 2019). Navigation API is a specific type of API providing a suite of geolocation API and mapping building blocks that enables software developers to retrieve the data they need to create a routing or navigation related application, from identifying locations and displaying maps, to providing directions and customizing journeys. Through examining the product page of a API such as Sygic API (Sygic API 2020), HERE API (HERE API 2020), MapQuest API (MapQuest API 2020), Google Maps API (Google Maps API 2020) and OpenstreetMap API (OpenStreetMap API 2020), it is understood that depending on the API provider, navigation APIs typically support use cases such as GPS navigation software, retail guidance and fleet management. A bus tracking and ETA app falls perfectly under the first use case: GPS navigation software, where the Navigation API is able to use the map data provided or hosted by the API, leveraging the historical data and real time information to deliver routing services, calculating an optimized routes using real time data, turn-by-turn navigation and estimate travel time through the respective API's algorithm. When using an API, the developer need not to consider the map data, the processes and algorithms required to calculate the ETA, the data are provided to the developer through the API. Accurate ETA might be able to address the long waiting time issue reported by users in (Thong et al. 2019). It is made known to this study that the shuttle bus tracking app developed from Thong et al.'s study is based on Google API service, however the ETA accuracy provided by the application is not considered accurate.

The lack of study that focuses on ETA accuracy in API, especially in shuttle bus tracking and ETA application motivates this study. This study also serves as evaluation of ETA accuracy for (Thong et al. 2019; Chit et al. 2017) as the application developed uses Google API to track the shuttle bus and provide ETA. The objective of this study is to compare selected navigation applications which implement different API, focusing on comparing from the aspect of ETA accuracy in order to determine the suitable API to be integrated in the development of a shuttle bus tracking and ETA application. The following sections in this study are organized as follows. Literature review will be briefly discussed in Sect. 2. Section 3 describes the methodology used for comparison study. In Sect. 4, the results of the work will be compared and discussed. Lastly, the conclusion and future work of the study will be in Sect. 5.

2 Literature Review

2.1 Shuttle Bus and ETA

For the selection of a suitable API for the development of a shuttle bus ETA and tracking app, there are many aspects to consider such as the number of app users, pricing, documentation, ease of use and the features. For a bus tracking and ETA app, the navigation APIs best fits the purpose, where generally, a navigation APIs feature functionalities such as real time location tracking, turn by turn navigation, calculation of ETA, routing and rerouting. However, for a shuttle bus service tracking and ETA app, the most important aspect to take into account is the real time location tracking and calculation of ETA. This is because shuttle bus service is characterized by fixed route and schedules (Yim and Ceder 2006), hence the turn by turn navigation and rerouting is not required. When the schedule is arranged, the ETA is roughly estimated. From a user's perspective, it is important to them to know the location of the bus at the moment as well as their ETA so they can plan their time efficiently for commuting (Watkins et al. 2011).

Besides the factor of uncertainty in time while waiting for the arrival of the bus (Stradling et al. 2007) found out that the bus riders are concerned about their safety issues and having anxiety while waiting for the bus in general. Research conducted by Stradling et al. (2007) and Dziekan and Kottenhoff (2007) have found that bus riders have experienced a decrease in perceived waiting time when given the bus's real time information to refer to while waiting at the bus stops. Real-time information such as location tracking and ETA is an important information for road users and travellers for decision making. It is easily accessible by anyone in existing navigation applications around the world, such as Google Maps, Waze, MapQuest, and others.

Hannon et al. (2019) made a comparison of five different map providers and applications which is Google Maps, HERE, Bing Maps, Waze and MapQuest, to compare and assess the quality of traffic information which is ETA and ATA in the quest to find out which has the shortest and accurate ETA using a web mining system to gather traffic data. Through their experiment, MapQuest appears to be the most accurate, while Bing Maps takes the position of being the least accurate when providing ETA. A group of researchers in Jordan (Alomari and Al-Omari 2020) conducted an ETA accuracy performance comparison between Google Maps, Waze and HERE WeGo. The study concluded that Google Maps and Waze over estimated ETA in general while HERE WeGo underestimated the ETA most of the time. While conducting ANOVA test, the statistic showed there are no significant differences between Google Maps and Waze in terms of mean error but HERE WeGo's ETA mean error differs significantly from the other two applications. Information such as the time of departure, day of the week, the location of the buses, number of intersections and traffic signals are part of the historical data in a traffic information management system (Li et al. 2011), when developing Bus-Arrival Time Prediction Model based on historical traffic patterns, Yu et al. (2013) admitted traffic light and traffic congest to be a crucial factor to be considered for accurate ETA prediction. Li, et al. (2011) and Yu et al. (2013) influenced this study to include traffic congestion and traffic light as part of the aspects to investigate.

For measuring the accuracy of the ETA predictions, there are two of the most common metrics used to measure accuracy for continuous variables: mean absolute error (MAE) and root mean squared error (RMSE). The MAE is suitable to describe uniformly distributed errors. Because model errors are likely to have a normal distribution rather than a uniform distribution, the RMSE is a better metric to present than the MAE for such type of data (Chai and Draxler 2014). There are often disputes between RMSE and MAE (Willmott and Matsuura 2005), when assessing the accuracy of the applications, it is found that the results found using both modelling metrics are minimal, however the difference did help the study for further choosing the most accurate algorithm.

i. MAE

n = number of test cases.
ATA = actual arrival time.
ETA = estimated arrival time.

To calculate the MAE, the sum of the total difference between ATA and ETA will be calculated. MAE of each application will be calculated and compared. MAE is only a metric to measure the error rate of the prediction model, the volume of the data does not affect the value. The smaller the value of MAE, the more accurate the ETA predicted is. Hence, RMSE and MAE will be compared separately.

ii. RMSE

n = number of test cases.
ATA = actual arrival time.
ETA = estimated arrival time.

To calculate the RMSE, the sum of the total difference between ATA and ETA will be calculated. The difference between the calculation if RMSE and MAE is RMSE is square rooted, therefore the result is presented as the same unit as the data, in this case, in units of minutes. The larger the dataset, the bigger the RMSE value. The smaller the value of RMSE, the more accurate the ETA predicted is.

iii. PE

Percentage Error (PE) is the error of percentage compared to the ATA. When the percentage is a negative value, it means the app is conservative on the ETA prediction where it predicts that a vehicle will arrive at the destination late. On the contrary, if the percentage is a positive value, the app predicts the ETA optimistically where it predicts the vehicle will arrive at destination in a shorter time compared to the actual arrival time.

2.2 Navigation API

Some of the most popular navigation applications have developed their own API containing the data and information they have collected such as the road condition, stop light location and map data to share to other developers where some are only subscription-based, some are free. Google Maps API is the one of the most popular platforms that provide APIs. Google Maps API has already divided Maps API into several APIs, making Google Maps a platform. However, in this study, this API will be referred to as Google Maps API as Google Maps API as more than one element in Google Maps platform namely Google Directions API and Maps Javascript API are required to carry out routing and traffic data functions respectively (Google Maps API 2020), where Directions API provides the routing and ETA function, Maps Javascript API includes a traffic data layer collected through Google Maps application. Waze is a subsidiary of Google company, Waze API;s documentation is available on Google Website. However, it is only available for members who successfully signed up for the Waze SDK program. The Waze API is able to retrieve ETA and routing points and Waze's real-time traffic and location data, calculating the fastest route and navigating the user (Waze 2020).Here API is a navigation API most known with its accuracy as it has a comprehensive coverage that is updated on a near daily basis. The features offered by HERE API include navigation with augmented reality (AR), fleet telematics, high-precision maps, location advertising, tracking, routing and map visualization (HERE 2020). Mapbox is a navigation API used by Facebook and Snapchat for mapping purposes. Its features include map data, live updating map data, location searches, navigation and custom map. The data fed to the API are from both open and proprietary sources (Mapbox 2020). MapQuest API provides many functionalities. In its Direction API various routing options such as route type, optimised routing and route matrix are provided. In the Traffic API, the traffic service provides real time traffic information related to markets, incidents, and flow. (MapQuest Business 2020) OpenStreetMap API is one of the most famous API in navigation. Works like Wikipedia, it can be edited for fetching and saving raw geo data from/to the OpenStreetMap database. However, it does not provide routing and ETA functionality. (OpenStreetMap 2020).

In a shuttle bus tracking and ETA application, the characteristics or features to look for in the API are whether traffic data is provided, whether the API provides origin-destination routing as well as providing an ETA, and whether the API has rich historical data in the region where the shuttle bus operates. If the API is able to select a route, the travel time in the route can be computed using a prediction algorithm. Traffic data and historical data are two of the factors that affect the ETA prediction result. (Chien et al. 2002).

Comparing API is not a popular topic. Bauer et al. (2019) in their studies have discussed several web mapping providers' API which is Google Maps, TomTom, Bing and HERE as a real-time traffic information source in the aspect of their capabilities, strengths and weaknesses. But through their studies, ETA is not an aspect that has been discussed, as they are focusing on the whole structure of API through the conduct of quantitative and qualitative analysis. Bauer et al. (2019) compared Google Maps API, HERE API and TomTom API in their functions of providing real time traffic data. Waze API was not selected as one of the API to study because it does not provide live traffic layer data in its API. While comparing Google Maps API and HERE API, it is found that HERE API provides the most detailed real time traffic information. HERE also has the widest scope of service and information content, but Google Maps API has the benefit of being affordable. Both Google Maps API and the HERE API are able to achieve good geographic accuracy which is useful for location tracking and travel duration which calculates the ETA. HERE API does support other features that are not available on Google Maps API such as incident and flow traffic data in the same API (Bauer et al. 2019). Katona (2019) conducted a comparison between Google Maps API and Waze API to examine the route planning performance of the navigation applications. The goal of this article was to give an idea for the government of Hungary on how they can improve their daily work through the implementation of routing features in navigation applications through its API. However, only Google Maps data has been analyzed as Waze is owned by Google.

To compare test the APIs, the navigation application developed by the API provider will be tested. Google Maps and Waze are charting top 2 under Navigation Category in Apple App Store and Google Play Store in Malaysia; Here WeGo is an alternative to Google Maps implemented as the default map in Huawei mobile phones. According to a statistic provided by Canalys, the top 5 smartphone vendors in Malaysia for the second quarter of 2020 are Vivo, Oppo, Samsung, Huawei and Xiaomi (Xiung et al. 2020), out of the the top 5 vendors, Huawei is the only vendors that does not offer Google services as the aftermath of US Sanctions, as a solution Huawei included Here WeGo app on its app gallery as a replacement for Google Maps (Huawei Community 2020). The large market share of Huawei locally and globally (Canalys 2020) is a significant factor affecting the decision of the study to include it in the experiment.

3 Methodology

For this study, an experiment has been conducted to further investigate and compare the accuracy of ETA provided by the selected navigation applications. The steps of the experiment are as follows:

Step 1: Three navigation applications are selected for the experiment, which are Google Maps, Waze, and HERE WeGo. Since the purpose of this study is to identify the suitable API for development of shuttle bus tracking and ETA app, it is important that the selected NA to be tested fulfill the following requirements:

(i) The developer of the studied navigation application must have a public navigation API available for other applications developers. According to the documentations, the API must be able to calculate the ETA between defined origin and destination (Google Maps API 2020; HERE API 2020; Waze 2020).

(ii) The navigation application must have a high number of users in the studied geographical area. Navigation application is a means to collect data for the API, in this paper, it is assumed that as the number of users of the navigation application increases, the volume of historical data collected to improve the NA service increases exponentially (HERE WeGo 2020; Google Privacy Terms 2020; Privacy Policy of Waze 2020).

Step 2: The navigation applications are installed in three Android smartphones, running on Android version 10. The applications are configured to follow the route which is taken by the bus as illustrated in Fig. 2, and the ETA to each stop and points 1 to 5 are taken. The points are added between stops, making a total of 8 points of data collection, in order to determine whether the ETA is recalculated according to the current traffic conditions such as traffic jams, and stop lights. Points between stops are selected based on the stop light or road branches. The experiment was conducted by two researchers by riding a university shuttle bus at three different time slots in the span of two days. The time slots chosen for the experiment are chosen based on the different traffic conditions at different times of the day which is from 12–3 pm. Three trips from the shuttle bus schedule were selected for each day making a total of six trips entailed in Table 1. Using Google Maps's future ETA predictive functions (Google Maps 2020), the Trips selected are based on the predicted total travel time and are categorised based on the level of traffic congestion: heavy, medium and low. The main recorded data throughout the experiment was the ETA provided by each application, as well as the ATA.

Table 1. Selected bus trips and traffic congestion level

Test cases/bus trips	Traffic congestion level according to google maps future traffic prediction
Test Case 1: 18th September 2020 12pm	Low
Test Case 2: 18th September 2020 1.30pm	Medium
Test Case 3: 18th September 2020 3pm	High
Test Case 4: 22nd September 2020 12pm	Low
Test Case 5: 22nd September 2020 1.30pm	Medium
Test Case 6: 22nd September 2020 3pm	High

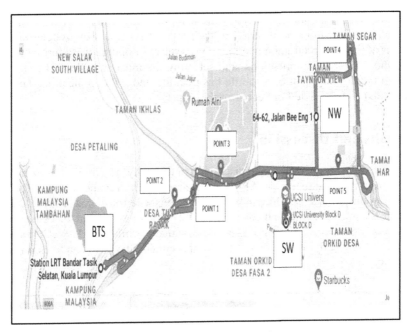

Fig. 1. Route map of shuttle bus

The details of each route segment are recorded in Table 2. Traffic Li et al. (2011)

Table 2. Route segments and description

Route Segments	Description
SW - Point 1	The bus departs from the bus stop and heads to Point 1
Point 1 - BTS	At Point 1, the route enters into an intersection and encounters the first stoplight. The route to BTS is also under construction and often encounters traffic congestion
BTS - Point 2	The route from BTS to Point 2 is straight
Point 2 - Point 3	At Point 2, the route enters into an intersection and encounters another stop light
Point 3 - NW	At Point 3, the route takes an entrance ramp into a highway before entering the residential area where NW is located
NW - Point 4	From NW to Point 4, the route exits the residential area into a highway
Point 4- Point 5	At Point 4, the route takes an entrance ramp into a highway
Point 5 - SW	At Point 5, the route enters another highway before entering a residential area where SW is located

Step 3: The recorded data was analyzed by using metric formulas MAE, RMSE, and PE, in order to determine the accuracy of the provided ETA, as well as determining the behaviour of the ETA prediction in either conservative or optimistic to further relate the ETA to the API of the applications, and selecting the most suitable API to be implemented in the development of a shuttle bus tracking and ETA application. The results are presented and discussed in Sect. 4 of this paper.

4 Results and Discussion

This section presents the results and discussion of the study. The three chosen navigation applications were used to test the API/ETA accuracy at different peak hours. The results show that amongst the three, Google Maps as seen on the leftmost image in Fig. 3 appears to provide the most accurate and conservative ETA, Waze as seen on the center in Fig. 3 ranks the second and predicts the ETA conservatively while HERE WeGo as seen on the rightmost image in Fig. 3 provides the least accurate ETA, often underestimating the travel time.

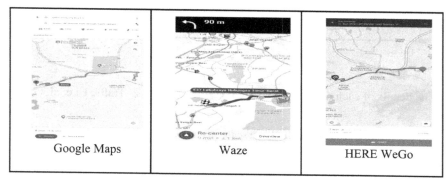

Fig. 2. Navigation apps interface

At each point, the ETA, which is displayed at the bottom of the navigation application interface as shown in Fig. 2, are recorded into Table 3. The data is then analyzed using MAE, RMSE and PE. Table 3 displays the method of data collection by this study, through the ride taken in a university shuttle bus on its fixed route, as displayed in Fig. 2 and described in Table 2. TBS, NW and SW are the stops, Point 1 falls between SW and TBS; Point 2 and Point 3 falls between TBS and NW; Point 4 and Point 5 falls between NW and SW. At each stop and point, the ETA to the next stop provided by Google Maps, Waze and Here WeGo app are recorded in two formats: remaining time to travel and time of arrival. The difference between the ATA and ETA are recorded in the column next to time. The time difference between ETA and ATA are later used to calculate the MAE and RMSE where it is known as error.

Table 3. Example of ETA and ATA data collected

	Google maps			Waze			Here WeGo		
	Remaining travel time (minutes)	ETA	Difference (minutes)	Remaining travel time (minutes)	ETA	Difference (minutes)	Remaining travel time (minutes)	ETA	Difference (minutes)
Depart Time	1.29								
SW - TBS	12	1.41	4	10	1.39	6	9	1.38	7
Point 1 - TBS	8	1.41	4	6	1.39	6	4	1.37	8
Actual Arrival time to TBS	1.45								
Depart Time	1.45								
TBS - NW	11	1.56	−3	8	1.53	0	8	1.53	0
Point 2 - NW	7	1.55	−2	5	1.53	0	5	1.53	0
Point 3 - NW	4	1.54	−1	3	1.53	0	3	1.53	0
Actual Arrival time to NW	1.53								
Depart Time	1.54								
NW - SW	9	2.03	−1	9	2.03	−1	10	2.04	−2
Point 4- SW	7	2.04	−2	6	2.03	−1	7	2.04	−2
Point 5 - SW	5	2.04	−2	4	2.03	−1	3	2.02	0
Actual Arrival time to SW	2.02								

Table 4. Applications ETA accuracy performance in RMSE metrics.

RMSE			
	Google Maps	Waze	HERE WeGo
In General (minutes)	13.34	14.49	18.28
With Stop Light (minutes)	0.49	0.58	0.58
With Traffic Jam (minutes)	0.46	0.38	0.62

Results (i) MAE

In Fig. 3, the general performance of ETA accuracy using MAE as the metric, Waze appears to be the most accurate app in terms of calculating ETA, the performance degrades while predicting ETA in route with stop light but returned to similar rate by a slight degrade during route with traffic jam. HERE WeGo has the most inaccurate ETA in general situations, in routes with stop light and performs even worse when encountering traffic jams. Google Maps ETA accuracy is not the best, in general, its performance is similar to HERE WeGo. Unlike HERE WeGo and Waze, Google Maps has the most consistent ETA predictability.

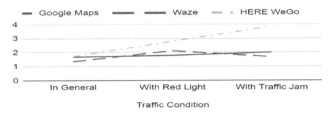

Fig. 3. Applications ETA accuracy performance in MAE metrics.

(ii) RMSE

In RMSE, the bigger the data, the larger the RMSE value. As the data size for each traffic condition is different, it is best to compare the RMSE between each navigation app of a traffic condition. In general, Google Maps has the best accuracy, slightly better than Waze while HERE WeGo has a considerably higher inaccuracy than the former. Same as the result in MAE, Google Maps has the best ETA accuracy in the route with stop light, while in the route section with traffic jams, Waze performs the best. In the route segments with stop light, Google Maps performs the best in terms of RMSE where Waze and HERE WeGo performs similarly in the metrics. The MAE of all navigation applications dropped significantly compared to the general performance. Google Maps is a clear winner when there is a traffic light situation where the ETA is closest to the ATA. MAE and RMSE results are consistent when measuring the accuracy of the ETA prediction in the route segment with traffic jams as presented in Table 3. On contraire to the general performance and the stop light situation, Waze has the highest accuracy when there is traffic congestion. According to MAE, it is clear that Waze performs better than how it did when encountering stop light while Google Maps performance dropped significantly when encountering traffic congestion. Under all route situations, HERE WeGo predicts the most inaccurate ETA, when the vehicle encounters traffic jams, the error in predicting the ETA is twice the error of Waze's.

(iii) PE

PE is examined to determine the behaviour of ETA prediction of the navigation applications as unlike MAE and RMSE, it does not present the error in absolute form. In terms of PE, Google Maps and Waze are far more negative compared to HERE WeGo, which means they predict the ETA in a very conservative way. This result is aligned with the discovery of (Alomari and Al-Omari 2020). Google Maps and Waze both displayed negative value while HERE WeGo is the only navigation app with positive value in PE. HERE WeGo achieves badly in terms and accuracy as well as being too optimistic on the ETA prediction indicates that the presence of stop light does not affect the ETA algorithms of the navigation app as it neglected the time a vehicle spent in the stop light.

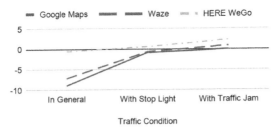

Fig. 4. Applications ETA accuracy performance in PE metrics

Discussion

HERE WeGo's performance in both traffic jams and stop lights indicates that HERE WeGo showed it weakness that it does not take traffic congestion and traffic light into consideration when predicting ETA resulting it to give the least accurate ETA as displayed in Fig. 3, Fig. 4 and Table 4 where its MAE, PE and RMSE value are much higher than its peers. Waze as a crowdsourcing map and traffic information has its strength in predicting the ETA based on the live information actively provided by its users. Referring to Fig. 3 and Table 4, Google Maps's ability to perform comparatively well during stop lights might be due to the civil information provided to the company by the government. HERE WeGo is a less popular but uprising choice for Malaysian users as result of the recent banning of Google Services on the second largest smartphone market worldwide (Canalys 2020). Through Bauer et al (2019), it is understood that HERE API provides incident and flow service which is useful in prediction ETA, however it was not effective in the studied area in this research as there is simply not enough historical data to support the service as seen from the experiment result of this study. Hence, even with less extra services, Google Maps API would still perform better in the studied area although HERE API has the services able to support better ETA prediction. Comparing the ETA provided by the API through their application is only one of the factors to evaluate the best choice of developing a shuttle bus tracking app, choosing the one that is suitable for the route conditions, budget, developer preferences and many other factors are equally important. HERE has an open source SDK providing various APIs such as Tracking and Routing where the former provides a fast, flexible way to add real-time and historical location to any IoT product and the latter provide precise instructions to a destination using various transport modes with detailed turn-by-turn instructions and graphical representation on top of the HERE map (HERE 2020). Google Maps open source SDK has a Direction API made for routing purposes where it calculates directions between locations using an HTTP request where it also takes traffic data in account but only with Google Maps Platform Premium Plan client ID. (Google 2020). Citing Armstrong (2015) in a study on forecasting, this study recommends forecasts to be more conservative rather than optimistic in order to have a higher level of trust with the user. In short, from the point of view of a developer, Google Maps API that has a rich set of historical data publicly available is the most suitable to be incorporated for a simple navigation app such as a shuttle bus tracking and ETA app. This is because Google Maps API can provide the consistent ETA prediction accuracy in all traffic situations encountered in the shuttle bus route, the error rate of ETA prediction is also comparatively low. Besides, the lowest starting development cost but does not sacrifice functionality and accuracy. While the lowest plan supports only 50,000 transactions per month, the plan is upgradable with a cost. Last but not least, include a live traffic data API provider. As discovered in this experiment and through literature review, the importance of a live traffic data is a key factor for accurate ETA prediction.

5   Conclusion

In conclusion, this paper discusses a comparison study that has been conducted to determine how accurate is the ETA provided by navigation applications, primarily focusing on how different APIs in different applications are able to provide an accurate ETA. In short, HERE WeGo is the least suitable API to be integrated to develop a shuttle bus tracking app while Google Maps is the most suitable API, as based on the outcome of this study, it provides the most accurate ETA prediction and it predicts ETA conservatively. This study provides an answer to which API potentially can provide the best ETA by comparing the three most popular applications which have their API available for developers. As regular navigation app road users, this group of people will also benefit from this paper by knowing this is the navigation app which suits their daily commute the best. The limitation of this study includes a limited set of data as only six trips are managed to be conducted in the provided time. In this study, the experiment was conducted only on Android smartphones, hence limiting the brands of the hardware, as well as the mobile OS tested. As API does not make up the application, there is a possibility that other techniques are implemented into the application to make it more usable which were unable to be identified in this study. Future work for this research includes implementing the tested APIs into a tracking and ETA application to isolate the issues and accuracy of the ETA prediction model used by the API, to increase the volume of data by conducting the experiment on a larger scale, that includes more trips at more time slots. With a larger volume of data, the result will be more accurate and there is a possibility to identify other factors that are affecting the ETA accuracy. To remove uncertainty of the result, testing the applications on identical hardware devices and mobile OS can be conducted; on the other hand, to identify whether hardware devices capabilities and mobile OS contribute to the performance of ETA accuracy, more variants of hardware devices can be added.

Acknowledgments.   The authors would like to thank CERVIE (Centre of Excellence for Research, Value Innovation and Entrepreneurship), UCSI University Kuala Lumpur, Malaysia for sponsoring this publication.

References

Aljedaani, W., Nagappan, M., Adams, B., Godfrey, M.: A comparison of bugs across the iOS and Android platforms of two open source cross platform browser apps. In: 2019 IEEE/ACM 6th International Conference on Mobile Software Engineering and Systems (MOBILESoft), pp. 76–86. IEEE, May 2019

Amin-Naseri, M., Chakraborty, P., Sharma, A., Gilbert, S.B., Hong, M.: Evaluating the reliability, coverage and added value of crowdsourced traffic incident reports from Waze. Transp. Res. Rec. **2672**(43), 34–43 (2018)

Anderson, K.J.: Mobile app recommendations: travel apps. Library Hi Tech News (2016)

Armstrong, J.S., Green, K.C., Graefe, A.: Golden rule of forecasting: be conservative. J. Bus. Res. **68**(8), 1717–1731 (2015)

Bauer, T.P., Edinger, J., Becker, C.: A qualitative and quantitative analysis of real time traffic information providers. In: 2019 IEEE International Conference on Pervasive Computing and Communications Workshops (PerCom Workshops), pp. 113–118. IEEE, March 2019

Bećirspahić, L., Karabegović, A.: Web portals for visualizing and searching spatial data. In: 2015 38th International Convention on Information and Communication Technology, Electronics and Microelectronics (MIPRO), pp. 305–311. IEEE, May 2015

Borhan, M.N., Ibrahim, A.N.H., Syamsunur, D., Rahmat, R.A.: Why public bus is a less attractive mode of transport: a case study of Putrajaya. Malaysia. Periodica Polytechnica Transp. Eng. **47**(1), 82–90 (2019)

Chai, T., Draxler, R.R.: Root mean square error (RMSE) or mean absolute error (MAE) – Arguments against avoiding RMSE in the literature. Geoscientific Model Dev. **7**(3), 1247–1250 (2014)

Cheung, P., Sengupta, U.: Analysis of journey planner apps and best practice features. Manchester Metropolitan University, Manchester, England (2016)

Chien, S.I.J., Ding, Y., Wei, C.: Dynamic bus arrival time prediction with artificial neural networks. J. Transp. Eng. **128**(5), 429–438 (2002)

Chit, S.M., Chaw, L.Y., Thong, C.L., Lee, C.Y.: A pilot study: Shuttle bus tracker app for campus users. In: 2017 International Conference on Research and Innovation in Information Systems (ICRIIS), pp. 1–6. IEEE, July 2017

Dziekan, K., Kottenhoff, K.: Dynamic at-stop real-time information displays for public transport: effects on customers. Transp. Res. Part A: Policy Practice **41**(6), 489–501 (2007)

Géza, K.: Analysis of the routing results and it's usage

Global smartphone market Q3 2020. (n.d.). https://www.canalys.com/newsroom/canalys-worldwide-smartphone-market-q3-2020

Goodall, N., Lee, E.: Comparison of Waze crash and disabled vehicle records with video ground truth. Transportation Research Interdisciplinary Perspectives, 100019 (2019)

Google Maps API (2020). https://developers.google.com/maps/documentation. Accessed Oct 2020

Google Maps (2020). https://www.google.com/maps

Google Play Store: Maps - Navigate & Explore- Apps on Google Play (2020A). https://play.google.com/store/apps/details?id=com.google.android.apps.maps. Accessed Oct 2020

Google Play Store: Waze - GPS, Maps, Traffic Alerts & Live Navigation - Apps on Google Play (2020B). https://play.google.com/store/apps/details?id=com.waze&hl=en. Accessed Oct 2020

Google Play Store: HERE WeGo – City Navigation - Apps on Google Play (2020C). https://play.google.com/store/apps/details?id=com.here.app.maps&hl=en. Accessed Oct 2020

Google Play Store. MAPS.ME – Offline maps, travel guides & navigation- Apps on Google Play (2020D). https://play.google.com/store/apps/details?id=com.mapswithme.maps.pro&hl=en. Accessed Oct 2020

Google Play Store. (2020E). MapQuest: Directions, Maps & GPS Navigation- Apps on Google Play. https://play.google.com/store/apps/details?id=com.mapquest.android.ace&hl=en. Accessed Oct 2020

Google Privacy Terms, How Google uses location information – Privacy & Terms. (2020). https://policies.google.com/technologies/location-data?hl=en-US

HERE API (2020). https://developer.here.com/. Accessed Oct 2020

HERE Technologies. (2020). https://www.here.com/. Accessed Oct 2020

HERE WeGo, HERE application or HERE Maps Privacy Supplement (updated): Legal, security, privacy and compliance (2020). https://legal.here.com/en-gb/privacy/here-wego-here-application-or-here-maps-privacy-supplement-updated

Hiroi, K., Imai, H., Kawaguchi, N.: Dynamic arrival time estimation model and visualization method for bus traffic. In: Mine, T., Fukuda, A., Ishida, S. (eds.) Intelligent Transport Systems for Everyone's Mobility, pp. 155–173. Springer, Singapore (2019). https://doi.org/10.1007/978-981-13-7434-0_9

HUAWEI Community: HERE WeGo: Your Google Maps alternative for Huawei and Honor phones. (n.d.). https://consumer.huawei.com/en/community/details/HERE-WeGo:-Your-Google-Maps-alternative-for-Huawei-and-Honor-phones/topicId_102513/

Kadam, A. J., Patil, V., Kaith, K., Patil, D., Sham.: Developing a smart bus for smart city using IOT technology. In: 2018 Second International Conference on Electronics, Communication and Aerospace Technology (ICECA) (2018)

Li, F., Yu, Y., Lin, H., Min, W.: Public bus arrival time prediction based on traffic information management system. In: Proceedings of 2011 IEEE International Conference on Service Operations, Logistics and Informatics (2011). https://doi.org/10.1109/soli.2011.5986581

Mapbox API (2020). https://docs.mapbox.com/api/. Accessed Oct 2020

MapQuest Business (2020). https://developer.mapquest.com/documentation/open/. Accessed Oct 2020

Maps.ME Mobile Offline Maps (2020). https://maps.me/#gsc.tab=0. Accessed Oct 2020

Morgul, E.F., et al.: Virtual sensors: Web-based real-time data collection methodology for transportation operation performance analysis. Transp. Res. Rec. 2442(1), 106–116 (2014)

Nair, D.J., Gilles, F., Chand, S., Saxena, N., Dixit, V.: Characterizing multicity urban traffic conditions using crowdsourced data. PLoS One 14(3), e0212845 (2019)

Noor, R.M., et al.: Predict Arrival Time by Using Machine Learning Algorithms to Promote Utilization of Urban Smart Bus (2020)

OpenStreetMap API. (2020). https://www.openstreetmap.org/#map=7/4.116/109.455. Accessed Oct 2020

Pant, K., Talukder, D., Biyani, P.: TrafficKarma: estimating effective traffic indicators using public data. In: Proceedings of the 2nd IKDD Conference on Data Sciences, p. 6. ACM (2015)

Petrovska, N., Stevanovic, A.: Traffic congestion analysis visualization tool. In: 2015 IEEE 18th International Conference on Intelligent Transportation Systems, pp. 1489–1494 (2015)

Petrovska, N., Stevanovic, A., Furht, B.: Visualization tools for traffic congestion estimation. In: Innovative Web Applications for Analyzing Traffic Operations, pp. 23–31. Springer, Cham (2016)

Privacy Policy of Waze, the GPS Navigation App. (2020). https://www.waze.com/legal/privacy#information-that-is-being-collected

Pylarinos, D., Pellas, I.: Incorporating open/free GIS and GPS software in power transmission line routine work: the case of Crete and Rhodes. Eng. Technol. Appl. Sci. Res. 7(1), 1316–1322 (2017)

Sangkhapan, S., Wannapiroon, P., Nilsook, P.: Smart Bus Management System Architecture Using Mesh App and Service Architecture. J. Softw., 130–137 (2020). https://doi.org/10.17706/jsw.15.5.130-137

Saputra, O.A., Ramdani, F., Saputra, M.C.: Comparison analysis of Google Maps, Wisepilot and Here-WeGo with user-centered design (UCD): approach & cartography. In: 2018 4th International Symposium on Geoinformatics (ISyG), pp. 1–5. IEEE (2018)

Sarraf, J., Priyadarshini, I., Pattnaik, P.K.: Real time bus monitoring system. In: Satapathy, S.C., Mandal, J.K., Udgata, S.K., Bhateja, V. (eds.) Information Systems Design and Intelligent Applications. AISC, vol. 433, pp. 551–557. Springer, New Delhi (2016). https://doi.org/10.1007/978-81-322-2755-7_57

Sharad, S., Sivakumar, P.B., Narayanan, V.A.: The smart bus for a smart city – A real-time implementation. In: 2016 IEEE International Conference on Advanced Networks and Telecommunications Systems (ANTS) (2016). https://doi.org/10.1109/ants.2016.7947850

Stradling, S., Carreno, M., Rye, T., Noble, A.: Passenger perceptions and the ideal urban bus journey experience. Transp. Policy **14**(4), 283–292 (2007)

Sygic API: (2020). https://www.sygic.com/developers/maps-api-services/javascript-map-api. Accessed October 2020

Tan, K., Wong, K.: Low-cost campus bus tracker using WiFi access points. In: 2016 IEEE International Conference on Consumer Electronics-Taiwan (ICCE-TW) (2016). https://doi.org/10.1109/icce-tw.2016.7520904

Thong, C.L., Chaw, L.Y., Chit, S.M., Lee, C.Y.: User evaluation on mobile application for shuttle bus service. In: SoMeT, pp. 422–429, September 2019

Watkins, K.E., Ferris, B., Borning, A., Rutherford, G.S., Layton, D.: Where Is My Bus? Impact of mobile real-time information on the perceived and actual wait time of transit riders. Transp. Res. Part A Policy Practice **45**(8), 839–848 (2011). https://doi.org/10.1016/j.tra.2011.06.010

Waze: About the Waze Transport SDK. Retrieved in October 2020, (2020). https://developers.google.com/waze/intro-transport

Willmott, C.J., Matsuura, K.: Advantages of the mean absolute error (MAE) over the root mean square error (RMSE) in assessing average model performance. Climate Res. **30**(1), 79–82 (2005)

Xiung, J., Xiung, J., Wong, A., Wong, A.: Canalys: Vivo overtakes Samsung as Malaysia's #1 smartphone vendor in Q2 2020, August 07 2020. https://www.soyacincau.com/2020/08/07/malaysia-top-5-smartphone-vendor-vivo-canalys-q2-2020/

Yim, Y.B., Ceder, A.: Smart feeder/shuttle bus service: consumer research and design. J. Public Transp. **9**(1), 5 (2006)

Yu, H., Xiao, R., Du, Y., He, Z.: A bus-arrival time prediction model based on historical traffic patterns. In: 2013 International Conference on Computer Sciences and Applications (2013). https://doi.org/10.1109/csa.2013.87

Yue, W.S., Hoy, C.W., Chye, K.K.: A preliminary survey analysis of school shuttle bus system towards smart mobility solutions. In: AIP Conference Proceedings, vol. 1891, No. 1, p. 020146. AIP Publishing LLC, October 2017

Zhou, P., Jiang, S., and Li, M.: Urban traffic monitoring with the help of bus riders. In: 2015 IEEE 35th International Conference on Distributed Computing Systems, 21–30 (2015). Author, F.: Article title. Journal **2**(5), 99–110 (2016)

A 2 × 2 Array Antenna for Multi-band Energy Harvesting for Biomedical Sensing Applications

Nebras Sobahi[1]([⊠]) [iD], Reda Ghoname[1] [iD], Marwa Mansour[2] [iD],
and Abdelhalim Zekry[3] [iD]

[1] Department Electrical and Computer Engineering, King Abdulaziz University, Jeddah,
Saudi Arabia
nsobahi@kau.edu.sa
[2] Microelectronics Department, Electronics Research Institute (ERI), Giza, Egypt
[3] Electronics and Communications Department, Faculty of Engineering, Ain Shams University,
Cairo, Egypt

Abstract. A novel multi-band planar 2 × 2 array loop antenna, with a frequency ranging from 0.5–4.5 GHz for energy harvesting applications is presented. The proposed loop antenna consists of an external strip loop and an internal banana strip connected to the external strip loop. The loop antenna occupies a small size of $62 \times 38 \, \text{mm}^2$, while the total area of the suggested array antenna is $164 \times 80 \, \text{mm}^2$. A prototype of the proposed 2 × 2 array antenna is fabricated, measured, and the results including return loss, efficiency, and gain, are obtained, and characterized. Therefore, excellent agreement was found between the measured and simulated results.

Keywords: 2 × 2 Array · Multi-band · Loop antenna · Planar antenna · Sensing · Biomedical applications

1 Introduction

In line with fast evolution of wireless communication systems, wide-band and multi-band antennas are widely studied and adopted for multi-standard applications. There is a crucial need to combine wireless services with small devices. Wide-band, multi-band, and compact structure antennas are significant requests for the multi- applications antenna design. For instance, monopole antennas [1], Inverted-F antennas (IFA) [2], and the many other design techniques are explained in [3]. Lately, the loop antennas could also provide excellent solutions for mobile range, and energy harvesting applications [4].

Conventional antennas used for 900 MHz frequency band are planar Inverted-F antennas (PIFA) [5], or monopole type [2] with direct feeding structure, but they have some drawbacks regarding their application to the multi-band small-sized applications. PIFA has a compact size, and it is easy to control impedance matching using the shorting pin. However, its impedance bandwidth is not wide enough for multiband operation [6].

© The Author(s), under exclusive license to Springer Nature Switzerland AG 2022
G. Salvendy and J. Wei (Eds.): HCII 2022, LNCS 13337, pp. 462–471, 2022.
https://doi.org/10.1007/978-3-031-05014-5_38

By disparity, a monopole has a more wideband characteristic than PIFA, but it is difficult to match with circuit board impedance [7].

Radio frequency energy signals are now ubiquitous, and they have indispensable features for RF energy harvesting systems. Compared to other energy sources such as thermal gradients, solar, and mechanical vibrations, the power density of RF energy is relatively low, but it is sufficient to charge some sensors or devices of harvested energy. Antennas are one of the essential parts of the developed energy harvesting system, and the performance of those antennas, such as their efficiency, gain and radiation patterns, is critical to improve overall performance. For this reason, it is very important to select suitable antennas based on their intended applications, such as in RFID, 5G and wireless sensor network, etc. However, antenna arrays with omnidirectional radiation patterns are dedicated to ambient RF energy harvesting systems, so signals can be received from all directions, improving the PCE of the system. Besides this, the backside radiation of antennas should be very low, as exemplified by wearable application.

In this paper, a new printed 2 × 2 array loop antenna for energy harvesting and wireless power transfer for biomedical sensing applications is proposed. The antenna has a planar structure and is easy to fabricate with a low cost printed circuit board (PCB). Moreover, the proposed 2 × 2 array antenna has the size of 164×80 mm^2, and produces radiation in six frequency bands for multi-standard applications.

The proposed loop antenna is composed of an external strip loop and an internal banana strip on the top layer, while its ground plane contains defective ground structure DGS. Furthermore, the DGS has the same shape as the internal banana strip. The external loop and internal banana strips support resonant modes for the proposed loop antenna. The first mode is created into a wide band at about 900 MHz to readily cover the energy harvesting, wireless power transfer, and GSM applications. The second mode covers a wide band around 1800 MHz to use for mobile and digital cellular system applications.

The loop antenna used to build the proposed 2 × 2 array antenna operates in six frequency bands from 0.4 to 5 GHz, achieves gain from 0.7 to 4 dB with a directivity between 3 and 8 dBi, and occupies an area of 164×80 mm^2. The proposed array antenna is designed and fabricated on FR4 material, and the radiation efficiency of the proposed array antenna is in the range between 35% and 71%.

The paper is organized in the following sections, loop antenna characteristics, the design considerations of the proposed antenna, the results of the proposed 2 × 2 array antenna, and finally conclusion.

2 Loop Antenna Characterization

The loop antennas are commonly classified according to their perimeter length into small loop antennas or large loop antennas [8]. Generally, the antenna is called a small loop antenna if its perimeter length is $\leq \frac{\lambda}{10}$, Where λ is the wavelength. The antenna is called a large loop antenna if its circumference length is around λ.

Figure 1(a) illustrates the rectangular loop antenna, where L and W are the length and width of the rectangular loop antenna, respectively. While $b1$ and $b2$ are the thickness and width of the driver, as shown in Fig. 1(a). The equivalent circuit of the loop antenna is displayed in Fig. 1(b) [9]. R_{rad} is the radiation resistance, which illustrates the energy

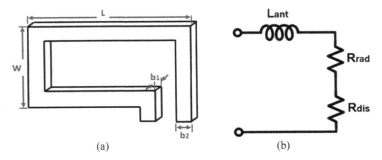

Fig. 1. (a) Structure of rectangular loop antenna, and (b) Equivalent circuit of the loop antenna.

radiated by the loop antenna, R_{dis} explains the energy dissipated by the Joule effect and L_{ant} is the inductance of the loop antenna [10]. The R_{rad}, R_{dis}, and L_{ant} are calculated by Eqs. 1, 2, and 3.

$$R_{rad} = 31171 \frac{N^2 S^2}{\lambda^4} \tag{1}$$

$$R_{dis} = \frac{W + L}{b_1 + b_2} \sqrt{\frac{\pi f \mu}{\sigma}} \tag{2}$$

$$L_{ant} = 2\mu \frac{a}{\pi} \left[Log \left(\frac{a}{b} \right) - 0.774 \right] \tag{3}$$

where N is the number of turns, σ is the conductivity of copper, f is the operating frequency, $S = WL$ is the surface area of the antenna, $a = \sqrt{LW}$, and $b = 0.35b_1 + 0.24b_2$ [9]. The inductance of the driver (L_1) is evaluated by:

$$L_1 = \frac{\mu a}{2} \tag{4}$$

The quality factor Q is given by [9]:

$$Q = \frac{2\pi f_r (L_{ant} + L_1)}{R_{rad} + R_{dis}} = \frac{f_r}{BW} \tag{5}$$

where BW is the bandwidth of the antenna and f_r is the resonance frequency. Then, the bandwidth of the antenna can be calculated by Eq. (6)

$$BW = \frac{f_r}{Q} \tag{6}$$

The radiation efficiency of the loop antenna is specified by the following equation:

$$\eta = \frac{R_{rad}}{R_{rad} + R_{dis}} \tag{7}$$

According to Eq. (7), the radiation efficiency relies basically on the dimensions of the loop antenna and the operating frequency. The benefits of the loop antenna are its small size and excellent directivity. While the drawbacks of the loop antenna are that its impedance matching may not always be good and that it has a very high resonance quality factor.

3   Antenna Design Consideration

The proposed antenna consists of an external strip loop with a regular width of 0.75 mm and an internal banana strip as clarified in Fig. 2. Figure 2(a) illustrates the top view geometry of the proposed antenna, and the bottom (ground plane) view geometry of the proposed antenna is shown in Fig. 2(b). The proposed antenna is designed on the top ungrounded section of dimension 62×15 mm^2. The proposed antenna is designed on 0.8 mm thick FR4 substrate with $\varepsilon_r = 4.5$ and loss tangent $= 0.025$. The simulation results are achieved by using CST microwave studio. The overall width and length of the proposed antenna are 62 mm and 38 mm, respectively. The first end of the external strip loop is the feeding line (direct feeding) of the proposed antenna, and the last end is connected to the ground plane through via as illustrated in Fig. 2.

Figure 3 depicts the simulation result of return loss for the proposed antenna illustrated in Fig. 2 and the case without DGS in the ground plane. In the absence of the DGS, there is only one mode (the second mode), at around 1800 MHz with acceptable matching impedance. at 900 MHz. On the contrary, with the insertion of the DGS in the ground plane, there is an additional mode (the third mode) with acceptable matching impedance, and the matching impedance of the first mode is also extremely improved.

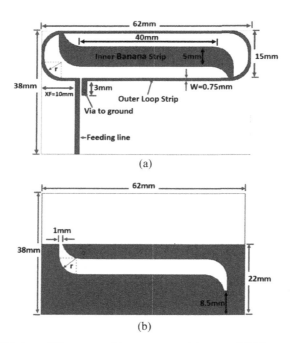

(a)

(b)

Fig. 2. 2D view of the proposed loop antenna, (a) top, and (b) bottom views.

Figure 4 illustrates the simulated return loss of the proposed antenna displayed in Fig. 2 and the cases without the internal banana strip.

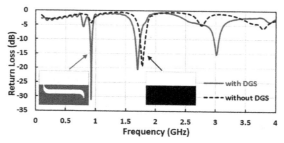

Fig. 3. Simulation results of return loss against frequency for the proposed antenna with and without DGS.

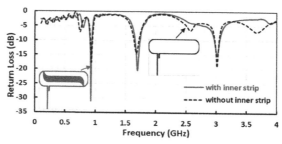

Fig. 4. Simulated return loss versus frequency of the proposed antenna with and without the inner banana strip.

The simulation result of return loss for the proposed antenna shown in Fig. 2 at different external strip loop width (W) is plotted in Fig. 5. The operating frequency at W = 0.75 mm is 900 MHz with perfect impedance matching. When W increases, the frequency band will increase to 3.1 GHz with a very good impedance matching.

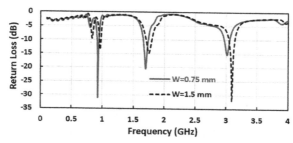

Fig. 5. Simulated return loss for the proposed antenna at different external strip loop width (W).

The simulation result of the return loss for the proposed antenna shown in Fig. 2 at different feeding line positions (X_F) is illustrated in Fig. 6. At $X_F = 10$ mm, the frequency is 900 MHz and when X_F increase, the frequency will increase.

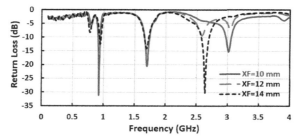

Fig. 6. Simulation result of return loss for the proposed antenna at different feeding line positions.

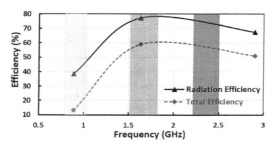

Fig. 7. Simulation result of the proposed antenna efficiency (%).

The simulated radiation efficiency and total efficiency of the proposed antenna are illustrated in Fig. 7. At 900 MHz, the radiation efficiency is about 38% and the total efficiency is around 13%.

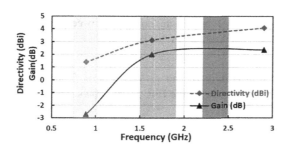

Fig. 8. Simulated antenna gain (dB) and directivity (dBi).

The proposed antenna gain is −2.71 dB and the antenna directivity is about 1.4 dBi, at 900 MHz. While for the DCS band ranges (1.7 GHz band), the antenna gain and directivity are 2 dB and 3.12 dBi, respectively, as illustrated in Fig. 8.

4 The Proposed 2 × 2 Array Antenna

The proposed 2 × 2 array antenna is composed of four loop antennas and are connected in a planer form as illustrated in Fig. 9. The separation between the two neighboring antennas must be greater than or equal to λ/4. The connection between face-to-face antennas is joined by the T connection as shown in Fig. 9(a). The proposed 2 × 2 array antenna has an overall width and length equal of 164 mm and 80 mm, respectively as illustrated in Fig. 9(a) and (b).

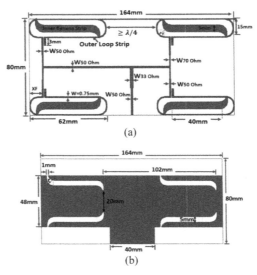

(a)

(b)

Fig. 9. 2D view of the proposed 2 × 2 array antenna, (a) top view, and (b) bottom (GND) view. The width of the feeding and all the transmission lines between the antennas are 0.8, 1.32 and 2.5 mm for $W_{70\Omega}$, $W_{70\Omega}$ and $W_{70\Omega}$, respectively.

The prototype photography of the proposed 2 × 2 array is shown in Fig. 10. Figure 10(a) shows the top view, while Fig. 10(b) shows the bottom view.

(a)   (b)

Fig. 10. Photo of the proposed 2 × 2 array antenna, (a) top, (b) bottom views.

Figure 11 illustrates the measured and simulated return loss of the proposed array antenna. The perfect agreement between the measurement and simulation is displayed in Fig. 11.

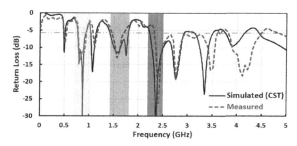

Fig. 11. Measured and simulated return loss of the proposed 2 × 2 array antenna.

The six resonant modes with acceptable matching impedance, measured at −6 dB return loss, are presented. The first mode operates at 500 MHz frequency and the second mode is a wideband with a bandwidth of 170 MHz (760–930 MHz), making it suitable for GSM applications. The third mode at 1 GHz frequency, and the fourth mode has a bandwidth of 250 MHz (1.46–1.71 GHz), DCS application. The fifth mode from 2.3 GHz to 3.6 GHz has a bandwidth of 1.3 GHz, and the sixth mode has a bandwidth of 0.7 GHz, from 3.8 to 4.5 GHz.

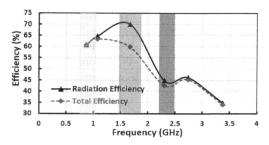

Fig. 12. Simulation result of the radiation efficiency and total efficiency for the proposed 2 × 2 array antenna.

The simulation results of radiation efficiency and total efficiency for the proposed array antenna are displayed in Fig. 12. For the energy harvesting and GSM applications, at 900 MHz frequency band, the efficiency is better than 61% in the range between 60.5% and 65%; for the GPS, DCS, PCS, and UMTS bands, the band between 1.4 GHz to 1.8 GHz, the maximum radiation efficiency is greater than 70%; and for 2.4 GHz frequency band, the WLAN band, the efficiency equals 45%.

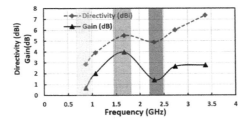

Fig. 13. Simulation result of the antenna gain (dB) and directivity (dBi) for the proposed 2 × 2 array antenna.

Table 1. 2 × 2 array and single loop antennas comparison.

Proposed antenna (Size, mm²)	Freq. bands (GHz)	Gain (dB)	Directivity (dBi)	Radiation eff (%)	Total eff (%)
2 × 2 array (164 × 80)	6wide bands	0.8–4	3–8	35–71	35–65
Single loop (62 × 38)	3narrow bands	−3–2	1–4	38–79	10–60

Figure 13 displays the simulated antenna gain (dB) and directivity (dBi). Over the energy harvesting and GSM bands, at 900 MHz frequency band, the proposed antenna gain is about 1 dB and the antenna directivity is around 3.5 dBi, whereas, for the DCS band ranges (1.7 GHz band), the antenna gain and directivity are 4 dB and 5.51 dBi, respectively. Also, for the 2.4 GHz frequency band, the antenna gain and directivity equal 1.5 dB and 4.9 dBi, respectively. Table 1 shows the comparison between the performance of the proposed 2 × 2 array and the single loop antennas.

5   Conclusion

The planar multi-band 2 × 2 array loop antenna is analyzed, designed, and fabricated using a FR4 material for energy harvesting, wireless power transfer, GSM, and multi-standard applications. The proposed multi-band array antenna covers six wide-band modes of operation in frequency range between 0.5 and 5 GHz. The maximum antenna gain and directivity of the proposed array are 4 dB and 8 dBi, respectively. The proposed array antenna is designed and simulated using CST microwave studio and fabricated with an excellent agreement between the simulation and experimental results. The suggested 2 × 2 array antenna occupies area 164 * 80 mm². The maximum radiation efficiency of the presented array equals 71%, while the peak value of the total efficiency is 65%.

References

1. Wong, K.L., et al.: Printed single-strip monopole using a chip inductor for penta-band WWAN operation in the mobile phone. IEEE Trans. Antennas Propag. **58**, 1011–1014 (2010)
2. Wu, C.H., et al.: Ultrawideband PIFA with a capacitive feed for penta-band folder-type mobile phone antenna. IEEE Trans. Antennas Propag. **57**, 2461–2464 (2009)
3. Wong, et al.: On-board printed coupled-fed loop antenna in close proximity to the surrounding ground plane for penta-band WWAN mobile phone. IEEE Trans. Antennas Propag. **59**, 751–757 (2011)
4. Chi, Y., et al.: Quarter-wavelength printed loop antenna with an internal printed matching circuit for GSM/DCS/PCS/UMTS operation in the mobile phone. IEEE Trans. Antennas Propag. **57**, 2541–2547 (2009)
5. Wu, C., et al.: Ultrawideband PIFA with a capacitive feed for penta-band folder-type mobile phone antenna. IEEE Trans. Antennas Propag. **57**(8), 2461–2464 (2009)
6. Yeh, S.-H., et al.: Dualband planar inverted F antenna for GSM/DCS mobile phones. IEEE Trans. Antennas Propag. **51**(5), 1124–1126 (2003)
7. Tung, H.-C., et al.: Monopole antenna fed by a coaxial cable in slide phone for GSM/DCS/PCS operation. IEEE Proc. Antennas Propag. Soc. Int. Symp. **2008**, 1–4 (2008)
8. Niekerk, J.V., et al.: Loop Antenna Basics and Regulatory Compliance for Short-Range Radio. Microchip Tech. Inc. (2002)
9. Karoui, S., et al.: Study and design of a loop antenna for application of medical telemetry. In: 2004 IEEE International Conference Industrial Technology, 2004. IEEE ICIT 2004, Hammamet, Tunisia, vol. 3, pp. 1589–1595 (2004)
10. Niekerk, J.V.: Matching small loop antennas to rfpic device. Microchip Technologies Inc. (2002)

(AR)e These Products Making Sense? Resolving Product Schema-Incongruity with Augmented Reality

Camen Teh[1], Chee Wei Phang[1(✉)], Cheng Zhang[2], and Alain Yee Loong Chong[1]

[1] Nottingham University Business School China, University of Nottingham Ningbo China, Ningbo 315100, China
{Camen.Teh,CheeWei.Phang,Alain.Chong}@nottingham.edu.cn
[2] Department of Information Management and Information Systems, Fudan University, Shanghai 200433, China
zhangche@fudan.edu.cn

Abstract. This paper investigates two distinct yet potentially complementary issues that when put together, may be able to solve each other. First, businesses are pressured to roll out innovative products to stay ahead of the competition, but product innovation is risky as it can sometimes violate consumer expectations due to schema incongruity. Second, while augmented reality (AR) technology has been examined in adoption studies in retail and advertising, and in practice, we have seen the occasional application of AR in marketing campaigns, AR remains a blackbox, in that both researchers and practitioners have little understanding of how the unique AR attributes can be maximised as well as in what contexts. Our study brings these two dilemmas together by examining how AR product presentations can be designed to improve consumer evaluations of innovative, yet schema-incongruent products. We propose the design of a field experiment that leverages two key attributes of AR, namely the superimposition of virtual items into real-life environments and the controllability of these virtual items. We propose to investigate how the styles of the virtual items (cartoon vs. realistic) and the levels of controllability (with control vs. without control) within an AR product presentation can facilitate incongruity resolution for schema-incongruent products, which could lead to positive product evaluations and behavioural intentions. We anticipate the findings of our experiment to provide novel insights into cognitive processes pertaining to the use of AR and to provide practical implications for the design of AR for incongruity resolution.

Keywords: Augmented reality · Schema incongruity · Incongruity resolution

1 Introduction

"After conditioning consumers for 124 years to expect ketchup to be red, the H.J. Heinz company pivoted suddenly on July 10, 2000, and gave the condiment a colourful makeover. The Heinz EZ Squirt debuted with Blastin' Green ketchup as a promotion in support of the first "Shrek" movie [1]."

G. Salvendy and J. Wei (Eds.): HCII 2022, LNCS 13337, pp. 472–490, 2022.
https://doi.org/10.1007/978-3-031-05014-5_39

Heinz's EZ Squirt Blastin' Green Ketchup was an initial hit due to its ergonomically-designed packaging for kids with its plastic, squeezable bottle and a narrow nozzle; combined with its timely launch in support of the animated film starring a green ogre as the protagonist named Shrek. However, its success was essentially short-lived and the product was pulled off the shelves almost as quickly as it got rolled out. In 2011, Business Insider even named Heinz's EZ Squirt Ketchup one of the biggest food flops of all time [2]. Many have attributed the fall of EZ Squirt to the inability for consumers to make sense of the product anymore [3, 4]. As soon as the buzz of the Shrek movie died down, consumers could no longer make sense of the product. Ketchup is red because it is made from tomatoes and this made sense because tomatoes are red. Without the connection to Shrek the green ogre, green ketchup simply spiraled into being an odd food fad. As the opening quote aptly points out, expectations of ketchup being red is hard-wired into our heads, and researchers, such as Jhang et al. [5] and Noseworthy et al. [6], has substantiated that the more discrepant an innovation is from conventional expectations, the more likely it is to fail.

The importance of product innovation for business growth has been reiterated by a rich stream of literature, particularly its impact on business growth and product performance [7, 8], and companies are continuously pressured to produce innovative products [9]. Yet, this is a risky pursuit for businesses as new products can sometimes violate existing schemas and are incongruent with consumer expectations [10]. As exemplified by Heinz's "innovative" product, not all product innovations end up with success, especially when the innovative product is highly schema-incongruent.

According to the schema congruity effect coined by Meyers-Levy and Tybout [11], new products that are extremely incongruent with consumers' schemas or expectations will result in lower evaluations in comparison to those of more congruent products. Subsequent studies have drawn from this finding to identify ways to improve consumers' evaluation and attitudes towards incongruent products, specifically in facilitating consumers' ability to resolve incongruity (e.g. Jhang et al. [5] and Noseworthy et al. [6]). This study intends to contribute to this stream of literature by focusing on how augmented reality (AR) can facilitate incongruity resolution.

One of the most-used definitions of AR is the one coined by Azuma [12] in his seminal work, where AR technology is defined as a system that combines the real and virtual, and is registered in three dimensions, as well as in real time. Among its many applications in different domains, AR use in retail is starting to gain momentum in mainstream discussions, especially with applications such as virtual try-ons, in-store navigation and interactive product presentations [13, 14]. AR's ability to embed virtual information into real-world environments (i.e. in-store) in an interactive manner provides an opportunity for the delivery of product presentations that can enhance customer experience and increase product evaluation [15]. The embedding of virtual information into physical environments is particularly meaningful, as it has the potential to mitigate consumer problems typically associated with conventional brick-and-mortar retail, such as information asymmetry, where there is a pervasive knowledge gap between consumer and retailer about a product. For instance, in the case of Treasury Wine Estates (one of the world's largest wine companies), AR labels were used on their wine bottles to bring customers informative content, including the history of the vineyard from which the wine originated, among other information [16]. AR has the potential to mitigate product uncertainty, through vivid and interactive AR product presentations and information that allow users to make connections and bridge product knowledge gaps. In this study, we investigate whether AR-enabled product presentations can assist consumers in making connections between disparate schemas elicited by a schema incongruent product in the same way.

Despite the potentials of AR, not all businesses view AR's promises as worthy of a big-budget investment, particularly with concerns about what is needed for an AR experience to run reliably [17]. However, this may well be concerns of the past as not only is the consumers' appetite for a differentiated shopping experience growing, more than 1 billion mobile smartphones and tablet devices can deliver AR experiences today and these are supported by ever-improving network bandwidth [18]. Nevertheless, businesses remain unsure about how they can maximise the benefits of AR, and in what context would AR be useful for. In addition, as it currently stands, and, to the best of the authors' knowledge, studies on the design of AR experiences in the context of retail and advertising, and how different AR designs can lead to positive product evaluations and increased purchase remain under-researched. The answer to the question of "What is so special about AR?" eludes us still.

We argue that the value of AR for businesses can be ascertained and maximised by examining how the unique properties of AR can be designed to achieve meaningful outcomes, which in this study, would be incongruity resolution for innovative but schema-incongruent products. Against this backdrop, we propose a study on the two core properties of AR, namely the superimposition of virtual objects into real-world environments and its controllability. Specifically, we plan to examine the realism of virtual items (cartoon vs. realistic) and the different levels of controllability (with control vs. no control) of an AR product presentation; and how these two features of AR can lead to incongruity resolution for a schema-incongruent product in a between-group design field experiment. This paper details the conceptual background of this study and discusses the design of a field experiment to test our hypotheses.

2   Conceptual Background

2.1   Schema-Incongruity Resolution

In a well-established framework by Mandler [19], it was proposed that the level of congruity between a new product and an existing category schema of the product influences cognitive processing of individuals, leading to the evaluation of the new product. Based on this proposition, Meyers-Levy and Tybout [11] coined the schema congruity effect. The basis of this concept is that information perceived as schema congruent allow for comfort of familiarity and requires little cognitive processing, whereas schema incongruent information lead to surprise and unfamiliarity, in turn causing extensive cognitive processing in order for individuals to make sense of the incongruence [11].

A general consensus from prior literature on schema-incongruent products and consumer evaluation [5, 6, 10], is when consumers can successfully make sense of incongruent products, their evaluation of the product are likely to be more positive; on the other hand, if the consumers are unable to make sense of such products, the adverse effect occurs. This study adopts the same assumption in that successfully resolving schema discrepancies can result in a positive response (i.e. the positive affect accompanied by the "lightbulb", "Oh, I get it" response) that works similar to a psychological reward mechanism, which in turn enhances product evaluations [11, 19]. It has also been empirically tested that successful resolution of incongruity also has a positive effect on behavioural intentions [20]. In this study, we investigate whether incongruity resolution can also lead to purchase intention and WOM intention.

Several studies have investigated solutions for increasing evaluation for incongruent products through different mechanisms [5, 6]. Noseworthy et al. [6] specifically investigated the use of feature-based association by incorporating an enabler. For instance, the colour green, can help consumers make sense of a semantically-related feature like "vitamin enriched" of a perceived incongruent product, which is a green, vitamin-enriched coffee. In the study, it was found that two "wrongs" (i.e. the features "green" and "vitamin-enriched"), which are both incongruent with our understanding of coffee, made a "right", in that matching these two semantically-related feature to an incongruent coffee product, was able to help consumers make sense of the incongruent feature and led to more positive evaluations. In another study by Jhang et al. [5], on the other hand, the authors tested consumers' acceptance of incongruent products using strategies that facilitated cognitive flexibility. The authors Jhang et al. [5] found that priming for cognitive flexibility increased the likelihood for consumers to make associative links across disparate schemas, therein resolving the incongruence, which similar to the study by Noseworthy et al. [6], led to better evaluations. However, instead of using semantic enablers, Jhang et al. [5] manipulated cognitive flexibility using positive affect, a future (vs. past) launch description and a prime of cognitive flexibility by generating multiple explanations of a situation. For this study, we investigate how AR technology can be leveraged to resolve incongruity and increase evaluations for schema-incongruent products, drawing from the concepts and empirical evidence found in these key studies on incongruity resolution for schema-incongruent products.

2.2 Style of AR (Realism of AR)

A key feature of AR technology is the superimposition of virtual items into the real-world context. The virtual items embedded in an AR experience can range from unrealistic, cartoon items (e.g. of fictional characters in AR books) to textual information (e.g. customer reviews), as well as 3D virtual clothes presented in a realistic form, like in the Magic Mirror or virtual try-on applications of AR. Interestingly, prior literature on AR in retail have not given much attention to the level of realism of the virtual content superimposed into our real-world environments, and on the cognitive processes pertaining to it. Although these have not been investigated in the context of AR, prior studies in advertising have examined the use of cartoons and unrealistic visual content in traditional advertising.

A study by Heiser et al. [21], for instance, found that the use of cartoon or animated effects of spokespeople in print ads led to positive consumer advertising outcomes, such as attitude toward the ad, attitude toward brand, as well as the purchase intention of the advertised brand. Heiser et al. [21] found that the cartoon ads led to these positive outcomes through creativity and distinctiveness effect induced by cartoonised formats of the ad. In a conceptual work by Smith and Yang [22] on advertising creativity, the authors argue that one of the fundamental characteristics of ad creativity is divergence, whereby ads containing elements that are novel, different or unusual are deemed creative. Two factors were included in the list of determinants of divergence: (1) unusual perspective (i.e. seeing things from a different or unusual outlook); and (2) fantasy (i.e. the ability to generate non-real ideas, worlds or creations) [22]. Both factors included examples of the use of cartoons in ads, which departed from conventional advertising using real-world elements. This suggests that the use of cartoons can facilitate the effects of divergence, which can lead to flexible thinking and therefore supporting problem solving [23]. The effects of divergence and creativity are similar to the mechanisms of cognitive flexibility examined in Jhang et al. [5], in which it was found that priming for cognitive flexibility increased the likelihood for consumers to make associative links across disparate schemata, therein resolving the incongruence and thus led to better evaluations for schema-incongruent products.

Based on prior advertising literature that found that the use of cartoon or unrealistic elements in advertising can lead to creativity [21, 22], and by extension, flexible thinking [23], as well as extant literature on cognitive flexibility and incongruity resolution [5], it stands to reason that the use cartoon, unrealistic elements in AR can facilitate incongruity resolution of schema-incongruent products. Drawing from these and past literature on incongruity resolution leading to positive evaluations and behavioural intentions, we present our first hypothesis:

H1: Cartoon AR product presentations will lead to higher incongruity resolution of schema-incongruent products and thus, more positive product evaluations and behavioural intentions compared to realistic AR product presentations.

2.3 Controllability

Another unique feature of AR is the sensory experience of being able to touch and interact with virtual content. As McLean and Wilson [24] argue, the combination of manipulating the real, physical world and the virtual world is a unique attribute of AR, in that users can manipulate what they see. Some AR experiences can be designed in a way that allows users to control and manipulate the virtual content that is superimposed into their real-life environment, such as in the IKEA Place app, in which users can control where the virtual furniture would be projected into their physical environment through their smartphone camera simply by sliding or tapping their finger on their screen [24]. On the other hand, some AR experiences are lower in user controllability, or have none at all, in that users have little to no control of the virtual content overlaid into the real-world environment. For instance, in the case of Treasury Wine Estate's wine, users simply scan AR labels on the wine bottles as the only action on their part, and later passively watch and listen to the virtual character introduce the product [16]. In the former example, users are able to control the virtual items and the overall AR experience, whereas in the latter, users take on a passive role and have little to no control over the virtual items and experience low interactivity overall.

In one of the studies investigating incongruity resolution and acceptance of schema-incongruent products, Jhang et al. [5] speculated that there may be a difference in the process of incongruity resolution, in whether the resolution is self-generated or prompted by the marketer of the schema-incongruent product through message-driven approaches, such as providing rationales or explanations of why incongruity exists in advertisements. Drawing from the process-based account of incongruity resolution, the process of resolving the incongruence by oneself would result in positive affect that would lead to more favourable evaluations of the schema-incongruent product [5]. Jhang et al. [5] tested this hypothesis and found contradictory findings. They found that the external provision of incongruity rationale resulted in equally positive evaluations of the schema-incongruent product stimulus, even when the insight was not achieved from the process of resolving incongruity by oneself. In this study, the authors used a cognitive flexibility prime of asking participants to think of multiple possible explanation (with cognitive flexibility prime) vs. one explanation (no cognitive flexibility prime) to an ambiguous situation to induce self-generated incongruity resolution, and later requested participants to read an ad copy of a schema-incongruent stimulus that was manipulated to include or exclude an incongruity rationale.

It is plausible that the results found did not support the process-based account because the participants' involvement and their sense of control in the resolution process may not have been salient enough in the experiment setting. Further, other studies have provided empirical evidence that complements the process-based account. In a study on antecedents of consumer creativity in problem-solving contexts, Burroughs and Glen Mick [26] found that an individual's belief that events are within his or her control are more creative in their response to a consumption problem. Similarly, Schreier and Prugl [27, p. 337] found that individuals with strong beliefs that outcomes depend primarily on their own actions are more likely to "cope with new usage situations, and to challenge and appreciate improvements in existing products", while those with low control beliefs, tend to avoid new and difficult situations.

Leveraging AR's uniqueness of controllability, we propose that user involvement and control in the AR experience would be salient, particularly with the user's ability to control the virtual information that act as the rationalising link or insight that connects disparate schemata. An active role in controlling the virtual content provided to rationalise the incongruity elicited by the schema-incongruent product may result in a stronger feeling of resolving the incongruity by oneself, rather than relying on the provision of incongruity rationale by brands. As such, we argue that, for resolving schema incongruity, interactive AR product presentations with user controllability will perform better than AR product presentations without user controllability:

H2: AR product presentations with controllability will lead to higher incongruity resolution of schema-incongruent products and thus, more positive product evaluations and behavioural intentions compared to AR product presentations without controllability.

3   Experiment Design

To test our hypotheses, we propose a field experiment using different AR designs of a product presentation to introduce a schema-incongruent product. The schema-incongruent product stimulus we propose is a food product that has been found to be schema-incongruent based on public sentiment on mainstream media. We plan to conduct the experiment at a small grocery store located at a university campus's student living area that sells both packaged and fresh food products. The store owner has agreed to provide us access to their store as a field experiment site.

While we have the choice of conducting the experiment in a laboratory setting, we choose to conduct a field experiment because we believe that a field experiment would help us achieve higher ecological validity, in that it would allow us to replicate a retail experience that is as close to a natural retail setting as possible. When recruiting participants, we will introduce this experiment ambiguously as a study on consumer feedback regarding a new product that was added into the store. In doing so, participants will be less likely to guess the focus of the research or of the AR design manipulations used in the different treatment groups, which may affect their behaviour.

3.1 Stimulus Selection

To further enhance external validity, we will use a real product, JUST Eggs as our incongruent product stimulus for this study. JUST Eggs is a product of Eat Just, a California food technology start-up that offers plant-based alternatives to conventional egg products [28]. JUST Eggs are made entirely from plants and contrary to the name of the product, contains no actual, animal eggs. The product is in liquid form and stored in a bottle. While the product is claimed to be a safer and more sustainable alternative to conventional eggs [29–31], there is still some skepticism among consumers regarding this product. In an online article [30], a consumer wrote the following:

"I cracked open a bottle [of JUST Eggs] in the morning and was admittedly hesitant. I love eggs for breakfast, but something about eating eggs poured from a bottle has never appealed to me – even from a bottle of real eggs. Here, I was diving into the unknown world of mung bean eggs."

The initial hesitation described by the consumer was caused by what can be understood as feature-based incongruence, as has been pointed out in the study by Noseworthy et al. [6], in which the incongruent product stimulus used was green coffee. Green coffee was incongruent because the feature (colour) green is incongruent with our schema of coffee colours, which are typically black or brown. As the quote above aptly highlighted, eating eggs poured from a bottle is something the consumer found unappealing. In the same way that the green colour feature was mismatched with our schema of coffee, the feature of eggs being stored in a bottle was incongruent with our schema of eggs, which would assume that eggs are retrieved naturally from a round or oval shell. Thus, we deem this product to be an appropriate stimulus for this study as it captures the conceptual understanding of schema incongruence indicated in prior literature.

3.2 AR Product Presentation Design Manipulations

At the current stage of our research, we have designed the product presentations that will be the experiment manipulations for our study. Drawing from prior studies on cartoon effects in conventional print advertisements [21], we took original advertising materials such as promotional videos, images and nutritional information from JUST Eggs website as well as their official YouTube channel and digitally modified these to vary the execution of cartoon-realistic effect on the AR presentations (see Fig. 1). For the controllability manipulation, we vary between the presence and absence of four buttons that allowed users to: (1) play/pause; (2) skip segments; (3) go back to previous segment; and (4) go back to start (see Fig. 2).

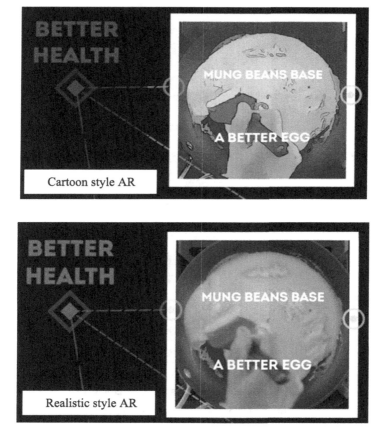

Fig. 1. AR cartoon-realistic style manipulations

With these, we have four versions of AR product presentations that make up our 2 (AR cartoon vs. AR realistic) x 2 (AR with control vs. AR no control) between-group experiment design. An AR presentation of one of four versions will appear when the participants scan a sticker code that will be stuck onto our product stimulus, corresponding to their assigned treatment group (see Fig. 3). The content and information of all four versions of the product presentation are kept consistent with only the cartoon-realistic effects and presence-absence of buttons as design manipulations.

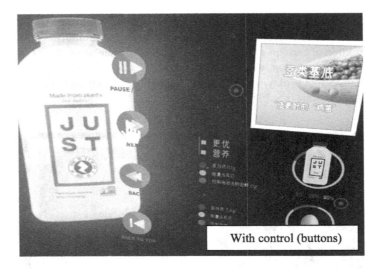

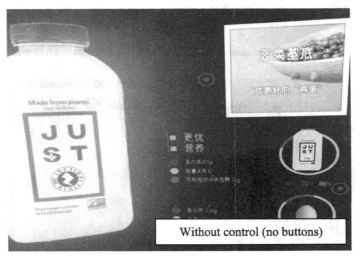

Fig. 2. AR controllability manipulation with the presence and absence of buttons

3.3 Participants

We plan to recruit undergraduate and master's students from a university in China to be participants for our field experiment. We chose university students participants for two reasons. First, the grocery store that has agreed for us to use their space as our experiment site is located in the university campus's student living area and having student participants living in close vicinity to the experiment site would greatly reduce the likelihood of participants dropping out of the experiment. Second, AR is a relatively new technology, and it has been found that users of AR applications tend to be young

Fig. 3. Mock-up of product stimulus with QR code that triggers AR product presentation

and educated [32]. Thus, we deem student participants as an appropriate population for our sample.

Participant recruitment advertisements will be circulated on Chinese social media platform, WeChat and on an online forum for students from the university that is operated independently by the university's students. In the ads, the study will be introduced as a study on consumer evaluation regarding a new product at the campus's grocery store. It will be stated that participation of this study consists of two parts. First is the pre-experiment survey part, where participants will be required to fill in an online questionnaire a week before the experiment. Second is the field experiment part, which will commence after participants meet the requirements of the survey. Participants will receive an email specifying the time allocated to them for the field experiment. Participants must complete both parts in order to receive the remuneration of 80 RMB. We intend to recruit at least 250 participants, in order to have at least 50 participants per treatment group.

3.4 Pre-experiment Survey

The pre-experiment survey is designed to resemble an online quiz, in which students will be required to watch 3 videos that shows the use of AR in retail and product packaging. Each video is less than 1.5 min long, and is followed by 3 multiple-choice questions, 9 questions in total. Students will be required to answer at least 7 out of the 9 questions correctly in order to proceed to the second part of our study, which is the field experiment. The purpose of this pre-experiment survey is to eliminate any novelty effects of AR that can produce noise to our measured variables. We take into consideration that AR is still a relatively new technology to some participants, and the novelty of the technology may influence the participants' behaviour as some of them may be exposed to the technology for the first time during the field experiment. With this quiz survey, participants will watch the video attentively to obtain at least the minimum score, and thus, be pre-exposed to the use of AR in retail and advertising settings prior to the field experiment. The questions in the survey are simple and are not phrased to be directed at AR technology (e.g. "In the video, the user scanned a code on a product to start the game. What was this product?"). Participants will be allowed to make unlimited attempts until they get the required score.

3.5 Field Experiment Procedure

Following the pre-experiment survey, we will allocate participants into the 4 treatment groups. The experiment schedule will consist of time slots, whereby each slot will be allocated a maximum of 4 participants, and all participants within a slot will receive the same treatment (i.e. one slot, one treatment group). Participants will be allocated a slot depending on the treatment group that they are randomised into. We plan to employ the same treatment within one time slot instead of different treatments within one slot to minimise the risk of participants guessing that there are different treatments being administered in the experiment.

When participants arrive at the store at their allocated time slots, they will be invited into the store to view a new product (our schema-incongruent product stimulus) promoted in the store. The participants will go in either alone or in a pair (a maximum of 4 participants at a time) and will be led into the store by one of two store assistants (one assistant attending 1 to 2 participants). The store assistant will lead participants to one of two corners of the store where the product will be displayed (see Fig. 4). This is to ensure that the store assistants, who are our research assistants, will be able to monitor the participants attentively and make sure they do not interact with each other.

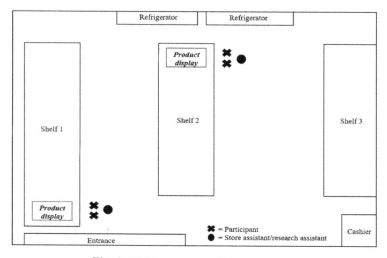

Fig. 4. Field experiment site's store layout

The store assistants will introduce the product stimulus as a new product that has just been introduced to the market and in the store. There will be a printed poster next to the products with very basic information of the product, including what the product is (plant-based eggs), its nutritional information and promotional price (see Fig. 5).

Fig. 5. Mock-up of product promotion poster

The participants will be given some time to look at the product and the poster. After a few minutes, the store assistant will request for the participants to fill up a short questionnaire that asks for participants' demographic information and measures their product knowledge, brand familiarity and initial schema incongruity resolution prior to receiving the AR treatments (see Table 1).

Table 1. Overview of variables and measurement items for pre-treatment questionnaire

Variable	Item/Scale	
Product knowledge (self-developed)	(1-Strongly disagree; 7-Strongly agree)	
	PK1	Before being introduced to this product today, you were familiar with other products that are similar to the product presented
	PK2	The product presented is new to you. (R)

(continued)

Table 1. (*continued*)

Variable	Item/Scale	
Brand familiarity (self-developed)	(1-Strongly disagree; 7-Strongly agree)	
	BF1	Before being introduced to this product today, you were familiar with the brand presented
	BF2	The brand of this product is new to you. (R)
Initial incongruity resolution (adapted from Jhang et al. [5])	(1- Makes no sense; 7-Makes sense)	
	PIR1	How does this product make sense to you?
	(1-Strongly disagree; 7-Strongly agree)	
	PIR2	I understand the logic of this product

R = reverse code items.

After the participants complete the first questionnaire, the store assistants will ask the participants to scan a QR code that leads them to a webpage. The webpage opens a web scanner that participants will use to scan the QR codes on the bottled product, which will trigger the AR product presentation according to their allocated treatment group. The participants will view or interact with (if they are in the with-controllability groups) the AR product presentation for 3 to 5 minutes. When the participants no longer want to view or interact with the AR product presentation, the store assistants will ask if they would like to pre-order the product at their own cost, outside of the participation remuneration of this study. Participants has no obligation to purchase the item, and purchase will be entirely on their own volition. Pre-orders will be measured as actual purchase.

Finally, the participants will fill in the post-treatment and final questionnaire that includes our manipulation checks, and measurements of our investigated variables, including perceived control, post-treatment incongruity resolution, product evaluation, purchase intention, word of mouth and other control variables (see Table 2).

Table 2. Overview of variables and measurement items for post-treatment questionnaire

Variable	Item/Scale	
Realism of AR (self-developed)	(1-Strongly disagree; 7-Strongly agree)	
	RE1	The visual content in the product presentation are realistic
	RE2	The visual content in the product presentation look lifelike

(*continued*)

Table 2. (*continued*)

Variable	Item/Scale	
Controllability (self-developed)	(1-Strongly disagree; 7-Strongly agree)	
	CO1	There are options for me to control the playing of parts of the product presentation content
	CO2	There are functions for me to control how the product presentation content is to be played
Perceived control (adapted from Park and Yoo [33])	(1-Strongly disagree; 7-Strongly agree)	
	PC1	I felt that I had a lot of control over my experiences when viewing the product presentation
	PC2	During the product presentation, I could choose freely what I wanted to see
	PC3	I am confident I can control the product presentation
	PC4	I feel a lot of personal control over the product presentation
	PC5	What I viewed was entirely up to me
Incongruity resolution (adapted from Jhang et al. [5])	(1- Makes no sense; 7-Makes sense)	
	IR1	How does this product make sense to you?
	(1-Strongly disagree; 7-Strongly agree)	
	IR2	I understand the logic of this product
Product evaluation (adapted from Jhang et al. [5])	(1- Very unfavourable; 7-Very favourable)	
	PE1	The product is…
	(1- Very unappealing; 7-Very appealing)	
	PE2	The product is…
Purchase intention (adapted from Bues et al. [34])	(1- Very unlikely; 7-Very likely)	
	PI1	Would the purchase of the demonstrated product be more likely or less likely given the presentation shown?
	PI2	How likely will you purchase this item in the future?
	PI3	Given the presentation, how likely is it that you would consider the purchase of the presented product?

(*continued*)

Table 2. (*continued*)

Variable	Item/Scale	
Word of mouth (Zeithaml et al. [35])	(1-Strongly disagree; 7-Strongly agree)	
	WOM1	I would say positive things about the product to other people
	WOM2	I would recommend the product to someone who seeks my advice
	WOM3	I would encourage friends and relatives to use the product
Need for change [a] (adapted from Wood and Swait [36])	(1-Strongly disagree; 7-Strongly agree) *Generally, your friend and/or family would describe you as a person who...*	
	NCH1	Always likes introducing new things to friends
	NCH2	When seeing a new or different brand on the shelf, you would often pick it up just to see what it is like
	NCH3	Often reads the information on product packages just out of curiosity
Need for cognition [a] (adapted from Lins de Holanda Coelho et al. [37])	(1-Strongly disagree; 7-Strongly agree) *Generally, your friend and/or family would describe you as a person who...*	
	NCOG1	Prefers complex problems more than simple problems
	NCOG2	Likes to have the responsibility of handling a situation that requires a lot of thinking
	NCOG3	Would rather do something that requires little thought than something that will challenge my thinking abilities. (R)
	NCOG4	Enjoys tasks that involve coming up with new solutions to problems
Health consciousness [a] (adapted from Chen [38])	(1-Strongly disagree; 7-Strongly agree) *Generally, the following statements apply to you:*	
	HC1	I consider myself very health conscious
	HC2	My health is so valuable to me that I am prepared to sacrifice many things for it
	HC3	I often ask myself whether something is healthy for me

(*continued*)

Table 2. (*continued*)

Variable	Item/Scale	
Dietary group attitude [a] (adapted from Povey et al. [39])	(1-Strongly disagree; 7-Strongly agree) *Generally, you...*	
	DGA1	Consciously avoid eating meat
	DGA2	Do not enjoy eating meat
	DGA3	Intend to have a vegetarian or vegan diet in the future
Food variety seeking [a] (adapted from Van Trijp and Steenkamp [40])	(1-Strongly disagree; 7-Strongly agree) *Generally, the following statements apply to you:*	
	FVS1	Usually, when I eat out, I like to try unusual items, even if I am not sure I would like them
	FVS2	I think it is fun to try out food items that one is not familiar with
	FVS3	I am curious about food products I am not familiar with

[a] = control variables
R = reverse code items.

4   Discussion and Outlook

We presented the design of a field experiment to investigate how AR technology can provide value in facilitating incongruity resolution in the context of introducing innovative products that can be schema-incongruent to consumers, based on the concept of schema incongruity, as well as prior literature on cartoon effects and control, in relation to incongruity resolution. We expect that certain designs of the AR experience can lead to positive outcomes, specifically that cartoon-style designs of AR and AR experiences that allows users to control its content will result in higher incongruity resolution, better evaluations and stronger purchase and WOM intentions. We propose to test these hypotheses in a realistic environment; a grocery store, and on a real product that has been indicated to be schema-incongruent.

We anticipate our investigation to have implications for both research and practice alike. For research, this study will provide novel insights on AR's unique properties of: (1) superimposing virtual items that can be designed in cartoon, distinctive styles into real-world environments and; (2) its interactivity that allows for users to have a stronger sense of control over the virtual items; and how these two features can lead to cognitive effects of incongruity resolution. While our investigated context is largely based on a retail environment and advertising as we are looking into product presentations, our findings has the potential to be extended to other AR research areas such as in communications (e.g. the study of AR designs to deliver incongruent messages or ideas) and education (e.g. investigating how different AR designs can facilitate problem-solving). This study also opens up avenues for future research within the same line of investigation. For instance, if our hypotheses are supported, it would be worth testing if different types of schema-incongruent products would lead to the same results (e.g. if it was a luxury product instead of a food product), and if other factors, such as product involvement and brand familiarity, can influence the effects we hypothesised.

In terms of practice, we expect that our findings will provide evidence on whether AR is a worthy investment for businesses. If we find that AR does indeed facilitate incongruity resolution and lead to higher evaluations and purchase, our study would indicate that designing and employing AR marketing campaigns to introduce a new product would be a small price to pay compared to the losses that can incur if the launch of a new product fails due to low consumer acceptance caused by conflicts in consumer expectation or schema-incongruity. Our study can also inform how AR can be designed (cartoon vs. realistic styles and with control vs. without control) to bring forth maximum benefits to stakeholders. In addition, similar to how our study can be extended to research in other domains, our findings may also be transferrable to other real-world contexts, such as organisational shifts or structural changes where discomfort is high, stemming from unfamiliarity (like with schema-incongruent products). For instance, stakeholders may use AR-delivered transformative campaigns or AR technology to deliver difficult announcements as it may lead to better outcomes compared to conventional modes of communication.

We plan to proceed with the experiment as described in this paper, and in the following steps to our ongoing research endeavour, we plan to explore possible boundary conditions, such as product involvement and brand familiarity, as previously mentioned.

References

1. Cox Media Group. https://www.wpxi.com/archive/this-day-july-10-2000-heinz-ez-squirt-colored-ketchup-debuts/YHSDWPPYBFEPXKVR5EUVY3H6YI/
2. Business Insider. https://www.businessinsider.com/major-food-flops-2011-1
3. Medium. https://medium.com/@kaeteepang/what-is-ez-squirt-ketchup-by-heinz-325d13bfb6e4
4. Fast Company. https://www.fastcompany.com/1779591/what-were-they-thinking-day-ketchup-crossed-line-perfect-purple
5. Jhang, J.H., Grant, S.J., Campbell, M.C.: Get It? Got It. Good! Enhancing new product acceptance by facilitating resolution of extreme incongruity. J. Mark. Res. **49**, 247–259 (2012). https://doi.org/10.1509/jmr.10.0428
6. Noseworthy, T.J., Murray, K.B., Di Muro, F.: When two wrongs make a right: using conjunctive enablers to enhance evaluations for extremely incongruent new products. J. Consum. Res. **44**, 1379–1396 (2017). https://doi.org/10.1093/jcr/ucx106
7. Utterback, J.M., Abernathy, W.J.: A dynamic model of process and product innovation. Omega **3**, 639–656 (1975). https://doi.org/10.1016/0305-0483(75)90068-7
8. Henard, D.H., Szymanski, D.M.: Why some new products are more successful than others. J. Mark. Res. **38**, 362–375 (2001). https://doi.org/10.1509/jmkr.38.3.362.18861
9. Gourville, J.T.: Eager sellers and stony buyers: understanding the psychology of new-product adoption. Harvard Bus. Rev. **84**, 98–106, 145 (2006)
10. Noseworthy, T.J., Di Muro, F., Murray, K.B.: The role of arousal in congruity-based product evaluation. J. Consum. Res. **41**, 1108–1126 (2014). https://doi.org/10.1086/678301
11. Meyers-Levy, J., Tybout, A.M.: Schema congruity as a basis for product evaluation. J. Consum. Res. **16**, 39–54 (1989). https://doi.org/10.1086/209192

12. Azuma, R.T.: A survey of augmented reality. Presence: Teleoperators and Virtual Environments 6, 355–385 (1997). https://doi.org/10.1162/pres.1997.6.4.355
13. Medium. https://medium.com/@inverita/5-applications-of-augmented-reality-in-the-retail-industry-4ae3e774e2c3
14. Harvard Business Review. https://hbr.org/2016/09/virtual-and-augmented-reality-will-reshape-retail
15. Spreer, P., Kallweit, K.: Augmented reality in retail: assessing the acceptance and potential for multimedia product presentation at the PoS. Trans. Mark. Res. 1, 20–25 (2014), https://doi.org/10.15764/MR.2014.01002
16. Treasury Wine Estates. https://www.tweglobal.com/media/news/twe-drives-consumer-engagement-to-wine-brands-through-innovative-use-of-augmented-reality-technology
17. Forbes. https://www.forbes.com/sites/nikkibaird/2019/03/20/what-consumer-adoption-of-augmented-reality-means-for-retail/
18. Deloitte. https://www2.deloitte.com/us/en/insights/topics/emerging-technologies/augmented-shopping-3d-technology-retail.html
19. Mandler, G.: The Structure of Value: Accounting For Taste. Psychology Press, Affect and Cognition (1981)
20. Abolhasani, M., Golrokhi, Z.: Eat to the beat: musical incongruity resolution in restaurant advertising. J. Int. Consum. Mark. 1–25 (2021). https://doi.org/10.1080/08961530.2021.2022061
21. Heiser, R.S., Sierra, J.J., Torres, I.M.: Creativity via cartoon spokespeople in print ads: capitalizing on the distinctiveness effect. J. Advert. 37, 75–84 (2008). https://doi.org/10.2753/JOA0091-3367370406
22. Smith, R.E., Yang, X.: Toward a general theory of creativity in advertising: examining the role of divergence. Mark. Theory 4, 31–58 (2004). https://doi.org/10.1177/1470593104044086
23. Zuo, B., Wen, F., Wang, M., Wang, Y.: The mediating role of cognitive flexibility in the influence of counter-stereotypes on creativity. Front. Psychol. 10, 105 (2019). https://doi.org/10.3389/fpsyg.2019.00105
24. McLean, G., Wilson, A.: Shopping in the digital world: examining customer engagement through augmented reality mobile applications. Comput. Hum. Behav. 101, 210–224 (2019). https://doi.org/10.1016/j.chb.2019.07.002
25. de Ruyter, K., Heller, J., Hilken, T., Chylinski, M., Keeling, D.I., Mahr, D.: Seeing with the customer's eye: exploring the challenges and opportunities of AR advertising. J. Advert. 49, 109–124 (2020). https://doi.org/10.1080/00913367.2020.1740123
26. Burroughs, J.E., Glen Mick, D.: Exploring antecedents and consequences of consumer creativity in a problem-solving context. J. Consum. Res. 31, 402–411 (2004). https://doi.org/10.1086/422118
27. Schreier, M., Prügl, R.: Extending lead-user theory: antecedents and consequences of consumers' lead userness. 25, 331–346 (2008). https://doi.org/10.1111/j.1540-5885.2008.00305.x
28. Crunchbase. https://www.crunchbase.com/organization/just-inc
29. Vox Media. https://www.vox.com/future-perfect/2020/2/6/21126419/eggs-just-sodexo-plant-based-protein
30. Thrillist. https://www.thrillist.com/news/nation/just-egg-vegan-eggs-review-ingredients
31. Plant Based News. https://plantbasednews.org/lifestyle/vegan-just-egg-whole-foods-stores-across-us/
32. Olsson, T., Salo, M.: Online user survey on current mobile augmented reality applications. In: IEEE International Symposium on Mixed and Augmented Reality (2011)
33. Park, M., Yoo, J.: Effects of perceived interactivity of augmented reality on consumer responses: a mental imagery perspective. J. Retail. Consum. Serv. 52, 101912 (2020). https://doi.org/10.1016/j.jretconser.2019.101912

34. Bues, M., Steiner, M., Stafflage, M., Krafft, M.: How mobile in-store advertising influences purchase intention: value drivers and mediating effects from a consumer perspective. Psychol. Mark. **34**, 157–174 (2017). https://doi.org/10.1002/mar.20981

35. Zeithaml, V.A., Berry, L.L., Parasuraman, A.: The behavioral consequences of service quality. J. Mark. **60**, 31–46 (1996). https://doi.org/10.2307/1251929

36. Wood, S.L., Swait, J.: Psychological indicators of innovation adoption: cross-classification based on need for cognition and need for change. J. Consum. Psychol. **12**, 1–13 (2002). https://doi.org/10.1207/S15327663JCP1201_01

37. de Holanda Coelho, G.L., Hanel, P.H.P., Wolf, L.J.: The very efficient assessment of need for cognition: developing a six-item version. Assessment **27**, 1870–1885 (2018). https://doi.org/10.1177/1073191118793208

38. Chen, M.F.: Attitude toward organic foods among Taiwanese as related to health consciousness, environmental attitudes, and the mediating effects of a healthy lifestyle. Br. Food J. **111**, 165–178 (2009). https://doi.org/10.1108/00070700910931986

39. Povey, R., Wellens, B., Conner, M.: Attitudes towards following meat, vegetarian and vegan diets: an examination of the role of ambivalence. Appetite **37**, 15–26 (2001). https://doi.org/10.1006/appe.2001.0406

40. Van Trijp, H.C.M., Steenkamp, J.-B.E.M.: Consumers' variety seeking tendency with respect to foods: measurement and managerial implications. Eur. Rev. Agric. Econ. **19**, 181–195 (1992). https://doi.org/10.1093/erae/19.2.181

Author Index

Printed in the United States
by Baker & Taylor Publisher Services